Introduction to Control Systems

Macmillan Series in Applied Systems Science

C. T. Leondes, Editor

Bruce O. Watkins

Introduction

UTAH STATE UNIVERSITY

to Control Systems

THE MACMILLAN COMPANY, NEW YORK
COLLIER-MACMILLAN LIMITED, LONDON

To the student in search of knowledge.

May he use it in the service of humanity.

First Printing

Library of Congress catalog card number: 68–13836

THE MACMILLAN COMPANY, NEW YORK
COLLIER-MACMILLAN CANADA, LTD., TORONTO, ONTARIO

Printed in the United States of America

Preface

Automatic control courses appeared in undergraduate engineering curricula around the end of World War II, and the text *Principles of Servomechanisms* by G. S. Brown and D. A. Campbell was one of the first to specialize in this area. Subsequently, the number of textbooks grew rapidly, and the original frequency analysis technique, based on the work of H. W. Bode, was followed shortly by the root-locus method of W. R. Evans, popularized by J. G. Truxal's classic *Control System Synthesis* in 1955. Since then a large number of works in control have appeared, and at this time at least a dozen excellent introductory textbooks are available. Most of these discuss analysis and design in terms of frequency analysis and root locus. A third and very promising procedure, the parameter plane method, introduced by D. Mitrović and advanced by D. D. Šiljak and G. J. Thaler, has not gained prominence, at least as yet.

Investigations into general system theory, utilizing time-domain analysis, came to the foreground in 1955, and this area developed rapidly. This approach, familiar in Europe (particularly Russia), became important in the United States through the efforts of R. E. Kalman, E. G. Gilbert, and R. Bellman, among others. L. A. Zadeh and C. A. Desoer brought out the rigorous text *Linear System Theory*, which collected state-space concepts, in 1963. About three years ago the author conceived the idea of including the state-space approach in an undergraduate text. At the time it seemed a splendid notion; however, the recent spate of books along these lines indicates that he was not alone. We can undoubtedly look forward to more effort along these lines, although specific directions may be hard to forecast.

This book is an attempt to provide an introduction to the control system area, such that upon completion the undergraduate student should be in a position to read the current literature without too much difficulty, to pursue advanced and specialized courses, or to move into design with little readjustment.

Most engineering instructors now realize that system theory in general, and control theory in particular, is interdisciplinary, cutting across all specialized engineering fields. Further, the feedback and system concepts have much wider application, for example, to social and economic problems. Hence the author attempts to set a broad horizon before the student. On the other hand, an inevitable specialization background shows up all too clearly; although the text exhorts the reader to be broad, the examples are concentrated in the electrical engineering spectrum. This may be unfortunate but is perhaps understandable. In the next generation perhaps we may achieve more unity.

Addressed to the average undergraduate, the text does not attempt to be overly rigorous. Hopefully, enough rigor has been introduced to provide clear understanding, but not so much as to discourage continuation and further exploration. A Laplace transform background is assumed, but a short appendix is provided for those without it. The author assumes less background in linear and matrix theory; thus the text gives a fairly extensive appendix on matrices and a chapter on state-space theory. The individual instructor will no doubt have certain sections he may wish to accentuate or skip, depending on the background of his students. To cover the entire book in detail probably would require almost one school year.

The book emphasizes the general theoretical nature of control system, and not the particular devices that may be used, although the examples do bring out the nature of some devices. For particulars on transducers, actuators, amplifiers, and so on, other books should be consulted.

Because the author has some difficulty reading the literature caused by differing terminology, alternative terminologies are provided frequently. Also, as examples usually appeal more to the average undergraduate than abstract relations, a large number of examples are furnished. Furthermore, the author's predeliction toward diagrams is quite apparent, and these may interest one type of engineer more than another. In particular, flow diagram concepts are widely used.

The author feels that the objective of engineering should be design, so the text has been slanted in this direction throughout. Only the design rudiments are discussed, however, and reference is made to the large number of texts that go into this matter in more detail. The emphasis here is more on the nature and philosophy of design.

A lengthy roll of supplementary texts is given at the end of each chapter. Some texts have been omitted inadvertedly and not purposely, and the author apologizes for these. Additional references will be found in those given, however.

Although effort has been made to keep errors down, errors unquestionably exist, and reports on such will be thankfully received.

Grateful acknowledgment is made to all those who assisted in the preparation of this book.

BRUCE O. WATKINS

Logan, Utah

Contents

1 Introduction

2 Equations Describing System Dynamics

3 Second-Order Systems

4 Signal Flow Diagrams and Computer Simulation

5 System Representation in State Space

6 Analysis in State Space

7 The Characteristic Equation and the Root Locus

8 Frequency Analysis

9 System Compensation—Conventional

10 Compensation—Modern

11 Discrete Time Systems

1 Introduction

1.1 Search for Control

In a very general sense, man's control of nature and himself constitutes the principal basis for differentiating man and animals. Through the use of science, man has become more and more successful in adapting nature to his ends. Civilization attests to progress in self-control also, although at the present time there is some question as to whether this aspect will develop as rapidly as man's destructive tendencies. Control as discussed in this book will of course be limited to a much narrower meaning, one which can be more rigorously defined in engineering and scientific terms, but it is perhaps worthwhile to briefly discuss control in this more general sense, particularly as the principles that have been developed by the control engineer now move into more and more areas outside the original boundaries of control for machines or processes. As only one example of many, feedback control ideas have been successfully used to simulate and explain the action of the heart and other organs. Economic problems also are being attacked using control ideas. It is not too much to say that control principles developed during and immediately after World War II, and now, being furthered by engineers and mathematicians, may offer one hope for the control of disruptive social forces. The student might ponder how control principles could be used in other areas as he studies control problems in specific cases.

In this general sense, then, we might look at a problem occupying man's attention, for example, how to grow more food. In attacking such a problem, one method of science is to isolate it from other problems and analyze the important factors, neglecting at first the secondary influences.

This is difficult to do with food growing, but we might attemp to collect all the processes concerned with this problem into a convenient box that we label a system, *S*. For example, the box might contain such items as land, workers, farm machinery, and seeds. Into this system go certain inputs, such as tillage, planting, fertilizer, direction of labor, and moisture, and from the system come outputs, or foods. Some of the inputs, such as water, for example, may not be particularly under our control, while others may be more so. Such a system might be represented by the box in Figure 1.1–1, containing all the interrelated components, into which go inputs, and out of which come outputs.

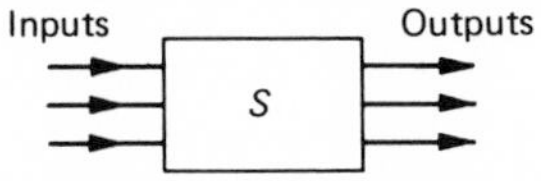

Figure 1.1–1. General system.

The system *S* was largely unknown in primitive times, but by putting in different inputs and observing the variation in the outputs, the system became better understood. Observation of the outputs led to further changes in the inputs; or a very crude feedback of output knowledge influencing input occurred. As man achieved increased cognizance of *S*, the specific details of the various division or subsystems of *S* were analyzed. At the same time, coupling, or influence from previously unsuspected sources, became evident, and *S* increased in size and complexity. At the present time, although man still has very incomplete ability to control the food system, he certainly has vastly more control than he had one hundred years ago.

We may, then, loosely define a system as a group of intercoupled components, from which one obtains certain outputs in response to particularized inputs. The more ability we have to predict the outputs, given the inputs, or, alternatively, the more effectively we can specify the required inputs to produce desired outputs, the better we know the system. For a more precise mathematical description of a system, we shall find it desirable to define in terms other than input-output relations, but this terminology will suffice here.

Another example that may be of more interest to the engineer concerns the process of prospecting for oil [1]. First the oil comes from the system *S* of Figure 1.1–1, and little is known about *S*. Then with geological developments, engineers and geologists ascertained that certain layers of earth are found with oil. A theory of the internal structure of *S* is hypothesized. Next, explosives are set off on the surface and the resulting earth disturbances examined. These results may cause revision of the theory.

We now may postulate several subsystems $S_1, S_2, \ldots, S_n$, where each subsystem may be defined by input-output relations. The internal structure of system S may now be that of Figure 1.1–2, where the arrows a, b, and c between the various subsystems S_n indicate the directions of information flow. Between S_3 and S_4 you note a backward flow c, which constitutes a feedback path of information from S_4 to S_3. In Figure 1.1–2 the information transmittal is instantaneous, although there may be delay in S_3 or S_4 in processing this information. Preferably S_1, S_2, S_3, and S_4 can be

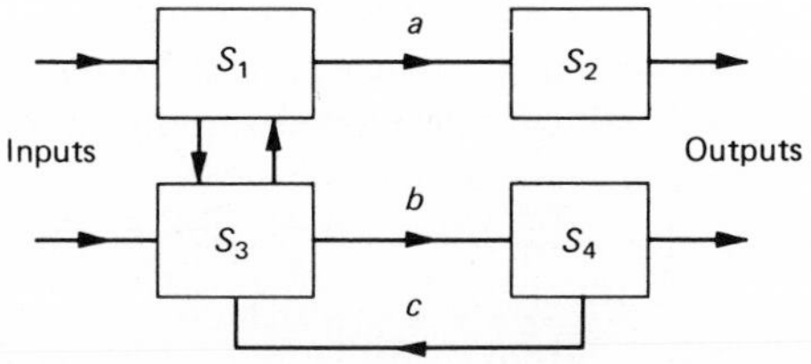

Figure 1.1–2. Information flow between subsystems.

described by mathematical relations, as it is through such relations that some hope exists for controlling the situation (finding oil). Some of the subsystems, such as S_3, may not be well known. However, if the couplings are known, S_3 may be postulated through the mathematical relations and the known outputs and inputs. New forms of inputs may be suggested by this model, and examination of the resulting outputs may refine it further.

The previous examples suggest a procedure as follows:

1. Set up a model of the physical system that approximates the operation in at least the gross effects. Try to describe this model with mathematical relations, using linear relations initially for simplicity.
2. Make tests on the model and compare the results with the known physical situation.
3. Revise the model in view of these tests.
4. Make other tests suggested by the new model, and refine the revised model.
5. Bring in couplings with other systems that may have been ignored in the initial model, and include the effects of these couplings.
6. Introduce more complex mathematical formulations (such as nonlinear equations) if necessary.
7. With the knowledge obtained, design new and better systems that will result in improved performance.

Procedures of this type have resulted in an immense expansion of knowledge in many seemingly unrelated areas.

1.2 Elementary Control Systems

To retreat from generalities to specifics, we start by reducing the scope of the attack. Our first illustrations will describe fairly simple systems having one or two inputs and one or two outputs. Also, as a first step it is necessary to isolate the system from couplings with other systems, that is, to ignore secondary effects. Primarily let us also consider linear systems, or systems to which one may apply the principle of superposition. The systems that we show first will be those controlling a fairly simple quantity, such as rotational position, linear displacement, voltage, current, temperature, or pressure. Such systems developed rapidly in World War II, and are called regulators and servomechanisms.

A few examples will clarify these ideas. One of the earliest and most familiar control efforts involves the control of heating for a residence. Figure 1.2–1a shows a situation in which a gas furnace provides the heat.

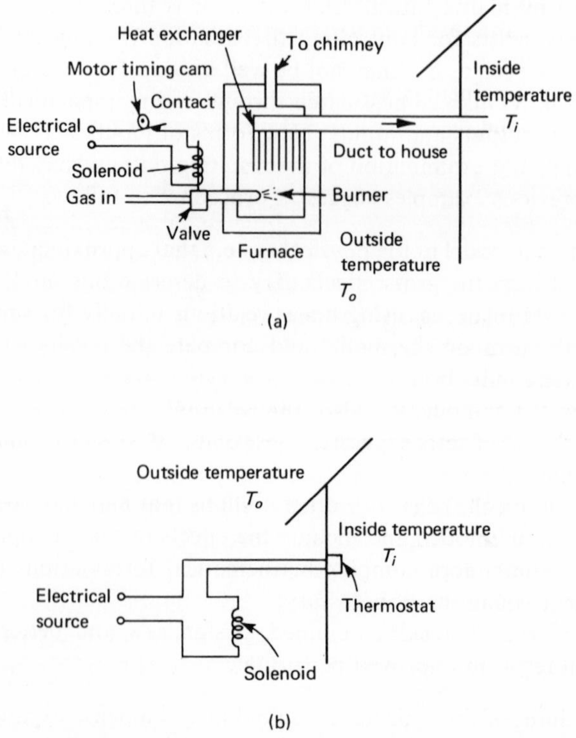

Figure 1.2–1. Control of house heating.

The gas enters the furnace through a valve, which is opened by an electric solenoid. A continually burning pilot light ignites the gas, which then heats the air in the furnace ducts. The electric solenoid might be operated by a timing motor and cam, so that a cyclic opening and closing of the gas line occurs, the length of each cycle being manually adjustable. For given outside and desired inside temperature, T_o and T_i, respectively, the cyclic rate can be adjusted so that the inside temperature remains within certain limits. This adjustment calibrates the controller. It is easy to see that this scheme will not be very satisfactory, for as soon as the outside temperature changes, the unchanging cyclic rate will result in either a too high or a too low inside temperature. The fundamental difficulty here resides in the fact that the control is independent of the desired output quantity, temperature T_i. Such a system is called an open-loop system.

If we had a man (or a robot) continually changing the cyclic on-off rate of the furnace in accordance with some previously determined program, dependent on the outside temperature, the results would be vastly improved. However, the latter scheme would still depend on a calibration and would not take into account changes in the furnace system, such as filter clogging or low gas pressure. Obviously a still better system results if we observe the inside temperature T_i and operate the solenoid accordingly. In Figure 1.2–1b a thermostat that may be set at a desired temperature value (set point) opens or closes the solenoid if the inside temperature departs from the desired value by an amount depending on the thermostatic sensitivity. This eliminates the timer. The thermostat senses the difference between the desired and actual temperatures, or the temperature error, and causes the system to operate. Accordingly, the thermostat is an error detector. In this system information concerning the output is fed back and compared with information concerning the desired result. Thus we have a feedback, or closed-loop, system.

The thermostatic system still cannot keep the temperature T_i constant, because there must be a temperature margin between contact opening and closing on the thermostat. Also, the solenoid either opens or closes the valve, so that the furnace is either completely off or on full, and, owing to a time lag in the heat exchanger, heat will continue to flow after the furnace shuts off, or, on the other hand, time will be consumed in getting heat into the room after the furnace starts. Thus, although the thermostatic on-off system is usually good enough for most purposes, it might be improved further by causing the flow of gas to be proportional to the temperature error $(T_o - T_i)$. This would require more elaborate equipment, such as a motor-operated gas valve with continuously changeable opening and a more refined error-sensing device.

Another example might be a washing machine that goes through a fixed cycle regardless of the cleanliness of the clothes (open loop). The loop is closed if the operator inspects the clothes and controls the cycling of the washing machine accordingly. Another case involving a human is the driving of an automobile. The driver watches the road, and as the automobile departs from the correct path, hopefully the driver observes the error and actuates the steering wheel for correction. The weakly powered steering signal is amplified by gears and levers to turn the car wheels. The driver in this case acts as an error detector and a low power actuator. Unfortunately, in too many cases the driver comprises the weak link, with results often fatal to the entire system. Thus, although the human brain is as yet unsurpassed in many respects by computers, automatic control by nonhuman components often results in faster, more precise, more economical, or more reliable control. The key word here is "automatic." It is desired that control systems operate automatically, and without human intervention.

A very common type of automatic control system adjusts the output angle of some rotatable equipment. This equipment may be a gun turret, an antenna, a mill roll, or it may take many other forms. In many cases the rotating device may have a very large mass and inertia, but we desire to make the output angle a very precise value. For example, a radio-telescope antenna may be several yards in diameter, but the necessary angular pointing precision may be within seconds of arc. Furthermore, we usually control the antenna from a remote position. Figure 1.2–2 shows a simplified version of a possible system.

In the system of Figure 1.2–2 the rotating input dial turns a potentiometer arm, whereas the antenna (which stands at a remote position) is geared to

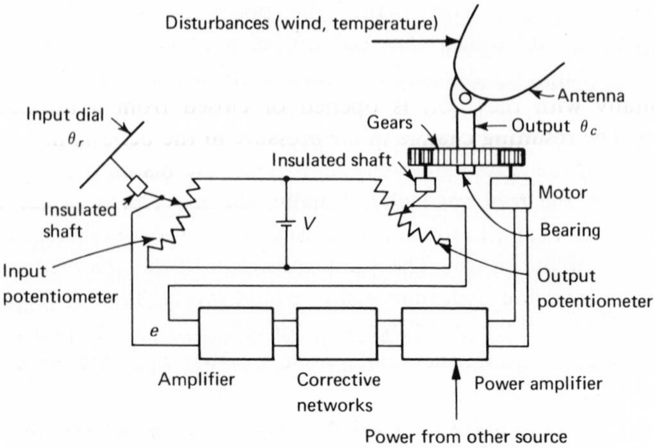

Figure 1.2–2. Antenna control system.

a similar potentiometer arm. If the two potentiometer arms are not at the same angular position, an error voltage e appears at the leftmost amplifier. The potentiometers are a form of error detector. The error signal is amplified, altered by corrective networks, and brought to a power amplifier, which drives a motor in the proper direction, bringing the antenna and the output potentiometer to the position that reduces the error to zero. The corrective networks alter the dynamic performance of the system and will be one of our major concerns. The antenna angle may not be the same as the input dial angle, owing to the gearing, but the angles are proportional. Although the system shown here uses electrical devices, other methods are often used. The power amplifier and motor could be hydraulic, and the error detector could be a differential gear assembly. As a matter of fact, the potentiometer scheme may not be too practical, because the antenna may rotate continuously in one direction. Figure 1.2–2 does, however, illustrate the general principles of many systems:

1. Using an error-detecting system, the actual output is compared with the desired or ideal output.
2. The difference is amplified.
3. The resulting signal is filtered or altered.
4. The altered signal controls the power to a motor or actuator.
5. The output is driven in a direction that will reduce the error.

Clearly this system is of the feedback type, as information concerning the output is fed back to the input. It is evident also that the motor or actuator must be reversible, and that the signal fed to the motor must be of the proper sign to cause corrective action to decrease, not increase, the error. Thus polarity is of utmost importance in any feedback scheme.

Figure 1.2–3 shows an air-oil control system [2]. The cutting tool moves horizontally along the work as the lathe rotates the work piece. The tracer moves with it and follows the contour of a prepared template. As the tracer arm changes its vertical position, the pilot valve (which also moves horizontally with the tool) is opened or closed from a normal or set position. The resulting change in air pressure in the bellows moves the oil spool valve up or down, allowing oil to enter the piston driving the tool, thus moving the tool vertically. Finally, the movement of the tool readjusts the pilot valve to the normal position, and the tool therefore follows the motion of the tracer. The pilot valve constitutes the error-detecting mechanism, and the hydraulic piston exerts several tons of force on the tool. Alteration of the error signal for desired dynamic response may be accomplished by using pneumatic devices rather than the electrical network of Figure 1.2–2.

The previous examples are chosen deliberately to illustrate the fact that control systems are made up of many different types of components. The control engineer may be called upon to deal with mechanical, hydraulic, electrical, pneumatic, thermal, biological, or other components. The control field synthesizes many specialities, and although basic control theory applies to all situations, the particular application may call for study in unfamiliar areas.

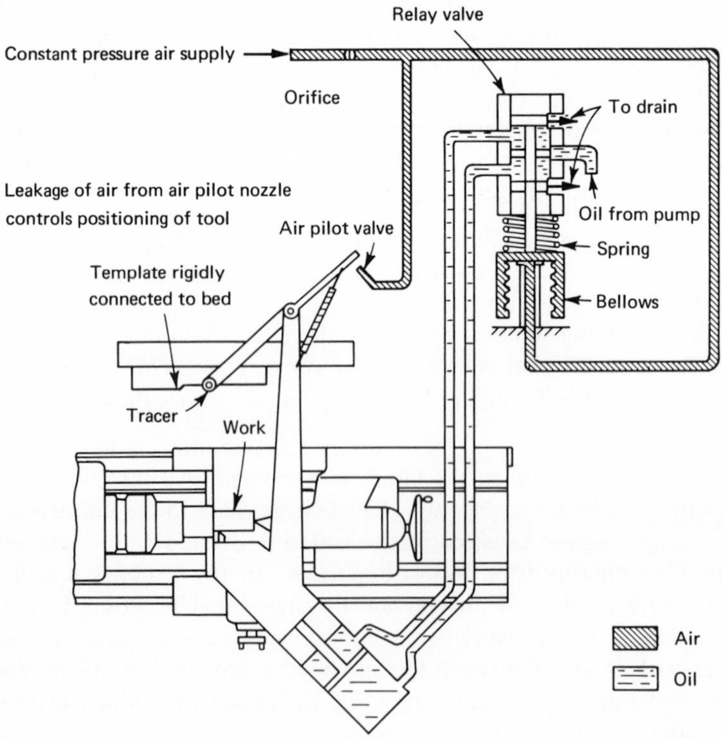

Figure 1.2–3. Contour-following lathe. (From Helm [2]; by permission of the author and the publisher.)

Recently automatic control has been attempted in much more complicated situations, for example, in the control of a refinery. In this application, there may be many inputs, and many outputs, and it may be desired to obtain a control resulting in the most economical process, or to maximize some other variable. This problem becomes very complex, because the interactions or couplings of the many subsystems cannot be neglected. Such controls often involve analog and digital computers as part of the feedback loop.

1.3 Some Terms and Definitions

Up to now we have spoken loosely, using words such as "linear" without precise definition. We need to make our nomenclature clearer; in fact, learning the terminology may be more than half the battle in most technical fields.

We begin by indicating that the input and output quantities previously discussed are generally functions of some common independent variable; in control systems this variable is almost always time. Thus an input m can be designated as $m(t)$ and an output y as $y(t)$. In many cases the function notation may be omitted if obvious. For the moment we shall also consider these to be continuous functions of time, as in Figure 1.3–1.

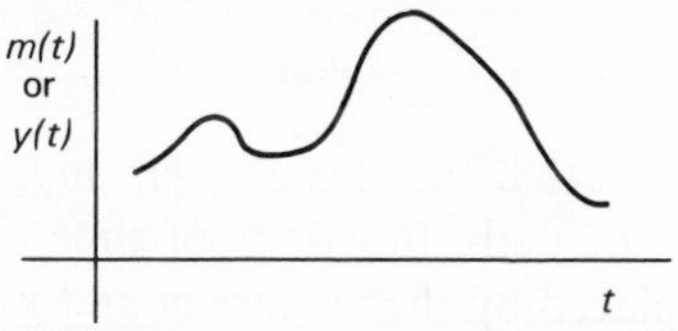

Figure 1.3–1. Continuous function of time.

In using the Laplace or other transforms, these quantities may be functions of an operator such as s, in which case m and y may be written $M(s)$ and $Y(s)$, or M and Y, respectively. The time functions often are called signals. In fact, the term "signal" applies to time functions inside the system (between elements or subsystems, such as a, b, and c in Figure 1.1–2).

A system or subsystem may now be defined on the basis of the input-output relations by using an operator S in the equation

$$y(t) = Sm(t) \qquad \textbf{(1.3–1)}$$

Equation (1.3–1) may be clarified by reference to Figure 1.3–2. S is an operator such that the output $y(t)$ results from the input $m(t)$ [3].*

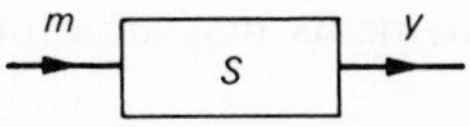

Figure 1.3–2. Operator *S*.

* The operator is such that $y(t)$ may depend not only on present values of $m(t)$, but past (and perhaps future) values of $m(t)$.

Now suppose that we have many inputs and outputs, as in Figure 1.1–1. We can still use Figure 1.3–2 and (1.3–1) if we take m to be an ordered array of inputs and y an ordered array of outputs. That is, let

$$\mathbf{m} = \begin{bmatrix} m_1 \\ m_2 \\ \cdot \\ \cdot \\ \cdot \\ m_n \end{bmatrix} \tag{1.3–2}$$

where now $m_1, m_2, \ldots, m_n$ are the inputs. The ordered array on the right side of (1.3–2) is a matrix (another name for an ordered array) of special characteristics: a $1 \times n$ matrix. (See Appendix B for a summary of the elements of matrix analysis.) Such a matrix is given the special name vector. We shall use boldface letters for a matrix. Thus (1.3–1) now becomes

$$\mathbf{y} = S\mathbf{m} \tag{1.3–3}$$

where you still understand that the elements $m_1, m_2, \ldots, m_n$ of **m** and the elements $y_1, y_2, \ldots, y_p$ of **y** are functions of time t. Figure 1.3–2 is still valid if m and y are replaced by the vectors **m** and **y**. This is simpler than Figure 1.1–1, which shows each separate input and output. In the situation described by (1.3–3), in general S will be a very complicated operator. However, if we limit the system to be linear, the operator S itself will be a matrix, or in this special case

$$\mathbf{y} = \mathbf{S}\mathbf{m} \tag{1.3–4}$$

We now need to define the terms "linear" and "time-invariant." For simplicity, we assume a single input-output system, as given by (1.3–1), although the results easily extend to the multi-input-output case. In Chapters 5 and 6 we shall discuss the latter situation in great detail.

We call a system "linear" if the principle of superposition applies. This principle states that if the output of a system is known for any particular input, then the output to the simultaneous application of any number of inputs will be the sum of the outputs resulting from each input acting alone. Furthermore, if any input is multiplied by a constant (independent of time), the output due to this input will be multiplied by the same constant.* In equation form these statements may be expressed as follows: If

$$y(t) = Sm(t)$$

and

$$S(\alpha m_1(t) + \beta m_2(t)) = \alpha S m_1(t) + \beta S m_2(t) \tag{1.3–5}$$

* Initial conditions in differential equations may be included as inputs.

where α and β are constants, the system is linear. If $\alpha = \beta = 1$, the previously stated additive law is obtained, whereas if $m_2 = 0$, the second, or multiplicative, property, which is called the attribute of homogeneity, appears.

Why concentrate so heavily on linear systems? The answer involves the philosophy of pragmatism: Linear systems can be treated by mathematical relations in a much simpler fashion than nonlinear systems. For example, look at the linear amplifier model illustrated by the straight line of Figure 1.3–3. In this case S is simply the slope of this line. If the input

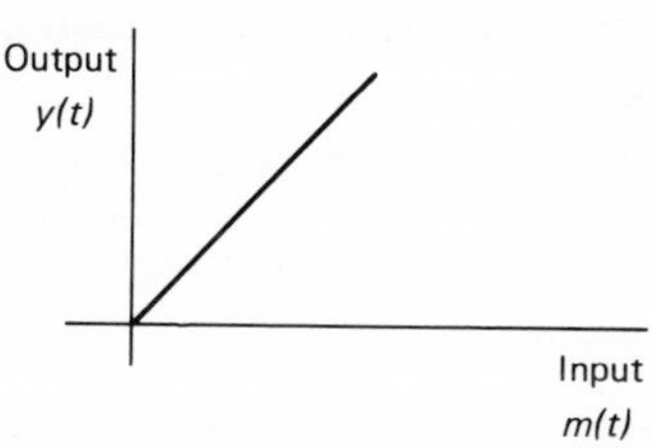

Figure 1.3–3. Linear operator.

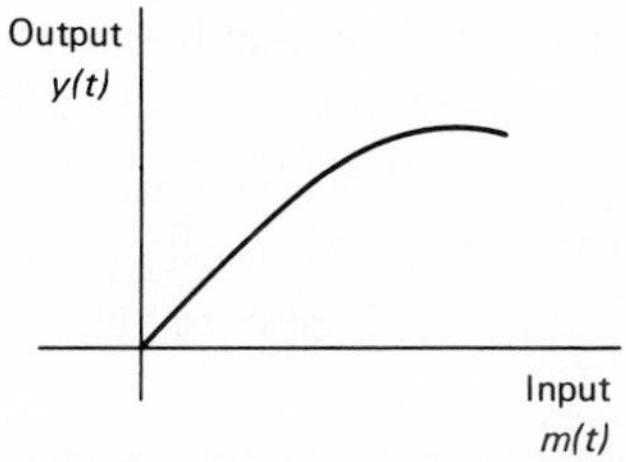

Figure 1.3–4. Nonlinear operator.

$m = K \sin \omega t$, then the output $y = S(K \sin \omega t)$. Clearly if K, the peak value of the input, increases, then the peak value of the output y, which is SK, increases proportionately, illustrating the homogeneity attribute. On the other hand, if S is an operator defined by the curve in Figure 1.3–4, then the mathematical operations become much more difficult, because, if m enters the nonlinear region, the peak output is no longer proportional to the peak input; in fact, worse yet, the output no longer has the same functional relation with time as it did in the linear case. Clearly, you can apply similar lines of argument for the case of two simultaneous inputs.

Linear theory, although greatly restricted, has nevertheless proved very useful in practical applications. In addition, linear theory can be extended to many nonlinear cases by either making an average linear approximation or by using a piecewise linear approximation to the actual characteristic. Hence, although natural phenomena are seldom linear, linear theory applies in many situations.

Although a system is linear, it may be time-varying; loosely that is, the operator is a function of the independent variable time. A non-time-varying system is also called fixed or stationary. If $y(t) = Sm(t)$, a stationary system may be defined in mathematical language by the relation

$$y(t - \tau) = Sm(t - \tau) \tag{1.3–6}$$

for any $m(t)$ and any τ, where τ is a constant (zero initial conditions). In different words, this indicates that the form of the response or output to any input is independent of the time of application of $m(t)$, or, alternatively, to the location of the origin of the time axis. We can therefore alter the independent (time) variable by any constant without affecting the character of the response.

The assumptions of linearity and stationarity greatly simplify the operator S and produce more tractable mathematical operations. These assumptions enable one to put the operator S either inside or outside other operations, such as summation ($\sum$), integration ($\int$), or differentiation (d/dt). You must be careful here to remember that S is an operator associated with m, and is similar, for example, to such operators as log, $\int$, and $\mathscr{L}$, and is not entity in itself.

Example 1.3–1

A system is described by the equation

$$y(t) = K_1 t m(t) + K_2 \frac{dm(t)}{dt} \tag{1.3–7}$$

Is it linear? Fixed?

Applying the left side of (1.3–5) to the first term on the right of (1.3–7), you obtain

$$K_1 t(\alpha m_1(t) + \beta m_2(t)) = K_1 t\alpha m_1(t) + K_1 t\beta m_2(t) = \alpha K_1 t m_1(t) + \beta K_1 t m_2(t)$$

For the second term,

$$K_2 \frac{d}{dt}[\alpha m_1(t) + \beta m_2(t)]$$
$$= K_2 \alpha \frac{d}{dt} m_1(t) + K_2 \beta \frac{d}{dt} m_2(t) = \alpha K_2 \frac{d}{dt} m_1(t) + \beta K_2 \frac{d}{dt} m_2(t)$$

The right sides of both equations satisfy the conditions of (1.3–5), and both equations may be added, so the system is linear.

If we apply an input $m(t-\tau)$ to the first term in (1.3–7), we obtain $S[m(t-\tau)] = K_1 t m(t-\tau)$. However, $y(t-\tau) = K_1(t-\tau)m(t-\tau)$, and this term is time-varying, because the conditions of (1.3–6) are not satisfied. The second term of (1.3–7) is fixed, but the complete system is not stationary.

Another definition needed is that of memory. A system or device has no memory if the output depends only on the present (instantaneous) input and not on any past or future input. An example of a system with no memory would be

$$y = K \sin m(t) \tag{1.3–8}$$

Thus the output at time t in a memoryless system is a function of the value of the input at the same time t and not of any past or future inputs. A physical illustration of a memoryless system might be a telephone switching scheme in which each digit is completely independent of previous or following digits and depends only on the position of a dial or push button. Another example of a system without memory is a tossed fair coin. By "fair" we mean that the probability of the coin coming up heads is 50 per cent. No matter how many heads come up in succession, the chances for the coin to come up heads on the next toss are still only 50 per cent; in other words, the coin does not remember past performance. The gambler who endows the coin (or dice) with memory, or more colloquially talks about a "streak of luck," may discover the true facts of life to his sorrow. (Alternatively, of course, the coin or dice might not be "fair.")

If a function of time is discrete rather than continuous, it may be dependent on the immediately previous value but not on any values prior to that. A simple illustration would be a flip-flop switch. The "off" position depends on the immediately previous position and an actuating signal. Such processes are sometimes called "Markov," and if the dependence extends to more events in the past than the immediately prior event, we have a "Markov chain." Whether finite or continuous, a system output at time t may depend on the previous inputs only in the interval $(t - t_1)$ to $t(t_1 \geq 0)$, in which case it has a memory interval of t_1. If the system has a memory, one also calls it dynamic. Most physical systems that we shall discuss will be of this type and have a memory interval of infinity. That is, all past inputs, as well as the immediate input, will contribute to the present output. Usually the more distant inputs will have less effect than the more recent; or a dynamic system has a memory that may be analogous to that of many students.

The concept of memory may also be expressed by differentiating a "function" and a "functional." A function $f(m)$ depends only on the immediate value of m. A functional, contrariwise, depends on past values of m as well as the immediate value. A simple functional, representing an infinite memory interval device, would be a capacitor, where the voltage $e(t)$ depends on all past values of the charge, or

$$e(t) = \frac{1}{C}\int_{-\infty}^{t} i(\tau)\, d\tau \qquad \textbf{(1.3-9)}$$

The term "functional" is somewhat confusing and has been defined in other ways, so we shall use it sparingly [4].

Finally, we need to define a physical or causal system. Such a system has a present output that does not depend on future inputs. Thus assume that an input over a certain interval t_1 to t_2 is $m_1(t)$, and the output

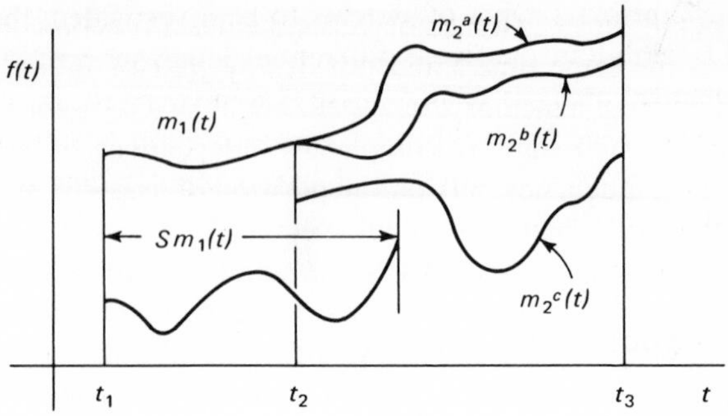

Figure 1.3–5. In a causal system, the output $Sm_1(t)$ is not altered by any $m_2(t)$.

corresponding to this input is $Sm_1(t)$, as in Figure 1.3–5. If we now have any input $m_2(t)$ extending from t_2 to t_3, $t_3 > t_2$, then the principle of causality states that the output $Sm_1(t)$ is unaltered by the function $m_2(t)$. This is illustrated in Figure 1.3–5.

Some wits have said, in irreverent language, "the system will not laugh before you tickle it," which is not as precise as the defining relations but more entertaining. You are so accustomed to the causal idea that you probably accept it without question and wonder why such a definition is necessary. On a macroscopic scale at least, no noncausal physical systems have been found. However, mathematical operations may not involve such concepts. In fact, to force a filter network developed from mathematical concepts to be causal requires considerable effort [5]. Also on the scale of the atom, some physicists now deny causality and substitute statistics, but this is a philosophical argument we had best avoid.

Primarily, the type of system with which we shall deal in this book will usually be described by differential equations if continuous (or difference equations if discrete). Each differential equation usually will be linear; that is, a function and its derivatives will be raised only to the first power, and the equation coefficients will not be functions of the dependent variable.

Furthermore, normally we shall deal with non-time-varying systems. This usually (but not always) means that the coefficients of the differential equation will be constants and not functions of the independent variable, time. The differential equations will be ordinary, which implies that the systems have lumped parameters, as contrasted to distributed parameter systems such as transmission lines, which must be described by partial differential equations. Finally, our system will almost always be causal and dynamic.

The preceding discussion has tacitly assumed that the operator S is known. For the primary types of systems to be investigated, the operator is delineated by simultaneous linear differential equations, and in Chapter 2 we make a detailed analysis of how these may be derived. In many cases, however, we may need to establish the operator by means of experiment, that is, by observation of outputs with given inputs. This is defined as the identification problem.

1.4 Classifications

Control systems may be classified in a variety of ways, some of which have already been mentioned. The classification may depend on the nature of the analysis, as well as the system itself. One differentiation is made by arranging the analysis into deterministic or stochastic. This categorization associated itself with the types of signals studied.

By a deterministic signal, we mean one that we can predict with little uncertainty. That is, if we write an input $m(t)$, say, as

$$m(t) = 50\sin(10t + 30°) \qquad t \geq 0 \tag{1.4–1}$$

we imply that at time $t = 0$ the value of the signal will be 25. Thus the signals, whether expressed by equations or graphs, are specified for all time. The actual value of the signal will be within a given tolerance, that is, the tolerance of the calculator device or the graph reader. Whatever this tolerance, it is sufficiently small that it does not influence the method of analysis, although we may attempt to improve the computational or measurement accuracy, if necessary.

The outstanding characteristic of a deterministic signal is its predictability and repeatability within some reasonable tolerance. If the value of the signal is not predictable within fairly narrow limits, then it is called random or stochastic [6]. For this type of signal we may have little idea as to its value at any particular instant, and the best we may be able to do is to specify the probability that the signal will lie within certain limits. In analyzing signals of this type, it becomes necessary to adopt a completely different kind of analysis, based on probability theory; such an analysis, or the system designed on the basis of this analysis, is termed stochastic. In this book we shall be concerned with deterministic signals and systems and assume that the variations of the signals from the specified values are relatively unimportant.

We may also classify systems as to whether the independent variable, time, is continuous or not. If the signal (which may be discontinuous) is a function of the continuous variable t, the system is termed "continuous-time," or, simply, continuous. For example, the signal of Figure 1.4–1

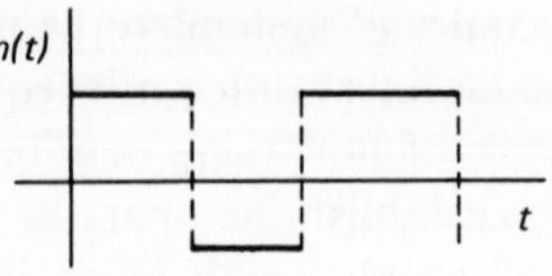

Figure 1.4–1. Continuous time function.

would be of the continuous-time variety if the value of the signal at any time t (except at dependent variable discontinuities) is specified.

Alternatively, if the signal is a function of time only at particular instants and is not known between these points in time, then it is a function of a discrete variable, or a system with such signals is said to be a discrete-time system. An example of such a system is indicated in Figure 1.4–2,

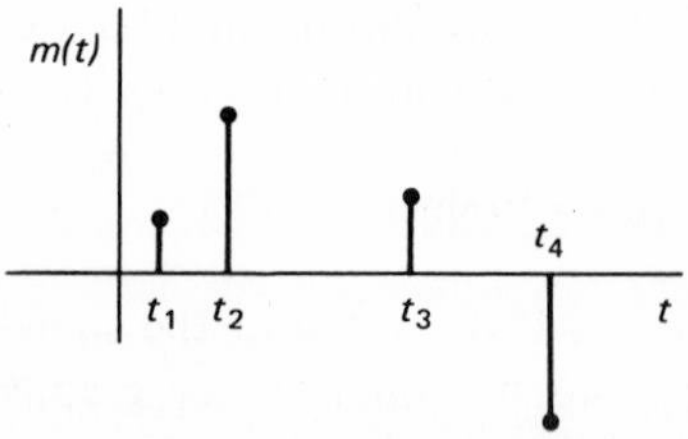

Figure 1.4–2. Discrete function of time.

where the values of the signal are known only at times $t_1, t_2, t_3, \ldots, t_n$, but not for times between t_1 and t_2, and so on. A signal that is such a function may be written

$$m = m(t_k)$$

or, more briefly,

$$m = m(k)$$

where k represents the instant at which the function is known.

One large class of discrete-time systems is termed "sampled-data systems." This terminology arises from the fact that we can assume the value of the signal at the kth instant to be derived from a continuous time signal followed by a sampling switch, as in Figure 1.4–3. The switch sw

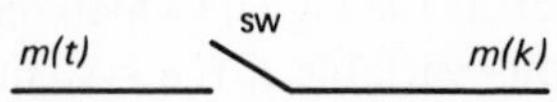

Figure 1.4–3. Sampler for a discrete function of time.

closes only for an instant, and the value of $f(t)$ at this instant is transmitted to the right side of the switch in Figure 1.4–3. In practice, the period between sampling instants is usually constant, so that in Figure 1.4–2 the time intervals (t_1, t_2) and (t_{n-1}, t_n) are the same. This kind of sampling easily can be approximated by a relay or a transistor, in which the time interval for taking the sample is finite but very short compared to the "off" time, so that the latter is taken as the sampling time interval.

Discrete systems arise naturally from many data-processing devices, as for example where a large number of signals may be examined by sampling each one in turn. Also, the digital computer is a discrete-time device, and, if such a computer is a part of a system, the signals must be discrete. Frequently a signal may be considered to be continuous, although it is actually discrete. Thus the digital computer again actually performs an integration of a continuous function by taking discrete intervals in time. If these time intervals become sufficiently short, the output of the computer (the integral) may be close enough to the precise value using a continuous function. However, if the intervals are too far apart, the result may be unusable. In this integration example, the proper time interval depends on how rapidly the continuous function changes and the accuracy required.

From our standpoint, an important distinction between continuous-time systems and discrete systems is that we shall characterize the former by differential equations, while the latter will be characterized by difference equations. Thus, for example, a continuous system might be defined by the differential equation

$$\frac{dy(t)}{dt} = f(y(t), m(t))$$

whereas a discrete system would be defined by the corresponding difference equation

$$y(k+1) = f(y(k), m(k))$$

If the sampling for the discrete system has a constant period, and the system is linear, we may solve difference equations by the Z-transform in a manner analogous to the solution of liner differential equations with the Laplace or Fourier transform. Most of the terminology and definitions discussed in Section 1.3 can be extended easily to the discrete case. Thus, for example, a non-time-varying system having an input-output relation

$$y(k) = Sm(k)$$

would be defined by the equation

$$y(k-n) = Sm(k-n)$$

for any m and any n. The definition of linearity is also found in (1.3–5) if the functions in that equation are considered discrete-time functions. In this book we shall concentrate on continuous time signals and systems.

We have already discussed another possible way that systems may be classified—as to whether they contain feedback or not. An implication has been made that the feedback variety is superior. If one explores this more deeply, this advantage rests on a form of uncertainty. Conceivably, if all signals were accurately known (deterministic), if we knew all the disturbances to which the system would be subjected, if we understood just how the system would age, and if we could express all these factors mathematically, theoretically an open loop (nonfeedback) system could be designed. As an example, in shooting an astronaut to the moon, the vehicle will be followed by radar tracking. The amount it is off course (the error) will be calculated, and corrective signals will be sent to cause local jets to bring the vehicle on course. Thus a feedback is established to revise the course. If all factors were precisely known, a program could be provided that would take care of all situations in the launch, and no vehicle jets would be required. In a sense, however, the uncertainties in the situation call for a feedback of information and remedial action. Even if all eventualities could be anticipated, the mathematical relations likely would be so complex as to preclude a solution. Thus our lack of omnipotence favors the feedback system. We shall discuss the feedback versus nonfeedback system in mathematical terms in Section 1.7.

Another classification of systems concerns the manner of transmitting the signals between the components and subsystems forming the complete system. Although electrical engineers are quite familiar with the fact that a low-frequency signal may be conveyed by means of a higher-frequency signal through a process called modulation, other engineers may not be so aware. Hence we spend a brief time on this question. Modulation usually implies that a high-frequency signal (termed a "carrier") is varied

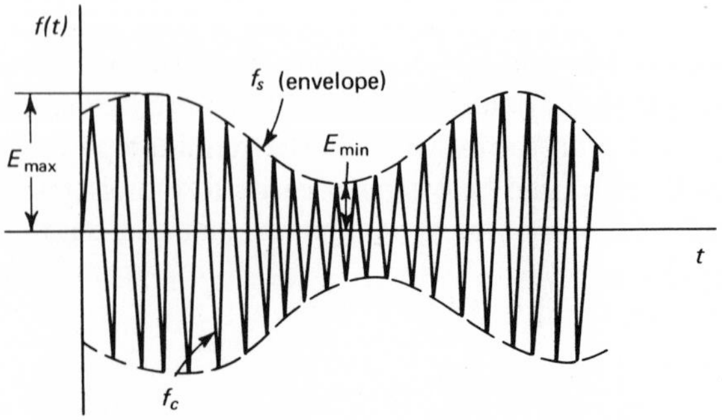

Figure 1.4–4. Amplitude-modulated carrier signal f_c.

in a distinct pattern that reflects the information contained in a lower-frequency signal. The earliest, and still a common method, is illustrated by the ordinary AM radio, where the letters "AM" stand for "amplitude modulation." This means that the amplitude of the high-frequency carrier is varied in accordance with the amplitude of the low-frequency signal (which contains the desired information), and this variation is at the rate of the variation of the low-frequency signal. Thus, if the signal has a frequency f_s cycles per second (hertz, or Hz) and the carrier has a frequency of f_c, where $f_c \gg f_s$, the amplitude modulation for one cycle is as shown in Figure 1.4–4. The frequency f_c is constant, the "envelope" of the carrier varies at a rate determined by f_s, and the amplitude varies with the amplitude of the modulating signal. Such a modulated carrier can be expressed mathematically by

$$f(t) = E \sin 2\pi f_c t + Em(\sin 2\pi f_c t \sin 2\pi f_s t) \tag{1.4–2}$$

where E is the value of the unmodulated carrier and m represents the per unit modulation, or the ratio of the peak to the average of the modulated carrier. In (1.4–2) we require $m \leq 1$ if $E_{\text{min}} \geq 0$ in Figure 1.4–4. Amplitude modulation is only one of the modulation possibilities. Many other types have been used, such as frequency, phase, pulse height, pulse width, and pulse code. In all cases the original signal is transmitted in some other form. To retrieve the signal on some point, a "detector" is needed, which may in many cases be quite complex. For the AM signal all we need is a diode that conducts only one way and an RC filter, as in Figure 1.4–5.

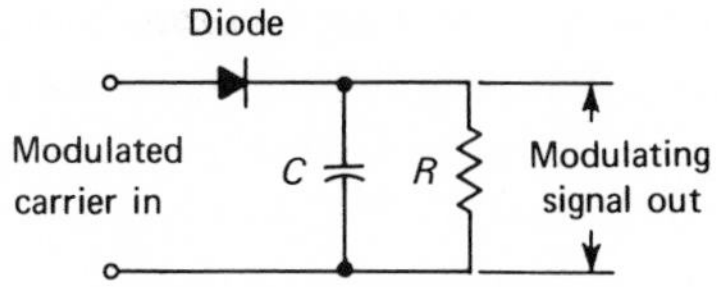

Figure 1.4–5. AM detector.

We now proceed to a more complicated signal than that illustrated by the envelope of Figure 1.4–4. You are familiar with the fact that theoretically any periodic signal satisfying certain requirements (which are not onerous) can be expressed by a sum of sinusoidal signals. Such a sum is called a Fourier series. Consequently if we assume that a signal is periodic, we can form this signal by adding sine waves of varying amplitude, frequency, and phase, or

$$f_1(t) = A_0 + \sum_{n=1}^{\infty} A_n \sin(2\pi f_n t + \phi_n) \tag{1.4–3}$$

where $A_0, A_1 \ldots, A_n$ are constants, and $\phi_1, \phi_2, \ldots, \phi_n$ are phase angles. Although the sum in (1.4–3) is infinite, terms with large n have small magnitudes A_n for most periodic $f_1(t)$, or the higher frequencies do not contribute as much to the signal as the lower frequencies. Hence usually $f_1(t)$ may be approximated as closely as required by terminating the summation on some finite value of n, say $n = k$. The frequency range $(0 - f_k)$ thus required is called the band of interest. It is clear that each term of (1.4–3) will modulate a carrier in the manner illustrated by Figure 1.4–4 and that the envelope of the combination will represent the summation of (1.4–3), except that if we transmit only in the frequency range 0 to f_k the upper sum limit will be k. (The period of the modulation signal can be extended, which results in more frequency terms in the summation, and in the limit one obtains a Fourier integral.)

If we avoid the sticky problems associated with a continuous frequency spectrum and assume that our signals do not change very rapidly, we are therefore interested in transmitting a band of signals from zero frequency to some frequency f_k. We may use these signals directly or modulate them on some sort of carrier. Much of the literature terms the system dealing with the former, or "direct," type of signal as "d-c", and the latter as "a-c." These are very confusing terms, and we prefer to use the terms "noncarrier" and "carrier," respectively, to distinguish such systems. In systems involving mechanical elements, the upper frequency f_k of the band requiring transmission rarely exceeds 20 Hz and is usually much less than this. Hence relatively low frequencies may be used as carriers. More specifically, 50- to 60-Hz frequencies, being readily available in power systems, can and are used extensively as carriers in the modulated carrier system. (In smaller or lighter systems, or on aircraft, 400 and 2,000 Hz may be advantageous.) These frequencies are far below the frequencies used for radio or television broadcasting but are adequate nevertheless for carrier-type control systems.

What are the advantages of the carrier system? If we examine the AM modulation equation (1.4–2), for one signal frequency f_s, by trigonometric substitution we see that this becomes

$$f(t) = E \sin 2\pi f_c t + \frac{mE}{2} \cos 2\pi(f_c - f_s)t + \frac{mE}{2} \cos 2\pi(f_c + f_s)t \quad \textbf{(1.4–4)}$$

or $f(t)$ is composed of a carrier and two "sideband" frequencies, one displaced f_s above the carrier and the other displaced f_s below. In a carrier-type system, for example, if the carrier were 60 Hz, and the maximum $f_k = 10$ Hz, then the frequency band to be transmitted would extend from 50 to 70 Hz. Such a frequency range can be very simply amplified by an *RC*-coupled electronic amplifier, whereas it is fairly difficult to amplify frequencies from 0 to 10 Hz, which would be the band transmitted by a noncarrier system. The difficulty lies in the "drift" of the direct-coupled amplifier, which is necessary to transmit zero frequency (d-c). (Fluid amplifiers give promise of overcoming some deficiencies in electronic amplifiers.) Another advantage is that the signal generated by very useful error-detecting systems is of the modulated type. One such system consists of two synchros, which generate a modulated voltage with an envelope proportional to their angular difference, and a second uses an E transformer, which generates a modulated voltage with an envelope proportional to a linear position. These simple devices are thus angular and linear positional error indicators. In these cases, the modulated carrier is of the "suppressed carrier" type, or of the form

$$f(t) = E \sin 2\pi f_c t \sin 2\pi f_s t \tag{1.4–5}$$

One cycle of this signal is shown in Figure 1.4–6, where

$$\omega_s = 2\pi f_s \qquad \omega_c = 2\pi f_c$$

It is to be noted that the envelope of Figure 1.4–6 changes sign each half-cycle of the frequency $\omega_s/2\pi$. This is in contradiction to the envelope of the normal amplitude-modulated signal of Figure 1.4–4, and implies that we need a special type of detector, known as a "phase-sensitive" detector.

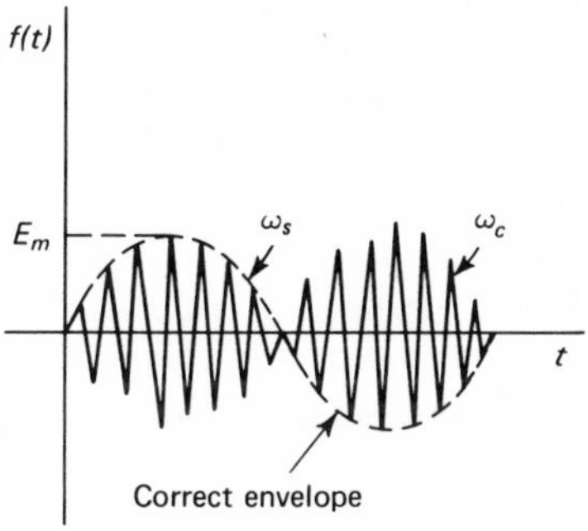

Figure 1.4–6. Suppressed carrier modulation.

Finally, the two-phase a-c motor is frequently used as a driver for mechanical systems, and this motor operates with signals of the type given by (1.4–5) on one phase, if the other phase is excited with a constant frequency f_c.

The previously discussed particulars relate to the hardware of some systems and are helpful to the beginner who might become confused when he encounters both carrier and noncarrier systems in practice and in the laboratory. We have given details on only one type of modulation; as previously indicated, many other types may exist. The more important point to be made here is that in discussing signal flow in systems, and in operating on such signals, we normally imply that the operation or alteration is made on the basic unmodulated or direct signal. If a corrective network is used as a subsystem, for example, it changes this basic signal. In some carrier systems the modulated carrier can be transformed to approximate the alterations desired in the information itself, but often the carrier may be demodulated, altered, and then remodulated, because envelope operations on the carrier are limited. Such operations will be discussed in Chapter 9.

Other classifications of systems are made. Some systems are known as "process" control systems. This implies that the control applies to some sort of processing, for example, gasoline refining or chemical manufacturing. Usually the factors that characterize process control are large numbers of inputs and outputs, very long time constants (or low frequencies), a wide range of implementing devices, high requirements for efficient processing, desire for a low-cost controller, and special terminology. Actually the same fundamental ideas pertain to process control as to any other control, and the same theory applies. The terminology that has grown up in the chemical and manufacturing process fields is different from that used by electrical or mechanical engineers, but once you overcome this terminology barrier, there is little difference in the control problem.

Sometimes systems are classified as to the type of operation, and this is particularly true of the process control industry. Thus we have such control terms as "proportional," "proportional plus derivative," and "proportional plus integral." In control theory these terms describe only particular types of controllers. We wish to explore control schemes in great generality and will illustrate specific examples, such as those mentioned, at the appropriate time.

Many other classifications are possible, but the previous discussion suffices for now to illustrate some of the terms used by control engineers.

1.5 Block Diagrams and Flow Diagrams

Signal flow diagrams and schematic block diagrams greatly assist in analyzing a control system. These diagrams graphically show the reactions between the various inputs and outputs of the subsystems and the relation of the variables of interest in the complete system. On the basis that one picture is worth a thousand words, the engineer habitually used diagrams of all sorts. Figures 1.1–1, 1.1–2, 1.2–2, and others are illustrations of diagrams used to aid in analysis. The first type of diagram usually drawn shows the various devices or subsystems in somewhat pictorial form, as in Figure 1.2–1, 1.2–2, or 1.2–3. The next step is to reduce these representations to a more abstract structure, which depicts the relationships between subsystems, shown as blocks with input and output signals, but with subsystems indicated by word descriptions rather than by drawing of the apparatus. Such a diagram might be termed a schematic block diagram and is illustrated by Figure 1.5–1, showing the antenna system of Figure

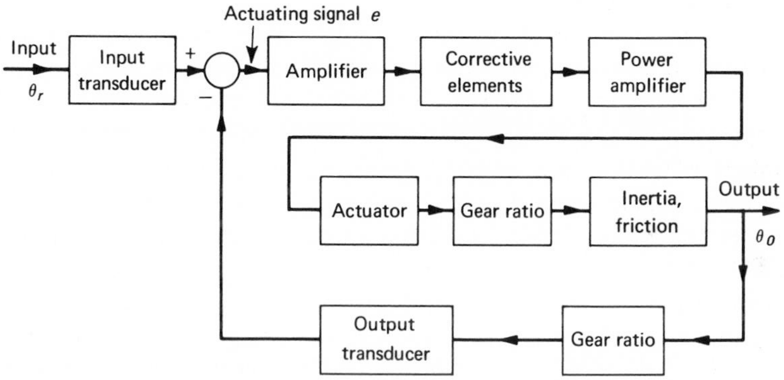

Figure 1.5–1. Schematic block diagram of antenna control system of Figure 1.2–2.

1.2–2 in more abstract form. In this diagram, there are two general rules: (1) The signals are assumed to flow unilaterally in the direction of the arrows, and (2) a block representing a subsystem is assumed not to load a preceding subsystem; for example, in Figure 1.5–1 the output of the first amplifier is taken to be independent of the corrective element subsystem following, and so on for succeeding subsystems to the right. You note that we have lost much of the detail; that is, the type of amplifier, actuator, types of connections (hydraulic, electrical, mechanical), and so on, are not given. The important concern is the flow of signals and the subsystem type in general terms; specific apparatus is not given. The error "wheel" shown isolated in Figure 1.5–2 indicates a subtraction of signal b from a to result in signal c. It is possible to have other signals coming into this

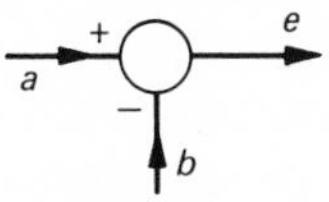

Figure 1.5–2. Error wheel.

wheel with appropriate sign. For this example the input and output transducers consist of the input and output potentiometers and the associated voltage V of Figure 1.2–2. These devices together form an error detector, which in this case alters an angular difference to a voltage. Frequently the schematic diagram may be simplified as to the error detector by lumping the input and output transducers into one error-detecting device, shown to the right of the error wheel in Figure 1.5–3, since the transducers often

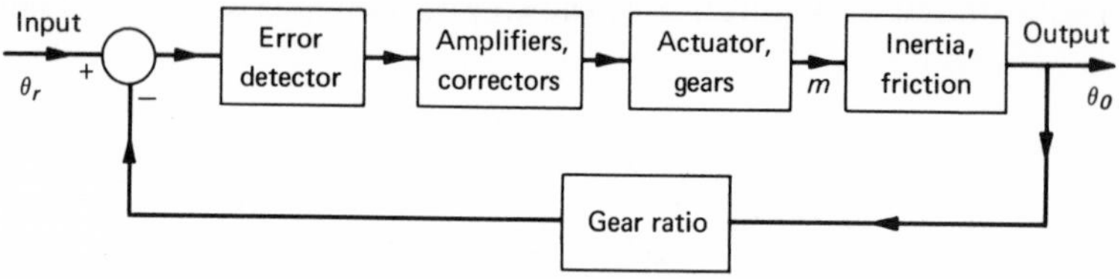

Figure 1.5–3. Reduction of block diagram of Figure 1.5–1.

have the same input-output characteristics. Also in this and in other cases, such as for example a synchro set, you can consider the error detector to be a single unit converting a mechanical positional error into an electrical signal. If, in addition, we combine the amplifiers and corrective elements, we can then reduce Figure 1.5–1 to a schematic such as Figure 1.5–3. This may be condensed still further into a schematic such as Figure 1.5–4,

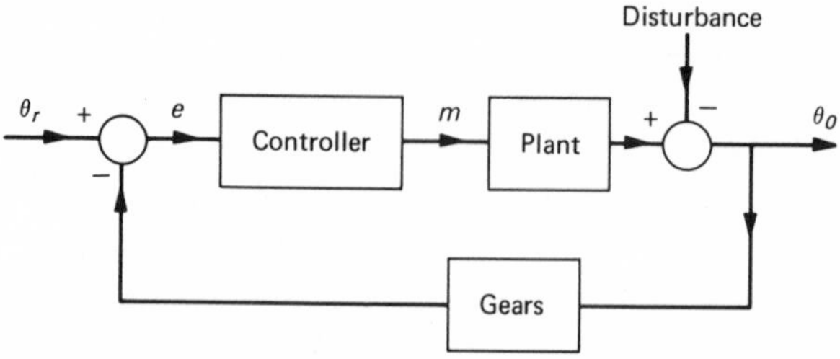

Figure 1.5–4. Further reduction of block diagram of Figure 1.5–1.

where all the devices in the forward path from e to m are called the "controller," and inertia and friction are called the controlled system, or the "plant."

Figure 1.5–4 also shows how load factors other than inertia and friction might be handled. These additional inputs are shown at the appropriate point and are called "disturbances." In the case of the antenna, a disturbance might be a wind; for a motor driving a roller in a steel mill, it might be the varying torque on the roller; with a voltage regulator, it might be a fluctuation of a power load on the regulator; in process control, it might be the temperature change of a coolant. In any case, the units of the disturbance must match the units of the other signals at the input point. Thus, in Figure 1.5–4, if the actual disturbance were a wind, an appropriate alteration or subsystem block would be necessary to convert the effect of the wind into an output angle disturbance.

Figure 1.5–4 illustrates a feedback system. A more general diagram could be shown in Figure 1.5–5, where the controller might be of any type. Furthermore, because we can have both multiinput and multioutput systems, the input-output quantities are depicted as vectors, or ordered arrays of signals.

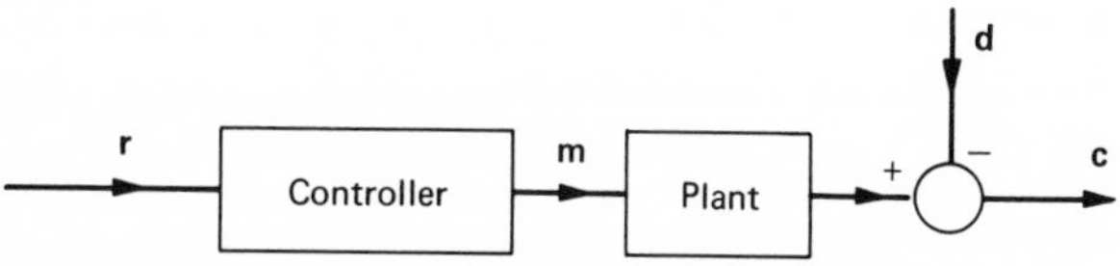

Figure 1.5–5. General control diagram.

In Figure 1.5–5 the plant is considered to be a system presented to the control engineer, together with specifications for its output in the face of given disturbances. Certain references $r_1, r_2, \ldots, r_n$ may also be given. The problem of the control engineer consists in designing a controller to meet the specifications. If feedback paths are desired, these are considered as part of the controller. Unfortunately, life is not as simple as this ideal situation. Frequently the division of the system into a plant and a controller may not be obvious and may require some arbitrary groupings. With these made, the plant characteristics may not be known very well and, far from being furnished to the engineer, may require many tests and assumptions on his part. Finally, the specifications may not provide the desired performance; that is, what represents a "good" system becomes most difficult to describe in precise terms and is a subject of considerable controversy, because, in the last analysis, "good" implies a great deal of subjectivity. These matters will become clearer as we continue: At the moment let us return to the ideal situation.

The diagrams of Figures 1.5–4 and 1.5–5 look very much like the diagrams used in Section 1.1 to define a system. This impels us to take another step and draw a functional block diagram, or a flow diagram, showing the

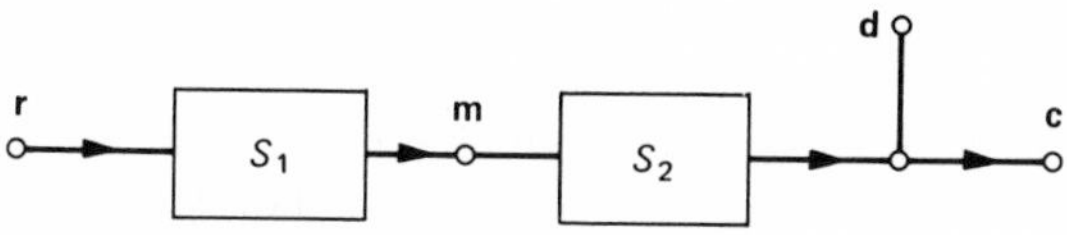

Figure 1.5–6. Functional diagram.

blocks as subsystems which operate on input signals and from which we obtain outputs providing inputs to other subsystems, and so on. Thus Figure 1.5–5 would become Figure 1.5–6. We see from Figure 1.5–6 that we have arrived in a backward manner to a diagram similar to Figure 1.3–2, which served in describing a system. We have made some slight changes; in particular, we have added some small round circles in Figure 1.5–6, called nodes. Nodes designate the variables used in the mathematical relations describing the system operation and represent system quantities of interest, such as voltage, current, position, angle, velocity, and pressure. Nodes are connected by subsystems, often called branches. From our definition of a system, and if we recall that signals flow only unilaterally in the direction of the arrows, a single branch connecting two nodes obviously represents the relation between the node at the output and the node at the input. This relation is an operator and in linear systems may be expressed by linear mathematical equations. In nonlinear systems the block or branch representation is still used, but it is now expressed by nonlinear equations or by graphs. It is understood that all signals entering a node are summed at the node, or that a signal leaving a node is the sum of all signals entering. As suggested previously, a second node dependent on a first node does not affect the value of the first node (unless there is feedback from the second to the first node). In engineering terms, a succeeding node does not load the previous node. (If such is not the case, the diagram must be redrawn with the loading effects included.)

The flow diagram is particularly useful, as will be seen in Chapter 4, in reducing the system to more manageable form. To discuss the flow diagram in a preliminary way here, let us return to single input-output subsystems. In this case, the subsystem operator may be called a branch, a transmittance, or, less frequently, a gain. In Figure 1.5–7 the relation

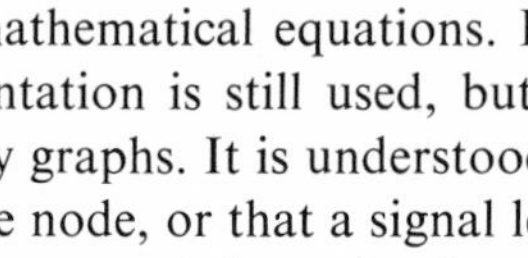

Figure 1.5–7. Simple flow diagram for $F = Ma$.

between force and acceleration (mass constant) is shown by a flow diagram and gives a graphical description of the relation $F = Ma$. That is, the node a (acceleration) is modified by the operator or transmittance M to produce the node F (force). The signal flows unilaterally in the direction of the arrows and we imply that the direction of flow into the branch operator is the same as that out of it. (In some cases only one arrow may be shown on the output, the other being implied.) As previously indicated, "signal" is used in a very broad sense. Alternatively, one might consider the arrows to represent the flow of energy in the system.

Summarizing the rules for drawing a flow diagram:

1. Signals flow unilaterally along the branches in the arrow direction.
2. A signal entering a branch is multiplied by the branch operator.
3. A node variable represents the sum of all signals entering the node.
4. All branches leaving a node transmit the variable represented by that node.

The complete combination of nodes and branches in a system gives a graphical representation of the mathematical equations or relations describing the system. These equations in general involve differentiations or integrations, but in any case the flow diagram gives no more information concerning the system than the equations describing it. The information may be in more understandable form, however, and the manipulation of the diagram is often easier, or more meaningful, than manipulation of the equations. Although the discussion here concerns single input-output systems, the flow diagram may be generalized to multi-input-output systems.

Our antenna system of Figures 1.5–1 and 1.5–3 might be shown by the flow diagram of Figure 1.5–8, where a branch without an enclosed operator is considered to have a transmittance of 1. The error wheel of Figures 1.5–2 to 1.5–5 is replaced by introducing a specific subtraction operator -1 between nodes f and e in Figure 1.5–8. This representation has an advantage in the reduction of flow diagrams, as will be discussed in Chapter 4.

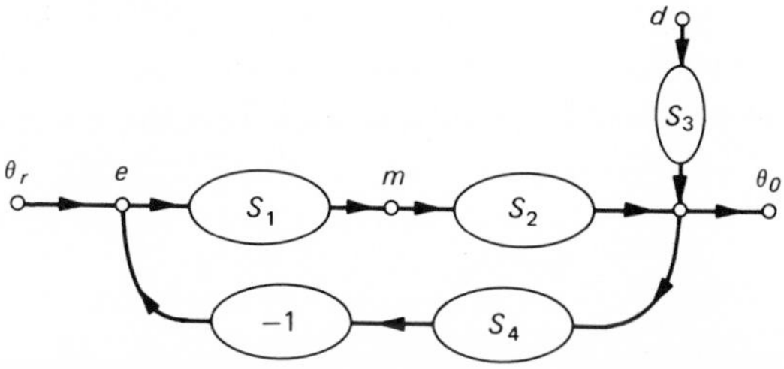

Figure 1.5–8. Flow diagram for antenna system of Figure 1.2–2.

Sometimes the person who draws the flow diagram omits the elliptical enclosure and writes the transmittance adjacent to the branch. These matters are of course details that may be altered by individual taste. We prefer the enclosed operators, because otherwise in a complicated diagram it may be difficult to associate an operator with the proper branch. Other texts call diagrams such as Figure 1.5–3 "block" diagrams. Usually in block diagrams, nodes are omitted, the error wheel is used, and the operators are shown in rectangular blocks. The block diagram and the flow diagram furnish the same information. The use of nodes, however, makes it somewhat easier to set down rules of logic for alteration of the diagram (which corresponds to elimination or changes of variables in the mathematical equations). If a linear operator involves integration or differentiation, it is frequently desirable to use the Laplace or Fourier transform and to depict the operator transmittance as a function in the complex s domain resulting from these transformations. Similarly, in a sampled-data system, the transmittance may be characterized by functions resulting from the Z transform.

Most importantly, the flow diagram gives an abstraction of the system, which is one of its most important features. In Figure 1.5–8, for example, the details of the equipment have been lost and we are free to concentrate on the relations between the system variables. These relations constitute the vital aspect of system analysis, although it is true that an important part of the engineering task resides in the development of practical, efficient, and economical hardware to furnish the required transmittance characteristics. Thus many different types of devices might result in the same flow diagram.

We close this section on flow diagrams by showing a combination schematic-flow diagram that will be basic to many of the systems considered.

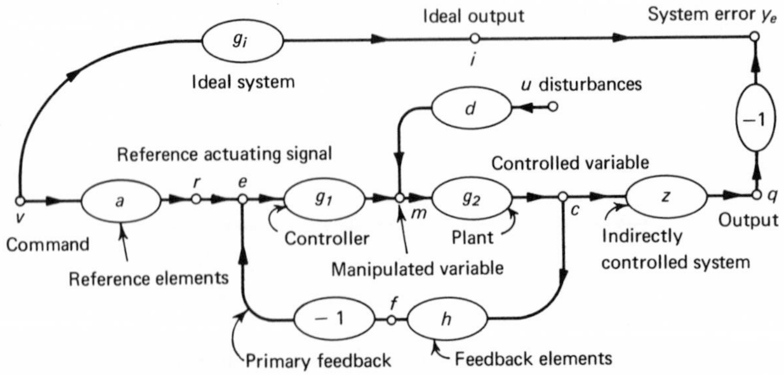

Figure 1.5–9. Single-output flow diagram defining system quantities.

Some definitions may be associated with the diagram of Figure 1.5–9 as follows [7]:

The command is an input independent of the control system.

The ideal output is the ouput one desires to obtain from the command. Usually it is directly proportional to the command and is often equal to it.

The reference signal is the standard of comparison for the system and is usually a simple function of the command.

The controller or control elements produce the manipulated variable m from the actuating signal e.

The plant or controlled system is the quantity or process to be controlled.

A disturbance is a signal other than the reference which affects the controlled variable.

The primary feedback is a signal depending on the controlled variable and which is compared with the reference signal to obtain the actuating signal. There may be other feedback loops, and these are called "internal" feedback paths.

The actuating signal is the reference signal minus the primary feedback.

The system error is the difference between the ideal output and the actual output. In many cases the transmittances of the feedback elements h, the reference elements a, and the ideal system g_i are all 1, and in this case the system error and the actuating signal are equal.

The control ratio is the ratio c/r with the feedback loops closed. We also term this the "closed loop function" (implying that the operation utilizes feedback).

The loop function is the product of all operators around a closed loop. Thus in Figure 1.5–9 the loop function is $-g_1 g_2 h$.

The open loop function is the product of all operators in a loop up to the feedback node f; that is, if we open the loop at f, the open loop function is f/e, or $g_1 g_2 h$ in Figure 1.5–9. Alternatively, the open loop function is the absolute value of the loop function, where by absolute value we mean changing the sign of the loop function to positive if it is negative. This is also termed the "return ratio" [8].

It already has been indicated that in many actual systems it may be difficult to isolate the operators or transmittances as neatly as shown by Figure 1.5–9. Some arbitrary decisions become necessary to decide where the controller leaves off and the plant starts. The plant may be a device or process not under the jurisdiction of the control designer, and it may be difficult to identify precisely although its general nature is known; the example of prospecting for oil in Section 1.1 is a case in point. In other more fortunate cases, the controls designer may have some opportunity to influence the plant design, which usually results in happier designers.

It is clear that larger and more complicated systems with many outputs and inputs may be depicted by combining and coupling in various ways the simple system of Figure 1.5–9. Thus the construction of multi-input-output systems from smaller subsystems is fairly straightforward. However, the tearing down of a large system into its components does not constitute such an easy task, and in general several alternative solutions may be possible.

1.6 Test Signals

In analyzing systems, both theoretically and in the laboratory, certain signals have been found to be useful. The criteria for the serviceability of a signal are (1) the extent to which the signal will assist in the design, (2) the adequacy of performance of the system so designed under operating conditions, and (3) the practicality of generating the signal in a field or laboratory situation. To these three points might be added the desirability for simplicity in the mathematical operations engendered by the signal. We shall confine the subsequent discussion to deterministic signals.

The sine-wave signal is perhaps the oldest signal used in analysis, owing to the fact that amplifier design started (and continues) with such a base. This signal is described by

$$m(t) = A_k \sin(\omega_k t + \phi_k) \tag{1.6–1}$$

where $\omega_k = 2\pi f_k$ and f_k is the frequency in hertz (Hz).

In (1.6–1), $t = 0$ usually is assumed to have occurred far in the past; that is, $t \gg 0$, so that we have essentially steady-state conditions and no transients. The philosophy behind design using the sine wave is contained in (1.4–3); that is, the actual signal to which the system will be subjected is assumed to be made up of a Fourier series of such terms as (1.6–1), and, if the system performs adequately for each one of these terms, it presumably will perform adequately for the actual signal. Owing to the fact that in practical design the Fourier series must be terminated at some finite number, we can only approximate this ideal. The difficulty with this design becomes obvious if we recall that the Fourier series is based on the premise that $f_1(t)$ in (1.4–3) is periodic. If the actual $f(t)$ changes fairly slowly, the Fourier series description may suffice; however, if $f(t)$ changes rapidly, it may not, because we may terminate the series too soon for adequate description.

The previous discussion does not exhaust the subject, of course. Rigorous integral relations (the Fourier transform) exist that allow determination of the system response to almost any signal if the sinusoidal response for all frequencies is known. Many papers have been written exploiting these relations, but unfortunately the application of these techniques becomes tedious and not too practical for design work, at least in the preliminary stages. This will be discussed further in Chapter 8. In spite of many handicaps, sinusoidal analysis is still important, for in many situations a solution using such techniques will be simple and adequate. Perhaps of greater importance is the superiority of the sine wave in the third category; that is, the sine-wave signal is easy to instrument, and the characteristics of

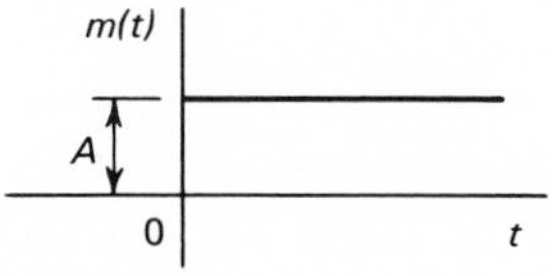

Figure 1.6–1. Step function $Au(t)$.

an existing system often can be determined most easily and exactly using such signals.

Following the sine wave in importance is the step function, shown in Figure 1.6–1, and described mathematically by

$$m(t) = \begin{cases} 0 & t < 0 \\ A & t \geq 0 \end{cases} \tag{1.6–2}$$

The unit step function, that is, where $A = 1$, is usually given the designation $u(t)$. Thus a time function $m(t) = 0$, $t < t_1$, and $m(t) = A$, $t \geq t_1 (t_1 > 0)$ can be described by the equation

$$m(t) = Au(t - t_1)$$

which is the step function of Figure 1.6–1 displaced t_1 units along the t axis.

The output of a system to a step input provides a basis for many important performance indices of system operation, and hence partially meets criterion 1 and 2 given at the beginning of the section. It is easy to generate and meets criterion 3 well. The identification of an existing system using a step-function input usually is not as satisfactory as applying other signals, and adequate performance for a step-function input does not always mean good performance for other inputs.

The step function is a special case of the polynomial function

$$m(t) = m_0 + m_1 t + m_2 t^2 + \cdots \qquad t \geq 0 \tag{1.6–3}$$

where only the first term is retained. If we use only the second term we get the ramp function, and if we use only the third term we get the parabolic function, and so on. Alternatively, if $m(t)$ is the integral $\int_0^t g(x)\,dx$, then the ramp function is this integral applied to a step $g(x)$, and the parabolic function is this integral applied to a ramp $g(x)$, and so on. Thus the unit ramp function is

$$m(t) = 0 \qquad t < 0 \tag{1.6–4a}$$

$$m(t) = t \qquad t \geq 0 \tag{1.6–4b}$$

and the unit parabolic function is

$$m(t) = 0 \qquad t < 0 \tag{1.6–5a}$$

$$m(t) = \tfrac{1}{2}t^2 \qquad t \geq 0 \tag{1.6–5b}$$

and both are shown in Figure 1.6–2.

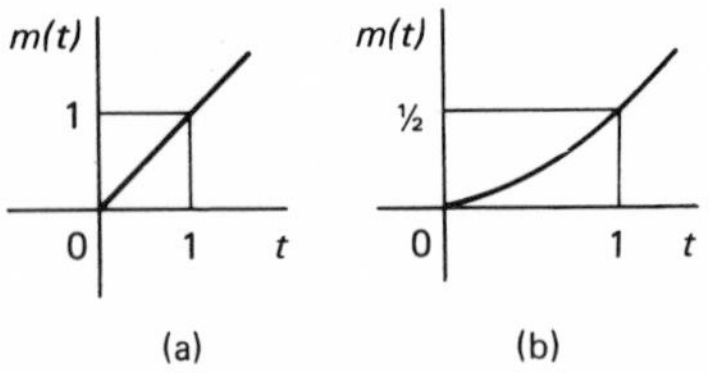

Figure 1.6–2. Ramp function $tu(t)$ and parabolic function $1/2t^2u(t)$.

Ramp and parabolic functions are useful in testing the velocity and acceleration respectively of a positioning system, for example.

Because ramps and other higher-order terms in a polynomial may be obtained by integration of a preceding term, we are tempted to differentiate a unit step function to obtain a new signal, which we term a unit impulse or delta function, $\delta(t)$, and this might be used as a definition of the unit impulse. The unit impulse, however, is well known to be a very tricky function. In fact, it is not a function in the ordinary sense at all, and to understand it thoroughly, one should apply the theory of distributions introduced by Schwartz [9, 10]. Because we do not have the space (and conceivably the patience) to pursue this here, perhaps a reasonable and yet understandable definition for the impulse function consists of the equations

$$\int_{-\infty}^{\infty} \delta(t - t_1) f(t)\, dt = f(t_1) \tag{1.6–6a}$$

$$\delta(t - t_1) = 0 \qquad t \neq t_1 \tag{1.6–6b}$$

$$\delta(t - t_1) = \delta(t_1 - t) \tag{1.6–6c}$$

where $f(t)$ is an arbitrary function, continuous at $t = t_1$. Equations (1.6–6) indicate that $\delta(t - t_1)$, together with the integral, acts such that the value $f(t_1)$ is "sifted out" of the function $f(t)$ by the integration performed on the left of the equation. The delta function is thus better defined by the results it produces than as an entity in itself.

The delta function $\delta(t)$ is a special form of a distribution which may be obtained as a generalized limit of a series of several more ordinary functions.* One that is well known to engineers is

$$f(t) = \lim_{\lambda \to 0} \frac{1}{\lambda}[u(t) - u(t - \lambda)] \tag{1.6–7}$$

where the limit represents the limit of the series of functions represented on the right side of (1.6–7) as λ becomes smaller. This is illustrated in Figure 1.6–3, where we have a step function of value $1/\lambda$ followed by a

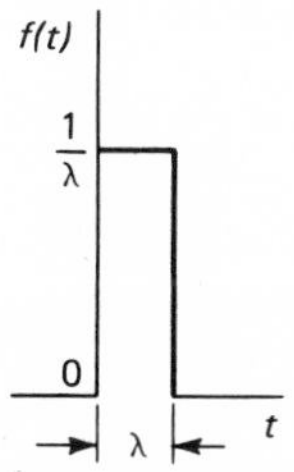

Figure 1.6–3. One possible δ function is a limit of the sequence of $f(t)$'s as $\lambda \to 0$.

negative step of the same value translated in time by λ. The area of the rectangle equals $(1/\lambda)(\lambda)$, or 1. Then (1.6–7) is sometimes described as allowing λ to approach zero in Figure 1.6–3 while the area remains constant. If we follow this to the limit, we have some visualization difficulty, which emphasizes the fact that $\delta(t)$ is not an ordinary function. $\delta(t - t_1)$ is $\delta(t)$ delayed t_1 units in time.

Two other functions that might serve as delta functions are shown in the following two equations:

$$\delta(t) = \lim_{\lambda \to 0} \frac{\epsilon^{-t^2/\lambda}}{\sqrt{\lambda\pi}} \tag{1.6–8}$$

$$\delta(t) = \lim_{\omega \to \infty} \frac{\sin \omega t}{\pi t} \tag{1.6–9}$$

where again both limits are to be taken in the sense of limits of a series of functions [10]. In certain cases, it is also necessary to adopt the definition

$$f(t)\delta(t) = f(0)\delta(t) \tag{1.6–10}$$

if $f(t)$ is continuous at $t = 0$ [11].

* A distribution assigns a number $N[\phi(t)]$ to a test function $\phi(t)$. The test function $\phi(t)$ must meet certain requirements.

If we visualize (1.6–7) as a very sharp long spike as $\lambda \to 0$, then (1.6–6) may become more meaningful. Thus when we plot $\delta(t-t_1)$ in Figure 1.6–4, which is just $\delta(t)$ delayed by time t_1 and consider $\delta(t-t_1)$ as a

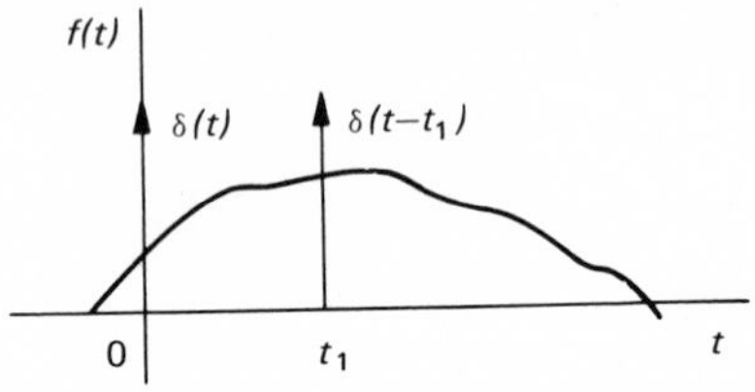

Figure 1.6–4. Sifting property of a δ function.

weighting function for $f(t)$, it is clear from (1.6–6b) that the only value where $f(t)$ is not weighted to zero is at t_1. At this point $f(t)=f(t_1)$, a constant that can be brought outside the integral, and the left side of (1.6–6a) becomes

$$\int_{-\infty}^{\infty} \delta(t-t_1) f(t)\, dt = f(t_1) \int_{-\infty}^{\infty} \delta(t-t_1)\, dt \qquad \textbf{(1.6–11)}$$

The integral on the right side of (1.6–11) is 1 if we meet the definition given by (1.6–6a). Therefore $\int_{-\infty}^{\infty} \delta(t)\, dt = 1$. Further and more rigorous treatment shows that the relation $\delta(t) = du(t)/dt$ is indeed true in the distribution sense.

The delta function $\delta(t)$ and the polynomial functions are extremely useful in theoretical work. For example, the Laplace transforms of the polynomial type functions are

$$\mathscr{L}\tfrac{1}{2}t^2u(t) = \frac{1}{s^3} \qquad \textbf{(1.6–12a)}$$

$$\mathscr{L}\,tu(t) = \frac{1}{s^2} \qquad \textbf{(1.6–12b)}$$

$$\mathscr{L}\,u(t) = \frac{1}{s} \qquad \textbf{(1.6–12c)}$$

$$\mathscr{L}\,\delta(t) = 1 \qquad \textbf{(1.6–12d)}$$

which provide very simple operations in the complex frequency, or s, domain.

In the time domain, if the impulse response is known, the response to most other signals can be found by the superposition integral. Without going into detail here, you can see from Figure 1.6–5 that a reasonably

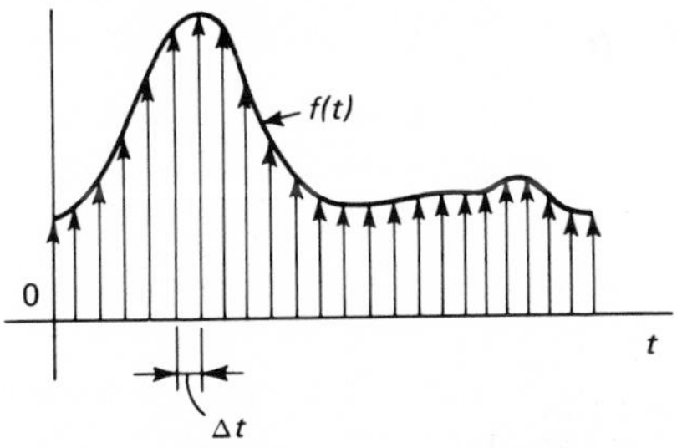

Figure 1.6–5. Approximating an $f(t)$ by means of impulses.

well-behaved signal may be approximated by a series of impulse functions $A\delta(t)$ that may be equally spaced Δt in time and of differing values of A. By reducing Δt, $m(t)$ may be approximated as closely as desired. It seems reasonable, then, that a linear system response due to an input $m(t)$ can be approximated by some sort of summation of the responses due to each impulse, and that in the limit as $\Delta t \to 0$, the response can be represented by an integral.

Thus, if the system is linear, causal, and fixed, one may show rigorously that the following convolution equations hold [12]:*

$$y(t) = \int_0^t h(\lambda)m(t-\lambda)\,d\lambda \qquad \textbf{(1.6–13a)}$$

$$y(t) = \int_0^t m(\lambda)h(t-\lambda)\,d\lambda \qquad \textbf{(1.6–13b)}$$

where $h(t)$ is the impulse response (zero initial conditions) and $y(t)$ is the output due to the system input $m(t)u(t)$. Taking the Laplace transform of either (1.6–13a) or (1.6–13b), convolution goes over into a product in the s domain, or

$$Y(s) = M(s)H(s) \qquad \textbf{(1.6–14)}$$

Hence the ratio of the output to input in the s domain becomes simply

$$\frac{Y(s)}{M(s)} = H(s) \qquad \textbf{(1.6–15)}$$

* The convolution integral is the special case of the superposition integral for fixed systems.

The left side of (1.6–15) is called the transfer function between output and input. Hence the transfer function constitutes an operator S in the s domain that we calculate by finding $h(t)$, or the transform of the response to an impulse occurring at $t = 0$ with zero initial conditions (impulse response). Since $\mathscr{L}\delta(t) = 1$ from (1.6–12d), the transfer function becomes very easy to obtain.

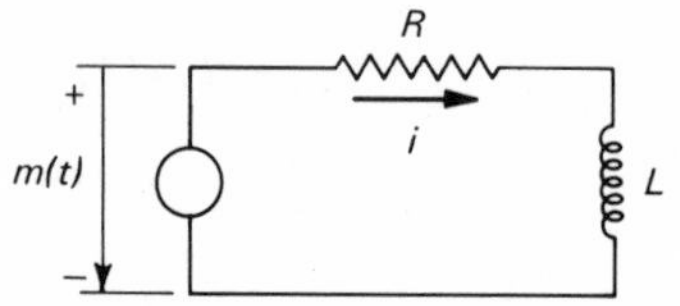

Figure 1.6–6. Figure for Example 1.6–1.

Example 1.6–1

Find the output $i(t)$ in Figure 1.6–6 if $m(t) = 10\epsilon^{-2t}u(t)$ with $i(0_-) = 0$.

Solution: To find the impulse response, let us first find the step response; that is, let $m(t) = u(t)$. The result may be written down from elementary differential equation theory, or

$$i(t) = \frac{1}{R}(1 - \epsilon^{-(R/L)t})u(t)$$

The impulse response for a fixed system is the derivitive of the step response [13]. Hence for an impulse input,

$$i(t) = h(t) = \left(\frac{1}{L}\epsilon^{-(R/L)t}\right)u(t) + \delta(t)\left[\frac{1}{R}(1 - \epsilon^{-(R/L)t})\right]_{t=0}$$

Observe that $i(0_+) = 1/L$, or $i(0_+) \neq 0$. This seems to violate the dictum that flux linkages (iL) must be continuous or cannot change instantaneously, since $i(0_-) = 0$. However, the impulse input implies an instantaneous insertion of energy into the system, which is physically not possible. Thus again we show that $\delta(t)$ is a strange, but useful, theoretical mathematical device. Using (1.6–13a), for $m(t) = 10\epsilon^{-2t}u(t)$,

$$i(t) = \int_0^t \frac{1}{L}\epsilon^{-(R/L)\lambda}(10\epsilon^{-2(t-\lambda)})\,d\lambda$$

$$= \frac{10}{R - 2L}(\epsilon^{-2t} - \epsilon^{-(R/L)t})u(t)$$

The transfer function is

$$H(s) = \mathscr{L}\left[\frac{1}{L}\epsilon^{-(R/L)t}\right] = \frac{1}{L}\frac{1}{(s + R/L)}$$

This may also be found directly from Figure 1.6–6 if one takes the initial condition (zero) to be just after $t = 0$ but just before application of the impulse. Then

$$Y(s) = \frac{10}{s+2}\left[\left(\frac{1}{L}\right)\frac{1}{s+R/L}\right] = \frac{10}{R-2L}\left(\frac{1}{s+2} - \frac{1}{s+R/L}\right)$$

or

$$y(t) = i(t) = \frac{10}{R-2L}(\epsilon^{-2t} - \epsilon^{-(R/L)t})u(t)$$

The example illustrates the occasional difficulty in finding the initial condition, a difficulty that can be detoured by taking the integrals in (1.6–13) from $-\infty$ to ∞, introducing the appropriate step functions in the integral and considering the discontinuity at $t = 0$ [14]. The initial condition taken previously should also be justified to your satisfaction, however, by examining Problem 1.14.

On the question of the generation of an impulse, $\delta(t)$ does not fare so well. Physically, you would require the input of a very large amount of energy in a very short period of time, and in the limit this clearly becomes impossible. However, an impulse $A\delta(t)$ could be approximated by using a rectangular pulse similar to Figure 1.6–3, whose height was $A(1/\lambda)$ and whose width λ was very small compared to all other time constants in the system. This may be very possible in many systems. In an experiment involving inertia, for example, a short, heavy blow from a hammer on a mass much larger than the hammer could approximate an impulse. In an electrical circuit, a pulse having a duration of less than 1/10 the smallest time constant would approximate an impulse.

Last, the exponential function

$$f(t) = A\epsilon^{\gamma t} \tag{1.6–16}$$

is useful, where γ may be a complex quantity. If $\gamma = j\omega$, then

$$f(t) = A\epsilon^{j\omega t}$$

or

$$f(t) = A(\cos \omega t + j \sin \omega t) \tag{1.6–17}$$

If we take the real or imaginary part of (1.6–17), we have back the cosine or sine function, respectively. The sine-wave signal is thus a special case of the exponential. If

$$\gamma = -\sigma + j\omega$$

then

$$f(t) = A\epsilon^{-\sigma t}\epsilon^{j\omega t}$$

or $$f(t) = A\epsilon^{-\sigma t}(\cos \omega t + j \sin \omega t) \qquad \textbf{(1.6–18)}$$

and the real or imaginary parts are damped sinusoids.

The sine wave, impulse, step, ramp, and parabolic functions are the functions most frequently used in deterministic control design. In addition, to check static output, we may also use a very simple unvarying input.

1.7 Why Feedback?

The system of Figure 1.7–1 is clearly a feedback type of system. Systems are classified into feedback and open loop (nonfeedback) systems, as shown previously by several examples. It was also stated that feedback systems might result in better control than nonfeedback systems. In many cases nonfeedback control may be good enough; it will usually be less costly and require less engineering design. Specifically what does feedback

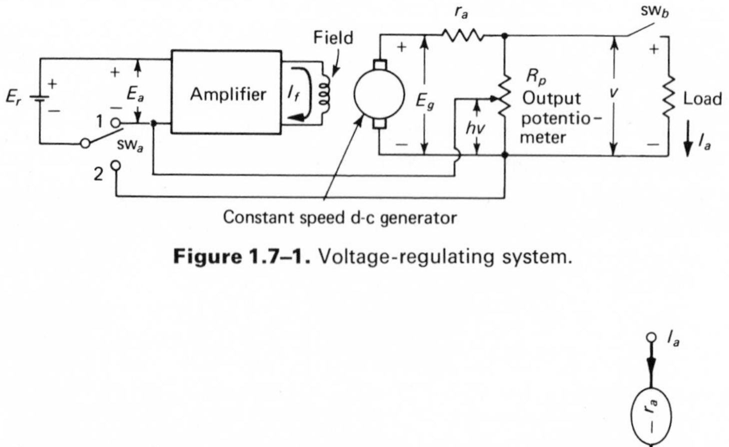

Figure 1.7–1. Voltage-regulating system.

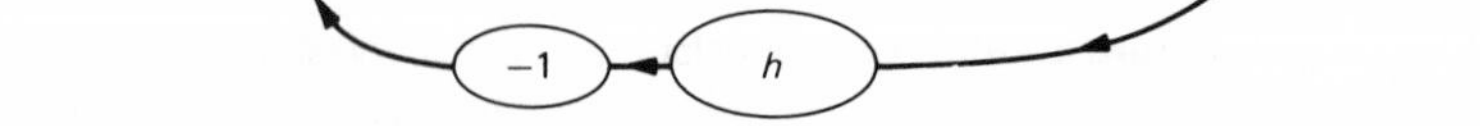

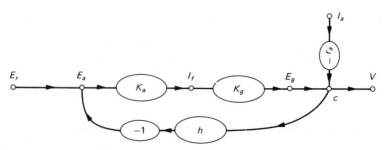

Figure 1.7–2. Flow diagram for Figure 1.7–1.

have to offer? To answer this question, consider the simple voltage regulating system of Figure 1.7–1. With switch sw_a in position 2, the flow diagram can be drawn as in Figure 1.7–2. In Figures 1.7–1 and 1.7–2 the amplifier gain K_a and the generator gain K_g are assumed constant, and the linear output potentiometer is set at some fraction h and draws negligible current.

Then

$$K_a = \frac{I_f}{E_a} \tag{1.7–1}$$

$$K_g = \frac{E_g}{I_f} \tag{1.7–2}$$

$$E_a = E_r - hV \tag{1.7–3}$$

$$V = E_g - I_a r_a \tag{1.7–4}$$

The effect of the drop $I_a r_a$ on the voltage V is most easily shown by a second (disturbance) input at node c. Combining relations in the previous equations we obtain

$$V = (E_r - hV)K_a K_g - I_a r_a \tag{1.7–5}$$

or

$$V = \frac{K_a K_g}{1 + hK_a K_g} E_r - \frac{I_a r_a}{1 + hK_a K_g} \tag{1.7–6}$$

Equation (1.7–6) may be plotted in Figure 1.7–3 to show the variation in V with I_a, E_r constant. The first term on the right side of (1.7–6) represents the effect of the input E_r on V, and the second represents the effect of the input I_a on V. If I_a is zero, then V depends only on h, K_a, and E_r.

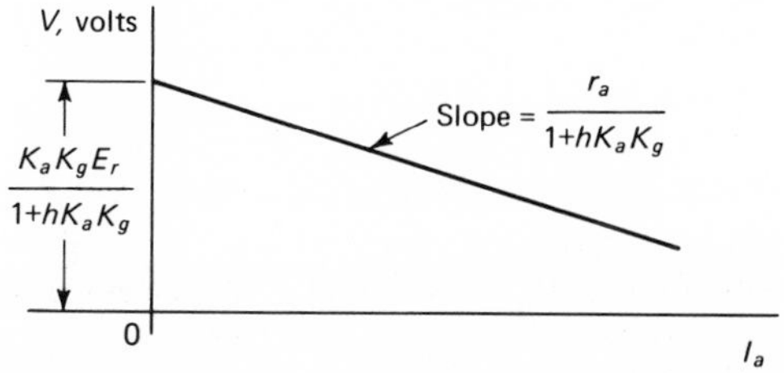

Figure 1.7–3. Variation of output voltage V with I_a.

Example 1.7–1

Let

$$h = \tfrac{1}{4}$$

$$K_a = 4 \text{ amps/volt}$$

$$K_g = 100 \text{ volts/amp}$$

$$V = 400 \text{ volts}$$

Then

$$V = K_a K_g E_a \qquad \text{or} \qquad E_a = 1 \text{ volt}$$

$$E_r = E_a + hV = 1 + 400/4 = 101 \text{ volts}$$

From (1.7–6), the change in V due to I_a is given by

$$\frac{\partial V}{\partial I_a} = \frac{-r_a}{1 + hK_a K_g} \tag{1.7–7}$$

Now let $I_a = 20$ amp and $r_a = 1$ ohm. The change in voltage V as given by (1.7–7) is then

$$\frac{-1}{1 + \frac{1}{4}(400)} = \frac{-1}{101} \text{ volt/amp}$$

or, for 20 amp, -0.198 volt. The reduction in voltage V is therefore 0.198/400, or about 0.05 per cent.

If in Figure 1.7–1, sw_a is put to position 1, then in Figure 1.7–2 the feedback path with $-h$ is open and the result is a nonfeedback system. Equation (1.7–3) no longer holds, and we now get

$$V = K_a K_g E_r - I_a r_a \tag{1.7–8}$$

$$\frac{\partial V}{\partial I_a} = -r_a \tag{1.7–9}$$

For the same no-load output voltage V, either E_r or $K_a K_g$ can be reduced. If $V = 400$ volts with $I_a = 0$ and $E_r = 101$ volts, as previously, $K_a K_g$ can be made 400/101, or a reduction of about 100. From (1.7–9) the change of voltage V is 1 volt/amp, or with the previous load of 20 amp, the percentage reduction in voltage V is 20/400, or 5 per cent. Obviously the feedback system is vastly superior to the open loop system in respect to variations due to disturbances. As discussed previously, if we knew precisely just when these disturbances would occur, and their values, the nonfeedback system would serve nicely, because we could program E_r (or $K_a K_g$) to change accordingly. The point is, however, that we seldom know these factors accurately in advance.

Again look at (1.7–6) and assume that I_a is zero. Then $V/E_r = K_a K_g/(1 + hK_a K_g)$. If $hK_a K_g$ (the open loop function between nodes E_a

and f) is large compared to 1, then $V/E_r \simeq 1/h$, and the voltage V is practically independent of $K_a K_g$. The feedback device h can be constructed of high-quality nonaging elements, because this path normally carries little energy. Hence the elements in the forward transmittance path $K_a K_g$ may vary considerably without affecting V. In the open loop system, however, the output V directly depends on $K_a K_g$, and any change varies V proportionately.

The variation of one quantity when another changes may be called the sensitivity of the first with respect to the second. One quantitative definition of sensitivity is that of Bode [15], as follows:

$$\mathscr{S}^T_\alpha = \frac{d \ln T}{d \ln \alpha}$$

or

$$\mathscr{S}^T_\alpha = \frac{\alpha}{T}\frac{dT}{d\alpha} \tag{1.7–10}$$

Definition (1.7–10) states that the sensitivity $\mathscr{S}$ of some transmittance T with respect to an element α equals the rate of change of T with respect to α (evaluated at the "nominal" value of α), times α/T, where α and T are again the nominal values. The α/T factor puts the evaluation on a per unit basis for α and T. The "nominal" value is the number used in a computation, which may be an average value, an assumed value, or a value at a certain temperature, pressure, or age, and so on.

Applying (1.7–10) to Example 1.7–1 with $T = V/E_r$ and $\alpha = K_a K_g$, from (1.7–6) we find that for $I_a = 0$,

$$\mathscr{S}^{V/E_r}_{K_g K_a} = \frac{(K_g K_a)(1 + hK_g K_a)}{K_g K_a} \frac{1 + hK_a K_g - K_a K_g h}{(1 + hK_a K_g)^2} = \frac{1}{1 + hK_a K_g} \tag{1.7–11}$$

For the nonfeedback case,

$$\mathscr{S}^{V/E_r}_{K_g K_a} = \frac{K_a K_g}{K_a K_g}(1) = 1 \tag{1.7–12}$$

The sensitivity of the closed loop transmittance of (1.7–11) can be made very small compared to the sensitivity of the open loop transmittance of (1.7–12) by making $hK_a K_g$ large. In the previous example,

$$\mathscr{S}^T_{K_g K_a} = \frac{1}{1 + \frac{1}{4}(4)(100)} = \frac{1}{101}$$

in the feedback case but $=1$ in the open loop case. Practically, the feedback system allows very wide changes in K_a and K_g in Figure 1.7–2, or in the forward path gain in general, with only slight changes in the overall system input-output relations. Thus aging of transistors, alteration in motor characteristics, temperature, and other environmental effects will have inconsequential results in a properly designed system.

It is also interesting to investigate the sensitivity with respect to the feedback factor h in Figure 1.7–2. Using (1.7–10) with $a = h$ and following the same procedure as before we get

$$\mathscr{S}_h^{V/E_r} = \frac{1 + hK_a K_g}{-hK_a K_g} \tag{1.7–13}$$

and, using the values of the example,

$$\mathscr{S}_h^{V/E_r} = \frac{-100}{101} = -1$$

or the system is very sensitive to changes in the feedback element. This is not serious, however, as the feedback path carries little power or energy, and the designer may therefore specify precision and nonsensitive elements, or make some special provision, constant temperature say, at relatively low cost. In many cases $h = 1$, so that the feedback path becomes a most insensitive direct connection.

What do we pay for the startling improvements shown by feedback? For one thing, obviously we pay in gain. The feedback system in the example requires a $K_a K_g = 400$, while the nonfeedback system needs a gain of only 400/101, or only about 1/100 as much. Gain, however, is easy and inexpensive to obtain, particularly if the gain is made at low power levels. Thus low-cost electrical, pneumatic, or hydraulic amplifiers with gains in the thousands are commonplace. The situation cannot be this easy, however; you know that rarely does one get something for nothing. The catch lies in the fact that in Figure 1.7–2 we have omitted an important consideration—that the transmittances are not constant but change with frequency. The system gain at high frequencies may render the system inoperable, in that the output will increase and be limited only by the nonlinearity of the elements for large signal flows. This condition is called instability, and design to retain feedback benefits but to prevent instability becomes one of the chief problems of the systems engineer.

The use of feedback also appeals in a philosophical sense to the designer, in that this seems intuitively the best approach. In fact, feedback has become so prevalent that danger lies in losing sight of the possibilities of simpler and less expensive designs using nonfeedback systems.

1.8 Next Steps

Whatever apparatus, devices, or quantities are to be controlled, we are faced with dynamic as well as static operation. That is, transient conditions assume very great importance. It is therefore necessary to attempt to form a model to describe the dynamic operation of the system, and this in turn means the use of differential or difference equations, as discussed in Section 1.3. In general these equations may be obtained in one of two ways: (1) application of known laws to known components, and (2) measurement of dynamic responses.

Although the performance equations for many devices can be predicted from physical laws, in other cases it may be almost impossible to do this. For example, the dynamic characteristics of an airplane or a ship may not be amenable to computation, and the only alternative is measurement. This identification problem may be very difficult in a large multi-input-output system. In case 1, measurement is usually desirable after computation to check the results and to refine the model.

As pointed out in Section 1.3, in a first attempt to solve a controls problem, the differential equations are assumed to be linear, because linear theory is highly developed. Although few devices follow linear laws, it is worth stressing that linear theory directs the design of the majority of controls systems and that these operate remarkably well. If strictly linear theory fails, the next step is to design for piecewise linearity. Finally, nonlinear ideas may be applied. A vast amount of work now goes forward in the nonlinear area, although it is not likely that the design of nonlinear systems will ever be as straightforward as that of linear systems. Finally, as previously indicated, in this book we shall deal primarily with non-time-varying systems. Thus the operators S_n described in Section 1.3 (or the transmittances of the flow graph) will be described by ordinary differential equations with constant coefficients for continuous-time systems.

Systems are characterized by mathematical symbols in two general ways: (1) using functions of time, and (2) using functions of complex frequency. By "complex frequency," as mentioned before, we imply the symbol s as utilized in the Laplace transform (see Appendix A). In other words, we may employ either the time domain or the frequency domain for the mathematical equations necessary for engineering analysis and synthesis. In the time domain the differential equations of the system become the principal tool, while in the frequency domain we apply transfer functions. First, we shall describe briefly the transfer function and then the time-domain approach.

The transfer function expresses the ratio of the input of a system or subsystem to the output in the complex frequency domain with initial conditions taken as zero, as shown in Example 1.6–1. As another example, in Chapter 2 the differential equation for the output angle of a servomechanism such as shown in Figure 1.2–2 will be found to be of the form

$$J\frac{d^2c_M}{dt^2} + F\frac{dc_M}{dt} + K_1c_M = Kr(t) \tag{1.8–1}$$

where J is the equivalent load inertia, F the equivalent friction, K_1 is hK, K is the total amplifier-motor gain, c_M the output shaft angular position, $r(t)$ the input angular position, and h the feedback constant. The Laplace transform replaces dc_M/dt by $sC_M(s)$ and d^2c_M/dt^2 by $s^2C_M(s)$. Thus, taking all initial conditions as zero, we obtain from (1.8–1),

$$(Js^2 + Fs + K_1)C_M(s) = KR(s) \tag{1.8–2}$$

where $C_M(s)$ and $R(s)$ are the Laplace transforms of c_M and r. Then

$$\frac{C_M(s)}{R(s)} = \frac{K}{Js^2 + Fs + K_1} \tag{1.8–3}$$

The right side of (1.8–3) is the transfer function between R and C_M already discussed in Section 1.6. When we set the denominator of (1.8–3) to zero, we obtain the characteristic equation of the system, and the roots of this equation determine much of the system performance. If these roots are complex, s takes on complex values—hence the term "complex frequency." Figure 1.8–1 shows graphically relation (1.8–3) in terms of a

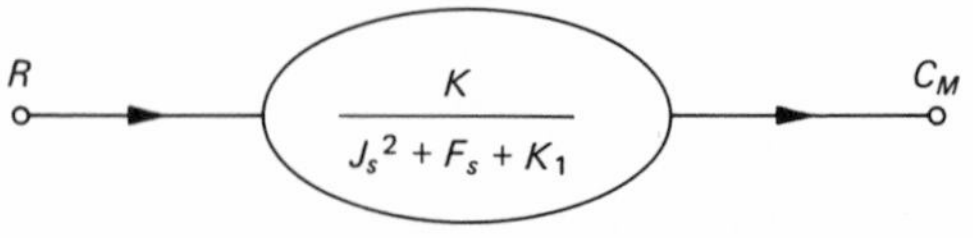

Figure 1.8–1. Flow diagram for Equation (1.8–3).

flow diagram, where $K/(Js^2 + Fs + K_1)$ is the operator transmittance between graph nodes R and C_M. In complex frequency analysis, the operator is therefore the transfer function shown in the block of Figure 1.8–1 or on the right of (1.8–3).

As previously discussed, in a flow diagram a transmittance following (in the direction of the arrow) a node does not affect that node (unless we have a feedback path from the second transmittance). Thus in Figure 1.8–2,

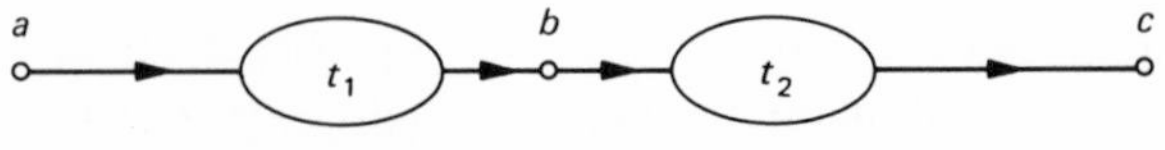

Figure 1.8–2. Two operators in series.

$b = t_1 a$ and $c = t_2 b$, or a is independent of b or c and b is independent of c. Hence we can state that $c = t_1 t_2 a$, or the total transmittance is the product of the serial transmittances. If there is a loading effect of c on b, then the flow diagram of Figure 1.8–2 is not correct, and it is necessary to find $t_1 t_2$ as a whole. Thus in drawing flow diagrams you must choose nodes such that the loading effect can be assumed to be negligible in the problem at hand. This is not a serious matter, as a special unilateral device (for example, a cathode follower) may be inserted, if necessary. At any rate, if the nodes are correctly chosen to fulfill the requirements, it is clear from Figure 1.8–2 that if t_1 and t_2 depict two series transfer function operators, then the overall transfer function is the product of the two transfer functions. Rules involving more complex combinations of transfer functions will be demonstrated later. The point to be made here is that subsystem transfer functions are easily combinable into transfer functions representing larger systems, thus making the assembly of such systems easy to portray in mathematical language. Transfer functions of systems having more than one input and output may be grouped into an array or matrix. Note that the Laplace transform applies only to linear differential equations with either constant or time-varying coefficients. The Z transform similarly applies to linear difference equations. Hence the transfer function cannot be used for nonlinear problems, although some of the nonlinear relations still may be depicted on a flow diagram.

The time-domain approach utilizes the differential or difference equations directly and applies to nonlinear as well as linear situations, although the solution in the former case is much more difficult. The time-domain technique is actually much older than the frequency method but lagged due to the difficulty of solving the equations, or, more precisely, to the difficulty of improving performance by altering the equations. Stimulated by World War II, frequency-domain analysis rapidly evolved, and it is probably safe to say that most control systems are designed by this method and will be for some time. Interest in time-domain analysis now has revived, owing to a number of factors, among them the following:

1. Further investigation of nonlinear problems.
2. An increasing number of multi-input-output problems.
3. Desire to make the performance of the system optimal in some sense.
4. Desire to make design more "scientific" (less subject to engineering intuition).
5. The advent of high-speed large-scale computing equipment, enabling rapid solution of problems and pointing toward computer control.

A majority of the research to advance control application now lies in the time domain, and ability to read the current literature requires a background in this field. On the other hand, we do not throw away the frequency-domain approach, as not only is this method useful in its own right but transfer function ideas assist in time-domain analysis.

In Chapter 2 we shall introduce methods of obtaining the linear constant-coefficient differential equations to be used in either time-domain or frequency-domain analysis for continuous-time systems. Chapter 3 will take up solutions of the second-order system as described by (1.8–1). The second-order system is important not only as an introduction to the general subject, but because a great deal of design is based on an approximation of the actual system to a second-order system, or at least upon assumptions as to how the characteristics of the actual system will differ from those of a second-order system. Chapter 4 will continue the subject of flow diagrams, which will be important in condensing subsystems into larger systems or reducing the number of variables in a system. Chapters 5 and 6 will go into modern methods of attacking system problems and will be largely concerned with time-domain solutions. Chapters 7 and 8 will explore the more conventional methods of the frequency-domain approach; Chapter 7 will discuss the root locus method of analysis, and Chapter 8 will take up the frequency analysis method. In Chapter 9 we will discuss some practical methods for compensation, based on the previous two chapters. Toward the end of the text we shall discuss such topics as optimality and discrete time systems. The control field is so broad that it is of course impossible to cover all aspects of it in one book. If we can introduce you to some of the principles and stimulate you toward further investigation, we shall have achieved our objective.

PROBLEMS

1.1. A motor vehicle has one front wheel and two rear wheels (front view, Figure P1.1). Devise a control system to keep the seat level in this view if

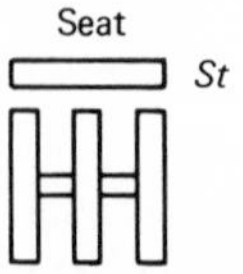

Figure P1.1.

one rear wheel goes over a bump or the vehicle goes around a sharp curve. Indicate your error detector, actuator devices, and so on. Draw a flow diagram.*

* See Y. T. Li, J. L. Meiry, and W. G. Roeseler, An Active Roll Mode Suspension System for Ground Vehicles, Preprints, 1966 Joint Automatic Control Conference, University of Washington, Seattle, pp. 390–399.

1.2. It is desired to control the thickness of steel in a rolling mill. The steel goes through two rollers, one of which may move up or down. Devise a detector system and a control device.

1.3. Devise a system to brake an automobile if it comes within a distance y of another vehicle, y to depend on the speed of approach.

1.4. Design a system to keep a platform level in one direction in a tumbling spacecraft. Discuss how this might be extended to three directions.

1.5. Diagram the relations showing an eight-year-old child desiring to obtain a bicycle from his parents. Show possible feedback paths and controls the child might apply.

1.6. Determine whether the systems described by the following equations are (1) linear or (2) stationary. The input is $m(t)$ and the output is $y(t)$.

(a) $y(t) = 3m(t) + 6\,\dfrac{dm(t)}{dt} + 5\displaystyle\int_{-\infty}^{t} m(\lambda)\,d\lambda.$

(b) $y(t) = 2m(t^2) + t\,\dfrac{d^2m(t)}{dt^2}.$

(c) $y(t) = [m(t)]^2.$

(d) $y(t) = 5 + m(t)\cos\omega t.$

(e) $y(t) = 0,\ t < 6;\ = m(t),\ t \geq 6.$

(f) $\dfrac{d^3y(t)}{dt^3} + 3\,\dfrac{d^2y(t)}{dt} + 6\,\dfrac{dy(t)}{dt} + 8y(t) = m(t).$

(g) $t\,\dfrac{dy(t)}{dt} + y(t) = m(t) + 3\,\dfrac{dm(t)}{dt}.$

1.7. If in Figure P1.7 the output is $y(t)$ and the input is $x(t)$, is the system causal? What if the roles of x and y are interchanged as input-output relations?

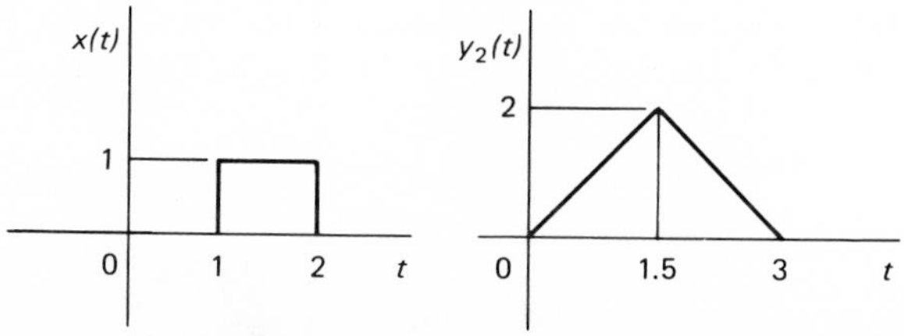

Figure P1.7.

1.8. (a) If two linear stationary systems S_1 and S_2 are in series and give an output $y(t)$ for some input $m(t)$: (1) Is the system linear? (2) Will the same output result is S_1 and S_2 are interchanged?

(b) Repeat (a) if S_1 and S_2 are linear and time-varying.

(c) Repeat (a) if S_1 is linear and S_2 nonlinear, both being stationary.

1.9. Draw a flow diagram for the system shown in Figure 1.7–1.

1.10. Draw flow diagrams for Problems 1.2 and 1.3.

1.11. Find the Fourier series for the half-wave rectifier output shown in Figure P1.11. How many terms should be retained in the series if the root-mean-square value of the series is to be within 2 per cent of the root-mean-square value of the original function?

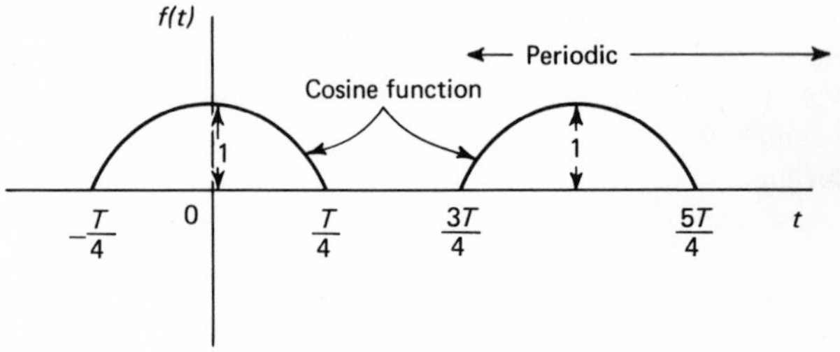

Figure P1.11.

1.12. (a) Find the overall transfer function $E_o(s)/E_i(s)$ for Figure P1.12 in the Laplace s domain, with initial conditions zero.

(b) Compare this transfer function with the product of the transfer functions of circuits (a) and (b) separately.

(c) Indicate the relationship of the component values if, in your opinion, the product (approximate) transfer function (b) is sufficiently close to the exact transfer function (a), and indicate the basis of your judgment.

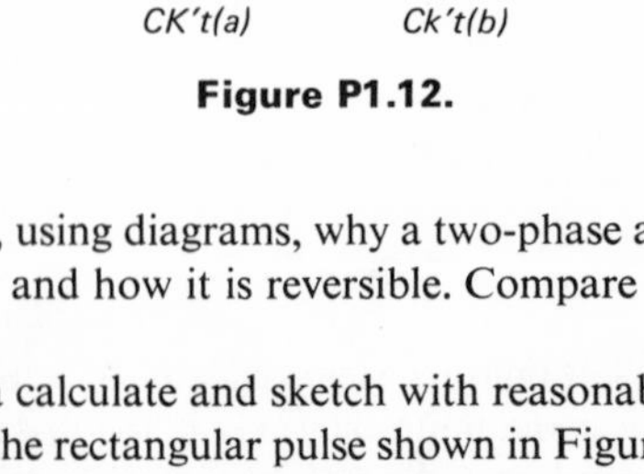

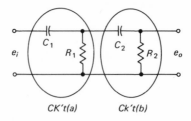

Figure P1.12.

1.13. Discuss in detail, using diagrams, why a two-phase a-c motor has a starting torque, and why and how it is reversible. Compare with a single-phase a-c motor.*

1.14. In Figure P1.14a calculate and sketch with reasonable accuracy the output voltage v_c if e is the rectangular pulse shown in Figure P1.14b. Superimpose on this a sketch of v_c if e is an impulse. Compare the two outputs at $t = 0.1\tau$.

* See, for example, A. E. Fitzgerald and C. Kingsley, *Electric Machinery*, McGraw-Hill, New York, 1952.

(Zero initial conditions exist in each case.) Repeat for a pulse with the same area but height $100/\tau$ and width 0.01τ, except compare outputs at $t = 0.01\tau$.

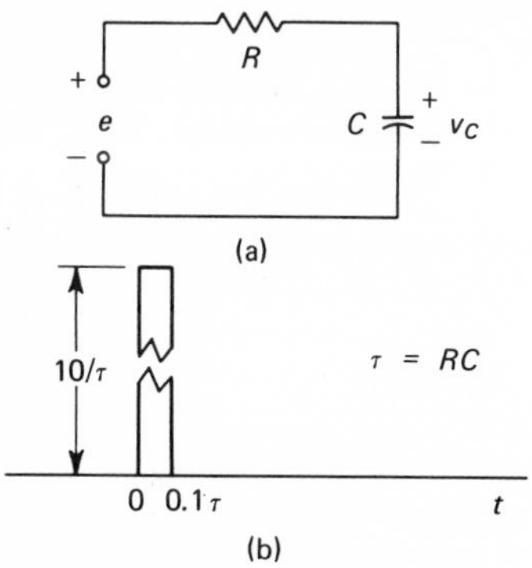

Figure P1.14.

1.15. Show that $f(t) = \int_0^\infty \dot{f}(\lambda) u(t - \lambda)\, d\lambda$ if $f(t) = 0$, $t < 0$.

1.16. Find the impulse response $h(t)$ for the system described by

$$\frac{d^2y}{dt^2} + 3\frac{dy}{dt} + 2y = m(t)$$

[$h(t)$ implies that all initial conditions at $t = 0_-$ are zero.]

1.17. Find the response $y(t)$ in Problem 1.16 if $m(t) = 5\epsilon^{-3t}$: (a) using the results of Problem 1.16 and the convolution integral, and (b) using the Laplace transform method directly.

1.18. Convolution may be performed graphically. For example if Figure P1.18a represents two functions $x(t)$ and $y(t)$ to be convolved, then Figure P1.18b shows that by (a) folding one function about the $f(\tau)$ axis, (b) translating this function forward t units, (c) multiplying the two functions together, and (d) finding the area under the resulting curve, the convolution integral may be evaluated at $\tau = t$. By repeating this for all possible values of t, the output

$$v(t) = x(t)*y(t) = \int_0^t x(t - \tau)y(\tau)\, d\tau = \int_0^t y(t - \tau)x(\tau)\, dt$$

may be evaluated. (From the preceding convolution relations, either function may be folded and translated.) This method is very easy if the functions $x(t)$ and $y(t)$ are simple, and analytic solutions may be obtained

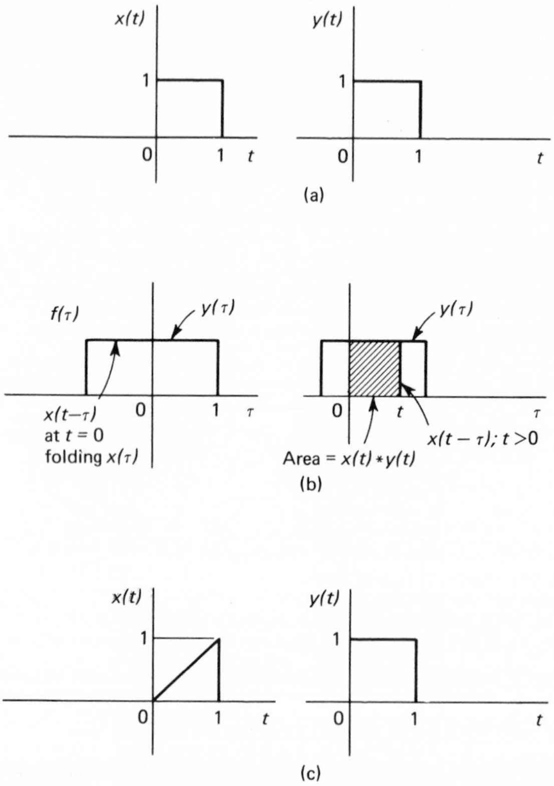

Figure P1.18.

by expressing the area of (d) in terms of t and the other constants. Find $v(t) = x(t)*y(t)$ analytically for the functions of Figure P1.18a and Figure P1.18c, and sketch $v(t)$ in each case.

1.19. For a time-varying system, the impulse response is a function of time, that is, $h = h(t, \tau)$, where τ is the time the impulse is applied. Then the simple convolution integral does not apply. Why? Suggest a substitute integral. How is the Laplace transform affected if the system is time-varying?

1.20. In Figure 1.7–1, let the amplifier gain be 1 amp output (I_f) for 1 volt input (E_a), the generator gain be 50 volts (E_g) for 1 amp I_f. Let $r_a = 1.5$ ohms, $R_p = 10^7$ ohms, and $h = 0.25$. (a) sw$_a$ is at 2 (feedback position) and sw$_b$ is open. (a) If $E_g = 300$ volts, find E_r. (b) With conditions as in (a), find the change in V with sw$_b$ closed, and with a load current $I_a = 30$ amp. (c) If sw$_a$ is at 1 (no feedback), find E_r for $V = 300$ volts, sw$_b$ open, all other conditions as before. (d) With conditions as in (c), find V if sw$_b$ is closed and $I_a = 30$ amp. (e) With conditions as in (d), find E_r to make $V = 300$ volts.

1.21. It is easy to show that in Figure P1.21,

$$T(s) = \frac{Y(s)}{R(s)} = \frac{KG_1(s)}{1 + KG_1(s)H(s)}$$

where $T(s)$ is the overall system transfer function.

(a) Assume that $G_1(s) = K_2$ and $H(s) = K_3$. Find the Bode sensitivity $\mathcal{S}$ of T with respect to K, that is, $\mathcal{S}_K^T$.

(b) If at some other value of s than in (a), if K_2 is reduced by 10 and K_3 reduced by 2, find the new sensitivity $\mathcal{S}_K^T$ in terms of the value found in (a).

(c) Repeat (a) and (b) for $\mathcal{S}_H^T$.

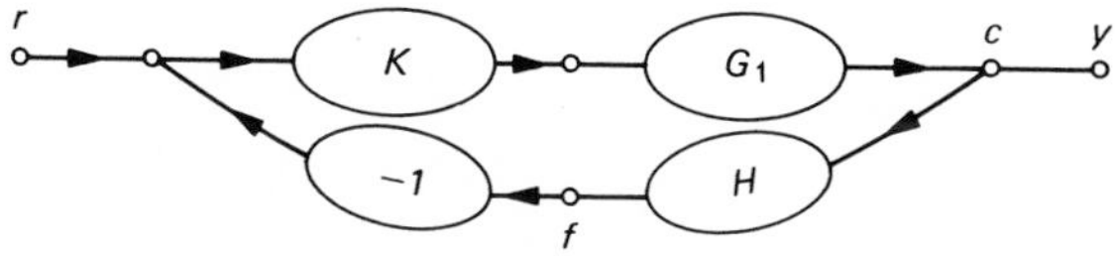

Figure P1.21.

REFERENCES AND FURTHER READING

[1] R. Bellman, Is Science Big Enough to Cope with Society? *Saturday Rev.*, June 5, 1965, pp. 53–44.

[2] H. A. Helm, The Frequency-Response Approach to the Design of a Mechanical Servo, *Trans. ASME*, **76** (1954), 1195–1214.

[3] R. J. Schwarz and Bernard Friedland, *Linear Systems*, McGraw-Hill, New York, 1965, pp. 1–5.

[4] G. M. Kranc and P. E. Sarachik, An Application of Functional Analysis to the Optimal Control Problem, *J. Basic Eng.*, A.S.M.E. **85** (1963), 143–150.

[5] G. C. Newton, Jr., L. A. Gould, and J. K. Kaiser, *Analytical Design of Linear Feedback Controls*, Wiley, New York, 1957, pp. 140–159.

[6] *Ibid.*, pp. 78–85.

[7] V. Del Toro and S. R. Parker, *Principles of Control Systems Engineering*, McGraw-Hill, New York, 1960, pp. 5–8.

[8] H. W. Bode, *Network Analysis and Feedback Amplifier Design*, Van Nostrand, Princeton, N.J., 1945, pp. 44–50.

[9] L. Schwartz, *Theorie des distributions*, Hermann, Paris, 1950–1951.

[10] A. Papoulis, *The Fourier Integral and Its Applications*, McGraw-Hill, New York, 1962, pp. 269–282.

[11] R. J. Schwarz and B. Friedland, *Linear Systems*, McGraw-Hill, New York, 1965, p. 71.

[12] M. F. Gardner and J. L. Barnes, *Transients in Linear Systems*, Wiley, New York, 1942, pp. 228–236.

[13] Reference [3], pp. 79–80.
[14] R. Bracewell, *The Fourier Transform and Its Applications*, McGraw-Hill, New York, 1965.
[15] Reference [8], pp. 52–53.

Some Control Texts (Primarily Conventional Treatment)

Texts marked * contain more advanced material.

[16] I. A. Greenwood, J. V. Holden, and D. MacRae, *Electronic Instruments*, MIT Rad. Lab., Vol. 21, McGraw-Hill, New York, 1947.
[17] M. M. James, N. B. Nichols, and R. S. Philips, *Theory of Servomechanisms*, MIT Rad. Lab. Series, Vol. 25, McGraw-Hill, New York, 1947, and Dover, New York, 1965.
[18] G. S. Brown and D. A. Campbell, *Principles of Servomechanisms*, Wiley, New York, 1948.
[19] W. R. Ahrendt and J. Taplin, *Automatic Feedback Control*, McGraw-Hill, New York, 1951.
[20] F. E. Nixon, *Principles of Automatic Controls*, Prentice-Hall, Englewood Cliffs, N.J., 1953.
[21] G. J. Thaler and R. G. Brown, *Servomechanisms Analysis*, McGraw-Hill, New York, 1953.
[22] J. C. West, *Textbook of Servomechanisms*, Macmillan, New York, 1953.
[23] W. R. Evans, *Control System Dynamics*, McGraw-Hill, New York, 1954.
[24] G. H. Fett, *Feedback Control Systems*, Prentice-Hall, Englewood Cliffs, N.J., 1954.
[25] R. A. Bruns and R. M. Saunders, *Analysis of Feedback Control Systems*, McGraw-Hill, New York, 1955.
[26]* J. G. Truxal, *Automatic Feedback Control System Synthesis*, McGraw-Hill, New York, 1955.
[27] G. J. Murphy, *Basic Automatic Control Theory*, Van Nostrand, Princeton, N.J., 1957.
[28] J. L. Bower and P. M. Schultheiss, *Introduction of the Design of Servomechanisms*, Wiley, New York, 1958.
[29] D. P. Eckman, *Automatic Process Control*, Wiley, New York, 1958.
[30]* E. M. Grabbe, S. Ramo, and D. Wooldridge, *Handbook of Automation, Computation, and Control*, Vol. 1, Wiley, New York, 1958.
[31] P. H. Hammond, *Feedback Theory and Its Applications*, Macmillan, New York, 1958.
[32] C. J. Savant, Jr., *Basic Feedback Control System Design*, McGraw-Hill, New York, 1958.
[33]* O. J. Smith, *Feedback Control Systems*, McGraw-Hill, New York, 1958.
[34] H. Chestnut and R. W. Mayer, *Servomechanisms and Regulating System Design*, Vol. 1, Wiley, New York, 2nd ed., 1959.
[35] V. Del Toro and S. R. Parker, *Principles of Control System Engineering*, McGraw-Hill, New York, 1959.
[36] Gordon Murphy, *Control Engineering*, Van Nostrand, Princeton, N.J., 1959.
[37] J. J. D'Azzo and C. Houpis, *Control System Analysis and Synthesis*, McGraw-Hill, New York, 1960.
[38]* G. J. Thaler and R. G. Brown, *Analysis and Design of Feedback Control Systems*, McGraw-Hill, New York, 2nd ed., 1960.

[39] C. H. Wilts, *Principles of Feedback Control*, Addison-Wesley, Reading, Mass., 1960.
[40] L. D. Harris, *Introduction to Feedback Systems*, Wiley, New York, 1961.
[41]* E. M. Grabbe, S. Ramo, and D. E. Wooldridge, *Handbook of Automation, Computation and Control*, Vols. 2 and 3, Wiley, New York, 1961.
[42] R. N. Clark, *Introduction to Automatic Control Systems*, Wiley, New York, 1962.
[43] Y. H. Ku, *Analysis and Control of Linear Systems*, International Textbook, Scranton, Pa., 1962.
[44] B. C. Kuo, *Automatic Control Systems*, Prentice-Hall, Englewood Cliffs, N.J., 1962.
[45] G. Lago and L. M. Benningfield, *Control System Theory*, Ronald, New York, 1962.
[46] E. C. Barbe, *Linear Control Systems*, International Textbook, Scranton, Pa., 1963.
[47]* I. M. Horowitz, *Synthesis of Feedback Systems*, Academic Press, New York, 1963.
[48] H. L. Harrison and J. G. Bollinger, *Introduction to Automatic Controls*, International Textbook, Scranton, Pa., 1963.
[49] P. S. Buckley, *Techniques of Process Control*, Wiley, New York, 1964.
[50]* J. C. Gille, M. J. Pelegrin, and R. Decauline, *Feedback Control Systems*, McGraw-Hill, New York, 1964.
[51] C. J. Savant, Jr., *Control System Design*, McGraw-Hill, New York, 2nd ed., 1964.
[52] A. W. Langill, Jr., *Automatic Control Systems Engineering*, Vol. 1, Prentice-Hall, Englewood Cliffs, N.J., 1965.
[53]* J. J. D'Azzo and C. H. Houpis, *Feedback Control System Analysis and Synthesis*, McGraw-Hill, New York, 2nd ed., 1966.
[54] R. C. Dorf, *Modern Control Systems*, Addison-Wesley, Reading, Mass., 1967.

2 Equations Describing System Dynamics

2.1 Introduction

By dynamic performance we mean the operation of a system when changing from one state to another, as opposed to steady-state operation. The steady-state performance is of utmost importance, because unless the system produces the proper output under quiescent conditions, it is no good. Often, obtaining satisfactory steady-state conditions raises difficult problems (usually caused by nonlinearities, such as stiction), and some of these problems will be examined in Chapter 9. The dynamic performance, however, causes equally serious problems and forms the basis of complications concerning stability, for example. To study the dynamic performance we need to write the differential equations of motion for the system and to put these in various forms convenient for the desired analysis. Initially, these equations of motion will be considered to be linear, as departures from linearity can best be considered after establishing a good base in linear theory.

In adopting certain equations describing a system, at the same time we form a model of the system. The model selected may depict the system adequately for our purpose. On the other hand, the model may characterize the system only in the grosser aspects, if at all. Proper operation of the physical system depends inherently on the model we select for design, and remodeling may become necessary at times. The linear model, sufficient for many situations, may be almost useless in others.

Because the system engineer deals with a wide variety of devices, it is necessary to understand dynamic equations applying to many fields. System design cuts across all engineering (and other) specialties and tends to unify much of what otherwise may seem disconnected. Exploring dynamic operations in other engineering disciplines does not turn out to be as difficult as you might think, because you will soon see that the differential equations, although varying in detail, are remarkably similar in general form, so that in fact one may often verify dynamical operation in new areas by analogy to familiar situations. Although derivation of dynamic equations by analogy is hazardous, differences in systems often primarily entail nomenclature, terminology, and units. We shall not be able to cover the vast number of possible systems; illustrations of a few, however, should enable you to attack other systems.

We shall aim at systems that are extensively applied in control theory. In many special situations much more sophisticated theory may be necessary, in which case the designer will have to educate himself in the field, or enlist the aid of other experts. In this chapter we shall first deal with simple subsystems, later using an illustration of an assembly of subsystems into an overall system.

2.2 Electrical Systems

Electrical systems often may be approximated by using the lumped, linear, bilateral, elementary models of resistance, inductance, capacitance, and source. Resistance, R, is diagrammed as in Figure 2.2–1, and defined by the associated equation

$$v = iR \tag{2.2–1}$$

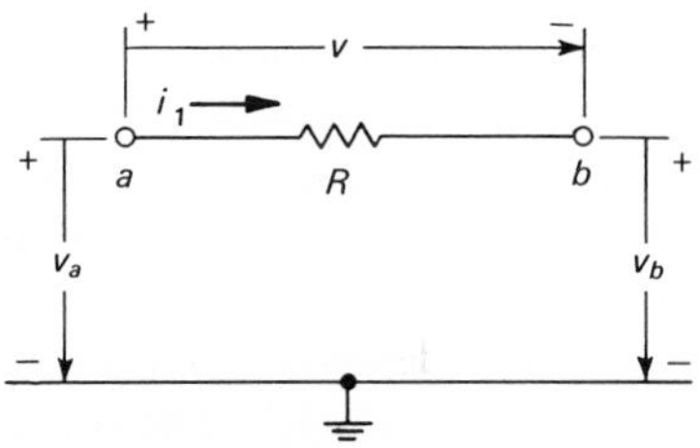

Figure 2.2–1. Resistance.

If v is in units of volts and i in units of amperes, the unit of R is the ohm. On interpreting (2.2–1) it must be related to Figure 2.2–1 in regard to the reference directions of v, voltage, and i, current. That is, what we mean by the symbols v and i in (2.2–1) is shown by the references of

Figure 2.2–1, where the arrow shows the flow direction of i, and the + and − signs and the arrow show the polarity of v. When the element is placed in a circuit containing other elements and sources, the numerical solution for i may result in a negative number. This simply means that positive current flows opposite to our reference direction. From (2.2–1) v would also be a negative quantity in this case. The voltage v is the voltage or potential difference across R or between points a and b, or

$$v = v_a - v_b \tag{2.2–2}$$

where v_a and v_b are voltages with respect to a common reference, say ground (zero potential). The (+) terminal of R is at a higher voltage than the (−) terminal, implying that external energy must be supplied to carry charge from the minus (−) to the plus (+) terminal. As the plus (+) terminal implies a minus (−) terminal, the minus sign could be omitted. Rather than use the (+) and (−) signs, we can use the arrow of Figure 2.2–1, where the direction of the arrow represents a voltage drop, or a voltage reduction in the arrow direction. We shall adopt this convention in this text, possibly adding the (+) and (−) signs at times, although the use of both conventions contains redundant information. As Figure 2.2–1 is purely a convention to enable communication, we could just as well reverse the v arrow direction to indicate the meaning of v in the related equations. If we did so, however, for R positive, (2.2–1) would then become

$$v = -iR \tag{2.2–3}$$

Some texts use a (+) sign alone, some use the arrow alone, and in some the arrow direction represents a rise in voltage and in others a drop. The reader must make clear to himself the meaning of the symbols used.

The voltage v and its defining arrow represents an "across" variable; that is, the potential v exists between or across two points, and the reference potential of b is lower than that of a in Figure 2.2–1. The current i arrow represents a "through" variable; that is, we imagine current as being something that flows *through* the element. The fact that in the case of current, something physical—namely electrons—is thought to flow from a to b has little to do with our definition, which is nothing but a mathematical artifice. The physical flow of electrons (water, air, and so on, in other cases) may reinforce our understanding, however. The designation of through and across variables will be utilized in Chapter 5.

We have dwelt rather lengthily on the subject of references, but unless the symbols in the mathematical equation are referenced on a diagram, or in some other way, you will become hopelessly confused in any complex problem, as will become evident in some of the examples. To reiterate, the reference arrow on the current indicates that we have agreed to call the current positive when it flows in this direction, and this is the meaning of the symbol i in the related equation. A similar statement applies to the arrow for v. Physically, a resistance might be a conductor that impedes the flow of current through it.

Inductance, L, has the defining equation

$$v = L\frac{di}{dt} \tag{2.2–4}$$

where L is in henrys, with v and i as before. Equation (2.2–4) is referenced by Figure 2.2–2, where positive di/dt is in the same direction as i and we omit the terminal letters and the voltages to ground, these being understood. This model approximates a coil through which current flows, setting up a magnetic flux that links with this current.

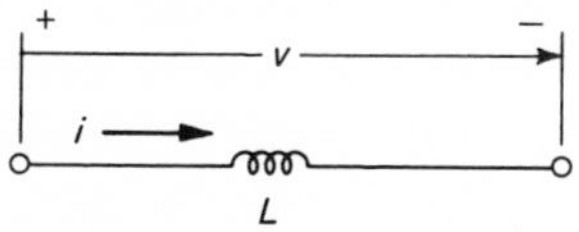

Figure 2.2–2. Inductance.

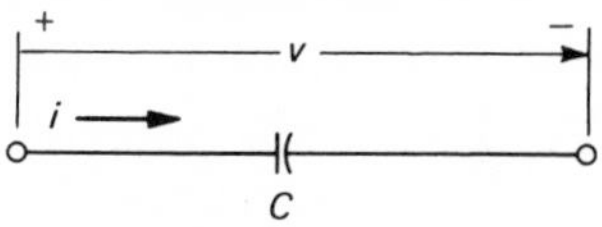

Figure 2.2–3. Capacitance.

Capacitance C is defined and symbolized by (2.2–5) and Figure 2.2–3, where the capacitance is in farads, other units as before:

$$i = C\frac{dv}{dt} \tag{2.2–5}$$

C approximates a charge storage device that physically might consist of two large thin plates seperated by a nonconductor.

A source may be defined as a model of an apparatus producing electrical energy from some energy form. Two sources may be defined, a current source and a voltage source. The current source in Figure 2.2–4 maintains a constant current i_g no matter what is connected to its terminals, while the voltage source in Figure 2.2–5 maintains a constant voltage v_g across

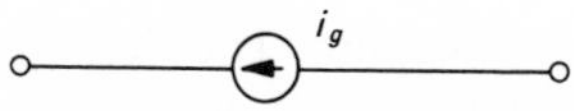

Figure 2.2–4. Current source.

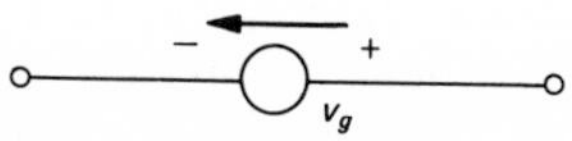

Figure 2.2–5. Voltage source.

its terminals regardless of what devices connect to its terminals. The usual physical source may be more closely approximated by combining the model source and the model resistance R as in Figure 2.2–6. (In some cases a still better model might include L and C.)

Electrical circuit equations are written by using Kirchhoff's laws, which have been found to hold in our situation. The current law states that the summation of currents into a junction is zero, while the voltage law states

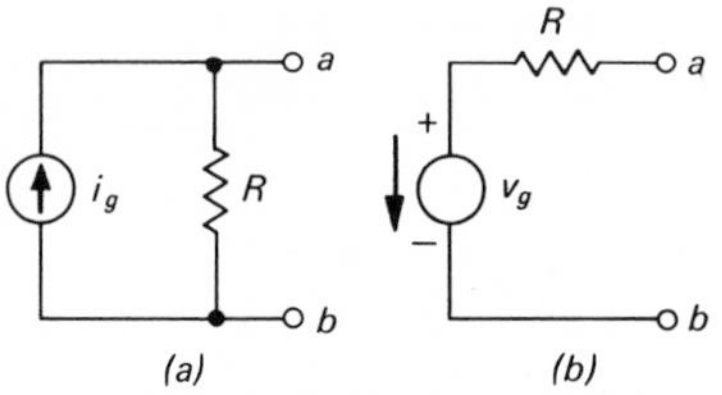

Figure 2.2–6 Practical sources.

that the summation of voltages around a closed path (loop) is zero. A junction (or node) is an intersection of two or more branches, where a branch is an element with two terminals. The current law proceeds from the assumption that positive or negative charge cannot accumulate at a node, and because current is rate of charge flow, obviously charge must flow out of a node as rapidly as it flows in. In Figure 2.2–7 the current law at node a gives

$$i_1 - i_2 - i_3 + i_4 = 0 \tag{2.2–6}$$

where i_2 and i_3 are subtracted, since they flow out of the node. The voltage law is based on the assumption of conservation of energy. As voltage

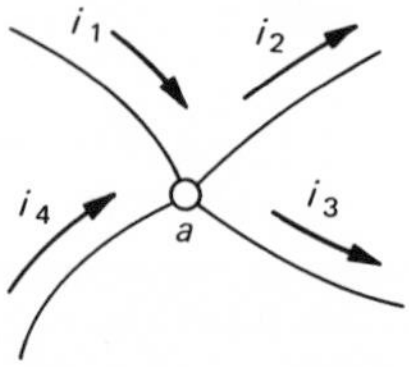

Figure 2.2–7. Currents entering a node.

represents energy per unit charge, the summation of voltages from a point around a loop back to this same point must be zero. The closed loop taken in applying the voltage law may be around a series of branches in the circuit but in some cases may not include a branch. In Figure 2.2–8, proceeding clockwise around loop $abcd$, the voltage law gives the equation

$$-v_g + v_1 + v_2 = 0 \tag{2.2–7a}$$

while proceeding around the loop *abefd* gives

$$-v_g + v_1 + v_3 + v_4 = 0 \qquad \text{(2.2–7b)}$$

Because there is no electrical connection between terminals *e* and *f*, $i_3 = 0$ and $i_1 = i_2$. Hence $v_2 = v_4$.

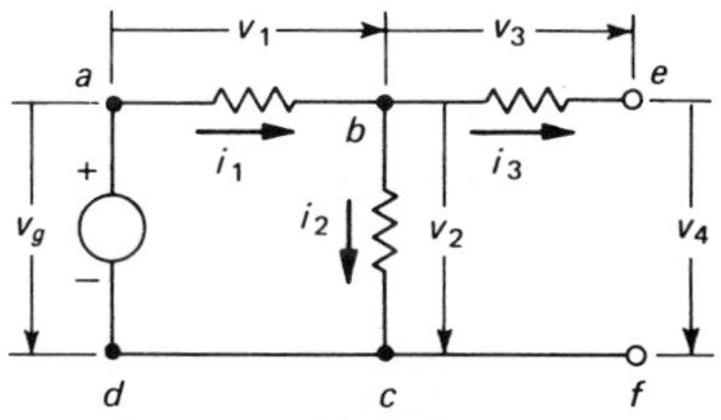

Figure 2.2–8 Electrical circuit.

Using Kirchhoff's laws and the previous definitions, we now show that Figures 2.2–9a and 2.2–9b illustrate equivalent sources with respect to devices connected to terminals *a* and *b*. From Kirchhoff's current law and (2.2–1), Figure 2.2–9a gives

$$i = i_g - \frac{v}{R_1} \qquad \text{(2.2–8a)}$$

or

$$v = R_1 i_g - R_1 i \qquad \text{(2.2–8b)}$$

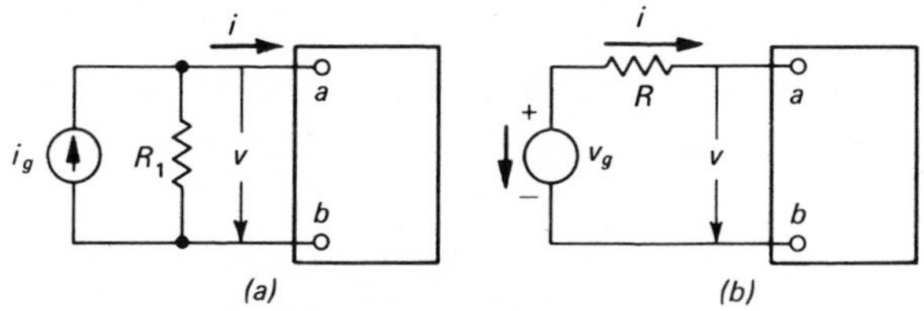

Figure 2.2–9. Equivalent sources.

From Kirchhoff's voltage law and (2.2–1), we get from Figure 2.2–9b,

$$v = v_g - iR \qquad \text{(2.2–9)}$$

For the sources to give the same *v* and *i* at terminals *ab*, we must equate (2.2–8b) to (2.2–9), or

$$v_g - iR = R_1 i_g - R_1 i \qquad \text{(2.2–10a)}$$

$$(v_g - R_1 i_g) + i(R_1 - R) = 0 \qquad \text{(2.2–10b)}$$

If $i \neq 0$, then for (2.2–10b) to be true, $R_1 = R$ and $v_g = i_g R_1$. Hence the sources of Figs. 2.2–9a and 2.2–9b are equivalent if $R_1 = R$ and $v_g = i_g R$, or $i_g = v_g/R$. Substitution of L or C in place of R produces analogous equations but containing derivatives or integrals of i.

We need more elements in our bag of models, and one of these is a mutual inductance M. When two inductances are close to each other, such that the magnetic field of one links the other, if current changes in one, a voltage is produced in the other, and vice versa.

Using Figure 2.2–10, we may define the mutual M by connecting a voltage source through a switch sw to the left terminals and an infinite resistance voltmeter v on the right terminals, as in Figure 2.2–11.

When the switch sw is closed, the current i_1 increases and

$$v_2 = M\frac{di_1}{dt} \tag{2.2–11}$$

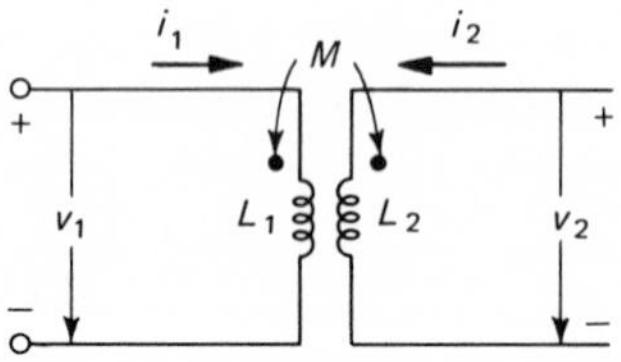

Figure 2.2–10. Mutual inductance.

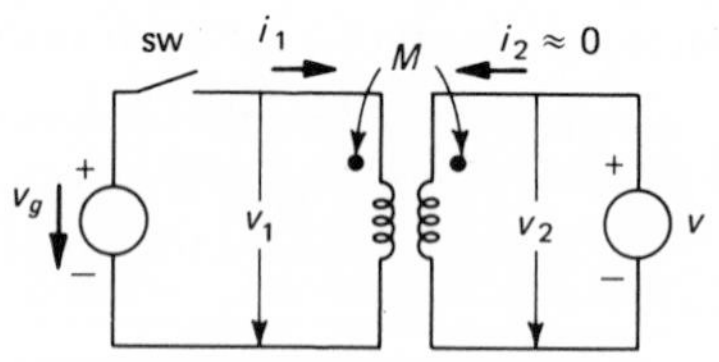

Figure 2.2–11. Mutual polarity.

The dots in Figure 2.2–11 relate to the polarity of the observed voltage v_2 are are shown for the case that the voltmeter deflects upscale. If the voltmeter deflects downscale, the dot on one of the coils should be moved to its lower side. In this latter case (2.2–11) should be written

$$v_2 = -M\frac{di_1}{dt}$$

if the reference direction for v_2 in Figure 2.2–11 is retained. Thus when one dot is positive with respect to the other end of its coil terminal, the other dot is simultaneously positive.

If $M = \sqrt{L_1 L_2}$, then all the magnetic flux linking L_1 also links L_2, or we have perfect coupling. This results in a "perfect" transformer, where

$$\frac{v_2}{v_1} = \sqrt{\frac{L_2}{L_1}}$$

If L_1 and L_2 become very large (approaching infinity), we have the "ideal" transformer of Figure 2.2–12, where

$$v_2 = nv_1 \tag{2.2–12a}$$

$$i_2 = -\frac{i_1}{n} \tag{2.2–12b}$$

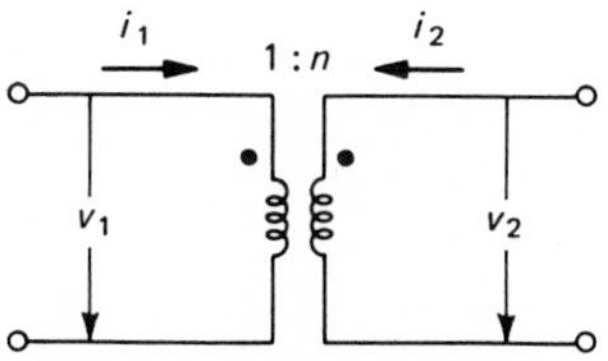

Figure 2.2–12. Transformer.

and where $n = \sqrt{L_2/L_1}$ is the winding ratio of coil 2 to coil 1. The polarity dots show that if an applied voltage v_1 increases, v_2 will increase (no sources applied to the right side). A physical transformer may be represented by the model of Figure 2.2–12 in combination with the previous models. Mutual capacitance (coupling of electrostatic fields) does not exist.

We are now ready to put the elementary models together to form a more complex model—an electric circuit.

In the first example, Figure 2.2–13, the voltage v is across and common to all elements. From Kirchhoff's current law at node 1, with node 2 as reference,

$$i_g = i_C + i_L + i_R \tag{2.2–13}$$

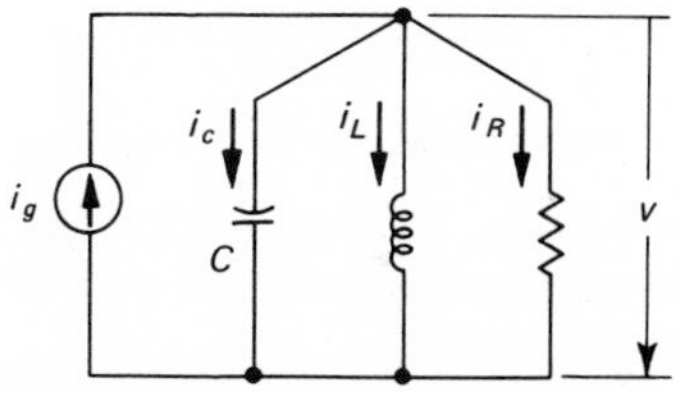

Figure 2.2–13. Electrical system.

From (2.2–1), $i_R = v/R$; from (2.2–5), $i_C = C(dv/dt)$. Rearranging (2.2–4) we obtain

$$v\,dt = L\,di_L$$

and integrating both sides we see that

$$\int di_L = \frac{1}{L}\int v\,dt$$

or, finally,

$$i_L = \frac{1}{L}\int v\,dt \qquad \textbf{(2.2–14)}$$

Relation (2.2–14), with v as the dependent variable, is called the dual of (2.2–4), where i is the dependent variable.

Substitution in (2.2–13) results in

$$i_g = C\frac{dv}{dt} + \frac{v}{R} + \frac{1}{L}\int v\,dt \qquad \textbf{(2.2–15)}$$

Differentiating (2.2–15) with respect to t gives the final differential equation,

$$\frac{di_g}{dt} = C\frac{d^2v}{dt^2} + \frac{1}{R}\frac{dv}{dt} + \frac{1}{L}v \qquad \textbf{(2.2–16)}$$

and if the driving (source) current is zero at all times the result is the homogeneous equation

$$C\frac{d^2v}{dt^2} + \frac{1}{R}\frac{dv}{dt} + \frac{1}{L}v = 0 \qquad \textbf{(2.2–17)}$$

Figure 2.2–14 shows a more complicated circuit.

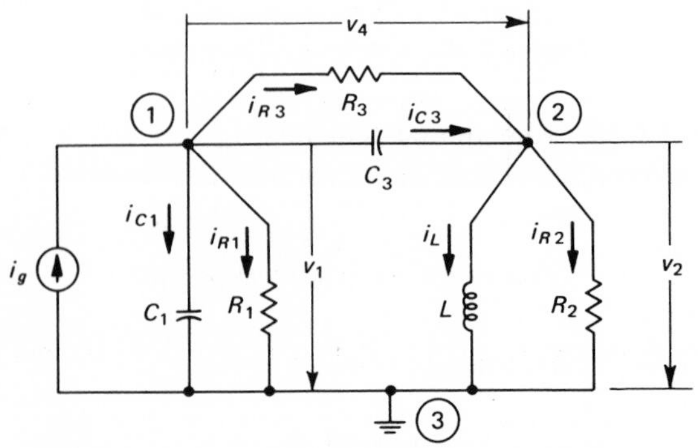

Figure 2.2–14. More complicated electrical system.

Using Kirchhoff's voltage law around loop 1, 2, 3, you will find that

$$v_4 + v_2 - v_1 = 0$$

or

$$v_4 = v_1 - v_2 \tag{2.2–18}$$

Now apply the current law at node 1 and then at node 2 (node 3 is reference). The results are

$$i_g = C_1 \frac{dt}{dv_1} + \frac{v_1}{R_3} + \frac{1}{R_1} v_1 + C_3 \frac{dv_1}{dt} - \frac{v_2}{R_3} - C_3 \frac{dv_2}{dt}$$

$$0 = \frac{1}{L} \int_0^t v_2\, dx + i_L(0) + \frac{v_2}{R_2} + \frac{v_2}{R_3} + C_3 \frac{dv_2}{dt} - \frac{v_1}{R_3} - C_3 \frac{dv_1}{dt}$$

Differentiating and simplifying, we get

$$\frac{di_g}{dt} = (C_1 + C_3) \frac{d^2 v_1}{dt^2} + \left(\frac{1}{R_1} + \frac{1}{R_3}\right) \frac{dv_1}{dt} - C_3 \frac{d^2 v_2}{dt^2} - \frac{1}{R_3} \frac{dt}{dv_2} \tag{2.2–19a}$$

$$0 = -C_3 \frac{d^2 v_1}{dt^2} - \frac{1}{R_3} \frac{dv_1}{dt} + C_3 \frac{d^2 v_2}{dt^2} + \left(\frac{1}{R_2} + \frac{1}{R_3}\right) \frac{dv_2}{dt} + \frac{1}{L} v_2 \tag{2.2–19b}$$

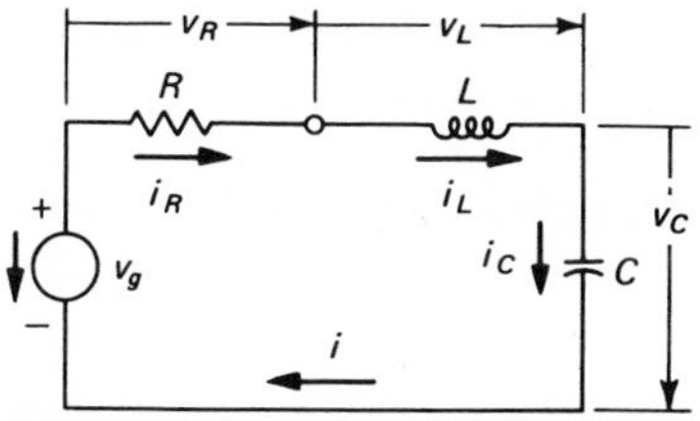

Figure 2.15. Another electrical system.

In Figure 2.2–15, from the current law, $i_R = i_L = i_C = i$; applying the voltage law around the circuit loop produces the equation

$$v_g = v_R + v_L + v_C \tag{2.2–20}$$

From (2.2–1), $v_R = iR$; from (2.2–4), $v_L = L(di/dt)$; and from (2.2–5), $v_C = (1/C) \int i_C\, dt$. Substituting in (2.2–20) gives

$$v_g = iR + L \frac{di}{dt} + \frac{1}{C} \int i\, dt$$

Charge $q = \int i\,dt$, so this takes the form

$$v_g = L\frac{d^2q}{dt^2} + R\frac{dq}{dt} + \frac{q}{C} \tag{2.2–21}$$

Inspection of (2.2–21) reveals a startling similarity to (2.2–16). In (2.2–16) v is the dependent variable, whereas in (2.2–21) q is the dependent variable. The equations are called duals.

Figure 2.2–16 shows a loop circuit with a mutual M. Assume that L_1 and L_2 include the self-inductance of the coupled coils. Proceeding clockwise around each loop, we find

$$\text{Loop 1:}\quad v_g = L_1\frac{di_1}{dt} + R_1 i_1 - M\frac{di_2}{dt} \tag{2.2–22a}$$

$$\text{Loop 2:}\quad 0 = -M\frac{di_1}{dt} + L_2\frac{di_2}{dt} + R_2 i_2 + \frac{1}{C_2}\int i_2\,dt \tag{2.2–22b}$$

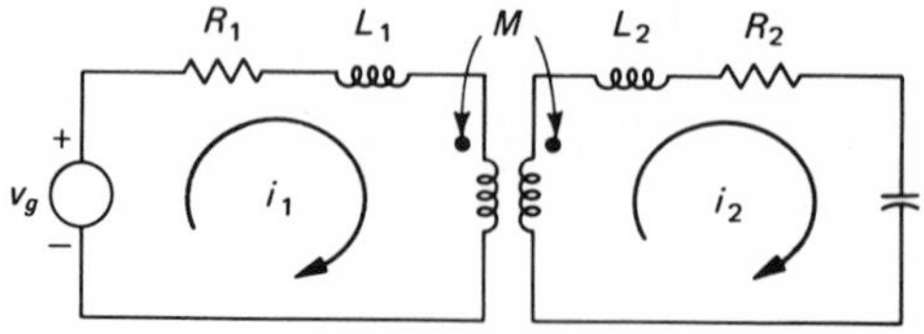

Figure 2.2–16. Electrical system with mutual coupling.

The sign of the mutual voltage drop [last term in (2.2–22a)] can be determined by taking the reference direction of di_2/dt in the same direction as i_2. Then the dot on the right coil is negative with respect to the other end, and, from the dot convention, the dot on the left coil is simultaneously negative for the induced voltage. Adding voltages clockwise around loop 1, the mutual drop becomes negative. The sign in (2.2–22b) may be determined similarly.

If Figure 2.2–16 contains an ideal transformer as shown in Figure 2.2–17, then around loop 2,

$$v_2 = -L_2\frac{di_2}{dt} - R_2 i_2 - \frac{1}{C_2}\int i_2\,dt$$

and around loop 1,

$$v_g = L_1\frac{di_1}{dt} + R_1 i_1 + v_1$$

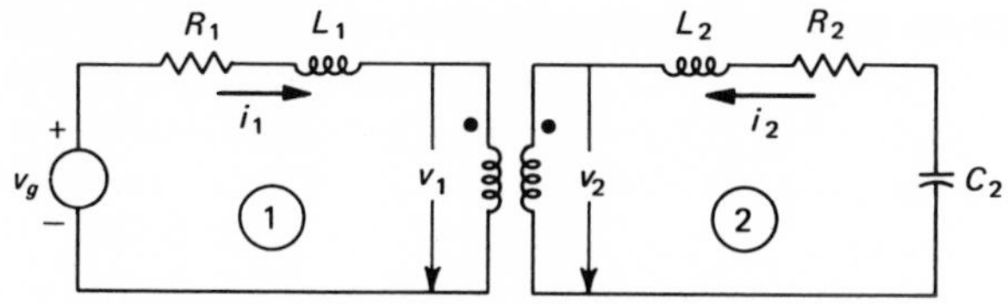

Figure 2.2–17. Electrical system with transformer.

But from (2.2–12), $v_2 = nv_1$ and $i_2 = -i_1/n$. Hence

$$v_g = L_1 \frac{di_1}{dt} + R_1 i_1 + \frac{v_2}{n}$$

$$= L_1 \frac{di_1}{dt} + R_1 i_1 - \left(\frac{L_2}{n}\frac{di_2}{dt} + \frac{R_2}{n} i_2 + \frac{1}{C_2 n}\int i_2\, dt\right)$$

or

$$v_g = \left((L_1 + \frac{L_2}{n^2}\right)\frac{di_1}{dt} + \left(R_1 + \frac{R_2}{n^2}\right) i_1 + \frac{1}{C_2 n^2}\int i_1\, dt \qquad \textbf{(2.2–23)}$$

From (2.2–23) the constants in the second loop have been altered by the transformer ratio squared, or we say that the source v_g "sees" the elements in loop 2 as changed by the factor $1/n^2$. We also often express this effect as "matching" loops 1 and 2.

Another model that we shall use is an amplifier. Figure 2.2–18 shows a quantity entering the amplifier from the left, and another quantity $y = Kx$

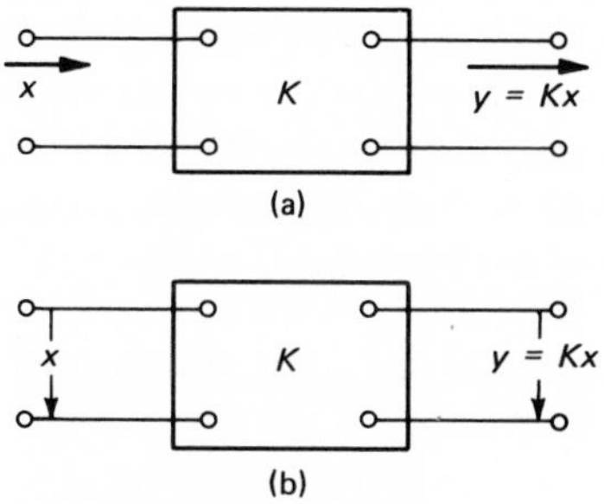

Figure 2.2–18. Amplifiers.

appearing at the output. Figure 2.2–18a shows a current amplifier and Figure 2.2–18b a voltage amplifier. In other situations x may be a current and y a voltage, or vice versa. Thus K contains the units y/x, and may be greater, less, or equal to 1. In still other devices the entering and leaving quantities may be of a completely different nature, such as mechanical-electrical. In some cases energy may be supplied from a source external to the circuit, such that y becomes a larger source of energy than x; or it is closer to the ideal sources of Figures 2.2–4 and 2.2–5. The power or energy amplifier is unilateral, in that x cannot be obtained from y. The amplifier differs from the transformer in that the energy output of the ideal transformer is identical to the input, whereas the amplifier energy output may be greater than the input, the excess being supplied from an external source.

If external energy is not supplied, Figure 2.2–18 can be the model of a transducer, a device that deals with weak signals and transforms one quantity into another, usually with some energy loss. A more realistic description of a transducer will require the addition of some of the other simple models aleady discussed.

The examples make it clear that any complicated electrical circuit can be described by a set of simultaneous differential equations, and that with the model assumptions taken, the equations are linear with constant coefficients (stationary). You choose the dependent variable such that the equations may be written easily. The substitution of an equivalent source or use of a transformer relation often assists in simplification. Very much the same procedure will now be used for other types of systems.

2.3 Mechanical Systems

After spending considerable time on electrical systems, we now hope to use these concepts to shorten our study of other systems. Mechanical systems may be divided into two categories: translational and rotational. Consider first the translational system of Figure 2.3–1. Here a force $f_g(t)$ accelerates a mass M and is opposed by a spring and a viscous friction force f_B. Positive displacement x and velocity $v = dx/dt$ are to the right. Following the electrical prelude, we set up symbols for the mass, spring, and viscous friction as in Figure 2.3–2, defined as follows:

(a) $$f_M = M\frac{dv}{dt} \qquad \textbf{(2.3–1a)}$$

(b) $$v = \frac{1}{K}\frac{df_s}{dt} \qquad \textbf{(2.3–1b)}$$

(c) $${}_{B} = Bv \qquad \textbf{(2.3–1c)}$$

(d) force source

(e) velocity source

where f is the force in newtons, M the constant mass in kilograms, v the velocity in meters per second, K the compliance (spring constant) in

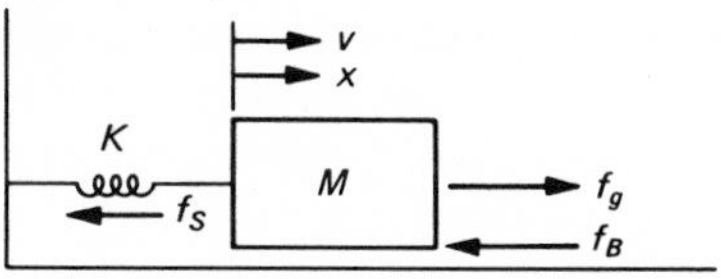

Figure 2.3–1. Mechanical system (translational).

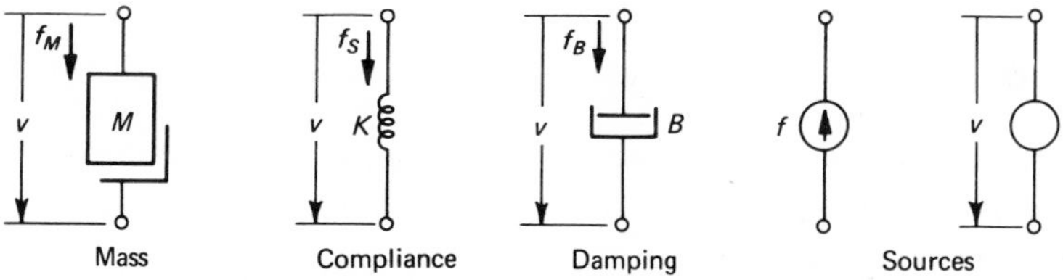

Figure 2.3–2. Translational mechanical symbols.

newtons per kilogram, and B the damping (viscous friction constant) in kilograms per meter per second. Physically, the viscous friction B could be a piston moving in a fluid-containing cylinder, with provision for adjustable leakage of the fluid through an orifice in the piston. Equation (2.3–1a) represents one of Newton's laws of motion, which in the more general form is $f_M = d(Mv)/dt$. In these mechanical systems, v is the across variable and f the through variable, corresponding to v and i for the electrical systems.

From Figure 2.3–1 we construct the related diagram by the following rules:

1. Find the terminals of each element.
2. Connect at a common node those terminals that move together.
3. Connect to a reference node terminals that remain stationary.
4. Connect the source with the direction of force or polarity of velocity indicated.
5. Write the equations of motion using D'Alambert's principle, which states that the summation of forces leaving a node must be zero. [The force producing mass acceleration, given by (2.3–1a), is included.]

Following these rules with Figure 2.3–1, Figure 2.3–3 is obtained. The source (forcing function) f_g is drawn in the direction shown because the reference for v in Figure 2.3–1 indicates that increasing f increases v. Integrating (2.3–1) we get for the spring

$$f_s = K \int v \, dt = Kx$$

Then following D'Alambert's principle we obtain

$$M\frac{d^2x}{dt^2} + B\frac{dx}{dt} + Kx = f_g \tag{2.3–2}$$

where x is displacement measured from a reference position.

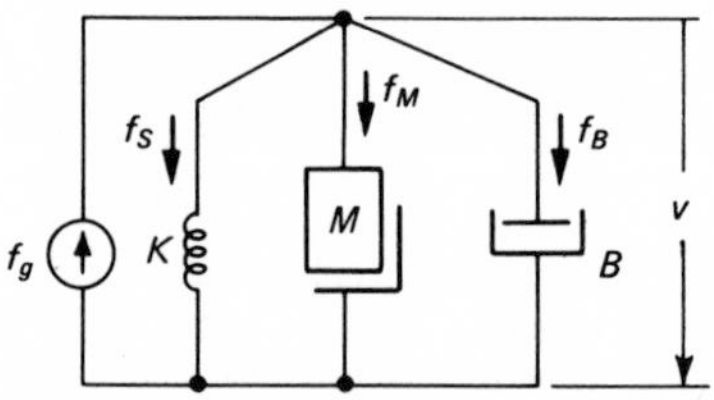

Figure 2.3–3. Equivalent diagram for Figure 2.3–1.

The system of Figure 2.3–4 gives the diagram of Figure 2.3–5, from which you can write (node 3 as reference)

$$\text{Node 1:}\quad M_1\frac{dv_1}{dt} + B_1v_1 + \int K_1v_1\,dt - B_2(v_2 - v_1) - K_2\int(v_2 - v_1)\,dt = 0$$

$$\text{Node 2:}\quad -K_2\int(v_1 - v_2)\,dt - B_2(v_1 - v_2) + M_2\frac{dv_2}{dt} = f_g$$

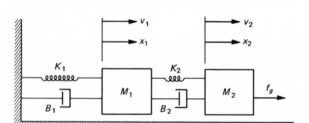

Figure 2.3–4. Two-mass system.

Putting the velocities in terms of distance x, and collecting like quantities we obtain

$$M_1\frac{d^2x_1}{dt^2} + (B_1 + B_2)\frac{dx_1}{dt} + (K_1 + K_2)x_1 - B_2\frac{dx_2}{dt} - K_2x_2 = 0 \tag{2.3–3a}$$

$$-B_2\frac{dx_1}{dt} - K_2x_1 + M_2\frac{d^2x_2}{dt^2} + B_2\frac{dx_2}{dt} + K_2x_2 = f_g \tag{2.3–3b}$$

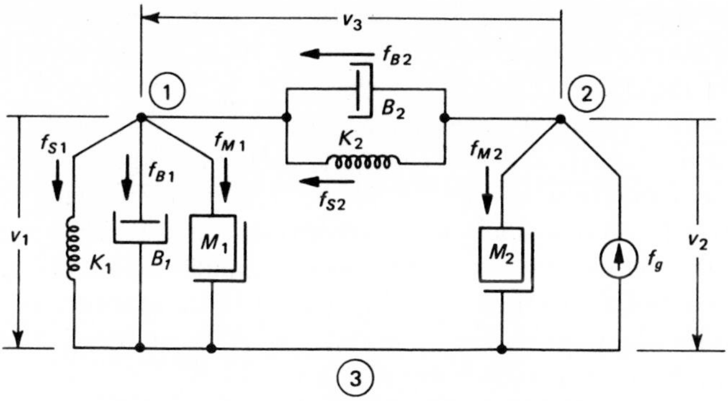

Figure 2.3–5. Force-velocity diagram for Figure 2.3–4.

The similarity of these to (2.2–19a) and (2.2–19b) is obvious. The analog of the loop equation also exists in the mechanical realm. In this case the summation of the velocities around a closed loop must equal zero.

The mechanical transformer consists of a lever as in Figure 2.3–6 and can be symbolized as in Figure 2.3–7. Here

$$v_2 = v_1 n$$

$$f_2 = -\frac{f_1}{n}$$

where $n = b/a$. The arrows in Figure 2.3–6 indicate the positive reference directions for (f_1, v_1) and (f_2, v_2).

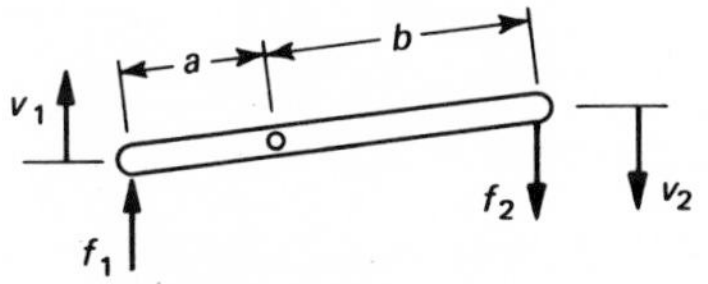

Figure 2.3–6. Lever.

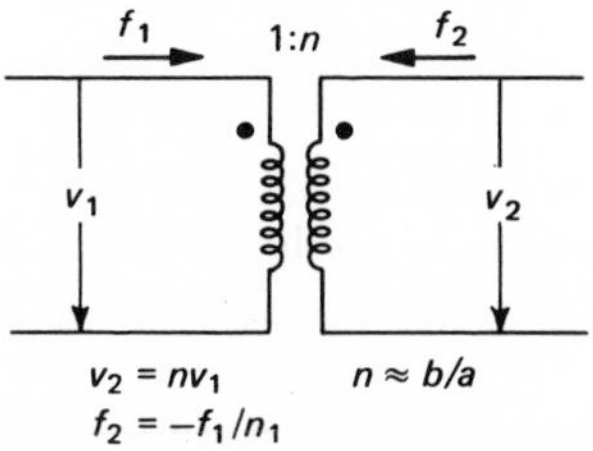

Figure 2.3–7. Diagram for Figure 2.3–6.

The models of a spring and transformer in the mechanical system represent physical components more closely than do the corresponding models in the electrical system.

Rotational systems proceed on a very similar basis, with torque τ analogous to force f; angular velocity $\omega = d\theta/dt$ analogous to velocity v, and inertia J analogous to mass M, where θ represents an angle. Torque τ is the through variable and angular velocity ω comprises the across variable. Spring and viscous frictional torques are similar to the corresponding forces in translational motion. The rotational transformer, of course, consists of a gear train. Consequently we can set up symbols for rotational elements rather easily, as in Figure 2.3–8.

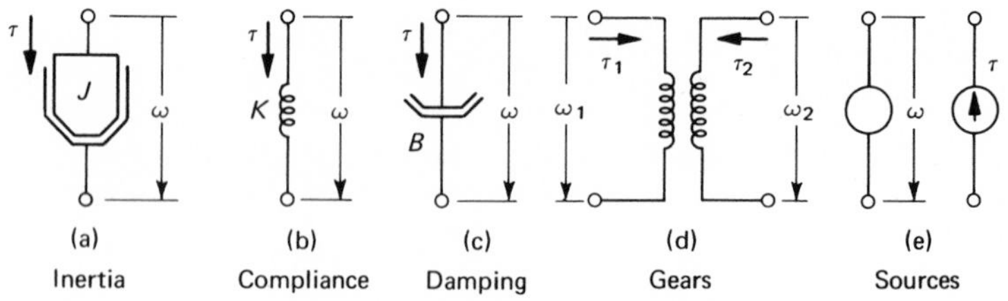

Figure 2.3–8. Rotational symbols.

The defining equations are:

(a) $$\tau = J\frac{d\omega}{dt} \tag{2.3–4a}$$

(b) $$\omega = \frac{1}{K}\frac{d\tau}{dt} \tag{2.3–4b}$$

(c) $$\tau = B\omega \tag{2.3–4c}$$

(d) $$\omega_2 = n\omega_1 \tag{2.3–4d}$$

(e) $$\tau_2 = -\frac{\tau_1}{n} \tag{2.3–4e}$$

(f) angular velocity source

(g) torque source

where τ is in newton-meters, J in kilogram-meters^2, K in newton-meters per radian, B in newton-meter-seconds, ω in radians per second, and n is the gear ratio, with $n = n_1/n_2$, where n_1 and n_2 are the number of teeth on gear 1 and gear 2, respectively. In a train of gears, an odd number of gears leads to an output angular velocity in the same direction as the input angular velocity, and an even number of gears leads to an opposite output angular velocity. We shall assume an odd number of gears or else reference the angular velocities to directions on a schematic diagram showing angular directions.

Physically the damping B might consist of a paddle wheel rotating in a fluid-filled cylinder, and K could be the spring force per radian in a twisted shaft. Usually mechanical shafts have such a large stiffness that this element may be neglected, just as you may neglect inductance in many electrical circuits. However, very large inertias may require a prohibitively heavy shaft to prevent twisting, in which case K must be considered. A gear train is an almost perfect transformer, but since the gears cannot mesh exactly, the teeth do not contact for a brief period when the gear reverses. This is called "backlash" and is one of the more obnoxious nonlinearities.

As an example of a rotational system, consider the inertia J_3 of Figure 2.3–9 driven through a gear train utilizing an even number of gears by a d-c motor, with a shaft spring and viscous friction both present. The positive directions of ω_2 and ω_3 are considered to be opposite to ω_1, as shown in Figure 2.3–9. The developed torque of a d-c motor in the linear region is given by

$$\tau_d = K_\tau \phi i_a \tag{2.3–5}$$

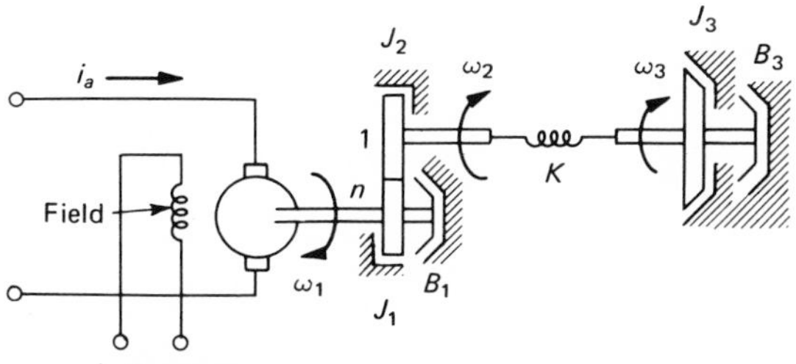

Figure 2.3–9. Electromechanical system.

where K_τ is a constant for a given motor, depending on the physical construction (number of poles, number of conductors, diameter, and so on), ϕ the magnetic flux per pole, and i_a the armature current. If i_f, the field current, is constant, then ϕ is approximately constant, and

$$\tau_d = K_1 i_a \tag{2.3–6}$$

where $K_1 = K_\tau \phi$. Actually the flux ϕ is influenced by armature reaction, and saturation occurs with large i_a, leading to a decrease of ϕ. This means nonlinear operation, which we neglect here. Taking the linear model the armature current and torque are related by the constant K_1, and this can be represented by an amplifier, as in Figure 2.3–10.

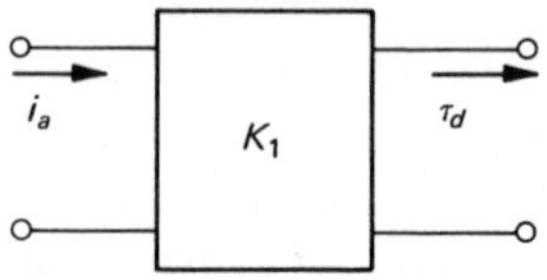

Figure 2.3–10. Linear model for motor.

The mechanical system with the source τ_d can be drawn as in Figure 2.3–11, where B_1 includes the viscous friction of the motor. Using D'Alambert's principle, the following equations can be written (with node 4 as the reference node):

$$\text{Node 1:}\quad J_1 \frac{d\omega_1}{dt} + B_1\omega_1 + \tau_3 = \tau_d \tag{2.3–7}$$

$$\text{Node 2:}\quad J_2 \frac{d\omega_2}{dt} + \tau_4 + K\int \omega_2\,dt - K\int \omega_3\,dt = 0 \tag{2.3–8}$$

$$\text{Node 3:}\quad J_3 \frac{d\omega_3}{dt} + K\int \omega_3\,dt - K\int \omega_2\,dt + B_3\,\omega_3 = 0 \tag{2.3–9}$$

$$\omega_2 = n\omega_1 \tag{2.3–10a}$$

$$\tau_4 = -\frac{\tau_3}{n} \tag{2.3–10b}$$

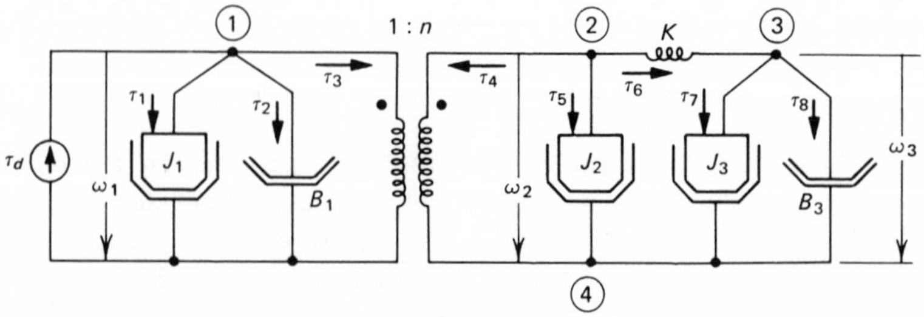

Figure 2.3–11. Symbolic representation of Figure 2.3–9.

With these five equations you can find the five unknowns. Considerable simplification results if we "refer" all quantities either to the motor shaft (node 1) or to the load shaft (node 3); that is, if the transformer (gear ratio) is eliminated. Multiply (2.3–8) by n and use (2.3–10b) to obtain

$$nJ_2 \frac{d\omega_2}{dt} + nK \int \omega_2 \, dt - nK \int \omega_3 \, dt = \tau_3 \tag{2.3–11}$$

Now let $\omega_3 = n\omega_3'$ and use (2.3–10a). The result is

$$n^2 J_2 \frac{d\omega_1}{dt} + n^2 K \int \omega_1 \, dt - n^2 K \int \omega_3' \, dt = \tau_3 \tag{2.3–12}$$

Similarly, multiply (2.3–9) by n and let $\omega_3 = n\omega_3'$ to get

$$n^2 J_3 \frac{d\omega_3'}{dt} + n^2 K \int \omega_3' \, dt - n^2 K \int \omega_1 \, dt + n^2 B_3 \omega_3' = 0 \tag{2.3–13}$$

Finally, combining (2.3–7) and (2.3–12) and differentiating the result (together with (2.3–13), with respect to time, we find that two equations replace the previous five:

$$(J_1 + n^2 J_2) \frac{d^2\theta_1}{dt^2} + B_1 \frac{d\theta_1}{dt} + n^2 K \theta_1 - n^2 K \theta_3' = \tau_d \tag{2.3–14}$$

$$-n^2 K \theta_1 + n^2 J_3 \frac{d^2\theta_3'}{dt^2} + n^2 B_3 \frac{d\theta_3'}{dt} + n^2 K \theta_3' = 0 \tag{2.3–15}$$

where $\theta_3 = n\theta_3'$.

In (2.3–14) and (2.3–15) all quantities are in terms of the motor shaft. We say that conditions have been referred to (or seen from) the motor. This is similar to the use of the transformer in the electrical case, where the impedances may be referred to either the source side or the load side of the transformer. Evidently to refer inertia, viscous friction, or spring constants from the load side of the gear train to the motor side, we multiply by n^2, where n = load speed/motor speed. Then the equivalent values from the viewpoint of the motor become $(J_M + n^2 J_L)$, $(B_M + n^2 B_L)$, and $(K_M + n^2 K_L)$, where the subscripts M and L refer to the motor and the load, respectively. Alternatively, all quantities could be referred to the load shaft. Table 2.3–1 summarizes these results.

After the solution of (2.3–14) and (2.3–15), the actual values of ω_3 and θ_3 are easily found by the relations $\omega_3 = n\omega_3'$ and $\theta_3 = n\theta_3'$. Usually n is a small number, as it is more practical and economical to construct a small, light, fast motor and to "match" its torque to that of the load inertia by means of a gear train. If the gear-train inertia, friction, and shaft spring are neglected, it is easy to show that maximum acceleration of the load inertia may be obtained by making $n^2 = J_M/J_L$. Similar situations occur in many mechanical devices such as the automobile.

Other mechanical devices analogous to electrical elements, such as mutual mass or inertia and amplifiers, also exist, but not being prevalent, are omitted here.

TABLE 2.3–1

Quantity	Equivalent Quantity Referred to Motor Shaft	Equivalent Quantity Referred to Load Shaft	
Inertia	$J_M + n^2 J_L$	$\frac{J_M}{n^2} + J_L$	
Viscous friction	$B_M + n^2 B_L$	$\frac{B_M}{n^2} + B_L$	$n = \frac{\text{load speed}}{\text{motor speed}}$
Spring constant	$K_M + n^2 L_L$	$\frac{K_M}{n^2} + K_L$	$= \frac{\text{motor gear teeth}}{\text{load gear teeth}}$
Torque	$\tau_M = n\tau_L$	$\tau_L = \frac{\tau_M}{n}$	
Angular velocity	$\omega_M = \frac{\omega_L}{n}$	$\omega_L = n\omega_M$	

2.4 Fluid Systems

Fluid systems may be divided into two types: hydraulic and pneumatic. Normally the hydraulic system uses oil or a noninflammable liquid similar to oil, whereas the usual pneumatic system operates with compressed air. In each case we may set up system models analogous to those discussed in the electrical and mechanical cases. As usual, these models correspond

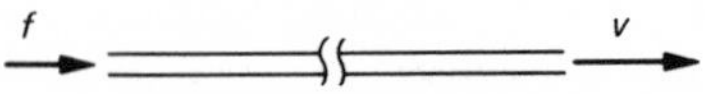

Figure 2.4–1. Fluid line.

to only a first approximation of physical devices. A liquid system contains the effects of turbulent flow, compressability, leakage, and so on, all of which lead to nonlinear operation. In addition, we have a phenomenon not discussed in the previous systems, which is called transport lag or delay time. In Figure 2.4–1 if we have a long pipe full of fluid with a piston on the left end, and push suddenly on the piston with a force f, the response on the right end will not be observed until some time later. Delay times also exist in electrical and mechanical systems, but in these cases the velocity of transmission is so fast that these times can be neglected, while in the fluid systems this may not be the case. It is possible to find equations for fluid devices that are valid in limited operating regions; that is, the device is piecewise-linearized. There are also techniques for considering delay time, as you will see later.

The hydraulic system has the advantage that hydraulic pistons or motors have very large force (or torque) to weight (or size) ratios compared to electrical motors, while the pneumatic system has the advantage that gas transmission lines are easily installed and pneumatic devices are simple and inexpensive. Low-power high-gain fluid amplifiers offer promise in that they require little maintenance and are unaffected by radiation.

Figure 2.4–2 shows the hydraulic symbols, which are defined by

(a) $$Q = C\frac{dh}{dt} \qquad \textbf{(2.4–1a)}$$

(b) $$h = RQ \qquad \textbf{(2.4–1b)}$$

(c) $$h = L\frac{dQ}{dt} \qquad \textbf{(2.4–1c)}$$

(d) $$h_2 = nh_1 \qquad \textbf{(2.4–1d)}$$

(e) $$Q_2 = -\frac{Q_1}{n} \qquad \textbf{(2.4–1e)}$$

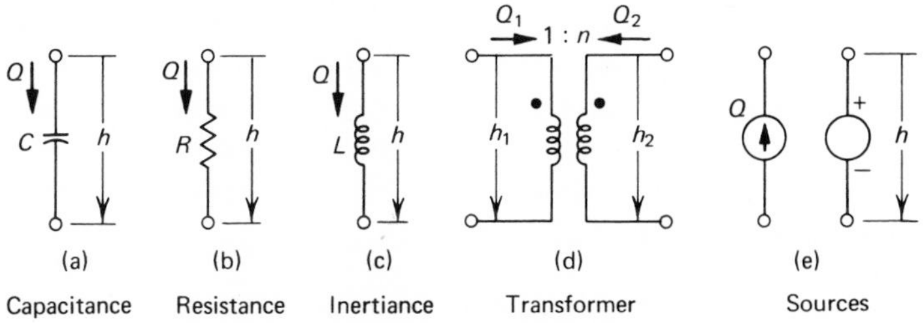

Figure 2.4–2. Hydraulic symbols.

where Q is the quantity of fluid in cubic meters per second, h the head in meter-newtons/kilogram, C the capacitance, R the resistance, L the inertiance in consistent units, Q the through variable, and h the across variable. Physically, the sources consist of a constant volume pump or a constant pressure pump, while the transformer might be a device similar to a hydraulic jack, with n the ratio of the piston areas.

The pneumatic symbols and defining equations are (see Figure 2.4–3)

(a) $$w = C\frac{dp}{dt} \tag{2.4–2a}$$

(b) $$p = Rw \tag{2.4–2b}$$

(c) $$p = L\frac{dw}{dt} \tag{2.4–2c}$$

(d) $$p_2 = np_1 \tag{2.4–2d}$$

(e) $$w_2 = -\frac{w_1}{n} \tag{2.4–2e}$$

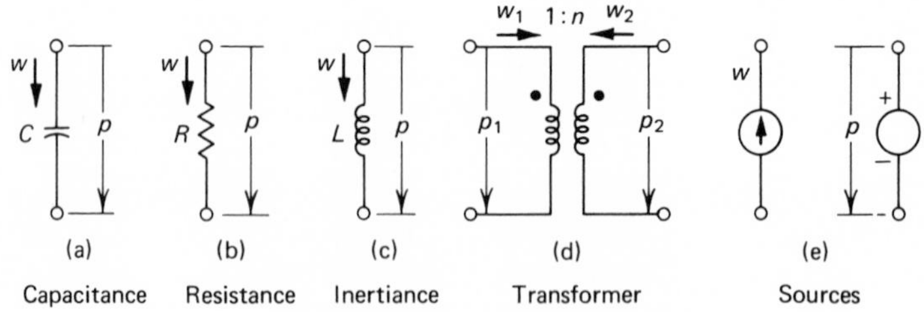

Figure 2.4–3. Pneumatic symbols.

where w is the mass of fluid flowing per second, p the pressure in newtons per meter squared, the other quantities being in consistent units as shown by the equations. Physically C represents a reservoir in the fluid systems, and R the frictional resistance of the conduit. Inertiance L is seldom used in a pneumatic system, although in a hydraulic system the inertia of the fluid might be appreciable. w is the through variable and p the across variable.

Some fluid texts use gravitational units. Thus the head h would be in meters and the pressure p would be in kilograms per square meter, where the kilogram of force is the force of gravity on a kilogram of mass. The flow w would then be a weight flow per second.

In Figure 2.4–4 we give an example of a fluid system involving feedback. Here it is desired to maintain the head h_2 constant with Q_2 changing. A float controls an actuator that varies Q_1 in proportion to the head h_2. We shall not go into the mechanics of the actuator and valve control but assume a relation $Q_1 = K(h_0 - h_2)$, where h_0 is the desired level of the head h_2.

Figure 2.4–5 might be one way of representing this system. From this figure, the following equations can be written:

$$\text{Node 1:}\quad C_1\frac{dh_1}{dt}+\frac{h_1}{R_1}-\frac{h_2}{R_1}=Q_1 \tag{2.4–3a}$$

$$\text{Node 2:}\quad \frac{h_2}{R_1}-\frac{h_1}{R_1}+C_2\frac{dh_2}{dt}=-Q_2 \tag{2.4–3b}$$

$$Q_1=K(h_0-h_2) \tag{2.4–3c}$$

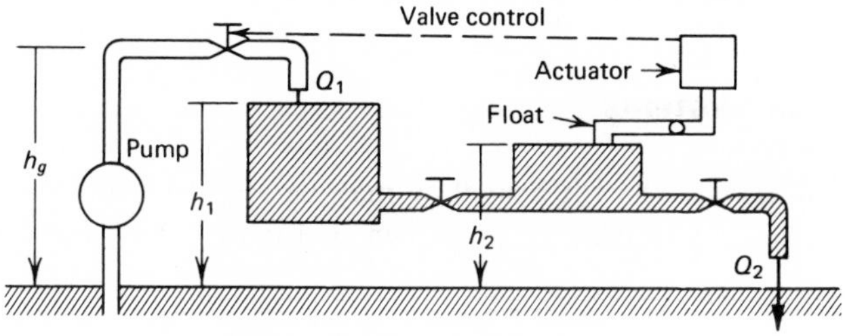

Figure 2.4–4. Hydraulic system.

Substituting (2.4–3c) into (2.4–3a), we get

$$R_1C_1\frac{dh_1}{dt}+h_1-(1-R_1K)h_2=R_1Kh_0, \tag{2.4–4a}$$

and from (2.4–3b) we get

$$h_2-h_1+C_2R_1\frac{dh_2}{dt}=-R_1Q_2 \tag{2.4–4b}$$

Combining (2.4–4a) and (2.4–4b) you get

$$R_1C_1C_2\frac{d^2h_2}{dt^2}+(C_1+C_2)\frac{dh_2}{dt}+Kh_2=Kh_0-\left(R_1C_1\frac{dq_2}{dt}+q_2\right) \tag{2.4–5}$$

Equation (2.4–5) may be easily obtained by using the Laplace transform on (2.4–4a) and (2.4–4b) with zero initial conditions. You may think of this system as having two inputs, h_0 and Q_2. It is a feedback system, since Q_1 depends on both h_0 and h_2. Q_2 may be considered a "disturbance" that affects h_2. This sort of system may be studied more easily by use of flow diagrams, as will be shown subsequently. Pneumatic systems give similar equations, but the physical reservoirs C must be enclosed.

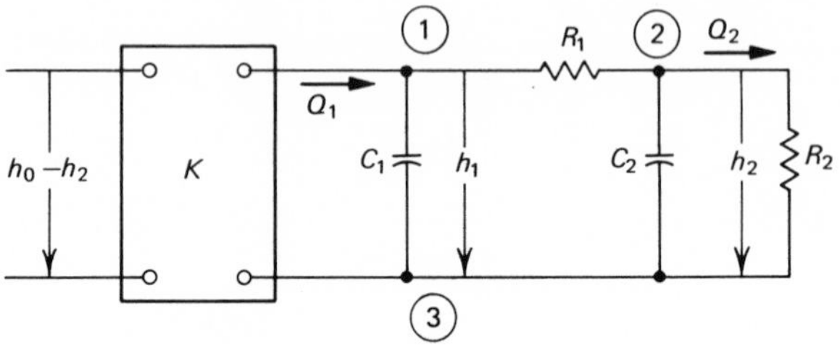

Figure 2.4–5. Symbolic representation of Figure 2.4–4.

2.5 Thermal Systems

Problems associated with heat flow may be studied using the symbols of capacitance and resistance, as shown in Figure 2.5–1 and defined in (2.5–1):

(a)
$$q = C\frac{dT}{dt} \tag{2.5–1a}$$

(b)
$$q = \frac{T}{R} \tag{2.5–1b}$$

where q is the heat flow in joules per second, T the temperature in degrees centigrade, and the other units as shown by the equations. R represents heat loss due to convection, conduction, or radiation, and C accounts for the increased energy of the system due to heat flow into it. As in other systems, the linear model may be only an approximation. A common situation in many chemical processes involves the heating of a fluid, as in Figure 2.5–2, where some sort of heater (shown here as electric) supplies

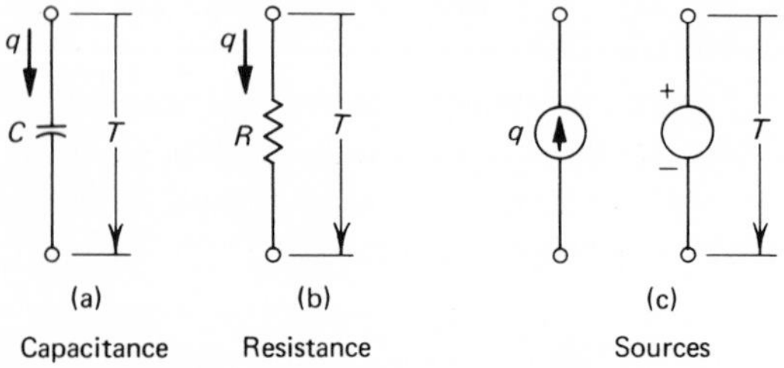

Figure 2.5–1. Thermal symbols.

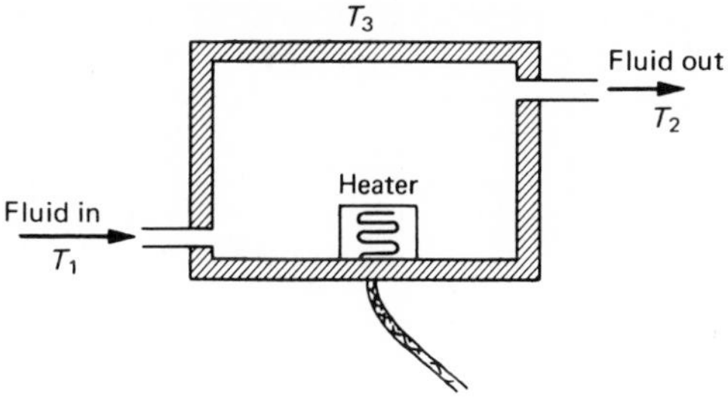

Figure 2.5–2. Thermal system.

a given amount of heat per second, and it is desired to provide a temperature increase $(T_2 - T_1)$ to the fluid, which completely fills the tank. Because the heat into the fluid is $q = QS(T_2 - T_1)$ calories per second, where Q is the fluid flow in cubic meters per second, and S is the specific heat of the fluid in calories per cubic meter per degree centigrade, it is possible to consider this heat as flowing through an equivalent resistance $R_1 = 1/QS$. Figure 2.5–3 depicts the equivalent diagram, with R_2 the thermal resistance of the insulation.

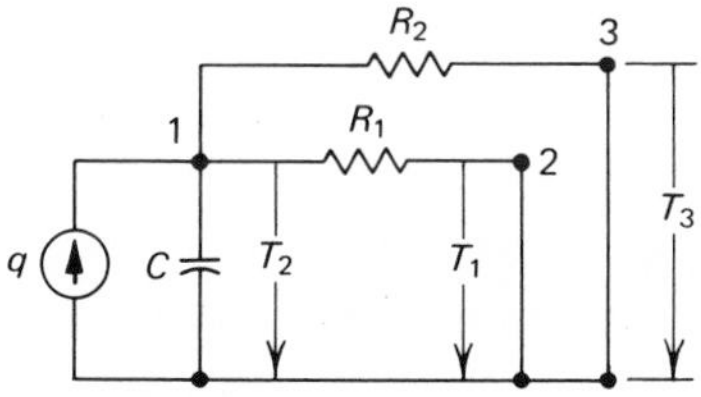

Figure 2.5–3. Symbolic representation of Figure 2.5–2.

2.6 Subsystem Combination and Feedback

One final example will be shown that will combine subsystems from different areas and will also involve feedback. We shall also give an example of how the constants of a device could be measured.

The system in Figure 2.6–1 might represent the antenna control discussed in Chapter 1. The potentiometers are identical and supplied by a constant voltage E_1. The motor has a constant field, and assuming linearity the developed torque τ_d is given by the equation

$$\tau_d = K_\tau i \tag{2.6–1}$$

where K_τ is the motor torque constant.

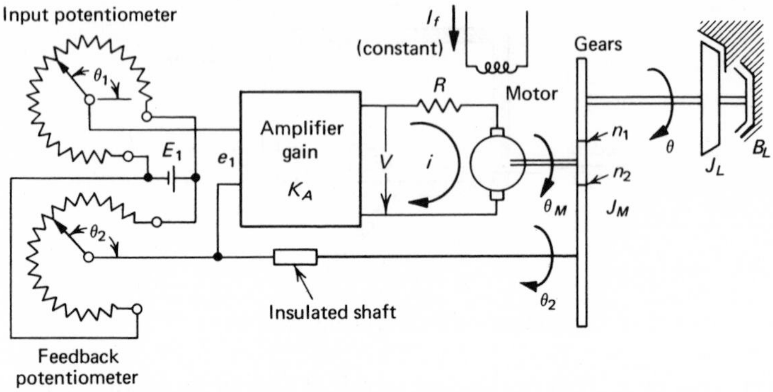

Figure 2.6–1. Possible system schematic of antenna control.

Using Kirchhoff's voltage law around the motor amplifier–output loop,

$$i = \frac{V - E}{R} \tag{2.6–2}$$

where

$$E = K_E \frac{d\theta_M}{dt} \tag{2.6–3}$$

E being the internally generated voltage of the motor (electromotive force, or emf) and K_E the emf constant. Then, substituting back in (2.6–1), you get

$$\tau_d = \frac{K_\tau V}{R} - \frac{K_\tau K_E}{R} \frac{d\theta_M}{dt} \tag{2.6–4}$$

Now imagine the motor connected to a dynamometer and running at constant speed. The developed torque τ_d then becomes absorbed in (1) motor viscous friction and (2) output torque τ to the dynamometer or

$$\tau = \tau_d - B_M n \tag{2.6–5}$$

where B_M is the motor viscous friction, and $n = d\theta_M/dt$, a constant. Putting (2.6–4) into (2.6–5) we get

$$\tau = \frac{K_\tau V}{R} - \left(\frac{K_\tau K_E}{R} + B_M\right) n \tag{2.6–6}$$

or

$$\tau = K_M V - Fn \tag{2.6–7}$$

where $K_M = K_\tau/R$ and $F = (K_\tau K_E/R) + B_M$. In other words, flux-cutting leading to an emf generated by the motor acts in the same manner as mechanical viscous friction.

Now, in the dynamometer experiment, if you keep V, the applied motor voltage, constant at a value V_1 and obtain τ for various values of n, you can plot (2.6–7) with τ as a function of n (steady-state conditions). The result will be the straight line shown in Figure 2.6–2. The slope of this

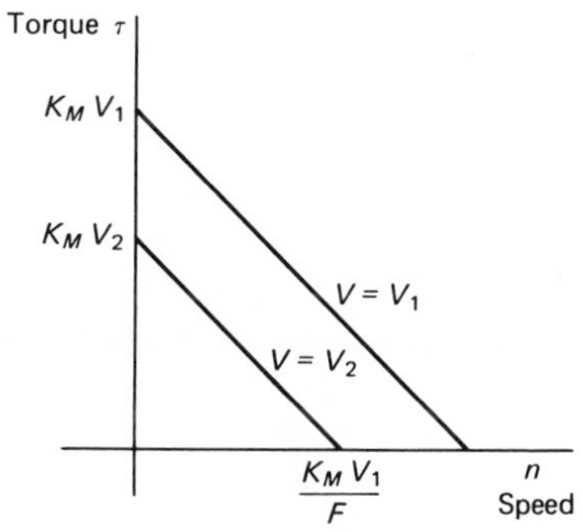

Figure 2.6–2. Torque-speed curves for motor.

line is $-F$ and the intersection at the τ axis is $K_M V_1$. If the voltage is held at some value V_2, a parallel line with the same slope is obtained (see Figure 2.6–2). Hence by making such measurements we can determine the equivalent viscous friction F (which includes the effect of the generated emf) and the motor torque constant K_M. F will have the units of torque per radian per second, and K_M will be in units of torque per applied volt.

We thus have a model of the motor in terms of the applied voltage V, a torque constant K_M, and an equivalent viscous friction constant rather than in terms of the motor current and a torque constant K_τ as in the example given in connection with Figure 2.3–9 and (2.3–5). In the present model the motor viscous friction is included with F, whereas in the previous model it was included with the mechanical shaft and gear friction B_1 of Figure 2.3–11. One of these models may serve better depending on the situation.

Equation (2.6–7) applies to a large variety of motors of different types. For example, the two-phase electric motor used in carrier systems would have an equation similar to this, where V would be the voltage applied to one phase (maintaining constant voltage on the other phase). It would also apply to a rotary hydraulic motor, where V would be the angle of the tilt plate, assuming constant oil pressure. The tests to determine the curves of Figure 2.6–2 are easy to make but will usually reveal curved rather than straight lines. This of course means that the device is non-linear, and to use a linear model we must use the line tangent to the curve at the operating point of interest.

Equation (2.6–7) shows that the developed torque at standstill is $K_M V$, K_M being determined by our experiment. Under dynamic conditions this torque will be "used up" in accelerating inertia, overcoming frictional type forces, and in springing the shaft. As shown previously, it is perhaps simplest to "refer" all quantities to the motor shaft or in terms of θ_M. Then, assuming the shaft spring negligible,

$$K_M V = (J_M + n_1^2 J_L) \frac{d^2\theta_M}{dt^2} + (F + n_1^2 B_L) \frac{d\theta_M}{dt} \qquad \textbf{(2.6–8)}$$

where $n_1 = \theta/\theta_M$.

Equation (2.6–8) implies that the gear inertias have been included in the first term in parentheses in (2.6–8) and the gear frictional effects in the second term. The amplifier input e_1 is given by the relations

$$e_1 = K_d(\theta_2 - \theta_1) \qquad \textbf{(2.6–9a)}$$

$$K_d = \frac{E_1}{\phi} \qquad \textbf{(2.6–9b)}$$

where E_1 is a constant voltage across the potentiometers, ϕ the total angle of each potentiometer winding, θ_1 the input shaft position, and $\theta_2 + n_2 \theta_M$. The amplifier output is given by the equation

$$V = K_A e_1 \qquad \textbf{(2.9–10)}$$

Hence, substituting in (2.6–8), you obtain

$$K_A K_M K_d(n_2 \theta_M - \theta_1) = (J_M + n_1^2 J_L) \frac{d^2\theta_M}{dt^2} + (F + n_1^2 B_L) \frac{d\theta_M}{dt} \qquad \textbf{(2.6–11)}$$

or $$J_1 \frac{d^2\theta_M}{dt^2} + D \frac{d\theta_M}{dt} + K_1\theta_M = K_2\theta_1 \qquad \textbf{(2.6–12)}$$

where

$$J_1 = (J_M + n_1^2 J_L)$$

$$D = F + n_1^2 B_L$$

$$K_1 = K_M K_A K_d n_2$$

$$K_2 = K_M K_A K_d$$

Since the output angle $\theta = n_1\theta_M$,

$$J_1 \frac{d^2\theta}{dt^2} + D \frac{d\theta}{dt} + K_1\theta = n_1 K_2 \theta_1 \tag{2.6–13}$$

which gives θ in terms of θ_1. Under steady-state conditions, the derivatives are zero, and

$$\theta = \frac{n_1}{n_2}\theta_2$$

and further if, $n_1 = n_2$,

$$\theta = \theta_1 \tag{2.6–14}$$

You see that (2.6–13) is a second-order differential equation of the form

$$\frac{d^2\theta}{dt^2} + A \frac{d\theta}{dt} + B\theta = C\theta_1 \tag{2.6–15}$$

If you let $x_1 = \theta$ and $x_2 = d\theta/dt$, then (2.6–15) becomes

$$\dot{x}_1 = x_2 \tag{2.6–16a}$$

$$\dot{x}_2 = -Bx_1 - Ax_2 + C\theta_1 \tag{2.6–16b}$$

$$\theta = x_1 \tag{2.6–16c}$$

where $\dot{x} = dx/dt$.

Equations (2.6–16) are the equivalent of (2.6–15) but expressed in phase-space form. The variables x_1 and x_2 are known as state variables and, when $\dot{x}_1 = x_2$, as phase variables. We shall discuss state-space variables in great detail in Chapters 5 and 6.

The performance of a system expressed either by (2.6–15) or (2.6–16) when θ_1 becomes some function of time is easily analyzed and will be the subject of Chapter 3. As previously indicated, the usual deterministic driving functions studied are the impulse, the step, the ramp, and the sinusoidal. In stochastic control, θ_1 would be a random function.

2.7 Conclusions

In a complete system there will be combinations of subsystems and systems that may contain any of the elements in the areas discussed. If the symbols and defining equations seem repetitious, this will emphasize the similarities between and the analogous nature of elements that are unlike superficially. While pointing out the similarities between the general form of the equations, perhaps you should be warned that obtaining the proper coefficients may not be so easy, and that the special characteristics of elements of one type may require a different development from those of another type. In still more complicated systems, there may be several inputs similar to θ_1 in Figure 2.6–1 and several outputs similar to θ_2. The number of outputs and inputs may not necessarily be equal, because in general there will be cross-coupling between subsystems and systems.

It is clear that differential equations for any combination of subsystems may be written using the appropriate models of the physical system; the symbolic representation may not be necessary with experience, as often the equations are obvious. Rather than continue with additional examples, more complicated combinations can be analyzed in a generalized and abstract fashion, using the flow diagram, as will be shown in Chapter 4. This is particularly useful when we have feedback. Of course, it would be hopeless to give the equations or mathematical models for every possible device. You will have to investigate each new situation as it arises.

In more complicated systems, the equations of Lagrange with generalized coordinates may result in a simpler and more rapid derivation than the laws heretofore mentioned. Lagrange's equations of motion are

$$\frac{d}{dt}\frac{\partial L}{\partial \dot{q}_i} - \frac{\partial L}{\partial q_i} + \frac{\partial F}{\partial \dot{q}_i} = Q_i \qquad \textbf{(2.7–1)}$$

where $L = L(\dot{q}_i, q_i) = [T_e(\dot{q}_i, q_i) - U(q_i)]$, T_e being the kinetic energy function, U the potential energy function, F the dissipation function, Q_i the driving function for the ith coordinate, q_i a generalized coordinate, and $\dot{q}_i = dq_i/dt$. The subscript i ranges from 1 to n, where n is the number of degrees of freedom of the system. Thus n second order differential equations result from (2.7–1). Table 2.7–1 gives a few of the expressions for T_e, U, and F corresponding to the subsystems we have studied. Lagrange's equations are particularly useful in complex systems, and we shall not go into these further here, except to remark that (2.7–1) again demonstrates the basic coherence of dynamic equations for all systems, with the reservation that the expressions for energy may require specialized consideration. [1, 2, 3.] Equation 2.7–1 is useful in expressing systems in terms of state variables. By adopting the generalized coordinates θ and $\dot{\theta}$, (2.6–16) can be found from (2.7–1) for the antenna example.†

† The state space equations may be found more directly by using the Hamiltonian function, which gives $2n$ first order differential equations. See references [1], [2], and [3], and Chapter 10.

In some cases the differential equations cannot be written from theoretical considerations. For example, it would be difficult to write equations describing the dynamic performance of a ship or an airplane. We could use experience obtained with other situations in some cases. In other cases, it might be desirable to make tests on the system, putting in

TABLE 2.7–1

System	Lagrange Functions: Loop Basis	Lagrange Functions: Node Basis
Mechanical		
M	$U=(\int f\,dt)^2/2M$	$T_3=1/2Mv^2$
B	$F=f^2/2B$	$F=1/2Bv^2$
K	$T_e=f^2/2K$	$U=1/2Kx^2$
J	$U=(\int \tau\,dt)^2/2J$	$T_e=1/2J\omega^2$
B	$F=\tau^2/2B$	$F=1/2D\omega^2$
K	$T_e=\tau^2/2K$	$U=1/2K\theta^2$
Electrical		
C	$U=(\int i\,dt)^2/2C$	$T_e=1/2Cv^2$
R	$F=1/2Ri^2$	$F=v^2/2R$
L	$T_e=1/2Li^2$	$U=(\int v\,dt)^2/2L$
Fluid		
C	$U=(\int Q\,dt)^2/2C$	$T_e=1/2Ch^2$
R	$F=1/2RQ^2$	$F=h^2/2R$
C	$U=(\int w\,dt)^2/2C$	$T_e=1/2Cp^2$
R	$F=1/2Rw^2$	$F=p^2/2R$
Thermal		
C		$T_e=1/2CT^2$
R		$F=T^2/2R$

test signals, and observing responses. As suggested in Chapter 1, we could postulate a model and, on the basis of tests, alter and improve the model. The basic pitfall encountered with such experiments consists in the impossibility of devising inputs and environments such that we can predict performance under all possible conditions. However, no alternative to actual testing may exist. Naturally, the final system design is proved by actual performance, which leads to accumulated experience as an important factor in design.

It has been pointed out that the models used are first approximations to physical elements. Some model imperfections have been indicated, and it is not amiss to discuss a few other deviations in actual situations and to outline the improvement of the model. For example, friction, both rotational and translational, may not be proportional to velocity.

Figure 2.7–1 shows a series of curves obtained by tests on frictional forces. Curve OB illustrates the simple viscous friction used in the linear

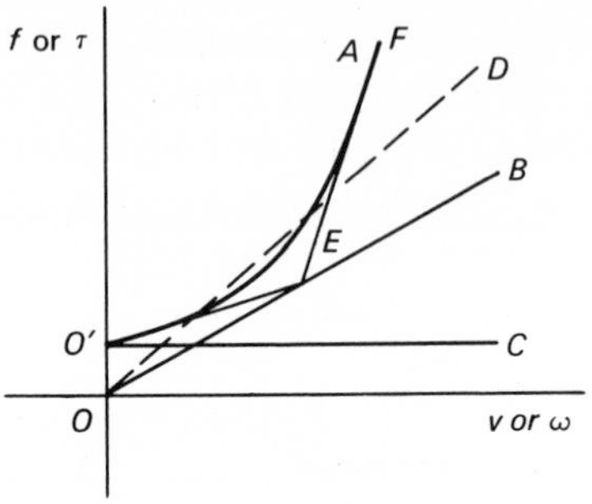

Figure 2.7–1. Frictional forces.

equations. A type of friction that exerts a force opposing the motion with no velocity, but no force with velocity, such as shown by OO', is sometimes called stiction, while a third type, offering a constant force, independent of velocity such as presented by $O'C$, is termed Coulomb friction. The actual friction may be a combination of these, plus some nonlinear portion, such as $O'A$ in Figure 2.7–1. It may be possible to obtain a closer approximation to the physical situation, while still using linear equations, to take an average curve, such as OD. Alternatively, two solutions might be prepared, one based on a curve $O'E$ and one based on a curve EF. This technique is called "piecewise" linearization. Even if the function is very nonlinear, linear assumptions may define at least the limits of operation. Similar approximations apply to the remaining nonlinearities discussed subsequently.

A spring, if stretched beyond its elastic limit, will not maintain a constant force per unit displacement. In fact, it may take a "set" and not return to the original position when the force is removed, as in Figure 2.7–2.

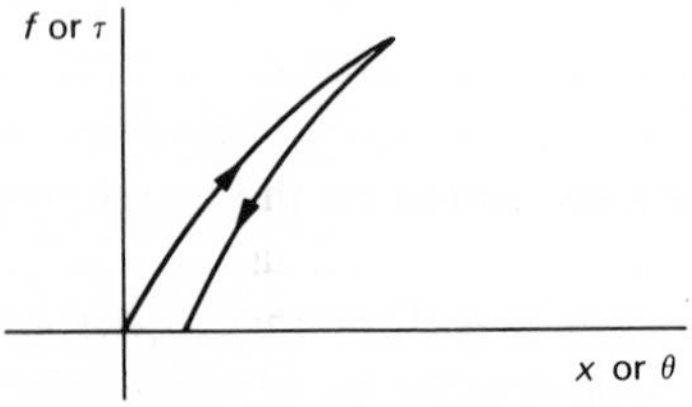

Figure 2.7–2. Spring characteristics.

Inductance L in electrical systems has no consistency, as shown in Figure 2.7–3, where ψ represents the flux linkages ($\psi = Li$). As i increases the curve OB becomes nonlinear, and the inductive coil is said to be "saturated"; that is, it becomes more difficult to obtain the same amount of flux per unit current as in the unsaturated region near the origin. Furthermore, if the current decreases from B, the flux linkages ψ do not follow the path OB but some other, such as to form a hysteresis loop as depicted in Figure 2.7–3. Such effects are quite prevalent with a ferro-

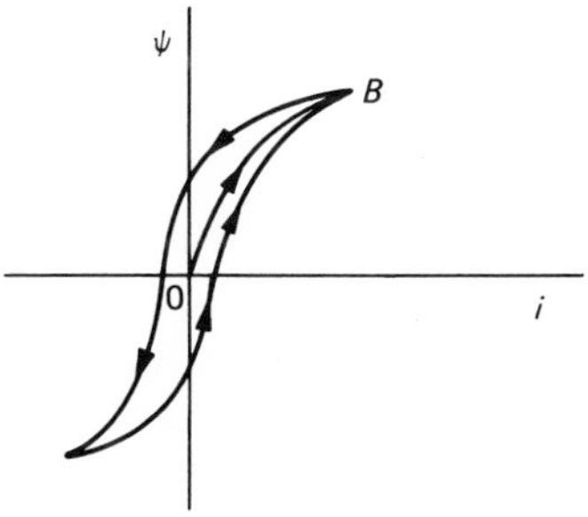

Figure 2.7–3. Magnetic hysterisis loop.

magnetic core, and it is difficult to obtain an inductance of any practical size without such a core. Owing to this and other considerations, inductances in corrective networks are avoided wherever possible, but of course inductance exists inherently in rotating or magnetic amplifiers. Resistance changes with temperature, and thus a curve of resistance voltage versus current might be very nonlinear unless special effort is made to maintain a constant temperature. Resistance may also contain inductance, and vice versa, but these effects can be represented by judicious combinations of the linear models. Capacitance is usually well behaved, except for aging in certain types of capacitors.

In the example of Section 2.6 we mentioned that the motor torque versus speed curves would not be straight lines. An actual test might give results more like Figure 2.7–4. In Figure 2.7–4 the torque is not proportional to the speed; also it is not proportional to the applied voltage V. Here we may take some average straight line whose slope approximates expected conditions, and whose intersection on the τ axis gives a reasonable torque constant K_M. Alternatively, we could use several different values of K_M and F and obtain the system performance under various conditions. The latter investigation would involve much more labor, so the preliminary design would undoubtedly be made on the basis of average values for K_M and F.

Fluid and thermal devices can be extremely nonlinear. As already pointed out, turbulence, for example, leads to nonlinearities. Some difficulties may be avoided with proper design. Thermal resistance, which

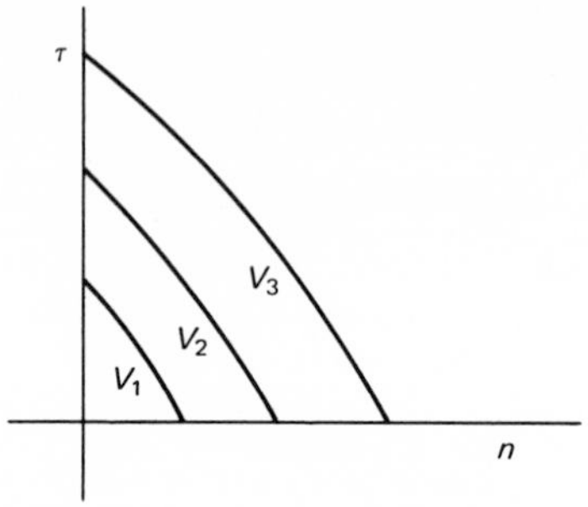

Figure 2.7–4. Practical motor characteristics.

symbolizes convection, radiation, or conduction heat losses may be anything but constant. Obtaining even an estimate for these losses may be difficult. However, useful results may frequently be obtained by the methods outlined previously for the case of friction. We only make a frontal attack on the nonlinear problem when linear solutions are not sufficiently good for our purpose.

Finally, the physical device may not be considered as lumped in space, but may be distributed. Illustration of distributed parameters are electrical transmission lines, hydraulic or pneumatic pipes, large chemical converters, and large diaphragms. In such instances, it is necessary to go back to the more fundamental partial differential equations. In such cases an equivalent lumped model may sometimes be fashioned.

We have only touched on the variations of lumped, linear models from the devices found in nature. If the variation becomes large, of course you can expect performance markedly different from predictions based on linear design. All is not so dark as this discussion might suggest, however. Returning to the analysis of sensitivity, you recall that if feedback is used, the system may be relatively insensitive to gain variation. Thus feedback will often cover a multitude of sins of omission and commision concerning parameter evaluation. Last, from a pragmatic viewpoint, we find linear theory most useful even if not precise.

A word might be said as to units. Up to now we have put our units in the MKS (meter, kilogram, second) system. In the United States and England, although the slug, foot, second system will no doubt die, it is all too likely that it will linger on for many years. Measurements are also made in inches, ounces, and other discouraging units. One of the more frustrating mechanical quantities in the English system is inertia J. If the mass unit is slugs, the units of inertia should be slug-feet squared, but it is frequently given in pound-feet squared. If the latter is the case, this figure should be divided by 32.2 to obtain slug-feet squared. Table 2.7–2 reviews

TABLE 2.7–2. UNIT SYSTEMS*

Quantity	Symbol	MKS Units	English Units
Mechanical, translational			
Force	f	newton = kg-m/sec^2	lb = slug-ft/sec^2
Distance	x	m	ft
Velocity	v	m/sec	ft/sec
Acceleration	a	m/sec^2	ft/sec^2
Mass	M	kg	slug
Compliance	K	nwt/m	lb/ft
Damping	B	nwt-sec/m	lb-sec/ft
Mechanical, rotational			
Torque	τ	nwt-m	lb-ft
Angle	θ	rad	rad
Angular velocity	ω	rad/sec	rad/sec
Moment of inertia	J	kg-m^2	slug-ft^2
Compliance	K	nwt-m/rad	lb-ft/rad
Damping	B	nwt-m-sec/rad	lb-ft-sec/rad
Fluid, hydraulic			
Flow	Q	m^3/sec	ft^3/sec
Head	h	nwt-m/kg	lb-ft/slug
Capacitance	C	kg-m^2/nwt	slug-ft^2/lb
Fluid, gas			
Flow	w	kg/sec	slug/sec
Pressure	p	nwt/m^2	lb/ft^2
Capacitance	C	kg-m^2/nwt	slug-ft^2/lb
Resistance	R	1/m-sec	1/ft-sec
Thermal			
Flow	q	joules/sec-watts	Btu/sec
Temperature	T	°C	°F
Capacitance	C	joules/°C	Btu/°F
Resistance	R	°C-sec/joule	°F-sec/Btu
Electrical			
Current	i	amperes (coulombs/sec)	
Voltage	v	volts	
Capacitance	C	farads	
Resistance	R	ohms	
Inductance	L	henrys	
Charge	q	coulombs	

* m, meters; kg, kilograms; nwt, newtons; sec, seconds; ft, feet; lb, pounds; rad, radians; C, centigrade; F, fahrenheit; Btu, British thermal units

the principal units used here from which other unit systems may be derived. In particular situations units other than those shown may be more convenient. For example, the hydraulic units imply a constant density fluid, because the energy per second is given by multiplying by the density in kilograms per meter cubed. In some cases h may be in meters or feet; in others, in kilograms per meter squared; and so on. Engineering specialties develop units and nomenclature peculiar to the situation that must be learned by the newcomer.

In Chapter 1 we pointed out the application of system theory to much broader situations, involving electrobiological, transportation, economic, and even social problems. We do not have space to go into these here, but the first step is to postulate a model of the system under consideration by writing equations describing the system. Obviously in such problems there usually will be many equations and the model will be most complicated. After building the model it must again be tested against observations made in the real world and the model revised. The principles involved are thus no different, but the details and the model improvement become much more difficult than in the case of engineering systems. Nevertheless, considerable progress has been made in setting up biological systems, for example. Opportunities in these more sophisticated areas will continue to increase.

PROBLEMS

2.1. (a) In Figure P2.1 find the differential equation involving e_o and e_i and their time derivatives.

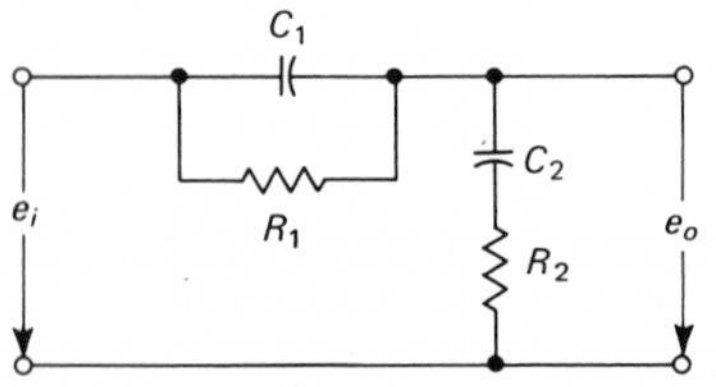

Figure P2.1.

(b) Obtain the transfer function $E_o(s)/E_i(s)$, $v_{c1} = v_{c2} = 0$ at $t = 0$, where $E_o(s) = \mathscr{L}e_o(t)$.

[*Note:* (a) may be done from (b).]

2.2. In Figure P2.2 find the differential equation involving e_i and i_L and their time derivatives, where $e_2 = K_1e_1$.

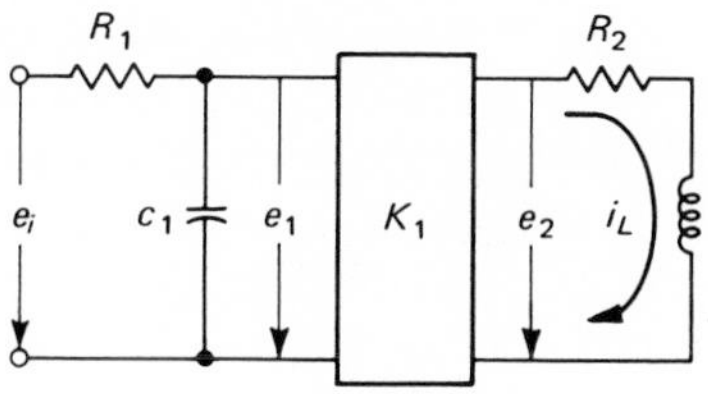

Figure P2.2.

2.3. (a) In Figure P2.3 find the differential equations involving i_1, i_2, e_i, and their derivatives. The element values are in the kiloohms, microfarads, and henrys.

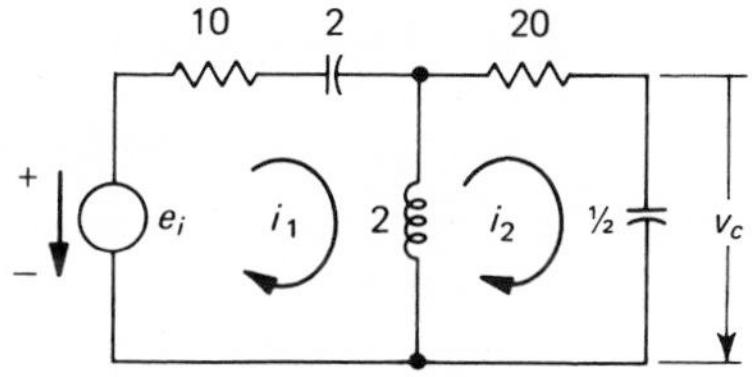

Figure P2.3.

(b) Find the transfer function $V_c(s)/E_i(s)$ (all initial conditions zero).

2.4. (a) In Figure P2.4 find the transfer function $V_2(s)/I_p(s)$. All elements are as in Problem 2.3.

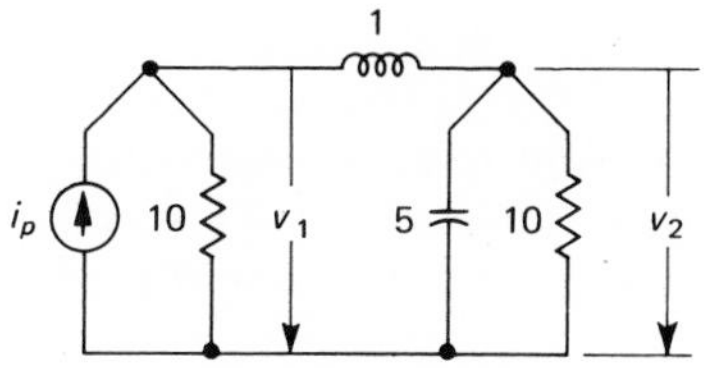

Figure P2.4.

(b) Find the differential equations involving v_1, v_2, and i_p and their derivatives.

(c) Put (b) in phase-space form.

2.5. (a) In Figure P2.5, element values are in ohms and farads. If $i_1 = i_2$ and $e_o = -100e_1$, all initial conditions zero, show that

$$\frac{E_o(s)}{E_i(s)} = \frac{-10^3}{2.02s + 11.01}$$

(b) Find $E_o(s)/E_i(s)$ if $K = e_o/e_1 = +100$.

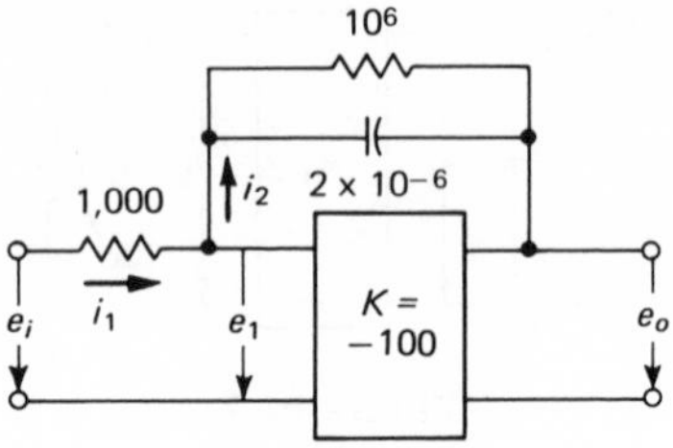

Figure P2.5.

2.6. In Figure P2.6, let

$$J = 15 \text{ lb-ft}^2$$

$$B = 2 \text{ lb-ft/rad/sec}$$

$$K = 30 \text{ lb-ft/rad}$$

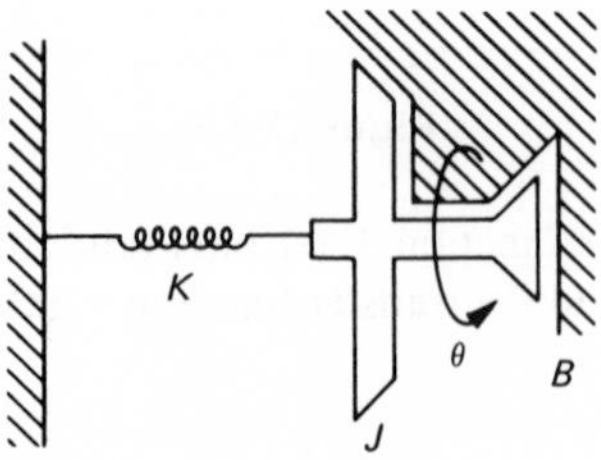

Figure P2.6.

The inertia J is displaced from the equilibrium position 0.1 rad. Find $\theta(t)$ after release. What is the value of B for critical damping [$\zeta = 1$ in the characteristic polynomial $(s^2 + 2\zeta\omega_n s + \omega_n^2)$]? (*Note:* Be careful of units here.)

2.7. Develop equations of motion for Figure P2.7, assuming that frictional forces of M_1 with respect to the container are negligible but that M_1 remains horizontal.

2.8. (a) Develop equations of motion for Figure P2.8 assuming that the bar M does not move horizontally and θ is small ($\sin\theta = \theta$, $\cos\theta = 1$). M has a mass of m kilograms per meter and a length l meters.

(b) Repeat (a) if viscous frictional forces B_1 and B_2 are in parallel with K_1 and K_2, respectively.

2.9. Find approximate linear equations of motion for Figure P2.9, where θ is small and the mass of the rod (length l) is negligible. (*Hint:* Take the cart M and the rod and mass m as two free bodies with associated horizontal and vertical forces. Write equations in terms of θ and $\dot{\theta}$, $\cos\theta$, and $\sin\theta$, neglect product terms, and finally let $\sin\theta = \theta$ and $\cos\theta = 1$.)

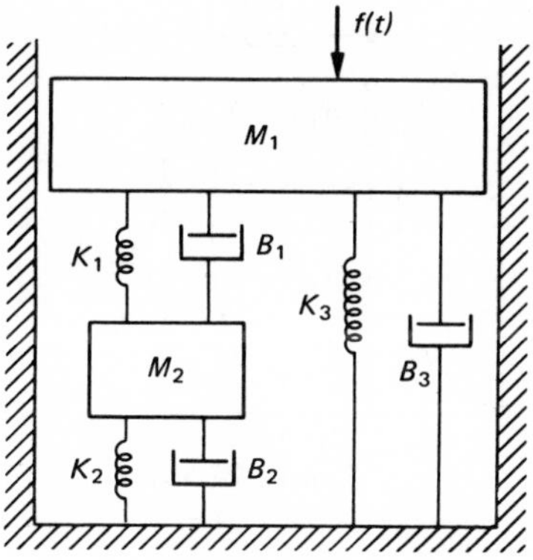

Figure P2.7.

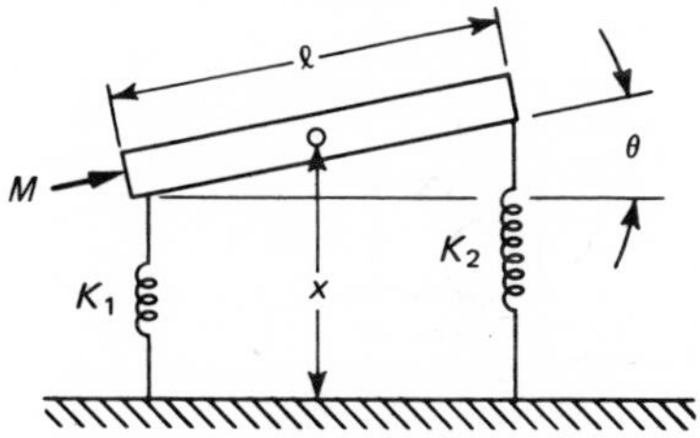

Figure P2.8.

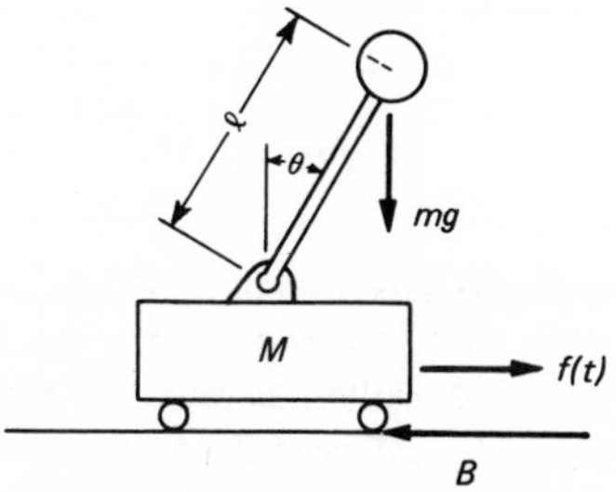

Figure P2.9.

2.10. In Figure P2.10 find $E_f(s)/E_i(s)$ (no initial conditions). The motor constants are K_t newton-meters per ampere and K_E volts per radian per second. (*Hint:* Write equations in terms of the loop currents i_1 and i_2. Write a loop equation involving e_f, and eliminate i_1 and i_2. Discuss any peculiarities you may notice concerning the zeros of the numerator of this function.)

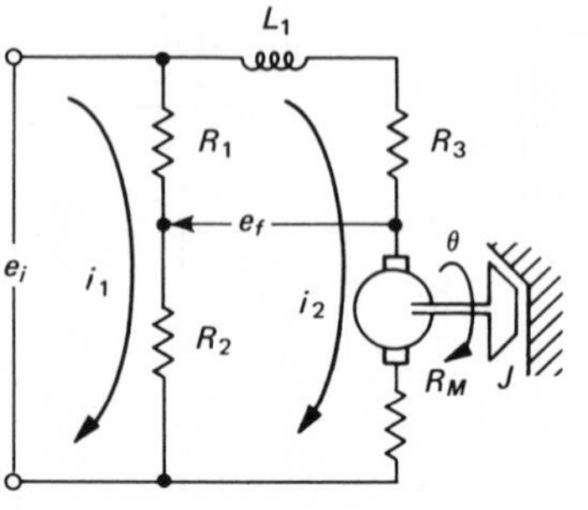

Figure P2.10.

2.11. The system of Figure P2.11 is proposed for a motor speed control; that is, $\omega = d\theta/dt$ is to be proportional to e_r under steady-state conditions. Assume that the generator G has a constant of K_g volts per ampere of field

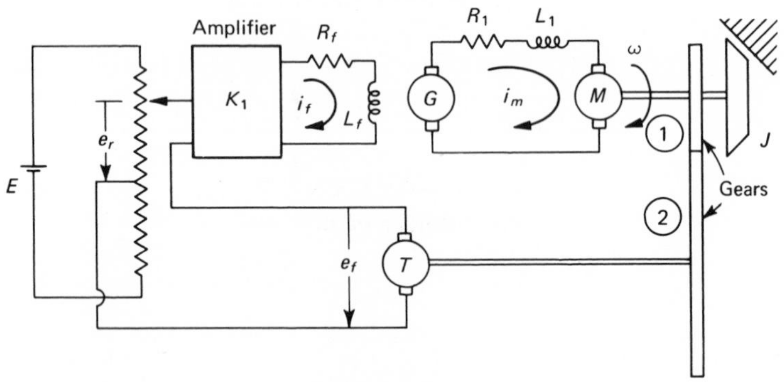

Figure P2.11.

current i_f, the motor M has constants of K_t newton-meters torque per ampere and K_e volts emf per radian per second, and the tachometer (generator) T produces K_f volts per revolution per minute. The amplifier gain is K_1 volts per volt and gear 2 has twice as many teeth as gear 1. Friction and shaft bending are negligible. Assume the polarity of e_f is proper for negative feedback conditions.

(a) Find a differential equation involving ω and e_r and their derivatives.

(b) Find ω in terms of e_r under steady-state conditions.

(c) If $L_1 = 0$, $R_1 = L_f = K_e K_T = K_g K_T = R_f = 1$, $J = 10$, and $K_1 = 100$, all in proper units, find K_f to give critical damping, if possible.

2.12. In Figure P2.12, G is defined by $0.004(dc/dt) + c = 80e$ and H is defined by $0.002(df/dt) + f = Kc$. Write the differential equation relating c and r.

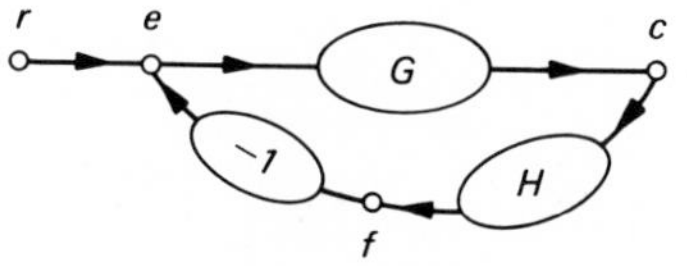

Figure P2.12.

2.13. (a) In Figure P2.13 find a differential equation relating h_2 and q_1 and their derivatives.

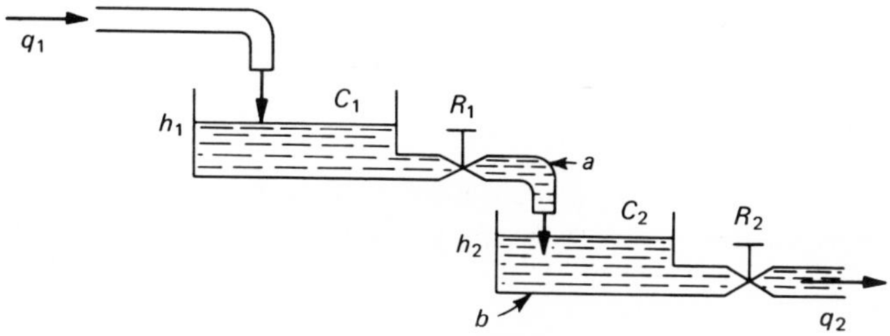

Figure P2.13.

(b) Repeat if pipe a connects into the bottom of reservoir b with no leakage.

2.14. In Figure P2.14 write the equation of motion for the inertia J if τ is a unit doublet (Laplace transform $= s$), all initial conditions zero. If $J = B = 1$,

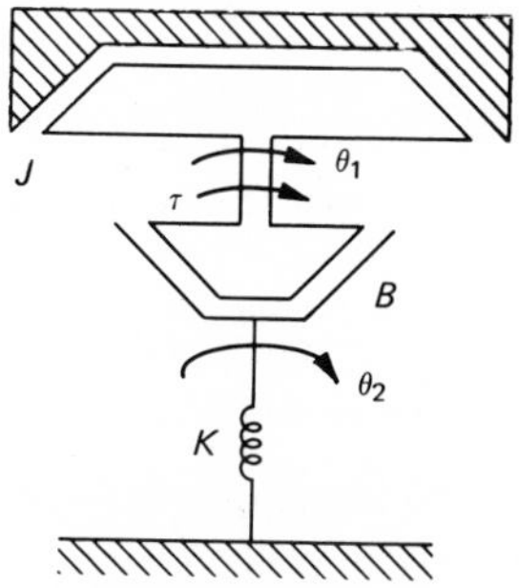

Figure P2.14.

find K to make the damping factor ζ of the characteristic polynomial $s^2 + 2\zeta\omega_n s + \omega_n^2$ equal to 0.5.

2.15. In Figure P2.15 show that the transfer function

$$\frac{\hat{\theta}_2(s)}{\hat{\tau}(s)} = \frac{10}{(100J_1 + J_2)s^2 + (100B_1 + B_2)s + 100K_1}$$

where τ is a torque applied to J_1.

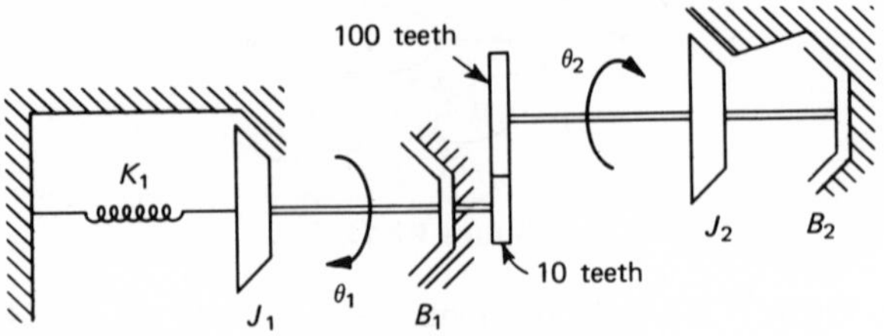

Figure P2.15.

REFERENCES AND FURTHER READING

[1] S. Seely, *Dynamic Systems Analysis*, Reinhold, New York, 1964.

[2] H. Goldstein, *Classical Mechanics*, Addison-Wesley, Reading, Mass., 1950.

[3] S. W. McCuskey, *An Introduction to Advanced Dynamics*, Addison-Wesley, Reading, Mass., 1959.

[4] J. T. Tou, *Modern Control Theory*, McGraw-Hill, New York, 1964.

[5] A. G. J. MacFarlane, *Engineering Systems Analysis*, Addison-Wesley, Reading, Mass., 1964, and G. G. Harrap & Co., London.

[6] C. R. Wylie, Jr., *Advanced Engineering Mathematics*, McGraw-Hill, New York 1966, pp. 144–180.

[7] H. E. Koenig, Y. Tokad, and H. K. Kesavan, *Analysis of Discrete Physical Systems*, McGraw-Hill, New York, 1967.

Most of the introductory control texts listed at the end of Chapter 1 contain material discussed in this chapter. For texts emphasizing components and testing, see also the following:

[8] W. R. Ahrendt and C. J. Savant, Jr., *Servomechanism Practice*, McGraw-Hill, New York, 2nd ed., 1960.

[9] J. E. Gibson and F. B. Tuteur, *Control Systems Components*, McGraw-Hill, New York, 1958.

[10] C. J. Savant, Jr., *Control System Design*, McGraw-Hill, New York, 2nd ed., 1964.

[11] I. A. Greenwood, J. V. Holden, and D. MacRae, *Electronic Instruments*, MIT Rad. Lab. Series, Vol. 21, McGraw-Hill, New York, 1947 (see also Dover edition).

[12] G. K. Tucker and D. M. Wills, *A Simplified Technique of Control System Engineering*, Minneapolis-Honeywell Regulator Co., Philadelphia, 1960.

[13] E. M. Grabbe, S. Ramo, and D. E. Wooldridge, *Handbook of Automation Computation and Control*, Vol. 3, Wiley, New York, 1961.

3 Second-Order Systems

3.1 Introduction

Up to now we have been involved in some necessary but rather dry definitions, some fairly simple dynamic equations, and some broad generalities. To keep you from becoming bored with the entire subject of controls, we shall now plunge into a discussion of a specific control system—one of second order. A system described by an equation where the second derivative of the controlled quantity, but no derivative of higher degree, becomes involved is a second-order system by definition. This type of system, which has importance in its own right for many applications, contains greater implication in that much control design, particularly in the frequency domain, is based on second-order-system analysis. Thus, if the system is of higher order (as it usually is), you either approximate it as a second-order system or you predict the response in terms of departures from the performance of a second-order system. We confine the discussion to linear, fixed systems.

We shall explore some performance indices for the second-order system and some simple techniques for system improvement, which we lump under the term "compensation." Conventional design may be said to rest on an understanding of second-order systems; optimal or state-space design, less so. These matters will become more clear as we proceed.

3.2 Antenna-Control-System Example

In Chapter 2 we derived some relations for a second-order system involving the control of an antenna. For convenience, we redraw the flow diagram of this system but with the added complication of a disturbance torque (wind) on the load. As discussed previously, the error-detector system usually can be lumped into one gain unit. Thus Figure 3.2–1

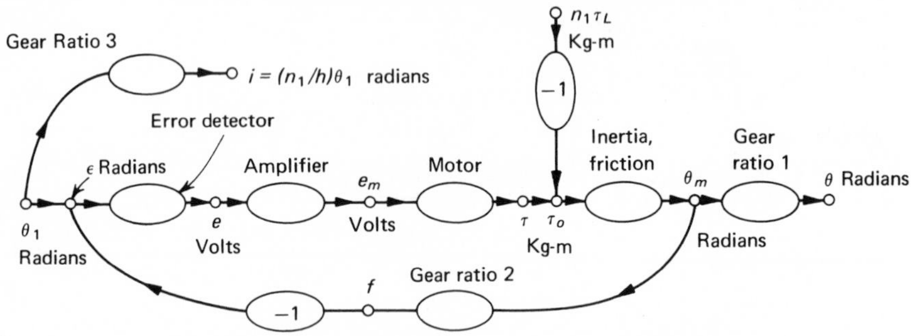

Figure 3.2–1. Schematic diagram for antenna control system.

represents the schematic diagram of the system, slightly altered to include the effect of the load disturbance, shown here as a torque $n_1\tau_L$ that is combined with the motor torque to result in the output torque τ_0, where n_1 is the gear ratio between the output shaft position θ and the motor shaft position θ_M and τ_L is the output shaft disturbance torque, assumed to oppose the motor torque τ ($\tau_0 = \tau - n_1\tau_L$). Usually n_1 is less than 1, so that the motor shaft torque is less than the load shaft torque, whereas the motor shaft speed is greater than the load shaft speed.

Let N_M = speed of the motor shaft
N_L = speed of the output shaft
N_f = speed of the error-detector shaft
n_1 = N_L/N_M, gear ratio 1
h = N_f/N_M, gear ratio 2
K_d = error-detector constant, volts/rad
K_A = amplifier constant, volts/volt
K_M = motor torque constant, newton-m/volt
J_1 = equivalent inertia referred to motor shaft Kg-m^2 ($J_M + n_1^2 J_L$; J_M and J_L are as defined in Section 2.6)
D = equivalent friction referred to motor shaft, newton-m/rad/sec (B_M + emf effect + $n_1^2 B_L = F + n_1^2 B_L$; F, B_M, and B_L are as defined in Section 2.6)
K_s = shaft bending torque, assumed negligible
τ = motor torque to load

Let $\tau_L = 0$ temporarily. Then $\tau_0 = \tau$, and

$$\tau = J_1 \frac{d^2\theta_M}{dt^2} + D\frac{d\theta_M}{dt} \tag{3.2–1}$$

Taking the Laplace transform of (3.2.–1), and assuming zero initial conditions, we obtain

$$\hat{\tau}(s) = (J_1 s^2 + Ds)\hat{\theta}_M(s) \tag{3.2–2}$$

or

$$\frac{\hat{\theta}_M(s)}{\hat{\tau}(s)} = \frac{1}{s(J_1 s + D)}$$

$$= \frac{1}{J_1 s[s + (D/J_1)]} \tag{3.2–3}$$

Equation (3.2–2) relates $\hat{\theta}_M(s)$ and $\hat{\tau}(s)$, and the quantity $J_1 s[s + (D/J_1)]$ is therefore an operator in the complex frequency domain. The operator $1/J_1 s[s + (D/J_1)]$ of (3.2–3) is called a transfer function. The reciprocal of D/J_1 (the term J_1/D) is called the time constant of the motor, its units being seconds.

If the desired output $i = (n_1/h)\theta_1$, as implied by Figure 3.2–1, then the quantity ϵ is not the error but is directly proportional to it. With this understanding we can omit the desired output i. Thus the flow diagram for the system may be depicted as in Figure 3.2–2, if we put the operators

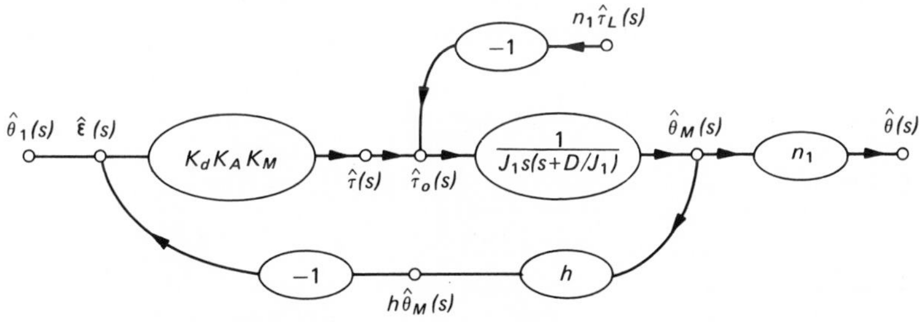

Figure 3.2–2. Flow diagram for antenna control system.

in transfer function form with the variables shown as functions of s.

From Figure 3.2–2, if $\tau_L = 0$,

$$(K_d K_A K_M)\hat{\epsilon}(s)\left(\frac{1}{s(J_1 s + D)}\right) = \hat{\theta}_M(s) \tag{3.2–4}$$

But

$$\hat{\epsilon}(s) = \hat{\theta}_1(s) - h\hat{\theta}_M(s) \tag{3.2–5}$$

Hence

$$K_d K_A K_M\,\hat{\theta}_1(s) = \hat{\theta}_M(s)(J_1 s^2 + Ds + K_1)$$

or

$$\frac{\hat{\theta}_M(s)}{\hat{\theta}_1(s)} = \frac{K_d K_A K_M}{J_1[s^2 + (D/J_1)s + (K_1/J_1)]} \tag{3.2–6}$$

where $K_1 = hK_d K_A K_M$. In differential equation form this becomes

$$J_1 \frac{d^2\theta_M}{dt^2} + D\frac{d\theta_M}{dt} + K_1\theta_M = K_2\theta_1 \qquad \textbf{(3.2–7)}$$

where θ_M and θ_1 are functions of time t and $K_2 = K_d K_A K_M$.

This is identical to (2.6–12) but was derived from the transfer function concept.†

Again from Figure 3.2–2,

$$\hat{\theta}_M(s) = \hat{\tau}_0(s)\left[\frac{1}{J_1 s[s + (D/J_1)]}\right] \qquad \textbf{(3.2–8)}$$

But if $\theta_1 = 0$, $\tau_0 = \tau - n_1\tau_L$, or

$$\hat{\tau}_0(s) = (-hK_d K_A K_M)\hat{\theta}_M(s) - n_1\hat{\tau}_L(s)$$

and hence

$$-hK_d K_A K_M \hat{\theta}_M(s) - n_1\hat{\tau}_L(s) = \hat{\theta}_M(s)(J_1 s[s + (D/J_1)]$$

or

$$\hat{\theta}_M(s) = \frac{-n_1\hat{\tau}_L(s)}{J_1[s^2 + (D/J_1)s + (K_1/J_1)]} \qquad \textbf{(3.2–9)}$$

Using the principle of superposition,

$$\hat{\theta}_M(s) = \frac{(K_2)\hat{\theta}_1(s)}{J_1[s^2 + (D/J_1)s + (K_1/J_1)]} - \frac{n_1\hat{\tau}_L(s)}{J_1[s^2 + (D/J_1)s + (K_1/J_1)]} \qquad \textbf{(3.2–10)}$$

Note that from (3.2–10) if we make K_2 large compared to n_1, then $\hat{\theta}_M(s)$ will be influenced more by $\hat{\theta}_1(s)$ than by $\hat{\tau}_L(s)$. Hence to lower the effect of disturbance, the gain of the forward path between the reference input and the disturbance should be made as large as possible. Furthermore, from the second term of (3.2–10), the larger K_1 becomes, the less the effect of the disturbance for very small s (low complex frequency). To find the output $\hat{\theta}$ only involves the application of the gear ratio n_1, or

$$\hat{\theta}(s) = n_1\hat{\theta}_M(s) \qquad \textbf{(3.2–11)}$$

For purposes of generality, you may find it instructive to rederive (3.2–10) by using the idea of operators directly. That is, let Figure 3.2–3

† The gear ratio h here is the same as n_2 in Section 2.6.

represent the system in terms of the general operators S_1, S_2, S_3, and S_4. The operator -1 will be shown explicitly.

The dependent variables θ_1, ϵ, τ, θ_M, and θ will be functions of an

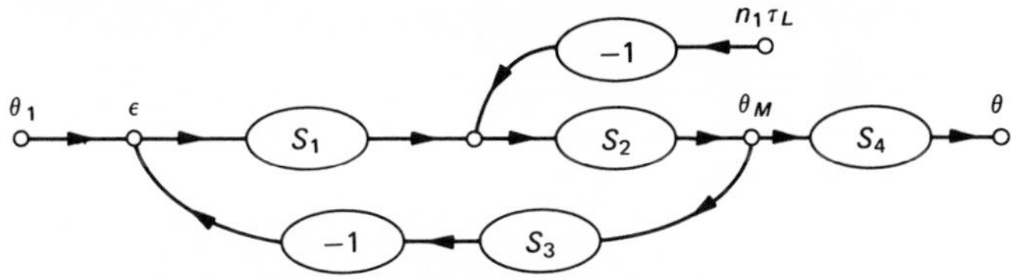

Figure 3.2–3. General flow diagram for Figure 3.2–1.

independent variable that will hinge on the type of operator. Then if we can select operators such that

$$\theta_M = S_2[S_1(\epsilon)] = S_2\, S_1(\epsilon) \tag{3.2–12}$$

or, in words, the operator that is the product of two operators gives the same result as the second operator working on the result of the first operation, we can produce some conclusions that will be general. Thus, if $\tau_L = 0$, from Figure 3.2–3 and the definition of an operator,

$$\theta_M = S_2\, S_1 \epsilon$$

But

$$\epsilon = \theta_1 - S_3\, \theta_M \tag{3.2–13}$$

Hence

$$\theta_M = S_2\, S_1(\theta_1 - S_3\, \theta_M)$$

$$= S_2\, S_1\, \theta_1 - S_2\, S_1\, S_3\, \theta_M$$

or

$$(I + S_2\, S_1 S_3)\theta_M = S_2\, S_1 \theta_1 \tag{3.2–14}$$

where the identity operator I is defined by the relations

$$I\theta_M = \theta_M = \theta_M\, I$$

Now define an inverse operator S^{-1} such that $SS^{-1} = S^{-1}S = I$. Then

$$\theta_M = (I + S_2\, S_1 S_3)^{-1} S_2\, S_1 \theta_1 \tag{3.2–15}$$

Further, if

$$(I + S_2 S_1 S_3)^{-1} = \frac{1}{I + S_2 S_1 S_3}$$

then

$$\theta_M = \frac{S_2 S_1}{I + S_2 S_1 S_3} \theta_1 \tag{3.2–16}$$

Similarly,

$$\theta_M = \frac{-S_2}{I + S_2 S_1 S_3} n_1 \tau_L \tag{3.2–17}$$

Also, from (3.2–13), if $\tau_L = 0$,

$$\epsilon = \frac{1}{I + S_2 S_1 S_3} \theta_1 \tag{3.2–18}$$

provided S_2, S_1, and S_3 commute.

If you use the transfer functions found with the Laplace transform as an operator (see Figure 3.2–2), substitution in (3.2–16) and (3.2–17) gives the same results as (3.2–10), as transfer functions obey the law set up by (3.2–12) and also commute. For this case $I = 1$, and operators such as transfer functions found by the Laplace, Fourier, and Z transforms may be placed in the form of equations similar to (3.2–16) or (3.2–17).† Other operators may not be placed in these forms, as operators such as matrices do not commute, and division by such an operator may not be defined.

3.3 Solution of the Second-Order Linear Equation

We now need to solve equations such as (3.2–7). To put this in a more general form, let us get the output in terms of θ, the output angle of Figure 3.2–2, where $\theta = \theta_M n_1$, and then replace θ by q and θ_1 by r. (The symbols q and r tie the system to the general diagram of Figure 1.5–9.) Doing this we obtain the equation

$$\frac{d^2q(t)}{dt^2} + A \frac{dq(t)}{dt} + Bq(t) = Er(t) \tag{3.3–1}$$

† The variables in these equations will be functions of s in the Laplace transform case.

(where τ_L has been ignored for the moment). In the antenna example being followed here, the coefficients in (3.3–1) are

$$A = \frac{D}{J_1} \qquad B = \frac{K_1}{J_1} \qquad E = \frac{n_1 K_d K_A K_M}{J_1}$$

The solution to this equation for most $r(t)$ may be obtained by either the classical approach or the Laplace transform approach. In the former case, the solution is known to be of the form

$$q(t) = C_1 \epsilon^{\alpha_1 t} + C_2 \epsilon^{\alpha_2 t} + C_3 r_1(t) \tag{3.3–2}$$

where α_1 and α_2 are the roots of the characteristic equation

$$s^2 + As + B = 0 \tag{3.3–3}$$

and C_1 and C_2 are constants determined by the initial conditions. C_3 is a constant determined such that (3.3–1) is satisfied when $r_1(t)$ has the same functional form as $r(t)$. The first two terms on the right side of (3.3–2) are called the transient (complementary) solution, and the last term is called the steady-state solution (particular integral).

Primarily we are interested in three cases for $r(t)$, as follows:

Case 1, unit step function:

$$r(t) = 0 \qquad t < 0$$

$$r(t) = 1 \qquad t \geq 0 \tag{3.3–4}$$

or

$$r(t) = u(t)$$

Case 2, unit ramp function:

$$r(t) = 0 \qquad t < 0$$

$$r(t) = t \qquad t \geq 0 \tag{3.3–5}$$

or

$$r(t) = tu(t)$$

Case 3, unit sinusoidal function:

$$r(t) = \sin \omega t \qquad \text{for all } t \tag{3.3–6}$$

In (3.3–4) and (3.3–5), the initial conditions are taken as zero,† while in

† In this book, zero initial conditions will be assumed when an input $r(t)$ exists unless otherwise indicated.

(3.3–6) we shall be interested in the steady-state solution for $t \gg 0$. In a linear system, if the actual driving function has K units, the solution will be that determined from the corresponding unit function multiplied by K. We have taken the initial time as $t = 0$, although more generally the initial time could be taken as $t = t_0$.

The Laplace transform of (3.3–1) for zero initial conditions on the function q and its derivative gives

$$(s^2 + As = B)Q(s) = E\mathscr{L}r(t) \tag{3.3–7}$$

or

$$Q(s) = \frac{E\mathscr{L}r(t)}{s^2 + As + B} \tag{3.3–8}$$

As before, the inverse transform that gives $q(t)$ depends on the roots of the characteristic equation $s^2 + As + B = 0$. From the quadratic formula these roots are

$$s = \frac{-A \pm \sqrt{A^2 - 4B}}{2} \tag{3.3–9}$$

and they may be real and unequal, real and equal, or complex. The complex root situation promises the most interest and it is helpful to introduce two new parameters ζ and ω_n by writing the characteristic equation in the form

$$s^2 + As + B = s^2 + 2\zeta\omega_n s + \omega_n^2 = 0 \tag{3.3–10}$$

ζ is called the "damping factor" and ω_n the "natural angular velocity" (or sometimes "natural frequency"). If the roots are complex, $\zeta < 1$, and

$$s_1 = -\zeta\omega_n + j\omega_n\sqrt{1 - \zeta^2} \tag{3.3–11a}$$

$$s_2 = -\zeta\omega_n - j\omega_n\sqrt{1 - \zeta^2} \tag{3.3–11b}$$

The symbol $\sqrt{x}$ will be taken to mean the positive root unless otherwise indicated.

We see that these roots may be shown in the complex plane as in Figure 3.3–1, where ω_n is the length of a line from the origin to s_1 or s_2, $\zeta\omega_n$ the real part, and $\zeta = \cos \phi$, where ϕ is measured from the negative real axis. Sin $\phi = \sqrt{1 - \zeta^2}$, and hence the imaginary part of s_1 is $\omega_d = \omega_n\sqrt{1 - \zeta^2}$.

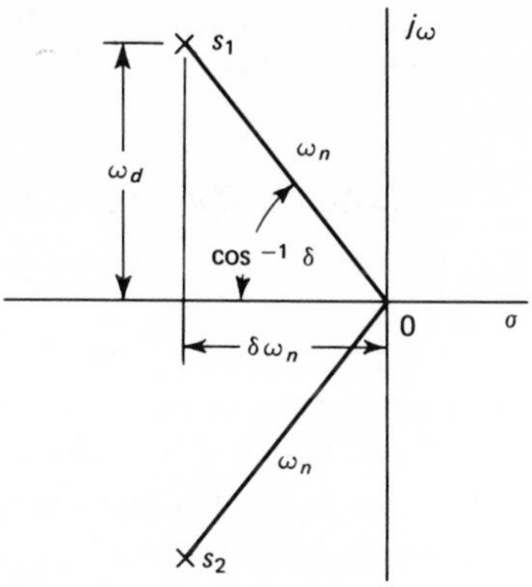

Figure 3.3–1. Pair of complex poles in the *s* plane.

If $r(t)$ is the unit step function of (3.3–4), $\mathscr{L}r(t) = 1/s$. Then for zero initial conditions,

$$q(t) = \mathscr{L}^{-1}\left[E\frac{1}{s[(s+\zeta\omega_n)^2 + \omega_n^2(1-\zeta^2)]}\right] \tag{3.3–12}$$

or

$$q(t) = E\left[\frac{1}{\omega_n^2} - \frac{1}{\omega_n^2\sqrt{1-\zeta^2}}\epsilon^{-\zeta\omega_n t}\sin[\omega_n(\sqrt{1-\zeta^2})t + \psi]\right] \qquad t \geq 0, \quad 1 > \zeta \geq 0 \tag{3.3–13a}$$

where

$$\psi = \tan^{-1}\frac{\sqrt{1-\zeta^2}}{\zeta} \tag{3.3–13b}$$

In the particular case of Figure 3.2–2,

$$\omega_n^2 = \frac{hK_d K_A K_M}{J_1} \qquad \zeta = \frac{D}{2\sqrt{hK_d K_A K_M J_1}} \qquad E = \frac{n_1 K_A K_d K_M}{J_1}$$

$\tau_L = 0$; hence $E/\omega_n^2 = n_1/h$. If the desired output $i(t) = (n_1/h)u(t)$, then the relative or normalized output is

$$\frac{q(t)}{n_1/h} = 1 - \frac{1}{\sqrt{1-\zeta^2}}\epsilon^{\zeta\omega_n t}\sin[\omega_n(\sqrt{1-\zeta^2})t + \psi] \qquad t \geq 0, \quad 1 > \zeta \geq 0 \tag{3.3–14}$$

where ψ is defined in (3.3–13b).

The difference between the desired output and the actual output is the error. Hence the error in terms of $i(t)$ is

$$y_e(t) = \frac{1}{\sqrt{1-\zeta^2}} \epsilon^{\zeta\omega_n t} \sin[\omega_n(\sqrt{1-\zeta^2})t + \psi] \qquad t \geq 0, \quad 1 > \zeta \geq 0 \tag{3.3–15}$$

If ζ reaches the limit of 1, then (3.3–14) and (3.3–15) become indeterminate. We can use L'Hospital's rule, but perhaps it is more revealing to return to (3.3–10), which shows that if $\zeta = 1$, the characteristic equation has two real equal roots. This is termed the degenerate case, and the solution with the previous conditions becomes

$$\frac{q(t)}{n_1/h} = 1 - \epsilon^{\omega_n t}(1 + \omega_n t) \tag{3.3–16}$$

This has theoretical, but not much practical interest, as it is unlikely in practice that the roots will be exactly the same.

If ζ reaches the limit of 0, then (3.3–14) becomes

$$\frac{q(t)}{n_1/h} = \begin{cases} 1 - \sin(\omega_n t + 90°) \\ 1 - \cos(\omega_n t) \end{cases} \tag{3.3–17}$$

or the system oscillates perfectly (with an added direct component). It then has zero damping, which in a practical linear system rarely can be accomplished.

The characteristic equation giving real roots results in two exponentially decaying terms and is said to be overdamped. Such a system has little use because of its sluggish transient response. The system with complex roots is said to be underdamped, and a lighter damping corresponds to a smaller ζ. The system with two equal real roots lies on the boundary and is said to be critically damped.

If the input $r(t)$ is a ramp function, (3.3–5), then $r(t) = 1/s^2$. The output for zero initial conditions is then

$$q(t) = \mathscr{L}^{-1}\left[E\frac{1}{s^2[(s+\zeta\omega_n)^2 + \omega_n^2(1-\zeta^2)]}\right] \tag{3.3–18}$$

You can work out the inverse transform of the right side of (3.3–18) without much difficulty. In this chapter we shall be interested primarily in the solution for this case as $t \to \infty$.

If the input $r(t)$ is a sinusoidal function with angular velocity ω, interest focuses on the steady-state condition ($t \gg 0$). Ordinary a-c analysis can be used, or, alternatively, the Laplace transform can be applied, where $r(t) = \omega/(s^2 + \omega^2)$ and the transient terms are neglected. The solution is

$$q(t) = \frac{E}{\omega_n^2} \frac{1}{[(1 - (\omega/\omega_n)^2)^2 + 4\zeta^2(\omega/\omega_n)^2]^{1/2}} \sin(\omega t - \theta) \qquad t \gg 0 \tag{3.3–19a}$$

where

$$\theta = \tan^{-1}\left[\frac{2\zeta(\omega/\omega_n)}{1 - (\omega/\omega_n)^2}\right] \tag{3.3–19b}$$

and, for our example, if the desired output is $(n_1/h)\sin \omega t$, then the normalized output is

$$\frac{q(t)}{n_1/h} = \frac{1}{[(1 - (\omega/\omega_n)^2)^2 + 4\zeta^2(\omega/\omega_n)^2]^{1/2}} \sin(\omega t - \theta) \tag{3.3–20}$$

In (3.3–19) and (3.3–20) $\theta = \theta(\omega)$ is a phase angle, not a shaft angle.

3.4 Performance Specifications

Before we analyze in detail equations (3.3–14), (3.3–15), and (3.3–20), we desire to discuss system specifications and indices of performance. To define a "best" system you must set up certain specific performance criteria for comparing systems, and what may be good criteria in one situation may not be good criteria in another. Writing or defining specifications for a control system is a task requiring as much or more understanding and ingenuity as designing.

Criteria for performance perhaps may be divided into two general categories: (1) criteria associated with classical analysis, and (2) criteria associated with modern analysis. This does not imply that these criteria do not overlap. However, it will be convenient to follow this classification because of historical development. In this chapter we shall take up the first classification, reserving the second classification for later chapters.

Performance criteria developed with classical analysis, which is primarily analysis in the frequency domain, grew up with the development of controls during World War II. These are based on experience with operating systems and usually are associated with single-output systems as in Figure 1.5–8. The first requirement is that the static error (difference between actual output and desired output) for no change in reference be less than a specified amount. Unless this basic requirement can be met, the system is obviously no good. The static error may be found by comparing the output with the desired output for some input as $t \to \infty$ and will depend on the input function. However, if the error is expressed as a function of the complex frequency s, it is often simpler to use the final value theorem of Laplace transformation theory, which is

$$\lim_{t\to\infty} y_e(t) = \lim_{s\to 0} s\,Y_e(s) \tag{3.4–1}$$

Equation (3.4–1) holds for $y_e(t)$ if $Y_e(s)$ represents a stable system. This approach is particularly useful if the error is $\hat{\varepsilon}(s)$ (Figure 3.2–2) or is proportional to it. Using the Laplace transform transfer function in (3.2–18),

$$\hat{\epsilon}(s) = \frac{1}{1 + S_1 S_2 S_3} R(s) \tag{3.4–2}$$

where $S_1 S_2 S_3$ is the transfer function around the loop, or for the antenna example

$$S_1 S_2 S_3 = \frac{h\hat{\theta}_M(s)}{\hat{\epsilon}(s)} = \frac{hK_d K_A K_M}{J_1 s(s + D/J_1)}$$

Using the terminology of Figure 1.5–9, the actual error is $y_e(t) = i(t) - q(t)$. For the antenna example (Figure 3.2–1) then,

$$Y_e(s) = I(s) - Q(s) = \frac{n_1}{h} R(s) - \frac{n_1}{h} \frac{S_1 S_2 S_3}{(1 + S_1 S_2 S_3)} R(s)$$

$$= \frac{n_1}{h}\left(1 - \frac{S_1 S_2 S_3}{1 + S_1 S_2 S_3}\right) R(s)$$

then

$$Y_e(s) = \left(\frac{n_1}{h}\right) \hat{\epsilon}(s) \tag{3.4–3}$$

In the example the actuating signal is

$$\hat{\epsilon}(s) = \frac{1}{1 + \{hK_d K_A K_M / J_1 s[s + (D/J_1)]\}} R(s) \tag{3.4–4}$$

and if $R(s) = 1/s\ [r(t) = u(t)]$,

$$\lim_{t\to\infty} \epsilon(t) = \lim_{s\to\infty} s \frac{1}{s} \frac{J_1 s(s + (D/J_1))}{J_1 s[s + (D/J_1)] + hK_d K_A K_M}$$

or

$$\lim_{t\to\infty} \epsilon(t) = 0$$

If $R(s) = 1/s^2$ $[r(t) = tu(t)]$,

$$\lim_{t\to\infty} \epsilon(t) = \lim_{s\to\infty} s \frac{1}{s^2} \frac{J_1 s[s + (D/J_1)]}{J_1 s[s + (D/J_1)] + hK_d K_A K_M}$$

or

$$\lim_{t\to\infty} \epsilon(t) = \frac{D}{hK_d K_A K_M} \tag{3.4-5}$$

D is usually not under the control of the designer, and h is determined by other considerations; hence the larger we make $K_d K_A K_M$, the smaller the static error of this system on a ramp input. The static error of this system on a step input is zero, which indicates no error after infinite time in this case. Figure 3.4–1 shows the ramp input and a typical output for this

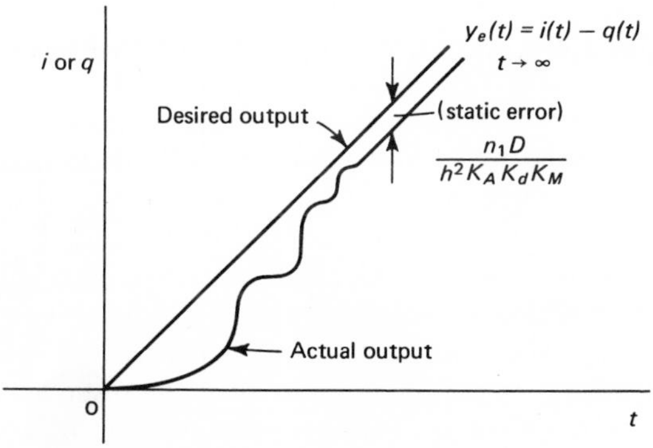

Figure 3.4–1. Output of a ramp input.

system which indicates that the output will proceed at the same rate as the input after the transients have disappeared, but the actual output lags behind the desired output by the amount of the static error. This amount is one criterion used for a static performance index (see Chapter 9). You can readily show that the static error on a parabolic input $r(t) = t^2u(t)$ is infinite for the system of the example.

Following the static specification, we have performance indices based on simple functional changes in the reference or the desired output. The functions used are usually (1) the step, (c) the ramp, (3) the parabolic, and (4) the sinusoidal. These functions are easy to generate, and experience has shown that response to them is often indicative of response to more complicated functions. Probably the step is the most widely used and is

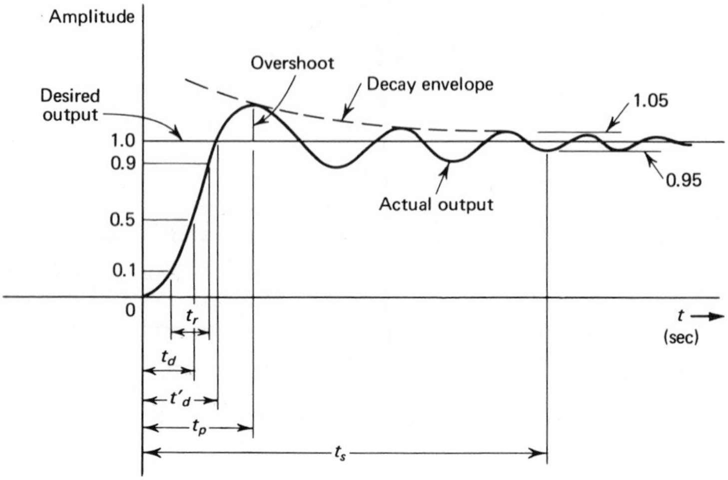

Figure 3.4–2. Performance indices based on step function.

shown in Figure 3.4–2 with the desired output normalized for convenience. With a step change in the desired output, some of the criteria are:

1. Per cent overshoot on the first reversal of the output.
2. 10 to 90 per cent rise time, t_r.
3. 50 per cent rise time (delay time), t_d.
4. Delay time t_d', where output first equals the desired value.
5. Settling time, t_s, or the time required for the response reach and to remain within a certain tolerance band (shown as ± 5 per cent in Figure 3.4–2).
6. Final error e in percentage.
7. Frequency of oscillation during settling.
8. Decay rate during settling.

The ramp function output has already been shown in Figure 3.4–1, and many similar criteria may be applied in this case.

The sinusoidal function has criteria of gain and phase angle (ratio of output to desired output in magnitude and phase). These criteria are usually plotted as a function of angular velocity. Figure 3.4–3 shows the magnitude ratio as a function of sinusoidal angular velocity ω using logarithmic scales. The magnitude criteria are bandwidth BW, peak response M_p (either in per unit or decibels), the angular velocity of the peak ω_p, and the final slope n (in decibels per decade). The phase-angle plot has less interest and often is not made. The frequency plot, Figure

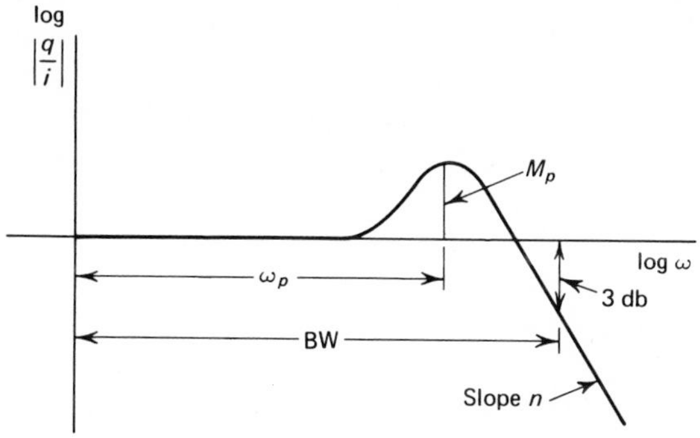

Figure 3.4–3. Performance indices based on sinusoidal function.

3.4–3, and the time-response plot, Figure 3.4–2, are connected through the Laplace and Fourier transforms.

A measure of performance that has received more recent attention is the integral of the squared error [1]. It would seem reasonable that some sort of index could be based on the area under the error curve, which is associated with some specified reference input, as in Figure 3.4–4. Such an expression might be

$$J = \int_0^T [y_e(t)]^2 \, dt \tag{3.4–6}$$

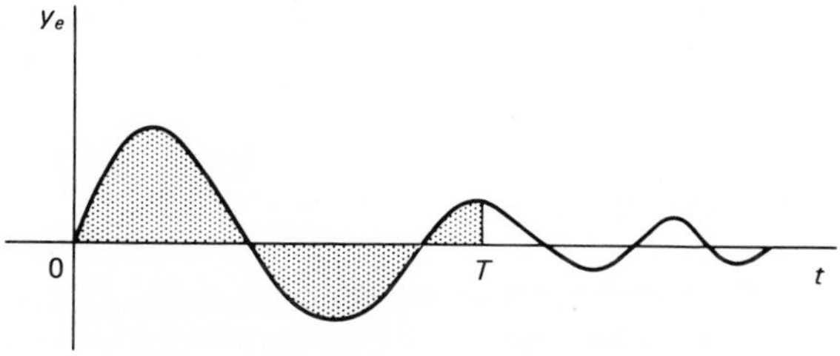

Figure 3.4–4. Error as a function of time.

where J is a performance index (a number) and the time $t = 0$ represents the time of application of the reference input, while $t = T$ is a specified upper limit. Usual reference inputs are step or ramp functions, and the upper limit is usually $T = \infty$ if the integral converges. Equation (3.4–6) has been exploited both algebraically and graphically and will be discussed subsequently. Systems designed for such a performance index may or may not result in "good" performance as measured by the previous indices.

Much the same criteria can be used with respect to a disturbance. The yardsticks often applied consist of: steady-state error in per unit of desired output, percent overshoot with application of a step disturbance, settling time, integral of the squared error, and so on. For the example under consideration, the equation is the same as (3.3–1) except that $E = n_1^2/J_1$ and $r(t)$ becomes $\tau_L(t)$. The solutions are thus of the same form as before but with different constants.

Very similar criteria are employed with discontinuous time and sampled-data systems. However, if the control signals become random, it is necessary to adopt other criteria; for example, that the mean-square error be the least [2].

Coming back to the simple performance measures already listed for deterministic systems, we would like to achieve the following:

1. Static error:
   a. As small as possible for all inputs.
2. Step input criteria:
   a. Rise time as fast as possible.
   b. Overshoot as small as possible.
   c. Settling time as small as possible.
   d. Decay rate as fast as possible.
   e. Delay times as small as possible.
   f. Frequency of oscillation as low as possible.
   g. Integral of the squared error for a given time and input as small as possible.
3. Sinusoidal criteria:
   a. Bandwidth small enough to exclude noise.
   b. Cutoff slope n as large as possible.
   c. M_p, peak response, as low as possible.

You note the term "as possible" occurring in most cases, and this follows from the fact that we cannot achieve all these things simultaneously. The designer finds it necessary to trade improvement in one region for deterioration in another. The traditional dilemma of the engineer becomes: What factors are the most important, and how much can I trade in one area to gain in another? For example, to achieve low static error, a high loop gain is required, but this high gain leads to a large overshoot and long settling time on step input. The fast rise time requires a large natural frequency ω_n (for the second-order system), and this means a large bandwidth, which is bad from a noise standpoint. The specification writer must determine which of the constituents have the greater importance and which the lesser importance.

In the realm of specifications art displaces science, and decisions are made on the basis of judgment and experience. The "best" system will depend to a large extent on the purpose of the system, and the success of the design must be judged on a pragmatic basis, which means the judge's prejudices are involved. Ultimately, arguments about specifications involve philosophical foundations and are thus not easily resolved. Often the designer may feel that the specifications are not suitable for the desired system, but he may have difficulty in convincing the specifying agency. Usually, we shall assume in this book that the specifications are given, but it is well to remember that you may at some time be required to write, alter, or at least criticize these specifications.

3.5 Second-Order-System Performance

Equation (3.3–14) gives the output in terms of the desired step output or a normalized output $(h/n_1)q(t)$ for a unit step reference $[r(t) = u(t)]$. It is convenient to use $\omega_n t$ as a normalized time scale, and doing this we obtain Figure 3.5–1. Examining Figure 3.5–1, you see that the overshoot depends only on the damping factor ζ. This can be made explicit by differentiating (3.3–14), which gives†

$$\frac{d}{dt}\frac{q(t)}{i(t)} = \frac{1}{\omega_n\sqrt{1-\zeta^2}}\,\epsilon^{-\zeta\omega_n t}\sin[\omega_n(\sqrt{1-\zeta^2})t] \tag{3.5–1}$$

The first (and peak) overshoot occurs when $\omega_n(\sqrt{1-\zeta^2})t = \pi$, or

$$\omega_n t = \frac{\pi}{\sqrt{1-\zeta^2}} \tag{3.5–2}$$

Substituting (3.5–2) back in (3.3–15), the maximum per cent overshoot becomes

$$\%\ \text{overshoot} = 100\epsilon^{-\zeta\pi/\sqrt{1-\zeta^2}} \tag{3.5–3}$$

Equation (3.5–3) is plotted in Figure 3.5–2, which shows the variation of the overshoot with ζ. To keep the per cent overshoot below 20 per cent, which is a fairly high value, the damping factor must be kept above 0.45. The settling time t_s also varies with ζ. It can be shown that for tolerance bands of 5 to 10 per cent $\omega_n t_s$ reaches a minimum of around 2.8 at a damping factor of about 0.7. For lower damping factors, the settling time

† Multiply the right side of (3.3–12) by s and transform.

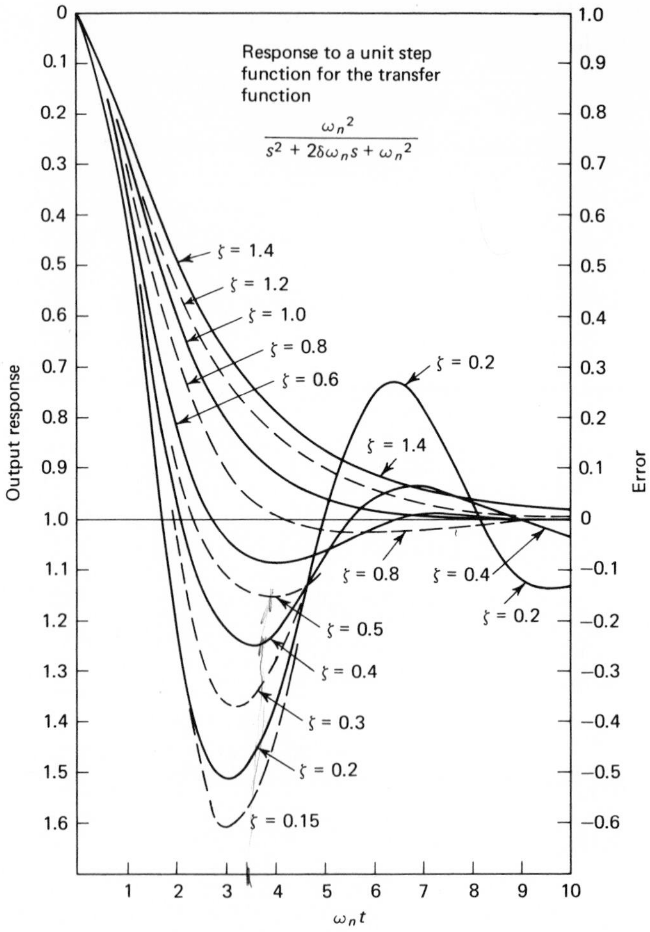

Figure 3.5–1. Response to a unit step function for a second-order system.

increases rather rapidly, while for higher factors, a less rapid increase occurs [3].

The rise time and delay time depend on both ζ and ω_n. To prevent too sluggish a system, a slight overshoot is customary. Alternatively, as you have seen, a very large overshoot results in a long settling time, both of which are usually undesirable. Hence the damping factor ζ is usually given a value somewhere between 0.5 and 0.9. Following this recipe (which might not be advisable in certain applications), we see from Figure 3.5–1 and Table 3.5–1 that the 10 to 90 per cent rise time does not change greatly with ζ but is inversely proportional to ω_n. Hence you can hold the overshoot to a reasonable value and reduce rise time by increasing ω_n, which also simultaneously reduces the settling time.

TABLE 3.5–1. APPROXIMATE 10 TO 90 PER CENT TIME t_r (IN SECONDS) IN TERMS OF ω_n

ζ	$\omega_n t_r$
0.4	1.45
0.5	1.58
0.6	1.86
0.7	2.16
0.8	2.55
1.0	3.47

Figure 3.5–1 shows curves for $\zeta > 1.0$, for which (3.3–14) does not apply. Referring to (3.3–10), if $\zeta = 1$, the roots of the characteristic equation become real and equal, while, if, $\zeta > 1$, the roots are real and unequal. The system does not oscillate in either case, as shown by the $\zeta \geq 1$ curves of Figure 3.5–1. Strictly speaking, the damping factor ζ is not defined for values greater than 1.

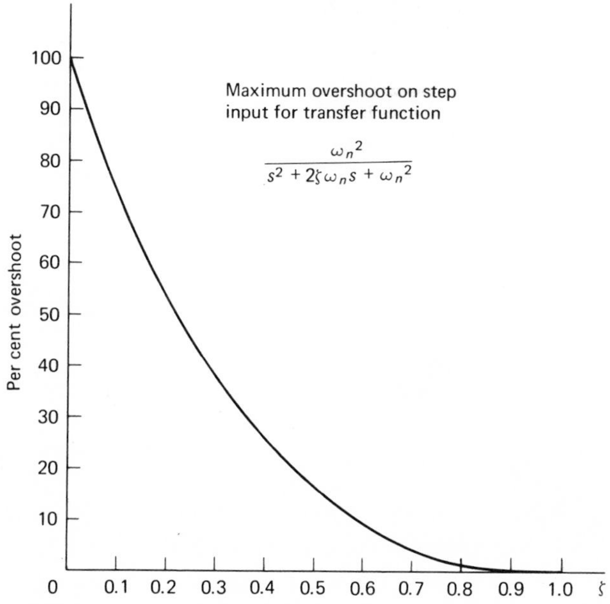

Figure 3.5–2. Maximum overshoot of response to step input.

Turning to the sinusoidal response, (3.3–20) gives the steady output in terms of the desired output. This equation can be plotted in two parts: (1) the magnitude or gain and (2) the phase. That is, the output will have the same angular velocity ω as the input, but the magnitude (either peak value or root-mean-square value) of the output compared to the desired output will be given by

$$\left|\frac{q}{i}\right| = \frac{1}{\{[1-(\omega/\omega_n)^2]^2 + 4\zeta^2(\omega/\omega_n)^2\}^{1/2}} \tag{3.5–4}$$

while the output will lag the desired output by the angle

$$\theta = \tan^{-1}\left[\frac{2\zeta\omega/\omega_n}{1-(\omega/\omega_n)^2}\right] \tag{3.5–5}$$

To plot these curves we adopt the normalized independent variable ω/ω_n, and Figure 3.5–3 shows the magnitude variation while Figure 3.5–4 shows the phase variation. The frequency scale is logarithmic, and the magnitude scale is also logarithmic. These curves are termed Bode plots [4].

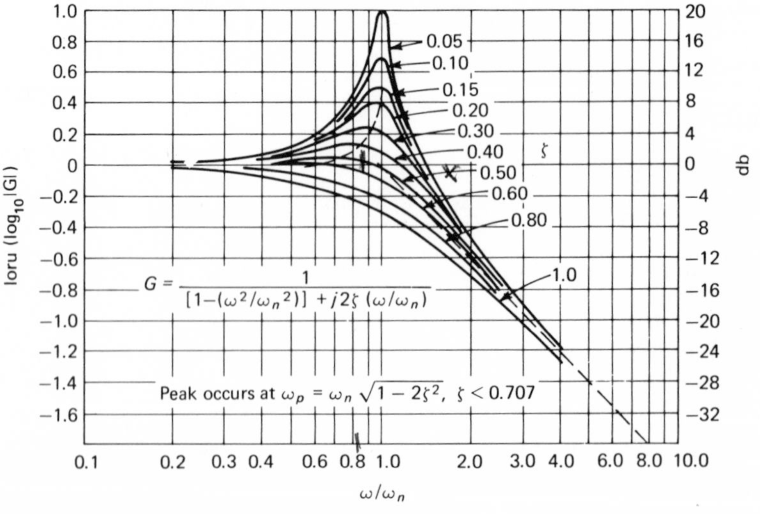

Figure 3.5–3. Response of second-order system to sinusoidal input of angular velocity ω – magnitude.

The peak value of the gain curve M_p, and the value of angular velocity ω_p at which it occurs, can be found by differentiating (3.3–19) with respect to ω and setting the zero. The result is

$$\omega_p = \omega_n\sqrt{1-2\zeta^2} \qquad 0 > \zeta > \tfrac{1}{2}\sqrt{2} \tag{3.5–6}$$

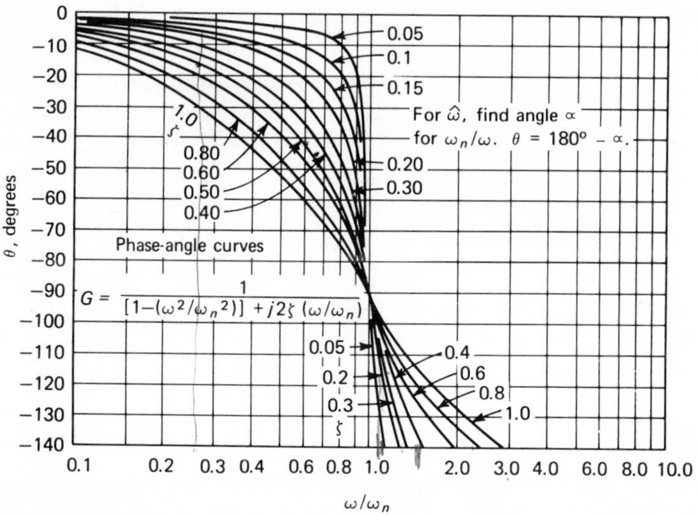

Figure 3.5–4. Response of second-order system to sinusoidal input of angular velocity ω – phase angle. $\hat{\omega} = \omega/\omega_n$ when $\omega/\omega_n \geq 1$ or $\hat{\omega}$ is ω/ω_n in the 1.0 to 10.0 region.

Substituting this back into (3.5–4),

$$M_p = \frac{1}{2\zeta\sqrt{1-\zeta^2}} \qquad 0 < \zeta \leq \tfrac{1}{2}\sqrt{2} \tag{3.5–7}$$

Equations (3.5–6) and (3.5–7) apply only if $0 < \xi \leq \frac{1}{2}\sqrt{2}$, since for $\zeta > \frac{1}{2}\sqrt{2}$, Equation (3.5–6) becomes imaginary, or no peak occurs, and the magnitude curve slope is negative for $\omega > 0$.

The gain curve at high values of ω falls off at a rate of 40 db per decade, where the unit db is defined by the relation

$$\text{db} = 20 \log_{10} \left| \frac{q}{i} \right| \tag{3.5–8}$$

and a decade is a tenfold change in angular velocity.† This conclusion readily follows from (3.5–4), since as ω/ω_n becomes very large

$$\left| \frac{q}{i} \right| \simeq \frac{1}{(\omega/\omega_n)^2}$$

You can see that an intimate relation exists between the time response due to a step function and the frequency response. Mathematically this

† This is not the normal definition of a decibel.

connection, which is particularly simple in the case of the second-order system, is that between the time domain and the complex frequency domain, as expressed by the Fourier and Laplace transforms. This association assists not only in a theoretical way but is also useful experimentally. Thus knowledge of the frequency response tells us the time response. In the laboratory, the frequency response often results in more accurate system analysis than the time response from a step, say, because changes in the system show up more clearly in the former. If the system becomes of high order, the exact time response is obtainable only through complicated integral relations, which can be practically solved only by graphical techniques or computer methods. However, the following example illustrates the simplicity of the relation in the second-order case.

Example 3.5–1

In the instance of the control system being discussed, assume that a sinusoidal test signal of various fequencies is applied. If the test apparatus produces an electrical signal, as is the usual situation, the signal is most easily applied in series with the loop of Figure 3.2–1, just prior to the amplifier, and with θ_1 held constant. (A mechanical signal could be applied at θ_1 but this would be more difficult to measure.) The output θ can be measured electrically by means of a small auxilliary tachometer generator, or directly by a camera or other means. Assume that the frequency response curve of Figure 3.5–5 shows the normalized magnitude response. We observe

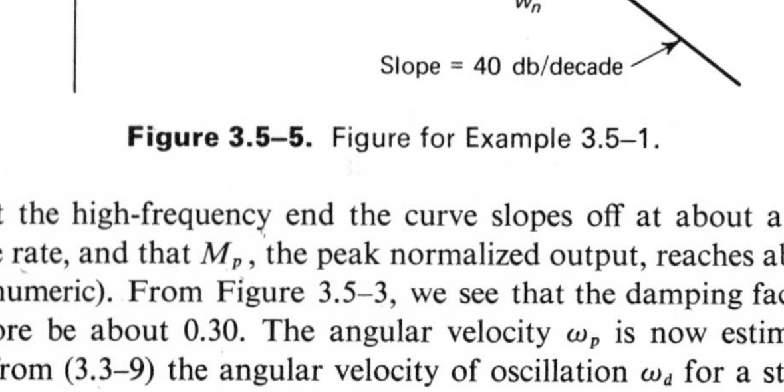

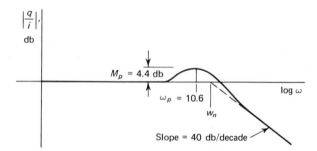

Figure 3.5–5. Figure for Example 3.5–1.

that at the high-frequency end the curve slopes off at about a 40 db per decade rate, and that M_p, the peak normalized output, reaches about 4.4 db (1.66 numeric). From Figure 3.5–3, we see that the damping factor ζ must therefore be about 0.30. The angular velocity ω_p is now estimated, and, since from (3.3–9) the angular velocity of oscillation ω_d for a step input is

$$\omega_d = \omega_n\sqrt{1-\zeta^2} \text{ rad/sec} \tag{3.5–9}$$

then, from (3.5–9),

$$\omega_d = \omega_p \frac{\sqrt{1-\zeta^2}}{\sqrt{1-2\zeta^2}} \tag{3.5–10}$$

Thus from Figure 3.5–5, the angular velocity

$$\omega_d = 10.6 \frac{\sqrt{1-(0.30)^2}}{\sqrt{1-2(0.30)^2}}$$

$$= 11.15 \text{ rad/sec}$$

The value of ω_n may be checked by projecting the 40-db slope back to the 0-db axis, as shown in Figure 3.5–5. In case the peak M_p is not well defined, or if $\zeta \geq \frac{1}{2}\sqrt{2}$, This would be the method for finding ω_n and ω_d.

Once ζ and ω_n are known, we now turn to Figure 3.5–1 and can predict the step response in all aspects. The step response (or impulse response) can then be used to find the response to any reasonably well-behaved deterministic signal by using the convolution integral.

These rather elementary relations form the basis of a great deal of classical design. More specifically, we select a pair of complex poles (resulting in a second-order system) to meet the specifications as well as possible. Then additional poles and zeros are added if necessary. The original pair of complex poles are often called "dominant" poles, in the sense that they presumably dominate the system characteristics. Design following this procedure becomes cut and try to a large extent, although direct synthesis methods have been developed (see Chapter 9).

Let us now investigate some compensation methods and the effect of adding additional poles and zeros to the system.

3.6 Simple Compensation of a Second-Order System

In using transfer functions in a flow diagram for control systems, the operators in a forward path are usually labeled G, and those in a feedback path as H. Thus Figure 3.2–3 can be represented (using the general input-output symbols) by Figure 3.6–1, where initially G_c, the compensation, is 1, and $D(s) = n_1\tau_L(s)$.

From (3.2–16) and (3.2–17),

$$C(s) = \frac{G_1G_2}{1+G_1G_2H} R(s) - \frac{G_2}{1+G_1G_2H} n_1\hat{\tau}_L(s) \tag{3.6–1}$$

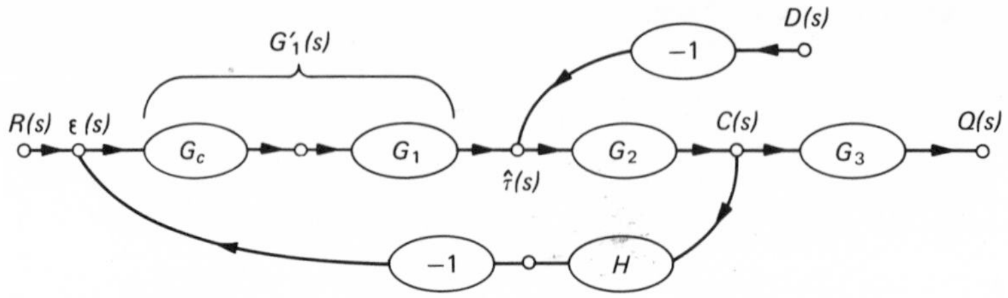

Figure 3.6–1. Tandem compensation in control system.

Letting $\hat{\tau}_L$ be zero for a time, then

$$\frac{C(s)}{R(s)} = \frac{G_1G_2}{1 + G_1G_2H} \tag{3.6–2}$$

where G_1, G_2, and H are functions of the complex variable s. G_1G_2H, or the open-loop transfer function, is also often called the return ratio. $1 + G_1G_2H$ is also termed the return difference, while C/R is called the control ratio [5]. The word "difference" in return difference stems from the fact that the returned quantity is usually subtracted from the input, or normally negative feedback conditions exist.

If G_1 and G_2 are representable in the time domain by linear differential equations with constant coefficients, then from the work we have done on the example, which you can easily extend to higher-order systems, it is clear that G_1 and G_2 are each a ratio of polynomials in s. Thus

$$G_1 = \frac{P_1(s)}{Q_1(s)} = \frac{b_m s^m + b_{m-1}s^{m-1} + \cdots + b_0}{s^n + a_{n-1}s^{n-1} + \cdots + a_0} \tag{3.6–3}$$

or in factored form,

$$G_1 = \frac{K\prod_{i=1}^{m}(s + z_i)}{\prod_{j=1}^{n}(s + p_j)} \tag{3.6–4}$$

where $\prod_{j=1}^{n}$ means: Take the product of n factors $(s + p_j)$, $j = 1, 2, \ldots, n$; K is a constant. The quantities $-p_j$ are called the poles of G_1 and the quantities $-z_i$ are called the zeros of G_1. The degree m of the numerator for a physical control system is usually at least 2 less than the degree n of the denominator and often consists only of the b_0 term.

The forward path operator G_1G_2 will be given by

$$G_1G_2 = \frac{P(s)}{Q(s)} \tag{3.6–5}$$

where $P(s) = P_1(s)P_2(s)$ and $Q(s) = Q_1(s)Q_2(s)$, and P and Q are thus new polynomials in s.

Similarly,

$$H(s) = \frac{U(s)}{V(s)} \tag{3.6–6}$$

where U and V are polynomials in s. Substituting (3.6–5) and (3.6–6) in 3.6–2) you obtain

$$\frac{C(s)}{R(s)} = \frac{P(s)/Q(s)}{1 + P(s)U(s)/Q(s)V(s)} \tag{3.6–7}$$

and, clearing fractions,

$$\frac{C(s)}{R(s)} = \frac{P(s)V(s)}{P(s)U(s) + Q(s)V(s)} \tag{3.6–8}$$

If $H(s)$ is a constant h, then (3.6–8) becomes

$$\frac{C(s)}{R(s)} = \frac{P(s)}{hP(s) + Q(s)} \tag{3.6–9}$$

and, if $h = 1$, you get

$$\frac{C(s)}{R(s)} = \frac{P(s)}{P(s) + Q(s)} \tag{3.6–10}$$

For positive feedback (no -1 operator in the feedback loop of Figure 3.6–1), (3.6–8), and (3.6–10) become

$$\frac{C(s)}{R(s)} = \frac{P(s)V(s)}{Q(s)V(s) - P(s)U(s)} \tag{3.6–11}$$

$$\frac{C(s)}{R(s)} = \frac{P(s)}{Q(s) - P(s)} \tag{3.6–12}$$

respectively.

The denominator of (3.6–8) or (3.6–10) produces a new polynomial in s but, whereas $P(s)$, $Q(s)$, $U(s)$, and $V(s)$ are usually known in factored form, because they have been derived from knowledge of the components and subsystems, the denominator $P(s)U(s) + Q(s)V(s)$ must be factored before the poles of $C(s)/R(s)$ are known, or we must find the roots of the characteristic equation

$$P(s)U(s) + Q(s)V(s) = 0 \tag{3.6–13}$$

You well know that finding the roots of a polynomial of over the second degree is a difficult task. This can be done readily by a modern digital computer at the cost of some time and expense. However, of even greater importance is the question "How do we manipulate the factors for $P(s)$, $Q(s)$, $U(s)$, and $V(s)$ to obtain the desired roots of the characteristic equation (3.6–13)?" If we find roots by some process, and these are unsatisfactory, what do we alter to get satisfactory ones? In still different language, what changes do you make in the open loop operator G_1G_2H to obtain a desired closed loop operator or control ratio as given by (3.6–8)? This is the classical design problem for single input-output systems, and one on which we shall spend much time in later chapters. At this point, let us take a few cases which will illustrate the situation in low-order systems.

First, let us see what happens if we add a zero to G_1 in the antenna example. From Figure 3.2–2 in the forward gain path we have $G_1 = K_d K_a K_M$ and $G_2 = 1/J_1 s(s + D/J_1)$. Then, if we insert a factor $(s + z_1)$ in G_c (Figure 3.6–1), we get $G_1' = K_d K_A K_M(s + z_i)$. However, it has previously been noted that the static error is determined by the transfer function as $s \to 0$. Hence, to maintain the static error prior to insertion of the zero, we should make $G_1' = (K_d K_A K_M/z_1)(s + z_1)$. Then, from (3.6–9),

$$\frac{C(s)}{R(s)} = \frac{(1/z_1)K_d K_A K_M(s + z_1)}{(h/z_1)K_d K_A K_M(s + z_1) + J_1 s[s + (D/J_1)]} \tag{3.6–14}$$

In the antenna example, $Q(s)$ is directly proportional to $C(s)$ and $I(s)$ is similarly proportional to $R(s)$; hence $C(s)/R(s)$ gives all the information needed on transient variations.

If we examine the denominator of (3.6–14), we see that whereas previously the characteristic equation was

$$J_1\left(s^2 + \frac{D}{J_1}s + \frac{K_1}{J_1}\right) = 0 \tag{3.6–15}$$

where $K_1 = hK_d K_A K_M$, we now have

$$J_1\left[s^2 + \left(\frac{D}{J_1} + \frac{K_1}{J_1 z_1}\right)s + \frac{K_1}{J_1}\right] = 0 \tag{3.6–16}$$

Thus $c(t)$ has been altered not only by the factor in the numerator (the zero $-z_1$) but the characteristic equation has also been changed, so that the poles are different. From (3.6–16), the equation is still of second order, and the angular velocity ω_n is the same, but the damping factor ζ is greater due to the second term of (3.6–16). [This assumes that $z_1 > 0$, or the zero of the equation $(s + z_1) = 0$ is in the left-half s plane.] The addition of the zero is a form of compensation G_c and the term in the $(s + z_1)$ factor in the numerator results in differentiation in the time domain. In process control a system with a derivative and direct proportion term in $G_1 G_2$ is often called a "proportional plus derivative" system [6].

If we add a pole in G_c and maintain the previous static error, we obtain

$$G_1' G_2 = \frac{p_1 K_d K_A K_M}{(s + p_1)[J_1 s(s + (D/J_1)]}$$

$$\frac{C(s)}{R(s)} = \frac{p_1 K_d K_A K_M}{J_1\{s^3 + [(D/J_1) + p_1]s^2 + (p_1 D/J_1)s + hp_1 K_d K_A K_M} \tag{3.6–17}$$

You see that the addition of the open loop pole at $-p_1$ $(p_1 > 0)$ makes the closed loop system $[C(s)/R(s)]$ of higher order. The factorization of the characteristic equation is no longer trivial; furthermore, since p_1 occurs in three terms, it is not obvious what its value should be to give the desired poles of the control ratio of C/R.

A system where $G_1' G_2$ contains a term $[(1/s) + k]$ multiplies the loop operator by a $1/s$ factor or adds a pole at the origin. Since $1/s$ represents integration in the time domain, this is sometimes called a "proportional plus integral" system [6]. This also increases the order of the characteristic equation.

The compensation may consist of both a pole and a zero, or, in more complex situations, several poles and zeros, and can be constructed physically using electrical, mechanical, or fluid elements. For complicated compensation, an electrical network is usually simple, light in weight, inexpensive, and easily constructable, although for relatively simple compensation, fluid or mechanical devices may be superior in performance or, depending on the other system elements, less expensive. In any case, so far in our discussion the compensation has been placed in the forward loop. In other words, $G_1' = G_1 G_c$, where G_1 is the new operator after the insertion of a series compensator G_c.

We might ask if some sort of feedback compensation might be used, as H_1 in Figure 3.6–2. The combination G_2 and the internal feedback H_1 can be replaced by a new operator

$$G_2' = \frac{G_2}{1 + G_2 H_1}$$

As G_2' is a ratio of polynomials of the form of (3.6–3) and (3.6–4), and $G_1' G_2$ is also a ratio of polynomials, it is clear that we can make $G_1 G_2' = G_1' G_2$, or, in other words, that the internal feedback H_1 can be adjusted

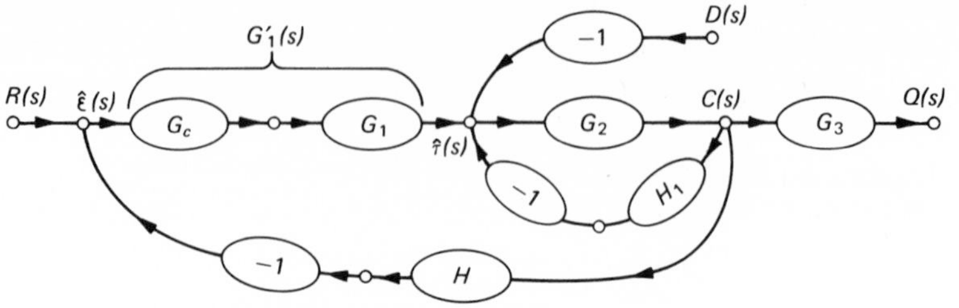

Figure 3.6–2. Feedback compensation in control system.

such that the same forward loop operator results as from a series compensator G_c. Alternatively, part of the compensation could be placed in a series compensator, and part in an internal feedback compensator H_1. This argument holds for the first term of (3.6–1), that is, for $C(s)/R(s)$, since the numerator of this function is $G_1 G_2$ (or $G_1' G_2'$ after compensation). For the second term [involving $C(s)/\hat{\tau}_L(s)$], however, you observe that the numerator is only G_2' after compensation. Therefore, by using an internal feedback H_1, it is possible to adjust $C(s)/R(s)$ somewhat independently of $C(s)/\hat{\tau}_L(s)$. Thus we might reduce the effect of the external torque and at the same time maintain the response to the desired input within specification. Practically, an internal feedback may also have advantages, because (1) as in any feedback system, it reduces the effect of variations in the forward path operators enclosed by the feedback loop, and (2) it can be made of small precise elements, owing to the low energy flow in the feedback path.

In our antenna example, we now examine a very simple but frequently used feedback compensator H_1 that is a small generator (called a tachometer) producing a voltage proportional to its speed. Physically, this can be a permanent pole d-c generator, or in the case of a carrier-type system, an a-c generator connected to the motor shaft. The output of the generator usually would be taken to a stage of the amplifier that precedes the motor of Figure 3.2–1.

Figure 3.6–3 shows a possible physical arrangement for the feedback path H_1 of Figure 3.6–2. Let the tachometer generate a voltage K_4 volts

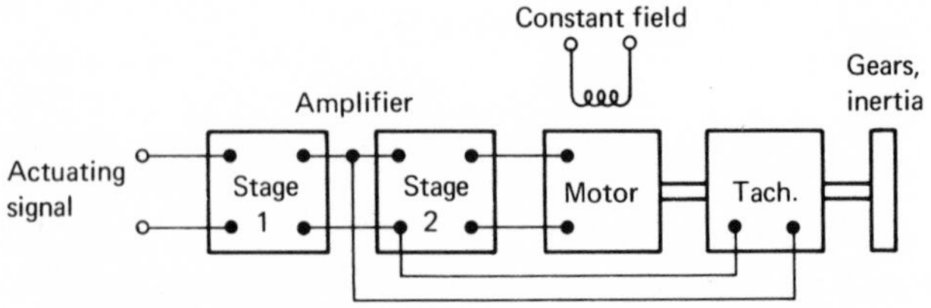

Figure 3.6–3. Schematic for internal tachometer feedback.

for each radian per second that its shafts rotates. Then the equation for the tachometer output V_t in terms of its shaft angle is

$$V_t = K_4 \frac{d\theta_m}{dt}$$

or the transfer function becomes

$$\frac{V_t}{\theta_M} = K_4 s$$

Let the amplification constant of stage 2 of the amplifier be K_B and the motor constant K_M, as before. Translating the schematic diagram of Figure 3.6–3 into the flow diagram of Figure 3.6–2, because the internal feedback enters the node $\hat{\tau}$, we see that H_1 includes the tachometer constant K_4, the amplification constant of stage 2 of the amplifier K_B, and the motor torque constant K_M. The -1 operator reminds us that the feedback must be such as to oppose the output of G_1. Then in Figure 3.6–2 for the antenna example

$$H_1 = K_4 K_B K_M s$$

or

$$H_1 = K_3 K_4 s$$

where $K_3 = K_M K_B$.

Then, using (3.6–8),

$$U(s) = K_3 K_4 s$$

$$V(s) = 1$$

$$G'_2(s) = \frac{1}{(K_3 K_4 s) + J_1 s[s + (D/J_1)]}$$

$$= \frac{1}{J_1 s\{s + [(D + K_3 K_4)/J_1]\}} \qquad \textbf{(3.6–18)}$$

You see that in this example the velocity feedback of the tachometer lowers the time constant of the motor from J_1/D to $J_1/(D + K_3 K_4)$. (If the internal feedback were positive, the time constant would be increased.) With the new G'_2, the overall function is

$$\frac{C(s)}{R(s)} = \frac{K_d K_A K_M}{hK_d K_A K_M + J_1 s\{s + [(D + K_3 K_4)/J]\}}$$

$$= \frac{K_d K_A K_M}{J_1\{s^2 + [(D + K_3 K_4)/J]s + (K_1/J_1)\}} \qquad \textbf{(3.6–19)}$$

You note that compared to (3.6–15) the characteristic equation of this system has been altered in a manner similar to that of (3.6–16), where the zero was introduced in the forward circuit but that the numerator of (3.6–19) does not contain the zero. (Special internal feedback devices could insert the zero.)

The response $C(s)$ to a disturbance torque is now given by

$$C(s) = \frac{-n_1 \hat{\tau}_L(s)}{J_1\{s^2 + [(D + K_3 K_4)/J_1]\, s + (K_1/J_1)\}} \tag{3.6–20}$$

Further compensation in either the internal feedback path or in the forward path could vary the response $C(s)$ to $R(s)$ in an independent manner from that of $C(s)$ to $\hat{\tau}_L(s)$.

As a final example, we look at a simple mechanical compensation. This consists of two inertias coupled through a viscous fluid, as in Figure 3.6–4.

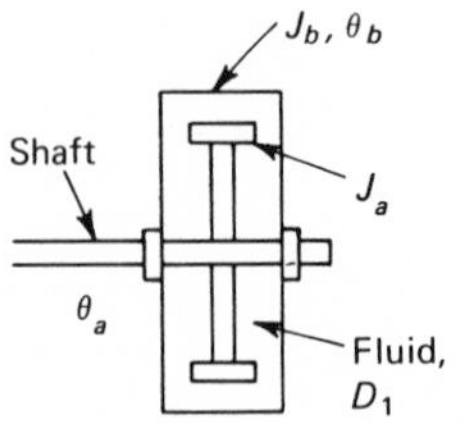

Figure 3.6–4. Mechanical compensator.

The inner inertia, J_a is connected to the motor shaft either directly or through gearing, while the outer inertia J_b rotates freely on the shaft. The space between the two inertias is filled with fluid. The equations of motion are

$$\tau_a(t) = J_a \frac{d^2\theta_a}{dt^2} + D_1\left(\frac{d\theta_a}{dt} - \frac{d\theta_b}{dt}\right)$$

$$0 = D_1\left(\frac{d\theta_b}{dt} - \frac{d\theta_a}{dt}\right) + J_b \frac{d^2\theta_b}{dt^2}$$

where τ_a is the shaft applied torque and D_1 is the viscous friction constant of the fluid. If you Laplace-transform these equations with all initial conditions taken as zero, then you get

$$\hat{\tau}_a(s) = \frac{s^2[J_a s + D_1(J_a + J_b)/J_b]}{s + (D_1/J_b)}\, \hat{\theta}_a(s) \tag{3.6–21}$$

If the inertias and friction constants of (3.6–21) are altered by the square of the gear ratio between the output shaft and motor shaft, the right term of (3.6–21) may be added to the right term of (3.2–2). After some algebra you then obtain

$$\frac{\hat{\theta}_M(s)}{\hat{\tau}(s)} = \frac{s + (D_1'/J_b')}{s[(J_1 + J_a)s^2 + \{[D_1'(J_1 + J_a' + J_b') + DJ_b']/J_b'\}s + (DD_1'/J_b')]}$$

(3.6–22)

where J_a', J_b', and D_1' are the constants altered by the square of the gear ratio. Usually, the previous inertias and J_a' are adjusted such that $(J_1 + J_a')$ is approximately equal to the previous J_1. Then

$$\frac{\hat{\theta}_M(s)}{\hat{\tau}(s)} = \frac{(s + D_1'/J_b)}{J_1 s\{s^2 + ([D_1'(J_1 + J_b') + DJ_b']/J_1 J_b')s + (DD_1/J_1 J_b')\}} \quad \textbf{(3.6–23)}$$

where J_1 has approximately the same value as in (3.2–3). Comparing (3.6–23) and (3.2–3) you see that the denominator of (3.6–23) is one degree higher than that for (3.2–3), and we have an added zero. Factoring the denominator into $(s + a)(s + b)$, where a and b may be complex, you observe that we have added both a zero and a pole to the open loop operator, and also probably altered the previous time constant (moved the previous pole). The system $C(s)/R(s)$ will now have a characteristic equation of third degree (or an additional pole) and a zero $s = -D_1'/J_b'$. The previous complex poles are altered. We leave the expression of the closed loop function to you as an exercise. By adjusting J_a, J_b, and D_1, you can change the location of the closed loop poles and the zero.

3.7 Effect of Added Poles or Zeros on the Time Response of a Second-Order System

In Section 3.6 we discussed various methods of compensation, which in the complex s domain reduced to adding poles and/or zeros to the existing system, of altering the existing complex poles. The addition of poles and zeros to the existing forward path G_1G_2 resulted in poles at different locations to the control ratio $C(s)/R(s)$. Most single input-output control systems usually have an overall feedback path of constant gain, which can be made 1 or -1 by flow diagram manipulation, and hence the closed loop zeros are the same as the open loop zeros. (With other devices, such as amplifiers, the overall feedback path may contain energy-storage devices, and this may not be the case.) What can we say about the effect of adding poles and zeros to the closed loop operator or control ratio $C(s)/R(s)$? Note that adding poles or zeros to C/R is not the same as adding poles or zeros to G_1G_2H, which was discussed in Section 3.6.

First look at the effect of adding a single zero to a second-order system, *assuming that the original complex poles remain fixed.* Then in the antenna example the normalized output on a step input becomes

$$\frac{q(t)}{n_1/h} = \mathscr{L}^{-1}\left[\frac{(1/z_1)\omega_n^2(s+z_1)}{s[(s+\zeta\omega_n)^2+\omega_n^2(1-\zeta^2)]}\right] \tag{3.7–1}$$

As discussed previously, the gain ω_n^2/z makes $sQ(s)(h/n_1) \to 1$ as $s \to 0$, or the response eventually equals the desired response for a step input. Figure 3.7–1 shows the s-plane pole-zero configuration.

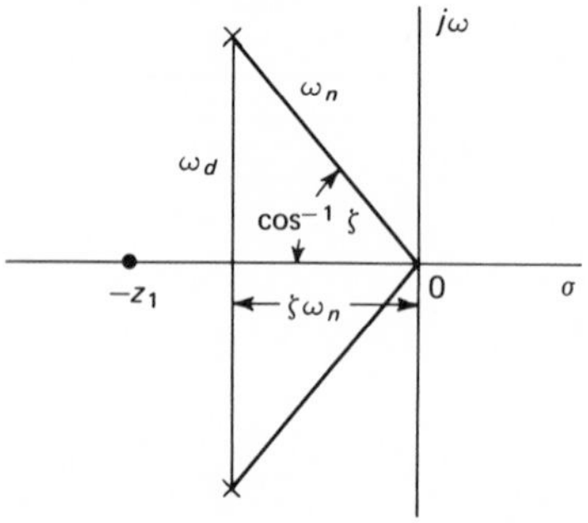

Figure 3.7–1. Zero added to complex pole pair.

Equation (3.7–1) indicates that the system will oscillate with the same angular velocity and have the same decay rate as previously, but the addition of the zero gives a faster rise time and a greater overshoot than with the complex poles alone. Figure 3.7–2 shows the per cent overshoot with the added zero plotted as a function of the distance of the zero relative to the real part of the complex poles. The curves are asymptotic at large z_1 to the situation without the zero, so we see that as the zero comes close to the origin, it has a very large effect on the overshoot (which also increases the settling time). The per cent overshoot increases from about 4 to 20 per cent when $(z_1/\zeta\omega_n)$ goes from a large number to 1 for $\zeta = \sqrt{2}/2$, while for $\zeta = \frac{1}{2}$ the per cent overshoot increases from about 15 to 69 per cent. Thus the overshoot roughly magnifies about five times as $z_1/\zeta\omega_n$ reaches 1. The rise time is lowered. This effect may be alternatively visualized by analogy to an electrostatic field in three dimensions, where the poles and zeros of Figure 3.7–1 represent the ends of line charges in such a field, the poles being lines charged positively and the zero lines charged negatively. The field in the region of the origin, as measured by the force on a hypothetical unit line charge, is clearly changed as z_1 comes closer to the origin [7]. The zero may be said to reduce the relative stability of the system.

In the sinusoidal response for fixed complex poles, the zero will increase the peak response M_p, increase the bandwidth, and cause the high-frequency slope to be 20 db per decade rather than the previous 40 db. This picture is somewhat misleading, as in practice an additional pole or poles usually accompany the zero and bring a return to the original slope at high frequencies. However, the high-frequency cutoff is not so sharp; thus an added zero increases the bandwidth and noise problems.

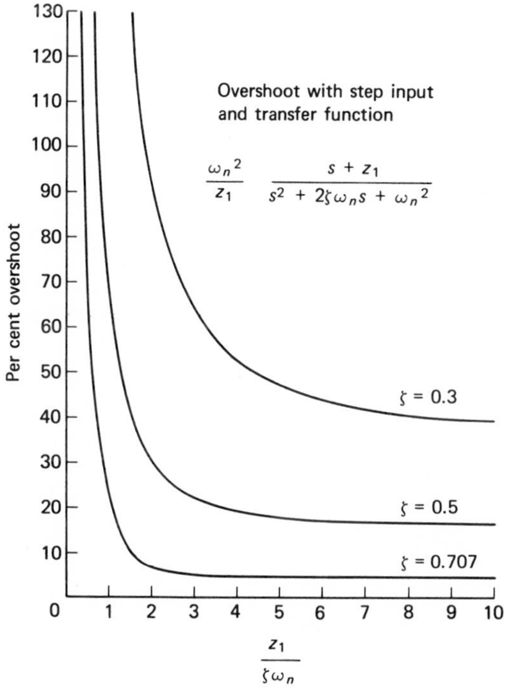

Figure 3.7–2. Per cent maximum overshoot of response to step input for second-order system with added zero.

An added pole stabilizes the second-order system or makes it more sluggish. It is not so easy to show the effect of the pole as we did that of the zero in Figure 3.7–2, but in general the real pole will add an exponentially decaying term and will also alter the magnitude and phase angle of the oscillating transient. The overshoot will be reduced, and the rise time will be increased. The equation for the step response in our antenna problem is

$$\frac{q(t)}{n_1/h} = \mathcal{L}^{-1}\left[\frac{p_1\omega_n^2}{s(s+p_1)[(s+\zeta\omega_n)^2+\omega_n^2(1-\zeta^2)]}\right] \tag{3.7–2}$$

The slope Δ of this step response is the same as the impulse response, which is

$$\Delta = \frac{d}{dt}\left[q(t)\frac{h}{n_1}\right] = \frac{\epsilon^{-p_1 t}}{(p_1 - \zeta\omega_n)^2 + \omega_d^2}$$

$$+ \frac{1}{\omega_d[(p_1 - \zeta\omega_n)^2 + \omega_d^2]^{1/2}}\epsilon^{-\zeta\omega_n t}\sin(\omega_d t - \psi) \qquad \textbf{(3.7–3)}$$

where $\omega_d = \omega_n\sqrt{1-\zeta^2}$ and $\psi = \tan^{-1}[\omega_d/(p_1 - \zeta\omega_n)]$. If $p_1 = \zeta\omega_n$, then the slope is

$$\Delta = \frac{\epsilon^{-p_1 t}}{\omega_d^2}[1 + \sin(\omega_d t - \psi)] \qquad \textbf{(3.7–4)}$$

Since $\sin(\omega_d t - \psi)$ is at most -1, the slope Δ is never negative. We conclude that if $p_1 \leq \zeta\omega_n$ there will be no overshoot in this system.† If $p_1 > \zeta\omega_n$, the exponent of the first term of (3.7–3) causes it to die out rapidly compared to the second term, while if this term $p_1 \leq \zeta\omega_n$, it will die out comparatively slowly.

If $p_1 \gg \omega_n$, then it will have little effect on the step function response. This may be shown from (3.7–2) by making $p_1 = 5\omega_n$. Then the inverse transform will give

$$\frac{h}{n_1}q(t) = 1 - \frac{5\omega_n^3\epsilon^{-5\omega_n t}}{5\omega_n[\omega_n^2(5-\zeta)^2 + \omega_n^2(1-\zeta^2)]}$$

$$+ \frac{5\omega_n^3\,\epsilon^{-\zeta\omega_n t}\sin(\omega_d t - \psi)}{\omega_n^2\sqrt{1-\zeta^2}[\omega_n^2(5-\zeta)^2 + \omega_n^2(1-\zeta^2)]^{1/2}} \qquad \textbf{(3.7–5)}$$

If $\zeta = 1$, then the second term of (3.7–5) is $\epsilon^{-5\omega_n t}/16$, while, if $\zeta < 1$, this term becomes even smaller. You can show that the third term is almost the same as the oscillatory term for the situation of the complex pole only. Compared to the third term, the second term has both a small initial value and a rapid decay due to the large exponent. It is therefore reasonable to say that a distant pole will have only a slight effect on the step-function response. The same conclusion follows if we use the potential analogy discussed before by viewing the effect of a distant line charge from the vicinity of the origin (see Figure 3.7–3).

As would be expected from the previous discussion, in the sinusoidal-frequency-response realm an added pole lowers M_p, reduces the bandwidth, and increases the cutoff rate.

† Clark [8] has sets of curves on the added pole problem.

If we have a zero and a pole close together in the configuration shown in Figure 3.7–3, the combination is called a "dipole." From the potential analogy, you see that the field at a distance from the dipole is disturbed only slightly, and you would expect very slight effect on the step-function response. This is true, but a close-in dipole with the zero nearest the origin, as in Figure 3.7–3, greatly reduces the static error on a ramp input for the system of our example. The reason for this will be shown subsequently, but you observe that a pole-zero configuration which improves static performance without much change in transient performance has much merit.

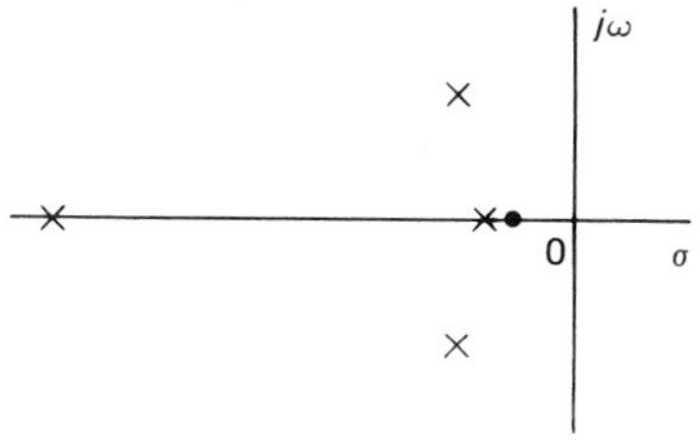

Figure 3.7–3. Complex poles, dipole, and a distant pole.

With both a pole and zero added to the original complex pair, the response becomes more complicated. One formula has been developed using the graphical definitions of Figure 3.7–4 [9]. This equation, representing the normalized step response, is

$$c(t) = 1 - \frac{\omega_n^2(z - p)}{z(\bar{a})^2}\,\epsilon^{-pt} + \frac{\bar{b}}{z}\,\frac{p}{\bar{a}}\,\frac{\omega_n}{\omega_d}\,\epsilon^{-\zeta\omega_n t}\sin(\omega_d t - \psi_1 + \psi_3 - \psi_4) \tag{3.7–6}$$

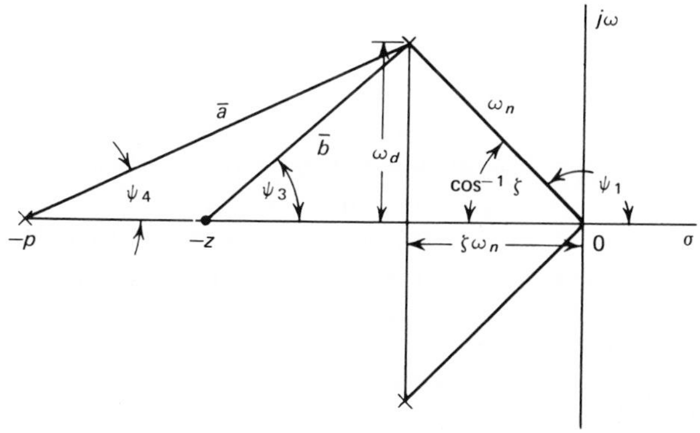

Figure 3.7–4. Figure for Equation (3.7–6). (Adapted from Grabbe, *et al.* [9].)

where $\bar{a}$, $\bar{b}$, p, and z are the magnitudes shown, the angles are as defined in Figure 3.7–4, and ω_d is as previously defined. If $p > 3\zeta\omega_n$, $t_p \simeq (\pi - \psi_3 + \psi_4)/\omega_d$ and $t_s \simeq 3/\zeta\omega_n$ (see Figure 3.4–2). A series of curves has been made up which can assist the designer in obtaining the performance indices for this particular configuration. [10, 11]. By using these curves, a pole-zero combination can be found to meet a set of specified indices. Additional distant poles and a dipole can be added without changing the transient response, as previously shown.

3.8 Second-Order System in State Space

In Chapter 2 you saw that a differential equation of second-order degree can be put into the form of two simultaneous differential equations of first degree. Applying this procedure to the second-order system of the antenna example, in (3.3–1) let $x_1(t) = q(t)$ and $x_2(t) = dq/dt$. Dropping the functional notation, you get

$$\dot{x}_1 = x_2 \tag{3.8–1a}$$

$$\dot{x}_2 = -Bx_1 - Ax_2 + Er \tag{3.8–1b}$$

$$q = x_1 \tag{3.8–1c}$$

or

$$\dot{x} = \mathbf{Wx} + \mathbf{Yr} \tag{3.8–2a}$$

$$\mathbf{q} = \mathbf{Cx} + \mathbf{Dr} \tag{3.8–2b}$$

where

$$\mathbf{x} = \begin{bmatrix} x_1 \\ x_2 \end{bmatrix} \qquad \mathbf{W} = \begin{bmatrix} 0 & 1 \\ -B & -A \end{bmatrix} \qquad \mathbf{Y} = \begin{bmatrix} 0 \\ E \end{bmatrix}$$

$$\mathbf{C} = [1 \quad 0] \qquad \mathbf{D} = \mathbf{0}$$

The matrix equations (3.8–2) are said to be in state-space form, and in this instance ($x_2 = \dot{x}_1$) in phase-variable form. The state-space variables are x_1 and x_2. No great advantage resides in the state-space form for a second-degree linear system; however, if the degree becomes very high, and we have more than one input and one output, the state-space approach becomes almost the only way of attacking the problem. Also, as we shall see in Chapter 4, solution by digital computer requires the equations to be of the form of (3.8–1), or of first degree only. The use of state-space variables carries us into modern control theory, as opposed to conventional control theory, which utilizes analysis in the complex s domain, The operators in modern linear control theory are thus matrices and usually exist in the time domain. In general, the expressions on the right of (3.8–1a) and (3.8–1b) may be time-varying and/or nonlinear. If time-varying, the matrices **W**, **Y**, **C**, and **D** become time-varying, rather than fixed, and if nonlinear, we cannot use matrix methods, although the state-variable concept still applies. In modern control theory, we also consider initial conditions, whereas conventional analysis usually assumes one transient dies out before the next one comes. Let us look at the example system in terms of a state-space representation.

First, examine the situation where $r(t) = 0$, or the driving function is zero. As will be shown in Chapters 5 and 6, the solution to (3.8–1) is straightforward and becomes

$$x_1(t) = \mathscr{L}^{-1}\left(\frac{s + 2\zeta\omega_n}{s^2 + 2\zeta\omega_n s + \omega_n^2} x_{10} + \frac{1}{s^2 + 2\zeta\omega_n s + \omega_n^2} x_{20}\right) \quad \textbf{(3.8–3a)}$$

$$x_2(t) = \mathscr{L}^{-1}\left(\frac{-\omega_n^2}{s^2 + 2\zeta\omega_n s + \omega_n^2} x_{10} + \frac{s}{s^2 + 2\zeta\omega_n s + \omega_n^2} x_{20}\right) \quad \textbf{(3.8–3b)}$$

where x_{10} and x_{20} are the values of x_1 and x_2 at $t = 0$ ($t_0 = 0$ here). Both x_1 and x_2 are therefore damped sinusoids decaying to zero as t approaches infinity. As the values of x_1 and x_2 continually decrease to zero, plotting x_2 versus x_1 on an $x_2 x_1$ plane results in a decreasing spiral curve, as in Figure 3.8–1. The curve crosses the axis infinitely many times, but the

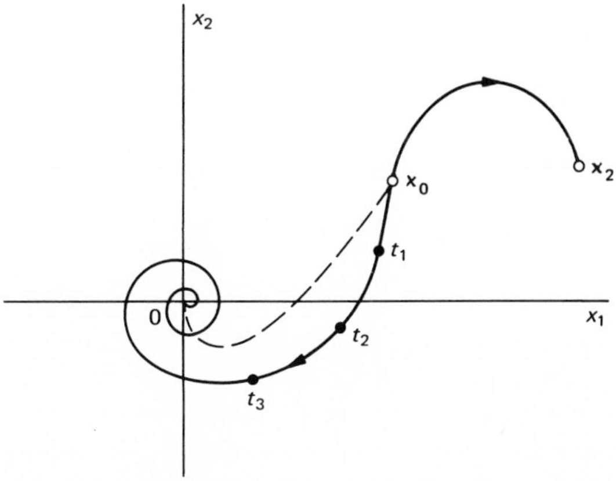

Figure 3.8–1. Underdamped trajectory for free second-order system in state space, and forced trajectory in state space.

system reaches the equilibrium point at the origin as $t \to \infty$. Practically, the curve gets very close to the origin within a few time constants, as you know. Reducing the damping factor makes the spiral larger, while if ζ becomes larger, the spiral gets tighter. At critical damping ($\zeta = 1$), the curve is no longer a spiral but may approach the origin directly without x_1 changing signs (dashed line in Figure 3.8–1). The locations of the state variables at different time are shown at t_1, t_2, and so on, on Figure 3.8–1.

To the solutions for x_1 and x_2 for initial conditions may be added the solutions with $r(t)$. These become

$$x_1(t) = \mathscr{L}^{-1}\left[\frac{ER(s)}{s^2 + 2\zeta\omega_n s + \omega_n^2}\right] \tag{3.8–4a}$$

$$x_2(t) = \mathscr{L}^{-1}\left[\frac{sER(s)}{s^2 + 2\zeta\omega_n s + \omega_n^2}\right] \tag{3.8–4b}$$

where $r = r(t)u(t)$.

The curves traced out by the state variables as time evolves are called trajectories in state space. A possible curve for some r might proceed from $\mathbf{x}_0$ to $\mathbf{x}_2$ in Figure 3.8–1. By a transformation of variables, for linear systems it is possible to make $\mathbf{x}_0$, or $\mathbf{x}_2$, the origin without loss of generality. Hence a step input (zero initial conditions) gives a spiral very much as in Figure 3.8–1 if the origin represents the final value and x_0 the initial value. For nonlinear systems, we may not be able to do this, as the system behaves in a dissimilar manner in different regions of the space.

Modern control theory concerns itself with trajectories in state space, where the space will be of dimension n, n being the number of state variables necessary to describe the system. In the case of two variables, as here, we could of course have reached the same conclusions regarding Figure 3.8–1 directly from the solution for (3.3–1). The present discussion points the way toward more advanced analysis, however.

3.9 Conclusions

Although we have followed a specific example (antenna control), the normalized response equations such as (3.3–14) and (3.3–20) are perfectly general. Coefficients of the differential equations will be determined by the devices used, but the equations themselves and the results as discussed in this chapter will depend only on the equations and not on the apparatus used. We have kept the discussion to operators that have the form of a ratio of polynomials when expressed in the complex frequency domain. Other operators exist which are more complicated and will be discussed later.

Design may be approached from two viewpoints: that of analysis and that of synthesis. In Section 3.6 we emphasized analysis, or what happens to the system when we insert compensating subsystems. Trial and error constitute a part of this design approach; that is, we insert a compensation G_c in series with the open loop operator $G_1 G_2 H$ and observe the results on the system operator C/R. The problem here then becomes: What changes need to be made in the open loop operator to produce the desired system operator or control ratio that will in turn meet the given performance specifications? The design is not entirely by trial and error, as powerful methods exist for predicting the system response operator given the open loop operator. These are largely graphical in nature and will be taken up in later chapters. These graphical tools, together with experience, reduce the number of tries in the analytic approach.

In synthesis, you select the control ratio initially and find the required open loop operator. The problem here is to select the control ratio properly and then to restrict the number of possible open loop operators to those that will result in simple and inexpensive compensation. In synthesis, many possible designs may result, so that considerations other than performance enter. The synthesis problem raises considerably more difficulties, and it may be necessary to confine attention to an approximate system of lower order than the actual system to obtain results at all. If we use a criteria of minimizing a performance index similar to that of (3.4–6), then the mathematics of the synthesis becomes more complicated, and for some performances indices may result in a very intricate and expensive controller. If we are willing to settle for a performance somewhere near the minimum (assuming the curve of the index is broad at this point), it may be possible to obtain a reasonably simple design. We explore some of these ideas in subsequent chapters.

PROBLEMS

3.1. If in the antenna control example of Section 3.2, $D = 2$, $J_1 = 3$, $K = 3.7$, all in consistent units, about how much, if any, will $\theta_M(t)$ overshoot its final value on its first reversal for a step input of $\theta_1(t)$ (disturbance torque zero)?

3.2. Using the antenna-control example of Section 3.2, it is desired that the maximum overshoot be no greater than 20 per cent, the sinusoidal bandwidth no greater than 10 Hz, but that the rise time be as small as possible consistent with these requirements. Find D and K, if $J_1 = 2$ (kg-m^2). Find the actual frequency of oscillation and the rate of damping ($\zeta\omega_n$). (*Hint:* See Figures 3.5–1 and 3.5–3.)

3.3. It is desired that a certain second-order control system have a 10 to 90 per cent rise time of 1 sec and a maximum overshoot on a step-function input of not more than 20 per cent. What must be the natural frequency ω_n? Repeat for a rise time of 0.3 sec. Find the angular velocity of oscillation ω_d in each case.

3.4. In Figure P3.4 find $\hat{\epsilon}(s)$ in terms of $R(s)$, $G(s)$, and $H(s)$. If $H(s) = 1$ and

$$G(s) = \frac{K}{s^m(s^n + A_{n-1}s^{n-1} + \cdots + A_1)}$$

find $\epsilon(t)$ as $t \to \infty$ if $r(t)$ is (a) $u(t)$, (b) $tu(t)$, and (c) $\frac{1}{2}t^2u(t)$, each for (1) $m = 0$, (2) $m = 1$, (3) $m = 2$, and (4) $m = 3$.

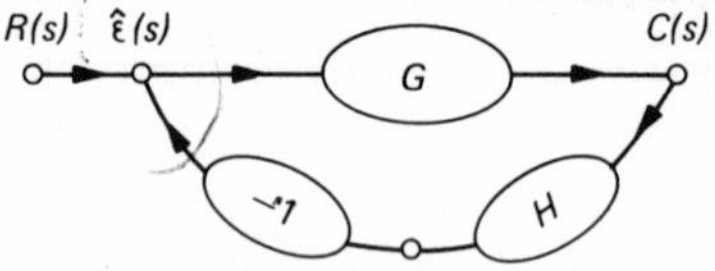

Figure P3.4.

3.5. Using a sinusoidal test in the laboratory a unity feedback control system shows second-order characteristics similar to those of Figure 3.5–5 except that $\omega_n = 6$ and $M_p = 2$ db (0.1 loru).
(a) What will be the per cent overshoot of the output on a step input? (b) The 10 to 90 per cent rise time? The oscillation frequency in hertz? (c) If at very low frequency the input equals the output, draw a flow diagram representing the system, and give all values. (d) Repeat (a), (b), and (c) if the conditions are changed such that at $\omega = \omega_n = 10$ the sinusoidal response is -2 db (-0.1 loru).

3.6. A second-order system shows a peak overshoot of about 50 per cent and an oscillation frequency of 3 Hz. What will M_p and ω_p have for the sinusoidal response? Find the phase angle at 1 Hz and 6 Hz.

3.7. In Figure P3.7 there is an internal feedback arrangement. If the internal feedback arrangement is open at F_2: (a) Find the maximum per cent overshoot of the output for a step input of $r(t)$ ($\hat{\tau}_L = 0$). (b) Repeat (a) except

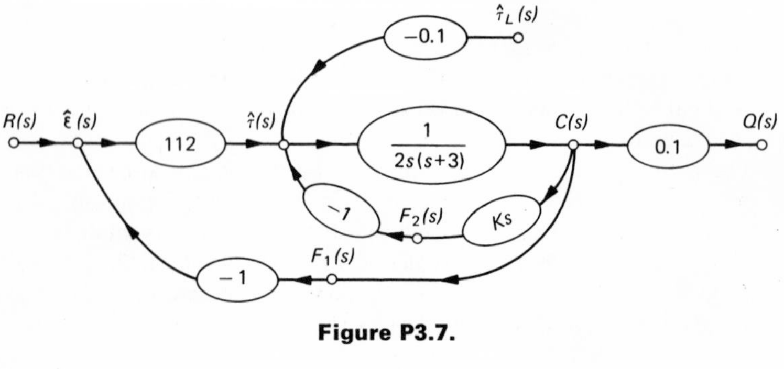

Figure P3.7.

for a step input of $\hat{\tau}_L(t)$ ($r = 0$). (c) Closing the $-Ks$ path at f_2, find the K necessary to reduce this overshoot to 20 per cent for a step $r(t)$ ($\hat{\tau}_L = 0$). (d) If $K_M K_B$ [as defined just prior to (3.6–18)] equals 50, what value should the tachometer constant K_4 have? (e) Find $\epsilon(t)$ as $t \to \infty$ for a unit input $r(t) = tu(t)$ ($\hat{\tau}_L = 0$) for the system with internal feedback and without. Repeat (e) with the forward path gain increased from 112 to 300, all other conditions being as before.

3.8. In Figure P3.8 let

$$G_1 = \frac{20}{5}\,\frac{s+5}{s+20}$$

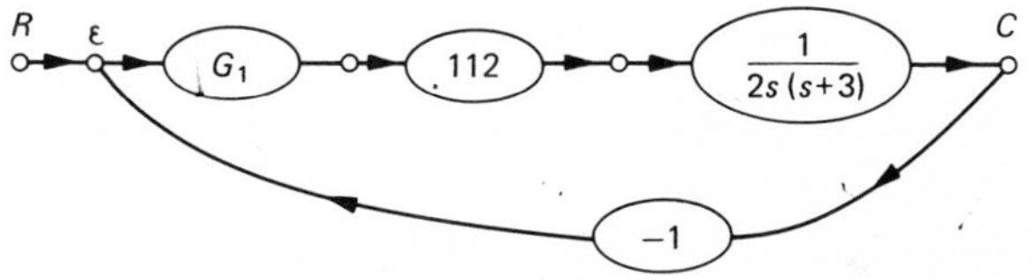

Figure P3.8.

Find and plot the system (C/R) poles and zeros. Find and sketch the response to a unit step input. Find the 10 to 90 percent rise time, the peak overshoot, and the oscillation angular velocity. Repeat for $G_1 = 1$. Find $\epsilon(t)$ as $t \to \infty$ for an input $tu(t)$ in each case.

3.9. In Figure P3.8 let $G_1 = (s + 0.25)/(s + 0.05)$ and repeat Problem 3.8.

3.10. Make a phase plane ($x_2 = \dot{x}_1$ versus x_1) plot for a second-order system with $\omega_n = 10$ and $\zeta = 0.5$ with a unit step input $u(t)$. The system starts at the origin with zero initial conditions and ends at $x_1 = 1$, $\dot{x}_1 = 0$. Indicate several time values along the state-space trajectory.

Digital computer aid is suggested for Problems 3.8, 3.9, and 3.10. If this is used, vary the compensation in Problems 3.8 and 3.9, and ζ and ω_n in Problem 3.10, and compare.

REFERENCES AND FURTHER READING

[1] S. S. L. Chang, *Synthesis of Optimum Control Systems*, McGraw-Hill, New York, 1961, pp. 11–35; see also reference [2].

[2] G. C. Newton, Jr., L. A. Gould, and J. F. Kaiser, *Analytical Design of Linear Feedback Controls*, Wiley, New York, 1957, pp. 77–186.

[3] V. Del Toro and S. R. Parker, *Principles of Control System Engineering*, McGraw-Hill, New York, 1959, p. 112.

[4] H. W. Bode, *Network Analysis and Feedback Amplifier Design*, Van Nostrand, Princeton, N.J., 1945, pp. 303–360.

[5] *Ibid.*, pp. 44–50.

[6] D. P. Eckman, *Automatic Process Control*, Wiley, New York, 1958, pp. 66–72.

[7] J. G. Truxal, *Automatic Feedback Control System Synthesis*, McGraw-Hill, New York, 1955, pp. 29–34.
[8] R. N. Clark, *Introduction to Automatic Control Systems*, Wiley, New York, 1962, pp. 140–145.
[9] E. M. Grabbe, S. Ramo, and D. E. Wooldridge, *Handbook of Automation, Computation and Control*, Vol. 1, Wiley, New York, 1958.
[10] C. R. Hausenbauer and C. V. Lago, Synthesis of Control Systems Based on Approximation to a Third Order System, *Trans. AIEE*, **77**, Part II (1958), 415–421.
[11] G. Lago and L. M. Benningfield, *Control System Theory*, Ronald, New York, 1962, pp. 436–456.

Introductory and Advanced State Space Textbooks

[12] L. K. Timothy and B. E. Bona, *State Space Analysis: An Introduction*, McGraw-Hill, New York, 1968.
[13] J. C. Hsu and A. V. Meyer, *Modern Control Principles and Applications*, McGraw-Hill, New York, 1968.
[14] O. I. Elgerd, *Control Systems Theory*, McGraw-Hill, New York, 1967.
[15] R. C. Dorf, *Time Domain Analysis and Design of Control Systems*, Addison-Wesley, Reading, Mass., 1965.
[16] J. T. Tou, *Modern Control Theory*, McGraw-Hill, New York, 1964.
[17] L. A. Zadeh and C. A. Desoer, *Linear System Theory*, McGraw-Hill, New York, 1963.
[18] S. C. Gupta, *Transform and State Variable Methods in Linear Systems*, Wiley, New York, 1966.

See also references for Chapters 6 and 10.

4 Signal Flow Diagrams and Computer Simulation

4.1 Introduction

We have already discussed signal flow diagrams to some extent in the previous chapters. In this chapter we investigate methods for altering the flow diagram, to find overall input-output relations utilizing the diagrams and the relation of the flow diagram to computer simulation, in particular to analog simulation.

Signal flow diagrams are schematic diagrams that assist in analyzing system performance. They are particularly helpful when feedback exists. The diagrams become very useful in translating a system to the "bread-board" stage and determining analog simulations of the system. The diagrams give no more information than the algebraic or differential equations defining the system, but they may be more descriptive to the engineer who normally utilizes diagrams for visualization and inspiration for alterations. As discussed in Chapter 1, block diagrams and flow diagrams give the same information, but flow diagrams may be easier to manipulate.

4.2 Drawing the Signal Flow Diagram

A diagram consists of nodes and directed branches. A node (small circle) represents any variable quantity, such as voltage, current, force, torque, or pressure, as used in the system equations. The directed branches connect the nodes and are operators that express the relations between the system variables. "Signals" flow unilaterally along the branches, being converted by the branch operator. Figure 4.2–1 gives a simple example of two nodes and one directed branch. You may think of these signals as carrying power, energy, force, or, in abstract terms, information, which is utilized and altered by the system to accomplish the desired results. The entire diagram showing all nodes and branch operators represents the simultaneous

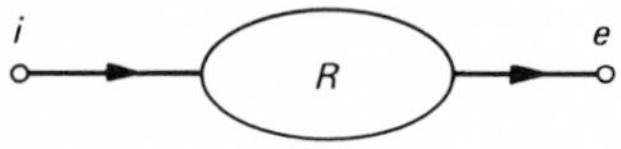

Figure 4.2–1. Flow diagram for $e = iR$.

equations of the system. An arrow on the branch indicates the unilateral direction of information flow, and in most cases the predominate flows are from left to right, and from top to bottom, as in most written languages of the western civilizations. A node a is assumed not to affect a preceding node b unless there is a feedback path from b to a. By "preceding" we mean in a sense opposite to that of the flow of information. Thus any "loading" effect must either be disregarded by an approximation or described fully by the equations (thus possibly setting up additional nodes). As a very simple example, consider Figure 4.2–2, which shows a

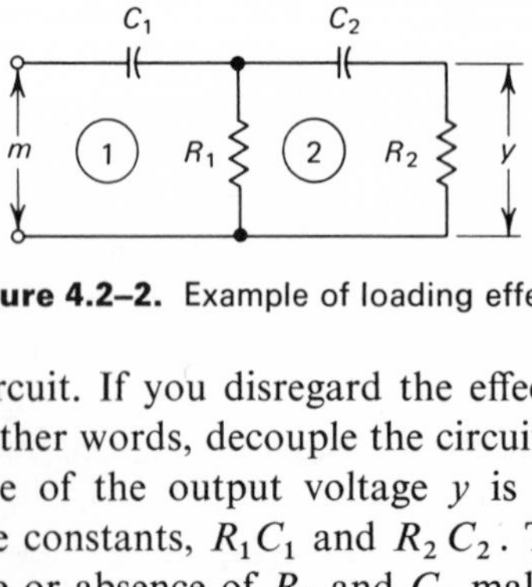

Figure 4.2–2. Example of loading effect.

two-loop electrical circuit. If you disregard the effect of loop (2) on the resistance R_1 (or, in other words, decouple the circuits), we could say that the transient response of the output voltage y is related to the input voltage x by two time constants, R_1C_1 and R_2C_2. This might be almost correct if the presence or absence of R_2 and C_2 makes little difference in the voltage across R_1. However, if addition of the second circuit changes the voltage across R_1 by an unacceptable amount, then you must use Kirchhoff's laws and write two equations for the circuit. Thus, using the Laplace transform and assuming all initial conditions are zero, from Figure 4.2–2,

$$\frac{y(t)}{m(t)} = \mathscr{L}^{-1}\left[\frac{R_1R_2C_1C_2s^2}{R_1R_2C_1C_2s^2 + (R_1C_1 + R_1C_2 + R_2C_2)s + 1}\right] \quad \textbf{(4.2–1)}$$

Assuming no loading effect on R_1,

$$\frac{y(t)}{m(t)} = \mathscr{L}^{-1}\left(\frac{R_1C_1s}{R_1C_1s+1}\,\frac{R_2C_2s}{R_2C_2s+1}\right)$$

$$= \mathscr{L}^{-1}\left[\frac{R_1R_2C_1C_2s^2}{R_1R_2C_1C_2s^2 + (R_1C_1 + R_2C_2)s + 1}\right] \qquad \textbf{(4.2–2)}$$

Thus (4.2–2) represents the system of Figure 4.2–2 only if R_1C_2 is small compared to $(R_1C_1 + R_2C_2)$.

Very often approximations are necessary to reduce the system to manageable form. For example, we normally neglect the effect of the armature current on the total field in a motor, the bending in a short shaft, the inductance in a resistor, the pressure drop in a hydraulic line, and so on. At other times, however, these effects may be very important and lead to system oscillations that otherwise would not be predicted. In such cases the equations may have to contain more terms, or additional equations become necessary. The engineer must make a judgement, which may be subject to later revisions, as to how much approximation he can tolerate.

A node variable represents the sum of all signals entering the node, and all branches leaving a node transmit the variable represented by that node. Let us now give an example.

Figure 4.2–3 represents the equations

$$\begin{aligned} q_1 &= -3q_2 - 5q_4 + m_2 \\ q_2 &= 5q_1 \\ q_3 &= q_2 - 4q_4 + m_1 \\ q_4 &= 15q_3 \\ y &= q_4 + m_1 \end{aligned} \qquad \textbf{(4.2–3)}$$

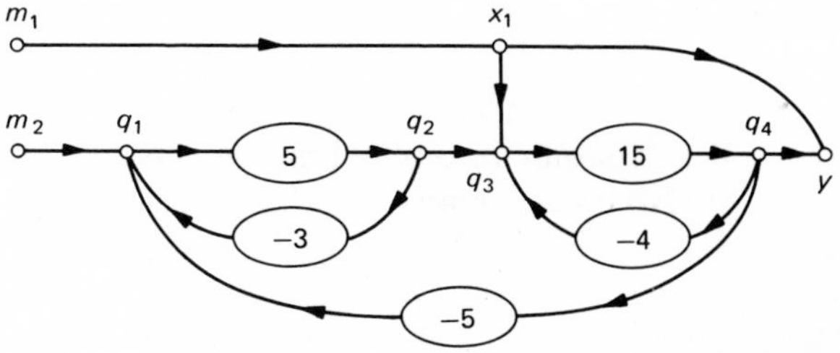

Figure 4.2–3. Simple flow diagram.

In Figure 4.2–3 it is understood that the operator of the directed branch is 1 if it is not shown. Note, for example, that $q_3 = q_2 + m_1 - 4q_4$. From the previous discussion, q_2 is independent of q_3, as is q_1 (except for the relation through q_4), that q_4 is independent of y, q_1 independent of m_1, and so on. Usually we first write the equations and later draw the flow diagram to delineate the equations graphically. Then by proper manipulation of the diagram, the solution of the equations may be found. Before continuing with these matters, let us make some precise definitions that will be useful.

Flow Diagram Definitions

1. Operator (transmittance)
   a. Branch: The relation between the node into which the branch is directed and the node from which it leaves, neglecting all other branches. In Figure 4.2–1 this is R. In Figure 4.2–3 the branch between q_1 and q_2 has 5 as an operator. The branch operator is considered to be 1 if it is not shown.
   b. System: The relation between any two nodes designated as system output and input, respectively.
   c. Loop: The product of all operators (the total transmittance) around a closed loop. In Figure 4.2–3 there is a loop from q_1 through q_2 back to q_1, where the loop operator is $(-3)(5) = -15$, and another loop from q_1 through q_4 back to q_1, where the loop operator is -375. There is a final loop of -60 from q_3 through q_4 back to q_3.
   Note: In feedback systems we distinguish the loop operator from the open loop operator or function. The open loop function is also called the return ratio (see Chapter 1), but the former designation has more prevalence in control literature. In the normal system, the feedback signal is subtracted from the reference to form the error. In this case, the open loop function is the negative of the loop function. For the positive feedback case, the two functions are identical.
2. Nodes
   a. Source: Nodes independent of other nodes.
   b. Sink: Nodes with only incoming branches.
   c. Dependent: Nodes depending on other nodes.
3. Forward path P_{ab}: The product of all branch operators (total transmittance) in going from node a (often a source) to another node b (often a sink), disregarding all loops, and proceeding only once through any node along the path.

The nodes a and b must be designated or understood, and in general there may be more than one such path between them. Thus in Figure 4.2–3 there are two forward paths between m_1 and y, so that for these nodes, $P_1 = 1$ and $P_2 = 15$. Between m_2 and y there is only one forward path, with $P = 75$. There is a forward path between q_4 and q_1 of $P = -5$, but there is no forward path between y and m_1, or y and m_2. In following a forward path or a loop, any node may be encountered once and only once.

4. Touching and nontouching loops and paths: Any loop that passes through or connects to a node lying along a forward path P is said to "touch" the path. If a loop does not involve any node along P it is "nontouching." Similarly, loops may be "touching" or "nontouching." In Figure 4.2–3 the two loops with operators -15 and -375 through q_1 are touching, and the two loops with operators -60 and -375 through q_4 are touching, but the loop operator -15 through q_1 does not touch the loop operator -60 through q_4. The forward path from m_1 to y with $P = 1$ does not touch any loop, while all other forward paths touch loops. The forward path from m_2 to y touches all loops.

In this chapter we concern ourselves with operators that commute; that is, $G_1G_2(x) = G_2G_1(x)$. If the operators did not commute, it would be necessary to be more careful in maintaining the proper order of tandem operators. Also we shall utilize operators whose inverse is the algebraic inverse; that is, $H^{-1} = 1/H$. Among the operators satisfying these requirements, as already discussed, are those found by using Laplace, Fourier, and Z transforms with the system equations, and are termed transfer functions. In the case of these transforms, the transfer function is found by writing the relation between two nodes assuming all initial conditions are zero. For example, if we have the equation

$$5\frac{dy}{dt} + 3y = m \tag{4.2-4}$$

and we use the Laplace transform,

$$(5s + 3)Y(s) = M(s) + y(0_+) \tag{4.2–5}$$

If $y(0_+) = 0$,

$$\frac{Y(s)}{M(s)} = \frac{1}{5s + 3} \tag{4.2–6}$$

and this can be depicted as in Figure 4.2–4. The nodes can also be shown as functions of time, or $u(t)$ and $y(t)$ in Figure 4.2–4, if we properly interpret the branch operator. Hence in this convention an integrator would be shown as $1/s$ and a differentiator as s. It is thus possible to extend the flow

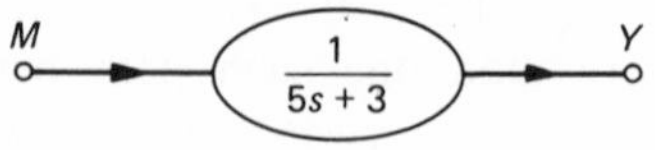

Figure 4.2–4. Flow diagram with transfer function operator.

diagram from simple algebraic equations such as (4.2–3) to differential equations. For simultaneous differential equations, the operators become matrices, and problems of commutivity and inverse relations arise, but the flow diagram still has great utility. The diagrams may also be helpful in illustrating nonlinear systems, but the direct use of the diagram in obtaining solutions becomes very restricted.

With practice you may draw the flow diagram directly from the electromechanical system symbols as shown in Chapter 2, properly connected. However, we advised the beginner to write out the equations in detail, as otherwise it is easy to omit necessary nodes and branches. To obtain nontrivial solutions, there must be exactly as many equations as dependent variables, as you know from the solution of simultaneous equations. The independent variables are usually the system inputs, and the dependent variables are the quantities describing the system operation. As discussed in Chapter 2, we may use nodal analysis, mesh analysis, or some combination of these in depicting the system. Thus the flow diagram is not unique, and in fact by judicious use of system variables, one flow diagram may be much simpler than another, although both properly delineate the system.

4.3 Alteration of the Flow Diagram

We use the flow diagram to reduce the system to simpler terms, eliminate unwanted internal variables, or alter the system to different terms. You can assume instantaneous signal flow (unless we introduce a delay operator). The diagram may be altered by very simple operations and reduced piece by piece. However, there are powerful methods of obtaining large-scale reductions rapidly. Let us take up the simple alterations first, using the transfer-function type of operation [1].

Figure 4.3–1 shows a feedback system that is frequently encountered. Then

$$Y = G(1 - L - L^2 - L^3 - \cdots)M \tag{4.3–1}$$

where L is the open loop operator GH. Using the formula for the sum of a geometric series,

$$Y = \frac{GM}{1 + L} \tag{4.3–2}$$

or

$$\frac{Y}{M} = \frac{G}{1 + GH} \tag{4.3–3}$$

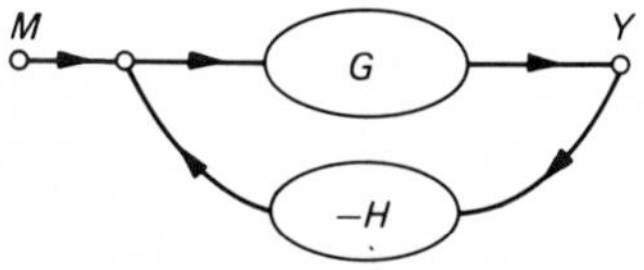

Figure 4.3–1. Flow diagram with feedback.

and finally, if $H = 1$.

$$\frac{Y}{M} = \frac{G}{1 + G} \tag{4.3–4}$$

Thus Figure 4.3–1 may be replaced by Figure 4.3–2. This result we have already obtained by other methods.

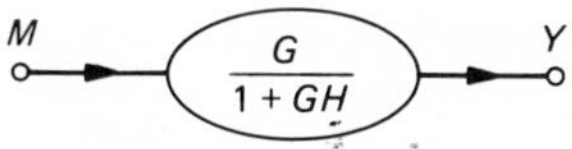

Figure 4.3–2. Equivalent of Figure 4.3–1.

In Figure 4.3–1, following the definitions given previously, GH is the open loop function and $-GH$ the loop function. The subtraction operator of -1, previously shown separately in the diagrams of the preceding chapters, has been combined with the feedback path operator here.

Two tandem operators reduce to their product, as in Figure 4.3–3, while parallel operators reduce to their sum, as in Figure 4.3–4.

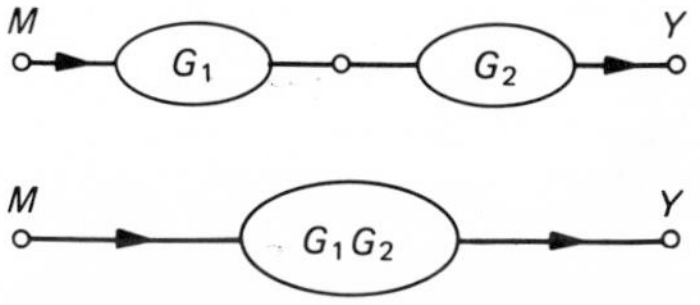

Figure 4.3–3. Series equivalents.

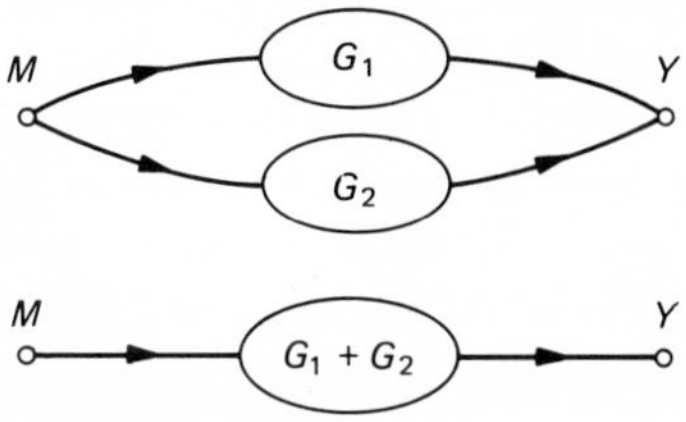

Figure 4.3–4. Parallel equivalents.

It is frequently desirable to reduce a feedback system with operator H to one with unity operator. Rearranging (4.3–3) we obtain

$$\frac{Y}{M} = \frac{1}{H}\frac{GH}{1 + GH} \tag{4.3–5}$$

Equation (4.3–5) suggests reduction of Figure 4.3–5a to 4.3–5b, which has unity feedback. Hence we can derive many relations for a negative

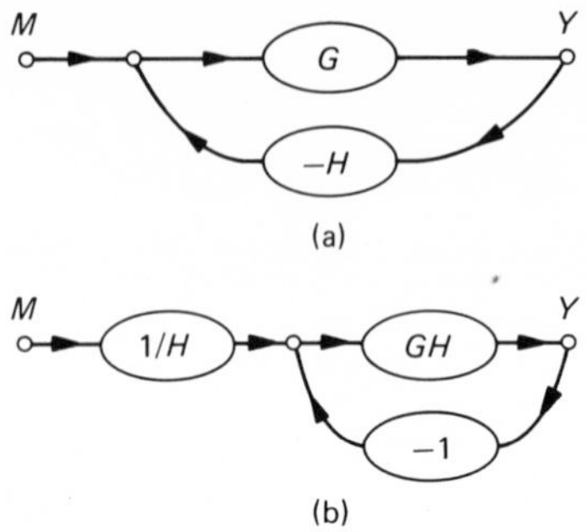

Figure 4.3–5. Obtaining a unity feedback system.

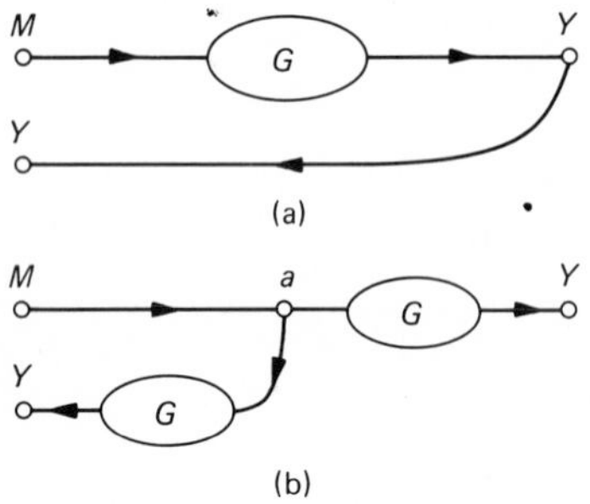

Figure 4.3–6. Alteration of the flow diagram.

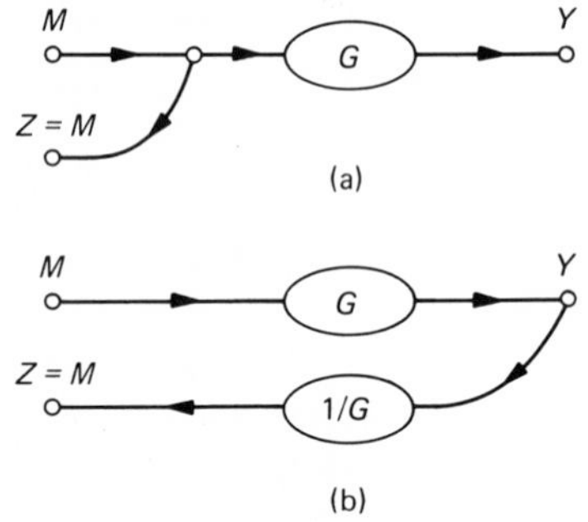

Figure 4.3–7. Alteration of the flow diagram.

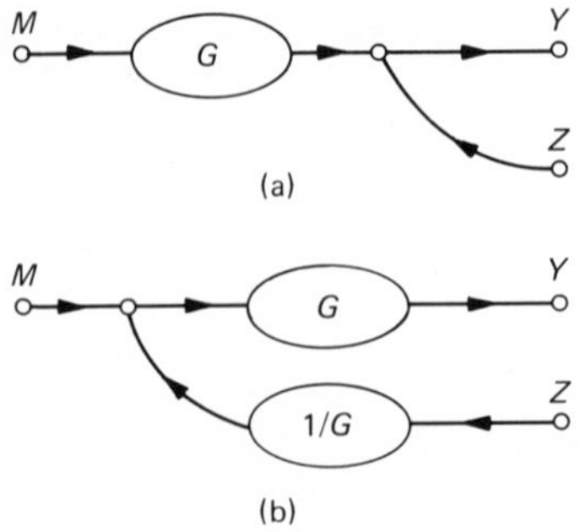

Figure 4.3–8. Alteration of the flow diagram.

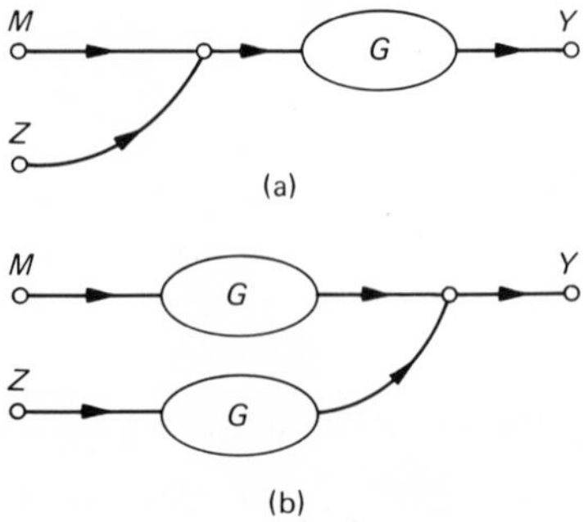

Figure 4.3–9. Alteration of the flow diagram

feedback system that will be valid by simple alteration for a system with $-H$ feedback. [If the feedback is positive, the sign of GH or G alters in the denominators of (4.3–3) (4.3–4), and (4.3–5).]

It is also frequently possible to simplify the feedback loop or a forward path by moving a branch to a new node point. For example, in Figure

4.3–6a we may introduce node a in front of G. Then Figure 4.3–6b gives the same results. Alternatively, we may move a branch beyond an operator, as in Figure 4.3–7. Figures 4.3–8 and 4.3–9 show similar alterations, except with incoming signals. By combinations of these alterations, you can reduce a complicated diagram to a simpler one.

Example 4.3–1

Figure 4.3–10a may be simplified by first reducing the inner loops, and finally the outer loop, as shown. Figure 4.3–10c shows the final result. Mason's rule, soon to be discussed, obtains this in one step.

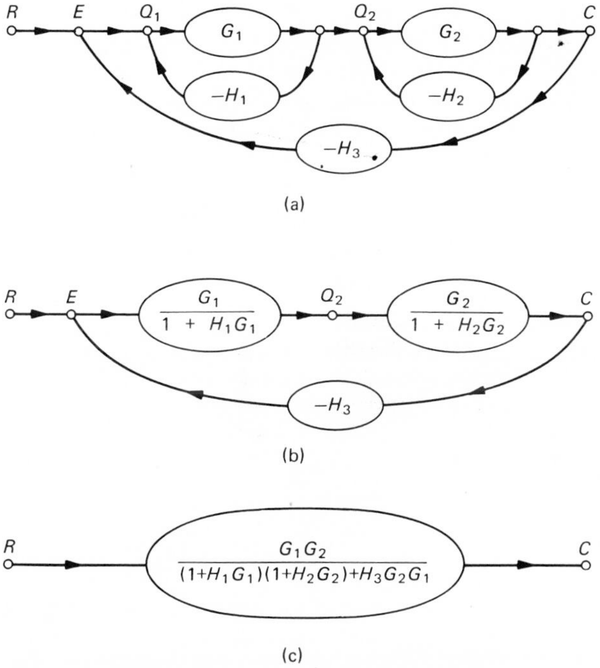

Figure 4.3–10. Reduction of inner loops.

Example 4.3–2

You may desire to isolate a single branch operator, such as H_1 in Figure 4.3–10a. Using that figure, reduce the second inner loop as in Figure 4.3–11a. Next, move the starting end of the branch $-H_1$ to C as in part (b). Now, move the termination of the top branch to a new node Q_3 between R and E as in part (c). Combine the feedback branch $-H_3$, separate out the operator H_1, and finally obtain a diagram isolating H_1 as in part (d).

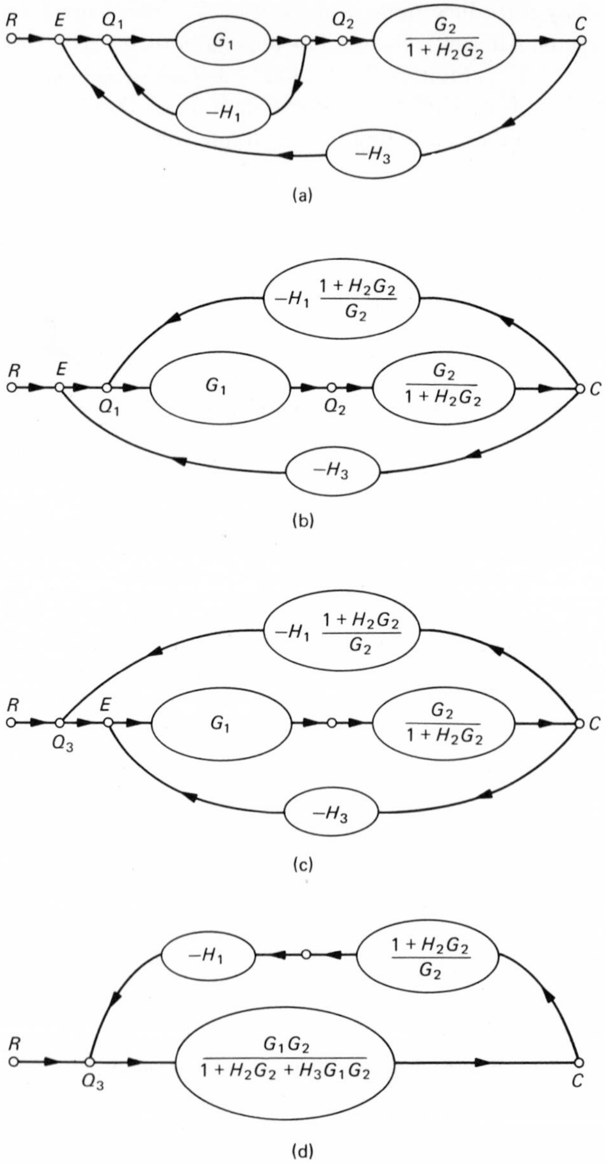

Figure 4.3–11. Isolation of an operator.

In a multiinput system, it is often required to obtain a diagram for each input separately. For example, if there is a disturbance, it may be desired to obtain a diagram for the desired input and one for the disturbance.

Example 4.3–3

In Figure 4.3–12a, if we make $R = 0$, then part (b) represents the flow diagram with D as input. This reduces to part (c). If $D = 0$, then part (d) represents the flow diagram with R as input. Note that the denominator of the branch is the same in each case, but that the numerators are different.

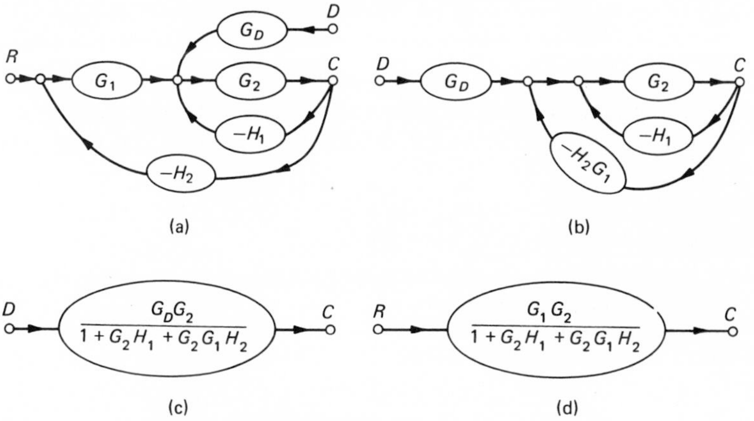

Figure 4.3–12. Alteration of the flow diagram.

It is possible to eliminate internal nodes step by step by shifting branch terminations and to reduce the diagram to a single input-output variety. This is, however, a lengthy process subject to errors, and so we now take up Mason's rule, a method of obtaining overall input-output relations rapidly. The previous reduction rules are usually sufficient for most control work requiring simple alterations.

4.4 Reduction of the Flow Diagram—Mason's Rule

In obtaining a solution for simultaneous linear equations, one method is to use determinates, If we have the equations

$$\begin{aligned} a_{11}y_1 + a_{12}y_2 + \cdots + a_{1n}y_n &= b_1 \\ a_{21}y_1 + a_{22}y_2 + \cdots + a_{2n}y_n &= b_2 \\ a_{i1}y + a_{i2}y_2 + \cdots + a_{in}y_n &= b_i \\ a_{n1}y_1 + a_{n2}y_2 + \cdots + a_{nn}y_n &= b_n \end{aligned} \tag{4.4–1}$$

it is well known that the solution by Cramer's rule is

$$y_k = \frac{\Delta_k}{\Delta} \qquad k = 1, n \tag{4.4–2}$$

where Δ is the determinate of the a_{ij} coefficients; that is,

$$\Delta = \begin{vmatrix} a_{11} & a_{12} \cdots a_{1n} \\ \vdots & \vdots \\ a_{n1} & \cdots \quad a_{nn} \end{vmatrix} \tag{4.4-3}$$

and Δ_k is the same as Δ, except with the kth column of Δ replaced by the column of b_i's.

It is assumed that Δ exists; that is, it is nonsingular. Mason's rule allows us to find Δ and Δ_k from the flow diagram directly. One proof is based on topological arguments, and we refer the reader to Mason's papers [2, 3].

As usual, we first make some definitions. Assume input node i and output node j, and let

Δ = the graph determinant

P_k = the kth forward path between i and j.

Δ_k = the path factor or graph determinant Δ when *all* loops touching the kth path are deleted

Then Mason's rule is

$$T_{ij} = \frac{\sum_{k=1}^{n} P_k \Delta_k}{\Delta} \tag{4.4-4}$$

where T_{ij} is the input-output relation between nodes i and j, n is the total number of forward paths, and

$$\begin{aligned} \Delta = 1 &- (\textstyle\sum \text{ all different loops}) \\ &+ (\textstyle\sum \text{ all different products of pairs of nontouching loops}) \\ &- (\textstyle\sum \text{ all different products of triplets of nontouching loops}) \\ &+ \cdots \end{aligned} \tag{4.4-5}$$

The relation for Δ is an infinite series but for most systems terminates after a few terms, because there are seldom nontouching loops of order greater than 3. In fact, for many systems Δ consists of only one of two terms. We can best illustrate Mason's rule by a few examples.

Example 4.4–1

In Figure 4.4–1 let us find Δ, the flow diagram determinate. There are five loops: *ac*, *gi*, *abd*, *ghj*, and *gfae*. There are four pairs of nontouching loops: *ac* and *gi*, *abd* and *ghj*, *ac* and *ghj*, and *gi* and *abd*. There are no nontouching loops in order of three (triplets) or higher. Then

$$\begin{aligned} \Delta = (1 - ac - gi - abd - ghj - gfae) \\ + (ac)(gi) + (abd)(ghj) + (ac)(ghj) + (gi)(abd) \end{aligned} \tag{4.4-6}$$

Now to find any input-output operator T_{ij}, this Δ applies. Let us find T_{12} and T_{13}. For T_{12}, there are two forward paths

$$P_1 = 2ab$$

$$P_2 = 3gfab$$

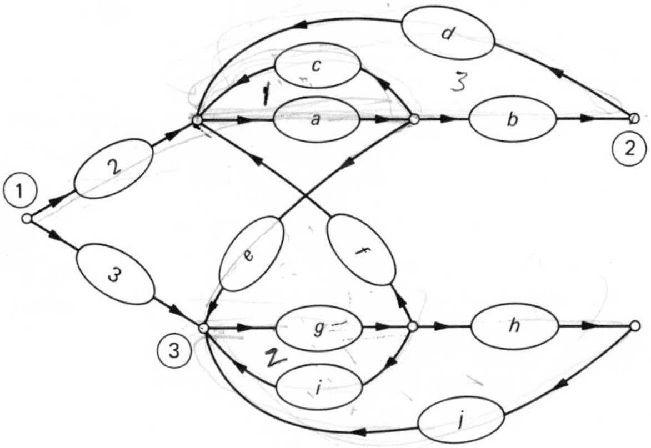

Figure 4.4–1. Flow diagram for Example 4.4–1.

For the path P_1, if we eliminate all loops touching this path, then

$$\Delta_1 = (1 - gi - ghj)$$

while the path P_2 touches all loops, hence

$$\Delta_2 = 1$$

Then

$$T_{12} = \frac{2ab(1 - gi - ghj) + 3gfab(1)}{\Delta} \tag{4.4–7}$$

Similarly,

$$T_{13} = \frac{3(1 - ac - abd) + 2ae(1)}{\Delta} \tag{4.4–8}$$

Normally Δ is easily calculated by (4.4–5), but in some cases keeping track of loop doublets, triplets, and so on, may be difficult. In these cases, an existing interior node may be split or an artificial node inserted and split [4].

Example 4.4–2

In Figure 4.4–2a insert node 3 and split this node as in Figure 4.4–2b. Then

$$\Delta = \Delta^{\circ} - \sum_{k} L_k \Delta_k \tag{4.4–9}$$

where Δ° is the graph determinate with the jth node opened, using one part of this node as a source and the other part as a sink (in this case 3′ is the

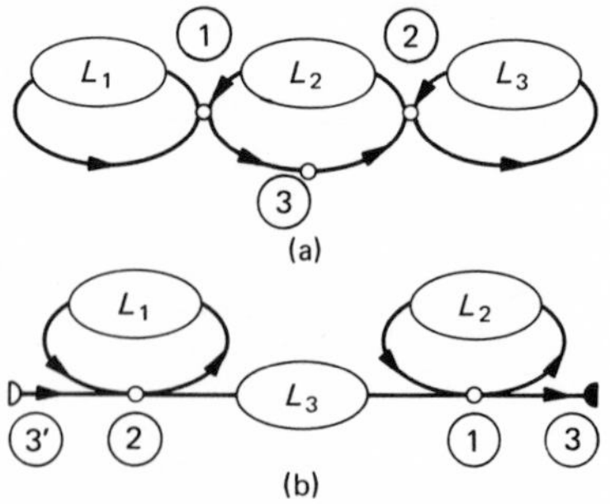

Figure 4.4–2. Node splitting.

source, 3 the sink). L_k is the kth opened loop resulting from splitting the jth node. Δ_k is the path factor for L_k. In Figure 4.4–2b, then

$$\Delta^{\circ} = 1 - (L_1 + L_2) + (L_1 L_2)$$

$$L_k = L_3$$

$$\Delta_k = 1$$

Then

$$\Delta = 1 - (L_1 + L_2) + (L_1 L_2) - L_3$$

$$= 1 - (L_1 + L_2 + L_3) + (L_1 L_2) \tag{4.4–10}$$

This result can be obtained more easily from (4.4–5), but in other situations involving many isolated loops, (4.4–9) may be simpler.

Example 4.4–3

Let us now use the flow diagram with Figure 4.4–3, which shows a transistor circuit in (a) and the low-frequency small-signal equivalent pi circuit in (b). In (b), $g_m = 0.100$, the π resistance is 1000, and the "base" resistance is neglected. From Figure 4.4–3 we obtain the following equations:

$$i_1 = \frac{v_1 - v_2}{2000}$$

$$v_a = 1000 i_1$$

$$v_b = -500(0.1 v_a)$$

$$v_2 = 500(0.1 v_a + i_1 - 0.1 v_b) + i_2(500)$$

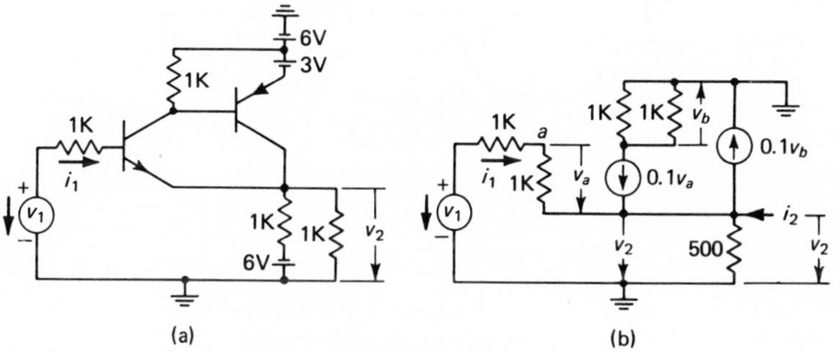

Figure 4.4–3. Transistor circuit.

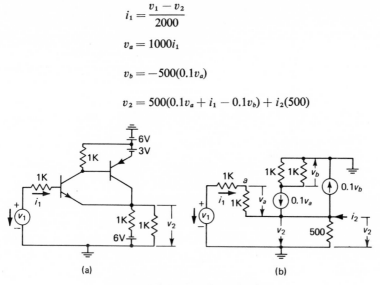

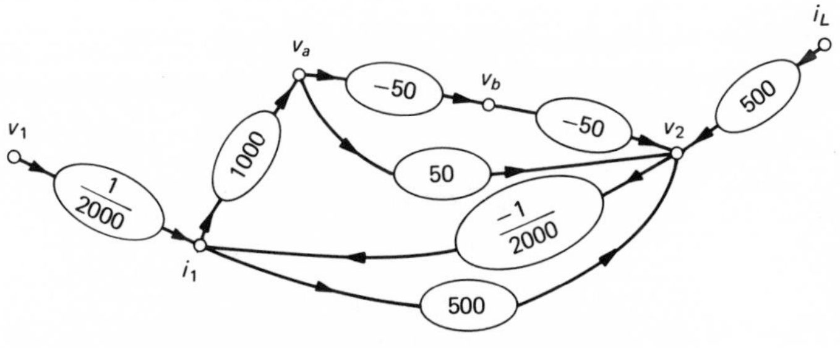

Figure 4.4–4. Flow diagram for Figure 4.4–3.

From these equations draw the flow diagram of Figure 4.4–4. Find (a) the voltage gain v_2/v_1 when $i_2 = 0$, (b) the looking-back impedance v_2/i_2 when $v_1 = 0$, and (c) the looking-in impedance v_1/i_1 when $i_2 = 0$.

Solution:

$$\Delta = 1 - \left[-\frac{500}{200} - \frac{1000}{2000}(50 + 2500) \right]$$

$$= 1 + 1275$$

$$= 1276$$

For v_2/v_1, $i_L = 0$,

$$P_1 = \frac{1}{2000}(500) \qquad \Delta_1 = 1$$

$$P_2 = \frac{1}{2000}(1000)(2500) = 1250 \qquad \Delta_2 = 1$$

$$P_3 = \frac{1}{2000}(1000)(50) = 25 \qquad \Delta_3 = 1$$

Then

$$\frac{v_2}{v_1} = \frac{0.25 + 1250 + 25}{1276} \simeq 1$$

For v_2/i_L, $v_1 = 0$

$$P_1 = 500 \qquad \Delta_1 = 1$$

or

$$\frac{v_2}{i_L} = \frac{500}{1276} \simeq 0.392 \text{ ohm}$$

For i_1/v_1, $i_L = 0$,

$$P_1 = \frac{1}{2000} \qquad \Delta_1 = 1$$

$$\frac{i_1}{v_1} = \frac{1}{(2000)(1276)}$$

or

$$\frac{v_1}{i_1} = 2.55 \times 10^6 \text{ ohms}$$

Thus the circuit has a very high input impedance, a very low looking-back impedance, and a gain of about 1 at no load. The variables used in Fig. 4.4–4 are not unique. Other analysis might be used, resulting in a different flow diagram.

If we wish to find the same quantities at higher frequencies, it is easy to add a capacitance c_1 to Figure 4.4–3 between a and b and c_2 between b and c. Additional equations involving these capacitors are written and the flow diagram altered. If the gain is wanted as a function of sinusoidal angular velocity ω, then $s = j\omega$, and the computation carried through with complex quantities. Rather than continue with this, let us apply the flow diagram to a more complicated system.

Example 4.4–4

Figure 4.4–5a shows vacuum-tube amplifier that is set up to reduce the variations in output due to the effect of tube heater temperature. In this figure assume that the two tubes are alike, or $eh_1 = eh_2$, and the characteristics are the same. Figure 4.4–5b depicts one low-frequency small-signal equivalent diagram.

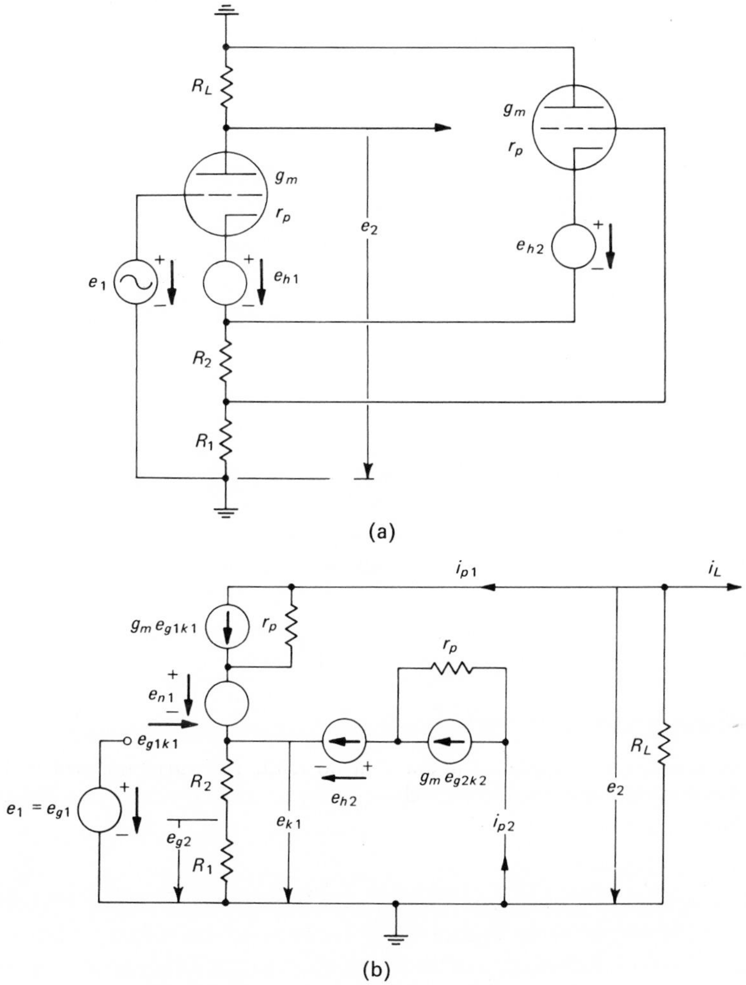

Figure 4.4–5. Circuit to balance heater voltages.

For Figure 4.4–5b one possible set of equations is

$$e_{g1k1} + e_{k1} - e_1 + e_{h1} = 0$$

or

$$e_{g1k1} = e_1 - e_{k1} - e_{h1} \tag{4.4–11a}$$

$$i_{p1} - g_m e_{g1k1} - (e_2 - eh_1 - e_{k1})\frac{1}{r_p} = 0$$

or

$$i_{p1} = g_m e_{g1k1} + (e_2 - e_{k1} - e_{h1})\frac{1}{r_p} \tag{4.4–11b}$$

$$e_{k1} = (i_{p1} + i_{p2})(R_1 + R_2) \tag{4.4–11c}$$

$$e_{g2k2} = -e_{h2} - \frac{R_2}{R_1 + R_2} e_{k1} \tag{4.4–11d}$$

$$e_2 = i_{p1}R_L - i_L R_L \tag{4.4–11e}$$

$$i_{p2} = g_m e_{g2k2} - (ek_1 + eh_2)\frac{1}{r_p} \tag{4.4–11f}$$

Figure 4.4–6 shows the flow diagram corresponding to (4.4–11) if $i_L = 0$.

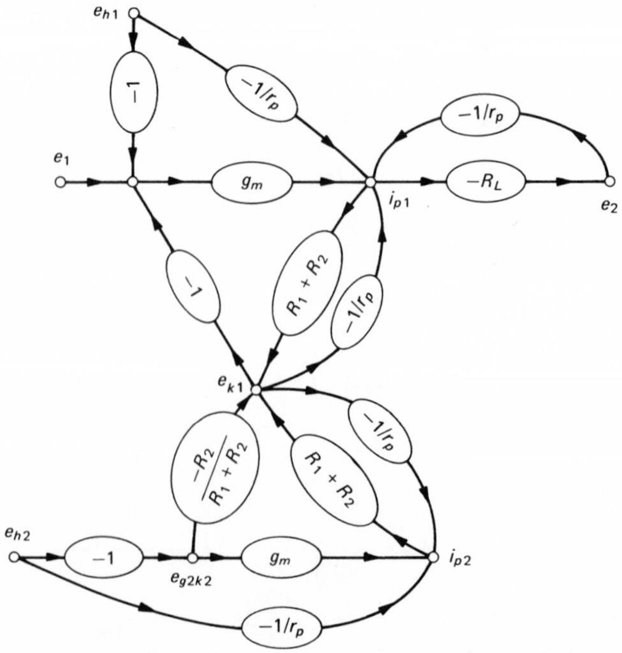

Figure 4.4–6. Flow diagram for Figure 4.4–5.

Using Mason's rule on Figure 4.4–6,

$$T_1 = \frac{e_2}{e_{h1}}\bigg|_{e_1=e_{h2}=0} = \frac{R_L[g_m + (1/r_p)]}{\Delta}\left\{1 - \left[-\frac{R_1 + R_2}{r_p} - \frac{g_m R_2}{R_1 + R_2}(R_1 + R_2)\right]\right\}$$

$$T_2 = \frac{e_2}{e_{h2}}\bigg|_{e_1=e_{h1}=0} = \frac{-R_L(R_1 + R_2)[g_m + (1/r_p)][g_m +)1/r_p)]}{\Delta}$$

To balance the heater effect, set $T_1 = -T_2$. Then

$$1 + \frac{R_1 + R_2}{r_p} + g_m R_2 = (R_1 + R_2)\left(g_m + \frac{1}{r_p}\right)$$

or

$$R_1 = \frac{1}{g_m} \tag{4.4–12}$$

In this example, it was unnecessary to find Δ. The problem was reduced to fairly simple terms by a judicious selection of variables so as to cause as many touching loops as possible. Algebraic solution by simultaneous equations would be difficult.

Finally, let us use the flow diagram in a control problem.

Example 4.4–5

In Figure 4.4–7, the operators are found by using the Laplace transform on the differential equations describing the components with initial conditions taken as zero, as previously discussed. Find Q/R.

Solution:

$$\Delta = 1 - \left[\frac{-10s}{2s(s+6)} - \frac{500}{2s(s+6)}\right]$$

$$= 1 + \frac{10s + 500}{2s(s+6)}$$

$$= \frac{2s^2 + 12s + 10s + 500}{2s(s+6)}$$

$$= \frac{2s^2 + 22s + 500}{2s(s+6)}$$

$$P_1 = 10(\tfrac{1}{10})\frac{500}{2s(s+6)} \qquad \Delta_1 = 1$$

Then

$$\frac{Q}{C} = \frac{500}{2s^2 + 22s + 500} = \frac{250}{s^2 + 11s + 250} \tag{4.4–13}$$

To find the differential equation relating R and C, from (4.4–13), $(s^2 + 11s + 150)Q = 250C$, or in the time domain†

$$\frac{d^2q(t)}{dt^2} + 11\frac{dq(t)}{dt} + 250q(t) = 250c(t) \tag{4.4–14}$$

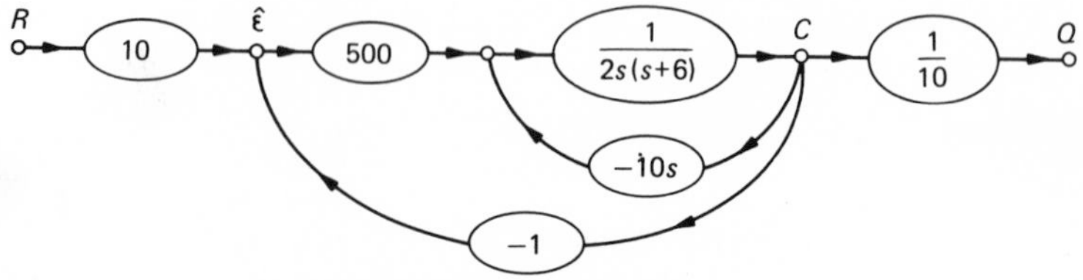

Figure 4.4–7. Control system flow diagram.

Thus we can find the overall differential equation rather easily from the flow diagram. A warning note might be sounded here: If the algebraic manipulation of the transfer function type of operator results in cancellations, the resulting differential equations will not reveal certain important aspects of the system. We shall further discuss this under the topics of observability and controllability and the topic of stability. At this point we only observe that cancellation implies a certainty about a pole or zero value that is rarely true in practice.

Although most of our examples have dealt with electrical systems, you clearly see that the same procedures are available with any set of simultaneous linear equations. Mason's rule is perhaps most useful in reducing complex subsystems to a desired overall input-output relation. Again, the rule accomplishes no more than a solution by some other means but the visualization offered by the flow diagram often may be suggestive of alterations and improvements to the engineer. As the system becomes more complicated, Mason's rule has less utility, and the numerical solution of simultaneous equations on the digital computer may become necessary if you require all the details. Otherwise, simplifying assumptions are in order.

4.5 Normal Forms and State-Space Representation

As the flow diagram is not unique, or, alternatively, there is a wide choice of possible system variables, you might ask, Is there any method

† Rigorously, the variable s as obtained from the Laplace transform should not be confused with the variable $p \equiv d/dt$. This becomes particularly important in time-varying systems (see reference [5]). Since we deal with fixed systems, we shall be somewhat loose.

of representing a differential equation that may be simpler than others, at least in some respects? Let us consider the differential equation

$$\frac{d^3y}{dt^2} + 6\frac{d^2y}{dt^2} + 5\frac{dy}{dt} + 50y = 4\frac{d^2m}{dt^2} + 3\frac{dm}{dt} + 2m \qquad \textbf{(4.5–1)}$$

and apply the Laplace transform, with all initial conditions zero. From (4.5–1) we get

$$(s^3 + 6s^2 + 5s + 50)\,Y = (4s^2 + 3s + 2)M$$

or

$$\frac{Y(s)}{M(s)} = \frac{4s^2 + 3s + 2}{s^3 + 6s^2 + 5s + 50} \qquad \textbf{(4.5–2)}$$

Divide the numerator and denominator of (4.5–2) by s^3 to get

$$\frac{Y(s)}{M(s)} = \frac{4/s + 3/s^2 + 2/s^3}{1 + 6/s + 5/s^2 + 50/s^3} \qquad \textbf{(4.5–3)}$$

In (4.5–3) the denominator looks remarkably like the Δ of Mason's rule—in fact, we can devise some simple configurations that give exactly this denominator by causing all loops to touch. One such configuration is shown in Figure 4.5–1a. Now we can obtain the numerator by forming forward paths, all of which have $\Delta_k = 1$, and add these on to obtain

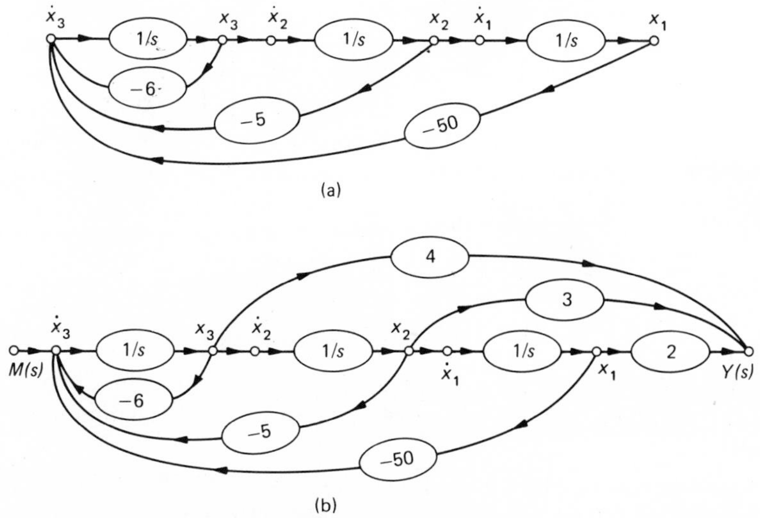

Figure 4.5–1. Flow diagram for Equation (4.5–3).

Figure 4.5–1b. You see that Figure 4.5–1 does represent (4.5–3), and hence (4.5–2). The internal variables, X_1, X_2, and X_3, are somewhat arbitrary. Since $1/s$ represents integration in the time domain, $\dot{X}_1$, $\dot{X}_2$, and $\dot{X}_3$ depict the transformed time derivatives of x_1, x_2, and x_3. Using Figure 4.5–1, we can rewrite (4.5–1) in the state-space or normal form, where all derivatives are involved to only the first power.

Converting to time variables,

$$\dot{x}_1 = x_2 \tag{4.5–4a}$$

$$\dot{x}_2 = x_3 \tag{4.5–4b}$$

$$\dot{x}_3 = -50x_1 - 5x_2 - 6x_3 + m \tag{4.5–4c}$$

$$y = 2x_1 + 3x_2 + 4x_3 \tag{4.5–4d}$$

where

$$\dot{x} = \frac{dx}{dt}$$

Equations (4.5–4) can be reduced to a simpler form by letting the variables $\dot{\mathbf{x}}$ and $\mathbf{x}$ be 3×1 matrices, then

$$\dot{\mathbf{x}} = \mathbf{A}\mathbf{x} + \mathbf{B}m \tag{4.5–5a}$$

$$y = \mathbf{C}\mathbf{x} + \mathbf{D}m \tag{4.5–5b}$$

where

$$\mathbf{A} = \begin{bmatrix} 0 & 1 & 0 \\ 0 & 0 & 1 \\ -50 & -5 & -6 \end{bmatrix} \qquad \mathbf{B} = \begin{bmatrix} 0 \\ 0 \\ 1 \end{bmatrix}$$

$$\mathbf{C} = [2 \quad 3 \quad 4] \qquad \mathbf{D} = \mathbf{0}$$

$$\mathbf{x} = \begin{bmatrix} x_1 \\ x_2 \\ x_3 \end{bmatrix} \qquad \dot{\mathbf{x}} = \begin{bmatrix} \dot{x}_1 \\ \dot{x}_2 \\ \dot{x}_3 \end{bmatrix}$$

Equations (4.5–5) are equations in state space and the x's are the state variables. We have already discussed this representation in Chapter 3, and the following two chapters will take up this type of equation in more detail.

It is easy to generalize on this procedure, and obtain two forms for any single input-output system, where the highest derivative of the input is of lesser degree than the highest derivative of the output. (This is the situation in most control systems.) These two forms are sometimes known as Kalman forms [6]. Thus given

$$\frac{Y(s)}{M(s)} = \frac{a_n s^{n-1} + a_{n-1}s^{n-2} + \cdots + a_1}{s^n + b_n s^{n-1} + b_{n-1}s^{n-2} + \cdots + b_1} \quad \textbf{(4.5–6)}$$

we may obtain equations of the form

$$\begin{aligned} \dot{\mathbf{x}} &= \mathbf{Ax} + \mathbf{Bm} \\ \mathbf{y} &= \mathbf{Cx} + \mathbf{Dm} \end{aligned} \quad \textbf{(4.5–7)}$$

through Figure 4.5–2 or Figure 4.5–3. If you consider the $1/s$ operators integrators, the variables may be shown as functions of time, as shown. Equations (4.5–8) give the matrices associated with Figure 4.5–2, while (4.5–9) are associated with Figure 4.5–3.

1st Kalman form

$$\mathbf{A} = \begin{bmatrix} 0 & 1 & 0 & \cdots & 0 \\ 0 & 0 & 1 & \cdots & 0 \\ \cdot & & & & \\ \cdot & & & & \\ \cdot & & & \cdots & 1 \\ -b_1 & -b_2 & -b_3 & \cdots & -b_n \end{bmatrix} \qquad \mathbf{B} = \begin{bmatrix} 0 \\ 0 \\ \cdot \\ \cdot \\ \cdot \\ 1 \end{bmatrix} \quad \textbf{(4.5–8)}$$

$$\mathbf{C} = [a_1 \quad a_2 \quad \cdots \quad a_n] \qquad \mathbf{D} = \mathbf{0}$$

2nd Kalman form

$$\mathbf{A} = \begin{bmatrix} 0 & 0 & \cdots & & -b_1 \\ 1 & 0 & \cdots & & -b_2 \\ 0 & 1 & 0 & & -b_3 \\ \vdots & & & & \vdots \\ 0 & 0 & \cdots & 1 & -b_n \end{bmatrix} \qquad \mathbf{B} = \begin{bmatrix} a_1 \\ a_2 \\ a_3 \\ \vdots \\ a_n \end{bmatrix} \quad \textbf{(4.5–9)}$$

$$\mathbf{C} = [0 \quad 0 \quad \cdots \quad 1] \qquad \mathbf{D} = \mathbf{0}$$

If n represents the highest derivative of y, then in both (4.5–8) and (4.5–9) the matrices have the following dimensions: **A** is $n \times n$, **B** is $n \times 1$, **C** is $1 \times n$, and **D** is 1×1.

If the highest derivative of the input has a degree equal to the highest derivative of the output, a flow diagram is still possible. For example, look at

$$\frac{d^2y}{dt^2} + 6\frac{dy}{dt} + 5y = 4\frac{d^2m}{dt^2} + 3\frac{dm}{dt} + 2m \quad \textbf{(4.5–10)}$$

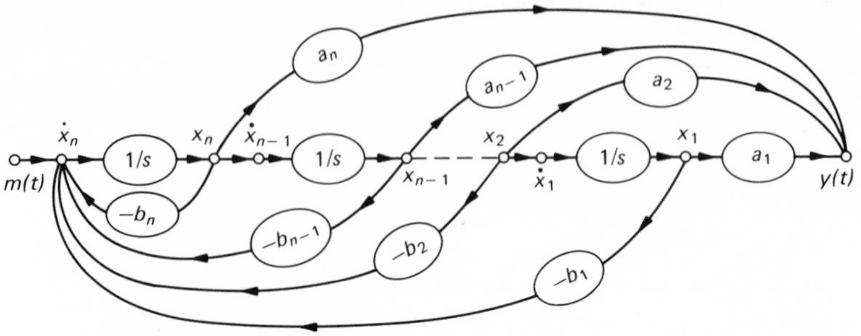

Figure 4.5–2. First Kalman form. $1/s$ represents integration.

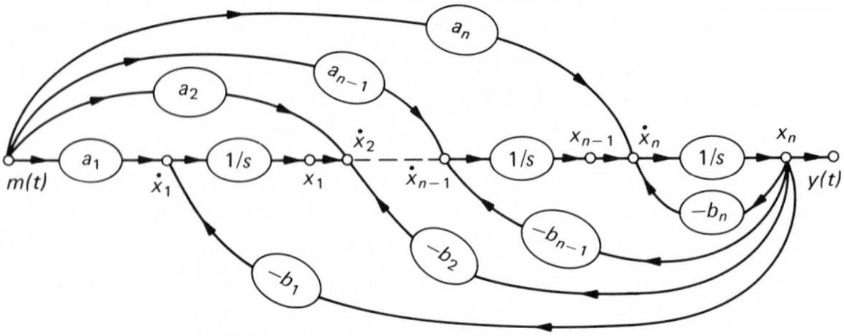

Figure 4.5–3. Second Kalman form. $1/s$ represents integration.

and consider the flow diagram of Figure 4.5–4, where we omit the functional notation. Using Mason's rule for Figure 4.5–4

$$\Delta = 1 + \frac{6}{s} + \frac{5}{s^2}$$

$$P_1 = \frac{a}{s^2} \qquad \Delta_1 = 1$$

$$P_2 = \frac{b}{s} \qquad \Delta_2 = 1$$

$$P_3 = c \qquad \Delta_3 = 1 + \frac{6}{s}$$

Hence

$$\frac{Y(s)}{M(s)} = \frac{a/s^2 + b/s + c(1 + 6/s)}{1 + 6/s + 5/s^2}$$

$$= \frac{cs^2 + (b + 6c)s + a}{s^2 + 6s + 5} \qquad \textbf{(4.5–11)}$$

From (4.5–10) (zero initial conditions),

$$\frac{Y(s)}{M(s)} = \frac{4s^2 + 3s + 2}{s^2 + 6s + 5} \tag{4.5–12}$$

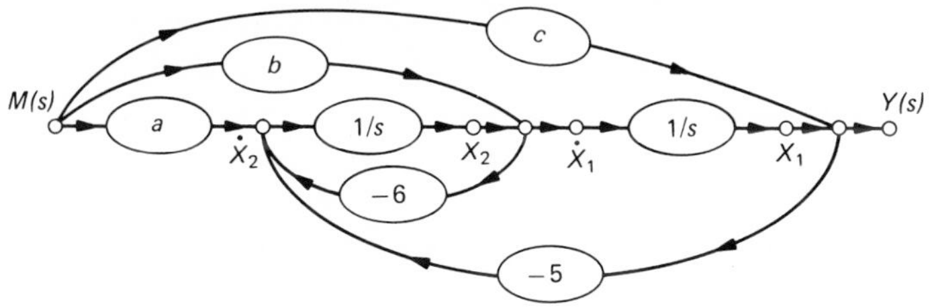

Figure 4.5–4. Flow diagram for Equation (4.5–10).

Comparing (4.5–11) with (4.5–12), if

$$c = 4$$

$$a = 2$$

$$b = -21$$

the flow diagram represents (4.5–10). From Figure 4.5–4 you may convince yourself that the state-space matrices of (4.5–5) in this case are

$$\mathbf{A} = \begin{bmatrix} 0 & 1 \\ -5 & -6 \end{bmatrix} \qquad \mathbf{B} = \begin{bmatrix} -21 \\ 108 \end{bmatrix}$$

$$\mathbf{C} = [1 \quad 0] \qquad \mathbf{D} = 4$$

4.6 Computer Simulation—Analog

Engineers have found computers to be very useful in analyzing systems of all kinds. In fact, modern systems are often so complex that solutions would be impossible without computer asistance. Also, obviously it is much less costly and time consuming to simulate system operation on a computer, and to make corrections in the design, than to build a trial physical system. The reader should be warned, however, that no computer will do any thinking for him. The best computer is only an aid, not a designer. You should never approach a computer without much preliminary paper and pencil work, and a clear plan of action.

We may divide computers into two general areas—digital and analog. The digital computer works in a serial way; that is, computations proceed step by step, and normally only one quantity can be handled at any instant. By virtue of this, and the fact that it requires finite time to compute each result, the digital computer must find the solution at discrete intervals, and if time is the independent variable this means discrete time intervals. The simulated system is thus a discrete time system as defined in Chapter 1. However, if the time intervals are sufficiently short, the results will very closely approximate a continuous time system. Large memory and high accuracy also characterize the digital computer. On the other hand, it is not easy to alter quantities in a problem; that is, any change in data, such as altering system constants, requires rerunning the computer program from the start. Programming may automate this to some extent, but the designer normally likes to see results from one alteration before proceeding to another. This requires some kind of output that may require time for interpretation, after which it may require more time to get the program back on the computer, as by then it will be processing other data. Larger and faster computers will alleviate this time lag but probably never eliminate it. The digital computer performs all computations by proper combination of the four basic operations of addition, subtraction, multiplication, and division.

The modern analog computer employs electronic components and works in a parallel fashion; in other words, many quantities may be available at the same time. It is characterized by a small memory and low accuracy, and the variables (voltages) are continuous functions of time. It is easy to change a parameter on this computer, because this only involves turning potentiometers, which in some computers may be done from a remote console. The outputs may be observed while the solution proceeds and the designer may stop the solution at any point to check the results. Many engineers therefore feel a closer rapport with the analog computer; it seems less remote perhaps. Some methods now involve using both computers together in a hybrid system, appropriately exploiting the advantages of each. You may expect to see much new development in this area in the next few years.

Let us discuss analog simulation first. Modern analog computers for the purpose of control simulation utilize electronic amplifiers, potentiometers, connections, and other electrical devices. Most students have at least a superficial knowledge of the operation of this computer. Appendix C discusses the details briefly for review purposes and lists references giving more complete coverage.

On examining Figures 4.5–2 and 4.5–3, you see that the diagrams contain several branch operators representing integrators in the time domain, and, if you look at Appendix C, you see that these diagrams are very similar to those given for the analog computer solution of differential equations. There are only a few differences: (1) The output of each amplifier in an electronic analog computer reverses the polarity of the input in addition to other operations, (2) in an analog computer you must usually time scale and magnitude scale the variables; and (3) it is necessary to put an initial condition on each variable. In the analog computer you accomplish this by initially charging the feedback capacitor of each integrator until the integrator output has the required value. Items (1) and (2) are essentially limitations imposed by the particular equipment used for the simulation. Item (3), the initial condition, can be depicted on the flow diagram, or understood. Thus, except for practical considerations (1) and (2), a flow diagram is essentially an analog computer representation. The Kalman canonical diagrams are computer simulations using only integrators. Although electronic amplifiers can serve as differentiators, this operation raises special problems, and we prefer to simulate with integrators throughout. Usually, although not always, we find it possible to accomplish this by adoption of the proper variables. The Kalman graphs illustrate two possibilities; there may be many others. If the variables are altered from the original, it is necessary to obtain the values of the computer variables in terms of variables that are physically measureable in the system. This is particularly true of the initial conditions on the integrators, which must be known to obtain a correct simulation.

Example 4.6–1

Find the first Kalman form for the system described by the differential equation

$$\frac{d^3y}{dt^3} + 5\frac{d^2y}{dt^2} + 6\frac{dy}{dt} = \frac{d^2m}{dt^2} + 4\frac{dm}{dt} + 2m \tag{4.6–1}$$

and obtain the relation between the state variables and the original variables.

Using (4.5–8) we obtain

$$\dot{x}_1 = x_2 \tag{4.6–2a}$$

$$\dot{x}_2 = x_3 \tag{4.6–2b}$$

$$\dot{x}_3 = -6x_2 - 5x_3 + m \tag{4.6–2c}$$

$$y = 2x_1 + 4x_2 + x_3 \tag{4.6–2d}$$

From the last equation,

$$\dot{y} = 2\dot{x}_1 + 4\dot{x}_2 + \dot{x}_3$$

Substituting the values for $\dot{x}_1$, $\dot{x}_2$, and $\dot{x}_3$ from the state equations,

$$\dot{y} = -4x_2 - x_3 + m$$

Differentiating,

$$\ddot{y} = -4\dot{x}_2 - \dot{x}_3 + \dot{m}$$

and substituting again,

$$\ddot{y} = x_3 + 6x_2 - m + \dot{m}$$

Solving the equations for x_1, x_2, and x_3, you get

$$x_1 = \tfrac{1}{2}(y + \dot{y} - m) \tag{4.6–3a}$$

$$x_2 = \tfrac{1}{2}(\dot{y} + \ddot{y} - \dot{m}) \tag{4.6–3b}$$

$$x_3 = -3\dot{y} - 2\ddot{y} + 2\dot{m} + m \tag{4.6–3c}$$

Example 4.6–2

In the system described by (4.5–1), find the second Kalman form and obtain the initial conditions on the integrators in terms of the variables m and y and their derivatives. Set up the analog computer diagram. From (4.5–6) and (4.5–9) you obtain

$$\dot{x}_1 = 50x_3 + 2m \tag{4.6–4a}$$

$$\dot{x}_2 = x_1 - 5x_3 + 3m \tag{4.6–4b}$$

$$\dot{x}_3 = x_2 - 6x_3 + 4m \tag{4.6–4c}$$

$$y = x_3 \tag{4.6–4d}$$

From (4.6–4d),

$$x_3 = y$$

Hence

$$\dot{x}_3 = \dot{y}$$

Substituting this result in (4.6–4c), you find

$$\dot{y} = x_2 - 6y + 4m$$

or

$$x_2 = \dot{y} + 6y - 4m$$

and thus

$$\dot{x}_2 = \ddot{y} + 6\dot{y} - 4\dot{m}$$

Substituting this in turn in (4.6–4b),

$$\ddot{y} + 6\dot{y} - 4\dot{m} = x_1 - 5y + 3m$$

or

$$x_1 = \ddot{y} + 6\dot{y} + 5y - 4\dot{m} - 3m$$

Thus the change in variables becomes

$$x_3 = y \qquad \textbf{(4.6–5a)}$$

$$x_2 = \dot{y} + 6y - 4m \qquad \textbf{(4.6–5b)}$$

$$x_1 = \ddot{y} + 6\dot{y} + 5y - 4\dot{m} - 3m \qquad \textbf{(4.6–5c)}$$

and the initial values of x_1, x_2, and x_3, or the initial conditions on each integrator, are known in terms of the initial values of y, $\dot{y}$, $\ddot{y}$, m, and $\dot{m}$. Next, because each integrator has a reversed sign output, we can start by assuming that the output of the left-most integrator of Figure 4.5–3 has $-x_1$ as output. Then rewrite (4.6–4) as

$$\dot{x}_1 = 50x_3 + 2m$$

$$-\dot{x}_2 = -x_1 + 5x_3 - 3m$$

$$\dot{x}_3 = x_2 - 6x_3 + 4m$$

Figure 4.6–1 is now an electronic analog computer simulation. It requires two additional amplifiers to be used for sign reversal. (The last reversal to obtain $+y$ is usually not necessary.) The initial conditions are also shown

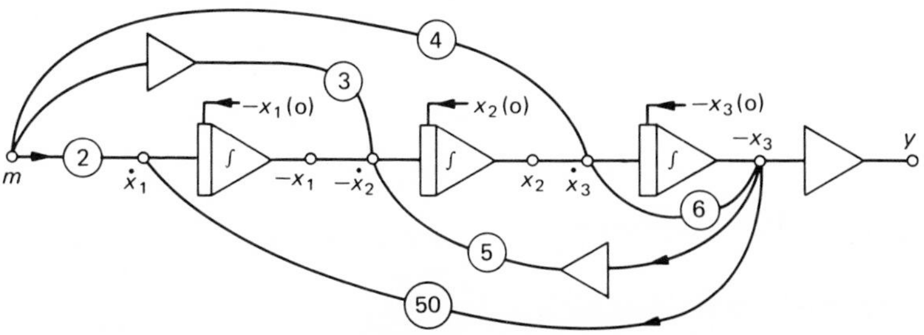

Figure 4.6–1. Analog computer simulation for Equation (4.5–1).

with $t_0 = 0$. The gains on the amplifiers are 1, which is not practical. It remains to time- and magnitude-scale the problem by introducing still new variables, x_1', x_2', and x_3', to avoid overloading the amplifiers, maintain a good signal to noise ratio, and obtain the required solution speed. These factors are discussed briefly in Appendix C and more fully in the references given there, and we do not pursue this here.

It is obvious that the symbolization of differential equations by means of a flow diagram using the variable s portrays an analog simulation of the system except for the details previously mentioned. We shall therefore employ this simulation scheme when required in the future. The initial condition on each integrator may be either shown explicitly, or understood; but in either case initial conditions (some or all of which may be zero) must always exist.

If the differential equation does not involve any derivatives of the input, one analog simulation may be found easily, as shown in the following example.

Example 4.6–3

Consider the equation

$$\frac{d^3y}{dt^2} + 6\frac{d^2y}{dt^2} + 5\frac{dy}{dt} + 50y = 2m \tag{4.6–6}$$

This is the same as (4.5–1) without the derivatives of the input x. Let

$$x_1 = y$$

$$x_2 = \dot{y}$$

$$x_3 = \ddot{y}$$

Then from (4.6–6) we obtain the normal form

$$\begin{aligned} \dot{x}_1 &= x_2 \\ \dot{x}_2 &= x_3 \\ \dot{x}_3 &= -6x_3 - 5x_2 - 50x_1 + 2m \\ y &= x_1 \end{aligned} \tag{4.6–7}$$

The state-variable matrices are

$$\mathbf{A} = \begin{bmatrix} 0 & 1 & 0 \\ 0 & 0 & 1 \\ -50 & -5 & -6 \end{bmatrix} \qquad \mathbf{B} = \begin{bmatrix} 0 \\ 0 \\ 2 \end{bmatrix} \tag{4.6–8}$$

$$\mathbf{C} = [1 \quad 0 \quad 0] \qquad \mathbf{D} = 0$$

and are very similar to those for one of Kalman's forms.

To see how the initial conditions can be included in the flow diagram, assume that $m = 0$ and we have initial conditions x_{10}, x_{20}, and x_{30} as the values of x_1, x_2, and x_3 at $t = 0$. Laplace-transforming (4.6–7), you obtain

$$sX_1(s) = X_2(s) + x_{10}$$

$$sX_2(s) = X_3(s) + x_{20}$$

$$sX_3(s) = -6X_3(s) - 5X_2(s) - 50X_1(s) + x_{30}$$

$$Y(s) = X_1(s)$$

Dropping the functional symbolism and solving, you obtain

$$X_1 = \frac{X_2}{s} + \frac{x_{10}}{s}$$

$$X_2 = \frac{X_3}{s} + \frac{x_{20}}{s}$$

$$X_3 = \frac{1}{s}(-6X_3 - 5X_2 - 50X_1) + \frac{x_{30}}{s}$$

Thus the initial condition may be shown in the flow diagram by an input at each state-variable node of that state-variable initial condition value divided by s. Hence at node X_1 we have an input of x_{10}/s, and so on. The complete

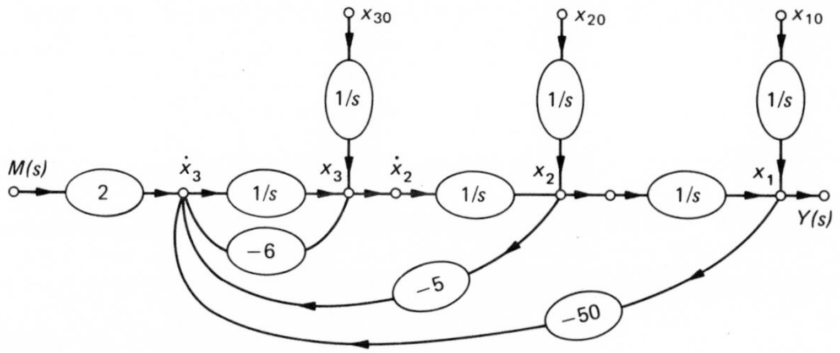

Figure 4.6–2. Representation of initial conditions in flow diagram for Equation (4.6–6).

flow diagram is shown in Figure 4.6–2. The initial conditions x_{10}, x_{20}, and x_{30} must be obtained in terms of y_{10}, y_{20}, and y_{30} as before, but the relations in this case are particularly simple.

The previous methods of analog simulation are sometimes termed "direct programming," and the following technique "parallel programming" [7]. In this procedure, we put the function $Y(s)/M(s)$ in the form of a partial fraction expansion.

Example 4.6–4

The partial fraction expansion of the Laplace-transformed (4.6–1) with zero initial conditions is

$$\frac{Y(s)}{M(s)} = \frac{1/3}{s} + \frac{-1/3}{s+3} + \frac{1}{s+2} \tag{4.6–9}$$

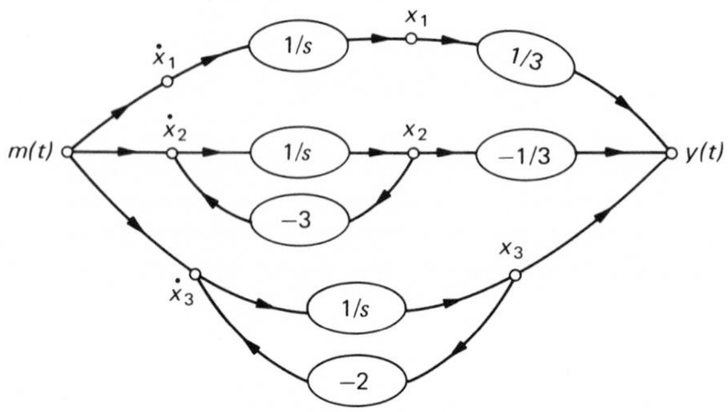

Figure 4.6–3. Parallel programming. $1/s$ represents integration.

From (4.6–9) Figure 4.6–3 may be drawn, where we show the variables in the time domain, and $1/s$ represents time integrations. The state equations are

$$\dot{\mathbf{x}} = \mathbf{A}\mathbf{x} + \mathbf{B}m$$

$$y = \mathbf{C}\mathbf{x} + \mathbf{D}m$$

where

$$\mathbf{A} = \begin{bmatrix} 0 & 0 & 0 \\ 0 & -3 & 0 \\ 0 & 0 & -2 \end{bmatrix} \qquad \mathbf{B} = \begin{bmatrix} 1 \\ 1 \\ 1 \end{bmatrix} \tag{4.6–10}$$

$$\mathbf{C} = [\tfrac{1}{3} \ -\tfrac{1}{3} \ 1] \qquad \mathbf{D} = \mathbf{0}$$

The initial conditions on x_1, x_2, and x_3 are understood in Figure 4.6–3, and the variables, x_1, x_2, and x_3 may be found in terms of y and its derivatives and m and its derivatives.

The equations depicted by (4.6–10) contain special interesting features. You see that

$$\dot{x}_1 = 0x_1 + m$$

$$\dot{x}_2 = -3x_2 + m$$

$$\dot{x}_3 = -2x_3 + m$$

or each equation contains only one state variable and is therefore very easy to solve, Thus, if $m = 0$,

$$x_1 = k_1$$

$$x_2 = k_2 \epsilon^{-3t}$$

$$x_3 = k_3 \epsilon^{-2t}$$

We call this procedure "decoupling" the system and term **A** a diagonalized matrix. Such a matrix has a special symbol $\mathbf{\Lambda}$, indicating that it is diagonalized. Moreover, note that the values along the main diagonal are the roots of the characteristic equation $s(s + 3)(s + 2) = 0$, or the poles of the transfer function

$$\frac{Y(s)}{M(s)} = \frac{s^2 + 4s + 2}{s^3 + 5s^2 + 6s}$$

These diagonal values are called "eigenvalues," "characteristic values," or "proper values." The eigenvalues are equivalent in most cases to the poles of the overall transfer function. If the numerator of the transfer function has a degree equal to that of the denominator, $\mathbf{D} \neq 0$. If the system has more than one input or output, the numerator becomes a matrix. If the eigenvalues are complex, the diagonalization still has validity, but computer simulation of a single complex root by one integrator is not possible.

Another technique is termed "iterative programming" [7]. Here the numerator of the transfer function is factored.

Example 4.6–5

From (4.6–1) we get

$$Z(s) = \frac{Y(s)}{M(s)} = \frac{1}{s} \frac{s + 2 + \sqrt{2}}{s + 3} \frac{s + 2 - \sqrt{2}}{s + 2} \qquad \textbf{(4.6–11)}$$

Then Figure 4.6–4 can be used for simulation.

From Figure 4.6–4 the state equations are

$$\dot{x}_1 = m$$

$$\dot{x}_2 = x_1 - 3x_2$$

$$\dot{x}_3 = (-1 + \sqrt{2})x_2 + x_1 - 2x_3$$

$$\begin{aligned} y &= (2 - \sqrt{2})x_3 + (-1 + \sqrt{2})x_2 + x_1 - 2x_3 \\ &= -\sqrt{2}x_3 + (-1 + \sqrt{2})x_2 + x_1 \end{aligned}$$

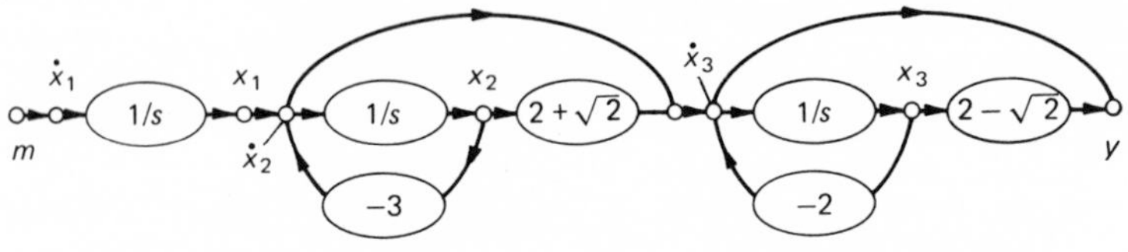

Figure 4.6–4. Iterative programming. $1/s$ represents integration.

Note that in the examples connected with (4.6–1) the output would grow continuously, with certain inputs. This would represent driven instability in a control system.

The simulations of Figure 4.6–3 and Figure 4.6–4 assume that the roots of the characteristic equation are real and distinct. Complex roots lead to quadratic factors in the characteristic polynomial. The partial fraction expansion thus gives terms such as $(a_1 s + a_0)/(s^2 + b_1 s + b_0)$. This factor may be simulated by one of the Kalman normal forms, leading to two state variables for each such branch in Figure 4.6–3. In these simulations the characteristic equation must be factored, which is a disadvantage compared to other forms.

It should be clear that a system described by simultaneous differential equations, that is, a multi-input-output system, may be simulated by working with each equation in turn by any of the methods previously described, or any combination thereof. Alternatively, if the system is described in state-space form, the **A**, **B**, **C**, and **D** matrices lead directly to a possible simulation. These matrices can be altered by linear matrix transformations to result in many other simulation possibilities. We shall discuss this further in the following chapters.

The generation of forcing functions is a requirement frequently met in simulation. Because fundamentally the electronic analog computer is a differential analyzer, any function that can be represented by a differential equation is easily simulated. The most commonly used functions are (1) polynomial, (2) step, (3) ramp, (4) exponential, and (5) sinusoidal. The polynomial

$$r = r_0 + r_1 t + r_2 t^2 + \cdots + r_{n-1} t^{n-1} \qquad t \geq 0 \tag{4.6–12}$$

may be expressed in the form of a differential equation by making $x_1 = r$. Then let

$$x_2 = \dot{x}_1 = r_1 + 2r_2 t + \cdots + (n-1)r_{n-1}t^{n-2}$$

$$x_3 = \dot{x}_2 = 2r_2 + 6r_3 t + \cdots + (n-1)(n-2)r_{n-2}t^{n-3}$$

and so on, to

$$\dot{x}_{n-1} = x_n$$

$$\dot{x}_n = 0$$

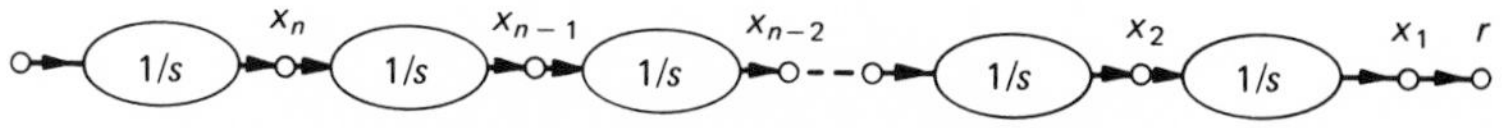

Figure 4.6–5. Simulation of a polynomial.

The state variables $x_1, x_2, \ldots, x_n$ can now be connected so as to generate the polynomial as in Figure 4.6–5. The initial conditions $x_k(0)$ at $t = 0_+$ are given by the previous equations with $t = 0$, or

$$\begin{aligned} x_1(0) &= r_0 \\ x_2(0) &= r_1 \\ x_3(0) &= 2r_2 \\ &\vdots \\ x_k(0) &= r_{k-1}(k-1)! \\ &\vdots \\ x_n(0) &= r_n(n-1)! \end{aligned}$$

The step and ramp are special cases of the polynomial. Thus for the step, we take one term of (4.6–12), and for the ramp, two terms. The step simulation is shown in Figure 4.6–6 and the ramp by Figure 4.6–7. In some cases a parabolic function consisting of three terms might be desired, and this extension is obvious.

Figure 4.6–6. Simulation of a step input; $x_1(0) = 0$.

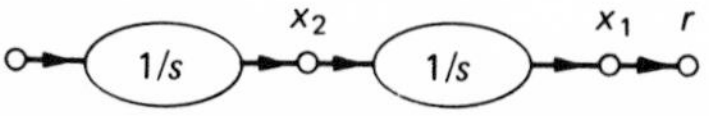

Figure 4.6–7. Simulation of a ramp input; $x_1(0) = 0$, $x_2 = r_1$.

In all polynomial cases the input of the leftmost integrator in the figures must be zero, which can be obtained by grounding this input.

The impulse function is difficult to generate. Theoretically we could differentiate a step, but the use of differentiation is discouraged. Furthermore, the amplifier for this purpose would saturate. Mechanically, an impulse can be approximated by a sharp hard blow, but, unless this is applied to a constructed portion of the system connected to the computer, it would be difficult to simulate. A diode arrangement that would deliver a pulse whose duration was short compared to the system time constants, and whose height was large compared to other variables, would give a satisfactory impulse approximation in some cases. Another reasonable approach might be to apply a step to the system, and differentiate the system output (linear, time-invariant system).

The exponential

$$r = r_0 \epsilon^{-at}, \qquad t \geq 0 \qquad a \geq 0, \tag{4.6–13}$$

is easy to simulate by letting $r = x_1$. Then

$$\dot{x}_1 = -ar_0 \epsilon^{-at} = -ax_1$$

The initial condition is obviously $x_1(0) = r_0$. The simulation is shown in Figure 4.6–8. If $a < 0$, the integrating amplifier will saturate in a short time.

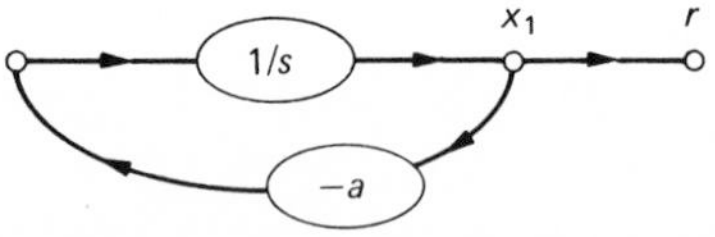

Figure 4.6–8. Simulation of an exponential function; $x_1(0) = r_0$.

The sine and cosine functions are formed from

$$\ddot{y}_1 + \omega^2 y_1 = 0 \qquad t \geq 0 \tag{4.6–14}$$

Let

$$\dot{y}_1 = \dot{x}_1 = \omega x_2$$

$$\dot{x}_2 = -\omega x_1$$

The initial conditions are $x_1(0)$ and $x_2(0)$. The outputs r_1 and r_2 in Figure 4.6–9 are then $r_1 = x_1(0)\cos \omega t$ and $x_2 = x_1(0)\sin \omega t$ if $x_2(0) = 0$.

In all the previous figures for forcing functions the sign inversions and time-magnitude scaling are not considered. A general function may be simulated by diodes and resistors (see Appendix C).

In some cases the forcing function may be eliminated by changing the initial conditions.

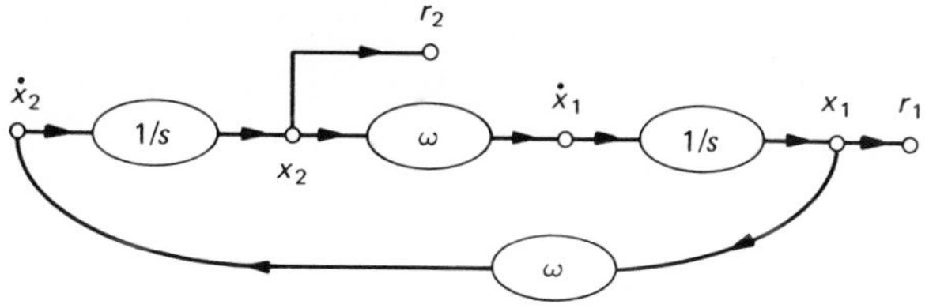

Figure 4.6–9. Simulation of a sinusoidal function.

Example 4.6–6

Examine the equations

$$-\dot{x}_1 = -x_2$$

$$\dot{x}_2 = -x_2 - kx_1 + m$$

and let m be a unit step function, $u(t)$.

These equations are simulated in the computer diagram of Figure 4.6–10. The node e is the error in a particular control system. Clearly the same results can be achieved by eliminating the first integrator and making the initial condition on the third integrator equal to $x_1(0) - m(0)$, since m is a unit step function. This could be extended to any polynomial if there were sufficient integrators [8].

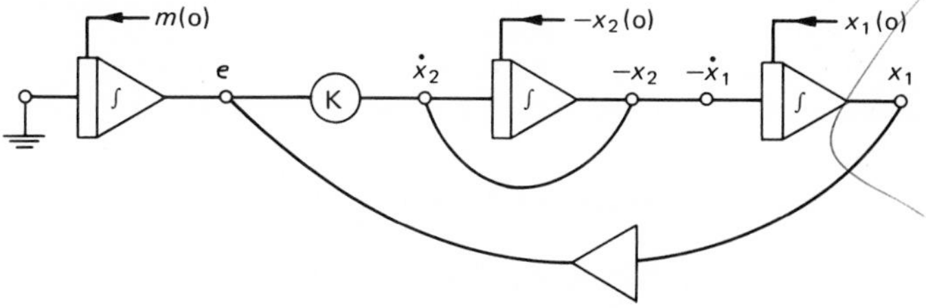

Figure 4.6–10. Analog computer connections for Example 4.6–6.

The simulation of nonlinear and discontinuous systems in the analog computer is straightforward. A nonlinear device simulating the actual function is connected in the proper branch in the simulation. Many such devices have been invented and are shown in the references of Appendix C. The sampled-data system can be simulated by the introduction of a relay closing and opening a contact at the proper rate. Multiplication of variables, resolution from polar to rectangular coordinates, and vice versa, and many other desired operations are now easily performed on the electronic analog computer.

4.7 Computer Simulation—Digital

Except for programs requiring high efficiency (fast execution time or low memory space), modern digital computers are usually programmed by using an algebraic-oriented language such as Fortran or Algol. Such program languages are particularly adapted to the engineer, who usually can learn the rudiments without difficulty. This reduces the simulation to the preparation of an adequate logic diagram, which is simply a step by step graphical description of the solution process. (See Figure 4.7–1 for a possible method for finding the roots of a quadratic). This also comes fairly naturally to the engineer. You may, however, have little knowledge of particular methods used to solve problems on a digital computer. These employ difference equations, polynomial approximations, iteration techniques, and many other approaches, all of which are lumped under the general title of "numerical analysis," which implies obtaining specifically numerical and not general analytical results. Frequently methods are used for which existence solutions cannot be proved rigorously but which work most of the time. In digital computer application you also need to become aware of the possible errors in the output. An eight-digit accuracy seems like heaven to the slide rule engineer, but a printed eight-digit answer often means less than three-digit accuracy after hundreds of iterations in the computer.

The routine for solving a problem on a digital computer is frequently called an "algorithm." System simulation means using algorithms to solve differential equations. There are a number of methods for attacking such equations digitally, but perhaps the most used methods involve (1) Runge-Kutta, and (2) predictor-corrector formulas. We shall not go into all the derivation details here, but give the results for a few cases [9]. First look at the first-order scalar equation

$$\dot{x} = f(x, t) \tag{4.7–1}$$

Let $x(t)$ be a solution, and expand $x(t)$ in a Taylor's series about some point (x_m, t_m). Then

$$x(t) = x_m + \dot{x}_m(t - t_m) + \frac{\ddot{x}_m}{2}(t - t_m)^2 + \cdots \tag{4.7–2}$$

where $\dot{x}_m$ means "evaluate $\dot{x}(t)$ at t_m."

Let $t = t_{m+1} = t_0 + ih$, where i is an integer and h a positive constant $(t_{m+1} - t_m)$. Then (4.7–2) becomes

$$x_{m+1} = x_m + h\dot{x}_m + \frac{h^2}{2}\ddot{x}_m + \cdots \tag{4.7–3}$$

From (4.7–1),

$$\dot{x}_m = f(x_m, t_m)$$

$$\ddot{x}_m = \frac{\partial f}{\partial t}(x, t) + f(x, t)\frac{\partial f}{\partial x}(x, t)$$

$$= f_t + f f_x$$

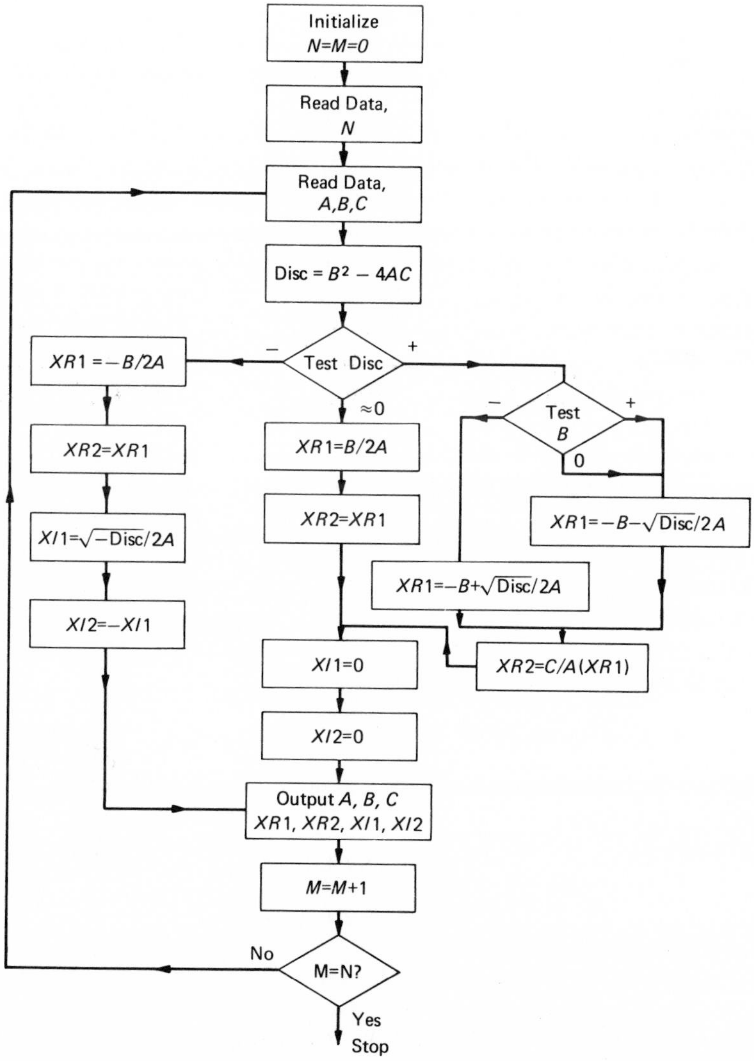

Figure 4.7–1. Algorithm logic diagram for obtaining the roots of the quadratic $Ax^2 + Bx + C = 0$.

where $f_x = \partial f/\partial x$, $f_t = \partial f/\partial t$, and all functions are evaluated at x_m and t_m. Hence (4.7–3) becomes

$$x_{m+1} = x_m + h[f + \frac{h}{2}(f_t + ff_x) + \cdots]$$

The Euler method truncates the Taylor series, so that

$$x_{m+1} = x_m + hf$$

or

$$x(t+h) = x(t) + hf(x, t) \qquad \textbf{(4.7–4)}$$

Interpreted geometrically, (4.7–4) requires us to find the slope at the point (x_m, t_m), multiply by the time interval h, and add x_m to get x_{m+1}. The method therefore assumes that the slope of the curve remains essentially constant over the interval h. Euler's method is inaccurate and the solutions may be unstable. A more accurate method might consist of taking the average of the slopes at (x_m, t_m) and $(x_{m+1}, t_m + h)$. This technique agrees with the Taylor series expansion out to three terms and is one Runge-Kutta method.

The averaging concept may be extended so that we get the equivalent of a Taylor series out to more terms, and this becomes the basis of the more accurate Runge-Kutta formulas [9, 10]. Perhaps the most used Runge-Kutta formula is the one-third rule, which is as follows (and see Figure 4.7–2):

$$x(t+h) = x(t) + \Delta x \qquad \textbf{(4.7–5a)}$$

with

$$\Delta x = \tfrac{1}{6}(a_1 + 2a_2 + 2a_3 + a_4) \qquad \textbf{(4.7–5b)}$$

where

$$a_1 = f(x, t)h$$

$$a_2 = f(x + \tfrac{1}{2}h, t + \tfrac{1}{2}a_1)h$$

$$a_3 = f(x + \tfrac{1}{2}h, t + \tfrac{1}{2}a_2)h$$

$$a_4 = f(x + h, t + a_3)h$$

You start at the initial conditions (x_0, t_0), and compute Δx by (4.7–5b). Then $x_1 = x_0 + \Delta x$, Now using (x_1, t_1), a new Δx_1 is computed to give $x_2 = x_1 + \Delta x_1$. Thus the function $x(t)$ evolves step by step. Interestingly enough, if f is a function of t only, (4.7–5) reduces to Simpson's rule. The error is of the order of h^5, and hence the formula is quite accurate for small h. Decreasing h beyond a certain point does not improve accuracy, because more computer-roundoff errors occur.

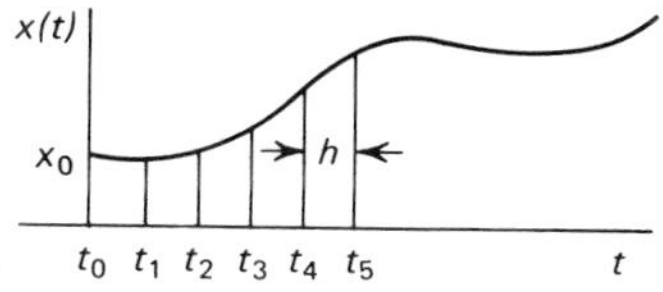

Figure 4.7–2. Solving a differential equation at discrete time intervals uniformly separated by h.

The method is readily extended to n simultaneous equations, because then we have n equations of the form

$$\dot{x}_k = f_k(x_1, x_2, \ldots, x_k, \ldots, x_n, t) \qquad k = 1, n \tag{4.7–6}$$

For each equation we compute a Δx_k by (4.7–5b), except using the right side of (4.7–6) in place of $f(x, t)$. All Δx_k, $k = 1, 2, \ldots, n$ are computed before moving on to the next step. This takes much more time, because not only do we have n equations for which we must find Δx_k, but the function f_k is much more complicated. The function f_k is not restricted to being linear but must be reasonably well behaved. [Among other things the $x_k(t)$ should be continuous and have finite derivatives.] Discontinuities can be handled if their occurrence in time is known. You have already seen that differential equations of any order may be reduced to simultaneous equations of the first order by a change of variable. Hence it is almost always possible to get the system in the form of (4.7–6).

The objection to the Runge-Kutta method is that four function computations must be made for each x_k and for each time step h. Other methods attempt to reduce the number of computations and are based on approximating $x_k(t)$ by a polynomial. The Milne method uses a predictor and a corrector. Assume that four points have been computed, perhaps by the Runge-Kutta algorithm. Then one Milne predictor is based on a quadratic:

$$x_k^{n+1} = x_k^{n-3} + \frac{4h}{3}(2\dot{x}_k^n - \dot{x}_k^{n-1} + 2\dot{x}_k^{n-2}) + 1792T \tag{4.7–7}$$

where the superscript n refers to the nth time interval (that is, at the start, n represents t_3 in Figure 4.7–2, and the value of x_k at t_4 is being computed), and the remainder $T = h^5 x_k^{(5)}/5760$. The fifth derivative, $x_k^{(5)}$ is to be evaluated at a point between x_k^{n+1} and x_k^n and, not being known, the last term is omitted. The various values of $\dot{x}_k$ are found from (4.7–6).

The value of x_k^{n+1} ascertained from (4.7–7) may be corrected by a cubic polynomial approximation, as follows:

$$x_k^{n+1} = \frac{1}{8}(x_k^n + 7x_k^{n-1}) + \frac{h}{192}(65\dot{x}_k^{n+1} + 243\dot{x}_k^n + 51\dot{x}_k^{n-1} + \dot{x}_k^{n-2}) - 75T \tag{4.7–8}$$

Thus once a tentative figure of x_k^{n+1} is obtained in (4.7–7), a more accurate value can be found from (4.7–8) (again omitting the last term). This can be repeated until the change in x_k^{n+1} is less than some preassigned amount, but if iterations of this kind are necessary, the advantage of the polynomial approximation is lost. The remainders in (4.7–7) and (4.7–8) may be used for an accuracy test. Assume that the right sides of these equations without the remainders give the same result and subtract (4.7–8) from (4.7–7), giving $\delta = 1717T$, where δ is the difference between the predictor and corrector values. Now divide this by the remainder in (4.7–8), giving a remainder R for truncation error in (4.7–8) of about $R \approx -\delta/23$. Assume that we have eight-digit accuracy on the digital computer (a common number) and allow two digits for roundoff error. Then to have no more than one unit of truncation error in the sixth significant figure in (4.7–8) we make $\delta < 23 \times 10^{-6}$. The predictor and corrector truncation errors are of the order of h^5; hence if we halve the step size h, the truncation error decreases by $\frac{1}{32}$, while if we double the step size, the truncation error increases by 32. This sets up a test for halving or doubling the step size. If the step size is to be halved, it is necessary to find previous intermediate values by an interpolation polynomial. Kunz [10] gives one possible set of relations as follows:

$$\dot{x}_k^{n-3/2} = \tfrac{1}{16}[9(\dot{x}_k^{n-2} + \dot{x}_k^{n-1}) - (\dot{x}_k^{n-3} + \dot{x}_k^n)] + R_1 \tag{4.7–9a}$$

$$\dot{x}_k^{n-1/2} = \tfrac{1}{16}[15\dot{x}_k^{n-1} + 5(\dot{x}_k^{n-2} - \dot{x}_k^n) + \dot{x}_k^{n-3}] + R_2 \tag{4.7–9b}$$

The test previously suggested assumes that $x^{(5)}$ in both (4.7–7) and (4.7–8) to be the same. Even if it is, the test does not, of course, take care of the accumulated error in $x(t)$, although some techniques exist to estimate this. An alternative method is to work the problem with no remainder testing but with a given h; repeat this with $h/2$, and compare results. (This is one way of checking the Runge-Kutta step size.) Such a comparison does not guarantee answers, but it does supply some confidence. Another check is to integrate the equations out to some point and then integrate backward in time and observe the error in the solution at the initial time. In any case, no way exists to be absolutely sure of the results, but these methods improve the probability of correctness.

It is clear that we have only skimmed over the surface of the very large subject of numerical analysis, which is the basis for digital computer application. If the designer plans to use such a computer, he must either learn something about the subject himself or employ the aid of an expert. It is hoped that we have given enough here to arouse your interest and to warn that results found by digital computer are not necessarily correct just because eight significant figures may be printed out. You are referred to the many excellent texts on this subject [9, 10, 11].

4.8 Conclusions

We have briefly explored flow diagrams and computer simulation. Simulation furnishes an important tool to the designer. For one thing, computer simulation is not restricted to linear systems. In a flow diagram it is quite easy to show a nonlinear operator. Figure 4.8–1a depicts a system with a nonlinear operator representing a saturation characteristic. The characteristic is given in more detail in Figure 4.8–1b, where the

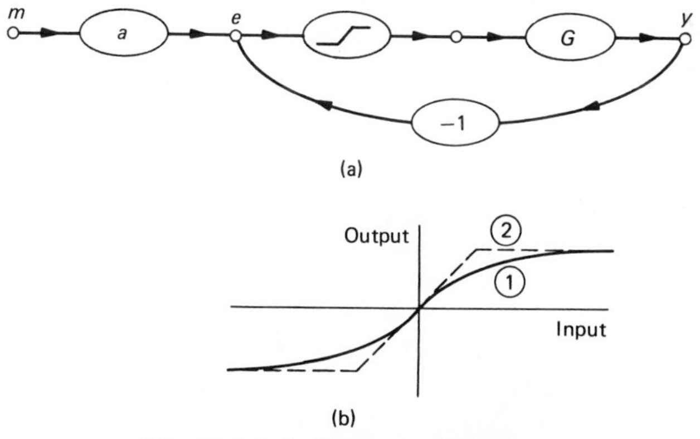

Figure 4.8–1. Nonlinear simulation.

horizontal axis gives the magnitude of the input and the vertical axis the corresponding magnitude of the output. The actual saturation curve (1) usually may be approximated with sufficient accuracy by a piecewise linear curve such as (2). The simulation on an analog computer may be made with a network of diodes or in some other way. On the digital computer, nonlinear equations are little more difficult than linear equations, as previously discussed.

The ease of obtaining computer solutions frequently leads the neophite designer to think of carrying everything to a computer. Some results may be obtained by cut and try techniques using the computer, but much expensive computer time may be used to no purpose unless the engineer has explored the problem in some depth before going to the machine. Sometimes, also, computer programs written in the past may stultify creative ideas for a fresh approach.

We have also pointed out the intimate connection between the flow diagram and the equations describing the system and how flow diagrams may be used to obtain alternative equations in state-variable form, or, on the other hand, how different system descriptions lead to alternative computer simulations. There are thus many possible ways to describe a system mathematically or simulating it, and some methods may be preferable to others in any given situation. We explore these ideas further in succeeding chapters.

PROBLEMS

4.1. In Figure P4.1 find E_0/E_i ($i_2 = 0$) using the flow diagram. Find the impedance $Z = E_0/-I_2$, ($e_i = 0$). Find the impedance $Z_1 = E_i/I_i$ ($i_2 = 0$). (*Hint:* Find $1/Z_1$.)

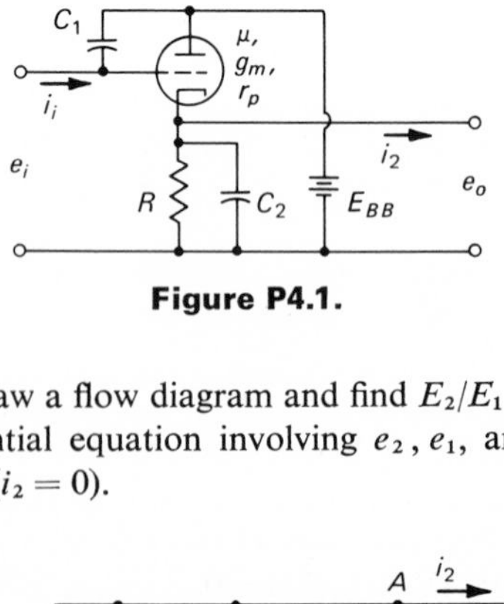

Figure P4.1.

4.2. In Figure P4.2 draw a flow diagram and find E_2/E_1 ($i_2 = 0$), $Z = E_2/-I_2$. Write the differential equation involving e_2, e_1, and their derivatives in state-space form ($i_2 = 0$).

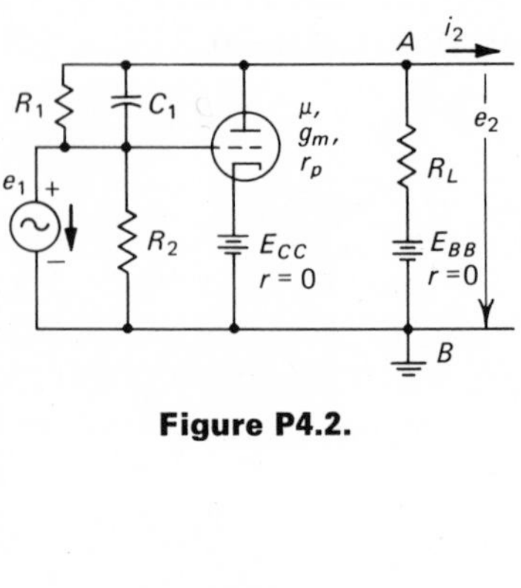

Figure P4.2.

4.3. Figure P4.3a represents one small signal equivalent transistor diagram. Draw a signal flow diagram for Figure P4.3b. (*Note:* This problem illustrates how complex the flow diagram may become.)

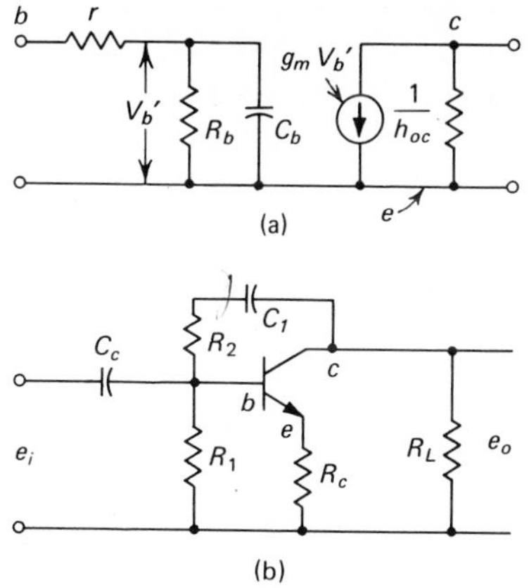

Figure P4.3.

4.4. Given a system equation

$$\frac{d^3c}{dt^3} + 10\frac{d^2c}{dt^2} + 80\frac{dc}{dt} + 128c = 5\frac{dr}{dt} + 6r$$

Find the first Kalman form and draw a flow diagram. Write the state-space equations. Find the initial conditions of the state variables in terms of c, r, and their derivatives.

4.5. Repeat Problem 4.4 for the second Kalman form.

4.6. Given the system equation

$$\frac{d^3y}{dt^3} + 9\frac{d^2y}{dt^2} + 26\frac{dy}{dt} + 24y = 15r$$

put the equation in partial fraction form, and draw a flow diagram representing this form. From this diagram, write the state-space equations and find the diagonalized matrix Λ.

4.7. In Figure P4.7 find the transfer function $C(s)/R(s)$ with $D(s) = 0$. Find the differential equation involving $c(t)$ and $r(t)$ and their derivatives. Find the transfer function $C(s)/D(s)$, $R(s) = 0$.

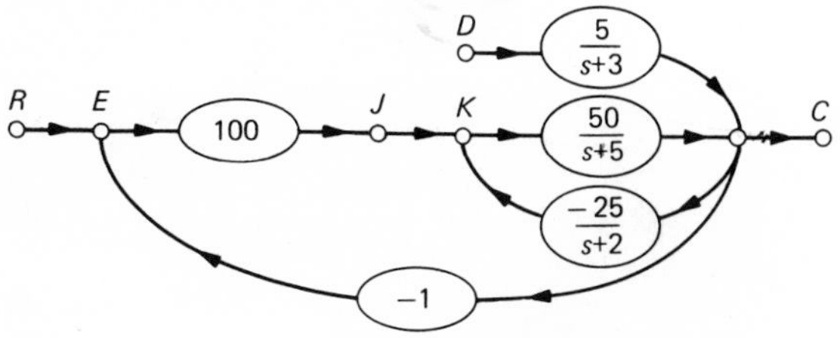

Figure P4.7.

4.8. In Figure P4.8, $6(dc/dt) + 10c = 20e$, $20(df/dt) + 5f = 10c$, $r = 10m$. Find the transfer function $C(s)/M(s)$, and the differential equation involving $c(t)$, $m(t)$, and their derivatives. Find the transfer function $E(s)/M(s)$.

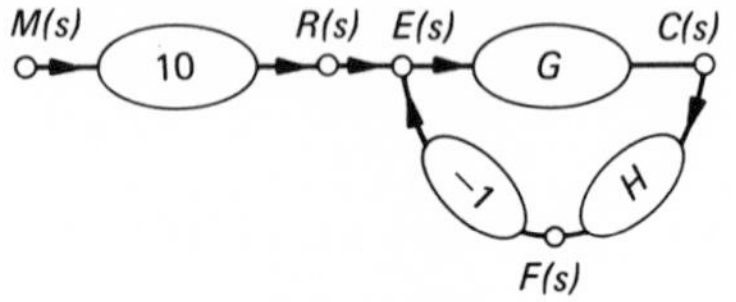

Figure P4.8.

4.9. A system is represented in state-space form as

$$\dot{\mathbf{x}} = \mathbf{A}\mathbf{x} + \mathbf{B}\mathbf{r}$$

$$\mathbf{y} = \mathbf{C}\mathbf{x} + \mathbf{D}\mathbf{r}$$

where

$$\mathbf{A} = \begin{bmatrix} 3 & 0 & 0 \\ 1 & 5 & 2 \\ 0 & 0 & 1 \end{bmatrix} \qquad \mathbf{B} = \begin{bmatrix} 1 & 0 \\ 2 & 0 \\ 0 & 5 \end{bmatrix}$$

$$\mathbf{C} = \begin{bmatrix} 2 & 0 & 1 \\ 6 & 2 & 0 \end{bmatrix} \qquad \mathbf{D} = \mathbf{0}$$

and

$$\mathbf{x} = \begin{bmatrix} x_1 \\ x_2 \\ x_3 \end{bmatrix} \qquad \mathbf{r} = \begin{bmatrix} r_1 \\ r_2 \end{bmatrix} \qquad \mathbf{y} = \begin{bmatrix} y_1 \\ y_2 \end{bmatrix}$$

(a) Draw a flow diagram representing this system.
(b) Using this flow diagram, find the transfer functions Y_1/R_1, Y_1/R_2, Y_2/R_1, and Y_2/R_2 and write the transfer function matrix $\mathbf{H}$, where $\mathbf{y} = \mathbf{H}\mathbf{r}$.

4.10. Given the differential equation

$$\frac{d^2y}{dt^2} + 3\frac{dy}{dt} + 5y = 0 \qquad y(0) = 1 \quad \dot{y}(0) = 0$$

put this in state-space form and obtain digital computer solutions using (a) the Euler method, and (b) the Runge-Kutta method.
Use different values of h and compare results with the correct analytic solution out to $t = 5$.

4.11. After completing Problem 4.10, do a computer solution for the equation

$$\frac{d^2y}{dt^2} + 3\frac{dy}{dt} + 5y^2 = 0$$

Let y and $\dot{y}$ take on various initial values.

REFERENCES AND FURTHER READING

[1] J. G. Truxal, *Automatic Feedback Control System Synthesis*, McGraw-Hill, New York, 1955, pp. 88–160.

[2] S. J. Mason, Feedback Theory: Some Properties of Signal Flow Graphs, *Proc. IRE*, **41** (1953), 1144–1156.

[3] S. J. Mason, Feedback Theory: Further Properties of Signal Flow Graphs, *Proc. IRE*, **44** (1956), 920–926.

[4] W. A. Lynch and J. G. Truxal, The Significance of Sensitivity in Feedback System Studies, *Res. Rept. PIBMRI 860–66*, June 1, 1961. Microwave Research Institute of Brooklyn, Brooklyn, New York; see also W. A. Lynch and J. G. Truxal, *Signals and Systems in Electrical Engineering*, McGraw-Hill, New York, 1962.

[5] P. M. De Russo, R. J. Roy, and C. M. Close, *State Variables for Engineers*, Wiley, New York, 1965, pp. 146–153.

[6] R. E. Kalman, Mathematical Description of Linear Dynamical Systems, *J. Soc. Ind. Appl. Math. Control*, **A1** (2) (1963), 152–192.

[7] J. T. Tou, *Modern Control Theory*, McGraw-Hill, New York, 1964, pp. 62–90.

[8] A. W. Langill, Jr., *Automatic Control Systems Engineering*, Vol. I, Prentice-Hall, Englewood Cliffs, N.J., 1965, pp. 111–135.

[9] D. D. McCracken and W. S. Dorn, *Numerical Methods and Fortran Programming*, Wiley, New York, 1964, pp. 311, 330.

[10] K. S. Kunz, *Numerical Analysis*, McGraw-Hill, New York, 1956, pp. 167–189 and 192–213.

[11] R. W. Hamming, *Numerical Methods for Scientists and Engineers*, McGraw-Hill, New York, 1962.

[12] R. S. Ledley, *Fortran IV Programming*, McGraw-Hill, New York, 1966.

[13] R. S. Ledley, *Digital Computer and Control Engineering*, McGraw-Hill, New York, 1960.

[14] N. R. Scott, *Analog and Digital Computer Technology*, McGraw-Hill, New York, 1960.

[15] G. A. Korn and T. M. Korn, *Electronic Analog Computers*, McGraw-Hill, New York, 2nd ed., 1956.

[16] G. A. Korn and T. M. Korn, *Electronic and Hybrid Computers*, McGraw-Hill, New York, 1964.

5 System Representation in State Space

5.1 Introduction

As discussed in Chapters 1 and 3, the more recent research in control systems involves direct solutions of the differential equations, usually in the time domain. To accomplish this it is necessary to adopt some systematic techniques, as otherwise the designer becomes overwhelmed with the immensity of the task. Matrix methods for solving linear equations have been known for some time, and it was only natural that this technique should be applied to general multi-input-output systems. Such systems cause a breakdown in the conventional methods that worked reasonably well with the single input-output system. The use of matrices is based upon the concept of a vector in a multidimensional space, the "length" and "angle" of the vector representing the solution. It is easy to visualize a vector in a two- or three-dimensional space, but when the dimensions exceed three, visualization is possibly only by analogy.

In Figure 5.1–1 we have a vector P in the familiar two-dimensional Euclidian space where the coordinate axis depict the dependent variables x and y. Each of these two variables represents a quantity of interest, such as an angle, a position, or a voltage. The independent variable in our case is usually time t. The vector at a particular time t_1 can be described by the projections on the coordinate axis or by its length l and angle θ. If the axis are orthogonal, $l = \sqrt{x_1^2 + y_1^2}$ and $\tan\theta = y_1/x_1$. As time goes on, the point P will describe a curve or trajectory in two-dimensional space, as shown by Figure 5.1–2. This space is called state-space and it is the

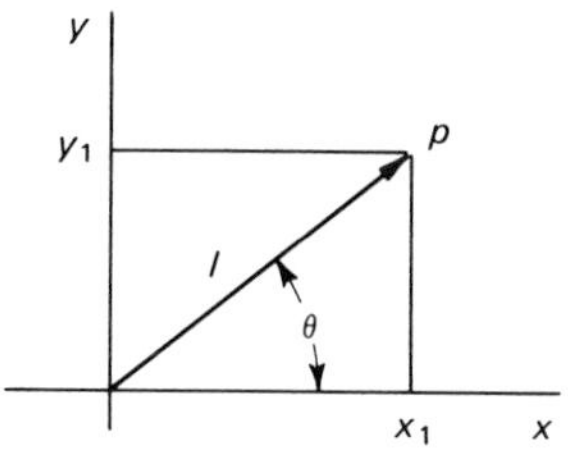

Figure 5.1–1. Vector.

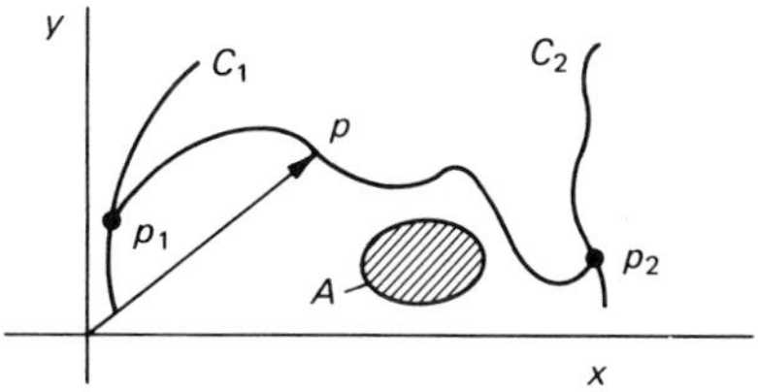

Figure 5.1–2. Trajectory traced by a vector that is a function of time.

trajectory in this space that is of concern, as the problem of control is to obtain a satisfactory trajectory. The word "satisfactory" in the design of a control system implies various subsets of the problem involving value judgments. Some of these are listed as follows:

1. Given the end points P_1 and P_2 of a trajectory, proceed from P_1 to P_2:
   a. In any way possible.
   b. In the least total time.
   c. With the least expenditure of energy.
   d. With the least possible maximum value of some variable.
2. Given some desired trajectory from P_1 to P_2, proceed from P_1 to P_2:
   a. Such that the error (difference between the desired trajectory and the actual trajectory) does not exceed a given value.
   b. Such that the integral with respect to time of the square of the error is a minimum.
   c. Such that the actual trajectory comes within a given distance to the given trajectory in the least possible time.
3. Repeat any of the previous requirements, but given input variables are not allowed to exceed specified values (input constraints).
4. Repeat any of the previous requirements, but the trajectory is not allowed in a specified region of state space (such as area A in Figure 3.1–2; state-space constraints).

The end points of the trajectory may not be defined as P_1 and P_2; that is, we may be required to go from a surface C_1 to a surface C_2 in Figure 5.1–2 under any of the previous restrictions. This is a problem of variable end points. Also we may be given the total time and P_1, to find P_2 with given constraints and required specifications on energy, maximum size of variables, error, and so on.

You note in the previous specifications that in general we make an effort to maximize or minimize some quantity subject to certain constraints. Thus we have somewhat more precise specifications than used in the conventional design methods as illustrated in Chapter 3 for the second-order system. More to the point, the object is to provide specifications that lead naturally to a mathematical synthesis rather than analysis. In the conventional method, if the analysis results in an unsatisfactory system, compensation is introduced, and a new analysis made, or we have a cut and try technique. Some synthesis methods utilizing the frequency domain have been developed, as shall be shown subsequently, but the optimal control problem implied by the previous specifications proposes to get the "best" system by maximizing some specific quantity determined by the requirements.† This does not relieve the designer of making some value judgments, but it does clarify what judgments are made and at what point they are made. The price paid for this sort of a "best" system is mathematical complexity and difficulty in achieving the results economically (or at all). In general, three methods exist for solving maximizing problems: (1) variational calculus, (2) Pontryagin's principle, and (3) dynamic programming. All these involve rather sophisticated mathematics, and solutions usually can be obtained in a reasonable time only with the aid of a computer. The solution, if obtainable, then may require elaborate equipment to effectuate the required operations.

These ideas, sketched rapidly here, hopefully will become clearer as you proceed. Before we go on to the maximizing problem, we need to understand the basic definitions, operations, and techniques of time-domain analysis. These are taken up in this chapter.

5.2 Vector Spaces

In time-domain analysis the differential equations, which may be of any order, are rewritten as differential equations of the first order. Thus one nth-order equation gives n first-order equations, and so on. We have shown in Chapters 3 and 4 some methods for accomplishing this and will give others in Section 5.7. Briefly, for example, if we take the equation

$$\frac{d^2v}{dt^2} + u\frac{dv}{dt} + wv = 0 \tag{5.2–1}$$

† Some doubt can exist as to the adequacy of a single performance index.

and let

$$x_1 = v \qquad x_2 = \dot{v} \qquad \text{where } \dot{v} = \frac{dv}{dt} \tag{5.2–2a}$$

we get

$$\dot{x}_1 = x_2$$

$$\dot{x}_2 = -wx_1 - ux_2 \tag{5.2–2b}$$

where $\dot{x} = dx/dt$. However, if we let $x_1 = -\dot{v}$, $x_2 = v$, then

$$\dot{x}_1 = wx_2 - ux_1 \tag{5.2–3a}$$

$$\dot{x}_2 = -x_1 \tag{52.–3b}$$

Equations (5.2–2) or (5.2–3) are called state equations and x_1 and x_2 state variables. As previously discussed, for a two-variable case if one variable is the derivative of the other, as in (5.2–2), the variable plane $x_2 x_1$ is termed a "phase" plane (space). We use the more general term "state space" here.

Further, as you have already seen in Chapter 4, (5.2–2) can be put into matrix notation as

$$\begin{bmatrix} \dot{x}_1 \\ \dot{x}_2 \end{bmatrix} = \begin{bmatrix} a_{11} & a_{12} \\ a_{21} & a_{22} \end{bmatrix} \begin{bmatrix} x_1 \\ x_2 \end{bmatrix}$$

or

$$\dot{\mathbf{x}} = \mathbf{A}\mathbf{x} \tag{5.2–4a}$$

where

$$\mathbf{A} = \begin{bmatrix} 0 & 1 \\ -w & -u \end{bmatrix} \tag{5.2–4b}$$

The $n \times 1$ column matrices designated $\dot{\mathbf{x}}$ and $\mathbf{x}$ are considered to represent the components of vectors on some abstract coordinates in a linear vector space, and are frequently called "column" vectors or, more simply, vectors.

The purpose of introducing state equations is that there is a powerful and growing mathematical theory connected with vector spaces. You can see that if the equations are linear, we may use operators such as matrices in connection with the solutions. Such logical arrangements as the matrix bring order to problems that might otherwise become hopelessly complicated. More important, the theory permits generalizations that may answer many problems at one time. The detailed solution by hand will be just as time consuming as before, but today we have powerful analog, digital, or hybrid computers to do the pick and shovel work. Even if the equations are nonlinear, the concept of a vector space becomes crucial in sophisticated control problems. Let us see what we mean by state and vector space, confining most of the discussion to linear equations. Space defines a collection of objects, and vector space means a collection of vectors. Linear, of course, implies that we deal with linear relations. You are familiar with the use of vectors in solving problems in mechanics, and in the two-dimensional physical space used in mechanics you know that a point P in this space may be represented by a vector. For example, suppose that we set up a coordinate system in the plane of the paper with orthogonal axis OA and OB, as in Figure 5.2–1, with O as origin. Then the vector X from O to P describes the point P in this space. To put X into algebraic symbols, one method is to define X as $\{x_1, x_2\}$, where the braces enclose an ordered pair of numbers (scalars), which are the coordinates of the point P. In terms of vector space, x_1 and x_2 are components of X on the axis OA and OB, respectively. To get a unit of measure for x_1 and x_2, we set up vectors e_1 and e_2 of unit length along the axis. Vectors e_1 and e_2 are called basis vectors, and in this case are orthonormal; that is, they are both orthogonal and of unit length.

The orthonormal set e_1, e_2 are also called the initial basis. In a set of simultaneous equations that will be described in vector notation, an initial set of basis vectors is specified or assumed. This does not mean that the initial basis vectors are unique; they are quite arbitrary in that we may (1) select the origin anywhere we please, (2) we may put e_1 and e_2 in any orientation in the plane (for example, in Figure 5.2–1 interchange e_1 and

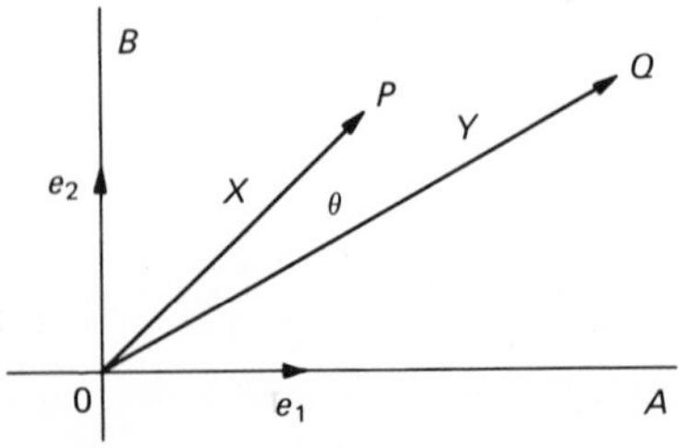

Figure 5.2–1. Vectors in two-dimensional space.

e_2), and (3) we may make the length unit any desired size. Thus the selection of an initial basis vector set is entirely at our discretion, and if we do not deal with two- or three-dimensional physical space, the basis vectors are in fact abstract. They have, however, properties of length and direction in a sense that we shall delineate further. The space shown in Figure 5.2–1 is a Euclidean space; that is, the initial basis vectors are orthogonal and a vector length is measured by taking the square root of the sum of the squares of its components. The dimension of the space is $n = 2$.

It is desired to set up a general system that extends the notion of a vector space to more than three dimensions but will reduce to the familiar physical spaces when $n \leq 3$. The generalized space will contain lines, planes, surfaces, angles, and in particular vectors, but of course these quantities must be defined in an abstract sense. We require the vectors to have direction and magnitude, but again these terms are redefined. Vector spaces can describe a wide range of functions, but we shall give most of our attention to spaces used with control problems.

We start by setting up axioms for adding and multiplying in an abstract space $\mathscr{A}$ and state that any two elements X and Y of the set of elements in $\mathscr{A}$ may be added to result in an element Z also in $\mathscr{A}$. That is, $X + Y = Z$ also belongs to the set of elements in $\mathscr{A}$. Furthermore, any element X of the set multiplied by a scalar (real or complex number) α produces an element in $\mathscr{A}$, or $\alpha X = W$, where W also belongs to the set. The operations of addition and scalar multiplication must then obey the following axiomatic rules:

Addition:

$$\text{Commutative, or } X + Y = Y + X \tag{5.2–5a}$$

$$\text{Distributive, or } (X + Y) + Z = X + (Y + Z) \tag{5.2–5b}$$

Multiplication by a scalar:

$$\text{Commutative, or } (\alpha\beta)X = (\beta\alpha)X \tag{5.2–5c}$$

$$\text{Associative, or } \alpha(\beta X) = (\alpha\beta)X \tag{5.2–5d}$$

$$\text{Distributive, or } \alpha(X + Y) = \alpha X + \alpha Y \tag{5.2–5e}$$

Also we set up a special element, the null element $\hat{0}$ and a special scalar 1, such that

$$\hat{0} + X = X \tag{5.2–5f}$$

$$X + (-X) = \hat{0} \tag{5.2–5g}$$

$$(1)X = X \tag{5.2–5h}$$

Any set of elements that follows axioms (5.2–5) is said to establish a vector space $\mathscr{A}$.

Many different sets of objects may satisfy the axioms of (5.2–5), or exist in a vector space. As examples, consider (1) the set of all real numbers, (2) the set of all polynomials of the form $a_n X^n + a_{n-1} X^{n-1} + \cdots + a_0$, (3) the set of directed line segments existing in a space having three dimensions (length, breadth, height), or (4) solutions of differential equations of the form $y^{(n)} + a_1 y^{(n-1)} + \cdots + a_{n-1} y^1 + a_n y = 0$. The name "vector" furnishes a geometric interpretation that is familiar to us in example 3, and assists in visualization.

If we narrow the space to a Euclidean space E and describe X by a set of numbers in an ordered array $\{x_1 x_2 x_3 \cdots x_n\}$, where the x_i may be considered the components of X on some coordinate system and are scalars, then

$$X + Y = \{x_1 + y_1, x_2 + y_2, \ldots, x_n + y_n\}$$

and

$$\alpha X = \{\alpha x_1, \alpha x_2, \ldots, \alpha x_n\}$$

In Hilbert space n approaches infinity, but we shall deal with a finite n here. Further, the x_i and y_i may be complex (vectors over a complex field) but for the sake of simplicity we usually take them as real (vectors over a real field). It is clear that this definition of X satisfies the general axioms and furthermore, if $n \leq 3$, these operations become just those performed on directed line segments in mechanics problems.

5.3 Linear Independence and Basis Vectors

A set of vectors X_i in a vector space $\mathscr{A}^n$ is said to be linearly dependent if

$$\alpha_1 X_1 + \alpha_2 X_2 + \cdots + \alpha_n X_n = \hat{0} \qquad \textbf{(5.3–1)}$$

where not all scalars $\alpha_i = 0$ and $\hat{0}$ is the null vector. If (5.3–1) is true only for all $\alpha_i = 0$, then $X_1, X_2, \ldots, X_n$ are linearly independent. If n vectors X_i in $\mathscr{A}^n$ are linearly independent, then $n + 1$ vectors X_i in $\mathscr{A}^n$ are dependent. If a set of vectors is linearly dependent, at least one may be expressed as a linear combination of the others.

Example 5.3–1

If $\alpha X + \beta Y = \hat{0}$ in Figure 5.2–1, then $X = -(\beta/\alpha) Y = \gamma Y$; whence $\theta = 0$, and X and Y lie along the same line.

A test for linear dependence of n vectors in $\mathscr{A}^n$ may be made as follows:

1. For each vector X_i form a column of ordered components (an $n \times 1$ matrix) of its components (all relative to an initial basis).
2. Form an $n \times n$ matrix $\mathbf{A}$ of all n columns.
3. If $\det \mathbf{A} \neq 0$, then the n vectors X_i are linearly independent.

Proof: A determinant is zero if and only if a linear combination of its columns gives a column of zeros (null vector).

Example 5.3–2

From step 1 suppose the resulting matrices are

$$\text{for } X_1, \begin{bmatrix} 1 \\ 2 \\ 3 \end{bmatrix} \qquad \text{for } X_2, \begin{bmatrix} 1 \\ 1 \\ 1 \end{bmatrix} \qquad \text{for } X_3, \begin{bmatrix} 2 \\ 3 \\ 1 \end{bmatrix}$$

all on the same orthonormal basis. Then

$$\mathbf{A} = \begin{bmatrix} 1 & 1 & 2 \\ 2 & 1 & 3 \\ 3 & 1 & 1 \end{bmatrix}$$

$\det \mathbf{A} = 3$, and hence X_1, X_2, and X_3 are linearly independent.

A set of vectors $X_1, X_2, \ldots, X_k$ determines or spans a space $\mathscr{A}^k$ if every vector Y in $\mathscr{A}^k$ can be represented as a linear combination of $X_1, X_2, \ldots, X_k$, that is, if

$$Y = \alpha_1 X_1 + \alpha_2 X_2 + \cdots + \alpha_k X_k \qquad \textbf{(5.3–2)}$$

where the α_i are scalars.

The vectors X_i, $i = 1, k$ constitute a set of basis vectors or form a basis if they meet requirement (5.3–2) and are also linearly independent. The space is said to have dimension k. It can be shown that any set of $k + 1$ vectors in a k-dimensional space $\mathscr{A}^k$ is linearly dependent, or that the maximum number of linearly independent vectors in $\mathscr{A}^k$ is k. If vectors in $\mathscr{A}^k$ are also in $\mathscr{A}^n$, $\mathscr{A}^k$ is said to be a subspace of $\mathscr{A}^n$ if $k \leq n$. (Some authors distinguish a subspace and a manifold [1].)

Example 5.3–3

If $n = 3$, a plane in three-dimensional Euclidean space is a subspace if it goes through the origin (includes the null vector). So also is a line through the origin. A plane that does not include the origin is known as a "hyper-plane."

Example 5.3–4

If the space includes all real polynomials of degree $\leq n$, then X^0, X^1, $X^2, \ldots, X^n$ form a basis.

In such a space we desire to have a measure of "length," or a metric. To define this quantity, first examine the concept of an "inner product." An inner product for a real vector space satisfies the axioms

$$(X, Y) = (Y, X) \tag{5.3–3a}$$

$$(X, Y+Z) = (X, Y) + (Y, Z) \tag{5.3–3b}$$

$$(\alpha X, Y) = \alpha(X, Y) \qquad (\alpha \text{ a scalar}) \tag{5.3–3c}$$

$$(X, X) \geq 0 \tag{5.3–3d}$$

A real vector space for which a real vector product is defined is termed a Euclidean space. (A complex vector space having a complex inner product is called a unitary space.) There are other possible vector products, such as integrals, but we shall be primarily interested in Euclidean spaces [2].

Next we define the length or norm of a vector X as $\|X\|$, where

$$\|X\| = [f(X, X)]^{1/2} \tag{5.3–4}$$

where f denotes a function. A norm must satisfy the following axioms:

$$\|X\| > 0 \quad X \neq \hat{0} \qquad \|X\| = 0 \quad X = \hat{0} \tag{5.3–5a}$$

$$\|\alpha X\| = |\alpha| \ \|X\|, \tag{5.3–5b}$$

where α is a scalar.

$$\|X + Y\| \leq \|X\| + \|Y\| \tag{5.3–5c}$$

Many possible norms may exist. For example, if we have an ordered array $\{a_1, a_2, \ldots, a_n\}$, then $X = \max a_i$, $i = 1, n$ would be an acceptable norm. At this time, however, we shall be interested in the Euclidean space norm.

Look at two vectors X and Y in a real space $\mathscr{A}^n$, where

$$X = \alpha_1 W_1 + \alpha_2 W_2 + \cdots + \alpha_n W_n$$

$$Y = \beta_1 Z_1 + \beta_2 Z_2 + \cdots + \beta_n Z_n$$

where the W_i and Z_i are linearly independent and thus form basis vectors in the space. Then, from (5.3–3b),

$$(X, Y) = \sum_{i=1}^{n} \sum_{j=1}^{n} \alpha_i \beta_j (W_i, Z_j) \qquad \textbf{(5.3–6)}$$

Furthermore, if W_i and Z_j are orthonormal, then by definition

$$(W_i, Z_j) = \delta_{ij} \qquad \textbf{(5.3–7)}$$

where

$$\begin{aligned} \delta_{ij} &= 0 \qquad i \neq j \\ &= 1 \qquad i = j \end{aligned}$$

and (5.3–6) becomes

$$(X, Y) = \sum_{i=1}^{n} \alpha_i \beta_i \qquad \textbf{(5.3–8)}$$

where α_i and β_i are components on the orthonormal basis. If α_i and β_i are complex, the complex conjugate of α_i develops in (5.3–8).

We now define our norm in Euclidean space E^n as

$$\|X\| = (X, Y)^{1/2} \qquad \textbf{(5.3–9)}$$

The angle θ between X and Y is then defined by the relation

$$\cos\theta = \frac{(X, Y)}{\|X\| \ \|Y\|} \qquad \textbf{(5.3–10)}$$

and the vectors X, Y are said to be orthogonal if $\cos\theta = 0$, or if $(X, Y) = 0$. Equations (5.3–9) and (5.3–10) give X a magnitude and direction if Y is adopted as reference, and hence we have accomplished part of the task of defining the "vector" X. It is clear from Figure 5.1–1 that in two-dimensional plane geometry the norm becomes the familiar square root of the sum of the squares on the two components of X and the scalar product is the familiar dot product. There is no definition for a cross product in linear vector space, however, although it is possible to have opposing orientations.

Two important inequalities hold in vector space: (1) the Schwartz inequality and (2) the triangle inequality. The Schwartz inequality states that given any two real vectors X, Y in an n-dimensional space E^n,

$$(X, Y)^2 \leq \|X\|^2 \ \|Y\|^2 \qquad \textbf{(5.3–11)}$$

This may be proved in Euclidean space by looking at the obviously true equation

$$\sum_{i=1}^{n} (\alpha_i - \lambda\beta_i)^2 \geq 0 \tag{5.3–12}$$

where the α_i and β_i are components of X and Y on the same basis and λ is a real number. To find some λ for which the left side of (5.3–12) is a minimum, differentiate with respect to λ. Then

$$2\sum_{i=1}^{n} (\alpha_i - \lambda\beta_i)\beta_i = 0$$

or

$$\lambda = \frac{\sum_{i=1}^{n} \alpha_i \beta_i}{\sum_{i=1}^{n} \beta_2^i}$$

Substituting this λ in (5.3–12), with some algebraic manipulation you will find that

$$\sum_{i=1}^{n} \alpha_i^2 - \frac{(\sum_{i=1}^{n} \alpha_i \beta_i)^2}{\sum_{i=1}^{n} \beta_i^2} \geq 0$$

or

$$\sum_{i=1}^{n} \alpha_i^2 \sum_{i=1}^{n} \beta_i^2 \geq (\sum_{i=1}^{n} \alpha_i \beta_i)^2$$

from which (5.3–11) follows. Equality holds only in the case that $Y = \gamma X$, where γ is a scalar.

Example 5.3–5

Let $X = \{3, 4\}$, $Y = \{5, 3\}$, both on the same orthonormal basis. Then

$$\|X\|^2 \|Y\|^2 = (25)(34) = 850$$

$$(X, Y)^2 = (27)^2 = 729$$

$$\cos\theta_{X,Y} = \frac{729}{850}$$

If

$$Y = \{6, 8\}, \text{ then } \|X\|^2 \|Y\|^2 = 4(25)(25) = 2500$$

$$(X, Y)^2 = 2500$$

The triangle inequality states that

$$\|X+Y\| \leq \|X\| + \|Y\| \tag{5.3–13}$$

where equality holds if $Y = \gamma X$. Both the Schwartz and triangle inequalities can be shown to hold in general [3].

From the development of (5.3–8), vector space $\mathscr{A}^n$ will be a Euclidean space E^n only if the initial basis vectors X_i are orthonormal.

If the vector space $\mathscr{A}^n$ is defined on some given basis vectors X_1, X_2, ..., X^n, where the X_i are linearly independent, then an orthonormal basis may be constructed by the Schmidt process.

Let

$$e_1 = \frac{X_1}{\|X_1\|}$$

Then e_1 is a vector in the direction of X_1 but of unit length. To obtain a vector Y_2 orthogonal to e_1, apply (5.3–10), or make $(Y_2, e_1) = 0$. If $Y_2 = X_2 - (X_2, e_1)e_1$, then Y_2 fulfills these requirements, since, using the axioms,

$$\begin{aligned}(Y_2, e_1) &= (X_2, e_1) - [(X_2, e_1)e_1, e_1] \\ &= (X_2, e_1) - (X_2, e_1)(e_1, e_1) \\ &= 0\end{aligned}$$

To obtain a vector unit length,

$$e_2 = \frac{Y_2}{\|Y_2\|}$$

This process is continued until all e_i up to and including e_n are found.

The previous operations are graphically depicted in Figure 5.3–1 for two-dimensional space. In Figure 5.3–1 first we obtain a unit vector e_1 in

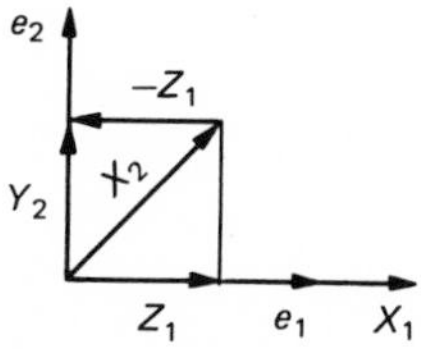

Figure 5.3–1. Obtaining an orthonormal set of vectors from a linearly independent set.

the direction of X_1. Then we subtract from X_2 a vector Z_1, which is formed by the orthogonal projection of X_2 on X_1 to get Y_2. Finally, Y_2 is normalized to get e_2. Clearly the orthonormal basis is not unique, because it depends on the order in which the basis set X_i is taken. To accomplish the Schmidt process algebraically, the lengths and directions of the X_i would have to be known, or an initial basis must be taken.

Another view of the example in two-dimensional Euclidean space is to think of any two linearly independent vectors X_1 and X_2 as generating (defining) a two-dimensional vector space E^2, thus $X_2 \neq X_1$. All vectors in this space (in the plane) are linear combinations of the basis vectors. The basis vectors are not unique and may be orthonormal or not; if they are not orthonormal, basis vectors may be found if we establish a unit of length and a reference direction. Alternatively, we may start with initial orthonormal basis vectors e_1 and e_2 and obtain expressions for any vector in the space in terms of these and then establish new basis vectors, if desired. A three-dimensional vector does not necessarily lie in this space; that is, two vectors do not span a three-dimensional space. A subspace of E^2 is a subset of the vectors spanning E^2 and one example here would be the space established by αe_1, with α taking all values from 0 to ∞.

5.4 Linear Transformations and Change of Basis

A transformation A on a vector X results in a vector Y or points in the space E^n are mapped into other points in the same space. Following the definition in Chapter 1, the transformation is linear if $A(\alpha X) = \alpha AX$ and $A(X_1 + X_2) = AX_1 + AX_2$. We may have linear transformations in succession, such as $A(BX) = ABX = CX$, where $C = AB$, in that order. Suppose we have a space E^n with initial basis vectors $e_1, e_2, \ldots, e_n$, and let

$$\begin{aligned} Ae_1 &= a_{11}e_1 + a_{21}e_2 + \cdots + a_{n1}e_n \\ Ae_2 &= a_{12}e_1 + e_{22}e_2 + \cdots + a_{n2}e_n \\ &\vdots \\ Ae_n &= a_{1n}e_1 + a_{2n}e_2 + \cdots + a_{nn}e_n \end{aligned} \tag{5.4–1}$$

or the linear transformation on each basis vector becomes a linear combination of the basis vectors. Call the matrix of the coefficients on the right side of (5.4–1) $\mathbf{A}^T$.

If the vector

$$X = x_1e_1 + x_2e_2 + \cdots + x_ne_n$$

then

$$Y = \mathbf{A}X = x_1\mathbf{A}e_1 + x_2\mathbf{A}e_2 + \cdots + x_n\mathbf{A}e_n$$

where the x_i are the components of X on the basis vectors. Hence

$$Y = \sum_{k=1}^{n} y_k e_k = \sum_{i=1}^{n} x_i \mathbf{A} e_i = \sum_{i=1}^{n} \sum_{k=1}^{n} a_{ki} x_i e_k$$

Interchanging summations,

$$y_k = \sum_{i=1}^{n} a_{ki} x_i \tag{5.4–2}$$

If k takes on values from 1 to n, then this can be expressed in matrix form as

$$\begin{bmatrix} y_1 \\ y_2 \\ \vdots \\ y_n \end{bmatrix} = \begin{bmatrix} a_{11} & a_{12} & \cdots & a_{1n} \\ a_{21} & a_{22} & \cdots & a_{2n} \\ \vdots & & & \\ a_{n1} & a_{n2} & \cdots & a_{nn} \end{bmatrix} \begin{bmatrix} x_1 \\ x_2 \\ \vdots \\ x_n \end{bmatrix} \tag{5.4–3a}$$

or

$$\mathbf{y} = \mathbf{A}\mathbf{x} \tag{5.4–3b}$$

where $\mathbf{y}$ and $\mathbf{x}$ are the $n \times 1$ matrices in (5.4–3a) and $\mathbf{A}^T$ is defined by (5.4–1). Hence the matrix $\mathbf{A}$ defines the linear transformation A. By continuing this analysis, you can derive all the rules for matrix manipulation. However, we shall assume that these rules are known (see Appendix B).

How does a matrix of a linear transformation change with respect to different basis vectors? Let $a_1, a_2, \ldots, a_n$ represent a new basis and $e_1, e_2, \ldots, e_n$ the old basis, and let

$$\begin{aligned} a_1 &= c_{11}e_1 + c_{21}e_2 + \cdots + c_{n1}e_n \\ a_2 &= c_{12}e_2 + c_{22}e_2 + \cdots + c_{n2}e_n \\ &\vdots \\ a_n &= e_{1n}e_1 + c_{2n}e_2 + \cdots + c_{nn}e_n \end{aligned}$$

Then for a vector X the coordinates x_i on the old e_i basis are related to the coordinates x_i' on the new a_i basis by the matrix equation

$$\mathbf{x} = \mathbf{C}\mathbf{x}' \tag{5.4–4}$$

where

$$\mathbf{C} = \begin{bmatrix} c_{11} & c_{12} & \cdots & c_{1n} \\ c_{21} & c_{22} & \cdots & c_{2n} \\ \vdots & & & \\ c_{n1} & c_{n2} & \cdots & c_{nn} \end{bmatrix}$$

Solving for $\mathbf{x}'$,

$$\mathbf{x}' = \mathbf{C}^{-1}\mathbf{x} \tag{5.4–5}$$

If we have a transformation $Y = AX$, then

$$\mathbf{y} = \mathbf{A}\mathbf{x} \qquad \text{on the old basis,}$$

$$\mathbf{y} = \mathbf{A}\mathbf{C}\mathbf{x}' \tag{5.4–6}$$

Since on the new basis $\mathbf{y} = \mathbf{C}\mathbf{y}'$,

$$\mathbf{C}\mathbf{y}' = \mathbf{A}\mathbf{C}\mathbf{x}'$$

or

$$\mathbf{y}' = \mathbf{C}^{-1}\mathbf{A}\mathbf{C}\mathbf{x}' \tag{5.4–7}$$

Thus the coordinates y_i of the vector Y on the new basis are given by the right side of (5.4–7) and the transformation matrix on the new basis is $\mathbf{C}^{-1}\mathbf{A}\mathbf{C}$. $\mathbf{C}$ must have an inverse, as otherwise the new basis vectors a_i would be linearly dependent.

Example 5.4–1.

Let

$$a_1 = 3e_1 + 2e_2$$

$$a_2 = 4e_1 + 1e_2$$

Then

$$\mathbf{C}^T = \begin{bmatrix} 3 & 2 \\ 4 & 1 \end{bmatrix}$$

and

$$\mathbf{C} = \begin{bmatrix} 3 & 4 \\ 2 & 1 \end{bmatrix}$$

If on the initial basis

$$\mathbf{x} = \begin{bmatrix} x_1 \\ x_2 \end{bmatrix} = \begin{bmatrix} 8 \\ 3 \end{bmatrix}$$

then $\mathbf{x} = \mathbf{C}\mathbf{x}'$, or on the new basis, $\mathbf{x}' = \mathbf{C}^{-1}\mathbf{x}$
In this case

$$\mathbf{C}^{-1} = \frac{1}{-5}\begin{bmatrix} 1 & -4 \\ -2 & 3 \end{bmatrix}$$

and

$$\mathbf{x}' = \begin{bmatrix} -1/5 & 4/5 \\ 2/5 & -3/5 \end{bmatrix}\begin{bmatrix} 8 \\ 3 \end{bmatrix} = \begin{bmatrix} 4/5 \\ 7/5 \end{bmatrix}$$

The change of basis is shown in Figure 5.4–1. On the initial basis, the vector $X = 8e_1 + 3e_2$, and on the new basis the vector $X = (4/5)a_1 + (7/5)a_2$. The vector has not changed, but the basis has changed.

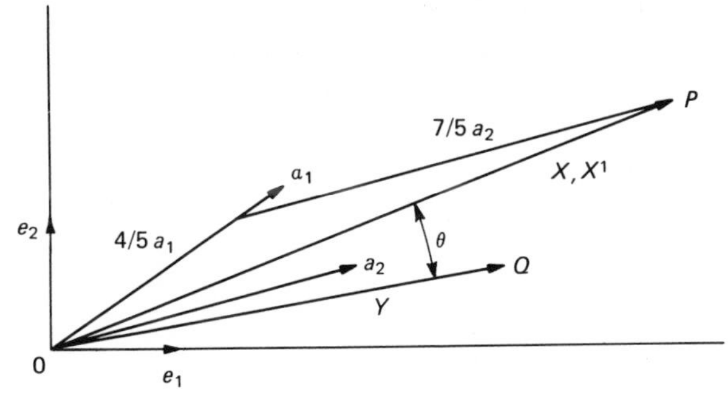

Figure 5.4–1. Change of basis for vector *X*, Example 5.4–1 ; linear transformation on *Y*.

Continuing Example 5.4–1, if the components of vector Y on the old basis is given by the matrix relation $\mathbf{y} = \mathbf{Ax}$, where

$$\mathbf{A} = \begin{bmatrix} 1/4 & 4/3 \\ 1/16 & 1/6 \end{bmatrix}$$

then

$$\begin{bmatrix} y_1 \\ y_2 \end{bmatrix} = \begin{bmatrix} 1/4 & 4/3 \\ 1/16 & 1/6 \end{bmatrix} \begin{bmatrix} x_1 \\ x_2 \end{bmatrix}$$

$$= \begin{bmatrix} 6 \\ 1 \end{bmatrix}$$

From (5.4–7),

$$\begin{bmatrix} y_1' \\ y_2' \end{bmatrix} = \begin{bmatrix} -1/5 & 4/5 \\ 2/5 & -3/5 \end{bmatrix} \begin{bmatrix} 1/4 & 4/3 \\ 1/16 & 1/6 \end{bmatrix} \begin{bmatrix} 3 & 4 \\ 2 & 1 \end{bmatrix} \begin{bmatrix} 4/5 \\ 7/5 \end{bmatrix}$$

You can verify that this gives the same results as $\mathbf{y}' = \mathbf{C}^{-1}\mathbf{y}$:

$$\begin{bmatrix} y_1' \\ y_2' \end{bmatrix} = \begin{bmatrix} -1/5 & 4/5 \\ 2/5 & -3/5 \end{bmatrix} \begin{bmatrix} 6 \\ 1 \end{bmatrix} = \begin{bmatrix} -2/5 \\ 9/5 \end{bmatrix}$$

Then $Y = -(2/5)a_1 + (9/5)a_2$ on the new basis (see Figure 5.4–1).

A set of n vectors V_i is said to be a reciprocal basis to a basis set of nU_i if $(V_i, U_j) = \delta_{ij}$, $i, j = 1, 2, \ldots, n$. If the original basis set U_i is orthonormal, the reciprocal set is also U_i.

A linear transformation from X to Y on the same basis is similar to a change of basis. Thus if we have a transformation $Y = AX$, then on the same basis, $\mathbf{y} = \mathbf{Ax}$, where $\mathbf{A}$ is the matrix of the transformation and Y is a vector representing X transformed. Alternatively, if $\mathbf{x}' = \mathbf{C}^{-1}\mathbf{x}$, where $\mathbf{C}$ is the transpose of the matrix relating the new basis to the old, we get a new representation of the vector X with components X_1' on the new basis. Clearly one operation gives the same results as the other. From one viewpoint we leave the vector X alone but express it on a different basis; from the other viewpoint we alter X on the same basis. A linear transformation thus corresponds to a deformation of the space (rotation, stretching or compressing, and so on). Again, comparing (5.4–3) and (5.4–7), we see that these are very similar. In fact, (5.4–7) represents the same alteration on basis a_1, a_2 as (5.4–3) on basis e_1, e_2. Thus matrix $\mathbf{S} = \mathbf{C}^{-1}\mathbf{AC}$ is said to be similar to $\mathbf{A}$, and det $\mathbf{S}$ = det $\mathbf{A}$. If linear transformations on the same basis fulfill our requirements, there is some advantage in staying on the same basis, as then we can identify the vector with its matrix; that is, let

$$X = \mathbf{x} = \begin{bmatrix} x_1 \\ x_2 \\ \vdots \\ x_n \end{bmatrix} \tag{5.4–8}$$

where the basis is specified or assumed. As already indicated, the initial basis is orthonormal.

Definition (5.4–8) is made in many control papers and texts in the United States. We have kept the vector X and the matrix $\mathbf{x}$ representing the vector separate until now because many other papers and texts do discuss basis changes, and you must be wary as to the notations of the writer [4]. A change of basis on (5.4–8) will cause difficulty unless care is taken to specify the new basis each time. You now see how the variables in a set of simultaneous equations, as shown by (5.2–4), for example, may be called "vectors." Obviously we can think of the solution as a vector space E^n composed of scalar components that may be varying with time.

So far we have discussed the matrix $\mathbf{A}$ as though it were an $n \times n$ matrix. This is not a restriction, because any $m \times n$ matrix can be made $n \times n$ by adding rows of zeros. Such a matrix will, of course, have a rank $m < n$. We can generalize and indicate then that all vectors Y resulting from the transformation A if they are still in space E^n will lie in a subspace of dimension m, $m \leq n$, where m is the rank of the matrix $\mathbf{A}$ defining A. [The rank m of a matrix is the largest $m \times m$ minor whose determinate is not zero, and also equals the maximum number of linearly independent rows (columns), if the row (column) coefficients are considered to be the coefficients of basis vectors.] The set of vectors for which the transformation

A is defined is called the domain of A, and the set of vectors Y is called the range of A. The null space of A is the space formed by $\mathbf{x}$, where $\mathbf{Ax} = \mathbf{0}$ and $\mathbf{A}$ is singular.

5.5 Eigenvalues and Quadratic Forms

The question now arises: Do any vectors $\mathbf{x}_i$ exist that have directions remaining unchanged (although the lengths may change) under the transformation $\mathbf{A}$? If so, a vector $\mathbf{x}$ of the set satisfies

$$\mathbf{Ax} = \lambda\mathbf{x} \tag{5.5–1}$$

where λ is a constant. Then

$$\mathbf{A}^2\mathbf{x} = \mathbf{A}(\mathbf{A})\mathbf{x} = \mathbf{A}\lambda\mathbf{x} = \lambda\mathbf{x} = \lambda\mathbf{Ax} = \lambda^2\mathbf{x}$$

and continuing,

$$\mathbf{A}^k\mathbf{x} = \lambda^k\mathbf{x} \tag{5.5–2}$$

Such vectors $\mathbf{x}_i$ are said to generate subspaces invariant under a transformation $\mathbf{A}^k$. (The directions of $\mathbf{x}_i$ are unchanged by $\mathbf{A}^k$.) Because many functions of $\mathbf{A}$ can be formed by a series containing terms of the form $\mathbf{A}^k$, this raises some interesting possibilities for simplification. The number λ, which may be complex in some cases, is called an eigenvalue (characteristic value, proper number). If we put (5.5–1) in the form of a set of simultaneous equations, since $(\lambda\mathbf{I} - \mathbf{A})\mathbf{x} = \mathbf{0}$,

$$\begin{aligned}(a_{11} - \lambda)x_1 + a_{12}x_2 + \cdots + a_{1n}x_n &= 0\\ a_{21}x_1 + (a_{22} - \lambda)x_2 + \cdots + a_{2n}x_n &= 0\\ &\vdots\\ a_{n1}x_1 + a_{n2}x_2 + \cdots + (a_{nn} - \lambda)x_n &= 0\end{aligned} \tag{5.5–3}$$

where x_j are the coordinates of $\mathbf{x}$ with respect to some basis vectors and

$$\mathbf{A} = \begin{bmatrix} a_{11} & a_{12} & \cdots & a_{1n}\\ a_{21} & a_{22} & \cdots & a_{2n}\\ \vdots & & & \\ a_{n1} & a_{n2} & \cdots & a_{nn}\end{bmatrix} \qquad \mathbf{I} = \begin{bmatrix} 1 & 0 & \cdots & 0\\ 0 & 1 & \cdots & 0\\ \vdots & & & \\ 0 & 0 & \cdots & 1\end{bmatrix}$$

From determinant theory you know that (5.5–3) will have a nonzero solution only if the determinant of the matrix of the coefficients is zero. Hence the solutions for λ are obtained by the equation

$$\det[\lambda\mathbf{I} - \mathbf{A}] = 0 \tag{5.5–4}$$

Equation (5.5–4) results in a polynomial in λ that, set to zero, is called the characteristic equation. This equation has n roots, the same as the degree of the polynomial. For each of the n roots λ_i, there exists a vector $\mathbf{x}_i$ that satisfies (5.5–1). If these vectors are linearly independent, they can form a basis for the space. The λ_i's are called the eigenvalues of the matrix and the vectors $\mathbf{x}_i$ are called the eigenvectors. In control systems the eigenvalues are also termed the "critical frequencies," because the factors of the characteristic polynomial determine the poles of the transfer function and hence the angular velocities of each component of the output. Thus the eigenvalues are equivalent to the familiar poles of the previously studied transfer functions. (Exceptions due to cancellations will be discussed later.)

Example 5.5–1

Find the eigenvalues and eigenvectors of the matrix

$$\begin{bmatrix} 5 & \sqrt{2} \\ \sqrt{2} & 4 \end{bmatrix}$$

Solution: Equation (5.5–1) gives

$$\left\{\begin{bmatrix} \lambda & 0 \\ 0 & \lambda \end{bmatrix} - \begin{bmatrix} 5 & \sqrt{2} \\ \sqrt{2} & 4 \end{bmatrix}\right\}\mathbf{x} = \mathbf{0}$$

or, from (5.5–4),

$$\det\begin{bmatrix} \lambda - 5 & -\sqrt{2} \\ -\sqrt{2} & \lambda - 4 \end{bmatrix} = 0$$

Then $(\lambda - 5)(\lambda - 4) - 2 = 0$, or

$$\lambda_2 - 9\lambda + 18 = 0$$

$$\lambda_1 = 6$$

$$\lambda_2 = 3$$

For $\lambda_1 = 6$, from (5.5–1),

$$\begin{bmatrix} 6 - 5 & -\sqrt{2} \\ -\sqrt{2} & 6 - 4 \end{bmatrix}\begin{bmatrix} x_1 \\ x_2 \end{bmatrix} = \mathbf{0}$$

or

$$1x_1 - \sqrt{2}_{x_2} = 0 \qquad x_1 = \sqrt{2}_{x_2}$$

$$-\sqrt{2}x_1 + 2x_2 = 0 \qquad x_1 = \sqrt{2}x_2$$

Note that both equations give the same result if no error has been made. Either x_1 or x_2 is arbitrary unless an eigenvector **u** of unit length is desired. In this case,

$$1 = x_1^2 + x_2^2$$

or

$$1 = 2x_2^2 + x_2^2$$

$$x_2 = \frac{1}{\sqrt{3}} \qquad x_1 = \sqrt{\frac{2}{3}} \qquad \text{or} \qquad \mathbf{u}_1 = [\sqrt{2/3} \quad 1/\sqrt{3}]^T$$

For $\lambda_2 = 3$,

$$\begin{bmatrix} 3-5 & -\sqrt{2} \\ -\sqrt{2} & 3-4 \end{bmatrix} \begin{bmatrix} x_1 \\ x_2 \end{bmatrix} = \mathbf{0}$$

$$-2x_1 - \sqrt{2}x_2 = 0 \qquad x_1 = \frac{-1}{\sqrt{2}} x_2$$

$$-\sqrt{2}x_1 - x_2 = 0 \qquad x_1 = \frac{-1}{\sqrt{2}} x_2$$

Normalizing,

$$\mathbf{u}_2 = [-1/\sqrt{3} \quad \sqrt{2}/\sqrt{3}]^T$$

Note that

$$(\mathbf{u}_1, \mathbf{u}_2) = \frac{-1}{\sqrt{3}} \sqrt{\frac{2}{3}} + \sqrt{\frac{2}{3}} \frac{1}{\sqrt{3}} = \frac{\sqrt{2}}{3} - \frac{\sqrt{2}}{3} = 0$$

or $\mathbf{u}_1$ and $\mathbf{u}_2$ are orthogonal in this case (**A** symmetric).

Note also that we could change the signs on both components of one or both eigenvectors and still meet the requirements of (5.5–1). We could also reverse $\mathbf{u}_1$ and $\mathbf{u}_2$ if we change the order of the λ values.

If the eigenvalues of **A** are all distinct, you may easily find the eigenvectors from the matrix $\mathbf{Adj}(\lambda\mathbf{I} - \mathbf{A})$ evaluated at $\lambda_1, \lambda_2, \ldots, \lambda_i$, and so on. Thus in Example 5.5–1,

$$\mathbf{Adj}(\lambda\mathbf{I} - \mathbf{A}) = \begin{bmatrix} \lambda - 4 & \sqrt{2} \\ \sqrt{2} & \lambda - 5 \end{bmatrix}^T$$

$$= \begin{bmatrix} \lambda - 4 & \sqrt{2} \\ \sqrt{2} & \lambda - 5 \end{bmatrix}$$

For $\lambda_1 = 6$,

$$\mathbf{Adj}(\lambda_1\mathbf{I} - \mathbf{A}) = \begin{bmatrix} 2 & \sqrt{2} \\ \sqrt{2} & 1 \end{bmatrix}$$

An eigenvector is proportional to either column, or

$$\begin{bmatrix} \sqrt{2} \\ 1 \end{bmatrix}$$

For $\lambda_2 = 3$,

$$\mathbf{Adj}(\lambda_2 \mathbf{I} - \mathbf{A}) = \begin{bmatrix} -1 & \sqrt{2} \\ \sqrt{2} & -2 \end{bmatrix}$$

or an eigenvector is

$$\begin{bmatrix} -1 \\ \sqrt{2} \end{bmatrix}$$

The matrix composed of eigenvectors as columns is called a modal matrix. Here one modal matrix is thus

$$\begin{bmatrix} \sqrt{2} & -1 \\ 1 & \sqrt{2} \end{bmatrix}$$

The matrix

$$\mathbf{T} = \begin{bmatrix} \dfrac{\sqrt{2}}{\sqrt{3}} & \dfrac{-1}{\sqrt{3}} \\ \dfrac{1}{\sqrt{3}} & \dfrac{\sqrt{2}}{\sqrt{3}} \end{bmatrix}$$

made up of the normalized vectors $\mathbf{u}_1$ and $\mathbf{u}_2$ has a special significance to be subsequently discussed.

It is not difficult to show that the eigenvalues of a real symmetric matrix are real and that the eigenvectors associated with distinct eigenvalues of a real symmetric matrix are orthogonal. For proof of the first statement, let

$$\mathbf{Ax} = \lambda \mathbf{x} \tag{5.5-5}$$

Then

$$\mathbf{Ax}^* = \lambda^* \mathbf{x}^*$$

$$(\mathbf{x}^*, \mathbf{Ax}) = \lambda(\mathbf{x}^*, \mathbf{x})$$

$$(x, A\mathbf{x}^*) = \lambda^*(\mathbf{x}, \mathbf{x}^*)$$

where $\mathbf{x}^*$ is the conjugate of $\mathbf{x}$.† If $\mathbf{A}$ symmetric, $\mathbf{A} = \mathbf{A}^T$; $(\mathbf{x}^*, \mathbf{Ax}) = (\mathbf{Ax}^*, \mathbf{x}) = (\mathbf{x}, \mathbf{Ax}^*)$. Then

$$(\lambda - \lambda^*)(\mathbf{x}, \mathbf{x}^*) = 0 \tag{5.5–6}$$

or

$$(\lambda - \lambda^*) = 0$$

Equation (5.5–6) cannot be true unless λ is real.

For proof of the second statement, let

$$\mathbf{Ax}_1 = \lambda_1 \mathbf{x}_1$$

$$\mathbf{Ax}_2 = \lambda_2 \mathbf{x}_2$$

Then

$$(\mathbf{x}_2, \mathbf{Ax}_1) = \lambda_1(\mathbf{x}_2, \mathbf{x}_1)$$

$$(\mathbf{x}_1, \mathbf{Ax}_2) = \lambda_2(\mathbf{x}_1, \mathbf{x}_2)$$

Since for a symmetric matrix $(\mathbf{x}_1, \mathbf{Ax}_2) = (\mathbf{Ax}_1, \mathbf{x}_2) = (\mathbf{x}_2, \mathbf{Ax}_1)$, and, if $\lambda \neq \lambda_2$,

$$(\mathbf{x}_1, \mathbf{x}_2) = 0 \tag{5.5–7}$$

Using these facts, let $\mathbf{T}$ be a matrix using the normalized eigenvectors of a symmetric matrix $\mathbf{A}$ as columns (modal matrix); that is, $\mathbf{T} = [\mathbf{u}_1 \mathbf{u}_2 \cdots \mathbf{u}_n]$, or

$$\mathbf{T} = \begin{bmatrix} u_1^1 & u_1^2 & \cdots & u_1^n \\ u_2^1 & u_2^2 & \cdots & u_2^n \\ \vdots & & & \\ u_n^1 & u_n^2 & \cdots & u_n^n \end{bmatrix} \tag{5.5–8}$$

where in (5.5–8) the superscript refers to the vector and the subscript to the component. Then for any entry C_{ij} in $\mathbf{T}^T\mathbf{T}$,

$$C_{ij} = \sum_{k=1}^{n} u_i^k u_k^j = \delta_{ij}$$

where δ_{ij} is the Kronecker delta defined in (5.3–7) or

$$\mathbf{T}^T\mathbf{T} = \mathbf{I} \tag{5.5–9}$$

† $(\mathbf{x}, \mathbf{y}) = \mathbf{y}^T\mathbf{x}^*$ if $\mathbf{x}$ and $\mathbf{y}$ are complex.

where **I** is the identity matrix. Matrices obeying (5.5–9) or the equivalent, $T^T = T^{-1}$, are called orthogonal.

From (5.5–8) and (5.5–1),

$$\mathbf{AT} = \begin{bmatrix} \lambda_1 u_1^1 & \lambda_2 u_1^2 & \cdots & \lambda_n u_1^n \\ \lambda_1 u_2^1 & \lambda_2 u_2^2 & \cdots & \lambda_n u_2^n \\ \vdots & & & \\ \lambda_1 u_n^1 & \lambda_2 u_n^2 & \cdots & \lambda_n u_n^n \end{bmatrix}$$

Hence for any entry D_{ij} in $\mathbf{T}^{-1}\mathbf{AT}$, $D_{ij} = \lambda_i \delta_{ij}$, or

$$\mathbf{T}^T\mathbf{AT} = \mathbf{\Lambda} = \begin{bmatrix} \lambda_1 & & & 0 \\ & \lambda_2 & & \\ & & \ddots & \\ 0 & & & \lambda_n \end{bmatrix} \tag{5.5–10}$$

Equation (5.5–10) demonstrates that a summetric matrix **A** is reduced to a diagonal form **Λ** by the transformation $\mathbf{T}^T\mathbf{AT}$.

Example 5.5–2

In Example 5.5–1

$$\mathbf{A} = \begin{bmatrix} 5 & \sqrt{2} \\ \sqrt{2} & 4 \end{bmatrix} \qquad \mathbf{T} = \begin{bmatrix} \sqrt{2}/\sqrt{3} & -1/\sqrt{3} \\ 1/\sqrt{3} & \sqrt{2}/\sqrt{3} \end{bmatrix}$$

Then

$$\mathbf{T}^T = \begin{bmatrix} \sqrt{2}/\sqrt{3} & 1/\sqrt{3} \\ -1/\sqrt{3} & \sqrt{2}/\sqrt{3} \end{bmatrix}$$

and you can verify that

$$\mathbf{\Lambda} = \mathbf{T}^T\mathbf{AT} = \begin{bmatrix} \sqrt{2}/\sqrt{3} & 1/\sqrt{3} \\ -1/\sqrt{3} & \sqrt{2}/\sqrt{3} \end{bmatrix} \begin{bmatrix} 5 & \sqrt{2} \\ \sqrt{2} & 4 \end{bmatrix} \begin{bmatrix} \sqrt{2}/\sqrt{3} & -1/\sqrt{3} \\ 1/\sqrt{3} & \sqrt{2}/\sqrt{3} \end{bmatrix} = \begin{bmatrix} 6 & 0 \\ 0 & 3 \end{bmatrix}$$

We shall not do so here, but it can be shown that any $n \times n$ matrix **A** with distinct eigenvectors $(\lambda_1, \lambda_2, \ldots, \lambda_n)$ can be diagonalized using the modal matrix **T** made up from the eigenvectors [5, 6]. Thus

$$\mathbf{\Lambda} = \mathbf{T}^{-1}\mathbf{AT} = \begin{bmatrix} \lambda_1 & & & 0 \\ & \lambda_2 & & \\ & & \ddots & \\ 0 & & & \lambda_n \end{bmatrix}$$

Note that if **A** is not symmetric, $\mathbf{T}^{-1} \neq \mathbf{T}^T$.

Example 5.5–3

From (5.2–2)

$$\dot{\mathbf{x}} = \mathbf{A}\mathbf{x}$$

where

$$\mathbf{A} = \begin{vmatrix} 0 & 1 \\ -w & -u \end{vmatrix}$$

Let $w = 6$, $u = 5$; then

$$\mathbf{A} = \begin{bmatrix} 0 & 1 \\ -6 & -5 \end{bmatrix}$$

The equation $\det|\lambda\mathbf{I} - \mathbf{A}| = 0$ gives $(\lambda + 2)(\lambda + 3) = 0$ or $\lambda_1 = -3$, $\lambda_2 = -2$. A set of corresponding eigenvectors (not normalized) are

$$\begin{bmatrix} 1 \\ -3 \end{bmatrix}, \begin{bmatrix} 1 \\ -2 \end{bmatrix}$$

Then

$$\mathbf{T} = \begin{vmatrix} 1 & 1 \\ -3 & -2 \end{vmatrix} \qquad \mathbf{T}^{-1} = \begin{bmatrix} -2 & -1 \\ 3 & 1 \end{bmatrix}$$

$$\mathbf{\Lambda} = \mathbf{T}^{-1}\mathbf{A}\mathbf{T} = \begin{bmatrix} -2 & -1 \\ 3 & 1 \end{bmatrix}\begin{bmatrix} 0 & 1 \\ -6 & -5 \end{bmatrix}\begin{bmatrix} 1 & 1 \\ -3 & -2 \end{bmatrix}$$

$$= \begin{bmatrix} -3 & 0 \\ 0 & -2 \end{bmatrix}$$

Then if $\mathbf{x} = \mathbf{T}_1\mathbf{y}$,

$$\dot{\mathbf{y}} = \mathbf{T}_1^{-1}\mathbf{A}\mathbf{T}_1\mathbf{y} = \mathbf{\Lambda}\mathbf{y}$$

or

$$\dot{y}_1 = -3y_1$$

$$\dot{y}_2 = -2y_2$$

(We use $\mathbf{T}_1$ here for a modal matrix with unnormalized eigenvectors.) The solutions are

$$y_1 = y_{10}\epsilon^{-3t}$$

$$y_2 = y_{20}\epsilon^{-2t}$$

where y_{10} and y_{20} are values of y_1 and y_2 at t_0, respectively. Since $\mathbf{y} = \mathbf{T}^{-1}\mathbf{x}$,

$$y_{10} = -2x_{10} - x_{20}$$

$$y_{20} = 3x_{10} + x_{20}$$

Then

$$\mathbf{x} = \mathbf{T}\mathbf{y}$$

or

$$x_1 = y_1 + y_2$$

$$x_2 = -3y_1 - 2y_2$$

or

$$x_1 = (-2x_{10} - x_{20})\epsilon^{-3t} + (3x_{10} + x_{20})\epsilon^{-2t}$$

Since $v = x_1$, $v_0 = x_{10}$, $\dot{v}_0 = x_{20}$, the above example gives the solution to the original equation (5.2–1) when $w = 6$, $u = 5$. Clearly it is possible to excite only one mode of oscillation at a time. Thus if $-2x_{10} - x_{20} = 0$, then only the ϵ^{-2t} mode will exist, whereas if $3x_{10} + 2x_{20} = 0$, only the ϵ^{-3t} mode will exist. Note that the eigenvectors need not be normalized to diagonalize the matrix **A**. If they are not normalized, the "length" of **y** differs from that of **x**, but this may not be relevant in the solution.

Example 5.5–4

Let $\mathbf{x} = \mathbf{A}\mathbf{x}$, where

$$\mathbf{A} = \begin{bmatrix} 4 & -3 \\ 3 & 4 \end{bmatrix}$$

Then $\lambda_1 = 4 + j3$, $\lambda_2 = 4 - j3$,

$$\mathbf{T} = \begin{bmatrix} 1 & 1 \\ -j & j \end{bmatrix} \qquad \mathbf{\Lambda} = \begin{bmatrix} 4 + j3 & 0 \\ 0 & 4 - j3 \end{bmatrix}$$

Then if

$$\mathbf{x} = \mathbf{T}\mathbf{y}$$

$$\dot{\mathbf{y}} = \mathbf{\Lambda} y$$

$$\dot{y}_1 = (4 + j3)y$$

$$\dot{y}_2 = (4 - j3)y$$

the solutions are

$$y_1 = y_{10}\,\epsilon^{4t}\epsilon^{j3t}$$

$$y_2 = y_{20}\,\epsilon^{4t}\epsilon^{-j3t}$$

Then $x_1 = y_{10}\epsilon^{4t}\epsilon^{j3t} + y_{20}\epsilon^{4t}\epsilon^{-j3t} = K\epsilon^{4t}(\cos 3t + \phi)$. The constants K and ϕ depend on the initial conditions (conditions at $t = 0_+$).

Note that in neither example are the eigenvectors orthogonal, because **A** is not symmetric. Complex angles may be defined, if desired.

If an $n \times n$ matrix **A** is of the special (canonical) form

$$\mathbf{A} = \begin{bmatrix} 0 & 1 & 0 & 0 \cdots\cdots\cdots & \\ 0 & 0 & 1 & 0 \cdots\cdots\cdots & \\ \cdots & \cdots & \cdots & \cdots\cdots\cdots & \\ 0 & 0 & 0 & 0 \cdots\cdots\cdots & 1 \\ a_{1n} & a_{2n} & a_{3n} & \cdots & a_{nn} \end{bmatrix} \tag{5.5–11}$$

and it has distinct eigenvectors $\lambda_1, \lambda_2, \ldots, \lambda_n$, then it is diagonalizable by a Vandermode-type matrix [7]†:

$$\mathbf{V} = \begin{bmatrix} 1 & 1 & \cdots & 1 \\ \lambda_1 & \lambda_2 & \cdots & \lambda_n \\ \lambda_1^2 & \lambda_2^2 & \cdots & \\ \cdots & \cdots & \cdots & \cdots \\ \lambda_1^{n-1} & \lambda_2^{n-1} & \cdots & \lambda_n^{n-1} \end{bmatrix} \tag{5.5–12}$$

Thus the state equation

$$\dot{\mathbf{x}} = \mathbf{A}\mathbf{x} + \mathbf{B}\mathbf{m} \tag{5.5–13}$$

may be altered to

$$\dot{\mathbf{z}} = \mathbf{\Lambda}\mathbf{z} + \mathbf{V}^{-1}\mathbf{B}\mathbf{m} \tag{5.5–14}$$

where

$$\mathbf{z} = \mathbf{V}^{-1}\mathbf{x}$$

Each column of **V** may be normalized, if desired.

Example 5.5–5

Diagonalize

$$\mathbf{A} = \begin{bmatrix} 0 & 1 & 0 \\ 0 & 0 & 1 \\ -4 & -6 & -4 \end{bmatrix}$$

† Also see Appendix B.

The eigenvalues are $\lambda_1 = -2$, $\lambda_2 = -1 + j1$, $\lambda_3 = -1 - j1$. Hence

$$\mathbf{V} = \begin{bmatrix} 1 & 1 & 1 \\ -2 & -1+j1 & -1-j1 \\ 4 & -2j & 2j \end{bmatrix}$$

Tou gives a method for finding $\mathbf{V}^{-1}$ in this case as follows [7]. Find

$$P_i(z) = \prod_{\substack{j=1 \\ j \neq i}}^{n} \frac{z - \lambda_j}{\lambda_i - \lambda_j} \qquad i = 1, \ldots, n \tag{5.5–15}$$

Then the element a_{ij} of T^{-1} is the coefficient of the z^{j-1} term of the polynomial $P_i(z)$.

Example 5.5–6

Find $\mathbf{V}^{-1}$ of Example 5.5–5.

Solution:

$$P_1(z) = \frac{(z + 1 - j1)(z + 1 + j1)}{(-2 + 1 - j1)(-2 + 1 + j1)}$$

$$P_2(z) = \frac{(z + 1 + j1)(z + 2)}{(-1 + j1 + 1 + j1)(-1 + j1 + 2)}$$

$$P_3(z) = \frac{(z + 1 - j1)(z + 2)}{(-1 - j1 + 1 - j1)(-1 - j1 + 2)}$$

Simplifying,

$$P_1(z) = \frac{z^2 + 2z + 2}{2}$$

$$P_2(z) = \frac{z^2(1 + j) + (2 + 4j)z + 4j}{-4}$$

$$P_3(z) = \frac{z^2(1 - j) + (2 - 4j)z - 4j}{-4}$$

Then

$$\mathbf{V}^{-1} = \begin{bmatrix} 1 & 1 & \frac{1}{2} \\ -j & -(\frac{1}{2} + j) & \frac{-(1+j)}{4} \\ j & -(\frac{1}{2} - j) & \frac{-(1-j)}{4} \end{bmatrix}$$

Note that each column contains two complex conjugates. Thus if one row is found, another row follows immediately.

If the matrix **A** in (5.5–13) is of the form (5.5–11), the state equations are said to be in phase-variable form. Several papers demonstrate how to get the state equations of a controllable system into this form [8].

The examples of diagonalization may not be impressive, because solutions of the original equations are so simple. However, if the size of the matrix **A** gets large, or the differential equation is of high degree, diagonalization may offer advantages. More particularly, the diagonal matrix becomes very important in theoretical developments. The practical difficulty in diagonalization lies in obtaining the eigenvalues and eigenvectors. Methods other than solving a polynomial can be used to find the eigenvalues and eigenvectors, as will be shown.

In some cases there may be repeated roots of the characteristic equation, but the eigenvectors corresponding to a multiple-valued eigenvector may be linearly independent.

Example 5.5–7

If

$$\mathbf{A} = \begin{bmatrix} 1 & 0 \\ 0 & 1 \end{bmatrix}$$

$\lambda_1 = 1$ is an eigenvalue of multiplicity 2, but

$$\mathbf{u}_1 = \begin{bmatrix} 1 \\ 0 \end{bmatrix} \qquad \mathbf{u}_2 = \begin{bmatrix} 0 \\ 1 \end{bmatrix}$$

are linearly independent and span the space.

If λ_i is a repeated characteristic root of order p, and the rank r of the $n \times n$ matrix **A** is $r = n - p$, then linearly independent eigenvectors may be found for the repeated eigenvalues. If $r > n - p$, then the matrix can still be reduced to a Jordan canonical form [9]. If the matrix **A** is symmetric, then each eigenvalue of order p produces p linearly independent eigenvectors. Actually most systems can be approximated with an **A** having distinct roots, because a slight alteration of the coefficients of a polynomial results in comparatively large variations of its zeros [10].

A quadratic form Q may be defined as

$$Q = \mathbf{x}^T\mathbf{A}\mathbf{x} \tag{5.5–16a}$$

$$Q = (\mathbf{x}, \mathbf{A}\mathbf{x}) \tag{5.5–16b}$$

where **A** may be symmetric without loss of generality. If we let $\mathbf{x} = \mathbf{T}\mathbf{y}$, where **T** is the matrix defined in (5.5–8) and derived from **A**, then

$$\begin{aligned} Q &= (\mathbf{Ty})^T\mathbf{ATy} \\ &= \mathbf{y}^T\mathbf{T}^T\mathbf{ATy} \\ &= \mathbf{y}^T\mathbf{\Lambda y} \end{aligned} \tag{5.5–17}$$

Equation (5.5–17) will have no cross-product terms and results in

$$Q = \lambda_1 y_1^2 + \lambda_2 y_2^2 + \cdots + \lambda_n y_n^2 \tag{5.5–18}$$

Equations such as (5.5–18) are much simpler than (5.5–16). Once **y** is known, then $\mathbf{x} = \mathbf{Ty}$. A quadratic form is said to be positive definite if $Q(\mathbf{x}) > 0$ for all **x** except **0**. It is said to be positive indefinite if $Q(\mathbf{x}) \geq 0$ for all $\mathbf{x} \neq 0$. Similar definitions hold for negative definite and negative indefinite. From (5.5–18) if all eigenvalues λ of the matrix **A** are positive, a quadratic form is positive definite, and if all are negative, it is negative definite. Corresponding to the quadratic form, the matrix **A** itself is also said to be a positive definite, and so on.

A quadratic form Q can be shown to be positive definite if all ordered principle minors of **A** are positive, or

$$a_{11} > 0, \quad \begin{vmatrix} a_{11} & a_{12} \\ a_{21} & a_{22} \end{vmatrix} > 0, \quad \begin{vmatrix} a_{11} & a_{12} & a_{13} \\ a_{21} & a_{22} & a_{23} \\ a_{31} & a_{32} & a_{33} \end{vmatrix} > 0, \ldots, |\mathbf{A}| > 0 \tag{5.5–19}$$

Example 5.5–8

Let the quadratic form Q be $3x_1^2 + 5x_1x_2 + 4x_2^2$. This may be written

$$[x_1 \quad x_2]\begin{bmatrix} 3 & 2 \\ 3 & 4 \end{bmatrix}\begin{bmatrix} x_1 \\ x_2 \end{bmatrix}$$

In this form the 2×2 matrix is not symmetric. However, if we let

$$z_1 = \frac{x_1}{2} \qquad z_2 = \frac{x_2}{2}$$

then $Q = 12z_1^2 + 20z_1z_2 + 16z_2$, or

$$[z_1 \quad z_2]\begin{bmatrix} 12 & 10 \\ 10 & 16 \end{bmatrix}\begin{bmatrix} z_1 \\ z_2 \end{bmatrix}$$

The principal minors are 12 and 92; hence the form is positive definite. The eigenvalues are approximately 24.2 and 3.80 and also indicate that the form

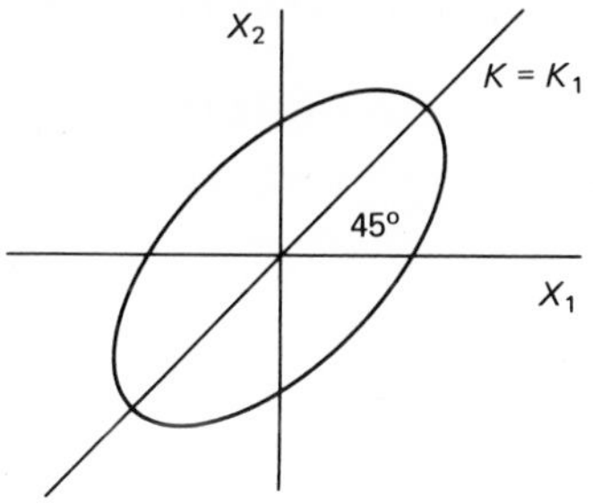

Figure 5.5–1. One ellipse of Example 5.5–1.

is positive definite, because $Q = 24.2y_1^2 + 3.8y_2^2$, where $\mathbf{z} = \mathbf{Ty}$ and the **T** matrix is formed by using the eigenvectors corresponding to the eigenvalues as columns.

Example 5.5–9

Given the quadratic form $(\mathbf{x}, \mathbf{Ax}) = K$, where

$$\mathbf{A} = \begin{bmatrix} 1 & -\sqrt{3}/4 \\ -\sqrt{3}/4 & 1 \end{bmatrix}$$

Draw the level curves for K having different values. Is the origin a maximum, minimum, or neither?

Solution:

The modal matrix (normalized) is

$$\mathbf{T} = \begin{bmatrix} 1/\sqrt{2} & 1/\sqrt{2} \\ -1/\sqrt{2} & 1/\sqrt{2} \end{bmatrix}$$

and the eigenvalues are

$$(1 + \sqrt{3}/2) \qquad (1 - \sqrt{3}/2)$$

Then if $\mathbf{x} = \mathbf{Ty}$,

$$(\mathbf{y}, \mathbf{\Lambda y}) = (1 + \sqrt{3}/2)y_1^2 + (1 - \sqrt{3}/2)y_2^2 = K$$

This obviously represents a family of ellipses with the major axis along y_2. Since **T** is a rotation of 45° counterclockwise, the original set of ellipses relative to the x_1x_2 axis has the major axis at 45° to x_1 (see Figure 5.5–1). The origin is a minimum, since as K gets smaller, the ellipse shrinks.

A quadratic form is said to have a singular point (equilibrium point, or stationary point) if $dQ/d\mathbf{x} = \text{grad}_{\mathbf{x}} Q = \mathbf{0}$. From Appendix B, $\text{grad}_{\mathbf{x}}\mathbf{Q} = 2\mathbf{A}\mathbf{x}$. Hence if $\mathbf{A} \neq \mathbf{0}$, then $\mathbf{x} = \mathbf{0}$ is a singular point. To find if the point is a maximum, minimum, or other, we take a second derivative, as in the scalar situation. This shows that the singular point will be a maximum if **A** is negative definite, a minimum if **A** is positive definite, and may be a saddle point if it is neither. (If **A** is negative definite, the signs of the principle minors alternate, starting with a negative sign for a_{11}.)

It may be shown that a real $Q = (\mathbf{x}, \mathbf{A}\mathbf{x})$ may be transformed to the form

$$x_1^2 + x_2^2 + \cdots + x_p^2 - x_{p+2}^2 - \cdots - x_r^2$$

where p is the number of positive eigenvalues and r is the rank of **A**. The number $(p - r)$ is called the signature of Q.†

5.6 Functions of a Matrix

Assume that the eigenvalues $\lambda_1, \lambda_2, \ldots, \lambda_n$ of a matrix are distinct but not necessarily real. If we let $p(\lambda)$ be a polynomial such that

$$p(\lambda_k) = f(\lambda_k) \qquad k = 1, 2, \ldots, n \tag{5.6–1}$$

then we define

$$f(\mathbf{A}) = p(\mathbf{A}) \tag{5.6–2}$$

In words, (5.6–1) indicates that the function $f(\lambda)$ equals $p(\lambda)$ at specific values of λ: $\lambda_1, \lambda_2, \ldots, \lambda_n$. Thus $p(\lambda)$ can be an interpolating polynomial. We are interested in functions $f(\mathbf{A})$, because solutions of differential equations can be given in terms of such functions, in particular, in terms of $\epsilon^{\mathbf{A}t}$.

One theorem of interest is the Cayley-Hamilton theorem, which states that every matrix **A** satisfies its own characteristic equation, or if

$$p(\lambda) = (\lambda - \lambda_1)(\lambda - \lambda_2) \cdots (\lambda - \lambda_n) = 0 \tag{5.6–3}$$

then

$$p(\mathbf{A}) = (\mathbf{A} - \lambda_1\mathbf{I})(\mathbf{A} - \lambda_2\mathbf{I}) \cdots (\mathbf{A} - \lambda_n\mathbf{I}) = \mathbf{0} \tag{5.6–4}$$

† Reference [26].

Example 5.6–1

If

$$\mathbf{A} = \begin{bmatrix} 5 & \sqrt{2} \\ \sqrt{2} & 4 \end{bmatrix}$$

then $f(\lambda) = p(\lambda) = \lambda^2 - 9\lambda + 18 = 0$. Then

$$P(A) = \mathbf{A}^2 - 9\mathbf{A} + 18\mathbf{I} = \begin{bmatrix} 5 & \sqrt{2} \\ \sqrt{2} & 4 \end{bmatrix}\begin{bmatrix} 5 & \sqrt{2} \\ \sqrt{2} & 4 \end{bmatrix} - 9\begin{bmatrix} 5 & \sqrt{2} \\ \sqrt{2} & 4 \end{bmatrix} + 18\begin{bmatrix} 1 & 0 \\ 0 & 1 \end{bmatrix}$$

You can easily verify that this results in a matrix with null column vectors. If repeated zeros of the characteristic equation exist, the theorem may be altered slightly [11].

You may prove the Cayley-Hamilton theorem for distinct eigenvalues as follows.

Let **A** be diagonalized by a modal matrix **T**, or

$$\mathbf{A} = \mathbf{T}^{-1}\mathbf{\Lambda}\mathbf{T}$$

Then

$$\mathbf{\Lambda} = \mathbf{T}^{-1}\mathbf{A}\mathbf{T}$$

$$\mathbf{\Lambda}^2 = (\mathbf{T}^{-1}\mathbf{A}\mathbf{T})(\mathbf{T}^{-1}\mathbf{A}\mathbf{T})$$

$$= \mathbf{T}^{-1}\mathbf{A}^2\mathbf{T}$$

Continuing, it is evident that

$$\mathbf{A}^k = \mathbf{T}\mathbf{\Lambda}^k\mathbf{T}^{-1}$$

Now examine

$$n(\mathbf{A}) = \mathbf{A}^n + d_1\mathbf{A}^{n-1} + \cdots + d_{n-1}\mathbf{A} + d_n\mathbf{I}$$

But

$$n(\mathbf{A}) = \mathbf{T}\begin{bmatrix} n(\lambda_1) & & & \\ & n(\lambda_2) & & \\ & & \ddots & \\ & & & n(\lambda_n) \end{bmatrix}\mathbf{T}^{-1}$$

where

$$n(\lambda) = \lambda^n + d_1\lambda^{n-1} + \cdots + d_{n-1}\lambda + d_n$$

and $\lambda_1, \lambda_2, \ldots, \lambda_n$ are the roots of $n(\lambda)$. If we choose $n(\lambda)$ to be the characteristic polynomial $p(\lambda)$ of $\mathbf{A}$, then

$$n(\lambda_1) = n(\lambda_2) = \cdots = n(\lambda_n) = 0$$

Hence $p(\mathbf{A}) = \mathbf{0}$ if

$$p(\lambda) = \det[\lambda\mathbf{I} - \mathbf{A}]$$

A method for finding a function $f(\mathbf{A})$ using the Cayley-Hamilton theorem may result in simplicity in many cases. Assume that $n(\mathbf{A})$ is a polynomial of higher degree than the order of $\mathbf{A}$. Then

$$\frac{n(\lambda)}{p(\lambda)} = q(\lambda) + \frac{r(\lambda)}{p(\lambda)} \tag{5.6–5}$$

where $p(\lambda)$ is a polynomial of lower degree than $n(\lambda)$ and $r(\lambda)$ is the remainder.

From (5.6–5),

$$n(\lambda) = q(\lambda)p(\lambda) + r(\lambda)$$

If we now let $p(\lambda)$ be the characteristic polynomial, $p(\lambda) = 0$ and

$$n(\lambda) = r(\lambda) \tag{5.6–6}$$

By the Cayley-Hamilton theorem, then

$$n(\mathbf{A}) = r(\mathbf{A}) \tag{5.6–7}$$

If, further, $f(\lambda)$ can be expressed by a power series of order n, again by the Cayley-Hamilton theorem, $f(\mathbf{A})$ can be delineated as a polynomial in the $n \times n$ matrix $\mathbf{A}$ of degree $n - 1$ (see subsequent examples). Then if

$$f(\lambda) = q(\lambda)p(\lambda) + r(\lambda)$$

$r(\lambda)$ will be a polynomial of degree $n - 1$, or

$$r(\lambda) = \alpha_0 + \alpha_1\lambda + \alpha_2\lambda^2 + \cdots + \alpha_{n-1}\lambda^{n-1} \tag{5.6–8}$$

and letting $p(\lambda)$ be the characteristic polynomial of $\mathbf{A}$,

$$f(\lambda) = r(\lambda) \tag{5.6–9}$$

Again following the previous argument,†

$$f(\mathbf{A}) = r(\mathbf{A}) \tag{5.6–10}$$

Example 5.6–2

Find $n(\mathbf{A}) = \mathbf{A}^4 + 2\mathbf{A}^3 + \mathbf{A}^2 + 3\mathbf{A} + \mathbf{I}$, where

$$\mathbf{A} = \begin{bmatrix} 0 & 1 \\ -3 & -4 \end{bmatrix}$$

The characteristic polynomial is $p(\lambda) = (\lambda + 3)(\lambda + 1)$. Then

$$\frac{n(\lambda)}{p(\lambda)} = \lambda^2 - 2\lambda + 6 + \frac{-15\lambda - 17}{\lambda^2 + 4\lambda + 3}$$

Hence

$$r(\lambda) = -15\lambda - 17$$

$$n(\mathbf{A}) = -15\mathbf{A} - 17\mathbf{I}$$

Example 5.6–3

Find $\epsilon^{\mathbf{A}t}$ for the $\mathbf{A}$ of Example 5.6–2,

$$f(\lambda_i) = \epsilon^{\lambda_i t} = \alpha_0 + \alpha_1 \lambda_i$$

Then

$$\epsilon^{-3t} = \alpha_0 - 3\alpha_1$$

$$\epsilon^{-t} = \alpha_0 - \alpha_1$$

whence

$$\alpha_0 = \tfrac{3}{2}\epsilon^{-t} - \tfrac{1}{2}\epsilon^{-3t}$$

$$\alpha_1 = \tfrac{1}{2}\epsilon^{-t} - \tfrac{1}{2}\epsilon^{-3t}$$

Then

$$f(\mathbf{A}) = \epsilon^{\mathbf{A}t} = \alpha_0 \mathbf{I} + \alpha_1 \mathbf{A}$$

$$= \begin{bmatrix} \tfrac{3}{2}\epsilon^{-t} - \tfrac{1}{2}\epsilon^{-3t} & \tfrac{1}{2}\epsilon^{-t} - \tfrac{1}{2}\epsilon^{-3t} \\ -\tfrac{3}{2}\epsilon^{-t} + \tfrac{3}{2}\epsilon^{-3t} & -\tfrac{1}{2}\epsilon^{-t} + 3\epsilon^{-3t} \end{bmatrix}$$

† The proof requires more rigorous evidence of analyticity. See reference [9], pp. 282–283.

Example 5.6–4

Find $\mathbf{A}^5$ for the $\mathbf{A}$ of Example 5.6–2:

$$f(\lambda_i) = \lambda^5$$

$$(-3)^5 = \alpha_0 - 3\alpha_1$$

$$(-1)^5 = \alpha_0 - \alpha_1$$

or

$$\alpha_0 = -\tfrac{3}{2} - \tfrac{1}{2}(-3)^5$$

$$\alpha_1 = -\tfrac{1}{2} - \tfrac{1}{2}(-3)^5$$

and

$$\mathbf{A}^5 = -[\tfrac{3}{2} + \tfrac{1}{2}(-3)^5]\mathbf{I} - [\tfrac{1}{2} + \tfrac{1}{2}(-3)^5]\mathbf{A}$$

A generalization of this procedure gives

$$f(\mathbf{A}) = \sum_{i=0}^{n-1} \alpha_i \mathbf{A}^i$$

where

$$\begin{bmatrix} f(\lambda_1) \\ f(\lambda_2) \\ \vdots \\ f(\lambda_n) \end{bmatrix} = \begin{bmatrix} 1 & \lambda_1 & \lambda_1^2 & \cdots & \lambda_1^{n-1} \\ 1 & \lambda_2 & \lambda_2^2 & \cdots & \lambda_2^{n-1} \\ \cdots & \cdots & \cdots & \cdots & \cdots \\ 1 & \lambda_n & \lambda_n^2 & \cdots & \lambda_n^{n-1} \end{bmatrix} \begin{bmatrix} \alpha_0 \\ \alpha_1 \\ \cdots \\ \alpha_{n-1} \end{bmatrix} \tag{5.6–11}$$

Note that we have again a form of the Vandermonde matrix.

If repeated roots occur, then (5.6–8) must be differentiated $(j-1)$ times with respect to λ to get equations for the α_i values related to an eigenvalue λ_i that is repeated j times.

Another method of finding $f(\mathbf{A})$ is to use a Taylor's series, which, if it converges absolutely and uniformly, may give a practical solution, particularly if a computer finds the matrix powers. Still another method is to use the Sylvester expansion theorem, which is based on Lagrange's interpolating polynomial [12, 13]. We show this without proof as follows:

$$f(\mathbf{A}) = \sum_{k=1}^{n} f(\lambda_k) \prod_{\substack{j=1 \\ j\neq k}}^{n} \frac{(\mathbf{A} - \lambda_j \mathbf{I})}{(\lambda_k - \lambda_j)} \tag{5.6–12}$$

where the λ_i values are distinct.

Example 5.6–5

Find $\epsilon^{\mathbf{A}t}$, where

$$\mathbf{A} = \begin{bmatrix} 5 & \sqrt{2} \\ \sqrt{2} & 4 \end{bmatrix} \qquad \lambda_1 = 6, \lambda_2 = 3$$

Then

$$\epsilon^{\mathbf{A}t} = \epsilon^{6t} \frac{\begin{bmatrix} 5 & \sqrt{2} \\ \sqrt{2} & 4 \end{bmatrix} - 3\begin{bmatrix} 1 & 0 \\ 0 & 1 \end{bmatrix}}{6-3} + \epsilon^{3t} \frac{\begin{bmatrix} 5 & \sqrt{2} \\ \sqrt{2} & 4 \end{bmatrix} - 6\begin{bmatrix} 1 & 0 \\ 0 & 1 \end{bmatrix}}{3-6}$$

$$= \epsilon^{6t} \frac{\begin{bmatrix} 2 & \sqrt{2} \\ \sqrt{2} & 1 \end{bmatrix}}{3} + \epsilon^{3t} \frac{\begin{bmatrix} -1 & \sqrt{2} \\ \sqrt{2} & -2 \end{bmatrix}}{3}$$

$$= \frac{1}{3}\begin{bmatrix} 2\epsilon^{6t} + \epsilon^{3t} & \sqrt{2}(\epsilon^{6t} - \epsilon^{3t}) \\ \sqrt{2}(\epsilon^{6t} - \epsilon^{3t}) & \epsilon^{6t} + 2\epsilon^{3t} \end{bmatrix} = \mathbf{B}$$

The solution of $\dot{\mathbf{x}} = \mathbf{A}\mathbf{x}$ will be $\mathbf{x} = \epsilon^{\mathbf{A}t}\mathbf{x}_0$, where $\mathbf{x}_0$ is the value of $\mathbf{x}$ at $t = 0_+$ (see Chapter 6). Hence if A is the matrix in this example, the solution is

$$\mathbf{x} = \mathbf{B}\mathbf{x}_0$$

You can verify that the same solution is obtained by solving

$$\dot{\mathbf{y}} = \mathbf{\Lambda}\mathbf{y}$$

where $\mathbf{x} = \mathbf{T}\mathbf{y}$ and

$$\mathbf{T} = \begin{bmatrix} \sqrt{2}/\sqrt{3} & -1/\sqrt{3} \\ 1/\sqrt{3} & \sqrt{2}/\sqrt{3} \end{bmatrix}$$

Example 5.6–6

Find $\mathbf{A}^\gamma$ where

$$\mathbf{A} = \begin{bmatrix} 5 & \sqrt{2} \\ \sqrt{2} & 4 \end{bmatrix} \qquad \lambda_1 = 6, \lambda_2 = 3$$

$$\mathbf{A}^\gamma = (2)6^{\gamma-1}\begin{bmatrix} 2 & \sqrt{2} \\ \sqrt{2} & 1 \end{bmatrix} - 3^{\gamma-1}\begin{bmatrix} -1 & \sqrt{2} \\ \sqrt{2} & -2 \end{bmatrix}$$

Then

$$\mathbf{A}^0 = \frac{1}{3}\begin{bmatrix} 2 & \sqrt{2} \\ \sqrt{2} & 1 \end{bmatrix} - \frac{1}{3}\begin{bmatrix} -1 & \sqrt{2} \\ \sqrt{2} & -2 \end{bmatrix} = \begin{bmatrix} 1 & 0 \\ 0 & 1 \end{bmatrix}$$

$$\mathbf{A}^2 = 12\begin{bmatrix} 2 & \sqrt{2} \\ \sqrt{2} & 1 \end{bmatrix} - 3\begin{bmatrix} -1 & \sqrt{2} \\ \sqrt{2} & -2 \end{bmatrix} = \begin{bmatrix} 27 & 9\sqrt{2} \\ 9\sqrt{2} & 18 \end{bmatrix}$$

$$\mathbf{A}^3 = 72\begin{bmatrix} 2 & \sqrt{2} \\ \sqrt{2} & 1 \end{bmatrix} - 9\begin{bmatrix} -1 & \sqrt{2} \\ \sqrt{2} & -2 \end{bmatrix} = \begin{bmatrix} 144 & 72\sqrt{2} \\ 72\sqrt{2} & 72 \end{bmatrix} - \begin{bmatrix} -9 & 9\sqrt{2} \\ 9\sqrt{2} & -18 \end{bmatrix}$$

$$= \begin{bmatrix} 153 & 63\sqrt{2} \\ 63\sqrt{2} & 90 \end{bmatrix}$$

$$\mathbf{A}^{1/2} = \frac{1}{\sqrt{3}}\begin{bmatrix} 2\sqrt{2}+1 & 2-\sqrt{2} \\ 2-\sqrt{2} & 2+\sqrt{2} \end{bmatrix}$$

$$\epsilon^{\mathbf{A}t} = \mathbf{A}^0 + A^1 t + \frac{\mathbf{A}^2 t^2}{2!} + \frac{\mathbf{A}^3 t^3}{3!} + \cdots$$

$$= \begin{bmatrix} 1 & 0 \\ 0 & 1 \end{bmatrix} + \begin{bmatrix} 5 & \sqrt{2} \\ \sqrt{2} & 4 \end{bmatrix} t + \begin{bmatrix} 27 & 9\sqrt{2} \\ 9\sqrt{2} & 18 \end{bmatrix}\frac{t^2}{2} + \begin{bmatrix} 153 & 63\sqrt{2} \\ 63\sqrt{2} & 90 \end{bmatrix}\frac{t^3}{6}$$

$$+ \begin{bmatrix} 891 & 405\sqrt{2} \\ 405\sqrt{2} & 486 \end{bmatrix}\frac{t^4}{24} + \begin{bmatrix} 5265 & 2511\sqrt{2} \\ 2511\sqrt{2} & 2754 \end{bmatrix}\frac{t^5}{120} + \cdots$$

(Obviously this is a poor way to find $\epsilon^{\mathbf{A}t}$.)

Example 5.6–7

Find $\log \mathbf{A}$:

$$\log \mathbf{A} = \frac{\log 6}{3}\begin{bmatrix} 2 & \sqrt{2} \\ \sqrt{2} & 1 \end{bmatrix} - \frac{\log 3}{3}\begin{bmatrix} -1 & \sqrt{2} \\ \sqrt{2} & -2 \end{bmatrix}$$

$\epsilon^{\mathbf{A}t}$ has usefulness in continuous time systems, while $\mathbf{A}^k$ has usefulness in discrete time systems. The Sylvester expansion theorem is useful for low-order matrices, but for higher orders the previous technique (Cayley-Hamilton) may be preferable.

Another approach to finding $\epsilon^{\mathbf{A}t}$ is through the spectral representation of a transformation.† Assume that the matrix $\mathbf{A}$ of a transformation has n distinct eigenvalues λ_i and n eigenvectors $\mathbf{u}_i$. Let $\mathbf{v}_i$, $i = 1, 2, \ldots, n$ be a

† Spectral representation is essentially diagonalization from another viewpoint; thus if time presses, this discussion may be disregarded.

reciprocal basis if the $\mathbf{u}_i$ are considered a basis, or $(\mathbf{v}_i, \mathbf{u}_j) = \mathbf{u}_i^T\mathbf{v}_j = \delta_{ij}$. Then a vector $\mathbf{x}$ can be delineated as

$$\mathbf{x} = \sum_{i=1}^{n} \alpha_i \mathbf{u}_i \tag{5.6–13}$$

Since the components α_k of $\mathbf{x}$ on the vectors $\mathbf{u}_i$ are given by

$$\alpha_k = (\mathbf{v}_k, \mathbf{x}) \qquad k = 1, 2, \ldots, n$$

then

$$\mathbf{x} = \sum_{i=1}^{n} (\mathbf{v}_i, \mathbf{x})\mathbf{u}_i \tag{5.6–14}$$

$$\mathbf{Ax} = \mathbf{A} \sum_{i=1}^{n} (\mathbf{v}_i, \mathbf{x})\mathbf{u}_i$$

$$= \sum_{i=1}^{n} (\mathbf{v}_i, \mathbf{x})\mathbf{Au}_i$$

$$\mathbf{Ax} = \sum_{i=1}^{n} (\mathbf{v}_i, \mathbf{x})\lambda_i\mathbf{u}_i \tag{5.6–15}$$

From the definition of the reciprocal basis vectors $\mathbf{u}_i$ and $\mathbf{v}_i$, we can form n equations to find the $\mathbf{v}_i$ if the $\mathbf{u}_i$ are known. Thus if we designate the components of $\mathbf{u}_i$ by $u_{1i}, u_{2i}, \ldots, u_{ni}$, from the definition we get

$$\mathbf{u}_1^T\mathbf{v}_1 = [u_{11} \quad u_{21} \quad \cdots \quad u_{n1}]\begin{bmatrix} v_{11} \\ v_{21} \\ \vdots \\ v_{n1} \end{bmatrix}$$

or continuing for all $\mathbf{u}_i$,

$$\begin{aligned} u_{11}v_{11} + u_{21}v_{21} + \cdots + u_{n1}v_{n1} &= 1 \\ u_{12}v_{11} + u_{22}v_{21} + \cdots + u_{n2}v_{n1} &= 0 \\ &\vdots \\ u_{1n}v_{11} + u_{2n}v_{21} + \cdots + u_{nn}v_{n1} &= 0 \end{aligned} \tag{5.6–16}$$

If we use the coefficients of the eigenvectors $\mathbf{u}_i$ as columns in a matrix $\mathbf{U}$, then

$$\mathbf{U} = \begin{bmatrix} u_{11} & u_{12} & \cdots & u_{1n} \\ u_{21} & u_{22} & \cdots & \\ \vdots & & & \vdots \\ u_{n1} & u_{n2} & \cdots & u_{nn} \end{bmatrix}$$

and (5.6–16) can be rewritten

$$\mathbf{U}^T\mathbf{v}_1 = \begin{bmatrix} 1 \\ 0 \\ \vdots \\ 0 \end{bmatrix}$$

Continuing with $\mathbf{v}_2$,

$$\mathbf{U}^T\mathbf{v}_2 = \begin{bmatrix} 0 \\ 1 \\ 0 \\ \vdots \\ 0 \end{bmatrix}$$

and so on, and if we form a matrix $\mathbf{V}$ with the coefficients of the $\mathbf{v}_i$ as columns, then

$$\mathbf{U}^T\mathbf{V} = \mathbf{I} \tag{5.6–17}$$

or

$$\mathbf{I} = \sum_{i=1}^{n} (\mathbf{u}_i \mathbf{v}_i^T)$$

$$\mathbf{I}\mathbf{x} = \mathbf{x} = \sum_{i=1}^{n} (\mathbf{u}_i \mathbf{v}_i^T)\mathbf{x}$$

Then, from (5.6–14),

$$\sum_{i=1}^{n} (\mathbf{v}_i, \mathbf{x})\mathbf{u}_i = \sum_{i=1}^{n} (\mathbf{u}_i \mathbf{v}_i^T)\mathbf{x} \tag{5.6–18}$$

Hence (5.6–15) becomes

$$\mathbf{A}\mathbf{x} = \sum_{i=1}^{n} \lambda_i(\mathbf{u}_i \mathbf{v}_i^T)\mathbf{x}$$

or

$$\mathbf{A} = \sum_{i=1}^{n} \lambda_i(\mathbf{u}_i \mathbf{v}_i^T) \tag{5.6–19}$$

Equation (5.6–19) is called the spectral representation of $\mathbf{A}$, and terms of the form $\mathbf{u}_i \mathbf{v}_i^T$ are called dyads and are similar to the dyadic operator in three-dimensional vector analysis.

In general, $(\mathbf{a}\mathbf{b}^T)\mathbf{x} = (\mathbf{b}, \mathbf{x})\mathbf{a}$, or a dyad maps all vectors $\mathbf{x}$ into a vector $\mathbf{a}$, to within a constant multiplier.

Figure 5.6–1 shows a possible set of eigenvectors $\mathbf{u}_1$ and $\mathbf{u}_2$ with the initial basis vectors e_1 and e_2. $\mathbf{v}_1$ is normal to $\mathbf{u}_2$ and $\mathbf{v}_2$ is normal to $\mathbf{u}_1$. $(v_1, u_1) = (v_2, u_2) = 1$. Now, given the equation

$$\dot{\mathbf{x}}(t) = \mathbf{A}\mathbf{x}(t) \tag{5.6–20}$$

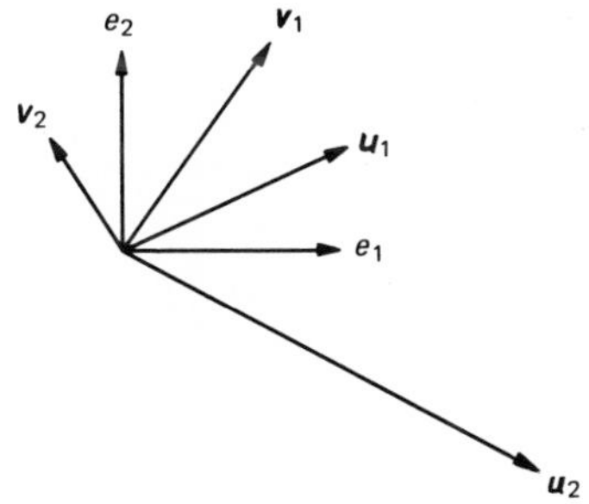

Figure 5.6–1. Reciprocal set of vectors **u** and **v**.

we can assume a solution

$$\mathbf{x}(t) = \sum_{i=1}^{n} \alpha_i(t)\mathbf{u}_i \tag{5.6–21}$$

where the α_i are components on the eigenvectors $\mathbf{u}_i$. Then from the definition of α_i and at $t = 0$,

$$\alpha_i(0) = (\mathbf{v}_i, \mathbf{x}_0)$$

where $\mathbf{x}_0 = \mathbf{x}(0)$.

Put (5.6–21) into (5.6–20) to get

$$\sum_{i=1}^{n} \dot{\alpha}_i \mathbf{u}_i = \mathbf{A} \sum_{i=1}^{n} \alpha_i \mathbf{u}_i$$

$$= \sum_{i=1}^{n} \alpha_i \lambda_i \mathbf{u}_i$$

Then

$$\dot{\alpha}_i = \lambda_i \alpha_i \qquad i = 1, 2, \ldots, n$$

$$\alpha_i = \epsilon^{\lambda_i t}\alpha_i(0)$$

$$= \epsilon^{\lambda_i t}(\mathbf{v}_i, \mathbf{x}_0)$$

Hence from (5.6–21)

$$\mathbf{x}(t) = \sum_{i=1}^{n} \epsilon^{\lambda_i t}(\mathbf{v}_i, \mathbf{x}_0)\mathbf{u}_i$$

$$= \sum_{i=1}^{n} \epsilon^{\lambda_i t}(\mathbf{u}_i\mathbf{v}_i^T)\mathbf{x}_0$$

We show in Chapter 6 that

$$\mathbf{x}(t) = \epsilon^{\mathbf{A}t}\mathbf{x}_0$$

Hence

$$\epsilon^{\mathbf{A}t} = \sum_{i=1}^{n} \epsilon^{\lambda_i t}(\mathbf{u}_i\mathbf{v}_i^T) \tag{5.6–22}$$

The $\mathbf{v}_1$ can be found from (5.6–17)

or

$$\mathbf{V} = (\mathbf{U}^T)^{-1} \tag{5.6–23}$$

Example 5.6–8

If $$\mathbf{A} = \begin{bmatrix} 5 & \sqrt{2} \\ \sqrt{2} & 4 \end{bmatrix} \qquad \lambda_1 = 6, \lambda_2 = 3$$

The eigenvectors (normalized) are

$$\begin{bmatrix} \sqrt{2}/\sqrt{3} \\ 1/\sqrt{3} \end{bmatrix} \begin{bmatrix} -1/\sqrt{3} \\ \sqrt{2}/\sqrt{3} \end{bmatrix}$$

or

$$\mathbf{U} = \frac{1}{\sqrt{3}} \begin{bmatrix} \sqrt{2} & -1 \\ 1 & \sqrt{2} \end{bmatrix}$$

Then

$$\mathbf{V} = \frac{1}{\sqrt{3}} \begin{bmatrix} \sqrt{2} & -1 \\ 1 & \sqrt{2} \end{bmatrix}$$

$$\epsilon^{\mathbf{A}t} = \epsilon^{6t} \frac{1}{\sqrt{3}} \begin{bmatrix} \sqrt{2} \\ 1 \end{bmatrix} \frac{1}{\sqrt{3}} [\sqrt{2} \quad 1] + \epsilon^{3t} \frac{1}{\sqrt{3}} \begin{bmatrix} -1 \\ \sqrt{2} \end{bmatrix} \frac{1}{\sqrt{3}} [-1 \quad \sqrt{2}]$$

$$= \epsilon^{6t} \frac{1}{3} \begin{bmatrix} 2 & \sqrt{2} \\ \sqrt{2} & 1 \end{bmatrix} + \epsilon^{3t} \frac{1}{3} \begin{bmatrix} 1 & -\sqrt{2} \\ -\sqrt{2} & 2 \end{bmatrix}$$

$$= \frac{1}{3} \begin{bmatrix} 2\epsilon^{6t} + \epsilon^{3t} & \sqrt{2}(\epsilon^{6t} - \epsilon^{3t}) \\ \sqrt{2}(\epsilon^{6t} - \epsilon^{3t}) & \epsilon^{6t} + 2\epsilon^{3t} \end{bmatrix}$$

The example illustrates the fact that if the eigenvectors are orthonormal, they form their own reciprocal basis; that is, $\mathbf{U} = \mathbf{V}$.

Actually, spectral representation and diagonalization are essentially the same approach but in slightly different terms [14]. If $\mathbf{A}$ has the canonical form of (5.5–11), then the Vandermonde matrix V of (5.5–12) and its inverse V^{-1} may be used to find the reciprocal basis sets.

5.7 Faddeeva's Method for Matrix Inversion

There are several methods for inverting a square matrix or finding $\mathbf{A}^{-1}$, the most preferable depending on the matrix itself. The most popular is probably the Gaussian elimination method, a variant of which is shown in Appendix B, and, if the matrix is not too ill-conditioned, usually gives a reasonable answer. We now show a method that gives the inverse and the characteristic equation simultaneously. The development follows Fadeeva [15, 16].†

Let the characteristic polynomial be

$$p_n(\lambda) = [\lambda^n + d_1\lambda^{n-1} + d_2\lambda^{n-2} + \cdots + d_n](-1)^n \tag{5.7–1}$$

and have zeros $\lambda_1, \lambda_2, \ldots, \lambda_n$.

Then

$$-d_1 = \lambda_1 + \lambda_2 + \cdots + \lambda_n$$

$$-2d_2 = \lambda_1^2 + \lambda_2^2 + \cdots + \lambda_n^2 + d_1(\lambda_1 + \lambda_2 + \cdots + \lambda_n)$$

$$-3d_3 = \lambda_1^3 + \lambda_2^3 + \cdots + \lambda_n^3 + d_1(\lambda_1^2 + \lambda_2^2 \cdots + \lambda_n^2) + d_2(\lambda_1 + \lambda_2 + \cdots + \lambda_n)$$

$$\cdots\cdots\cdots\cdots\cdots\cdots\cdots\cdots\cdots\cdots\cdots\cdots\cdots\cdots$$

or

$$-kd_k = S_k + d_1S_{k-1} + d_2S_{k-2} + \cdots + d_{k-1}S_1 \tag{5.7–2}$$

where

$$S_k = \sum_{i=1}^{n} \lambda_i^k$$

† We term this "Faddeeva's method," although Faddeeva gives credit to U. J. J. Leverreir and D. K. Faddeev [15].

Equation (5.7–2) is known as Newton's formula [17]. The characteristic equation is given by

$$\det[\lambda\mathbf{I} - \mathbf{A}] = 0 \tag{5.7–3}$$

where

$$\mathbf{A} = \begin{bmatrix} a_{11} & a_{12} & \cdots & a_{1n} \\ a_{21} & a_{22} & \cdots & a_{2n} \\ \cdots & \cdots & \cdots & \cdots \\ a_{n1} & a_{n2} & \cdots & a_{nn} \end{bmatrix}$$

If $\mathbf{A}$ is 2×2,

$$\begin{aligned} \det[\lambda\mathbf{I} - \mathbf{A}] &= (\lambda - a_{11})(\lambda - a_{22}) - a_{21}a_{12} \\ &= \lambda^2 - \lambda(a_{11} + a_{22}) + a_{11}a_{22} - a_{21}a_{12} \end{aligned}$$

From (5.7–1) the characteristic equation in this case is

$$\lambda^2 + d_1\lambda + d_2 = 0$$

Hence

$$-d_1 = a_{11} + a_{22}$$

By continuing this process, you can easily show that if $\mathbf{A}$ is $n \times n$,

$$-d_1 = a_{11} + a_{22} + \cdots + a_{nn}$$

The sum of the coefficients in the leading diagonal of $\mathbf{A}$ is called the trace of $\mathbf{A}$, or

$$\operatorname{tr} \mathbf{A} = a_{11} + a_{22} + \cdots + a_{nn}$$

Hence

$$-d_1 = \operatorname{tr} \mathbf{A} = \lambda_1 + \lambda_2 + \cdots + \lambda_n \tag{5.7–4}$$

By letting $\lambda = 0$ in (5.7–3) and (5.7–1),

$$(-1)^n d_n = \det \mathbf{A} = \lambda_1\lambda_2 \cdots \lambda_n \tag{5.7–5}$$

The eigenvalues of $\mathbf{A}$ are the eigenvalues of $\mathbf{\Lambda}$, the diagonal matrix formed from $\mathbf{A}$. The eigenvalues of $\mathbf{\Lambda}^k$ are $\lambda_1^k, \lambda_2^k, \ldots, \lambda_n^k$, hence we expect the eigenvalues of $\mathbf{A}^k$ to be the same [18]. Thus in general

$$\operatorname{tr} A^k = \lambda_1^k + \lambda_2^k + \cdots + \lambda_n^k \tag{5.7–6}$$

The following algorithm is proposed. Let

$$
\begin{array}{lll}
\mathbf{A}_1 = \mathbf{A} & \text{tr } \mathbf{A}_1 = -q_1 & \mathbf{B}_1 = \mathbf{A}_1 + q_1\mathbf{I} \\
\mathbf{A}_2 = \mathbf{A}\mathbf{B}_1 & \frac{1}{2} \text{ tr } \mathbf{A}_2 = -q_2 & \mathbf{B}_2 = \mathbf{A}_2 + q_2\mathbf{I} \\
\cdots\cdots & \cdots\cdots & \cdots\cdots \\
\mathbf{A}_{n-1} = \mathbf{A}\mathbf{B}_{n-2} & \dfrac{1}{n-1} \text{ tr } \mathbf{A}_{n-1} = -q_{n-1} & \mathbf{B}_{n-1} = \mathbf{A}_{n-1} + q_{n-1}\mathbf{I} \\
\mathbf{A}_n = \mathbf{A}\mathbf{B}_{n-1} & \dfrac{1}{n} \text{ tr } \mathbf{A}_n = -q_n & \mathbf{B}_n = \mathbf{A}_n + q_n\mathbf{I}
\end{array}
\tag{5.7–7}
$$

Since $-\text{tr } \mathbf{A} = d_1 = q_1$, assume that $d_2 = q_2 \cdots d_{k-1} = q_{k-1}$ and prove that

$$d_k = q_k$$

From the algorithm and the assumption

$$\mathbf{A}_k = \mathbf{A}^k + q_1\mathbf{A}^{k-1} + \cdots + q_{k-1}\mathbf{A} \tag{5.7–8a}$$

$$\mathbf{A}_k = \mathbf{A}^k + d_1\mathbf{A}^{k-1} + \cdots + d_{k-1}\mathbf{A} \tag{5.7–8b}$$

Again from the algorithm and (5.7–8),

$$\text{tr } \mathbf{A}_k = -kq_k = \text{tr } \mathbf{A}^k + d_1 \text{ tr } \mathbf{A}^{k-1} + \cdots + d_{k-1} \text{ tr } \mathbf{A} \tag{5.7–9}$$

Or, from (5.7–6),

$$\text{tr } \mathbf{A}_k = S_k + d_1 S_{k-1} + \cdots + d_{k-1} S_1 \tag{5.7–10}$$

Then, using (5.7–2) and (5.7–9),

$$kq_k = kd_k$$

or, finally,

$$q_k = d_k$$

Again from the algorithm

$$
\begin{aligned}
\mathbf{B}_n &= \mathbf{A}^n + d_1\mathbf{A}^{n-1} + \cdots + d_{n-1}\mathbf{A} + d_n\mathbf{I} \\
&= \mathbf{A}_n + d_n\mathbf{I}
\end{aligned}
\tag{5.7–11}
$$

However, from (5.7–8b), the right side of (5.7–11) satisfies the Cayley-Hamilton relation for the matrix **A** and its characteristic equation. Hence

$$\mathbf{B}_n = \mathbf{0}$$

$$\mathbf{A}_n = -d_n\mathbf{I}$$

Since

$$\mathbf{A}_n = \mathbf{A}\mathbf{B}_{n-1} \tag{5.7–12}$$

then

$$\frac{\mathbf{A}\mathbf{B}_{n-1}}{-d_n} = \mathbf{I}$$

$$\mathbf{A}^{-1} = \frac{-1}{d_n}\mathbf{B}_{n-1} \tag{5.7–13}$$

From (5.7–5), $(-1)^n d_n = \det(\mathbf{A})$ and $(-1)^{n-1}\mathbf{B}_{n-1}$ is **Adj A**. $\mathbf{A}\mathbf{B}_{n-1} = -d_n\mathbf{I}$ gives a check on the work in the algorithm described by (5.7–7) with $q_k = d_k$. This method is very slow but is insensitive to the matrix **A**. Note also that we do not need to factor the characteristic equation.

Example 5.7–1

Invert

$$\mathbf{A} = \begin{bmatrix} 1 & 2 & 3 \\ 2 & 1 & 3 \\ 3 & 2 & 1 \end{bmatrix}$$

$$-d_1 = 3 \qquad \mathbf{B}_1 = \begin{bmatrix} 1 & 2 & 3 \\ 2 & 1 & 3 \\ 3 & 2 & 1 \end{bmatrix} - \begin{bmatrix} 3 & & 0 \\ & 3 & \\ 0 & & 3 \end{bmatrix} = \begin{bmatrix} -2 & 2 & 3 \\ 2 & -2 & 3 \\ 3 & 2 & -2 \end{bmatrix}$$

$$\mathbf{A}_2 = \begin{bmatrix} 1 & 2 & 3 \\ 2 & 1 & 3 \\ 3 & 2 & 1 \end{bmatrix}\begin{bmatrix} -2 & 2 & 3 \\ 2 & -2 & 3 \\ 3 & 2 & -2 \end{bmatrix} = \begin{bmatrix} 11 & 4 & 3 \\ 7 & 8 & 3 \\ 1 & 4 & 13 \end{bmatrix}$$

$$-d_2 = 16 \qquad \mathbf{B}_2 = \begin{bmatrix} -5 & 4 & 3 \\ 7 & -8 & 3 \\ 1 & 4 & -3 \end{bmatrix}$$

$$-d_3 = 12 \qquad \mathbf{A}_3 = \begin{bmatrix} 1 & 2 & 3 \\ 2 & 1 & 3 \\ 3 & 2 & 1 \end{bmatrix}\begin{bmatrix} -5 & 4 & 3 \\ 7 & -8 & 3 \\ 1 & 4 & -3 \end{bmatrix}$$

$$= \begin{bmatrix} 12 & & 0 \\ & 12 & \\ 0 & & 12 \end{bmatrix} = 12\mathbf{I}$$

$$\mathbf{A}^{-1} = \frac{\begin{bmatrix} -5 & 4 & 3 \\ 7 & -8 & 3 \\ 1 & 4 & -3 \end{bmatrix}}{12}$$

The characteristic equation is

$$[\lambda^3 - 3\lambda^2 - 16\lambda - 12] = 0$$

Fadeeva also shows a method of using the previous **B** matrices and the eigenvalues to obtain the eigenvectors [19].

5.8 Obtaining Equations in State-Space Form

In Chapter 4 we studied some techniques for getting linear differential equations describing single input-output systems into state-space form. These were developed by writing the state-space equations from the flow diagram. If the Laplace type of transfer function from input to output is given by

$$\frac{Y}{M} = \frac{a_n s^n + a_{n-1}s^{n-1} + a_{n-2}s^{n-2} + \cdots + a_0}{s^n + b_{n-1}s^{n-1} + b_{n-2}s^{n-2} + \cdots + b_0} \tag{5.8–1}$$

then we may find state-space equations

$$\begin{aligned} \dot{\mathbf{x}} &= \mathbf{Ax} + \mathbf{Bm} \\ \mathbf{y} &= \mathbf{Cx} + \mathbf{Dm} \end{aligned} \tag{5.8–2}$$

Note that the polynomials in (5.8–1) are expressed somewhat differently than in Chapter 4. For $a_n = 0$, the Kalman normal forms are convenient. Still other forms for $a_n \neq 0$ may be obtained by algebraic comparison of (5.8–1) and (5.8–2) and an arbitrary selection of coefficients. One of these, sometimes called the "standard" form, is [20]

$$\mathbf{A} = \begin{bmatrix} 0 & 1 & 0 & \cdots & 0 \\ 0 & 0 & 1 & \cdots & 0 \\ \vdots & & & & \\ 0 & 0 & 0 & \cdots & 1 \\ -b_0 & -b_1 & -b_2 & \cdots & -b_{n-1} \end{bmatrix} \qquad \mathbf{B} = \begin{bmatrix} B_1 \\ B_2 \\ \vdots \\ B_n \end{bmatrix} \tag{5.8–3a}$$

$$\mathbf{C} = [1 \quad 0 \quad 0 \quad \cdots] \qquad \mathbf{D} = d \tag{5.8–3b}$$

where $B_1, \ldots, B_n$ and d are found from the equation

$$\begin{bmatrix} 1 & 0 & 0 & \cdots & 0 & 0 \\ b_{n-1} & 1 & 0 & \cdots & 0 & 0 \\ b_{n-2} & b_{n-1} & 1 & \cdots & 0 & 0 \\ \vdots & & & & & \\ b_1 & b_2 & b_3 & \cdots & 1 & 0 \\ b_0 & b_1 & b_2 & \cdots & b_{n-1} & 1 \end{bmatrix} \begin{bmatrix} d \\ B_1 \\ B_2 \\ \vdots \\ \\ B_n \end{bmatrix} = \begin{bmatrix} a_n \\ a_{n-1} \\ a_{n-2} \\ \vdots \\ \\ a_0 \end{bmatrix} \tag{5.8–3c}$$

If the characterization of the system requires simultaneous differential equations involving several variables, it becomes quite difficult to obtain a state-space description using the previous methods. Several techniques have been advanced [21, 22, 23]. A sophisticated and systematic approach will now be outlined. We omit proofs and confine the discussion to two-terminal elements.† As shown in Chapter 2, each element in a linear dynamic system is depicted by an equation involving two variables. For example, for the electrical elements, the variables are current and voltage; for the translational mechanical elements, the variables are force and distance; and so on. We made two classes of these variables: (1) through variables and (2) across variables. That is, if you look at the two nodes forming the terminals of an element, you find that one variable is an "across" quantity, or exists between one node and the other, while the other goes "through" the element. Obviously for the electrical case, the across variable is voltage, and the through variable is current, while for the rotational mechanical case the across variable is torque and the through variable is angular velocity, as already discussed in Chapter 2. The through variable is called a complement of the across variable and vice versa. As we seek equations involving only time derivatives, we chose the element description involving the derivative form and not the integral form. Then using the definitions in Chapter 2 in any system having e elements we immediately have e equations.

The connections of elements into a specific system then require certain constraint relations between the variables. These constraint equations were formed by using Kirchhoff's laws in the electrical network case. We now describe a more general technique based on these laws using electrical terminology for explanatory examples.

To assist in finding the constraint equations, we describe each element by two nodes with directed line between them. The nodes are identified by small letters and the line by a number. The direction of the arrow represents either the direction of the through variable or the polarity of the across variable. As discussed in Chapter 2, the polarity of the voltage across an element and the current through it are intimately associated with the element definition. Thus if the arrow in Figure 5.8–1 represents a current flow, in a passive element the potential of a is higher than b, or the foot of the arrow is at a positive (+) potential relative to the head of the arrow (−).

Again, as pointed out in Chapter 2, the current and potential directions are arbitrary and at our disposal, because they depict or define variables that will be used in the equations to be written. The exceptions to this

† The development here follows H. E. Koenig, who has done much to advance the technique of line graphs [24].

arbitrariness lie in the directivity of the forcing functions or source elements, which must be specified.

Figure 5.8–1 is somewhat like that for a flow diagram, but the definition is different. When we have a system, we put together the component line elements to form a line graph, again reminiscent of the flow diagram. The

Figure 5.8–1. Line graph for element.

purpose of the graph, however, is to aid in our bookkeeping on the constraint equations and not to find input-output relations. The line graph for an electrical network is almost the same as the network description, as shown in Figure 5.8–2.

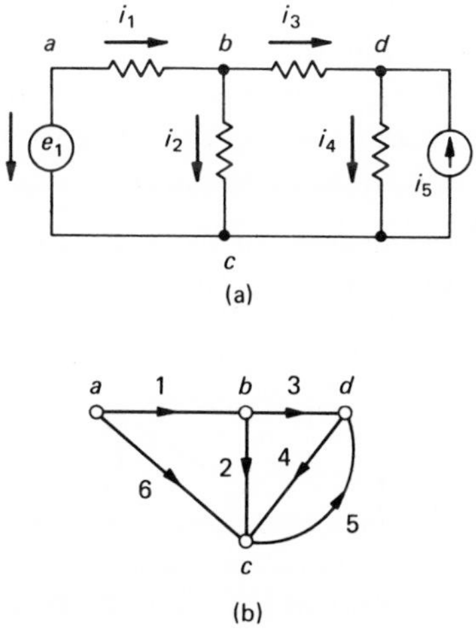

Figure 5.8–2. Line graph for electrical network.

We now define some important quantities, the first being a *path*.

1. A *path* is a subgraph by means of which one proceeds from one node to another.
2. A *loop* is a closed path going from one node back to the same node without proceeding through any node twice. Both a path and a loop

are similar to the same definitions as in a flow diagram, except that here we do not have to follow the arrows in taking a path or a loop (that is, the elements are bilateral and the arrow is a reference direction, not a flow of information as in the flow diagram).

3. A *tree* T of a graph G is a connected subgraph that contains all the nodes of G but has no loops. In some cases it may not be possible to connect all the nodes through line elements into a tree. In these cases it is possible to obtain two or more trees, which are then called a *forest*. Each tree in the forest may be treated separately, and we therefore continue the discussion with one tree T of a graph G_1. Each element in a tree is called a *branch*. A tree with n nodes contains $(n - 1)$ elements or branches.
4. The elements in a graph G, not contained in a tree T are called *links*. The set of elements constituting the links are the complement T' of T. When the links are added to the tree, loops are formed. There are e elements in G_1, and $(n - 1)$ elements in T, so there are $(e - n + 1)$ links or elements in T'. The orientation or reference direction r of a loop may be determined by drawing a directed arrow around the loop, the arrow being in the same direction as that of the chord (link) which causes the loop to close. The loop is said to be defined by this chord.
5. When we remove from the graph G_1 the minimum number of elements that leaves G_1 in exactly two parts, this set of elements is called a *cut set*. The set of $(n - 1)$ cut sets corresponding to any one tree T is defined as a *fundamental* cut set.

Suppose we now illustrate some of these ideas graphically. Let Figure 5.8–3 represent a line graph of some system with six elements. There are a

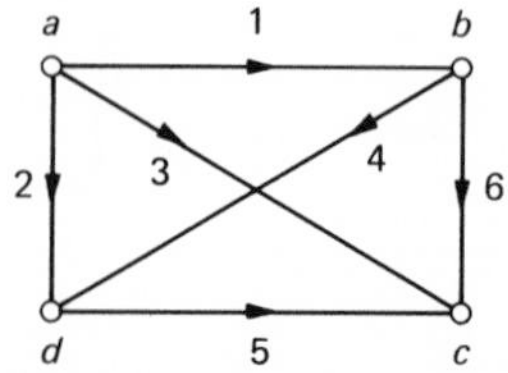

Figure 5.8–3. Six-element line graph.

number of possible trees. Thus in Figure 5.8–4, (a) shows one possible tree T, (b) shows the link set T', and (c) shows the loops. The set of $(e - n + 1)$ loops formed by each of the defining chords of T is called the fundamental set of loops. Figure 5.8–5 shows another possible tree, and the associated links and fundamental loops, and of course there are many other possible trees.

To find the fundamental cut sets associated with a given tree, draw closed lines that cut just *one* branch of the tree *T*, but divide the graph *G* into just two parts. The cut set is said to be defined by this branch. Thus

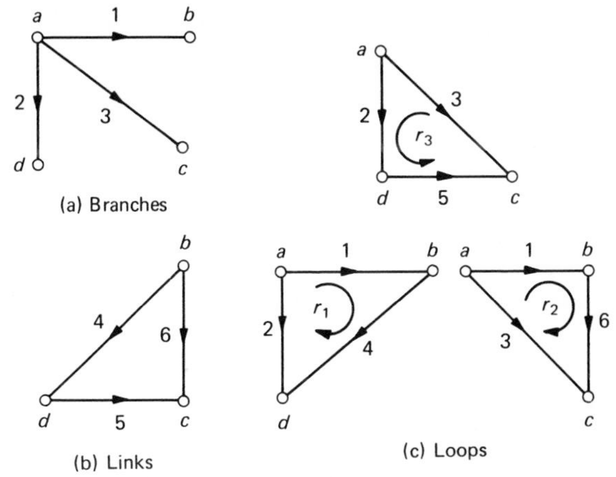

Figure 5.8–4. Possible set of branches, links, and loops for Figure 5.8–3.

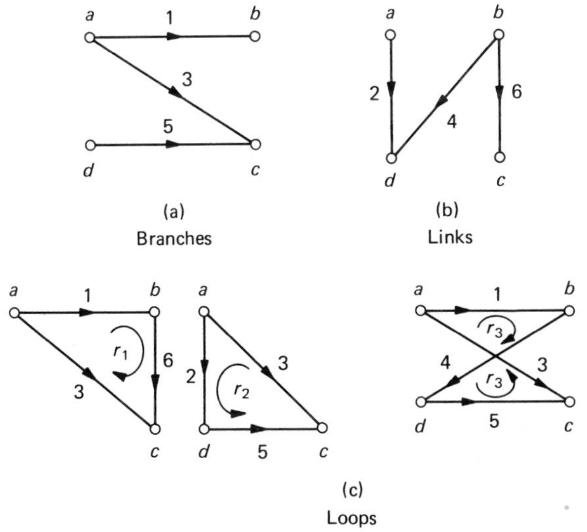

Figure 5.8–5. Another possible set of branches, links, and loops for Figure 5.8–3.

for the tree of Figure 5.8–5 the fundamental cut sets are (5, 4, 2), (1, 6, 4), and (3, 2, 6, 4), as shown in Figure 5.8–6 (an isolated node is considered a part). The orientation or direction of the cut set is taken to be the direction of the defining branch with respect to one of the parts. Corresponding to other trees, we have other fundamental cut sets.

The fundamental set of loops associated with a selected tree now stipulate a set of loop equations using the across variables. Let the across variables associated with the elements 1, 2, ..., e be $v_1, v_2, \ldots, v_e$ and

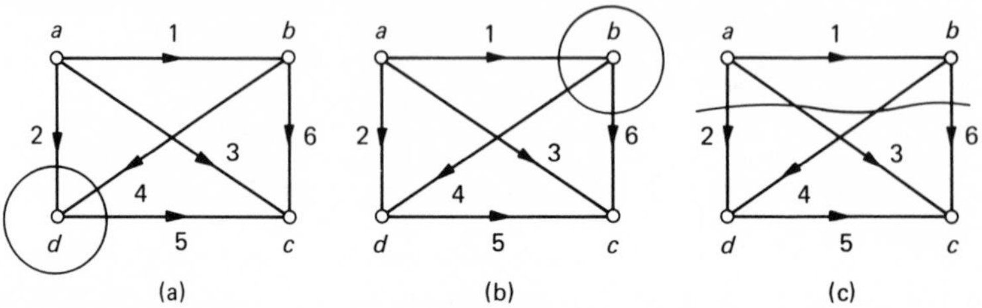

Figure 5.8–6. Method of obtaining fundamental cut sets associated with tree of Figure 5.8–5.

form a vector $\mathbf{v}$ with these components. The components are not necessarily in numerical order; later you will see that it is desirable that the branch across variables appear first, followed by the link variables. Thus in Figure 5.8–5, we might let

$$\mathbf{v} = \begin{bmatrix} v_1 \\ v_3 \\ v_5 \\ v_2 \\ v_4 \\ v_6 \end{bmatrix} = \begin{bmatrix} \mathbf{v}_b \\ \mathbf{v}_e \end{bmatrix} \tag{5.8–4}$$

where

$$\mathbf{v}_b = \begin{bmatrix} v_1 \\ v_3 \\ v_5 \end{bmatrix}$$

is the branch variable vector and

$$\mathbf{v}_e = \begin{bmatrix} v_2 \\ v_4 \\ v_6 \end{bmatrix}$$

is the link variable vector.

We now form a matrix **L** as follows:

1. List as headings of the columns the elements in the same order as selected for the vector **v**.
2. To the left of the matrix, list the fundamental loops in the same order as their defining chords in $\mathbf{v}_e$.
3. Fill in each row of the matrix by inserting a 1 in a column where the loop direction r is the same as the element direction, a (-1) in a column where the loop direction is opposite to that of the element direction, and a 0 if the column element is not part of the loop. Continue for all rows.

In Figure 5.8–5, we have, for example:

	Column					
Loop	**1**	**3**	**5**	**2**	**4**	**6**
2, 3, 5	0	−1	1	1	0	0
4, 5, 3, 1	1	−1	1	0	1	0
6, 3, 1	1	−1	0	0	0	1

With this choice of rows and columns, observe that

$$\mathbf{L} = [\mathbf{F} : \mathbf{I}] \tag{5.8–5}$$

Where in this example

$$\mathbf{F} = \begin{bmatrix} 0 & -1 & 1 \\ 1 & -1 & 1 \\ 1 & -1 & 0 \end{bmatrix}$$

Similarly, the fundamental set of cut sets associated with a selected tree stipulate a set of cut-set equations. Let the through variables associated with the elements 1, 2, ..., e be $i_1, i_2, \ldots, i_e$ and form a vector **i**, and let us list these in the same order as the across variables in the loop equations. We form a matrix **J** as follows:

1. List the heads of the columns the same as before.
2. To the left of the matrix list the fundamental cut sets in the order of the defining branches.
3. Fill in each row of the matrix by inserting a 1 in a column where the cut-set direction is the same as the element direction, a (-1) in a column where the cut-set direction is opposite to the element direction, and a 0 if the element is not part of the cut set.

In Figure 5.8–6, we have, for example:

	Column					
Cut set	**1**	**3**	**5**	**2**	**4**	**6**
1, 6, 4	1	0	0	0	−1	−1
3, 2, 6, 4	0	1	0	1	1	1
5, 4, 2	0	0	1	−1	−1	0

Now we note that

$$\mathbf{J} = [\mathbf{I} : -\mathbf{F}^T] \tag{5.8–6}$$

where $\mathbf{F}^T$ is the transpose of the $\mathbf{F}$ previously found. In general, if we select the through and across variables in the manner shown, then we shall obtain

$$[\mathbf{F} : \mathbf{I}] \begin{bmatrix} \mathbf{v}_b \\ \mathbf{v}_e \end{bmatrix} = \mathbf{0}$$

or

$$-\mathbf{F}\mathbf{v}_b = \mathbf{v}_e \tag{5.8–7}$$

and

$$[\mathbf{I} : -\mathbf{F}^T] \begin{bmatrix} \mathbf{i}_b \\ \mathbf{i}_e \end{bmatrix} = \mathbf{0}$$

or

$$\mathbf{F}^T\mathbf{i}_e = \mathbf{i}_b \tag{5.8–8}$$

where $\mathbf{F}$ and $-\mathbf{F}^T$ are obtained as demonstrated.

Since $\mathbf{F}^T$ is the transpose of $\mathbf{F}$, it is not necessary to write the cut-set equations as shown previously. However, you may find it desirable to do so as a check against the work. Equations (5.8–7) and (5.8–8) together with the original element defining equations, now form the basis of a state-space form. Although we have not proved (5.8–7) or (5.3–8), we note that (5.8–7) follows from Kirchhoff's voltage law and (5.8–8) from Kirchhoff's current law. In non-electrical cases, the analogous physical laws result in the same conclusions. In general $\mathbf{F}$ is not square as in the example.

To produce a state-space form, experience has shown that it helps to select the tree in a specific manner [22, 24]. We call the set of $(n - 1)$ *across* variables connected with the branches of a tree and the set of $(e - n + 1)$ through variables connected with the links *primary* variables and their complementary variables *secondary* variables. If possible, a tree is selected such that (1) the element defining equations for the dynamic components give the derivatives of the primary variables as explicit functions of the secondary variables, and (2) the defining equations for the energy-absorbing components and the forcing functions or sources show primary variables as explicit functions of the secondary variables, or of time t. Item (2) implies that each across type of source should be a branch of the tree and each through type source should be a link. Thus in the electrical network case, the tree should include all the capacitors and voltage sources and the links all the inductors and current sources if possible. Such a tree is called a "proper" tree [22].

Example 5.8–1

Given the network of Figure 5.8–7a. Find a set of state-space equations. Figure 5.8–7b shows a possible line graph. The element defining equations, in the order of numbering in Figure 5.8–7b, are

$$\frac{dv_1}{dt} = \frac{1}{C_1} i_1$$

$$\frac{dv_2}{dt} = \frac{1}{C_2} i_2$$

$$\frac{dv_3}{dt} = \frac{1}{C_3} i_3$$

$$\frac{di_4}{dt} = \frac{1}{L_1} v_4$$

$$\frac{di_5}{dt} = \frac{1}{L_2} v_5$$

$$v_6 = R_1 i_6$$

$$v_7 = R_2 i_7$$

$$i_8 = i_5$$

where all variables are functions of the independent variable time. The primary variables are to the left and the secondary variables are to the right in these equations. This set of equations can be expressed in matrix form as follows:

$$\frac{d}{dt}\begin{bmatrix} v_1 \\ v_2 \\ v_3 \end{bmatrix} = \begin{bmatrix} 1/C_1 & 0 & 0 \\ 0 & 1/C_2 & 0 \\ 0 & 0 & 1/C_3 \end{bmatrix} \begin{bmatrix} i_1 \\ i_2 \\ i_3 \end{bmatrix} \tag{5.8–9}$$

$$\frac{d}{dt}\begin{bmatrix} i_4 \\ i_5 \end{bmatrix} = \begin{bmatrix} 1/L_1 & 0 \\ 0 & 1/L_2 \end{bmatrix} \begin{bmatrix} v_4 \\ v_5 \end{bmatrix} \tag{5.8–10}$$

$$\begin{bmatrix} v_6 \\ v_7 \end{bmatrix} = \begin{bmatrix} R_1 & 0 \\ 0 & R_2 \end{bmatrix} \begin{bmatrix} i_6 \\ i_7 \end{bmatrix} \tag{5.8–11}$$

$$i_8 = i_s \tag{5.8–12}$$

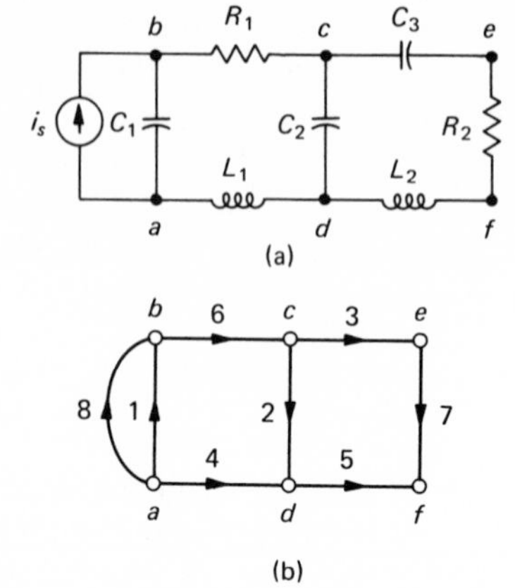

Figure 5.8–7. Network and line graph for Example 5.8–1.

By means of the constraint equations we desire to eliminate the secondary variables. With the tree of Figure 5.8–8, and taking $\mathbf{v}_b = [v_1 v_2 v_3 v_6 v_7]^T$ and $\mathbf{v}_e = [v_4 v_5 v_8]^T$,

$$\mathbf{F} = \begin{array}{c} \begin{matrix} 1 & 2 & 3 & 6 & 7 \end{matrix} \\ \begin{bmatrix} -1 & -1 & 0 & -1 & 0 \\ 0 & 1 & -1 & 0 & -1 \\ -1 & 0 & 0 & 0 & 0 \end{bmatrix} \end{array} \qquad \mathbf{F}^T = \begin{bmatrix} -1 & 0 & -1 \\ -1 & 1 & 0 \\ 0 & -1 & 0 \\ -1 & 0 & 0 \\ 0 & -1 & 0 \end{bmatrix}$$

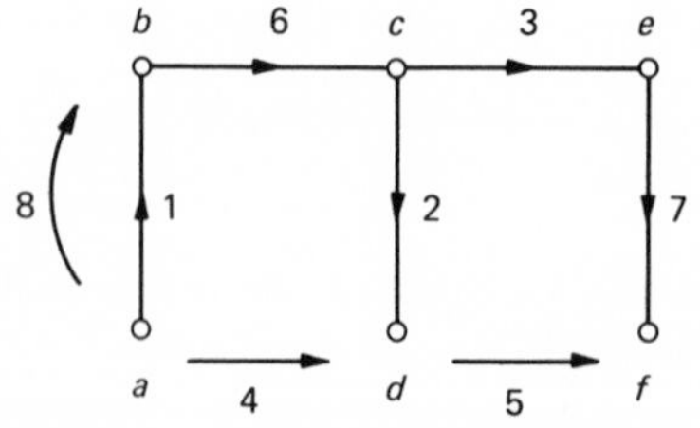

Figure 5.8–8. Tree and links for Example 5.8–1.

From (5.8–7), omitting v_8, which equals v_1,

$$\begin{bmatrix} v_4 \\ v_5 \end{bmatrix} = \begin{bmatrix} 1 & 1 & 0 & 1 & 0 \\ 0 & -1 & 1 & 0 & 1 \end{bmatrix} \begin{bmatrix} v_1 \\ v_2 \\ v_3 \\ v_6 \\ v_7 \end{bmatrix} \tag{5.8–13}$$

and, from (5.8–8),

$$\begin{bmatrix} i_1 \\ i_2 \\ i_3 \\ i_6 \\ i_7 \end{bmatrix} = \begin{bmatrix} -1 & 0 & -1 \\ -1 & 1 & 0 \\ 0 & -1 & 0 \\ -1 & 0 & 0 \\ 0 & -1 & 0 \end{bmatrix} \begin{bmatrix} i_4 \\ i_5 \\ i_8 \end{bmatrix} \tag{5.8–14a}$$

Equation (5.8–14a) gives the two equations

$$\begin{bmatrix} i_1 \\ i_2 \\ i_3 \end{bmatrix} = \begin{bmatrix} -1 & 0 & -1 \\ -1 & 1 & 0 \\ 0 & -1 & 0 \end{bmatrix} \begin{bmatrix} i_4 \\ i_5 \\ i_8 \end{bmatrix} \tag{5.8–14b}$$

$$\begin{bmatrix} i_6 \\ i_7 \end{bmatrix} = \begin{bmatrix} -1 & 0 & 0 \\ 0 & -1 & 0 \end{bmatrix} \begin{bmatrix} i_4 \\ i_5 \\ i_8 \end{bmatrix} \tag{5.8–14c}$$

Substituting (5.8–14b) into (5.8–9) you obtain

$$\frac{d}{dt}\begin{bmatrix} v_1 \\ v_2 \\ v_3 \end{bmatrix} = \begin{bmatrix} -1/C_1 & 0 & -1/C_1 \\ -1/C_2 & 1/C_2 & 0 \\ 0 & -1/C_3 & 0 \end{bmatrix} \begin{bmatrix} i_4 \\ i_5 \\ i_8 \end{bmatrix}$$

or

$$\frac{d}{dt}\begin{bmatrix} v_1 \\ v_2 \\ v_3 \end{bmatrix} = \begin{bmatrix} -1/C_1 & 0 \\ -1/C_2 & 1/C_2 \\ 0 & -1/C_3 \end{bmatrix} \begin{bmatrix} i_4 \\ i_5 \end{bmatrix} + \begin{bmatrix} -1/C_1 \\ 0 \\ 0 \end{bmatrix} i_8 \tag{5.8–15}$$

Substituting (5.8–13) into (5.8–10) results in

$$\frac{d}{dt}\begin{bmatrix} i_4 \\ i_5 \end{bmatrix} = \begin{bmatrix} 1/L_1 & 1/L_1 & 0 & 1/L_1 & 0 \\ 0 & -1/L_2 & 1/L_2 & 0 & 1/L_2 \end{bmatrix} \begin{bmatrix} v_1 \\ v_2 \\ v_3 \\ v_6 \\ v_7 \end{bmatrix} \tag{5.8–16}$$

Substituting (5.8–14c) into (5.8–11) you find

$$\begin{bmatrix} v_6 \\ v_7 \end{bmatrix} = \begin{bmatrix} -R_1 & 0 \\ 0 & -R_2 \end{bmatrix} \begin{bmatrix} i_4 \\ i_5 \end{bmatrix} \tag{5.8–17}$$

We have now eliminated all secondary variables. Next we eliminate the primary variables associated with the energy-absorbing elements. In this case these are v_6 and v_7.

From (5.8–16) you see that

$$\frac{d}{dt}\begin{bmatrix} i_4 \\ i_5 \end{bmatrix} = \begin{bmatrix} 1/L_1 & 1/L_1 & 0 \\ 0 & -1/L_2 & 1/L_2 \end{bmatrix}\begin{bmatrix} v_1 \\ v_2 \\ v_3 \end{bmatrix} + \begin{bmatrix} 1/L_1 & 0 \\ 0 & 1/L_2 \end{bmatrix}\begin{bmatrix} v_6 \\ v_7 \end{bmatrix}$$

Substituting (5.8–17) into the right-most term of this equation, there results

$$\frac{d}{dt}\begin{bmatrix} i_4 \\ i_5 \end{bmatrix} = \begin{bmatrix} 1/L_1 & 1/L_1 & 0 \\ 0 & -1/L_2 & 1/L_2 \end{bmatrix}\begin{bmatrix} v_1 \\ v_2 \\ v_3 \end{bmatrix} + \begin{bmatrix} -R_1/L_1 & 0 \\ 0 & -R_2/L_2 \end{bmatrix}\begin{bmatrix} i_4 \\ i_5 \end{bmatrix}$$

or

$$\frac{d}{dt}\begin{bmatrix} i_4 \\ i_5 \end{bmatrix} = \begin{bmatrix} 1/L_1 & 1/L_1 & 0 & -R_1/L_1 & 0 \\ 0 & -1/L_2 & 1/L_2 & 0 & -R_2/L_2 \end{bmatrix}\begin{bmatrix} v_1 \\ v_2 \\ v_3 \\ i_4 \\ i_5 \end{bmatrix} \quad \textbf{(5.8–18)}$$

Combining (5.8–15) and (5.8–18), we get

$$\frac{d}{dt}\begin{bmatrix} v_1 \\ v_2 \\ v_3 \\ i_4 \\ i_5 \end{bmatrix} = \begin{bmatrix} 0 & 0 & 0 & -1/C_1 & 0 \\ 0 & 0 & 0 & -1/C_2 & 1/C_2 \\ 0 & 0 & 0 & 0 & -1/C_3 \\ 1/L_1 & 1/L_1 & 0 & -R_1/L_1 & 0 \\ 0 & -1/L_2 & 1/L_2 & 0 & -R_2/L_2 \end{bmatrix}\begin{bmatrix} v_1 \\ v_2 \\ v_3 \\ i_4 \\ i_5 \end{bmatrix} + \begin{bmatrix} -1/C_1 \\ 0 \\ 0 \\ 0 \\ 0 \end{bmatrix} i_s$$

(5.8–19)

This is in a state-space form $\dot{\mathbf{x}} = \mathbf{Ax} + \mathbf{Bm}$, where $\dot{\mathbf{x}}$ is the vector on the left side of (5.8–10), $\mathbf{A}$ is the 5×5 matrix, and $\mathbf{B}$ is the 5×1 matrix, both on the right side. Note that in the beginning we could have omitted the source and carried the solution through, adding the source at the end, since it affects only one voltage, v_1, in this case. The state variable v_1 is the voltage of node a with respect to b_1, v_2, the voltage between nodes c and d, v_3, the voltage between nodes c and e, i_4 the current from node a to node d through L_1, and i_5 the current from node d to node f through L_2. All other variables may be found in terms of these.

If the source is not perfect, a current source may be converted to a voltage source, or vice versa, to comply with the requirements that a voltage source exist in a branch and a current source exist in a link. If the sources are perfect, it may not be possible to select a tree as suggested. In some cases a proper tree cannot be found even if source conversions are made.

Example 5.8–2

If in Figure 5.8–7 C_3 becomes an inductance L_3, we cannot make a tree containing all capacitors. We select a tree with the greatest number of capacitor branches. Then the defining equations become

$$\frac{d}{dt}\begin{bmatrix} v_1 \\ v_2 \end{bmatrix} = \begin{bmatrix} 1/C_1 & 0 \\ 0 & 1/C_2 \end{bmatrix}\begin{bmatrix} i_1 \\ i_2 \end{bmatrix}$$

$$\frac{d}{dt}\begin{bmatrix} i_4 \\ i_5 \end{bmatrix} = \begin{bmatrix} 1/L_1 & 0 \\ 0 & 1/L_2 \end{bmatrix}\begin{bmatrix} v_4 \\ v_5 \end{bmatrix}$$

$$\begin{bmatrix} v_3 \\ v_6 \\ v_7 \end{bmatrix} = \begin{bmatrix} L_3(d/dt) & 0 & 0 \\ 0 & R_1 & 0 \\ 0 & 0 & R_2 \end{bmatrix}\begin{bmatrix} i_3 \\ i_6 \\ i_7 \end{bmatrix}$$

$$i_8 = i_s$$

Note that one of the primary variables (v_3) is not in the desired form. The matrix **F** is as before; hence

$$\begin{bmatrix} i_1 \\ i_2 \\ i_3 \end{bmatrix} = \begin{bmatrix} -1 & 0 & -1 \\ -1 & 1 & 0 \\ 0 & -1 & 0 \end{bmatrix}\begin{bmatrix} i_4 \\ i_5 \\ i_8 \end{bmatrix}$$

and

$$\begin{bmatrix} v_4 \\ v_5 \end{bmatrix} = \begin{bmatrix} 1 & 1 \\ 0 & -1 \end{bmatrix}\begin{bmatrix} v_1 \\ v_2 \end{bmatrix} + \begin{bmatrix} 1 & 0 \\ 0 & 1 \end{bmatrix}\begin{bmatrix} v_6 \\ v_7 \end{bmatrix} + \begin{bmatrix} 0 \\ 1 \end{bmatrix} v_3$$

But

$$v_3 = L_3\frac{di_3}{dt} = -L_3\frac{di_5}{dt} \text{ from (5.8–14a)}$$

Hence

$$\begin{bmatrix} v_4 \\ v_5 \end{bmatrix} = \begin{bmatrix} 1 & 1 \\ 0 & -1 \end{bmatrix}\begin{bmatrix} v_1 \\ v_2 \end{bmatrix} + \begin{bmatrix} -R_1 & 0 \\ 0 & -R_2 \end{bmatrix}\begin{bmatrix} i_4 \\ i_5 \end{bmatrix} - \begin{bmatrix} 0 \\ L_3 \end{bmatrix}\frac{di_5}{dt}$$

Then

$$\frac{d}{dt}\begin{bmatrix} i_4 \\ i_5 \end{bmatrix} = \begin{bmatrix} 1/L_1 & 0 \\ 0 & 1/L_2 \end{bmatrix}\begin{bmatrix} 1 & 1 \\ 0 & -1 \end{bmatrix}\begin{bmatrix} v_1 \\ v_2 \end{bmatrix} + \begin{bmatrix} -R_1 & 0 \\ 0 & -R_2 \end{bmatrix}\begin{bmatrix} i_4 \\ i_5 \end{bmatrix} - \begin{bmatrix} 0 \\ L_3 \end{bmatrix}\frac{di_5}{dt}$$

or

$$\frac{d}{dt}\begin{bmatrix} i_4 \\ i_5 \end{bmatrix} = \begin{bmatrix} 1/L_1 & 1/L_1 & -R_1/L_1 & 0 \\ 0 & -\dfrac{1}{L_2+L_3} & 0 & -\dfrac{R_2}{L_2+L_3} \end{bmatrix}\begin{bmatrix} v_1 \\ v_2 \\ i_4 \\ i_5 \end{bmatrix}$$

Combining, we get

$$\frac{d}{dt}\begin{bmatrix} v_1 \\ v_2 \\ i_4 \\ i_5 \end{bmatrix} = \begin{bmatrix} 0 & 0 & 1/C_1 & 0 \\ 0 & 0 & 0 & 1/C_2 \\ 1/L_1 & 1/L_1 & -R_1/L_1 & 0 \\ 0 & -\dfrac{1}{L_2 + L_3} & 0 & -\dfrac{R_2}{L_2 + L_3} \end{bmatrix} \begin{bmatrix} v_1 \\ v_2 \\ i_4 \\ i_5 \end{bmatrix} + \begin{bmatrix} -1/C_1 \\ 0 \\ 0 \\ 0 \end{bmatrix} i_s$$

Note that $\mathbf{A}$ is 4×4, whereas previously it was 5×5.

The general procedure is then

1. Choose a tree such that the maximum number of defining equations give the derivatives of the primary variables as functions of the secondary variables.
2. Write the element-defining equations using the primary variables as functions of the secondary variables.
3. Using the constraint equations found from the loop and cut-set laws, eliminate the secondary variables.
4. Eliminate the primary variables associated with the energy-absorbing elements and the sources.
5. Put the equations into state-space form.

We complete this section with a mechanical example.

Example 5.8–3

In Figure 5.8–9 we have two rotating inertias J_1 and J_2 connected by a spring K_1 and damper B_1. Inertia J_2 is driven by a torque τ_s and is connected to the frame by a spring K_2. Write a state-space set of equations.

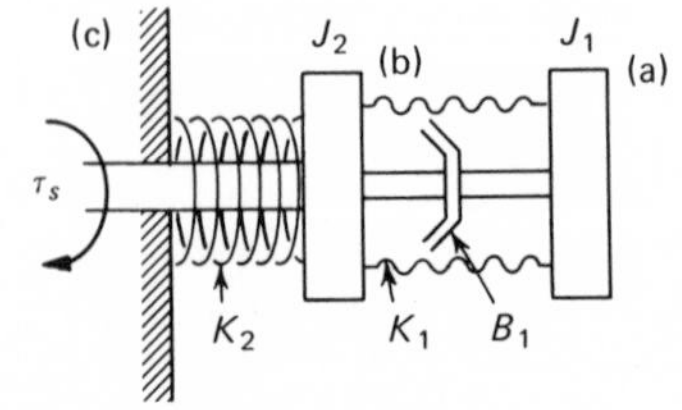

Figure 5.8–9. Mechanical system for Example 5.8–3.

Number the elements as follows: $1 \to J_1$, $2 \to K_1$, $3 \to B_1$, $4 \to J_2$, $5 \to K_2$, and $6 \to \tau_s$. Then a line graph might appear as in Figure 5.8–10a. We select a tree as shown in Figure 5.8–10b with links 2, 3, 5, and 6. The defining equations then are

$$\frac{d}{dt}\begin{bmatrix}\dot{\theta}_1\\ \dot{\theta}_4\end{bmatrix}=\begin{bmatrix}1/J_1 & 0\\ 0 & 1/J_2\end{bmatrix}\begin{bmatrix}\tau_1\\ \tau_4\end{bmatrix}$$

$$\frac{d}{dt}\begin{bmatrix}\tau_2\\ \tau_5\end{bmatrix}=\begin{bmatrix}K_1 & 0\\ 0 & K_2\end{bmatrix}\begin{bmatrix}\dot{\theta}_2\\ \dot{\theta}_5\end{bmatrix}$$

$$\tau_3 = B_1\dot{\theta}_3$$

$$\tau_6 = \tau_s$$

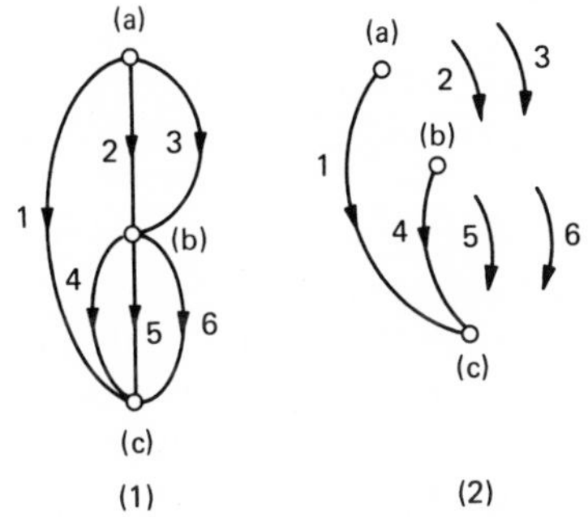

Figure 5.8–10. (a) Line graph for Figure 5.8–9. (b) Tree and links for Figure 5.8–9.

The **F** matrix is

e \ l	1	4	2	3	5	6
2	−1	1				
3	−1	1				
4	0	−1				
5	0	−1				

$$F^T=\begin{bmatrix}-1 & -1 & 0 & 0\\ 1 & 1 & -1 & -1\end{bmatrix}$$

Hence

$$\begin{bmatrix}\tau_1\\ \tau_4\end{bmatrix}=\begin{bmatrix}-1 & -1 & 0 & 0\\ 1 & 1 & -1 & -1\end{bmatrix}\begin{bmatrix}\tau_2\\ \tau_3\\ \tau_5\\ \tau_6\end{bmatrix}$$

$$\begin{bmatrix}\dot{\theta}_2\\ \dot{\theta}_5\end{bmatrix}=\begin{bmatrix}1 & -1\\ 0 & 1\end{bmatrix}\begin{bmatrix}\dot{\theta}_1\\ \dot{\theta}_4\end{bmatrix}$$

$$[\dot{\theta}_3]=[1 \quad -1]\begin{bmatrix}\dot{\theta}_1\\ \dot{\theta}_4\end{bmatrix}$$

Substituting, we get

$$\frac{d}{dt}\begin{bmatrix}\tau_2\\ \tau_5\end{bmatrix}=\begin{bmatrix}K_1 & -K_1\\ 0 & K_2\end{bmatrix}\begin{bmatrix}\dot{\theta}_1\\ \dot{\theta}_4\end{bmatrix}$$

$$\frac{d}{dt}\begin{bmatrix}\dot{\theta}_1\\ \dot{\theta}_4\end{bmatrix}=\begin{bmatrix}-1/J_1 & -1/J_1 & 0 & 0\\ 1/J_2 & 1/J_2 & -1/J_2 & -1/J_2\end{bmatrix}\begin{bmatrix}\tau_2\\ \tau_3\\ \tau_5\\ \tau_6\end{bmatrix}$$

From the last equation,

$$\frac{d}{dt}\begin{bmatrix}\dot{\theta}_1\\ \dot{\theta}_4\end{bmatrix}=\begin{bmatrix}-1/J_1 & 0\\ 1/J_2 & -1/J_2\end{bmatrix}\begin{bmatrix}\tau_2\\ \tau_5\end{bmatrix}+\begin{bmatrix}-1/J_1\\ 1/J_2\end{bmatrix}\tau_3+\begin{bmatrix}0\\ -1/J_2\end{bmatrix}\tau_6$$

Since

$$\tau_3=B_1\dot{\theta}_3=[B_1 \quad -B_1]\begin{bmatrix}\dot{\theta}_1\\ \dot{\theta}_4\end{bmatrix}$$

then

$$\frac{d}{dt}\begin{bmatrix}\dot{\theta}_1\\ \dot{\theta}_4\end{bmatrix}=\begin{bmatrix}-1/J_1 & 0\\ 1/J_2 & -1/J_2\end{bmatrix}\begin{bmatrix}\tau_2\\ \tau_5\end{bmatrix}+\begin{bmatrix}-B_1/J_1 & B_1/J_1\\ B_1/J_2 & -B_1/J_2\end{bmatrix}\begin{bmatrix}\dot{\theta}_1\\ \dot{\theta}_4\end{bmatrix}+\begin{bmatrix}0\\ -1/J_2\end{bmatrix}\tau_6$$

$$\frac{d}{dt}\begin{bmatrix}\dot{\theta}_1\\ \dot{\theta}_4\\ \tau_2\\ \tau_5\end{bmatrix}=\begin{bmatrix}-B_1/J_1 & B_1/J_1 & -1/J_1 & 0\\ B_1/J_2 & -B_1/J_2 & 1/J_2 & -1/J_2\\ K_1 & -K_1 & 0 & 0\\ 0 & K_2 & 0 & 0\end{bmatrix}\begin{bmatrix}\dot{\theta}_1\\ \dot{\theta}_4\\ \tau_2\\ \tau_5\end{bmatrix}+\begin{bmatrix}0\\ -1/J_2\\ 0\\ 0\end{bmatrix}\tau_6$$

Note that in Example 5.8–3 two of the variables are $\dot{\theta}_1$ and $\dot{\theta}_4$. Three and four terminal elements (transistors, transformers, and so on) may be included with little additional work.

State-space forms may also be found directly by applying the Euler-Lagrange canonical forms to energy functions or the Hamiltonian function, as mentioned in Chapter 2. The mechanical engineers exploit this technique more than other engineering disciplines. In the future this will likely become more widespread.

5.9 Control Systems in State Space

We have by no means exhausted the subject of vector spaces, but to avoid a premature exhaustion of the reader, let us see how to apply some of this material to the control problem, developing any additional theory as the need arises.

The object of control is to cause some observed output variables y_1, $y_2, \ldots, y_p$ to reach desired values within some reasonable time, the definition of reasonable depending on the variables and the specific required tasks. To obtain the wanted results, we have certain input variables $m_1, m_2, \ldots, m_l$. The input variables m_i constitute a vector **m** in some input space R^l, and the output variables y_i make up a vector **y** in some output space S^p. Some of the inputs m_i represent disturbances beyond our control. To obtain the outputs y_i using (or in some cases in spite of) the inputs m_i, we work with a subsystem (sometimes called a plant) containing dynamical components, that is, components storing and releasing energy.

The internal situation in the system can be described by numbers which specify the position and momentum of each component; these numbers at any instant represent the state of the system. The system is considered to be causal, or outputs are determined by the past history and inputs. In Figure 5.9–1, the internal state of the system is described by the n component vector **x**. As previously indicated, **x** is not unique, and the components x_i may not be accessible; we can only observe the inputs m_i and the outputs y_i. As outlined in Chapter 1, from these observations we can formulate a structure of the system, which may become more refined as our observations proceed. We can now define somewhat more rigorously a system as a structure with the following qualities [25]:

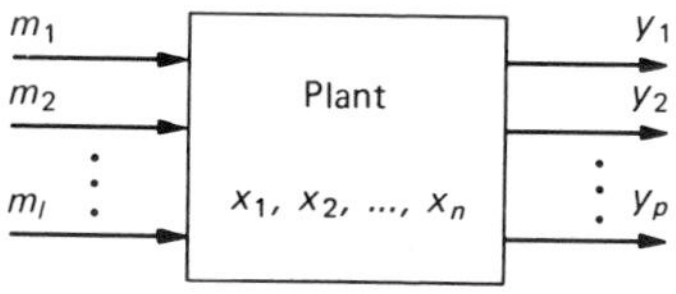

Figure 5.9–1. Multi-input-output system.

1. There is a given state space Σ^n and a set of values of time at which the behavior is defined.
2. There is a given input space R^l that contains the inputs to the system, and these are functions of the admissible time values.
3. For an initial time t_0 and an initial state $\mathbf{x}(t_0)$ in Σ^n, and an input **m** in R^l, the future states of the system are determined by a functional relation, or

$$\mathbf{x}(t) = F[\mathbf{x}(t_0), \mathbf{m}(t_0, t)] \tag{5.9–1}$$

4. The output $\mathbf{y}(t)$ of the system in space S^p is determined by the functional relation

$$\mathbf{y}(t) = E[\mathbf{x}(t_0), \mathbf{m}(t_0, t)] \tag{5.9–2}$$

5. The system is causal (nonanticipatory).

If the functional relations can be described by linear differential equations, then (5.9–1) and (5.9–2) become

$$\dot{\mathbf{x}}(t) = \mathbf{A}(t)\mathbf{x}(t) + \mathbf{B}(t)\mathbf{m}(t) \tag{5.9–3}$$

$$\mathbf{y}(t) = \mathbf{C}(t)\mathbf{x}(t) + \mathbf{D}(t)\mathbf{m}(t) \tag{5.9–4}$$

and if the system is stationary the transformations are time-independent, or

$$\dot{\mathbf{x}}(t) = \mathbf{A}\mathbf{x}(t) + \mathbf{B}\mathbf{m}(t) \tag{5.9–5a}$$

$$\mathbf{y}(t) = \mathbf{C}\mathbf{x}(t) + \mathbf{D}\mathbf{m}(t) \tag{5.9–5b}$$

where $\mathbf{A}$ is an $n \times n$ matrix, $\mathbf{B}$ is an $n \times l$ matrix, $\mathbf{C}$ is a $p \times n$ matrix, and $\mathbf{D}$ an $p \times l$ matrix. For our work, n represents the number of state variables necessary to represent the system or the sum of the highest degrees of the differential equations describing the system. The number of inputs is l, and the number of outputs is p. The matrix $\mathbf{D}$ is often $\mathbf{0}$, or there are no direct relations between input and output. Note that the output vector $\mathbf{y}$ is a linear combination of the state variables $\mathbf{x}_i$, $i = 1, n$. Hence fundamentally system operation is described by the state variable $\mathbf{x}$.

We shall deal with stationary systems, so (5.9–5a) and (5.9–5b) may be taken as definitions of a system. The functional dependence of $\mathbf{x}$, $\mathbf{y}$, and $\mathbf{m}$ on t may be omitted for brevity unless clarification is needed. $\mathbf{x}$ defines the state variable, and all vector quantities are on an initial orthonormal basis. This is a different definition than that given in Chapter 1, which was based on input-output considerations. The relation between the two definitions will be discussed in Chapter 6.

The problem of the control engineer is to manipulate $\mathbf{m}$ to produce the desired $\mathbf{y}$. The system with which the engineer accomplishes this is sometimes called the controller, it being assumed that he can specify the controller but usually has little or nothing to say about the plant. Furthermore, different objectives may govern in different cases. For example, it may be desired to bring the output $\mathbf{y}$ from an initial value to a given value in a minimum amount of time. Or it may be required that the output $\mathbf{y}$ should not overshoot the desired value with a specified input by more than a fixed percentage. It may also be required that these or other objectives be accomplished with a given amount of energy or a given amount of power. We are thus faced not only in building a system to produce certain results but in producing the "best" system in some sense.

In analysis, the engineer finds how a certain system will perform under certain conditions, that is, with given inputs. In synthesis, the engineer attempts to construct a system that will give the desired results. Synthesis is the much more difficult task, because there are a number of possible alternatives, one of which may be the best for a specific application. Usually in picking a system, the engineer must compromise among many requirements, and in the end it becomes necessary to use judgment in weighing these requirements. Obviously, for example, total mass and quantity of fuel require serious consideration for a space system but little or no consideration in a large power plant, whereas cost may be a major factor in the latter case but of minor importance in the former case. Picking number values for these weighting factors is more an art than a science, but experience with past systems at least forms a guide.

We have already discussed in a previous chapter many of the criteria used for conventional design, such as overshoot, rise time, and bandwidth. The philosophy of state-space design has developed from the desire to optimize some performance index. Thus the conventional criteria are guides but are rather vague when it becomes a question of system comparison. Furthermore, as we shall see, design in the complex frequency domain is cut and try to a large degree. Finally, the conventional criteria are difficult to use for multi-input-output systems. The objective, then, is to obtain performance indices that provide analytic solutions of the problem and remove the other objections mentioned.

The performance index J adopted is often an integral. In other words, we desire to minimize an integral of some function of the state, such as

$$J = \int_{t_0}^{t_f} F(\mathbf{x}, \mathbf{m}, \mathbf{y}_d, t)\, dt \tag{5.9–6}$$

where F is a function.

For example, in a single input-output case we might wish to minimize the square of the magnitude of the error, or if $e = (y - y_d)$, then J might be defined as

$$J = \int_{t_0}^{t_f} e^2\, dt \tag{5.9–7}$$

where t_0 and t_f are the initial and final times, respectively. In many cases $t_0 = 0$ and $t_f = \infty$, or

$$J = \int_{0}^{\infty} e^2\, dt \tag{5.9–8}$$

This type of index has already been mentioned in Chapter 3. Or it could be desired to minimize the square of the error plus some known weighting function times the effort, as

$$J = \int_{t_0}^{t_f} (e^2 + \omega m^2)\, dt \tag{5.9–9}$$

where ω is the weighting function.

In another case, we might wish to minimize the squared-error subject to a bound on the square of the effort m. This can be done by using an undetermined Lagrange multiplier λ, or by minimizing

$$J = \int_{t_0}^{t_f} (e^2 + \lambda m^2)\, dt \qquad \textbf{(5.9–10)}$$

An alternative criteria would be to minimize the final position (pursuit problem) as in

$$J = |y(t_f) - y_d(t_f)| \qquad \textbf{(5.9–11)}$$

In other cases, it might be required to minimize the control effort, or to maximize the range with performance indices

$$J = \int_{0}^{t_f} \|m\|^2\, dt \qquad \textbf{(5.9–12)}$$

or

$$J = \|x(t_f) - x(t_0)\| \qquad \textbf{(5.9–13)}$$

Many problems wish to minimize time, or

$$J = \int_{0}^{t_f} dt$$

$$= t_f \qquad \textbf{(5.9–14)}$$

All the previous minimizations may be subject to bounds on the control value m. Such bounds inevitably lead to nonlinear systems; hence we rapidly take evasive action and continue.

In general, the performance index can be written

$$J = \int_{t_0}^{t_f} [(\mathbf{y} - \mathbf{r})^T \mathbf{J} (\mathbf{y} - \mathbf{r}) + \mathbf{m}^T \mathbf{L} \mathbf{m}]\, dt \qquad \textbf{(5.9–15)}$$

where the reference **r** and the desired output are assumed to be identical, and **J** and **L** are matrices of coefficients. We now note that although we have consolidated the criteria into one performance index, we still have to determine the coefficients of **J** and **L**. In other words, the designer must still make a judgment as to the relative importance of various factors; he can be guided in the selection of these factors by experience, but he has few formulas for advance choice. Thus the machine may replace man in many respects, but in the matter of performance criteria the human element is difficult to eliminate.

Some differences in the philosophy of the two approaches may be noted. In the older methods, stability or relative stability are basic. A control with marginal stability (undamped oscillations) has never been considered satisfactory in most cases—thus the emphasis on overshoot, settling time, and so on. In the new state-space approach, stability becomes much less important, and the main aim is to minimize a performance index; in general, this means the response takes whatever form is necessary. Of course, instability of any state variable cannot be allowed, but usually the question of relative stability is secondary to minimization of the desired quantities. It does turn out that systems which minimize the integral of the squared error, for example, do have fast rise time and low overshoot on a step input, as would be suspected from a consideration of the area under the error magnitude curve.

You may wonder why we so often chose a squared quantity (say error), rather than perhaps the magnitude of the error as the integrand in the performance index. The answer is a pragmatic one; problems involving squared terms are much more tractable than other types. Thus the general performance index of (5.9–15) contains quadratic forms. These may result in analytic solutions. However, for some problems there may be a question as to whether a quadratic type of performance index does give the best performance, and computers may be used to find solutions for other indices. For example, rather than using a squared-error criterion for all time, it might seem preferable to deemphasize the error during the first stage of a change, when the error is inevitably large, and emphasize it for later stages. Again, if we compromise somewhat on the performance index, it may be possible to construct a much simpler system than otherwise but whose performance is only slightly different from the optimal one.

The synthesis attack with a performance index results in mathematical complexity, and analytic solutions may be obtained in only very simple cases. In fact, one of the chief criticisms of this approach is the difficulty of achieving a practical system. To retreat from the sky to the earth may require approximations to the exact solutions, but engineers are used to this; their job is to make the dreams of the mathematician and scientist practical.

PROBLEMS

5.1. For a given n, if V is the set of all polynomials with real coefficients and of degree $\leq n$, show that V forms a vector space.

5.2. Show that the set V of all solutions to a homogeneous differential equation with constant coefficients and of degree n constitutes a vector space.

5.3. Discuss the space of all points in a rectangular room with respect to one corner. Do these form a vector space?

5.4. Given the vectors $\mathbf{x}_1, \mathbf{x}_2$, and $\mathbf{x}_3$, denoted by $\{1, 2, 3\}$, $\{1, 1, 4\}$, and $\{0, 1, 3\}$, show whether or not these are linearly independent.

5.5. Show that the set of m vectors $\mathbf{x}_i$ having n components is linearly independent if

$$\det\begin{bmatrix} (\mathbf{x}_1, \mathbf{x}_1) & (\mathbf{x}_1, \mathbf{x}_2) & \cdots & (\mathbf{x}_1, \mathbf{x}_m) \\ (\mathbf{x}_2, \mathbf{x}_1) & (\mathbf{x}_2, \mathbf{x}_2) & \cdots & (\mathbf{x}_2, \mathbf{x}_m) \\ \cdots & \cdots & \cdots & \cdots \\ (\mathbf{x}_m, \mathbf{x}_1) & (\mathbf{x}_m, \mathbf{x}_2) & \cdots & (\mathbf{x}_m, \mathbf{x}_m) \end{bmatrix} \neq 0$$

This determinant is called the Gramiam. [*Hint:* In (5.3–1) let $n = m$ and take the inner product successively with respect to $\mathbf{x}_1, \mathbf{x}_2, \ldots, \mathbf{x}_m$, and examine the solutions of the resulting set of equations for $\alpha_1, \alpha_2, \ldots, \alpha_m$.]

5.6. Using the results of Problem 5.5, find if $\mathbf{x}_1$ and $\mathbf{x}_2$, denoted by $\{1, 5, 2\}$ and $\{2, 6, 3\}$, respectively, are linearly independent.

5.7. Using the results of Problem 5.5, find if x_1 and x_2, denoted by $\{1 + j, j, 2\}$ and $\{-j, 1, j - 2\}$, respectively, are linearly independent.

5.8. Given a set of vectors described by $\{1, 2, 3\}$, $\{2, 3, 1\}$, and $\{3, 2, 1\}$, form one orthonormal set of basis vectors.

5.9. Find the Euclidean norm of each vector of Problem 5.8 and the angles between them.

5.10. If

$$a_1 = 4e_1 + e_2$$

$$a_2 = 3e_1 + e_2$$

where e_1 and e_2 are basis vectors and $x = 6e_1 + 5e_2$, find x in terms of the new basis vectors a_1, a_2.

5.11. If in Problem 5.10 $Y = AX$, where the transformation A is represented by the matrix.

$$\mathbf{A} = \begin{bmatrix} 2 & 1 \\ 2 & 3 \end{bmatrix}$$

find Y on the old basis e_1, e_2 and on the new basis a_1, a_2.

5.12. If an $n \times n$ matrix $\mathbf{A}$ has eigenvalues $\lambda_1, \lambda_2, \ldots, \lambda_n$, show that

(a) $\mathbf{A}^{-1}$ has eigenvalues $1/\lambda_1, 1/\lambda_2, \ldots, 1/\lambda_n$.

(b) $\mathbf{A}^k$ has eigenvalues $\lambda_1^k, \lambda_2^k, \ldots, \lambda_n^k$.

(c) $\mathbf{A}^T$ has eigenvalues $\lambda_1, \lambda_2, \ldots, \lambda_n$.

5.13. For an $n \times n$ matrix $\mathbf{A}$ show that

(a) $\mathbf{A} + \mathbf{A}^T$ is symmetric.

(b) $\mathbf{A} - \mathbf{A}^T$ is skew symmetric.

(c) $(\mathbf{AB})^T = \mathbf{B}^T\mathbf{A}^T$.

(d) $\operatorname{tr}(\mathbf{A} + \mathbf{B}) = \operatorname{tr} \mathbf{A} + \operatorname{tr} \mathbf{B}$.

(e) $\operatorname{tr}(\mathbf{AB}) = \operatorname{tr}(\mathbf{BA})$.

5.14. Show that the eigenvalues of an orthogonal matrix ($A^T = A^{-1}$) have a magnitude of 1.

5.15. If

$$\mathbf{A} = \begin{bmatrix} 1 & 2 \\ 3 & 4 \end{bmatrix} \qquad \mathbf{B} = \begin{bmatrix} 1 & 4 \\ 3 & 2 \end{bmatrix}$$

find

(a) $\mathbf{A} + \mathbf{B}$.

(b) $\mathbf{A} - \mathbf{B}$.

(c) $\mathbf{AB}$ and $\mathbf{BA}$.

(d) $\mathbf{A}^T$, $\mathbf{B}^T$, $(\mathbf{AB})^T$, and $(\mathbf{BA})^T$.

(e) $\mathbf{A}^{-1}$, $\mathbf{B}^{-1}$, $(\mathbf{AB})^{-1}$, and $(\mathbf{BA})^{-1}$.

5.16. Find the conditions on a 2×2 matrix such that $\mathbf{AB} = \mathbf{BA}$.

5.17. Show that the inverse of

$$\mathbf{A} = \begin{bmatrix} 1 & 2 & 1 \\ 1 & 1 & 2 \\ 2 & 3 & 1 \end{bmatrix} \qquad \text{is} \qquad \mathbf{A}^{-1} = \frac{1}{k}\begin{bmatrix} -5 & 1 & 3 \\ 3 & -1 & -1 \\ 1 & 1 & -1 \end{bmatrix}$$

where k is to be calculated, by

(a) Finding the inverse directly.

(b) Showing that $\mathbf{AA}^{-1} = \mathbf{I}$.

5.18. If an $n \times n$ matrix $\mathbf{A}$ is partitioned

$$\mathbf{A} = \left[\begin{array}{c:c} \mathbf{A}_{11} & \mathbf{A}_{12} \\ \hdashline \mathbf{A}_{21} & \mathbf{A}_{22} \end{array}\right]$$

where $\mathbf{A}_{11}$ is $p \times p$, $\mathbf{A}_{12}$ is $p \times q$, $\mathbf{A}_{21}$ is $q \times p$ and $\mathbf{A}_{22}$ is $q \times q$, where $p + q = n$, and $\mathbf{B}$ is partitioned in the same manner, find $\mathbf{B}_{11}$, $\mathbf{B}_{12}$, $\mathbf{B}_{21}$, and $\mathbf{B}_{22}$ in terms of $\mathbf{A}_{11}$, $\mathbf{A}_{12}$, $\mathbf{A}_{21}$, and $\mathbf{A}_{22}$ such that $\mathbf{B} = \mathbf{A}^{-1}$ (see Appendix B).

5.19. Find the inverse of the $\mathbf{A}$ of Problem 5.17 using the partitioning method of Problem 5.18.

5.20. Find the inverse and the characteristic equation for the $\mathbf{A}$ of Problem 5.17 using Faddeeva's method (Section 5.7).

5.21. Given three simultaneous equations represented by $\mathbf{Ax} = \mathbf{b}$, or

$$a_{11}x_1 + a_{12}x_2 + a_{13}x_3 = b_1$$

$$a_{21}x_1 + a_{22}x^3 + a_{23}x_3 = b_2$$

$$a_{31}x_1 + a_{32}x_2 + a_{33}x_3 = b_3$$

multiply row 1 by a_{21}/a_{11} and subtract from row 2, and multiply row 1 by a_{31}/a_{11} and subtract from row 3. Next multiply row 2 by a_{32}^1/a_{22}^1 and subtract from row 3, where a_{32}^1 and a_{22}^1 are the results of the first two operations. The result is now the equation $\mathbf{Bx} = \mathbf{c}$, where $\mathbf{B}$ is an upper triangular matrix (all elements below the main diagonal zero). The elements of $\mathbf{x}$ may now be found in reverse order; x_3, x_2, and x_1. This is called the method of Gaussian elimination. Since $\mathbf{AA}^{-1} = \mathbf{I}$, to find $\mathbf{A}^{-1}$, let $\mathbf{d}_1, \mathbf{d}_2, \mathbf{d}_3$ be the columns of $\mathbf{A}^{-1}$ and $\mathbf{e}_1, \mathbf{e}_2, \mathbf{e}_3$ be the corresponding columns of $\mathbf{I}$;

$$\left(\mathbf{e}_1 = \begin{bmatrix} 1 \\ 0 \\ 0 \end{bmatrix}, \mathbf{e}_2 = \begin{bmatrix} 0 \\ 1 \\ 0 \end{bmatrix}, \mathbf{e}_3 = \begin{bmatrix} 0 \\ 0 \\ 1 \end{bmatrix}\right)$$

Then the solutions of $\mathbf{Ad}_1 = \mathbf{e}_1$, $\mathbf{Ad}_2 = \mathbf{e}_2$, and $\mathbf{Ad}_3 = \mathbf{e}_3$ give the columns of $\mathbf{A}^{-1}$. Find the inverse of the $\mathbf{A}$ of Problem 5.17 by this method.

5.22. Find a matrix $\mathbf{V}$ to diagonalize

$$\mathbf{A} = \begin{bmatrix} 0 & 1 & 0 \\ 0 & 0 & 1 \\ -6 & -11 & -6 \end{bmatrix}$$

and find $\mathbf{V}^{-1}$.

5.23. Given a Vandermonde matrix

$$\mathbf{V} = \begin{bmatrix} 1 & 1 & 1 \\ -1 & 4 & -2 \\ 1 & 16 & 4 \end{bmatrix}$$

find $\mathbf{V}^{-1}$ and an $\mathbf{A}$ in the phase variable form such that $\mathbf{V}$ will diagonalize $\mathbf{A}$.

5.24. Given

$$\mathbf{A} = \begin{bmatrix} 2 & -2 \\ -1 & 3 \end{bmatrix}$$

(a) Find **adj A**.
(b) Find the eigenvalues and (normalized) eigenvectors.
(c) Write the modal matrix **T**.
(d) Using the diagonalizing transformation $\mathbf{x} = \mathbf{Ty}$, find the solution to the differential equation $\dot{\mathbf{x}} = \mathbf{Ax}$ in terms of the initial values of $\mathbf{x}$, $x_1(0)$, and $x_2(0)$.

5.25. Find the eigenvalues, the normalized eigenvectors, the modal matrix, and the diagonal form for the matrix $\mathbf{A}$, where

$$\mathbf{A} = \begin{bmatrix} 4 & 3 & -2 \\ -2 & -1 & 3 \\ 4 & 4 & -1 \end{bmatrix}$$

5.26. Demonstrate that $\mathbf{PAP}^{-1}$ has the same eigenvalues as $\mathbf{A}$ in Problem 5.25, where $\mathbf{P}$ is any 3×3 matrix with an inverse. (Omit the trivial case where $\mathbf{P} = \mathbf{I}$.)

5.27. The Gaussian elimination method of solving a system of linear equations shown in Problem 5.21 is an application of elementary row transformations described in Appendix B. These, in turn, are equivalent to premultiplication by a slightly altered identity matrix. Premultiplication of $\mathbf{A}$ by a unit matrix with an added element k in the ith row and jth column ($i \neq j$) is equivalent to adding k times the jth row to the ith row of A. Find the premultiplying matrices to transform the $\mathbf{A}$ of Problem 5.17 into an upper triangular matrix. Another slightly altered identity matrix will interchange rows. What is it?

5.28. Given a vector

$$\mathbf{a} = \begin{bmatrix} 1 \\ 2 \\ 2 \end{bmatrix}$$

on an orthonormal basis. Express the components of $\mathbf{a}$ as two vectors, one parallel to

$$\mathbf{b} = \begin{bmatrix} 2 \\ 1 \\ 4 \end{bmatrix}$$

and one perpendicular to $\mathbf{b}$, where $\mathbf{b}$ is on the same basis.

5.29. Find the inner and outer products of

$$\mathbf{x} = \begin{bmatrix} 1 \\ 2 \\ -1 \end{bmatrix} \qquad \mathbf{y} = \begin{bmatrix} 3 \\ 1 \\ 2 \end{bmatrix}$$

5.30. Find the rank of

$$\mathbf{A} = \begin{bmatrix} 2 & -1 & 3 \\ 5 & 6 & 4 \\ 3 & 7 & 1 \end{bmatrix}$$

5.31. Given

$$\mathbf{A} = \begin{bmatrix} 2 & -2 \\ 1 & 5 \end{bmatrix}$$

find $\epsilon^{\mathbf{A}t}$ using

(a) Sylvester expansion formula.
(b) Cayley-Hamilton remainder technique.
(c) Spectral representation.

5.32. Repeat Problem 5.31 if

$$\mathbf{A} = \begin{bmatrix} 1 & -5/2 \\ 2 & -3 \end{bmatrix}$$

5.33. For the matrices of Problems 5.31 and 5.32, find $\mathbf{A}^4$, $\mathbf{A}^{1/2}$, and cos **A**, if possible.

5.34. Using the matrix of Problem 5.31, express $\mathbf{A}^4 + 2\mathbf{A}^3 + 3\mathbf{A}^2 + 4\mathbf{A}$ in terms of **A** and **I**.

5.35. If $Q = (\mathbf{x}, \mathbf{Ax})$, transform Q into $(\mathbf{y}, \mathbf{\Lambda y})$, and find the resulting curves for $Q = K$, where K is a constant for the following **A**. Is the origin a minimum, maximum, or neither? Sketch the curves relative to the original x axis.

(a) $\mathbf{A} = \begin{bmatrix} 5/4 & \sqrt{3}/4 \\ \sqrt{3}/4 & 7/4 \end{bmatrix}$ (b) $\mathbf{A} = \begin{bmatrix} 1/4 & -3\sqrt{3}/4 \\ -3\sqrt{3}/4 & -5/4 \end{bmatrix}$

(c) $\mathbf{A} = \begin{bmatrix} 1/2 & 1/2 \\ 1/2 & 1/2 \end{bmatrix}$ (d) $\mathbf{A} = \begin{bmatrix} \sqrt{3}/2 & 1/2 \\ -1/2 & \sqrt{3}/2 \end{bmatrix}$

5.36. If $\mathbf{A} = \begin{bmatrix} 3/\sqrt{2} & \sqrt{2} \\ -3/\sqrt{2} & \sqrt{2} \end{bmatrix}$ find a symmetric matrix **B** which gives the same Q; that is $(\mathbf{x}, \mathbf{Bx}) = (\mathbf{x}, \mathbf{Ax})$.

5.37. Write a digital computer program to invert a matrix (up to 20×20) using the Gaussian elimination method of Problem 5.21.

5.38. Write a digital computer program to invert a matrix and find the characteristic equation using the Faddeeva method. Compare results with Problem 5.37.

5.39. Write state-space equations for the systems described by

(a)
$$\ddot{y}_1 + 4\dot{y}_1 + 2y_1 = \dot{m}_1 + 2m_1 + m_2$$
$$\dot{y}_2 + 2y_2 = -2m_1 + 3m_2$$

(b)
$$\ddot{y}_1 + 3\dot{y}_1 + 4y_2 = m_1 + 3\dot{m}_2 + m_2$$
$$\ddot{y}_2 + 3\dot{y}_1 + 2y_2 = \ddot{m}_2 + 3\dot{m}_1 + m_1$$

[*Hint:* Draw a flow diagram for each system, label the nodes as new variables x_1, x_2, and write the corresponding vector-matrix equations (see also Chapter 4).]

5.40. Write state equations for the systems described by

$$\dddot{y}_1 + 3\ddot{y}_1 + 2y_1 - 6y_2 = m_1 - 5m_2$$
$$\dot{y}_2 - 3y_2 + 2y_1 = 2m_1 + 3m_2$$

5.41. Using flow diagrams, write the transfer function matrices (as functions of s) for the systems of Problem 5.39, that is, the relation between the output vector **y** and the input vector **m**.

5.42. (a) Redo Example 5.8–1 using a different tree.
(b) Redo Example 5.8–3 using a different tree.

5.43. In the antenna example of Chapter 3, find a state-space expression using the techniques of Section 5.8. Compare with a state expression found from the flow diagram.

REFERENCES AND FURTHER READING

[1] B. Friedman, *Principles and Techniques of Applied Mathematics*, Wiley, New York, 1956, pp. 12–13.
[2] D. T. Finkbeiner, II, *Introduction to Matrices and Linear Transformations*, Freeman, San Francisco, 2nd ed., 1966, pp. 187–196.
[3] *Ibid.*
[4] L. P. Huelsman, *Circuits, Matrices and Linear Vector Spaces*, McGraw-Hill, New York, 1963.
[5] Finkbeiner, *op. cit.*, pp. 144–148.
[6] R. Bellman, *Introduction to Matrix Analysis*, McGraw-Hill, New York, 1960, pp. 187–188.
[7] J. T. Tou, *Modern Control Theory*, McGraw-Hill, New York, 1964, pp. 51–53.
[8] L. M. Silverman, Transformation of Time Variable Systems to Canonical (phase variable) Form, *IEEE Trans. Auto. Control*, **11** (1966), 300–303; see also several papers in **11** (1966), 607–610.
[9] P. M. De Russo, R. J. Roy, and C. M. Close, *State Variables for Engineers*, Wiley, New York, 1965, pp. 254–262.
[10] Bellman, *op. cit.*, p. 198.
[11] L. A. Zadeh and C. A. Desoer, *Linear System Theory*, McGraw-Hill, New York, pp. 305–306, 593–596.
[12] Zadeh and Desoer, *op. cit.*, pp. 607–609.
[13] De Russo, Roy, and Close, *op. cit.*, pp. 276–280.
[14] De Russo, Roy, and Close, *op. cit.*, pp. 240, 244.
[15] V. N. Faddeeva, *Computational Methods of Linear Algebra*, Dover, New York, 1959, pp. 177–182.
[16] J. S. Frame, Matrix Functions and Applications, *IEEE Spectrum*, **1** (1964), 123–131.
[17] M. Bocher, *Introduction to Higher Algebra*, Macmillan, New York, 1907, pp. 240–244, and Dover, New York, 1964.
[18] Faddeeva, *op. cit.*, pp. 16–17, 46.
[19] Faddeeva, *op. cit.*, pp. 181–182.
[20] R. J. Schwarz and B. Friedland, *Linear Systems*, McGraw-Hill, New York, 1965, pp. 39–43.
[21] De Russo, Roy, and Close, *op. cit.*, pp. 329–340.
[22] T. R. Bashkow, The A Matrix, A New Network Description, *IRE Trans. Circuit Theory*, **4** (1957), 117–120.
[23] P. R. Bryant, The Explicit Form of Bashkow's A Matrix, *IRE Trans. Circuit Theory*, **9** (1962), 117–120.
[24] H. E. Koenig, Y. Tokad, and H. K. Kesavan, *Analysis of Discrete Physical Systems*, McGraw-Hill, New York, 1967, pp. 1–189.
[25] R. E. Kalman, Mathematical Description of Linear Dynamical Systems, *J. Soc. Ind. Appl. Math.* **A1** (2) (1963), 154–155.
[26] F. R. Gantmacher, *The Theory of Matrices*, Vols. I and II, Chelsea, New York, 1959.

6 Analysis in State Space

6.1 Undriven Systems

Solutions of equations using matrices follow very closely the analogous solutions of scalar equations in the time-invariant case. Time-varying parameters lead to nonanalogous solutions and to the use of the adjoint transformation. In the stationary case, look at the equation

$$\dot{\boldsymbol{\phi}}(t) = \mathbf{A}\boldsymbol{\phi}(t) \qquad \boldsymbol{\phi}(0) = \mathbf{I} \tag{6.1–1}$$

where $\mathbf{A}$ is a constant $n \times n$ matrix and $\boldsymbol{\phi}(t)$ is the solution, called the transition matrix. As in the scalar case, assume that

$$\begin{aligned} \boldsymbol{\phi}(t) &= \epsilon^{\mathbf{A}t} \\ &= \exp(\mathbf{A}t) \end{aligned} \tag{6.1–2}$$

where

$$\exp(\mathbf{A}t) = \mathbf{I} + \mathbf{A}t + \mathbf{A}^2t^2/2! + \cdots + \mathbf{A}^k t^k/k! + \cdots$$

Then

$$\begin{aligned} \frac{d}{dt}[\exp(\mathbf{A}t)] &= \mathbf{A} + \mathbf{A}^2 t + \mathbf{A}^3 t^2/2! + \cdots + \mathbf{A}^{k+1}t^k/k! + \cdots \\ &= \mathbf{A}\exp(\mathbf{A}t) \end{aligned}$$

Hence (6.1–2) is a correct solution to (6.1–1). Then given the undriven system

$$\dot{\mathbf{x}}(t) = \mathbf{A}\mathbf{x}(t) \tag{6.1–3}$$

$$\mathbf{x}(t_0) = \mathbf{x}_0$$

the solution is

$$\mathbf{x}(t) = \exp[\mathbf{A}(t - t_0)]\mathbf{x}_0 \qquad \textbf{(6.1–4)}$$

We anticipated this result in Chapter 5 in our zealous pursuit of exp($\mathbf{A}t$).

In Chapter 5 we investigated various techniques for finding exp($\mathbf{A}t$). To recapitulate, we list the methods here:

1. Cayley-Hamilton with remainder polynomial (Example 5.6–3).
2. Sylvester expansion formula (Example 5.6–5).
3. a. Spectral representation (Example 5.6–8).
   b. Diagonalization (Examples 5.5–5 and 5.5–6; this will be discussed in greater detail subsequently).

Let us now look at a method that utilizes the ideas presented in the Fadeeva method of inverting a matrix and at the same time employs the Laplace transform. If we apply the Laplace transformation to (6.1–3), let $t_0 = 0$ for convenience, and bring the initial condition vector $\mathbf{x}(0)$ to the right side of the equation we get

$$(s\mathbf{I} - \mathbf{A})\mathbf{X}(s) = \mathbf{x}(0) \qquad \textbf{(6.1–5)}$$

where the matrix $\mathbf{I}$ is necessary to maintain a matrix equation. The solution to (6.1–5) in the frequency domain becomes

$$\mathbf{X}(s) = (s\mathbf{I} - \mathbf{A})^{-1}\mathbf{x}(0) \qquad \textbf{(6.1–6)}$$

Hence (6.1–6) allows us to solve the equations in terms of s. An inverse transformation then gives $\mathbf{x}(t)$.

From (6.1–6) and (6.1–4),

$$\boldsymbol{\phi}(t) = \exp(\mathbf{A}t) = \mathscr{L}^{-1}[(s\mathbf{I} - \mathbf{A})^{-1}) \qquad \textbf{(6.1–7)}$$

Example 6.1–1

Let

$$\mathbf{A} = \begin{bmatrix} 5 & \sqrt{2} \\ \sqrt{2} & 4 \end{bmatrix}$$

in (6.1–3). Then

$$(s\mathbf{I} - \mathbf{A}) = \begin{bmatrix} s & 0 \\ 0 & s \end{bmatrix} - \begin{bmatrix} 5 & \sqrt{2} \\ \sqrt{2} & 4 \end{bmatrix} = \begin{bmatrix} s-5 & -\sqrt{2} \\ -\sqrt{2} & s-4 \end{bmatrix}$$

$$(s\mathbf{I} - \mathbf{A})^{-1} = \left(\frac{1}{\det(s\mathbf{I} - \mathbf{A})}\right) \begin{bmatrix} s-4 & \sqrt{2} \\ \sqrt{2} & s-5 \end{bmatrix}$$

Since $\det(s\mathbf{I} - \mathbf{A}) = s^2 - 9s + 18 = (s-6)(s-3)$,

$$(s\mathbf{I} - \mathbf{A})^{-1} = \frac{\begin{bmatrix} s-4 & \sqrt{2} \\ \sqrt{2} & s-5 \end{bmatrix}}{s^2 - 9s + 18}$$

and

$$\exp(\mathbf{A}t) = \mathscr{L}^{-1}\begin{bmatrix} \dfrac{s-4}{(s-6)(s-3)} & \dfrac{\sqrt{2}}{(s-6)(s-3)} \\ \dfrac{\sqrt{2}}{(s-6)(s-3)} & \dfrac{s-5}{(s-6)(s-3)} \end{bmatrix}$$

You can easily verify that this gives the same results as found in Example 5.6–5.

Evaluating $\boldsymbol{\phi}(t)$ then reduces to finding $\mathscr{L}^{-1}(s\mathbf{I} - \mathbf{A})^{-1}$. If

$$(s\mathbf{I} - \mathbf{A})^{-1} = \frac{\mathbf{B}(s)}{\det(s\mathbf{I} - \mathbf{A})} \tag{6.1–8}$$

the denominator $\det(s\mathbf{I} - \mathbf{A})$ is the same as the characteristic polynomial and $\mathbf{A}$ and with s substituted for λ.
Let

$$\det(s\mathbf{I} - \mathbf{A}) = d(s) = s^n + d_1 s^{n-1} + d_2 s^{n-2} + \cdots + d_n \tag{6.1–9}$$

$$\mathbf{B}(s) = s^{n-1}\mathbf{B}_0 + s^{n-2}\mathbf{B}_1 + \cdots + s\mathbf{B}_{n-2} + \mathbf{B}_{n-1} \tag{6.1–10}$$

Then, from (6.1–8),

$$\mathbf{I}(s^n + d_1 s^{n-1} + d_2 s^{n-2} + \cdots + d_n) = (s^{n-1}\mathbf{B}_0 + s^{n-2}\mathbf{B}_1 + \cdots + s\mathbf{B}_{n-2} + \mathbf{B}_{n-1})(s\mathbf{I} - \mathbf{A}) \tag{6.1–11}$$

Equation (6.1–11) requires that

$$\begin{aligned}
\mathbf{B}_0 &= \mathbf{I} \\
\mathbf{B}_1 &= \mathbf{A} + d_1\mathbf{I} \\
\mathbf{B}_2 &= \mathbf{A}\mathbf{B}_1 + d_2\mathbf{I} \\
&\vdots \\
\mathbf{B}_k &= \mathbf{A}\mathbf{B}_{k-1} + d_k\mathbf{I} \\
&\cdots\cdots\cdots\cdots \\
\mathbf{B}_{n-1} &= \mathbf{A}\mathbf{B}_{n-2} + d_{n-1}\mathbf{I} \\
\mathbf{0} &= \mathbf{A}\mathbf{B}_{n-1} + d_n\mathbf{I}
\end{aligned} \tag{6.1–12}$$

The **B** matrices given here are precisely those of the algorithm (5.7–7), where

$$
\begin{aligned}
-d_1 &= \operatorname{tr} \mathbf{A} \\
-d_2 &= \frac{1}{2} \operatorname{tr} \mathbf{A}\mathbf{B}_1 \\
&\vdots \\
-d_k &= \frac{1}{k} \operatorname{tr} \mathbf{A}\mathbf{B}_{k-1} \\
&\cdots\cdots\cdots\cdots \\
-d_n &= \frac{1}{n} \operatorname{tr} \mathbf{A}\mathbf{B}_{n-1}
\end{aligned}
\qquad \textbf{(6.1–13)}
$$

Hence

$$
(s\mathbf{I} - \mathbf{A})^{-1} = \frac{s^{n-1}\mathbf{B}_0 + s^{n-2}\mathbf{B}_1 + \cdots + s\mathbf{B}_{n-2} + \mathbf{B}_{n-1}}{s^n + d_1 s^{n-1} + d_2 s^{n-2} + \cdots + d_n} \qquad \textbf{(6.1–14)}
$$

where the $\mathbf{B}_k$ and d_k are defined by (6.1–12) and (6.1–13).

Example 6.1–2

Find

$$
(s\mathbf{I} - \mathbf{A})^{-1} \qquad \text{where} \qquad \mathbf{A} = \begin{bmatrix} 5 & \sqrt{2} \\ \sqrt{2} & 4 \end{bmatrix}
$$

Solution:

$$
\mathbf{B}_0 = \mathbf{I} \qquad \mathbf{A} = \begin{bmatrix} 5 & \sqrt{2} \\ \sqrt{2} & 4 \end{bmatrix}
$$

and $-d_1 = 9$,

$$
\mathbf{B}_1 = \begin{bmatrix} 5 & \sqrt{2} \\ \sqrt{2} & 4 \end{bmatrix} - \begin{bmatrix} 9 & 0 \\ 0 & 9 \end{bmatrix} = \begin{bmatrix} -4 & \sqrt{2} \\ \sqrt{2} & -5 \end{bmatrix}
$$

$$
\mathbf{A}\mathbf{B}_1 = \begin{bmatrix} 5 & \sqrt{2} \\ \sqrt{2} & 4 \end{bmatrix} \begin{bmatrix} -4 & \sqrt{2} \\ \sqrt{2} & -5 \end{bmatrix} = \begin{bmatrix} -18 & 0 \\ 0 & -18 \end{bmatrix}
$$

and $-d_2 = -18$

$$
\mathbf{A}\mathbf{B}_1 + d_2\mathbf{I} = \mathbf{0} \qquad \text{(check)}
$$

Then

$$
(s\mathbf{I} - \mathbf{A})^{-1} = \frac{\begin{bmatrix} s & 0 \\ 0 & s \end{bmatrix} + \begin{bmatrix} -4 & \sqrt{2} \\ \sqrt{2} & -5 \end{bmatrix}}{s^2 - 9s + 18}
$$

$$
= \frac{\begin{bmatrix} s-4 & \sqrt{2} \\ \sqrt{2} & s-5 \end{bmatrix}}{s^2 - 9s + 18}
$$

which checks Example 6.1–1.

The algorithm made up of (6.1–12) and (6.1–13), is easily programmed for a digital computer and is not limited to the case of distinct eigenvalues [1, 2].

The next job is to find $\mathscr{L}^{-1}(s\mathbf{I} - \mathbf{A})^{-1}$. This proceeds in a manner very similar to obtaining the inverse transform of a scalar; that is, we make a partial fraction expansion and take the inverse of this term by term. For distinct eigenvalues, the partial fraction expansion is easy; if multiple-valued eigenvalues occur, we have more difficult problems, just as in the scalar case.

First, we find the zeros of $\det(s\mathbf{I} - \mathbf{A}) = d(s)$ and put this polynomial in factored form, as $(s - \lambda_1)(s - \lambda_2) \cdots (s - \lambda_n)$, where some multiple zeros may occur. The elements of $\mathbf{B}(s)$ may have common factors that are also factors of $d(s)$. If so, these can be canceled, and (6.1–8) reduces to

$$(s\mathbf{I} - \mathbf{A})^{-1} = \frac{\mathbf{P}(s)}{p(s)} \tag{6.1–15}$$

where $(s - \lambda_k) \cdots (s - \lambda_l)p(s) = d(s)$; $\lambda_k, \ldots, \lambda_l$ being the zeros common to $d(s)$ and all elements of $\mathbf{B}(s)$ and $\mathbf{P}(s)$ being the reduced numerator matrix. $p(s)$ is called the minimal polynomial. The minimal polynomial of $\mathbf{A}$ is the polynomial $F(s)$ with a leading coefficient of 1 and the least degree such that $F(\mathbf{A}) = \mathbf{0}$. If the eigenvalues are all distinct, the minimal polynomial $p(s) = d(s)$.

We can now best describe the process by an example.

Example 6.1–3

Let

$$(s\mathbf{I} - \mathbf{A})^{-1} = \frac{\begin{bmatrix} (s+1)(s+2)(s+3) & (s+1)(s+4) \\ (s+1)(s+3) & (s+1)(s+2)(s+4) \end{bmatrix}}{(s+1)(s+1)(s+1)(s+2)(s^2+3s+9)}$$

An $(s + 1)$ common factor exists. Hence

$$\frac{\mathbf{P}(s)}{p(s)} = \frac{\begin{bmatrix} (s+2)(s+3) & s+4 \\ s+3 & (s+2)(s+4) \end{bmatrix}}{(s+1)^2(s+2)(s^2+3s+9)}$$

$$= \begin{bmatrix} a_{11} & a_{12} \\ a_{21} & a_{22} \end{bmatrix}$$

We now consider the inverse Laplace transforms of a_{11}, a_{12}, a_{21}, and a_{22}. First, look at the multiple pole at $s = -1$. This will give rise to two terms,

$[k_1/(s+1)^2]+k_2/(s+1)$. As shown in Appendix A, if $f(s)=P(s)/Q(s)$ has a pole of the order n at $s=s_k$, and $\phi(s)=(s-s_k)^n f(s)$, then

$$k_1 = \phi(s_k)$$
$$k_2 = \phi^1(s_k)$$
$$\vdots$$
$$k_j = \frac{\phi^{(j-1)} s_k}{(j-1)!}$$
$$\vdots$$
$$k_n = \frac{\phi^{(n-1)}(s_k)}{(n-1)}$$

where $\phi^{(n-1)}(s_k)$ means take the $(n-1)$st derivative of $\phi(s)$ with respect to s, and then evaluate at $s=s_k$. The inverse transform then becomes

$$\mathscr{L}^{-1}[f(s)] = \epsilon^{s_k t}\left[\frac{k_1 t^{n-1}}{(n-1)!} + \frac{k_2 t^{n-2}}{(n-2)!} + \cdots + \frac{k_j t^{n-j}}{(n-j)!} + \cdots + k_n\right]$$

For a_{11} and the pole at $s=-1$, then

$$k_1 = (s+1)^2 \left.\frac{(s+2)(s+3)}{(s+1)^2(s+2)(s^2+3s+9)}\right|_{s=-1} = \frac{-1+3}{1-3+9} = \frac{2}{7}$$

$$k_2 = \left.\frac{d}{ds}\frac{s+3}{s^2+3s+9}\right|_{s=-1} = \frac{5}{49}$$

We continue likewise for the other elements. For a_{11} and the pole at $s=-2$, $k_1=0$. For a_{12} and the pole at $s=-2$,

$$k_1 = \left.\frac{(s+4)}{(s+1)^2(s^2+3s+9)}\right|_{s=-2} = \frac{2}{7}$$

The complex poles may be handled likewise. However, it may be simpler in this case to find a numerator matrix for the quadratic factor (s^2+3s+9). Thus for a_{11},

$$\frac{s+3}{(s+1)^2(s^2+3s+9)} = \frac{2/7}{(s+1)^2} + \frac{5/49}{s+1} + \frac{k_3 s + k_4}{s^2+3s+9}$$

Expanding the right side and equating coefficients,

$$s+3 = \frac{2}{7}(s^2+3s+9) + \frac{5}{49}(s^3+4s^2+12s+9)$$
$$+ k_3(s^3+2s^2+s) + k_4(s^2+2s+1)$$

$$k_3 = -\frac{5}{49} \qquad k_4 = -\frac{24}{49}$$

If there is more than one quadratic factor, this technique becomes difficult. One method to find the constants in the partial fraction expansion on a digital computer is to apply the remainder theorem [3]. Continuing,

$$\frac{\mathbf{P}(s)}{p(s)} = \frac{\begin{bmatrix} \frac{2}{7} & \frac{3}{7} \\ \frac{2}{7} & \frac{3}{7} \end{bmatrix}}{(s+1)^2} + \frac{\begin{bmatrix} \frac{5}{49} & -\frac{17}{49} \\ -\frac{9}{49} & \frac{4}{49} \end{bmatrix}}{s+1} + \frac{\begin{bmatrix} 0 & \frac{2}{7} \\ \frac{1}{7} & 0 \end{bmatrix}}{s+2} + \frac{1}{49}\frac{\begin{bmatrix} -5s-24 & 3s-1 \\ 2s-3 & -4s-29 \end{bmatrix}}{s^2+3s+9} \tag{6.1–16}$$

The inversion is now fairly easy, so

$$\epsilon^{\mathbf{A}t} = t\epsilon^{-t}\left(\frac{1}{7}\right)\begin{bmatrix} 2 & 3 \\ 2 & 3 \end{bmatrix} + \epsilon^{-t}\left(\frac{1}{49}\right)\begin{bmatrix} 5 & -17 \\ -9 & 4 \end{bmatrix} + \epsilon^{-2t}\left(\frac{1}{7}\right)\begin{bmatrix} 0 & 2 \\ 1 & 0 \end{bmatrix}$$
$$+ \frac{\epsilon^{-(3/2)t}}{49}\left[\cos\frac{\sqrt{27}}{2}t - \frac{\sqrt{27}}{9}\sin\frac{\sqrt{27}}{2}t\right]\begin{bmatrix} -5 & 3 \\ 2 & -4 \end{bmatrix}$$
$$+ \frac{\epsilon^{-(3/2)t}}{49}\frac{2}{\sqrt{27}}\sin\frac{\sqrt{27}}{2}t\begin{bmatrix} -24 & -1 \\ -3 & -29 \end{bmatrix}$$

As indicated previously, the practical system will seldom have multiple poles; hence the partial fraction expansion is much easier than in the example. Laplace transform inversion becomes very tedious for matrices of any size. Approximate inversions suitable to a digital computer have been devised and are discussed in references [4], [5], and [6].

Another method of finding $\epsilon^{\mathbf{A}t}$ is by diagonalization, already discussed briefly in Chapter 5. Let

$$\dot{\mathbf{y}}(t) = \mathbf{\Lambda}\mathbf{y}(t_0) \tag{6.1–17}$$

where $\mathbf{\Lambda}$ is a diagonal matrix. The solution is obviously

$$\mathbf{y}(t) = \exp[\mathbf{\Lambda}(t - t_0)]\mathbf{y}_0 \tag{6.1–18}$$

But if we assume distinct eigenvalues,

$$\mathbf{\Lambda} = \begin{bmatrix} \lambda_1 & & & 0 \\ & \lambda_2 & & \\ & & \ddots & \\ 0 & & & \lambda_n \end{bmatrix} \tag{6.1–19}$$

$$\mathbf{\Lambda}^n = \begin{bmatrix} \lambda_1^n & & & 0 \\ & \lambda_2^n & & \\ & & \ddots & \\ 0 & & & \lambda_n^n \end{bmatrix} \tag{6.1–20}$$

Hence from the definition of exp($\mathbf{A}t$),

$$\exp[\mathbf{\Lambda}(t - t_0)] = \begin{bmatrix} \epsilon^{\lambda_1(t-t_0)} & & & 0 \\ & \epsilon^{\lambda_2(t-t_0)} & & \\ & & \ddots & \\ 0 & & & \epsilon^{\lambda_n(t-t_0)} \end{bmatrix} \tag{6.1–21}$$

Therefore, if we convert the system

$$\dot{\mathbf{x}}(t) = \mathbf{A}\mathbf{x}(t_0)$$

to diagonal form, we immediately get a solution.

As shown in Section 5.5, if the system is expressed in the normal form

$$\mathbf{A} = \begin{bmatrix} 0 & 1 & 0 & \cdots & 0 \\ 0 & 0 & 1 & \cdots & 0 \\ \cdot & \cdot & \cdot & \cdots & \cdot \\ 0 & 0 & 0 & \cdots & 1 \\ -b_0 & -b_1 & -b_2 & \cdots & -b_{n-1} \end{bmatrix} \tag{6.1–22}$$

as in the Kalman form of Chapter 4, or the standard form of (5.7–3), and has distinct eigenvalues, then **A** may be diagonalized by the Vandermonde matrix:

$$\mathbf{V} = \begin{bmatrix} 1 & 1 & \cdots & 1 \\ \lambda_1 & \lambda_2 & \cdots & \lambda_n \\ \lambda_1^2 & \lambda_2^2 & \cdots & \lambda_n^2 \\ \cdot & \cdot & \cdots & \cdot \\ \lambda_1^{n-1} & \lambda_2^{n-1} & \cdots & \lambda_n^{n-1} \end{bmatrix} \tag{6.1–23}$$

That is,

$$\mathbf{\Lambda} = \mathbf{V}^{-1}\mathbf{A}\mathbf{V} \tag{6.1–24}$$

Hence the state equation

$$\dot{\mathbf{x}} = \mathbf{A}\mathbf{x} + \mathbf{B}\mathbf{m}$$

becomes

$$\dot{\mathbf{z}} = \mathbf{\Lambda}\mathbf{z} + \mathbf{V}^{-1}\mathbf{B}\mathbf{m} \tag{6.1–25}$$

where

$$\mathbf{z} = \mathbf{V}^{-1}\mathbf{x}$$

Thus

$$\boldsymbol{\phi}(t) = \mathbf{V}\exp(\mathbf{\Lambda}t)\mathbf{V}^{-1} \tag{6.1–26}$$

Example 6.1–4

Let $\dot{\mathbf{x}} = \mathbf{A}\mathbf{x}$, $\mathbf{x}(t_0) = x_0$, where

$$\mathbf{A} = \begin{bmatrix} 0 & 1 \\ -2 & -3 \end{bmatrix}$$

$$\det(\lambda I - A) = \lambda^2 + 3\lambda + 2$$

$$\lambda_1 = -2$$

$$\lambda_2 = -1$$

Then

$$\mathbf{V} = \begin{bmatrix} 1 & 1 \\ -2 & -1 \end{bmatrix}$$

$$\mathbf{V}^{-1}\mathbf{A}\mathbf{V} = \begin{bmatrix} -1 & -1 \\ 2 & 1 \end{bmatrix} \begin{bmatrix} 0 & 1 \\ -2 & -3 \end{bmatrix} \begin{bmatrix} 1 & 1 \\ -2 & -1 \end{bmatrix}$$

$$= \begin{bmatrix} -2 & 0 \\ 0 & -1 \end{bmatrix}$$

Then

$$\boldsymbol{\phi}(t) = \begin{bmatrix} 1 & 1 \\ -2 & -1 \end{bmatrix} \begin{bmatrix} \epsilon^{-2t} & 0 \\ 0 & \epsilon^{-t} \end{bmatrix} \begin{bmatrix} -1 & -1 \\ 2 & 1 \end{bmatrix}$$

$$= \begin{bmatrix} -\epsilon^{-2t} + 2\epsilon^{-t} & -\epsilon^{-2t} + \epsilon^{-t} \\ 2\epsilon^{-2t} - 2\epsilon^{-t} & 2\epsilon^{-2t} - \epsilon^{-t} \end{bmatrix}$$

For a time-varying system, a general explicit analytical solution can be written only if the **A** matrix commutes, or if

$$\mathbf{A}(t_1)\mathbf{A}(t_2) = \mathbf{A}(t_2)\mathbf{A}(t_1) \qquad \text{for all } t_1 \text{ and } t_2 \tag{6.1–27}$$

Assuming (6.1–27) holds,

$$\boldsymbol{\phi}(t, \tau) = \exp \int_\tau^t \mathbf{A}(\lambda)\, d\lambda \tag{6.1–28}$$

$$\mathbf{x}(t) = \boldsymbol{\phi}(t, \tau)\mathbf{x}(\tau) \tag{6.1–29}$$

where τ is the initial condition time.

Unfortunately, **A** seldom satisfies (6.1–27), and some sort of computer solution becomes necessary [7].

Finally, for a nonlinear system, the equations usually cannot be shown with matrix coefficients, although the state-space form is nearly always possible. Solutions must be obtained by computer, as outlined in Chapter 4. Nevertheless, study of linear theory aids greatly in obtaining and understanding such solutions. The state-space equations become

$$\dot{\mathbf{x}}(t) = \mathbf{f}(\mathbf{x}, \mathbf{m}, t) \tag{6.1–30a}$$

$$\mathbf{y}(t) = \mathbf{g}(\mathbf{x}, \mathbf{m}, t) \tag{6.1–30b}$$

where **f** and **g** are general vector functions of **x**, **m**, and t. We can also write (6.1–30a) as

$$\dot{x}_i(t) = f_i(x_1, x_2, \ldots, x_n, m_1, m_2, \ldots, m_l, t) \qquad i = 1, 2, \ldots, n \tag{6.1–31}$$

6.2 Adjoint Transformations

The adjoint transformation constitutes an interesting transformation that has more application in time-varying systems than stationary systems. This transformation relates the solution at the initial time to that of some other time. If we take $t_0 = 0$ in (6.1–4) for convenience, then

$$\mathbf{x}(0) = \boldsymbol{\phi}^{-1}(t)\mathbf{x}(t) \tag{6.2–1}$$

Let $\boldsymbol{\psi}^T(t) = \boldsymbol{\phi}^{-1}(t)$. Then

$$\dot{\boldsymbol{\psi}}^T(t)\boldsymbol{\phi}(t) = \mathbf{I} \tag{6.2–2}$$

where $\boldsymbol{\psi}$ and $\boldsymbol{\phi}$ are both functions of t. Taking the derivative of (6.2–2), $\dot{\boldsymbol{\psi}}^T(t)\boldsymbol{\phi}(t) + \boldsymbol{\psi}^T(t)\dot{\boldsymbol{\phi}}(t) = \mathbf{0}$. Since $\dot{\boldsymbol{\phi}}(t) = \mathbf{A}\boldsymbol{\phi}(t)$,

$$[\dot{\boldsymbol{\psi}}^T(t) + \boldsymbol{\psi}^T(t)\mathbf{A}]\boldsymbol{\phi}(t) = \mathbf{0}$$

If $\boldsymbol{\phi}(t) \neq 0$,

$$\dot{\boldsymbol{\psi}}^T(t) = -\boldsymbol{\psi}^T(t)\mathbf{A}$$

$$\dot{\boldsymbol{\psi}}(t) = -\mathbf{A}^T\boldsymbol{\psi}(t) \tag{6.2–3}$$

Consider the system

$$\dot{\mathbf{z}}(t) = -\mathbf{A}^T\mathbf{z}(t) \tag{6.2–4}$$

where the transition matrix is $\boldsymbol{\psi}(t)$ from (6.2–3). Then

$$\mathbf{z}(t) = \boldsymbol{\psi}(t)\mathbf{z}(0)$$

From this development it is clear that the solution of (6.2–1) is related to the solution of (6.2–4); that is, $\boldsymbol{\phi}^{-1}(t)$ is the transpose of the transition matrix $\boldsymbol{\psi}(t)$ for (6.2–4). For stationary systems this saves a matrix inversion, but for time-varying systems it becomes much more important [8].

Example 6.2–1

Take the system

$$\dot{\mathbf{x}} = \mathbf{A}\mathbf{x} \qquad x(t_0) = x(0) \tag{6.2–5}$$

where

$$\mathbf{A} = \begin{bmatrix} 0 & 1 \\ -2 & -3 \end{bmatrix}$$

The set (6.2–4) is then

$$\dot{\mathbf{z}} = \begin{bmatrix} 0 & 2 \\ -1 & 3 \end{bmatrix}\mathbf{z}$$

Then

$$\boldsymbol{\psi}(t) = \mathscr{L}^{-1}\left(\begin{bmatrix} s & 0 \\ 0 & s \end{bmatrix} - \begin{bmatrix} 0 & 2 \\ -1 & 3 \end{bmatrix}\right)^{-1}$$

$$= \mathscr{L}^{-1}\frac{\begin{bmatrix} s-3 & 2 \\ -1 & s \end{bmatrix}}{(s-1)(s-2)}$$

or

$$\boldsymbol{\psi}(t) = \epsilon^{t}\begin{bmatrix} 2 & -2 \\ 1 & -1 \end{bmatrix} + \epsilon^{2t}\begin{bmatrix} -1 & 2 \\ -1 & 2 \end{bmatrix},$$

and

$$\boldsymbol{\phi}^{-1}(t) = \epsilon^{t}\begin{bmatrix} 2 & 1 \\ -2 & -1 \end{bmatrix} + \epsilon^{2t}\begin{bmatrix} -1 & -1 \\ 2 & 2 \end{bmatrix} \tag{6.2–6}$$

is the solution matrix for the equation

$$\mathbf{x}(0) = \boldsymbol{\phi}^{-1}(t)\mathbf{x}(t)$$

From (6.2–5),

$$\boldsymbol{\phi}(t) = \epsilon^{-t}\begin{bmatrix} 2 & 1 \\ -2 & -1 \end{bmatrix} + \epsilon^{-2t}\begin{bmatrix} -1 & -1 \\ 2 & 2 \end{bmatrix} \tag{6.2–7}$$

The product of $\boldsymbol{\phi}(t)$ from (6.2–7) and $\boldsymbol{\phi}^{-1}(t)$ from (6.2–6) is

$$\boldsymbol{\phi}(t)\boldsymbol{\phi}^{-1}(t) = \mathbf{I}$$

as it should be.

Since $\boldsymbol{\phi}(t) = \exp(\mathbf{A}t)$,

$$\boldsymbol{\phi}(t+\tau) = \exp[A(t+\tau)]$$

or

$$\boldsymbol{\phi}(t+\tau) = \boldsymbol{\phi}(t)\boldsymbol{\phi}(\tau) \tag{6.2–8}$$

If we let $\tau = -t$ in (6.2–8), then

$$\boldsymbol{\phi}(0) = \boldsymbol{\phi}(t)\boldsymbol{\phi}(-t)$$

But since

$$\boldsymbol{\phi}(0) = \mathbf{I}$$

$$\boldsymbol{\phi}(-t) = \boldsymbol{\phi}^{-1}(t) \tag{6.2–9}$$

Comparing (6.2–6) with (6.2–7), you see that Example 6.2–1 agrees with this result.

The adjoint transformation constitutes a sort of reverse time transformation, and we call the system of (6.2–4) the adjoint system. (This adjoint transformation is not the same as the adjoint matrix used with a matrix inversion. The word adjoin unfortunately is used in a great many contexts.)

If we have a one-dimensional system, the trajectory of which starts at state $\mathbf{x}_0$ at time t_0 and proceeds to $\mathbf{x}_T$ in T seconds, then if the adjoint system starts at $\mathbf{x}_T$ at time t_1, it will arrive at $\mathbf{x}_0$ in time $t_1 - T$ seconds.

In general, if the system is time-varying,

$$\boldsymbol{\phi}(t_0, t_1) = \boldsymbol{\phi}^{-1}(t_1, t_0) = \boldsymbol{\psi}^T(t_1, t_0) \tag{6.2–10}$$

The adjoint system is useful if the state is known at some later time, but not at an earlier time, or if boundary conditions at some time t_1 are given. It also becomes prominent in optimal systems [9, 10].

6.3 Driven Systems

Take the fixed state equation

$$\dot{\mathbf{x}}(t) = \mathbf{A}\mathbf{x}(t) + \mathbf{B}\mathbf{m}(t) \tag{6.3–1}$$

In the scalar case, the steady-state solution consists of a convolution integral. Let us assume this situation exists here, that is, that

$$\mathbf{x}(t) = \exp[\mathbf{A}(t - t_0)]\mathbf{x}_0 + \int_{t_0}^{t} \exp[A(t - \tau)]\mathbf{Bm}(\tau)\, d\tau \tag{6.3–2}$$

where $\mathbf{x}(t_0) = \mathbf{x}_0$. However,

$$\exp[\mathbf{A}(t - \tau)] = \exp(\mathbf{A}t)\exp(-\mathbf{A}\tau) \tag{6.3–3}$$

Hence (6.3–2) is equivalent to

$$\mathbf{x}(t) = \exp[\mathbf{A}(t - t_0)]\mathbf{x}_0 + \exp(\mathbf{A}t)\int_{t_0}^{t} \exp(-\mathbf{A}\tau)\mathbf{Bm}(\tau)\, d\tau \tag{6.3–4}$$

Differentiate (6.3–4) to get

$$\dot{\mathbf{x}}(t) = \mathbf{A}\exp[\mathbf{A}(t - t_0)]\mathbf{x}_0 + \mathbf{A}\exp(\mathbf{A}t)\int_{t_0}^{t} \exp(-\mathbf{A}\tau)\mathbf{Bm}(\tau)\, d\tau + \exp(\mathbf{A}t)\exp(-\mathbf{A}t)\mathbf{Bm}(t)$$

and, from (6.2–9),

$$\dot{\mathbf{x}}(t) = \mathbf{A}\left\{\exp[\mathbf{A}(t - t_0)]\mathbf{x}_0 + \exp(\mathbf{A}t)\int_{t_0}^{t} \exp(-\mathbf{A}\tau)\mathbf{Bm}(\tau)\, d\tau\right\} + \mathbf{Bm}(t) \tag{6.3–5}$$

We see that this satisfies (6.3–1). The initial condition is also satisfied, so (6.3–2) is a solution to (6.3–1). As a hand method of computation, (6.3–2) does not offer much hope unless the inputs $\mathbf{m}(t)$ are fairly simple. The integral can be evaluated by computer, however. We can also make the evaluation in the domain of the complex frequency s, as then the convolution integral goes over into a product of two transforms, and the inverse transform may be fairly easy to find. Thus for zero initial conditions where $\mathbf{M}(s)$ is the Laplace transform of $\mathbf{m}(t)$,

$$\mathbf{x}(s) = (s\mathbf{I} - \mathbf{A})^{-1}\mathbf{BM}(s) \tag{6.3–6}$$

Example 6.3–1

Find the solution to

$$\dot{\mathbf{x}}(t) = \mathbf{Ax}(t) + \mathbf{Bm}(t)$$

where

$$\mathbf{A} = \begin{bmatrix} 0 & 1 \\ -6 & -5 \end{bmatrix} \qquad \mathbf{B} = \begin{bmatrix} 0 & 0 \\ 0 & 1 \end{bmatrix} \qquad \mathbf{m} = \begin{bmatrix} 0 \\ 10 \sin 100t \end{bmatrix}$$

$$\mathbf{x}(1) = \begin{bmatrix} 4 \\ 5 \end{bmatrix}$$

Solution:

$$(s\mathbf{I} - \mathbf{A}) = \begin{bmatrix} s & -1 \\ 6 & s+5 \end{bmatrix}$$

The characteristic equation is $s^2 + 5s + 6 = 0$, the zeros of which are

$$s = -3, \; s = -2.$$

The transformed equation is then

$$\mathbf{X}(s) = (s\mathbf{I} - \mathbf{A})^{-1} \begin{bmatrix} x_{10} \\ x_{20} \end{bmatrix} + (s\mathbf{I} - \mathbf{A})^{-1} \begin{bmatrix} 0 \\ \dfrac{10^3}{s^2 + 100^2} \end{bmatrix}$$

where x_{10} and x_{20} are the values of $\mathbf{x}$ at $t = 0_+$. Shift the origin to $t = 1$; then

$$x_{10} = 4 \qquad x_{20} = 5$$

Then, with respect to the new origin,

$$\mathbf{X}(s) = \frac{\begin{bmatrix} s+5 & 1 \\ -6 & s \end{bmatrix}}{(s+3)(s+2)} \begin{bmatrix} 4 \\ 5 \end{bmatrix} + \frac{\begin{bmatrix} s+5 & 1 \\ -6 & s \end{bmatrix}}{(s+3)(s+2)} \begin{bmatrix} 0 \\ \dfrac{10^3}{s^2 + 100^2} \end{bmatrix}$$

$$= \frac{\begin{bmatrix} -2 & -1 \\ 6 & 3 \end{bmatrix}}{s+3} \begin{bmatrix} 4 \\ 5 \end{bmatrix} + \frac{\begin{bmatrix} 3 & 1 \\ -6 & -2 \end{bmatrix} \begin{bmatrix} 4 \\ 5 \end{bmatrix}}{s+2} + \frac{\begin{bmatrix} -2 & -1 \\ 6 & 3 \end{bmatrix} \begin{bmatrix} 0 \\ 10^3 \end{bmatrix}}{(s+3)(s^2 + 100^2)}$$

$$+ \frac{\begin{bmatrix} 3 & 1 \\ -6 & -2 \end{bmatrix} \begin{bmatrix} 0 \\ 10^3 \end{bmatrix}}{(s+2)(s^2 + 100^2)}$$

$$\mathbf{X}(s) = \frac{\begin{bmatrix} -13 \\ 39 \end{bmatrix}}{s+3} + \frac{\begin{bmatrix} 17 \\ -34 \end{bmatrix}}{s+2} + \frac{\begin{bmatrix} -10^3 \\ 3 \times 10^3 \end{bmatrix}}{(s+3)(s^2 + 100^2)} + \frac{\begin{bmatrix} 10^3 \\ -2 \times 10^3 \end{bmatrix}}{(s+2)(s^2 + 100^2)}$$

Transforming back to the time domain,

$$\mathbf{x}(t) = \epsilon^{-3t} \begin{bmatrix} -13 \\ 39 \end{bmatrix} + \epsilon^{-2t} \begin{bmatrix} 17 \\ -34 \end{bmatrix} + \epsilon^{-3t} \frac{10^3}{10^4 + 9} \begin{bmatrix} -1 \\ 3 \end{bmatrix}$$

$$+ \epsilon^{-2t} \frac{10^3}{10^4 + 4} \begin{bmatrix} 1 \\ -2 \end{bmatrix} + \frac{10^3 \sin(100t - \phi)}{(\sqrt{10^4 + 9})(100)} \begin{bmatrix} -1 \\ 3 \end{bmatrix}$$

$$+ \frac{10^3 \sin(100t - \alpha)}{(\sqrt{10^4 + 4})(100)} \begin{bmatrix} 1 \\ -2 \end{bmatrix}$$

where $\phi = \tan^{-1}(100/3)$, $\alpha = \tan^{-1}(100/2)$. Shifting the origin back to $t = 0$,

$$\mathbf{x}(t) = \epsilon^{-3(t-1)}\left(\begin{bmatrix}-13\\ 39\end{bmatrix} + \frac{10^3}{10^4+9}\begin{bmatrix}-1\\ 3\end{bmatrix}\right)$$

$$+ \epsilon^{-2(t-1)}\left(\begin{bmatrix}17\\ -34\end{bmatrix} + \frac{10^3}{10^4+4}\begin{bmatrix}1\\ -2\end{bmatrix}\right)$$

$$+ \frac{10}{\sqrt{10^4+9}}\sin[100(t-1)-\phi]\begin{bmatrix}-1\\ 3\end{bmatrix}$$

$$+ \frac{10}{\sqrt{10^4+4}}\sin[100(t-1)-\alpha]\begin{bmatrix}1\\ -2\end{bmatrix} \qquad t \geq 1$$

If a time-varying system has a driving function, or if

$$\dot{\mathbf{x}}(t) = \mathbf{A}(t)\mathbf{x}(t) + \mathbf{B}(t)\mathbf{m}(t) \tag{6.3–7a}$$

$$y(t) = \mathbf{C}(t)\mathbf{x} \tag{6.3–7b}$$

the transition matrix is $\boldsymbol{\phi}(t, \tau)$, and this replaces $\exp[\mathbf{A}(t - t_0)]$ and $\mathbf{B}$ becomes $\mathbf{B}(t)$ in (6.3–2). The adjoint system is given by

$$\dot{\mathbf{z}}(t) = \mathbf{A}(t)\mathbf{z}(t) + \mathbf{C}(t)\mathbf{m}(t) \tag{6.3–8a}$$

$$\mathbf{y}(t) = \mathbf{B}(t)\mathbf{z}(t) \tag{6.3–8b}$$

It is clear from Example 6.3–1 that hand solutions of systems of any size and with inputs of any complexity would be prohibitively lengthy and difficult. Chances for error would be so great that two persons would be necessary for constant check. For practical problem solutions, we are forced to computers. We also get an added bonus with the computer in that the solutions readily may be extended to time-varying nonlinear and discontinuous systems. Our time in developing matrix solutions has not been wasted, as state-space techniques are vital in obtaining general expressions; furthermore, it is important that we have some "feel" and understanding for the process. Computers will not do the thinking for us; they only remove the drudgery of calculation.

6.4 Computer Solutions in State Space

In Chapter 4 we discussed the simulation of systems with computers. To review this briefly, let us take a single input-output system depicted by the differential equation for the following example.

Example 6.4–1

$$\frac{d^3y}{dt^3} + 6\frac{d^2y}{dt^2} + 11\frac{dy}{dt} + 6y = 2\frac{d^2m}{dt^2} + 8\frac{dm}{dt} + 4m \qquad \textbf{(6.4–1)}$$

Then from Figure 4.5–2 we immediately get one possible analog simulation, as shown in Figure 6.4–1. In Figure 6.4–1, the amplifier inversions and time and magnitude scaling are not considered.

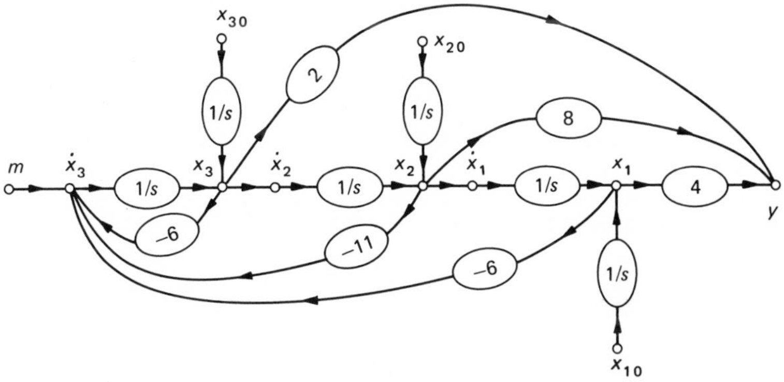

Figure 6.4–1. Analog simulation for Example 6.4–1.

From Figure 6.4–1 or (4.5–6), one state-space representation is thus

$$\dot{\mathbf{x}} = \mathbf{Ax} + \mathbf{Bm}$$

$$\mathbf{y} = \mathbf{Cx} + \mathbf{Dm}$$

where

$$\mathbf{A} = \begin{bmatrix} 0 & 1 & 0 \\ 0 & 0 & 1 \\ -6 & -11 & -6 \end{bmatrix} \qquad \mathbf{B} = \begin{bmatrix} 0 \\ 0 \\ 1 \end{bmatrix}$$

$$\mathbf{C} = [4 \quad 8 \quad 2] \qquad \mathbf{D} = 0$$

From the state-space equations,

$$\mathbf{y} = \mathbf{Cx}$$

$$= 4x_1 + 8x_2 + 2x_3$$

$$\dot{\mathbf{y}} = \mathbf{C}\dot{\mathbf{x}}$$

$$= \mathbf{CAx} + \mathbf{CBm}$$

$$= [-12 \quad -18 \quad -4]\mathbf{x} + 2m$$

$$\ddot{y} = \mathbf{CA}[\mathbf{Ax} + \mathbf{B}m] + \mathbf{CB}\dot{m}$$

$$= [24 \quad 32 \quad 6]\mathbf{x} - 4m + 2\dot{m}$$

or

$$\mathbf{z} = \mathbf{Fx} + \mathbf{G}m + \mathbf{H}\dot{m}$$

where

$$\mathbf{z} = \begin{bmatrix} y \\ \dot{y} \\ \ddot{y} \end{bmatrix} \qquad \mathbf{F} = \begin{bmatrix} 4 & 8 & 2 \\ -12 & -18 & -4 \\ 24 & 32 & 6 \end{bmatrix}$$

$$\mathbf{G} = \begin{bmatrix} 0 \\ 2 \\ -4 \end{bmatrix} \qquad \mathbf{H} = \begin{bmatrix} 0 \\ 0 \\ 2 \end{bmatrix}$$

$$\mathbf{x} = F^{-1}(\mathbf{z} - \mathbf{G}m - \mathbf{H}\dot{m}) \tag{6.4–2}$$

Equation (6.4–2) gives the initial conditions x_{10}, x_{20}, and x_{30} in terms of y, $\dot{y}$, and $\ddot{y}$ and m and $\dot{m}$. If all initial conditions on y are zero, then we may leave the initial condition values on x_{10}, x_{20}, and x_{30} zero and input $m(t)$ only.

The Vandermonde matrix is

$$\mathbf{V} = \begin{bmatrix} 1 & 1 & 1 \\ -1 & -2 & -3 \\ 1 & 4 & 9 \end{bmatrix}$$

$$\mathbf{V}^{-1} = -\tfrac{1}{2} \begin{bmatrix} -6 & -5 & -1 \\ 6 & 8 & 2 \\ -2 & -3 & -1 \end{bmatrix}$$

and the diagonalized equations for Example 6.4–1 then become

$$\dot{\mathbf{w}} = \begin{bmatrix} -1 & 0 & 0 \\ 0 & -2 & 0 \\ 0 & 0 & -3 \end{bmatrix} \mathbf{w} + \tfrac{1}{2} \begin{bmatrix} 1 \\ -2 \\ 1 \end{bmatrix} m \tag{6.4–3a}$$

$$\mathbf{y} = [-2 \quad -4 \quad -2]\mathbf{w} \tag{6.4–3b}$$

The resulting analog simulation for the diagonalized version is shown in Figure 6.4–2, with initial conditions omitted. You see that diagonalization effectively decouples the system so that each state variable is independent of the others. The actual diagonalization in a large system would require the aid of another computer (probably a digital machine), so the practicability of this transformation might be questionable. However the example does illustrate how other simulations might be made once the state equations are known.

In general, the transformation need not be one resulting in a diagonalized form. Some simulations may be simpler than others. If the matrices of Example 6.4–1 were

$$\mathbf{A} = \begin{bmatrix} a_{11} & a_{12} & a_{13} \\ a_{21} & a_{22} & a_{23} \\ a_{31} & a_{32} & a_{33} \end{bmatrix} \qquad \mathbf{B} = \begin{bmatrix} b_{11} \\ b_{12} \\ b_{13} \end{bmatrix}$$

$$\mathbf{C} = [c_{11} \quad c_{12} \quad c_{13}] \qquad \mathbf{n} = \mathbf{0}$$

then simulation would appear as in Figure 6.4–3. This becomes a rather complicated simulation, and it might be preferable to attempt to eliminate some of the couplings. Further, if the number of inputs and outputs increases, the general simulation indeed will become complex.

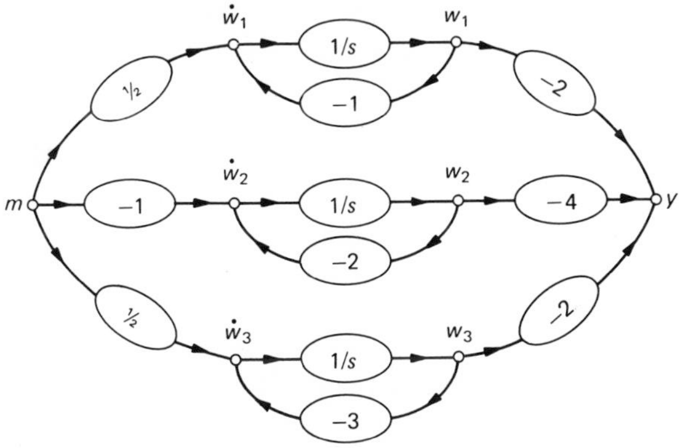

Figure 6.4–2. Diagonalized simulation for Example 6.4–1.

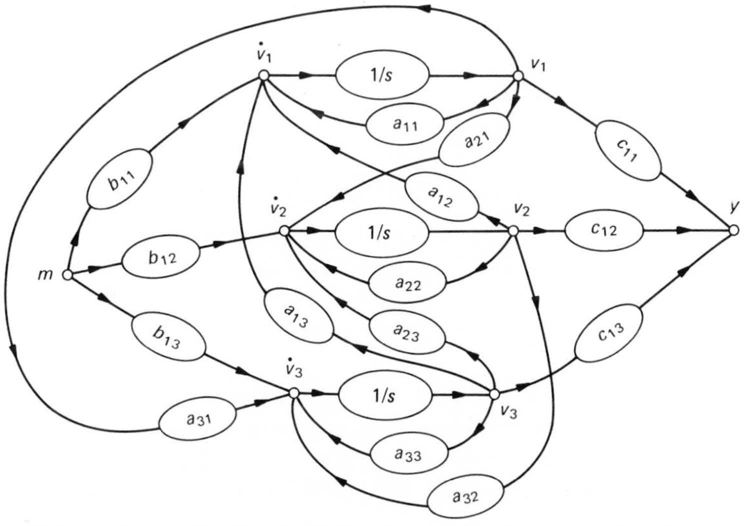

Figure 6.4–3. Possible simulation for a system in state-variable form.

Turning now to digital computer simulation, you see that once we have the equations in state-space form, the solution on the digital computer becomes straightforward. As shown in Section 4.7, solutions of simultaneous equation of the form

$$\dot{x}_i = f_i(x_1, x_2, \ldots, x_n) + g_i(m_1, m_2, \ldots, m_l) \qquad i = 1, \ldots, n \qquad \textbf{(6.4–4)}$$

are conceptually no more difficult than the solution of a single equation, although of course the computer memory and speed must be sufficient to obtain results in a reasonable time.

In recapitulation of these methods, we have repeatedly observed that the state variables are not unique, and these examples emphasize this point. Which set of variables might be the best constitutes a question often difficult to answer. From the standpoint of a computer simulation, one might be preferable to others, as already discussed. As another example, consider the Brachistochrone problem illustrated in Figure 6.4–4, and use a digital computer for solution. It is desired to allow a mass of unit value to proceed from the origin of the x_1x_2 plane to a line $x_1 = l$ under the influence of gravity and with no friction. What is the function $f(x_1, x_2)$ that will minimize the transit time?

This is a problem in the calculus of variations, and in terms of control theory we assume some control function $m(x_1, x_2)$ and with a digital computer we solve the state-space equations until $x_1 = l$, and find the time t_f required. A convenient control here is the angle m in Figure 6.4–4.

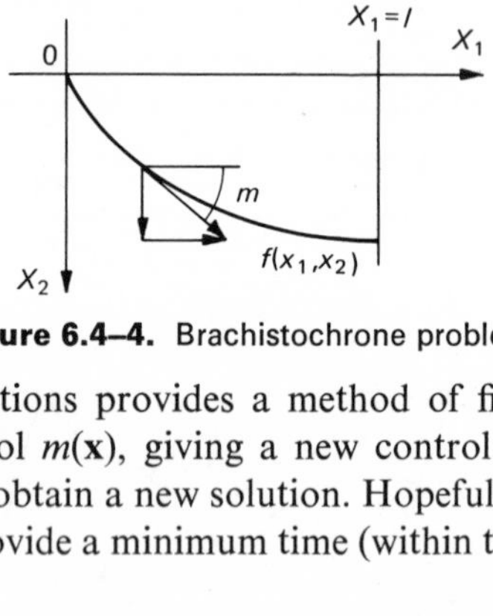

Figure 6.4–4. Brachistochrone problem.

The calculus of variations provides a method of finding a perturbation $\delta(x_1, x_2)$ in the control $m(\mathbf{x})$, giving a new control $m_1(\mathbf{x}) = m(\mathbf{x}) + \delta(\mathbf{x})$, which is then used to obtain a new solution. Hopefully after k iterations of this sort, $m_k(t)$ will provide a minimum time (within the required tolerance) [11].

If we let x_2 be positive downward for convenience, the kinetic energy at any one point must equal the change in potential energy. Hence if s is the curve length at any point (x_1, x_2), $\frac{1}{2}(\dot{s})^2 = gx_2$. But $\dot{x}_2 = \dot{s} \sin m$ and $\dot{x}_1 = \dot{s} \cos m$. Hence one possible set of state equations consists of

$$\dot{x}_1 = \sqrt{2gx_2} \cos m \qquad \textbf{(6.4–5a)}$$

$$\dot{z}_2 = \sqrt{2gx_2} \sin m \qquad \textbf{(6.4–5b)}$$

with t_f, the transit time, to be minimized. The difficulty with (6.4–5) is that at the origin m is about 90° and x_2 is zero. Hence (6.4–5a) has little immediate relevance and neither equation can be started on the integration process. The latter point could be obviated by providing a very small starting value (say 10^{-6}) or by shifting the origin. This proves to be unfeasible, owing to the large influence of (6.4–5b), the small effect of (6.4–5a), and the consequent large perturbations of δm in the vicinity of the origin. The iterations fail to converge.

Another approach is to minimize

$$\int_0^{s_f} \frac{1}{\sqrt{2gx_2}}\, ds$$

with the state equations

$$\frac{dx_1}{ds} = \cos m \tag{6.4–6a}$$

$$\frac{dx_2}{ds} = \sin m \tag{6.4–6b}$$

The difficulty with this is that near the lower limit of the integral the value of the integrand is very large, and slight changes of x_2 cause wild fluctuations in its value.

A third approach is to minimize t_f and let $x_3 = \dot{s}$. Then we have the set of equations

$$\dot{x}_3 = g \sin m \tag{6.4–7a}$$

$$\dot{x}_2 = x_3 \sin m \tag{6.4–7b}$$

$$\dot{x}_1 = x_3 \cos m \tag{6.4–7c}$$

This third set of equations overcomes the difficulties and provides converging iterations. The Brachistochrone problem can be solved analytically, but this discussion illustrates the point with regard to computer solutions.

In practical situations it is often desirable to obtain state variables that are measurable in the system as constructed, or at least some of them which are measurable. That is, the state variables are physical entities actually measurable by physical instruments. This provides a means for easily checking the design and for further refinement in identifying the system (ascertaining its characteristics). Unfortunately this is not always possible, and combinations of the state variables and their derivatives must be used for identification purposes. As soon as derivatives of functions must be obtained, Mephistophelean noise obscures the picture. This constitutes the reason problems simulated on computers avoid derivative operations and concentrate on integral operations and also one reason system identification may be a difficult task.

6.5 Multi-Input-Output Systems

In previous sections we have considered the derivation of state-space equations from the transfer function for single input-output systems, and computer simulation for such systems. Let us continue this for multi-input-output systems. The transfer function in this case is a matrix. As discussed in Chapter 3, the transfer function may be considered to be the transform of the response (output) of the system to an impulse input. In the general case, we apply at the jth input an impulse and observe the ith output as a function of time. This output is then element ij in the impulse response (weighting function) matrix $\mathbf{W}$ of a stationary system. Then if the system is at rest at $t = t_0$ (all initial conditions zero), for any input $\mathbf{m}(t)$,

$$\mathbf{y}(t) = \int_{t_0}^{t} \mathbf{W}(t - \tau)\mathbf{m}(\tau)\, d\tau \qquad \textbf{(6.5–1)}$$

and the transfer function is

$$\mathbf{Z}(s) = \mathscr{L}\mathbf{W}(t) \qquad \textbf{(6.5–2)}$$

where

$$\mathbf{y}(s) = \mathbf{Z}(s)\mathbf{M}(s)$$

If the stationary system equations are

$$\dot{\mathbf{x}}(t) = \mathbf{A}\mathbf{x}(t) + \mathbf{B}\mathbf{m}(t) \qquad \textbf{(6.5–3a)}$$

$$\mathbf{y}(t) = \mathbf{C}\mathbf{x}(t) \qquad \textbf{(6.5–3b)}$$

inspection of (6.5–1) and (6.5–2) indicates that

$$\begin{aligned} \mathbf{W}(t) &= \mathbf{C}\boldsymbol{\phi}(t)\mathbf{B} \qquad & t \geq t_0 \\ &= \mathbf{0} & t < t_0 \end{aligned} \qquad \textbf{(6.5–4)}$$

Hence the weighting function $\mathbf{W}$ may be found from the transition matrix if this is known.†

Experimentally, the weighting function matrix $\mathbf{W}$ can be found by sequentially applying known inputs and observing the outputs in turn.

† Reference [12], p. 121. If $D \neq 0$ and we have a time-varying system, then $\mathbf{W}(t, t_0) = \mathbf{C}(t)\boldsymbol{\phi}(t, t_0)\mathbf{B}(t_0) + \mathbf{D}\delta(t - t_0)$, $t \geq t_0$, where $\boldsymbol{\phi}(t, t_0)$ is time-varying.

Thus in Figure 6.5–1 $y_1, y_2, \ldots, y_p$ are observed for input m_1, all other inputs zero; then for input m_2; and so on. If the inputs are impulses, the outputs give **W** directly. Thus

$$\mathbf{W} = \begin{bmatrix} h_{11} & h_{12} & \cdots & h_{1l} \\ h_{21} & h_{22} & \cdots & h_{2l} \\ \cdots\cdots & & h_{ij} & \cdot\cdot \\ h_{p1} & h_{p2} & \cdots & h_{pl} \end{bmatrix} \tag{6.5–5}$$

where h_{ij} is the response at the ith output to an impulse at the jth input, all initial conditions and all other inputs zero.

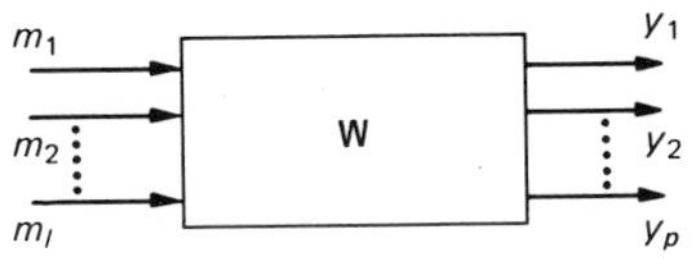

Figure 6.5–1. Multi-input-output system.

In a physical system this may not be so easy to accomplish, because it may be difficult to apply some of the inputs or observe some of the response outputs. Ideally, if we could continuously apply inputs and observe resulting outputs, continuous knowledge of **W** would be available, and corrective measured could be applied if **W** changed. The result would be an adaptive system; that is, one that would automatically adjust to changes in system parameters or external conditions. Continuous knowledge of the system is the keystone to design of the adaptive system, and we again encounter the "information problem." The measuring inputs must be such as not to disturb the system in its normal operation, the outputs (or state variables) must be monitored, and the responses due to the measuring inputs must be separated from the operating responses. A great deal of work has been done on this problem (one technique being the use of random signals), but continuing investigations indicate that it is not easily soluble. At least some knowledge of the system may usually be obtained by direct measurements, however.

Assuming we know **Z**(s), let us continue. If the number of inputs is 1 and the number of outputs is $p > 1$, and we can put **Z**(s) into the form

$$\mathbf{Z}(s) = \frac{1}{s^n + d_n s^{n-1} + \cdots + d_1} \begin{bmatrix} a_{1n} s^{n-1} + \cdots + a_{11} \\ \cdots\cdots\cdots\cdots \\ a_{pn} s^{n-1} + \cdots + a_{p1} \end{bmatrix} \tag{6.5–6}$$

then in the state-space equations (6.5–3a) and (6.5–3b) the matrices are†

$$\mathbf{A} = \begin{bmatrix} 0 & 1 & 0 & \cdots & 0 \\ 0 & 0 & 1 & \cdots & 0 \\ \cdots & \cdots & \cdots & \cdots & \cdots \\ 0 & 0 & 0 & \cdots & 1 \\ -d_1 & -d_2 & -d_3 & \cdots & -d_n \end{bmatrix} \tag{6.5–7a}$$

$$\mathbf{B} = \begin{bmatrix} 0 \\ 0 \\ \vdots \\ 1 \end{bmatrix} \tag{6.5–7b}$$

$$\mathbf{C} = \begin{bmatrix} a_{11} & a_{12} & \cdots & a_{1n} \\ a_{21} & a_{22} & \cdots & a_{2n} \\ \vdots & & & \vdots \\ a_{p1} & \cdots & \cdots & a_{pn} \end{bmatrix} \tag{6.5–7c}$$

If the number of outputs is 1 and the number of inputs >1 and

$$\mathbf{Z}(s) = \left[\frac{a_{n1} s^{n-1} + \cdots + a_{11}}{s^n + d_n s^{n-1} + \cdots + d_1} \cdots \frac{a_{nm} s^{n-1} + \cdots + a_{1m}}{s^n + d_n s^{n-1} + \cdots + d_1} \right]$$

then

$$\mathbf{A} = \begin{bmatrix} 0 & 0 & 0 & \cdots & 0 & -d_1 \\ 1 & 0 & 0 & \cdots & 0 & -d_2 \\ 0 & 1 & 0 & \cdots & 0 & -d_3 \\ \cdots & \cdots & \cdots & \cdots & \cdots & \cdots \\ 0 & 0 & 0 & \cdots & 1 & -d_n \end{bmatrix} \tag{6.5–8a}$$

$$\mathbf{C} = [0 \quad 0 \quad 0 \quad \cdots \quad 1] \tag{6.5–8b}$$

$$\mathbf{B} = \begin{bmatrix} a_{11} & a_{12} & \cdots & a_{1m} \\ a_{21} & a_{22} & \cdots & a_{2m} \\ \vdots & & & \vdots \\ a_{n1} & \cdots & \cdots & a_{nm} \end{bmatrix} \tag{6.5–8c}$$

If no common denominator can be found, then no simple general relation can be given.

If the number of inputs l and outputs p are arbitrary, and if the poles of $\mathbf{Z}(s)$ are all simple (order 1), then Kalman gives the following procedure (attributed to Gilbert) [13].

Let $\mathbf{Z}(s)$ have a total of q distinct poles $s_1, s_2, \ldots, s_q$. Let the residue matrices at each of these poles be $\mathbf{R}_1, \mathbf{R}_2, \ldots, \mathbf{R}_q$, and let

$$\mathbf{R}_k = \mathbf{C}_k \mathbf{B}_k \qquad k = 1, 2, \ldots, q$$

† To see this, draw the flow graph for (6.5–3) and find $y_1(s)$, $y_2(s)$, and so forth.

where $\mathbf{C}_k$ is a $p \times r_k$ matrix, $\mathbf{B}_k$ is a $r_k \times l$ matrix, and r_k is the rank of $\mathbf{R}_k$. Then

$$\mathbf{A} = \begin{bmatrix} s_1 \mathbf{I}_{r1} & \mathbf{0} & \cdots & \mathbf{0} \\ \mathbf{0} & s_2 \mathbf{I}_{r2} & \cdots & \mathbf{0} \\ \cdots & \cdots & \cdots & \cdots \\ \mathbf{0} & \mathbf{0} & \cdots & s_q \mathbf{I}_{r_q} \end{bmatrix} \tag{6.5–9a}$$

where $\mathbf{I}_{rk}$ is an identity matrix of the order r_k,

$$\mathbf{B} = \begin{bmatrix} \mathbf{B}_1 \\ \mathbf{B}_2 \\ \vdots \\ \mathbf{B}_q \end{bmatrix} \tag{6.5–9b}$$

$$\mathbf{C} = [\mathbf{C}_1 \quad \mathbf{C}_2 \quad \cdots \quad \mathbf{C}_q] \tag{6.5–9c}$$

A will be an $n \times n$ matrix, where $n = \sum_{k=1}^{q} r_k$.

Example 6.5–1 [13]

Let

$$\mathbf{Z}(s) = \begin{bmatrix} \dfrac{s+3}{(s+1)(s+2)} & \dfrac{s+4}{(s+2)(s+3)} \\ \dfrac{s+2}{(s+1)(s+4)} & \dfrac{s+5}{(s+1)(s+2)} \end{bmatrix}$$

The number of inputs $l = 2$, and the number of outputs $p = 2$. Then $s_1 = -1$, $s_2 = -2$, $s_3 = -3$, and $s_4 = -4$.

$$\mathbf{R}_1 = \begin{bmatrix} 2 & 0 \\ 1/3 & 4 \end{bmatrix} \qquad \mathbf{R}_2 = \begin{bmatrix} -1 & 2 \\ 0 & -3 \end{bmatrix}$$

$$\mathbf{R}_3 = \begin{bmatrix} 0 & -1 \\ 0 & 0 \end{bmatrix} \qquad \mathbf{R}_4 = \begin{bmatrix} 0 & 0 \\ 2/3 & 0 \end{bmatrix}$$

$r_1 = 2$, $r_2 = 2$, $r_3 = 1$, and $r_4 = 1$. Then making $\mathbf{R}_k = \mathbf{C}_k \mathbf{B}_k$,

$$\begin{bmatrix} 2 & 0 \\ \frac{1}{3} & 4 \end{bmatrix} = \begin{bmatrix} 1 & -\frac{6}{11} \\ \frac{13}{6} & 1 \end{bmatrix} \begin{bmatrix} 1 & 1 \\ -\frac{11}{6} & \frac{11}{6} \end{bmatrix}$$

$$\begin{bmatrix} -1 & 2 \\ 0 & -3 \end{bmatrix} = \begin{bmatrix} 1 & -1 \\ -2 & 1 \end{bmatrix} \begin{bmatrix} 1 & 1 \\ 2 & -1 \end{bmatrix}$$

$$\begin{bmatrix} 0 & -1 \\ 0 & 0 \end{bmatrix} = \begin{bmatrix} 1 \\ 0 \end{bmatrix} [0 \quad -1]$$

$$\begin{bmatrix} 0 & 0 \\ \frac{2}{3} & 0 \end{bmatrix} = \begin{bmatrix} 0 \\ \frac{2}{3} \end{bmatrix} [1 \quad 0]$$

and

$$\mathbf{A} = \begin{bmatrix} -1 & 0 & 0 & 0 & 0 & 0 \\ 0 & -1 & 0 & 0 & 0 & 0 \\ 0 & 0 & -2 & 0 & 0 & 0 \\ 0 & 0 & 0 & -2 & 0 & 0 \\ 0 & 0 & 0 & 0 & -3 & 0 \\ 0 & 0 & 0 & 0 & 0 & -4 \end{bmatrix}$$

$$\mathbf{B} = \begin{bmatrix} 1 & 1 \\ -\frac{11}{6} & \frac{11}{6} \\ 1 & 1 \\ 2 & -1 \\ 0 & -1 \\ 1 & 0 \end{bmatrix} \qquad \mathbf{C} = \begin{bmatrix} 1 & -\frac{6}{11} & 1 & -1 & 1 & 0 \\ \frac{13}{6} & 1 & -2 & -1 & 0 & \frac{2}{3} \end{bmatrix}$$

The matrix $\mathbf{A}$ will have distinct eigenvalues only if all $r_k = 1$. Kalman gives two methods for finding $\mathbf{B}$ and $\mathbf{C}$ [14]. An analog computer simulation may be made from these matrices. This analog computer setup may be easily checked if the weighting function is known; that is, we systematically insert inputs and observe the corresponding computer outputs to confirm the weighting function. The Gilbert realization is, of course, only one of the many possible.

As an alternative to finding the state equations from input-output relations, we may often write the state-space equations directly, as discussed previously (in particular, Section 5.8). In either case, using the state-space equations, we may form an analog simulation from which $\boldsymbol{\phi}(t)$ may be found directly. Thus, using (6.1–1) and (6.1–4), the solution of (6.1–3) is

$$\mathbf{x}(t) = \boldsymbol{\phi}(t)\mathbf{x}(0) \qquad \textbf{(6.5–10)}$$

for $t_0 = 0$, and where

$$\boldsymbol{\phi}(t) = \begin{bmatrix} \phi_{11}(t) & \phi_{1n}(t) \\ \cdots & \cdots \\ \phi_{n1}(t) & \phi_{nn}(t) \end{bmatrix} \qquad \textbf{(6.5–11)}$$

Hence

$$x_i(t) = \sum_{j=1}^{n} \phi_{ij}(t)x_j(0) \qquad i = 1, 2, \ldots, n \qquad \textbf{(6.5–12)}$$

and if $x_k(0) = 1$ but $x_j(0) = 0$, $j \neq k$, then

$$\phi_{ik}(t) = x_i(t) \tag{6.5–13}$$

Equation (6.5–13) states that element ϕ_{ik} in the $\boldsymbol{\phi}(t)$ matrix may be found at the output of the ith integrator if an initial condition of 1 is placed on the kth integrator, all other initial conditions zero. From Chapter 4 an initial condition of unity on an integrator is the same as a unit impulse $\delta(t)$ applied to the integrator input. To find ϕ_{ik} we therefore put a unit impulse at the input of the kth integrator and observe the output of the ith integrator, all connections being maintained and all other initial conditions zero. Whether the input-output connections are maintained is immaterial.†

Example 6.5–2

Given the analog simulation diagram of Figure 6.5–2, which represents the equations

$$\dot{\mathbf{x}} = \mathbf{A}\mathbf{x} + \mathbf{B}\mathbf{m}$$

$$\mathbf{y} = \mathbf{C}\mathbf{x} + \mathbf{D}\mathbf{m}$$

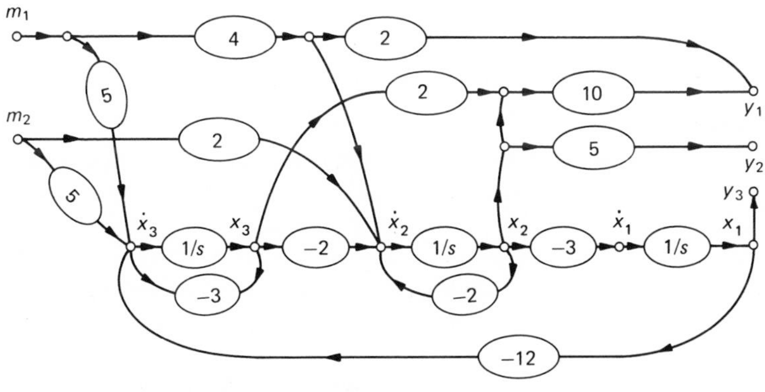

Figure 6.5–2. Analog simulation for Example 6.5–2.

where

$$\mathbf{A} = \begin{bmatrix} 0 & -3 & 0 \\ 0 & -2 & -2 \\ -12 & 0 & -3 \end{bmatrix} \qquad \mathbf{B} = \begin{bmatrix} 0 & 0 \\ 4 & 2 \\ 5 & 5 \end{bmatrix}$$

$$\mathbf{C} = \begin{bmatrix} 0 & 10 & 20 \\ 0 & 5 & 0 \\ 1 & 0 & 0 \end{bmatrix} \qquad \mathbf{D} = \begin{bmatrix} 8 & 0 \\ 0 & 0 \\ 0 & 0 \end{bmatrix}$$

† By integrator 1 we mean the integrator whose output is x_1, and so on.

Solution: Using the Laplace transform and applying Mason's rule, the graph determinant Δ is

$$\Delta = 1 - \left(-\frac{3}{s} - \frac{2}{s} - \frac{72}{s^3}\right) + \left(-\frac{3}{s}\right)\left(\frac{-2}{s}\right)$$

or

$$\Delta = \left(\frac{s^3 + 5s^2 + 6s + 72}{s^3}\right)$$

$$= \frac{(s+6)(s^2 - s + 12)}{s^3}$$

For ϕ_{11}, apply a unit impulse ($\mathscr{L}$ transform $= 1$) to the input of integrator 1, and find the output of 1. Then again using Mason's rule,

$$\phi_{11} = \mathscr{L}^{-1}\left\{\frac{1/s[1 - (-2/s - 3/s) + (2/s)(3/s)]}{\Delta}\right\}$$

$$= \mathscr{L}^{-1}\left(\frac{1}{s^3}\frac{s^2 + 5s + 6}{\Delta}\right)$$

Similarly, for ϕ_{12}, apply a unit impulse to the input of integrator 2 and observe the output of integrator 1. Then

$$\phi_{12} = \mathscr{L}^{-1}\left[\frac{(-3/s^2)(1 + 3/s)}{\Delta}\right]$$

Continuing,

$$\phi(t) = \mathscr{L}^{-1}\left[\frac{1}{(s+6)(s^2 - s + 12)}\right]\begin{bmatrix} s^2 + 5s + 6 & -3(s+3) & 6 \\ 24 & s^2 + 3s & -2s \\ -12s^2 & 36 & s^2 + 2s \end{bmatrix}$$

For systems that are not too large, this method may be less time consuming than using a matrix inversion.

So far we have assumed that the system may be described by input-output relations, using a transfer function $\mathbf{Z}(s)$, or by the state-space equations, using a transition matrix $\boldsymbol{\phi}(t)$. What is the relation between the system as obtained from the differential equations and the system obtained from the transfer function? This brings up the questions of controllability and observability, which we now discuss.

6.6 Controllability and Observability

There are several definitions of controllability. Let us adopt the following: Given that the system is at any state x_0 in the state space $\sum^n$ at

$t = 0$, then there exists some finite control $\mathbf{m}$ that will bring the system to any specified state $\mathbf{x}_1$ in the space $\sum^n$ within a finite length of time $t = t_f$. Observability is the dual of controllability. Thus the system is said to be observable if at any time $t_f > 0$ a knowledge of the output $\mathbf{y}$ and the system matrices enables us to determine the initial state $x(0)$. Controllability and observability have been studied extensively. Kalman and Gilbert divide any system into four parts: (1) completely observable and controllable, (2) observable and uncontrollable, (3) controllable and unobservable, and (4) uncontrollable and unobservable. Kalman gives the following example [15].

Example 6.6–1

In Figure 6.6–1 let x_1 be the magnetic flux linkages Li in the inductor and x_2 the electric charge $q = \int i\,dt$ on the capacitor. The inductor and capacitor values may vary with time but in any case $L/C = 1$. Let $m_1(t)$ be an ideal

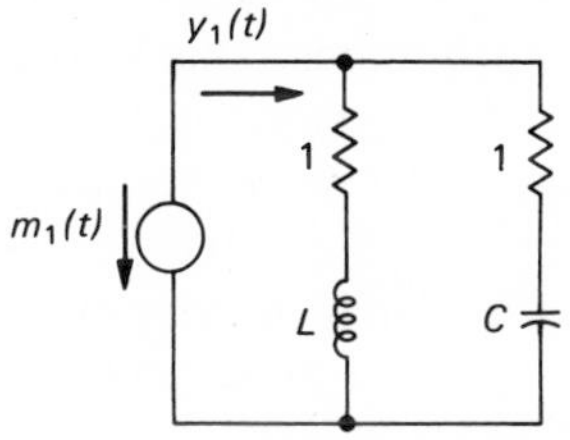

Figure 6.6–1. System for Example 6.6–1.

voltage source and $y_1(t)$ the current into the network. The equations are

$$\dot{x}_1 = -\frac{1}{L}x_1 + m_1$$

$$\dot{x}_2 = -\frac{1}{C}x_2 + m_1$$

$$y_1 = \frac{1}{L}x_1 + \dot{x}_2 \qquad \textbf{(6.6–1)}$$

$$= \frac{1}{L}x_1 - \frac{1}{C}x_2 + m_1$$

Now let

$$z_1 = \frac{x_1 + x_2}{2}$$

$$z_2 = \frac{x_1 - x_2}{2}$$

$$\frac{L}{C} = 1$$

Then (6.6–1) become

$$z_1 = -\frac{1}{L} z_1 + m_1$$

$$z_2 = -\frac{1}{L} z_2 \qquad \textbf{(6.6–2)}$$

$$y_1 = 2\frac{1}{L} z_2 + m_1$$

Then in (6.6–2) the state variable z_1 is controllable but not observable, while the state variable z_2 is observable but not controllable, or, in other words, z_2 is independent of m_1 while y_1 is independent of z_1. In still different language **y** is not coupled to some of the state variables, while some of the state variables are not coupled to **m**. These statements are equivalent to the original definitions. This is true because in this space $\sum^n$, $n = 2$, requiring two linearly independent vectors to span the space. Thus we cannot reach all points in the space, because the control m effects only one vector, z_1. The control can thus maneuver the state only in a subspace of one dimension, and the system is uncontrollable in two-dimensional space. Similar remarks pertain to observability.

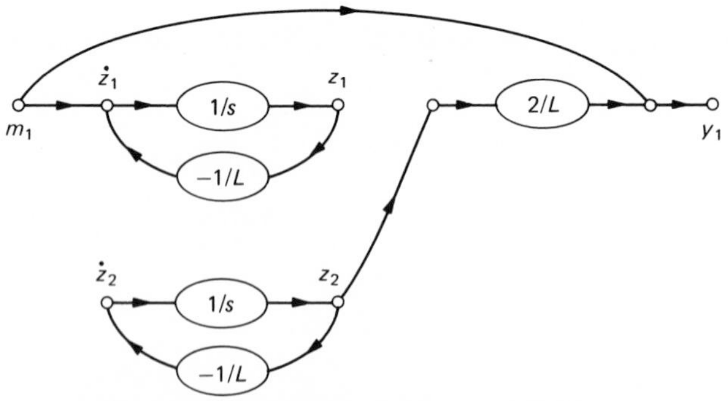

Figure 6.6–2. Flow diagram for Example 6.6.–1

Figure 6.6–2 shows a flow diagram for (6.6–2). It must be noted immediately that we have made a careful selection of constants to obtain this condition. Nevertheless, if the constants were not exactly as chosen, there still might be very weak coupling between variables, so that excursions of the state of the system would be only partially observed at the output, or alternatively large variations of some inputs would have little control of the state.

We can diagrammatically show the four parts of a system as in Figure 6.6–3. In this figure *A* represents the observable and controllable portion, *B* the controllable but unobservable portion, *C* the uncontrollable and unobservable portion, and *D* the observable but uncontrollable portion, respectively. Any or all of these may exist in any system.

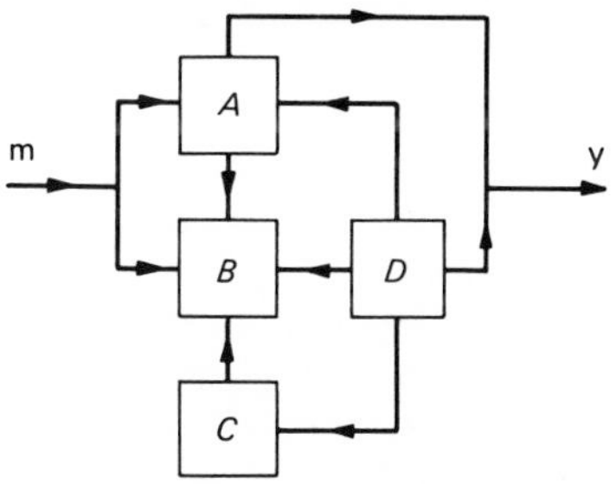

Figure 6.6–3. Four possible parts of a system.

The state variables $\mathbf{x}(t)$ are rather arbitrary, so how can we really tell whether or not we have uncontrollable or unobservable modes? Assume the system equations

$$\dot{\mathbf{x}} = \mathbf{Ax} + \mathbf{Bm} \qquad \textbf{(6.6–3a)}$$

$$\mathbf{y} = \mathbf{Cx} + \mathbf{Dm} \qquad \textbf{(6.6–3b)}$$

and let $\mathbf{A}$ have n distinct eigenvalues. Then you can find some matrix $\mathbf{T}$ such that $\mathbf{T}^{-1}\mathbf{AT} = \mathbf{\Lambda}$, a diagonal matrix. Multiply (6.6–3a) by $\mathbf{T}^{-1}$, or

$$\mathbf{T}^{-1}\dot{\mathbf{x}} = \mathbf{T}^{-1}\mathbf{Ax} + \mathbf{T}^{-1}\mathbf{Bm}$$

Let $\mathbf{x} = \mathbf{Tz}$. Then

$$\dot{\mathbf{z}} = \mathbf{\Lambda z} + \mathbf{B}_1\mathbf{m} \qquad \textbf{(6.6–4a)}$$

$$\mathbf{y} = \mathbf{C}_1\mathbf{z} + \mathbf{Dm} \qquad \textbf{(6.6–4b)}$$

where

$$\mathbf{\Lambda} = \mathbf{T}^{-1}\mathbf{AT}$$

$$\mathbf{B}_1 = \mathbf{T}^{-1}\mathbf{B}$$

$$\mathbf{C}_1 = \mathbf{CT}$$

$$\mathbf{\Lambda} = \begin{bmatrix} \lambda_1 & \cdots & \cdots & 0 \\ \cdot & \lambda_2 & \cdots & \cdot \\ \cdots & \cdots & \cdots & \cdots \\ 0 & \cdots & \cdots & \lambda_n \end{bmatrix}$$

Example 6.6–2

In (6.6–2)

$$\Lambda = \begin{bmatrix} -1/L & 0 \\ 0 & -1/L \end{bmatrix} \qquad \mathbf{B}_1 = \begin{bmatrix} 1 \\ 0 \end{bmatrix}$$

$$\mathbf{C}_1 = [0 \quad 2/L] \qquad \mathbf{D} = [1 \quad 0]$$

In (6.6–4) coordinates z_i corresponding to zero rows of B_1 are uncontrollable; they cannot be influenced by **m**. Coordinates z_i corresponding to zero columns of $\mathbf{C}_1$ are unobservable; they cannot be detected in the output **y**. Hence it is clear from (6.6–4) that the system described by (6.6–3) is completely controllable if and only if $\mathbf{B}_1$ has no zero rows, and completely observable if and only if $\mathbf{C}_1$ has no zero columns. In all cases, all coordinates z_i, $i = 1, 2, \ldots, n$ will belong to one of the four groups previously discussed. It is assumed here that system (6.6–3) has the minimum number of state variables and that the number of inputs has been reduced to the rank of **B**, and the number of columns **C** have been reduced so that the rank of **C** equals the number of outputs. A more complex analysis involving the Jordan cannonical form may also be applied to cases where the eigenvalues are not distinct, as indicated previously.

It may be difficult to make a diagonalization. Kalman gives an alternative procedure that will classify the variables into the four groups previously indicated. This algorithm, although straightforward, would require considerable justification, and we refer the interested reader to the basic article [16]. Athans and Falb show that for the linear time-invariant system, the system is completely controllable (all state-space variables can be affected by some input), if and only if the matrix

$$\mathbf{G} = [\mathbf{B} \vdots \mathbf{AB} \vdots \mathbf{A}^2\mathbf{B} : \cdots : \mathbf{A}^{n-1}\mathbf{B}] \tag{6.6–5}$$

has rank n. Similarly, the system is completely observable if and only if the matrix

$$\mathrm{H} = [\mathbf{C}^T : \mathbf{A}^T\mathbf{C}^T : (\mathbf{A}^T)^2\mathbf{C}^T : \cdots : (\mathbf{A}^T)^{n-1}\mathbf{C}^T] \tag{6.6–6}$$

has rank n [17].

An analog simulation of an uncontrollable or unobservable system made from the state equations will have state variables unconnected to the output, or not associated with the input, or both, as in Figure 6.6–2. Such a simulation would be unworkable.

Algebraic cancellations can occur in the transfer function $\mathbf{Z}(s)$, so the system represented by $\mathbf{Z}(s)$, or by simulations of differential equations derived from $\mathbf{Z}(s)$, as discussed in the previous sections, will not include the unobservable or uncontrollable modes of oscillation that may be present in actuality. In a physical system, even if exact cancellations do not occur, weak couplings may exist such that output modes will be obscured by noise and inputs may not demonstrate control. Thus the picture we get of the system by input-output measurements through the impulse response function may not be a correct representation. Better instrumentation and more sophisticated testing, particularly if some oscillatory modes are suspected, might clarify this picture, but such measurements may never reveal all the details. The system as defined from the impulse response function is therefore only part 1 of the system—the observable and controllable portion. Some authors refer to this as the "irreducible" portion; that is, the dimension n of the state space cannot be reduced below the value necessary to demonstrate the controllable and observable portion of the system. This n is given by Gilbert's theorem shown in (6.5–9).

Cancellations of numerator and denominator factors of $\mathbf{Z}(s)$ will lead to unobservable or uncontrollable state variables, or both, if the poles of $\mathbf{Z}(s)$ are simple. If the poles are multiple, as, for example, $(s + 1)^2$, cancellation of one $(s + 1)$ factor may not lead to such a situation.

Turning to the other side of the argument, should we have more faith in the differential equations (6.6–3), which, if you recall, define the system, than in an impulse response $\mathbf{W}(t)$ obtained by measurement? Not necessarily. In fact, if we follow one of the ideas of science—that theory must be checked by experiment—and if the differential equations were written from theoretical considerations, we might have some difficulty justifying them if experiment did not support the predictions. Perhaps we could explain away some of the discrepancies by poor instrumentation, nonlinearities, improper experimental procedure, and so on, but we might also suspect that perhaps our model was not correct. This would be particularly true if the experiment revealed more modes of oscillation than predicted by theory. On the other hand, we could have more state variables than necessary. Of course there is no real dilemma. The solution is that theory and practice must support each other. We postulate a model, make tests, revise the model, and continue to refine. Somewhere along the line, it becomes necessary to produce a result, then we say enough, and let the next investigator advance further.

Assuming that we have a reasonable model, and observe that cancellations do occur in $\mathbf{Z}(s)$, are they harmful? As a matter of fact, a considerable amount of design in the past has been based on just such cancellations. In design in the frequency domain, one of the techniques is to cancel out undesired poles in the transfer function and substitute desired poles or eliminate unwanted vibrational modes and put in wanted modes (see

Chapter 9). This is a very attractive procedure because it allows the designer to synthesize a system by selecting the desired input-output relations and to work backward to the required control device to be used with the given system. For example, if

$$Z(s) = \frac{K(s+\alpha)}{(s+a)(s+b)(s+c)}$$

is given and the desired

$$Z(s) = \frac{K_1(s+\alpha)}{(s+a)(s+b)(s+d)}$$

then a compensation device might have the transfer function

$$\frac{K_1(s+c)}{K(s+d)}$$

The zero of the compensation function cancels the undesired pole of the given system, and we might have a pole-zero configuration in the complex frequency plane as shown in Figure 6.6–4. Although the pole and zero

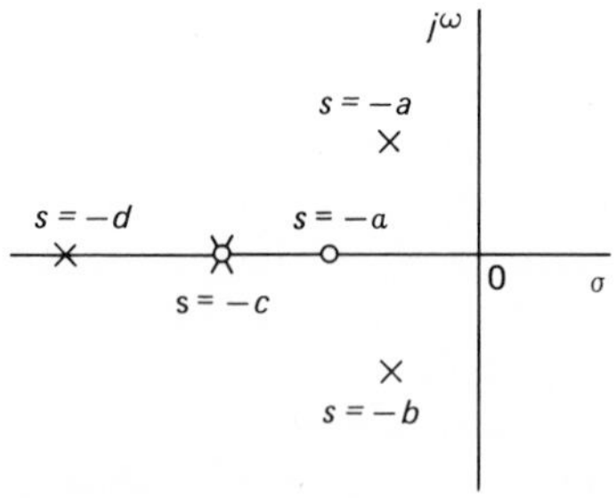

Figure 6.6–4. Compensation by cancellation.

are at $s = -c$, in any practical scheme they will be slightly separated, and we shall therefore have a weakly coupled system with respect to the vibration mode at $s = -c$. This may or may not be injurious. If the system is unobservable, say, a small rapidly decaying internal oscillation may only slightly affect the situation. On the other hand, if the pole at $s = -c$ is close to the origin, even a small error in cancellation might result in internal oscillations which could saturate system elements, leading to all sorts of other difficulties. Also it must be recognized that both the pole and zero at $s = -c$ will change with system aging and environment. Thus any pole considered for cancellation must be reasonably immune from drift. (It is relatively easy to keep the compensator poles and zeros within narrow bounds by using nonvarying elements.)

Assuming we could live with cancellations in the left-half s plane, could we do the same for the right-half plane? Obviously not, since any slight error in cancellation would result in a term of the form $\epsilon^{\sigma t}$ in one of the variables. This is a rapidly growing time function producing instability.

Example 6.6–3

Let

$$\mathbf{A} = \begin{bmatrix} 0 & 1 & 0 \\ -1 & 0 & 5 \\ 2 & 0 & -4 \end{bmatrix} \qquad \mathbf{B} = \begin{bmatrix} 0 \\ 0 \\ 1 \end{bmatrix}$$

$$\mathbf{C} = [-1 \quad 1 \quad 0] \qquad \mathbf{D} = \mathbf{0}$$

Then taking the Laplace transform in (6.6–3) and letting the initial conditions be zero,

$$\mathbf{X}(s) = \frac{\begin{bmatrix} s(s+4) & (s+4) & 5 \\ -s+6 & s(s+4) & 5s \\ 2s & 2 & s^2+1 \end{bmatrix}}{s^3+4s^2+s-6} \begin{bmatrix} 0 \\ 0 \\ M(s) \end{bmatrix} = \frac{\begin{bmatrix} 5M(s) \\ 5sM(s) \\ (s^2+1)M(s) \end{bmatrix}}{s^3+4s^2+s-6}$$

$$\mathbf{Y}(s) = [-1 \quad 1 \quad 0]\mathbf{x}(s)$$

$$Y(s) = -x_1(s) + x_2(s)$$

$$= \frac{-5M(s) + 5sM(s)}{s^3+4s^2+s-6}$$

$$\mathbf{Z}(s) = \frac{Y(s)}{M(s)} = \frac{5(s-1)}{(s-1)(s+2)(s+3)}$$

$$= \frac{5}{(s+2)(s+3)}$$

If

$$\mathbf{T} = \begin{bmatrix} 1 & 1 & 1 \\ 1 & -2 & -3 \\ \frac{2}{5} & 1 & 2 \end{bmatrix}$$

then

$$\mathbf{T}^{-1} = \frac{1}{12}\begin{bmatrix} 5 & 5 & 5 \\ 16 & -8 & -20 \\ -9 & 3 & 15 \end{bmatrix} \qquad \mathbf{\Lambda} = \begin{bmatrix} 1 & 0 & 0 \\ 0 & -2 & 0 \\ 0 & 0 & -3 \end{bmatrix}$$

$$\mathbf{B}_1 = \mathbf{T}^{-1}\mathbf{B} = \frac{1}{12}\begin{bmatrix} 5 \\ -20 \\ 15 \end{bmatrix} \qquad \mathbf{C}_1 = \mathbf{CT} = [0 \quad -3 \quad -4]$$

Then we see from $\mathbf{B}_1$ that the system is completely controllable but from $\mathbf{C}_1$ that the system is not completely observable. The mode corresponding to $(s - 1)$, which gives rise to a term $K\epsilon^t$, cannot be observed in the output of this single input-output system. If the system were simulated by an analog computer, one or more of the amplifiers would rapidly saturate.

Figure 6.6–5 shows one possible simulation of the system of Example 6.6–3 (clearly the first amplifier is superfluous in the transfer function). This reemphasizes the fact that we can simulate only the completely

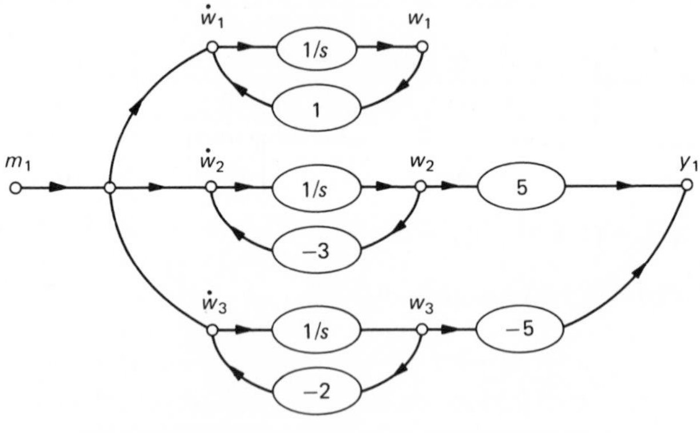

Figure 6.6–5. Flow diagram for Example 6.6—3.

observable and controllable part of the system. Gilbert shows that it is possible to obtain a system in which only the unstable modes are controllable and observable but in which some of the stable modes may not be controllable and observable [18].

The subject of uncontrollability and unobservability touches on the most basic philosophic concepts of control. In summary, if we define a system by a set of differential equations, then there may exist uncontrollable or unobservable modes of vibration not shown by the transfer function approach. Any physical simulation will reveal only the irreducible part of the system. In any system, particularly a multi-input-output system, lack of knowledge of these internal modes of vibration may lead to erroneous conclusions regarding stability, saturation, and other important questions. Obviously the designer must investigate these possibilities. We now turn to the subject of instability.

6.7 Stability

We can fairly safely say that stability, or at least relative stability, has been the chief concern of control designers using conventional methods (complex frequency domain methods). We shall define relative stability more rigorously in later chapters, but loosely this term implies a maximum value for the per unit deviation of the output variable $\mathbf{y}$ from its final value during some transient period. Although relative stability becomes of much less importance in the state-space approach, being secondary to the achievement of some performance index (which usually will indirectly effect relative stability), stability itself retains its importance. If the system is unstable, it is normally no good, regardless of its many other attributes. Therefore the designer likes to determine stability before he wastes much detail work on a proposed system. For a linear system determination of stability is comparatively easy, but for a nonlinear system this issue becomes very difficult—in fact, so difficult a computer simulation may be the only practical method. However, such investigations are never conclusive, because only a limited number of conditions can be investigated. Theoretical techniques that can avoid such a lengthy and expensive investigation are continually being developed. Although we are primarily concerned with linear systems, let us look at stability in a more general sense before taking up the linear case.

Rather than examine the output $\mathbf{y}$, it is more convenient to look at the state vector $\mathbf{x}$. First, we may define an equilibrium state as the state in which the system remains at rest with no input, or $\dot{\mathbf{x}} = \mathbf{0}$ when $\mathbf{m} = \mathbf{0}$ for all t. For the linear, stationary system, then

$$\mathbf{A}\mathbf{x}(t) = \mathbf{0} \qquad \textbf{(6.7–1)}$$

Obviously the null vector $\mathbf{x} = \mathbf{0}$ satisfies this definition. If $\det \mathbf{A} \neq 0$ ($\mathbf{A}$ nonsingular), then the origin is the only equilibrium point, but if $\mathbf{A}$ is singular, there are infinitely many such points. For a nonlinear system, the origin may or may not be an equilibrium point, and there may be either many or no other equilibrium points.

Now if we have the system in an equilibrium state $\mathbf{x}_e$ and displace it slightly, the state variable $\mathbf{x}$ will do one of three things: (1) return to a neighborhood of the equilibrium point, (2) will not return to this neighborhood but will remain a finite distance from the equilibrium point measured by change of the norm of $\mathbf{x}$, or (3) the norm of $\mathbf{x}$, will increase without bound. In case (1) the system is said to be stable, in case (2) unstable but bounded, and in case (3) unstable and unbounded. By the term "neighborhood" R_ϵ of $\mathbf{x}_e$ we mean the set of all $\mathbf{x}$ such that $\|\mathbf{x} - \mathbf{x}_e\| < \epsilon$, where ϵ is a specified constant greater than zero.

A bounded equilibrium state $\mathbf{x}_e$ may be more rigorously defined as follows: If a neighborhood of $\mathbf{x}_e$ exists such that if an initial state $\mathbf{x}_0$ is in this region, then $\|\mathbf{x}(t) - \mathbf{x}_e\| < \infty$ for all $t > t_0$ if the state is bounded.

An equilibrium state $\mathbf{x}_e$ is said to be stable in the sense of Lyapunov if to any neighborhood R_ϵ of $\mathbf{x}_e$ there corresponds some neighborhood R_δ such that if $\mathbf{x}_0$ lies within the latter neighborhood R_δ ($\|\mathbf{x}_e = \mathbf{x}_0\| < \delta$), then $\mathbf{x}(t)$ lies within the first neighborhood R_ϵ for all $t > t_0$. R_ϵ must contain R_δ. This definition of stability honors the Russian mathematician Lyapunov, who first worked out general tests for stability.

Lyapunov stability may be illustrated by Figure 6.7–1. This figure shows a two-dimensional space, with a third axis of time. This augmentation of

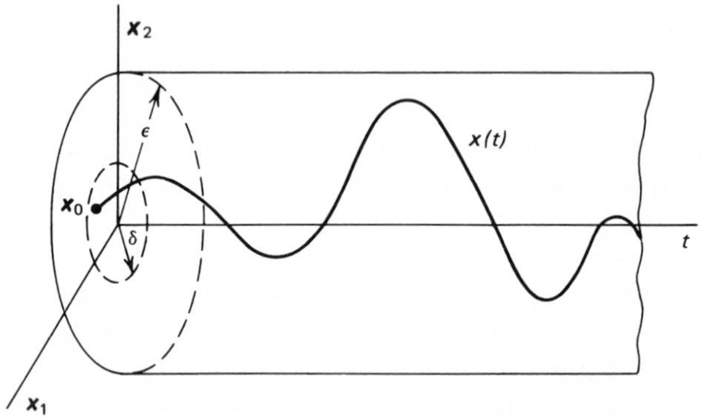

Figure 6.7–1. Lyapunov stability in a two-dimensional space.

state space by the time dimension is often convenient. The equilibrium point $\mathbf{x}_e$ is taken as the origin here ($\mathbf{x}_e = \mathbf{0}$). If you select some neighborhood R_ϵ of $\mathbf{x}_e$, and can find some neighborhood R_δ (ϵ, t_0) such that if the initial condition $\mathbf{x}_0$ lies within R_δ, $\mathbf{x}(t)$ will always lie within the neighborhood R_ϵ, The system is Lyapunov-stable. If δ is independent of t_0, then the system is uniformly stable. Thus a stationary stable system is uniformly stable.

The neighborhoods R_ϵ and R_δ are shown as circles with radii ϵ and δ, respectively, in Figure 6.7–1. Note that ϵ can be made arbitrarily small so long as it is greater than zero. Hence Lyapunov stability allows oscillations that may be made arbitrarily small. Contrariwise, a system may be defined as being *asymptotically stable* if it is stable in the Lyapunov sense, and if $\|\mathbf{x}(t) - \mathbf{x}_e\| \to 0$ as $t \to \infty$, for an initial condition $\mathbf{x}_0$ in the neighborhood

R_δ of $\mathbf{x}_e$. If in the previous definitions the neighborhood of the equilibrium point encompasses the entire state space, then $\mathbf{x}_e$ is said to be globally stable. Otherwise it is locally stable.

We might give a few illustrations of the previous definitions. A nonlinear system such as the Van Der Pol oscillator may describe a state-space trajectory that, after a short time, is retraced in cyclical fashion, regardless of the initial state. We call such a trajectory a "limit cycle." This corresponds to a bounded equilibrium state with respect to any point in the space. (See Figure 6.7–2.)

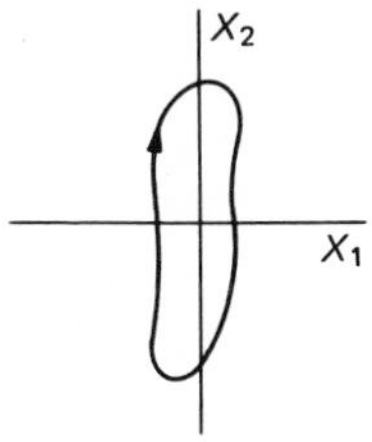

Figure 6.7–2. Limit cycle in nonlinear system.

Other nonlinear systems may have several possible limit cycles, the state vector proceeding to one or the other, depending on the initial state. In a conservative (lossless) linear system, the amplitude of oscillation depends on the initial conditions. Hence, if you furnish an $\epsilon > 0$, it is always possible to find a neighborhood δ for the initial condition such that the state vector stays closer than ϵ to the equilibrium point, and thus such a system is stable in the Lyapunov sense. An ideal multivibrator is unstable, because it goes from one state to another, these being separated by a finite and fixed distance. Thus one equilibrium state is more than an arbitrarily small distance from the other. Each equilibrium state is bounded, however. An unbounded linear system will either destroy some portion of itself as the state vector grows, or some part of it will saturate and the system will become nonlinear. In a system with mechanical parts, for example, a shaft could be broken by large changes in acceleration. More usually, an amplifier or motor will saturate; Thus for some input it will deliver maximum power and cannot deliver any more regardless of additional input.

A practical multivibrator is locally asymptotically stable, since, unless we apply a displacement of sufficient amount it will return to the initial state. It is not globally stable, since it will go to the other state if the initial displacement is large enough. It is still bounded in either state.

We can now derive some conditions for stability for linear systems and for linear stationary systems in particular. The first condition for stability in the Lyapunov sense for a linear system is that the norm of the transition matrix $\boldsymbol{\phi}(t, t_0)$ be finite for all $t > t_0$, or

$$\|\boldsymbol{\phi}(t, t_0)\| < K \qquad t > t_0$$

where K is some constant ($K < \infty$).

This is easily shown from the state equation with no input, $\dot{\mathbf{x}}(t) = \mathbf{A}(t)\mathbf{x}(t)$ to which the solution is (6.1–4) in the stationary case. In the non-stationary case the transition matrix is a function of t_0, so the solution is

$$\mathbf{x}(t) = \boldsymbol{\phi}(t, t_0)\mathbf{x}_0 \tag{6.7–2}$$

From (6.7–2),

$$\|\mathbf{x}(t)\| \leq \|\boldsymbol{\phi}(t, t_0)\| \; \|x_0\|$$

Assuming that

$$\|\boldsymbol{\phi}(t, t_0)\| < K \qquad t > t_0$$

then

$$\|\mathbf{x}(t)\| \leq K\|x_0\| \qquad t > t_0$$

Now if

$$\|x_0\| < \delta = \frac{\epsilon}{K}$$

then

$$\|\mathbf{x}(t)\| \leq \epsilon \qquad t > t_0$$

In the stationary case, δ will be independent of the time origin t_0, and hence the system is uniformly stable. Continuing the same line of reasoning, the system is asymptotically stable if it is stable and

$$\lim_{t \to \infty} \|\boldsymbol{\phi}(t, t_0)\| = 0 \qquad \text{for all } t_0$$

Proceeding to the non-time-varying case, which is of more interest to us here, a theorem of fundamental importance can now be derived. Letting $t_0 = 0$ in (6.1–4) for convenience (since the system is uniformly stable), then

$$\begin{aligned}\mathbf{x}(t) &= (\exp(\mathbf{A}t)(\mathbf{x}_0) \\ &= \boldsymbol{\phi}(t)\mathbf{x}_0 \\ &= \mathscr{L}^{-1}[(s\mathbf{I} - \mathbf{A})^{-1}\mathbf{x}_0]\end{aligned} \tag{6.7–3}$$

and by (6.1–15),

$$\mathbf{x}(t) = \mathscr{L}^{-1}\left[\frac{\mathbf{P}(s)}{p(s)} x_0\right] \tag{6.7–4}$$

where $p(s)$ is the minimal polynomial and $\mathbf{P}(s)$ is the numerator matrix. In inverting (6.7–4) we saw that if $p(s)$ has roots in the left-half s plane, that the resulting time function $\mathbf{x}(t)$ approaches zero as $t \to \infty$. For example, if the pole of $\mathbf{P}(s)/p(s)$ at $s = s_k$ is of multiplicity n, then the resulting time response has terms of the form $\mathbf{K}_q t^q \epsilon^{-s_k t}$, where $q = 0, 1, \ldots, n - 1$, and $\mathbf{K}_q$ is a matrix of constants. Clearly such terms approach zero as t approaches infinity. If the poles are in the right-half plane, then the time functions go to infinity because the exponents are positive. Finally, if the poles are on the $j\omega$ axis ($s_k = j\omega_k$), then the time function will be oscillatory and of the form $\mathbf{K}_q t_q \sin \omega_k t$. If we further restrict these poles to be simple, then the response is of the form $\mathbf{K} \sin \omega_k t$. The value of the elements of the constant $\mathbf{K}$ depends on the initial conditions, and as previously discussed, we can make the initial displacement from the equilibrium point $\mathbf{x}_e$ as small as we please. Finally, the roots of $p(s)$ are the eigenvalues of $\mathbf{A}$ [except for possible cancellations of $B(s)$ and $d(s)$]. Hence we can state that the system given by $\dot{\mathbf{x}} = \mathbf{A}\mathbf{x}$ (free system) is stable in the Lyapunov sense if all the eigenvalues of $\mathbf{A}$ have real parts equal to or less than zero and if the eigenvalues of $\mathbf{A}$ that are on the imaginary axis are simple zeros of $p(s)$. The system is asymptotically stable if the eigenvalues all have negative real parts.

Thus the test for stability in a linear stationary system reduces to locating the roots of the minimal polynomial $p(s)$. This may be done in a number of ways:

1. Factor $p(s)$.
2. Apply the Routh-Hurwitz test.
3. Plot a root locus.
4. Use the Nyquist criteria.

Factoring $p(s)$ is not a particularly easy task. Furthermore, it tells nothing about what changes to make in the system if it is not satisfactory. The Routh-Hurwitz test indicates whether the system is stable without factoring, but does not reveal relative stability, and is also subject to the previous criticism in regard to changes. The root locus and the Nyquist criteria give information concerning relative stability and guide the engineer in improving the design, as we shall discuss in more detail in later chapters.

It is easy to see that if we transform $\mathbf{A}$ to a diagonal matrix $\mathbf{\Lambda}$ and if the diagonal elements of $\mathbf{\Lambda}$ all have negative real parts, the system is asymptotically stable. This requires a factoring of the characteristic equation. The Fadeeva method can also be used, as shown in Section 5.7

The previous discussion of stability assumed no driving function $\mathbf{m}(t)$, or that the system was free (unforced). If a driving function exists and we again consider the state variable $\mathbf{x}$ and not the output $\mathbf{y}$, then

$$\dot{\mathbf{x}} = \mathbf{A}\mathbf{x} + \mathbf{B}\mathbf{m} \tag{6.7–5}$$

and we need a new definition of stability. One such definition is that a system is stable if the state is bounded ($\|\mathbf{x}(t)\| \leq K_1 < \infty$) when the input belongs to a bounded set ($\|\mathbf{m}(t)\| \leq K_2 < \infty$) for all $t > t_0$. Using this definition, theorems with regard to driven stability may be derived [19], [20]. If we adhere to the stationary system, and assume zero initial conditions, then from (6.3–2), the solution consists in a convolution of time functions. If we transform the time functions,

$$\mathbf{X}(s) = \mathbf{W}_1(s)\mathbf{M}(s) \tag{6.7–6}$$

where $\mathbf{W}_1(s)$ is the Laplace transform of the matrix relating the input $\mathbf{m}(t)$ to the state variable $\mathbf{x}(t)$.

Since

$$\mathbf{W}_1(s) = (s\mathbf{I} - \mathbf{A})^{-1}\mathbf{B}$$

it is clear that the state variable $\mathbf{x}(t)$ will be bounded with bounded input if the poles of $\mathbf{W}_1(s)$ [the roots of $\det(s\mathbf{I} - \mathbf{A})$] are in the left-half plane. [We cannot allow poles of $\mathbf{W}_1(s)$ on the imaginary axis in this case, because the convolution integral might go to infinity with certain inputs.] Hence if the transfer function $\mathbf{W}_1(s)$ is analytic in the right-half plane and on the imaginary axis, the driven stationary system is stable using the previous definition.

In using transfer functions to determine stability, it is necessary to keep in mind the discussion of controllability and observability in Section 6.4. Stability of nonlinear systems may be found by using Lyapunov functions and by Popov's theorem. Lyapunov functions may be very powerful in determining global stability, but unfortunately no straightforward technique has been developed for choosing an appropriate function. Popov's theorem is restricted to relatively simple systems but, being similar to the Nyquist criterion, has complex-plane experience in its favor [21]. If the system has uncontrollable or unobservable modes, some of these may be unstable, as pointed out in Section 6.6.

A stable and controllable fixed linear system may usually be brought to any desired point in state space if we assume an unlimited (linear) control. If the control is limited, we may have some difficulties. Many control problems are of the regulator type, where we desire the system outputs (and consequently the state variables) to remain at some fixed value (set point), which may be made the origin by proper choice of coordinates. Assuming a disturbance at $t = 0$ places the system at some point in state space $\mathbf{x}(0)$, the objective of the designer might consist of returning the system to $\mathbf{x} = \mathbf{0}$, or the origin, in the fastest possible time, given that the control quantities are limited.

Consider an nth-order system with a single control modeled by the equation

$$\dot{\mathbf{x}}(t) = \mathbf{\Lambda x}(t) + \mathbf{b}m(t) \tag{6.7–7}$$

where $|m(t)| \leq M < \infty$. The solution for the state variable x_i is then

$$x_i(t) = \epsilon^{\lambda_i t}[x_i(0) + \int_0^t \epsilon^{-\lambda_i \tau} b_i\, m(\tau)\, d\tau] \tag{6.7–8}$$

If $x_i(T) = 0,\ i = 1, 2, \ldots, n, \qquad T < \infty$, then

$$x_i(0) = -\int_0^T \epsilon^{-\lambda_i \tau} b_i\, m(\tau)\, d\tau \qquad i = 1, 2, \ldots, n \tag{6.7–9}$$

and, if $|m(t)| \leq M$,

$$|x_i(0)| = \left| \int_0^T \epsilon^{-\lambda_i \tau} b_i\, m(\tau)\, d\tau \right| \leq \int_0^T \epsilon^{-\lambda_i \tau} |b_i|\, |m(\tau)|\, d\tau \leq M \int_0^T \epsilon^{-\lambda_i \tau} |b_i|\, d\tau$$

$$= \frac{M|b_i|}{\lambda_i}(\epsilon^{-\lambda_i T} - 1) \tag{6.7–10}$$

Assuming that all λ_i are real, if one λ_i, say $\lambda_j > 0$ (system unstable), then from (6.7–10),

$$\epsilon^{-\lambda_j T} \leq 1 - \frac{\lambda_j |x_j(0)|}{M|b_j|} \tag{6.7–11}$$

Equation (6.7–11) cannot hold for $\lambda_j > 0$ and $T < \infty$ if

$$|x_j(0)| \geq \frac{M|b_j|}{\lambda_j} \tag{6.7–12}$$

On the other hand, if all $\lambda_i < 0$, then we may always find some $T < \infty$ such that (6.7–11) holds. This brief demonstration for real eigenvalues and one control may be extended to show that if the eigenvalues all have nonpositive real parts, the system can be forced to the origin from any point in state space and furthermore a mininum time trajectory exists, but, for an unstable system, the origin is accessible from only a limited set of initial conditions [22]. The system is therefore uncontrollable for points outside this set.

6.8 Linearization of Nonlinear Systems

Because of the introductory nature of this text, we have avoided detailed discussion of nonlinear systems. However, one attack on such systems consists of linearizing them in a region of interest, often around an equilibrium point. In some situations, if the operating point does not depart too far from the equilibrium point, the system designed on the basis of a linear model may perform satisfactorily.

As the word "equilibrium" carries some implication that the system is stable, we use the more general term "singular point" to describe the condition of state where no motion occurs. Let us discuss an autonomous system (one which is stationary and with, at most, a constant input). A general system may be described by

$$\dot{\mathbf{z}}(t) = \mathbf{f}(\mathbf{z}(t), \mathbf{m}) \tag{6.8–1}$$

The singular points are ascertained by a solution of

$$\dot{\mathbf{z}}(t) = \mathbf{0} \tag{6.8–2}$$

Let $\mathbf{z}_e$ be a singular point determined from (6.8–2) and

$$\mathbf{z}(t) = \mathbf{z}_e + \boldsymbol{\delta}z(t) \tag{6.8–3a}$$

$$\dot{\mathbf{z}}(t) = \mathbf{z}_e + \boldsymbol{\delta}\dot{\mathbf{z}}(t) \tag{6.8–3b}$$

$$\mathbf{m}(t) = \mathbf{m} + \boldsymbol{\delta}\mathbf{m}(t) \tag{6.8–3c}$$

where $\boldsymbol{\delta}\mathbf{z}(t)$, $\boldsymbol{\delta}\dot{\mathbf{z}}(t)$, and $\boldsymbol{\delta}\mathbf{m}(t)$ are variations around $\mathbf{z}_e$, $\dot{\mathbf{z}}_e$, and $\mathbf{m}$. Substituting (6.8–3) in (6.8–1), we get

$$\dot{\mathbf{z}}_e + \boldsymbol{\delta}\dot{\mathbf{z}}(t) = \mathbf{f}[\mathbf{z}_e + \boldsymbol{\delta}\mathbf{z}(t), \mathbf{m} + \boldsymbol{\delta}\mathbf{m}(t)] \tag{6.8–4}$$

If we can expand (6.8–4) in a Taylor's series about $\mathbf{x}_e$, then for the first state-space variable we get

$$\dot{z}_{e1} + \delta\dot{z}_1 = f_1(\mathbf{z}_e, \mathbf{m}) + \frac{\partial f_1}{\partial z_1}\,\delta z_1 + \frac{\partial f_1}{\partial z_2}\,\delta z_2$$

$$+ \cdots + \frac{1}{2}\,\frac{\partial^2 f_1}{\partial z_1^2}\,\delta z_2^1 + \frac{1}{2}\,\frac{\partial^2 f_1}{\partial z_2^2}\,\delta z_2^2 + \cdots$$

Continuing with all state variables in a like manner, dropping all terms of the order of δz^2 or higher, and recalling that $\dot{\mathbf{z}}_e = \mathbf{f}(\mathbf{z}_e, \mathbf{m})$, we obtain

$$\boldsymbol{\delta}\mathbf{z}(t) = J_z(\mathbf{z}_e, \mathbf{m})\boldsymbol{\delta} z(t) + J_m(\mathbf{z}_e, \mathbf{m})\boldsymbol{\delta}\mathbf{m}(t) \tag{6.8–5}$$

where J_z and J_m are the Jacobian matrices given by

$$\mathbf{J}_z(\mathbf{z}_e, \mathbf{m}) = \begin{bmatrix} \dfrac{\partial f_1}{\partial z_1} & \dfrac{\partial f_1}{\partial z_2} & \cdots & \dfrac{\partial f_1}{\partial z_n} \\ \dfrac{\partial f_2}{\partial z_1} & \dfrac{\partial f_2}{\partial z_2} & \cdots & \dfrac{\partial f_2}{\partial z_n} \\ \cdots & \cdots & \cdots & \cdots \\ \dfrac{\partial f_n}{\partial z_1} & \dfrac{\partial f_n}{\partial z_2} & \cdots & \dfrac{\partial f_n}{\partial z_n} \end{bmatrix}_{\mathbf{z}_e, \mathbf{m}} \tag{6.8–6}$$

$$\mathbf{J}_m(\mathbf{z}_e, \mathbf{m}) = \begin{bmatrix} \dfrac{\partial f_1}{\partial m_1} & \dfrac{\partial f_1}{\partial m_2} & \cdots & \dfrac{\partial f_1}{\partial m_l} \\ \dfrac{\partial f_2}{\partial m_1} & \dfrac{\partial f_2}{\partial m_2} & \cdots & \dfrac{\partial f_1}{\partial m_l} \\ \cdots & \cdots & \cdots & \cdots \\ \dfrac{\partial f_n}{\partial m_1} & \dfrac{\partial f_n}{\partial m_2} & \cdots & \dfrac{\partial f_n}{\partial m_l} \end{bmatrix}_{\mathbf{z}_e, \mathbf{m}} \tag{6.8–7}$$

The subscript $(\mathbf{z}_e, \mathbf{m})$ on the Jacobian matrices indicate that they must be evaluated at the point $\mathbf{z}_e$ and with the control $\mathbf{m}$. Equation (6.8–5) is now linear and we may attack it with any and all linear techniques.

Whether the linear model provides an adequate basis for design depends on the types of nonlinearities and the amount the system moves from the singular point. In process control, the assumption may be satisfactory even with a very nonlinear plant, because a relatively fixed operating point exists (providing the process can get started).

In particular, we can easily establish stability in the vicinity of a singular point. If the input $\mathbf{m}$ is a constant, then it merely shifts the singular point and does not affect the analysis. For example, the equilibrium point in the linear system

$$\dot{\mathbf{z}}(t) = \mathbf{A}\mathbf{z}(t) + \mathbf{B}\mathbf{m}(t)$$

is at

$$\mathbf{z}_e = -\mathbf{A}^{-1}\mathbf{B}\mathbf{m}$$

rather than at the origin, where it otherwise would be for $\mathbf{m} = \mathbf{0}$. Hence the results for a free system apply equally to a system with constant input but with a shifted singular point in the later case. If $\mathbf{m}$ varies with time ($\mathbf{m}(t)$), the situation is more difficult. However, stability for the autonomous system is of first importance.

Let the linearized equation for the system be

$$\boldsymbol{\delta}\dot{\mathbf{z}} = \mathbf{J}_z(\mathbf{z}_e)\boldsymbol{\delta}z \tag{6.8–8}$$

Then, from Section 6.7, if the eigenvalues of the linearized system all have negative real parts, the system is asymptotically stable in the neighborhood of the point $\mathbf{z}_e$. Furthermore the state-space trajectories in the vicinity of $\mathbf{z}_e$ will behave like the state-space trajectories of the linear system.

The previous concept has been widely used in studying second-order systems in phase space. Thus if the linearized system equation is

$$\ddot{y} + 2a\,|b|\,\dot{y} + b\,|b|\,y = 0 \tag{6.8–9}$$

we may put this in the state-space form utilizing phase variables as follows:

$$\begin{aligned} \dot{x}_1 &= x_2 \\ \dot{x}_2 &= -b\,|b|\,x_1 - 2a\,|b|\,x_2 \end{aligned} \tag{6.8–10}$$

In the linearized phase plane, x_2 versus x_1 the slope of a trajectory at any point is

$$\frac{dx_2}{dx_1} = \frac{\dot{x}_2}{\dot{x}_1} = \frac{-b\,|b|\,x_1 - 2a\,|b|\,x_2}{x_2} \tag{6.8–11}$$

Setting $\dot{x}_1 = \dot{x}_2 = 0$, the origin is the only singular point, as it should be. (Remember that the origin of the linearized phase plane is at one of the singular points $\mathbf{z}_e$ of the original space.) The behavior of the system depends on the eigenvalues or the roots of the characteristic equation $s^2 + 2a\,|b|\,s + b\,|b| = (s - \lambda_1)(s - \lambda_2) = 0$. If the eigenvalues λ_1 and λ_2 are in the left-half s plane, the system is stable, and so on. Figure 6.8–1 shows the general shapes of the trajectories for all combinations of eigenvalues, the arrows indicating the direction of motion as time increases.

In Figure 6.8–1, parts (b), (d), and (f), the original system is asymptotically stable (in the neighborhood of the singular point), whereas for the other cases it is not. For the case of eigenvalues on the $j\omega$ axis (linearized system), stability cannot be inferred by studying the linearized system alone [23]. The slope of a trajectory at any point in a plane z_1z_2 for a second-order system may be determined by obtaining dz_2/dz_1. Thus one method of locating trajectories in the original system consists of setting this slope to a constant γ_1, finding a number of points corresponding to this slope, and drawing lines (called isoclines) through these points. Other values of slope, γ_2, γ_3, and so on, may be selected. If sufficient slopes are known, trajectories may then be sketched by starting at any point and continuing with the proper slope [24]. In a phase plane, since $\dot{z}_1 = z_2$, the time along a trajectory between z_a and z_b may be computed from

$$t = \int_{z_a}^{z_b} \frac{dz_1}{z_2} \qquad \textbf{(6.8–12)}$$

Time also may be approximated graphically [25].

The general behavior of the trajectories in the vicinity of the singular points of the original nonlinear second-order equation may be inferred from Figure 6.8–1. Unfortunately we have difficulty in extending this concept to higher-order systems. We illustrate the use of this technique in the next example.

Example 6.8–1

Given the equation

$$\frac{d^2y}{dt^2} + 2\frac{dy}{dt} - 4y + 9y^3 = 0$$

find the singular points and determine their character.

Solution: Letting $z_1 = y$, $z_2 = \dot{y}$, we get the state-space equations in phase variable form as

$$\dot{z}_1 = z_2$$

$$\dot{z}_2 = 4z_1 - 2z_2 - 9z_1^3$$

At the singular points $\dot{z}_1 = \dot{z}_2 = 0$, or $z_2 = 0$; $z_1 = 0$, $z_1 = +2/3$, $z_1 = -2/3$. Thus the singular points are

$$\mathbf{z}_{e_1} = \begin{bmatrix} 0 \\ 0 \end{bmatrix} \qquad \mathbf{z}_{e_2} = \begin{bmatrix} \frac{2}{3} \\ 0 \end{bmatrix} \qquad \mathbf{z}_{e_3} = \begin{bmatrix} -\frac{2}{3} \\ 0 \end{bmatrix}$$

The Jacobian $\mathbf{J}_z$ is

$$\mathbf{J}_z = \begin{bmatrix} 0 & 1 \\ 4 - 27z_1^2 & -2 \end{bmatrix}_{\mathbf{z}_e}$$

Thus

$$\mathbf{J}_z(\mathbf{z}_{e_1}) = \begin{bmatrix} 0 & 1 \\ 4 & -2 \end{bmatrix}$$

$$\mathbf{J}_z(\mathbf{z}_{e_2}) = \mathbf{J}_z(\mathbf{z}_{e_3}) = \begin{bmatrix} 0 & 1 \\ -8 & -2 \end{bmatrix}$$

Hence at

$$\mathbf{z}_{e_1} = \begin{bmatrix} 0 \\ 0 \end{bmatrix}$$

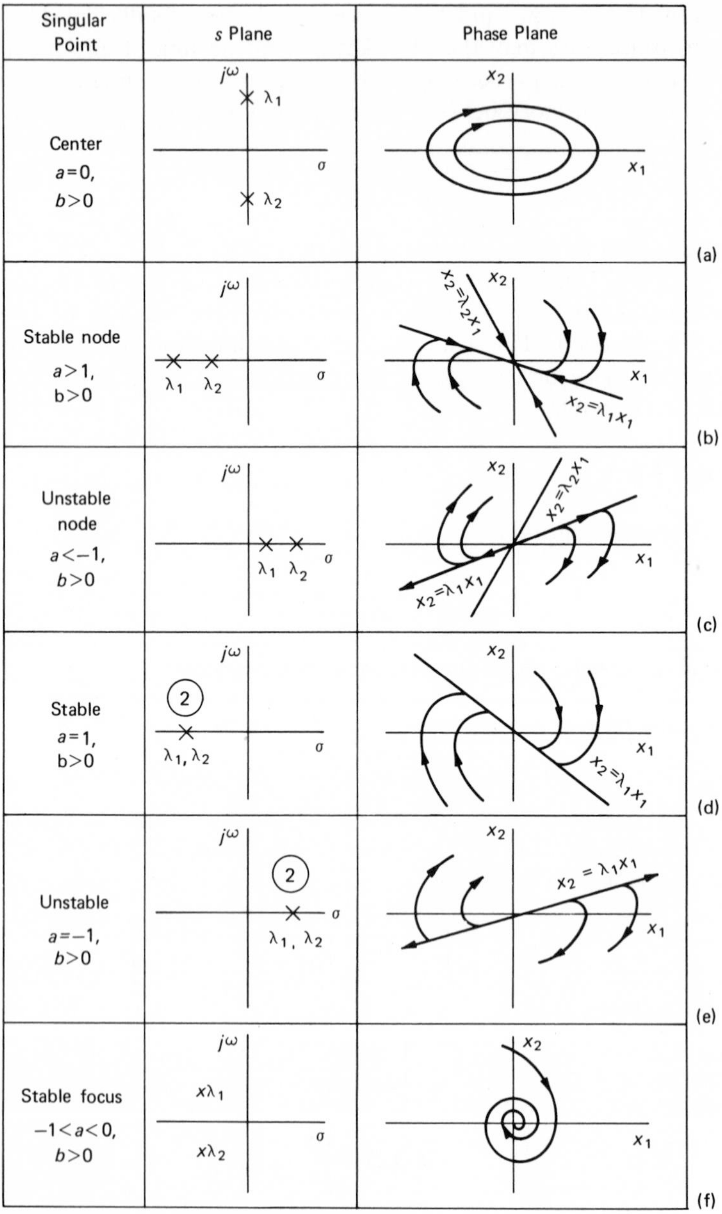

Singular Point
s Plane
Phase Plane
Center
a=0,
b>0
Stable node
a>1,
b>0
Unstable node
a<−1,
b>0
Stable
a=1,
b>0
Unstable
a=−1,
b>0
Stable focus
−1<a<0,
b>0
jω
σ
λ1
λ2
λ1, λ2
2
x2
x1
x2=λ1x1
x2=λ2x1
(a)
(b)
(c)
(d)
(e)
(f)

(a)

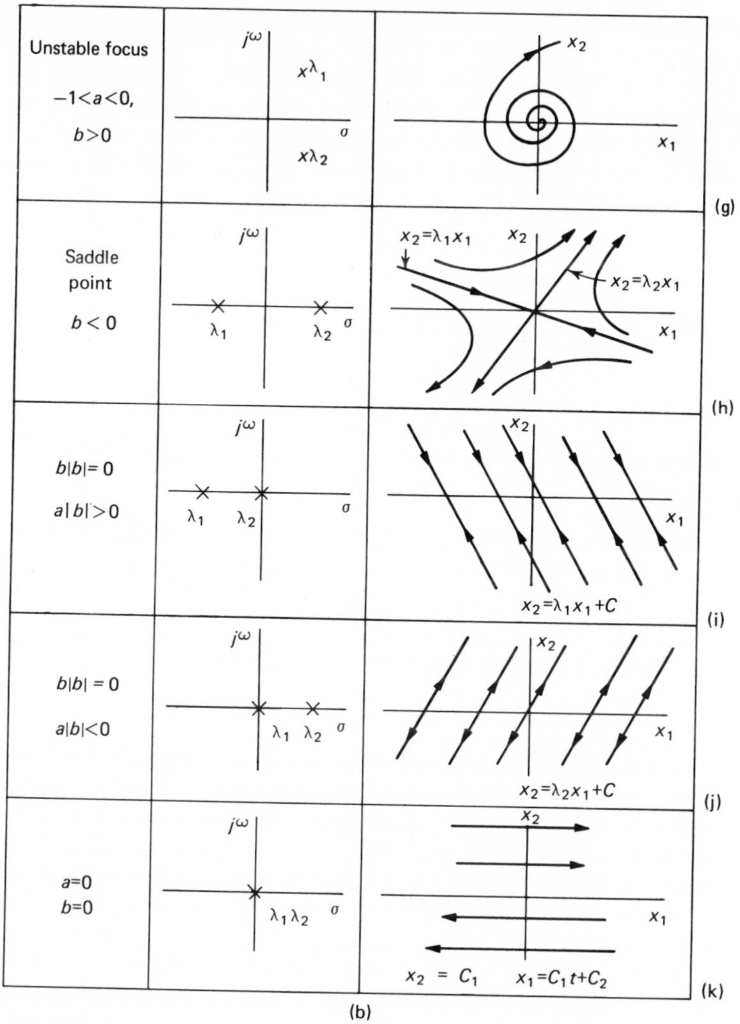

Figure 6.8–1. Possible singular points for nonlinear second-order differential equation shown in linearized phase plane (state variables x_1 and x_2 are with respect to singular point in **z** plane).

the linearized system characteristic equation is $s^2 + 2s - 4 = 0$, giving $a = \frac{1}{2}$ and $b = -2$ in (6.8–9). From Figure 6.8–1, the singular point is a saddle point and is unstable. At $\mathbf{z}_{e_2}$ and $\mathbf{z}_{e_3}$, the characteristic equation becomes $s^2 + 2s + 8 = 0$, resulting in $a = 1/\sqrt{8}$ and $b = \sqrt{8}$. From Figure 6.8–1 each of these singular points is a stable focus. The trajectories in the neighborhood of the singular points therefore will look similar to those of Figure 6.8–2. We could suspect from Figure 6.8–2 that for an initial condition to the right of the line $z_2 = (-1 - \sqrt{5})z_1$ the system would proceed to the stable point $z_1 = 2/3$, $z_2 = 0$, while to the left it would go to the stable

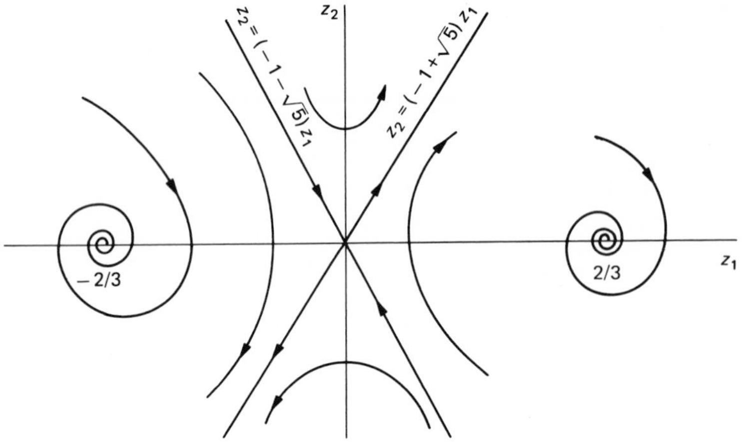

Figure 6.8–2. Trajectories in neighborhood of singular points for Example 6.8–1.

point $z_1 = -2/3$, $z_2 = 0$. This line is called the separatrix. Before we finally announce this conclusion, it might be best to compute and sketch in a few trajectories for the original system, however. A system that performs in this manner might make a good flip-flop device (although for rapidity of action stable nodes at $z_1 = \pm\frac{2}{3}$ would be preferable) but would not be a permissible control system unless we can guarantee no excursions near the separatrix. Thus a designer may not always require stability, because one designer's meat may be another's poison. Control designers, however, usually require meat.

Techniques of linearization other than by a Taylor's series are possible. As discussed in Chapter 2, we may simply assume an average linear characteristic for a known nonlinear device. Or we may approximate a nonlinear characteristic by two or three straight line segments, which means we need to investigate a number of linear systems. Nonlinear systems have also been studied by using the describing function, which essentially constitutes a form of linearization [26].

The present state of the science and art of control theory leads to the use of linear theory, at least in the beginning stages of design. The engineer must be aware of nonlinearities, however, and be prepared for some surprises in his first pilot system.

PROBLEMS

6.1. Given

$$\mathbf{A} = \begin{bmatrix} 0 & -3 \\ 2 & -5 \end{bmatrix}$$

Find $\epsilon^{\mathbf{A}t}$ using
(a) Sylvester expansion theorem.
(b) Cayley-Hamilton remainder technique.
(c) Spectral representation.
(d) Diagonalization.
(e) Laplace transform method.

6.2. Find $e^{\mathbf{A}t}$ for

$$\mathbf{A} = \begin{bmatrix} -2 & 1 \\ -2 & -4 \end{bmatrix}$$

6.3. Repeat Problem 6.2 for

$$\mathbf{A} = \begin{bmatrix} 0 & 2 & 0 \\ 0 & 0 & -4 \\ -1 & 3 & 6 \end{bmatrix}$$

6.4. Repeat Problem 6.2 for

$$\mathbf{A} = \begin{bmatrix} 0 & 1 & 0 \\ 0 & 0 & 1 \\ -6 & -11 & -6 \end{bmatrix}$$

6.5. Repeat Problem 6.2 for

$$\mathbf{A} = \begin{bmatrix} 0 & 1 \\ -5 & -3 \end{bmatrix}$$

6.6. Given the flow diagram shown in Figure P6.6:
(a) Write the equations in the state-variable form.
(b) Determine the **A**, **B**, **C**, and **D** matrices.
(c) Find the transition matrix $\boldsymbol{\phi}(t)$ by any of the methods of Problem 6.1, and check by finding $\mathscr{L}^{-1}[\hat{\boldsymbol{\phi}}(s)]$, where $\hat{\boldsymbol{\phi}}(s)$ is obtained from Figure P6.6 by applying impulses at each integrator, as shown in Example 6.5–2.

(d) Find $\mathbf{W}(t)$, the weighting function (impulse response) matrix from the transition matrix $\boldsymbol{\phi}(t)$ (Section 6.5) and check by finding $\mathbf{Z}(s) = Y(s)/M(s)$ directly from the flow diagram.

(e) If $m(t) = 3\epsilon^{-2t}u(t)$ and all initial conditions are zero, find $y(t)$ using the transition matrix.

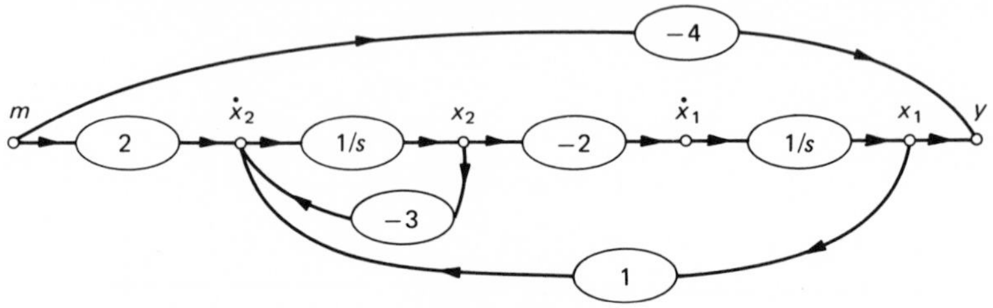

Figure P6.6.

6.7. Given the flow diagram of Figure P6.7:

(a) Write the equations in a state-space form and give the **A**, **B**, **C**, and **D** matrices.

(b) Find the characteristic equation and see if the system is stable by finding whether or not roots exist in the right-half s plane. (See also the Routh-Hurtwitz criterion, Chapter 7.)

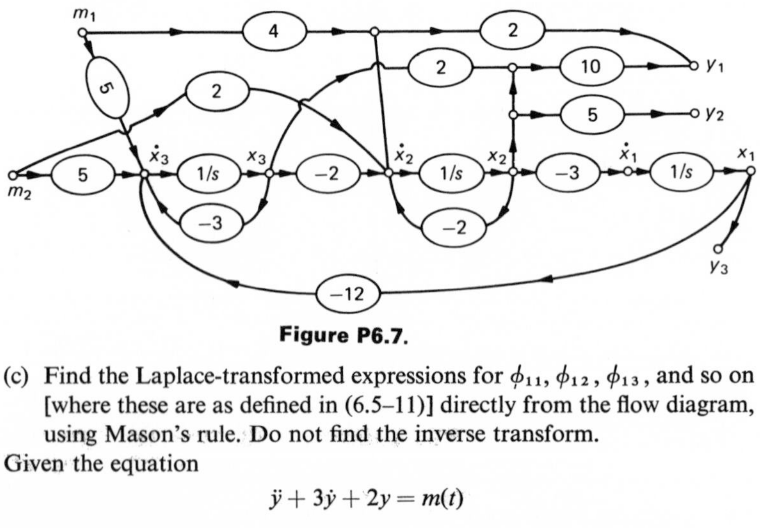

Figure P6.7.

(c) Find the Laplace-transformed expressions for $\phi_{11}, \phi_{12}, \phi_{13}$, and so on [where these are as defined in (6.5–11)] directly from the flow diagram, using Mason's rule. Do not find the inverse transform.

6.8. Given the equation

$$\ddot{y} + 3\dot{y} + 2y = m(t)$$

(a) Let $x_1 = y$, $x_2 = \dot{x}_1$, and find the characteristic vectors and the reciprocal basis vectors.

(b) Write the state-space equations.

(c) From (a) find the values of $x_1(0)$ and $x_2(0)$ such that only one mode will be excited at a time if $m(t) = 0$.

(d) Find $\boldsymbol{\phi}(t)$, the transition matrix.

6.9. Given the control system described by

$$\dot{\mathbf{x}} = \mathbf{A}\mathbf{x} + \mathbf{B}\mathbf{m}$$

$$\mathbf{y} = \mathbf{C}\mathbf{x} + \mathbf{D}\mathbf{m}$$

where

$$\mathbf{A} = \begin{bmatrix} 0 & 1 & 0 \\ 0 & 0 & 1 \\ -6 & -11 & -6 \end{bmatrix} \qquad \mathbf{B} = \begin{bmatrix} 1 \\ 1 \\ 1 \end{bmatrix}$$

$$\mathbf{C} = [0 \quad 1 \quad 1] \qquad \mathbf{D} = \mathbf{0}$$

(a) Find **V**, the matrix that diagonalizes **A** and $\mathbf{V}^{-1}$.
(b) Write the state-space equations in diagonalized form.
(c) Given that $x_1(0) = 1$, $x_2(0) = 2$, $x_3(0) = 3$, and **m** is $4u(t)$, find $y(t)$ using (b).
(d) Find $\mathscr{L}[\boldsymbol{\phi}(t)]$ for the original system.

6.10. Given the system of Problem 6.9 with the same **A** but

$$\mathbf{B} = \begin{bmatrix} 1 \\ 1 \\ -7 \end{bmatrix} \qquad \mathbf{C} = [4 \quad 1 \quad -3]$$

(a) Find the transfer function $\mathbf{Z}(s)$.
(b) Indicate which, if any, modes are uncontrollable and/or unobservable.

6.11. Given

$$\dot{\mathbf{x}} = \mathbf{A}\mathbf{x} + \mathbf{B}\mathbf{m}$$

$$\mathbf{y} = \mathbf{C}\mathbf{x} + \mathbf{D}\mathbf{m}$$

where

$$\mathbf{A} = \begin{bmatrix} 0 & 1 \\ -2 & -3 \end{bmatrix} \qquad \mathbf{B} = \begin{bmatrix} 1 & 2 \\ 3 & 2 \end{bmatrix}$$

$$\mathbf{C} = \begin{bmatrix} 2 & 3 \\ 1 & 4 \end{bmatrix} \qquad \mathbf{D} = \mathbf{0}$$

(a) Draw a simulation diagram.
(b) Find $\boldsymbol{\phi}(t)$, the transition matrix.
(c) Find $\mathbf{W}(t)$, the impulse response matrix from $\boldsymbol{\phi}(t)$.
(d) Find $\mathbf{Z}(s)$, the transfer function, from the simulation diagram, and check (c).
(e) Find $\mathbf{y}(t)$ if $x_1(0) = x_2(0) = 1$ and $m_1(t) = m_2(t) = u(t)$.

6.12. Given

$$\ddot{y} + (t + 1)\dot{y} + t^2 y = 0$$

(a) Put this into state-space form.
(b) Write the state-space form of the adjoint system using variables z_1 and z_2.
(c) Write the differential equation of a modified adjoint system in terms of $\mathbf{q} = [0 \quad 1]\mathbf{z}$ and its derivitives, where t is replaced by $(T - t_1)$.

6.13. (a) In Figure P6.13 write the state-space form with the variables shown.
(b) Find the impulse response matrix $\mathbf{W}(t)$ by two methods.

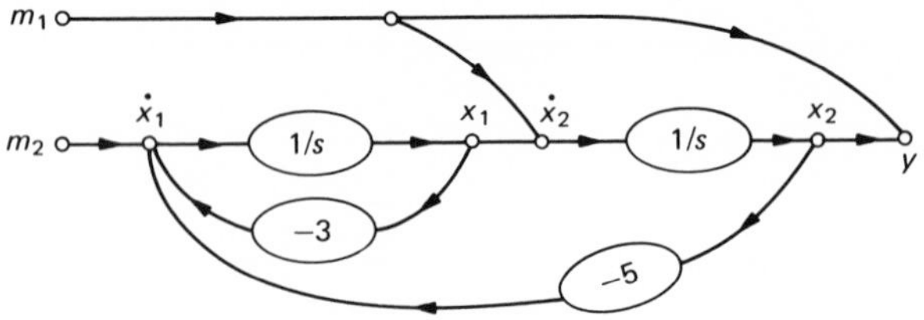

Figure P6.13.

6.14. Given

$$\dot{\mathbf{x}} = \mathbf{Ax} + \mathbf{Bm}$$

$$\mathbf{y} = \mathbf{Cx} + \mathbf{Dm}$$

$$\mathbf{A} = \begin{bmatrix} -1 & 1 \\ -1 & -2 \end{bmatrix} \qquad \mathbf{B} = \begin{bmatrix} 1 \\ 2 \end{bmatrix}$$

$$\mathbf{C} = [2 \quad 1] \qquad \mathbf{D} = 0$$

(a) Draw a simulation diagram.
(b) Using (a), find $\mathbf{Z}(s) = Y(s)/M(s)$.
(c) Check $\mathbf{Z}(s)$ by finding $\mathbf{W}(t)$ through $\boldsymbol{\phi}(t)$.

6.15. Using Figure P6.15:
(a) Write the differential equations of motion assuming M_1 and M_2 move only vertically.
(b) Let $x_1 = y_1, x_2 = \dot{y}_1, x_3 = y_2, x_4 = \dot{y}_2$, and write the state-space equations.
(c) If $f_1 = a \sin \omega t$, find K_2/M_2 in terms of ω and other constants to make $y_1 = 0$ as $t \to \infty$, if possible

6.16. Devise an unstable control system for which one mode is unobservable and one mode is uncontrollable.

6.17. Write a digital computer program for the Fadeeva method of finding $(s\mathbf{I} - \mathbf{A})^{-1}$ given $\mathbf{A}$.

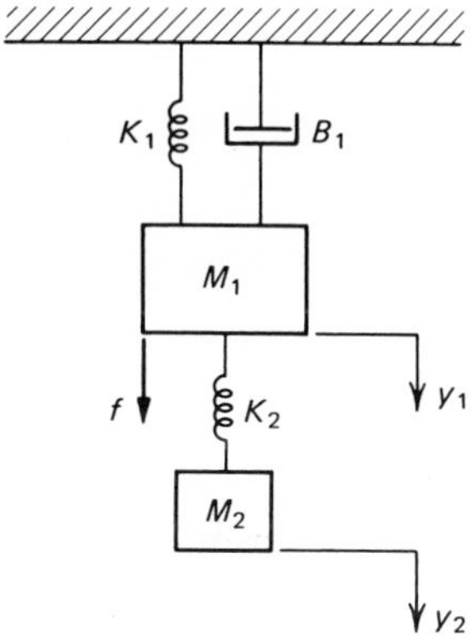

Figure P6.15.

6.18. Given the free system

$$\ddot{x} + x - 2x^3 = 0$$

let

$$x_1 = x \quad \text{and} \quad x_2 = \dot{x}_1$$

(a) Find the equilibrium points.
(b) Make a small region linearization at each point and determine its nature.
(c) Sketch isoclines for slopes of 0, 1, -1, and ∞.
(d) Sketch the phase portrait in the region $x_1 = \pm 2$, $x_2 = \pm 2$.

6.19. Repeat Problem 6.18 for the equation

$$\ddot{x} + b\dot{x} + Kb(x^2 - x - 2) = 0$$

for (a) $Kb > 0$
(b) $Kb < 0$.

6.20. Write a digital computer program to solve Problem 6.19 and see what initial conditions are necessary to obtain a root of $x^2 - x - 2 = 0$.

REFERENCES AND FURTHER READING

[1] V. N. Faddeeva, *Computational Methods of Linear Algebra*, Dover, New York, 1959, pp. 177–182.
[2] L. A. Zadeh and C. A. Desoer, *Linear System Theory*, McGraw-Hill, New York, pp. 303–306.
[3] J. G. Truxal, *Automatic Feedback Control System Synthesis*, McGraw-Hill, New York, 1955, pp. 21–26.

[4] R. E. Bellman, R. E. Kalaba, H. H. Kagiwada, and M. C. Prestrud, *Invarient Imbedding and Time-dependent Transport Processes*, Elsevier, Amsterdam, 1964, Chap. 1.
[5] H. V. Nordén, Numerical Inversion of the Laplace Transform, *Acta Acad. Aboensis Math. Phys.*, **22** (1961), 3–31.
[6] A. Papoulis, A New Method of Inversion of the Laplace Transform, *Quart. Appl. Math.*, **14** (1957), 405–414.
[7] P. M. De Russo, R. J. Roy, and C. M. Close, *State Variables for Engineers*, Wiley, New York, 1965, pp. 362–369.
[8] Zadeh and Desoer, *op. cit.*, pp. 369–375.
[9] De Russo, Roy, and Close, *op. cit.*, pp. 369, 375.
[10] M. Athans and P. L. Falb, *Optimal Control*, McGraw-Hill, New York, 1966, pp. 147–149.
[11] A. E. Bryson, Jr., and W. F. Denham, A Steepest Ascent Method for Solving Optimal Programming Problems, *J. Appl. Mech.*, **29** (2) (1962), 247–257 (also published by the Ratheon Co., Bedford, Mass., 1961); see also references in [10].
[12] R. J. Schwarz and B. Friedland, *Linear Systems*, McGraw-Hill, New York, 1965.
[13] R. E. Kalman, Mathematical Description of Linear Dynamical Systems, *J. Soc. Ind. Appl. Math. Control*, **A1** (2) (1963), 152–193; see also E. G. Gilbert, same issue.
[14] *Ibid.*
[15] *Ibid.*, p. 164.
[16] *Ibid.*
[17] Athans and Falb, *op. cit.*, pp. 200–211.
[18] E. G. Gilbert, Controllability and Observability in Multivariable Systems, *J. Soc. Ind. Appl. Math. Control*, **A1** (2) (1963), 128–152.
[19] Schwarz and Friedland, *op. cit.* pp. 378–382.
[20] Zadeh and Desoer, *op. cit.* pp. 385–392.
[21] J. C. Hsu and A. U. Meyer, *Modern Control Principles and Applications*, McGraw-Hill, New York, 1968, Chap. 10.
[22] L. S. Pontryagin, V. Boltyanski, R. Gamkrelidze, and E. Mishenko, *The Mathematical Theory of Optimal Processes*, Wiley (Interscience), New York, 1962, pp. 127–135.
[23] L. P. LaSalle and S. Lefschetz, *Stability by Lyapunov's Direct Method with Applications*, Academic Press, New York, 1961.
[24] G. J. Thaler and M. P. Pastel, *Analysis and Design of Nonlinear Feedback Control Systems*, McGraw-Hill, New York, 1962, pp. 66–71.
[25] Thaler and Pastel, *Ibid.*, pp. 82–86.
[26] J. G. Truxal, *Automatic Feedback Control System Synthesis*, McGraw-Hill, New York, 1955. Chap. 10.

Textbooks Using State-Space Methods

[27] W. W. Seifert and C. W. Steeg, Jr., *Control System Engineering*, McGraw-Hill, New York, 1960.
[28] L. A. Zadeh and C. A. Desoer, *Linear System Theory*, McGraw-Hill, New York, 1963.
[29] J. T. Tou, *Modern Control Theory*, McGraw-Hill, New York, 1964.
[30] P. M. De Russo, R. J. Roy, and C. M. Close, *State Variables for Engineers*, Wiley, New York, 1965.
[31] R. C. Dorf, *Time Domain Analysis and Design of Control Systems*, Addison-Wesley Reading, Mass., 1965.

[32] A. J. G. MacFarlane, *Engineering Systems Analysis*, Addision-Wesley, Reading, Mass., 1965.
[33] M. Athans and P. L. Falb, *Optimal Control*, McGraw-Hill, New York, 1966.
[34] G. J. Murphy, *Basic Automatic Control Theory*, Van Nostrand, Princeton, N.J., 2nd ed., 1966.
[35] O. I. Elgerd, *Control Systems Theory*, McGraw-Hill, New York, 1967.
[36] R. C. Dorf, *Modern Control Systems*, Addison-Wesley, Reading, Mass., 1967.
[37] H. E. Koenig, Y. Tokad, and H. K. Kesavan, *Analysis of Discrete Physical Systems*, McGraw-Hill, New York, 1967.
[38] K. Ogata, *State Space Analysis of Control Systems*, Prentice-Hall, Englewood Cliffs, N.J., 1967.
[39] L. K. Timothy and B. E. Bona, *State Space Analysis: An Introduction*, McGraw-Hill, New York, 1967.
[40] J. C. Hsu and A. U. Meyer, *Modern Control Principles and Applications*, McGraw-Hill, New York, 1968.

Textbooks on Nonlinear Systems

[41] A. A. Andronov and G. E. Chaikin, *Theory of Oscillations*, Princeton Univ. Press, Princeton, N.J., 1949.
[42] H. Chestnut and R. W. Mayer, *Servomechanisms and Regulating System Design*, Vol. II, Wiley, New York, 1955.
[43] R. L. Cosgriff, *Nonlinear Control Systems*, McGraw-Hill, New York, 1958.
[44] D. Graham and D. McRuer, *Analysis of Nonlinear Control Systems*, Wiley, New York, 1961.
[45] G. J. Thaler and M. P. Pastel, *Analysis and Design of Nonlinear Feedback Control Systems*, McGraw-Hill, New York, 1962.
[46] J. E. Gibson, *Nonlinear Automatic Control*, McGraw-Hill, New York, 1963.
[47] N. V. Butenin, *Elements of the Theory of Nonlinear Oscillations*, Ginn-Blaisdell, Boston, 1965.

7 The Characteristic Equation and the Root Locus

7.1 Introduction

In Chapter 6 you saw that the stability of a fixed system depends on the roots of the characteristic equation. (For purposes of simplicity we assume that the characteristic polynomial and the minimal polynomial are the same.) If these roots lie in the left-half plane, the system is assymptotically stable undriven and stable driven. Hence, if we can show that the roots are in the left-half plane, asymptotic stability, which will be our meaning of the word stability for fixed systems, is proved. The roots may be exactly located by factoring, but solving a polynomial of high degree becomes a most difficult task, as most engineers know. When the engineer has a computer terminal on his desk, it will be possible to obtain polynomial factors in a matter of seconds. Until that time, or until the invention of a small, low-cost polynomial solver, this method repels, not invites. The Routh-Hurwitz test is a fairly rapid test that indicates the existence of roots in the right-half plane but does not find exact values for roots. Thus it is a good tool for a quick check on stability. However, it does not offer much basis for design, because, unless you can narrow down the regions for the root locations, you know little about relative stability. Furthermore, design using either the root-solving method or the Routh-Hurwitz criteria consists of a matter of cut and try. That is, for each change made, a new location of roots is determined and the resulting performance checked. Such a procedure would be exasperating, and a good design would be a function of luck. The root locus provides a straightforward method for finding the roots of the characteristic equation as a function of some variable (such as gain) and is hence an excellent design tool. The root-locus technique was promulgated by W. R. Evans in 1948 and given further impetus by Truxal and Thaler [1, 2, 3].

We first discuss the Routh-Hurwitz criterion and then the root locus technique. In the latter case we shall assume a single input-output system that is both controllable and observable.

7.2 Routh-Hurwitz Test

The form of this test most suited to control systems is stated without proof [4].

Given the characteristic equation

$$d(s) = s^n + d_1 s^{n-1} + d_2 s^{n-2} + \cdots + d_n = 0 \qquad \textbf{(7.2–1)}$$

form a Routh array as follows:

$$\begin{array}{cccc} 1 & d_2 & d_4 & \cdots \\ d_1 & d_3 & d_5 & \cdots \\ a_1 & a_2 & a_3 & \cdots \\ b_1 & b_2 & b_3 & \cdots \\ c_1 & c_2 & c_3 & \cdots \\ \vdots & & & \end{array} \qquad \textbf{(7.2–2)}$$

where

$$a_1 = \frac{d_1 d_2 - (1)d_3}{d_1}, \quad a_2 = \frac{d_1 d_4 - (1)d_5}{d_1}, \quad a_3 = \frac{d_1 d_6 - (1)d_7}{d_1}, \quad \cdots$$

$$b_1 = \frac{a_1 d_3 - d_1 a_2}{a_1}, \quad b_2 = \frac{a_1 d_5 - d_1 a_3}{a_1}, \quad b_3 = \frac{a_1 d_7 - d_1 a_5}{a_1}, \quad \cdots \qquad \textbf{(7.2–3)}$$

$$c_1 = \frac{b_1 a_2 - a_1 b_2}{b_1}, \quad c_2 = \frac{b_1 a_3 - a_1 b_3}{b_1}, \quad \cdots$$

$$\vdots$$

Equations (7.2–3) are continued until the complete array of (7.2–2) contains $n + 1$ rows.

The Routh rule then states that the number of changes in sign in the first column of the array equals the number of roots of (7.2–1) with positive real parts. For stability, there must therefore be no changes in sign. (Again, by stability we imply asymptotic stability.)

Example 7.2–1

Given

$$s^5 + 3s^4 + 2s^3 + s^2 + 5s + 6 = 0 \tag{7.2–4}$$

find the number of roots with positive real parts.

From (7.2–2) the array becomes

$$\begin{array}{ccc} 1 & 2 & 5 \\ 3 & 1 & 6 \\ \frac{5}{3} & 3 & \\ -\frac{22}{5} & 6 & \\ \frac{116}{22} & & \\ 6 & & \end{array}$$

The table shows two sign changes in the first column; hence there are two roots in the right-half plane.

To avoid the fractional numbers in the example, any row may be multiplied or divided by any positive number. Thus the previous table might become

$$\begin{array}{ccc} 1 & 2 & 5 \\ 3 & 1 & 6 \\ 5 & 9 & \\ -11 & 15 & \\ 87 & & \\ 15 & & \end{array}$$

In some cases a first column term is zero. To avoid difficulty, let the term be a small positive quantity ϵ, and proceed as before.

Example 7.2–2

Given

$$s^4 + 3s^3 + s^2 + 3s + 1 = 0 \tag{7.2–5}$$

find the Routh table. We get, substituting ϵ for zero,

$$\begin{array}{rrr} 1 & 1 & 1 \\ 3 & 3 & \\ \epsilon & 1 & \\ 3 - \dfrac{3}{\epsilon} & & \\ 1 & & \end{array}$$

as $\epsilon \to 0$, in the first column, the third row term becomes a large negative number. Hence there are two roots with positive real parts.

If a row before the $(n + 2)$nd row has all zeros, roots of the characteristic equation exist that have the same magnitude but angles differing by π. To complete the table, we find a "subsidiary" function of the row preceding the row of zeros. Let this be the jth row and contain the numbers k_1, k_2, k_3, and so on. The subsidiary function is then

$$k_1 s^{n+1-j} + k_2 s^{n+1-j-2} + k_3 s^{n+1-j-4} + \cdots$$

Now take the derivative of this function with respect to s and proceed with the resulting coefficients as a row in place of the row of zeros.

Example 7.2–3

Find the Routh array for

$$s^6 + s^5 - 2s^4 - 3s^3 - 7s^2 - 4s - 4 = 0 \tag{7.2–6}$$

Proceeding as before we get

$$\begin{array}{rrrr} 1 & -2 & -7 & -4 \\ 1 & -3 & -4 & 0 \\ 1 & -3 & -4 & \\ 0 & 0 & 0 & \end{array}$$

The subsidiary function of row 3 ($j = 3$, $n = 6$) is

$$s^4 - 3s^2 - 4 \tag{7.2–7}$$

$$\frac{d}{ds}(s^4 - 3s^2 - 4) = 4s^3 - 6s$$

The table now continues with the fourth row as follows:

4	−6
−1.5	−4
−16.7	
−4	

There is one sign change in the first column, indicating one root with a positive real part. If we factor (7.2–7) we obtain

$$s^4 - 3s^2 - 4 = (s^2 + 1)(s^2 - 4)$$

which indicates that four roots of (7.2–6) are $s = \pm j1$ and $s = \pm 2$.

Roots on the $j\omega$ axis will always lead to a row of zeros, and if the subsidiary function is of not too high a degree, this function may be factored to give these values. Knowledge that some roots occur in pairs, one the negative of another, aids in this factoring. It is clear from the Routh array or consideration of (7.2–1) that if any d_i are negative, there will be roots in the right-half plane.

Using the Routh array it is possible to develop a general relation of coefficients, but for polynomials of order greater than 4, the equations become too complicated to be of much use. For the fourth-order equation

$$s^4 + A_1 s^3 + A_2 s^2 + A_3 s + A_4 = 0 \tag{7.2–8}$$

the Routh array gives the following requirements:

$$A_i > 0 \qquad i = 1, 2, 3, 4 \tag{7.2–9a}$$

$$(A_1 A_2 - A_3)A_3 - A_1^2 A_4 > 0 \tag{7.2–9b}$$

and for a third-order equation with $A_1 = 1$, we get

$$A_i > 0 \qquad i = 2, 3, 4 \tag{7.2–10a}$$

$$A_2 A_3 > A_4 \tag{7.2–10b}$$

If we have an equality sign in (7.2–9b) and (7.2–10b), some roots lie on the $j\omega$ axis.

Example 7.2–4

In Figure 7.2–1 find the value of K for which the system becomes unstable. The system transfer function is

$$\frac{Y(s)}{M(s)} = \frac{K}{s^3 + 6s^2 + 5s + K}$$

and the characteristic equation is $s^3 + 6s^2 + 5s + K = 0$

From (7.2–10),

$$A_2 = 6 \qquad A_3 = 5 \qquad A_4 = K \qquad 30 > K$$

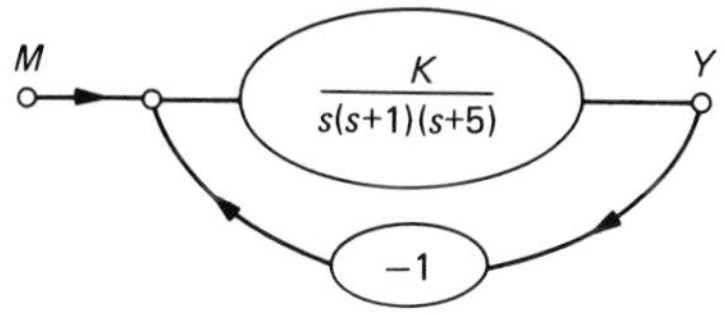

Figure 7.2–1. Unstable system for $K > 30$.

The system becomes unstable if $K > 30$. The characteristic equation will have imaginary roots if $K = 30$. Setting $K = 30$, we may find the location of the imaginary roots by the Routh array. The array becomes

1	5
6	30
0	0

Hence the subsidiary function is $6s^2 + 30 = (s + j\sqrt{5})(s - j\sqrt{6})$. Two roots are therefore $\pm j\sqrt{5}$ when $K = 30$.

7.3 Root Locus—Fundamentals

In a single input-output system of the form of Figure 7.3–1, the system transfer function is

$$\frac{C(s)}{R(s)} = \frac{G(s)}{1 + G(s)H(s)} \tag{7.3–1}$$

If

$$G(s) = \frac{P(s)}{Q(s)} = \frac{KP_1(s)}{Q(s)}$$

$$H(s) = \frac{U(s)}{V(s)}$$

where P, P_1, Q, U, and V are polynomials in s. We found in (3.6–8) that

$$\frac{C(s)}{R(s)} = \frac{P(s)V(s)}{P(s)U(s) + Q(s)V(s)} \tag{7.3–2a}$$

or

$$\frac{C(s)}{R(s)} = \frac{K_1 \prod_{k=1}^{m} (s + z_k)}{\prod_{k=1}^{n} (s + P_k)} \tag{7.3–2b}$$

where $-P_k$, $k = 1$ to n, are the poles and $-z_k$, $k = 1$ to m are the zeros of $C(s)/R(s)$. In terms of the characteristic functions, the $-P_k$'s are the eigenvalues or natural frequencies of the system. There will be n such frequencies if the poles are distinct, where n is the degree of the characteristic polynomial. m, the number of zeros, is less than n in most control systems.

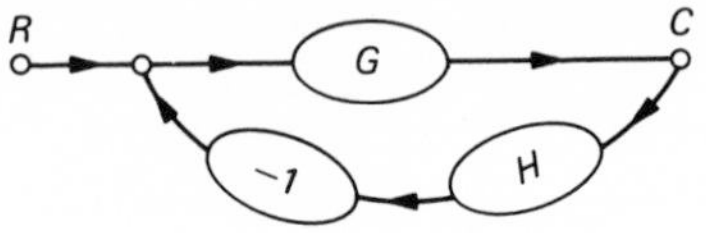

Figure 7.3–1. Feedback system.

K_1 is the constant remaining after $C(s)/R(s)$ has been put into the factored form shown in (7.3–3) and is considered to be positive; that is, $K_1 \geq 0$. The case for $K_1 \leq 0$ will be discussed later.

The open loop function may be written

$$G(s)H(s) = \frac{P(s)U(s)}{Q(s)V(s)} = \frac{K \prod_{i=1}^{m} (s + z_i)}{\prod_{j=1}^{n} (s + p_j)} \tag{7.3–3}$$

where $K \geq 0$.

We would like to find a reasonably simple method for finding the P_k from the p_j and z_i, which are known since normally $P(s)$, $Q(s)$, $U(s)$, and $V(s)$ are in factored form. In other words, we desire to locate the system poles given the open loop poles and zeros. [The system zeros are no problem—see (7.3–2).] From (7.3–2) and (7.3–3), the P_k are found by setting the characteristic polynomial $P(s)U(s) + Q(s)V(s) = 0$. Comparing (7.3–2) and (7.3–1) it is also clear that we could equally well set

$$1 + G(s)H(s) = 0 \tag{7.3–4}$$

Equation (7.3–4) is the basis of the root locus. To get this in a form more directly applicable, however, transfer the left term to the other side of the equation to obtain

$$G(s)H(s) = -1 \tag{7.3–5}$$

Now we recall that in the complex s plane this may be written

$$G(s)H(s) = |1| \epsilon^{j(2k+1)\pi} \qquad k = \text{integer} \tag{7.3–6}$$

In other words, roots of the characteristic equation lie in the s plane such that at each root $-P_k$, $k = 1, \ldots, n$,

$$|GH| = 1 \qquad \textbf{(7.3–7a)}$$

$$\arg GH = (2k+1)\pi \qquad k = \text{integer} \qquad \textbf{(7.3–7b)}$$

where arg GH means the angle of GH. To implement (7.3–7), look at Figure 7.3–2, which shows the location of open loop poles and zeros for

$$GH(s) = \frac{K(s+z_1)}{(s+p_1)(s+p_2)}$$

where $-z_1$ is the open loop zero and $-p_1$ and $-p_2$ are the open loop poles (usually known). Let s_1 be a root of the characteristic equation. We now draw lines from $-p_1$, $-p_2$, and $-z_1$ to s_1 as shown in Figure 7.3–2.

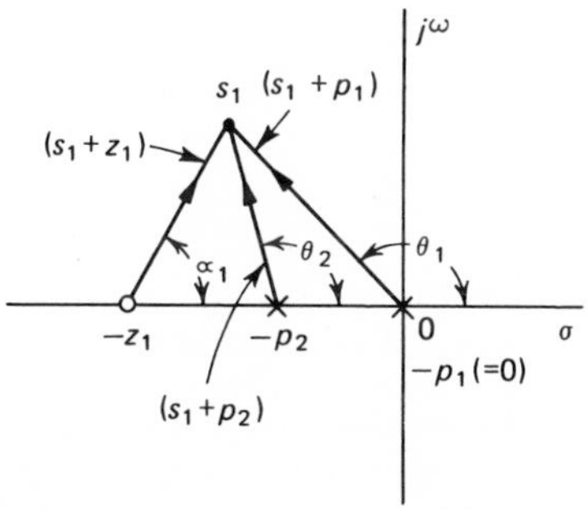

Figure 7.3–2. Magnitude and angle factors for $GH = K(s+z_1)/(s+p_1)(s+p_2)$, $p_1 = 0$.

In the s plane s_1 represents a vector from the origin to the point s_1. Hence these lines represent the vectors $(s_1 + p_1)$, $(s_1 + p_2)$, and $(s_1 + z_1)$, respectively. Putting these in polar form,

$$s_1 + p_1 = |s_1 + p_1| \epsilon^{j\theta_1} = r_1 \epsilon^{j\theta_1}$$

$$s_1 + p_2 = |s_1 + p_2| \epsilon^{j\theta_2} = r_2 \epsilon^{j\theta_2}$$

$$s_1 + z_1 = |s_1 + z_1| \epsilon^{j\alpha_1} = r_3 \epsilon^{j\alpha_1}$$

where r_k is the magnitude (length or norm) of the corresponding vector. Then (7.3–6) states that

$$\frac{K r_3 \epsilon^{j\alpha_1}}{r_1 r_2 \epsilon^{j\theta_1} \epsilon^{j\theta_2}} = |1| \epsilon^{j(2k+1)\pi}$$

or, from (7.3–7),

$$\alpha_1 - \theta_1 - \theta_2 = (2k+1)\pi \qquad k = \text{integer} \tag{7.3–8a}$$

$$\frac{Kr_3}{r_1 r_2} = 1 \tag{7.3–8b}$$

Thus if s_1 is a root of the characteristic equation, the algebraic sum of the angles of the vectors from the open loop poles and zeros to s_1 must be $(2k+1)\pi$, $k =$ integer.

The discussion of the example is easily extended to any number of open loop poles and zeros. Thus (7.3–7b) can be written

$$-\sum_{k=0}^{n} \theta_j + \sum_{k=1}^{m} \alpha_i = (2k+1)\pi \qquad k = \text{integer} \tag{7.3–9}$$

where the α_i are the angles of the lines from the zeros and the θ_j are the angles of the lines from the poles. Angles are always measured from the positive real axis, with a counterclockwise angle being positive by definition. Thus a locus of points may be drawn that satisfies (7.3–9), resulting in a curve or series of curves in the s plane. Turning to (7.3–7a), we note that for each of these points $|GH| = 1$. For any particular point s_1, the lengths of the vectors can be measured and are thus known. Hence in (7.3–3), K is the only unknown and is readily found by (7.3–7a). Thus the root locus represents the locus of points that satisfies the angle requirement (7.3–7b) or (7.3–9), and for which K is a variable. An example will illustrate a simple locus.

Example 7.3–1

Find the root locus of $GH(s) = K/s(s+4)$. The poles and zeros are shown in Figure 7.3–3. First we see that any point on the real axis between

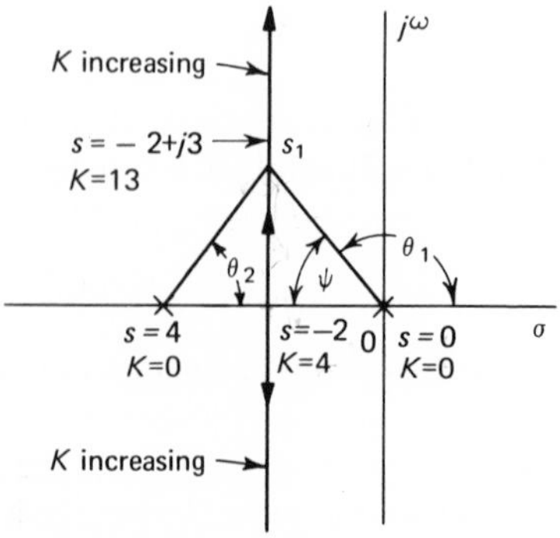

Figure 7.3–3. Root locus for $GH = K/s(s+4)$ negative feedback.

$s = 0$ and $s = -4$ satisfies the angle requirement, because the angle from the pole at $s = 0$ to such a point is π and from the pole at $s = -4$ to this point is zero. Next, for points above the real axis, we see that if we make an isosceles triangle with s_1 with the poles as a base, the angle requirement is also met, because in this case $\theta_2 = \pi - \theta_1$. Continuing this argument for all possible s values, branches of the locus therefore lie on a straight line through the point $s = -2$ and parallel to the $j\omega$ axis. Theoretically we now need to establish K values for each point on the locus, but obviously it is sufficient to first locate a few K values. Others can be found by interpolation, or later calculations, if necessary. The characteristic equation is

$$s^2 + 4s + K = 0$$

The root locus represents the roots of this equation as K varies, so clearly the open loop poles are the root points when $K = 0$. When $s = -2$, the vector from each loop pole has a magnitude $= 2$. Then from (7.3–7a), $K/(2)(2) = 1$, or $K = 4$. Between $s = 0$ and $s = -2$, and between $s = -4$ and $s = -2$, K goes from 0 to 4. For example, at $s = -1$, and at $s = -3$, $K = 3$, and so on. When $K > 4$, the roots become complex. When $s = -2 \pm j2$, the vector lengths are each $\sqrt{8}$, whence $K = 8$. Conjugate values of s obviously carry the same K values, as shown in Figure 7.3–3. The root locus is shown with heavy lines, with arrows pointing in the directions of increasing K. When $K \to \infty$, $s \to -2 \pm j\infty$. The loci thus give a graphical picture of the roots of the characteristic equation, which form the natural frequencies of oscillation of the system. This system is never unstable. Now suppose you desire to adjust K until the damping factor is 0.5. This means that $\cos \psi = 0.5$ or $\psi = 60°$. The $-P_1$ value will be where the line making an angle of 60° with the negative real axis crosses the locus, or, from Figure 7.3–3, at $s = -2 + j2\sqrt{3}$. The vector lengths are 4 and 4; hence $K = 16$ will give a closed loop system with a damping factor of 0.5. The oscillation frequency will be $\sqrt{3}/\pi$ Hz.

This example is very simple, and you can find the roots as easily by solving a quadratic, but, if the system is of higher order, the root locus becomes very informative, and, as seen from the establishment of K in the example, helpful in design. The procedure in design is to try to select a set of closed loop poles that will result in a satisfactory response. The root locus may be drawn with other variables than K, as will be discussed later.

7.4 Guidance Rules for the Root Locus

We see that to draw the root locus in practice we select a point s_1 in the complex s plane and check the angle criterion. If it is not met, we move the point and try again. The example of Section 7.3 was very simple, and it was easy to find the locus. In general, for high-order systems, such a cut and try process would be very time consuming and lead to frustration. We need some rules to show the approximate regions of the locus and using such rules you can sketch the locus. Often such a sketch shows that the design will be unsatisfactory. If more precise points are needed, the cut and try process has been greatly reduced. These rules will now be derived.

First, because GH is a ratio of polynomials in s with real coefficients, the characteristic equation will be a polynomial with real coefficients. The complex roots must therefore occur in conjugate pairs. Hence the locus in the lower half of the complex plane will be the mirror image of that in the upper half, and we need only draw the locus for positive $j\omega$ values.

Second, if $GH = K(G_1H_1) = -1$ on the root locus, then as $K \to 0$, $G_1H_1 \to \infty$. Hence the loci must start at the open loop poles (poles of G_1H_1) at a K value of zero. This has already been shown in Example 7.3–1. Since there are n open loop poles, where n is the order of the denominator polynomial of GH, n loci constitute the complete root locus. Third, alternatively to the second rule, as $K \to \infty$, $G_1H_1 \to 0$. Hence the loci terminate on the open loop zeros.

If we write GH as

$$GH(s) = \frac{K \prod_{i=1}^{m} (s + z_i)}{\prod_{j=1}^{n} (s + p_j)} \tag{7.4–1}$$

the number of finite zeros m is normally less than n, and hence we must include $q = n - m$ zeros at infinity. Now rewrite GH in the following manner:

$$GH(s) = \frac{K(s^m + a_1 s^{m-1} + \cdots)}{s^n + b_1 s^{n-1} + \cdots)} \tag{7.4–2}$$

$$GH(s) = \frac{K(s^m + a_1 s^{m-1} + \cdots)}{s^{m+q} + b_1 s^{m+q-1} + \cdots)}$$

$$= \frac{K}{s^q + (b_1 - a_1)s^{q-1} + \cdots} \tag{7.4–3}$$

For a moment suppose that $GH = K/s^q = -1$; then $s^q = -K$, which represents q vectors through the origin at angles to each other of $2\pi/q$. Two of these vectors are at angles of $\pm(\pi/q)$ to the positive real axis. Next suppose $GH = K/(s - r)^q = -1$. Following the previous argument, $(s - r)^q = -K$, which results in a series of vectors at the end of the vector r

and with angles as shown previously. Replace $(b_1 - a_1)$ in (7.4–3) by $-r$ to get

$$GH = \frac{K}{s^q - rs^{q-1} + \cdots} \tag{7.4–4}$$

Now $(s - r/q)^q = s^q - rs^{q-1} + \cdots$. Hence if s becomes large and we neglect powers of s lower than $(q - 1)$,

$$\underset{s \to \infty}{GH(s)} = \frac{K}{(s - r/q)^q} \tag{7.4–5}$$

Thus, from (7.4–5), for large s, q root loci become straight lines (vectors) at angles of $(2k + 1)\pi/q$ with the positive real axis, k taking on sufficient values to give q separate lines; these straight lines pass through the point $r/q = -(b_1 - a_1)/q$. From (7.4–2) b_1 is the negative of the sum of the zeros of the denominator polynomial, and a_1 is the negative of the sum of the finite zeros of the numerator. Also both b_1 and a_1 are real. Hence we see that $q = n - m$ root loci proceed to q zeros at infinity, asymptotically approaching straight lines at angles of $(2k + 1)\pi/q$, and that these straight lines pass through the point s_1 on the real axis, where

$$s_1 = -\frac{\sum_{i=1}^{n} p_i - \sum_{j=1}^{m} z_j}{n - m} \tag{7.4–6}$$

The fourth consideration concerns the portion of the real axis that constitutes part of the loci. In Figure 7.4–1 we plot a typical open loop pole-zero pattern and select a possible point s_1 on the real axis. First, we note that the vectors from the complex poles have angles θ_1 and θ_2. From the figure $\theta_1 - \psi_1 = 2\pi$ and $\theta_2 = -\psi_1$. Hence $\theta_1 + \theta_2 = 2\pi$, or the

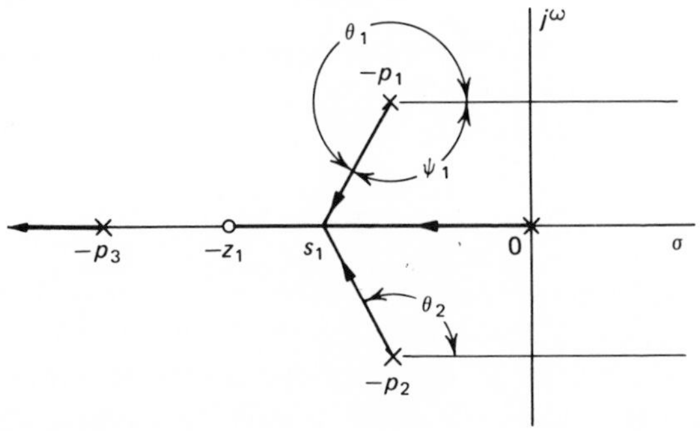

Figure 7.4–1. Root loci on real axis (negative feedback).

complex pole vectors do not contribute to arg GH if s_1 is real. Obviously the same would be true for any complex zeros. Next all vectors from poles or zeros to the left of s_1 have zero angle; hence only poles and zeros to the right of s_1 and on the real axis contribute to the angle. If there are an odd number of poles and zeros to the right of s_1, then the angle criterion is met. Hence the rule: Let the term "critical" frequencies include both poles and zeros; then the root locus lies on the real axis to the left of an odd number of critical frequencies.

Fifth, if the system becomes unstable with large K, then some of the loci will cross the $j\omega$ axis. The value of K at this crossing, and the value of ω there, may be found from Routh's rule applied to the characteristic equation (see Example 7.2–4). If the degree of this equation is high, this may be a difficult method of finding either K, or the point of crossing. Hence it may be easier to try values $s_1 = j\omega$, until the angle criteria is met.

Sixth, the angle of departure of the locus from a complex pole or the angle of arrival at a complex zero may be found from the angle criteria. Figure 7.4–2 illustrates this with a simple configuration of open loop poles and a zero. Rather than drawing vectors directly to the pole $-p_3$, we draw it to a point s_1 somewhere on a circle of radius ϵ around $-p_3$, as shown in Figure 7.4–2. If ϵ is small, the angles θ_1, θ_2, and α_1 will be the same as before (and are therefore known), and the angle of the vector

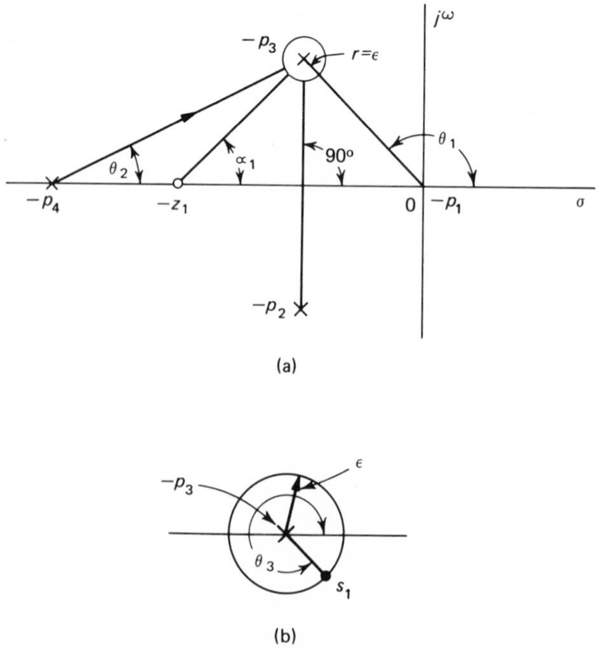

Figure 7.4–2. Angle of departure from pole.

from the conjugate pole will be 90°. Then $\pi/2 + \theta_1 + \theta_2 + \theta_3 - \alpha_1 = (2k + 1)\pi$, where the only unknown is θ_3. For example, if the complex poles in Figure 7.4–2 are at $s = -1 \pm j2$, one real pole is at $s = -4$, and the zero is at $s = -3$; then $\theta_1 = 116.5°$, $\theta_2 = 33.6°$, $\alpha_1 = 45°$, and we get $90 + 116.5 + 33.6 + \theta_3 - 45 = 180(3)$, or $\theta_3 = 345°$ ($\theta_3 = -15°$).

As a seventh factor, it helps to find possible multiple root points on the root locus. These will be points where the loci intersect at a common K value.

Let $1 + GH(s) = (s + s_1)^n f(s)$, where $-s_1$ is a zero of multiplicity n of $1 + GH = 0$. Then

$$\frac{d}{ds}(1 + GH) = \frac{d}{ds}(GH) = n(s + s_1)^{n-1} + (s + s_1)^n \frac{df(s)}{ds}$$

or

$$\left.\frac{d}{ds}(GH)\right|_{s=s_1} = 0 \qquad \textbf{(7.4–7)}$$

Also, since

$$\frac{d \ln GH}{ds} = \frac{1}{GH}\frac{dGH}{ds}$$

then

$$\frac{d \ln GH}{ds} = 0$$

at a multiple root value $-s_1$ or

$$\left.\frac{d}{ds}\left[\ln K + \sum_i \ln(s + z_i) - \sum_j \ln(s + p_j)\right]\right|_{s=s_1} = 0$$

or

$$\left.\left(\sum_i \frac{1}{s + z_i} - \sum_j \frac{1}{s + p_j}\right)\right|_{s=s_1} = 0 \qquad \textbf{(7.4–8)}$$

The multiplicity n of the root may be found by continued differentiation until

$$\left.\frac{d^n}{ds^n}(GH)\right|_{s=s_1} \neq 0$$

Equation (7.4–7) or (7.4–8) is the necessary condition for the existence of a multiple root point. The sufficient condition is that s_1 also be on the root locus. At a multiple root point s_1, the tangents to the branches of the root locus divide the space around s_1 into sectors of angle π/n each, with branches alternately entering and leaving s_1 [5].

In most cases if a multiple root exists, it will be of order 2 and lie on the real axis. It is then called a "breakaway" point.

In Example 7.3–1 there is a breakaway point at $s = -2$ or the characteristic equation is $(s+2)^2 = 0$ when $K = 4$. At this point the angles between the loci at $s = -2$ are at 90°; hence the loci leave the real axis at $\pm 90°$.

Equation (7.4–7) may be of high degree and thus difficult to solve. However, the values of any breakaway points $-s_1$ are usually known reasonably well by inspection. Hence a few trial divisions by $(s + s_1)$ will give the value of $-s_1$ as accurately as desired. An alternative procedure to find a breakaway point is to use the angle criterion. In Figure 7.4–3 it is

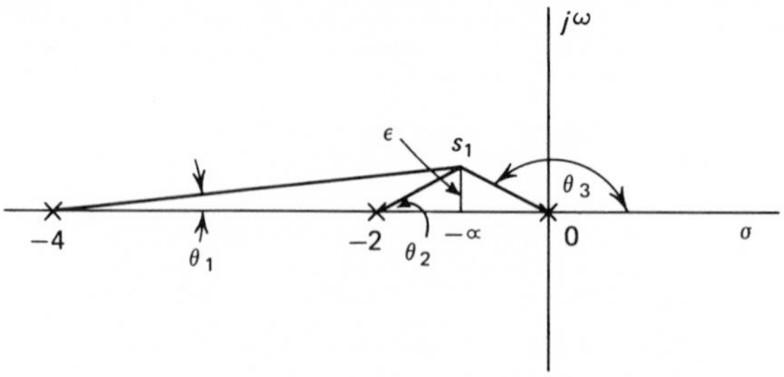

Figure 7.4–3. "Breakaway" point on real axis.

known that a breakaway point $-s_1$ must exist between the real axis poles at $s = 0$ and $s = -2$, because the real axis is part of the locus here. Assume a breakaway at $s = -\alpha$, with an associated value of K, and then increase K very slightly. The locus must move vertically a distance ϵ. The angular change must be zero if $-s_1$ is on the root locus. Hence in Figure 7.4–3

$$\theta_1 + \theta_2 - \theta_3 = 0$$

If ϵ is small, $\tan\theta \approx \theta$, and hence

$$\frac{\epsilon}{4-\alpha} + \frac{\epsilon}{2-\alpha} - \frac{\epsilon}{\alpha} = 0$$

or

$$\frac{1}{4-\alpha} + \frac{1}{2-\alpha} - \frac{1}{\alpha} = 0$$

Various values of α are tried until the equation is satisfied. From the figure, a starting value of $\alpha = 1$ can be used. Three tries gives $\alpha \approx 0.85$, which is close enough for most graphical work.

This procedure is readily extended to several real poles and zeros to give the formula

$$\sum_i \frac{1}{\alpha_i - z_i} = \sum_k \frac{1}{\alpha_k - p_k}$$

where the $-z_i$ are the finite real zeros and the $-p_k$ are the real poles, and the summations include all values of z_i or p_k. We see that this is the same equation as (7.4–8), but obtained by an alternative approach. If complex poles exist, the formula becomes complicated to use. An equivalent real pole may be found by drawing a right triangle as in Figure 7.4–4, with the assumed breakaway point as a vertex. Then $-p_k$ is an additional pole to be added to (7.4–9) and, since the complex poles exist in conjugate pairs, two such terms must be added.

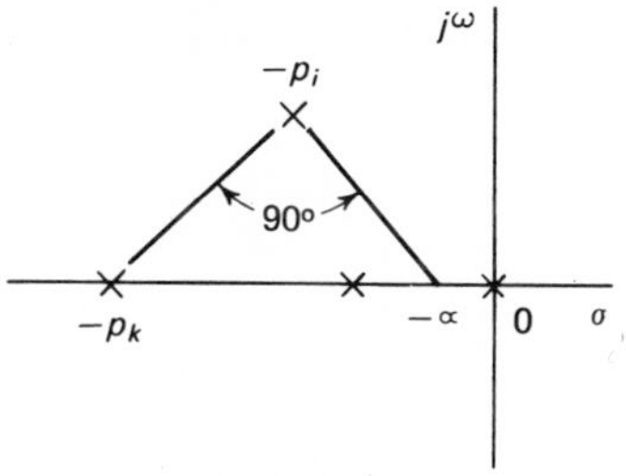

Figure 7.4–4. Equivalent real pole $-p_k$ to find breakaway point with complex pole $-p_1$.

Another method of locating a breakaway point is to note that $K = 0$ at the real poles, and a breakaway point is always located between two real poles. Thus the value of K with s real must be a maximum at a breakaway point. Thus calculating or plotting

$$|K| = \frac{\pi_j(s + p_j)}{\pi_i(s + z_i)}$$

for real values of s in the region of the suspected point reveals the breakaway point value when K is a maximum, as well as the corresponding K. Harris has derived formulas that assist in locating breakaway points, [6].

As a next rule, we see from (7.3–2) that the characteristic equation is

$$P(s)U(s) + Q(s)V(s) = 0$$

or, if the highest power of s is rationalized to 1,

$$s^n + d_1 s^{n-1} + \cdots + d_n = 0 \qquad \textbf{(7.4–9)}$$

Now $Q(s)V(s)$, the denominator of $G(s)H(s)$, is normally of higher power (by at least 2) than $P(s)U(s)$, the numerator (that is, $n \geq m + 2$). The gain factor K is contained in the $P(s)U(s)$ term; hence d_1 in (7.4–9) is independent of K. But d_1 is the negative of the sum of the zeros of (7.4–9), which are the poles $-P_j$ of the closed loop transfer function or the points on the root locus. Hence as some root loci go to the right, others must go to the left. Also if some root loci have been established, points on one or two remaining branches may be located by this rule. Note that d_1 in (7.4–9) is the same as b_1 in (7.4–2). It is also known that in (7.4–9)

$$d_n = \prod_{k=1}^{n} p_k \tag{7.4–10}$$

This sometimes helps to find a root or a K value at a root.

Finally, if we take the logarithm of GH in (7.4–1) and separate the real and imaginary parts,

$$\ln|G(s)H(s)| = \ln K + \sum_i \ln|s + z_i| - \sum_j \ln|s + p_j| \tag{7.4–11}$$

$$\arg[G(s)H(s)] = \sum_i \arg(s + z_i) - \sum_j \arg(s + p_j) \tag{7.4–12}$$

Equations (7.4–11) and (7.4–12) also will be found in describing a two-dimensional field due to line charges perpendicular to the field if opposite polarity line charges are placed at the pole and zero points $-p_j$ and $-z_i$. The potential lines correspond to (7.4–11) and the flow lines to (7.4–12). Obviously the root loci are special flow lines. Any familiarity with plotting electrostatic fields can thus be brought to bear on the root locus. This analogy will be exploited further for positive feedback, and for cases with $\arg GH = \theta$, where θ is any fixed angle [7].

The previous rules are listed in brief form and in different order in Table 7.4–1.

You should clearly understand that the rules discussed here only provide clues for the location of the loci. Any specific point not on the real axis must be checked by the angle rule. A device for rapidly checking the angle and also for computing the gain K is the Spirule [8]. Directions for operating the Spirule accompany the device, and the use of the Spirule may be learned within an hour or so. It should also be indicated, however, that the root locus has an advantage only if the designer can rapidly locate and sketch it. Rarely is a complete and accurate root locus exactly drawn, and then only toward the end of the design process.

The root locus may also be obtained using analytic techniques. One of these consists of varying K and finding the roots of the characteristic equation. Another makes a systematic search of the complex plane to

TABLE 7.4–1 RULES FOR ROOT LOCUS—NEGATIVE FEEDBACK

1. Plot the n open loop poles and m open loop zeros on a rectangular coordinate system comprising the complex plane. With K varying, the loci start at the open loop poles and terminate on the open loop zeros, with $n - m$ zeros being at infinity.
2. The asymptotes of the loci terminating at infinity intersect the real axis at the point $s_1 = -(\sum p_i - \sum z_i)/(n - m)$, and the asymptotes have angles with the real axis of $(2k + 1)\pi/(n - m)$, k = integer.
3. The real axis lying to the left of an odd number of critical frequencies is part of the root locus.
4. Some root loci cross the imaginary axis at the gain where instability impends. This may be located by using the Routh array.
5. The angles of departure from the poles and arrivals at the finite zeros must be such that the angle criteria are met.
6. Multiple roots may occur when $d(GH)/ds = 0$. In particular, multiple roots of order 2 frequently occur on the real axis. These breakaway points may be located and assist greatly in drawing the loci.
7. If the degree n of the numerator of GH is greater than the degree m of the denominator, such that $n \geq m + 2$, then $\sum_{k=1}^{n} p_k$ equals the coefficient of the $(n - 1)$st term in the characteristic polynomial (with the coefficient of the highest power being 1). Thus if some branches of the locus go to the left in the complex plane, others must go to the right.
8. If the open loop poles are considered positive line charges and the open loop zeros negative line charges, the root loci will coincide with some of the paths taken by a small positive test charge released in the field.

find points satisfying the angle requirement. Bendrikov and Teodorchik in Russia [9] and Krishman and others [10, 11] in the United States have devised analytic formulas for root loci. These techniques usually require a digital or analog computer for a system of any size.

7.5 Root–Locus Examples—Negative Feedback

To implement the preceding discussion, we give some examples of the root locus.

Example 7.5–1

Plot the root locus for $GH(s) = K/[s(s + 2)(s + 4)]$, negative feedback. Following Table 7.4–1:

1. The open loop poles are plotted at 0, −2, and −4 as in Figure 7.5–1. There are no finite zeros.
2. The asymptotes intersect at

$$s_1 = \frac{-2 - 4}{3} = \frac{-6}{3} = -2$$

The angle of the asymptotes are 60°, −60°, and 180°. These are drawn in lightly in Figure 7.5–1.

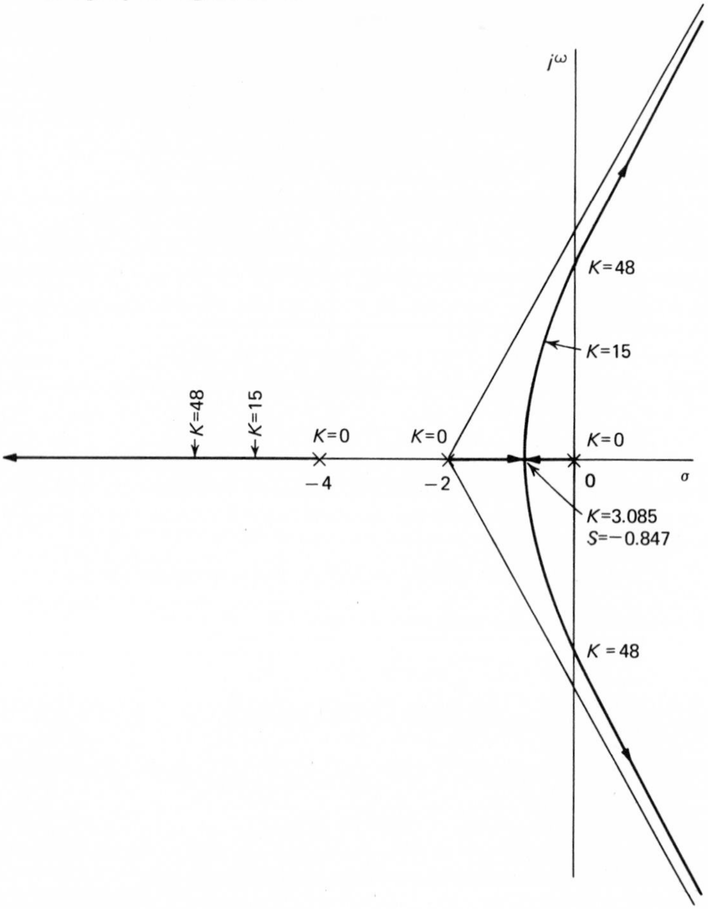

Figure 7.5–1. Root locus for $GH(s) = K/s(s+2)(s+4)$ negative feedback.

3. The real axis is part of the locus between 0 and −2, and from −4 to −∞. These branches are drawn in as heavy lines in Figure 7.5–1.
4. The characteristic equation is

$$s^3 + 6s^2 + 8s + K = 0$$

The Routh array is

$$\begin{array}{cc} 1 & 8 \\ 6 & K \\ \dfrac{48-K}{6} & \\ K & \end{array}$$

The root locus crosses the $j\omega$ axis when $K = 48$, or when the third row is 0. The $j\omega$ axis points are then roots of the subsidiary equation

$$6s^2 + 48 = 0$$

or

$$s = \pm j2\sqrt{2} \simeq \pm j2.83$$

5. There are no complex poles or zeros.

6.
$$\frac{d(GH)}{ds} = \frac{d}{ds}\frac{K}{s^3 + 6s^2 + 8s} = \frac{-K(3s^2 + 12s + 8)}{(s^3 + 6s^2 + 8s)^2} = 0$$

Hence

$$3s^2 + 12s + 8 = 0$$

or

$$s^2 + 4s + 8/3 = 0$$

Solving, we get $s \simeq -0.847$ or -3.15. The point at -0.847 is on the locus; hence it is a breakaway point. (The point at -3.15 is on a locus for $K < 0$.)

Alternatively in $GH(s)$, let $s = \sigma$, a real number. Then

$$\frac{K}{\sigma(\sigma + 2)(\sigma + 4)} = -1$$

on the real axis, or

$$\sigma^3 + 6\sigma^2 + 8\sigma + K = 0$$

which is the characteristic equation with s real. To find the point of maximum K, differentiate with respect to σ to get

$$3\sigma^2 + 12\sigma + 8 = 0$$

The solution is $\sigma \simeq -0.847$ or -3.15, as before. Putting $\sigma = -0.847$ back in the characteristic equation you get $K \approx 3.085$. If the characteristic equation is of high degree, it may be easier to plot K as a function of σ and to find the maximum K by inspection of this curve than to solve the differentiated equation.

7. The $\Sigma P_k = 6$, the coefficient of s^2 in this case. Select any point on the real axis to the left of -4, say $s = -5$. Then $P_1 = 5$ and the sum of the two other values $P_2 + P_3$ must equal $6 - 5 = 1$. From Figure 7.5–1 these roots must be on the complex root portion of the locus; hence each real part of P_2 and P_3 is $\frac{1}{2}$. The imaginary part may be found by the product rule, as will be shown subsequently. With the

locus drawn, this locates three roots corresponding to the same K. To find this K, use the characteristic equation with $s = -5$; thus

$$-125 + 150 - 40 + K = 0$$

or

$$K = 15$$

To find K values along the locus, use (7.3–7a). Draw lines to any point s_1 and measure the lengths r_1, r_2, and r_3. Then $K = r_1 r_2 r_3$ in Figure 7.5–1. In this particular example, K values may be easily found as shown previously. K may also be found by dividing the characteristic equation by a known factor. For example, at the breakaway point there is a double root of -0.847. Then we divide the characteristic polynomial by $(s + 0.847)^2 = s^2 + 1.694s + 0.719$, thus:

$$\begin{array}{r|l} & s + 4.306 \\ \hline s^2 + 1.694s + 0.719 & s^3 + 6s^2 \quad + 8s \quad + K \\ & s^3 + 1.694s^2 + 0.719s \\ \hline & \qquad 4.306s^2 + 7.281s + K \\ & \qquad 4.306s^2 + 7.29s + 3.085 \\ \hline \end{array}$$

Then $K \simeq 3.085$ at the breakaway point and the other root is at $s \simeq -4.306$. When $s = -5$,

$$(s + \tfrac{1}{2} + j\omega)(s + \tfrac{1}{2} - j\omega)(s + 5) = s^3 + 6s^2 + 8s + 15$$

From the product rule,

$$(\tfrac{1}{4} + \omega^2)(5) = 15$$

$$\omega \simeq 1.67$$

Hence the complex roots for $K = 35$ are at $s \simeq -0.5 \pm j1.67$. Algebraic procedures such as described for finding K values are not too useful if the system has a high degree or if K is involved in more than one term of the characteristic equation. They are only justified if the value of K needs to be more closely found in a particular case, or as the design narrows down.

Example 7.5–2

Plot the root locus for

$$GH = \frac{K(s + 3)}{s(s + 1)(s + 23)}$$

1. The open loop critical frequencies are plotted in Figure 7.5–2.
2. The asymptotes intersect at

$$s_1 = \frac{-1 - 23 + 3}{3 - 1} = -10.5$$

The angles of the asymptotes are $\pm 90°$.

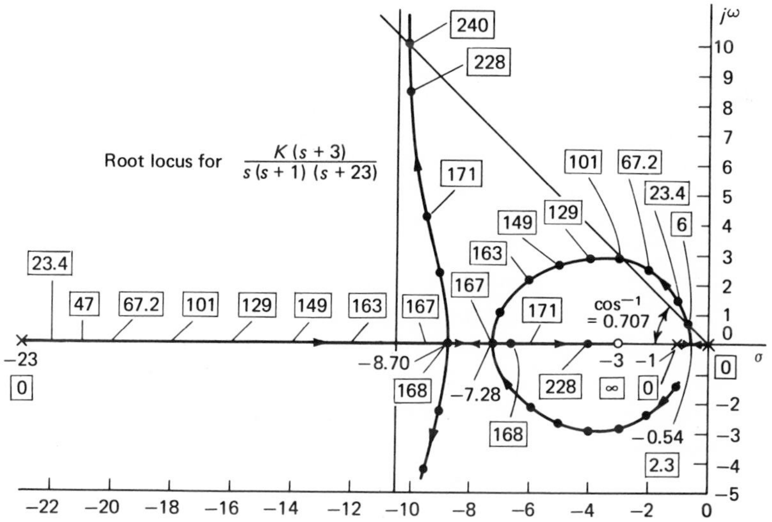

Figure 7.5–2. Root locus for $K(s+3)/s(s+1)(s+23)$, Example 7.5–2. Values of K : □.

3. The real axis is part of the locus between 0 and −1 and between −3 and −23.
4. By inspection the system is never unstable and there are no $j\omega$ axis crossings.
5. There are no complex open loop poles or zeros.
6. $$\frac{d(GH)}{ds} = \frac{d}{ds}\frac{K(s+3)}{s^3 + 24s^2 + 23s} = 0$$

or
$$2s^3 + 33s^2 + 144s + 69 = 0$$

By inspection there is a breakaway point very near −0.5. By trial division of the polynomial by $(s + \alpha)$, starting with $\alpha = -0.5$, the breakaway point is at about $s = -0.544$. (We take the figures out to three places here to obtain the remaining quadratic factor to reasonable accuracy.) From the division the remainder is $\simeq 2s^2 + 31.91s + 126.7$. The factors of this are about $(s + 7.28)$ and $(s + 8.70)$. Because −7.28 and −8.70 are real and the real axis is part of the root locus in this region, these are also multiple roots of order 2, or breakaway points.

7. By the sum and product rule, points on the locus may be found corresponding to various K values. Since the characteristic equation is $s^3 + 24s^2 + (23 + K)s + 3K = 0$, the use of these rules is not quite as simple as in the previous example. The Spirule is very useful in obtaining K values with the locus drawn, as the multiplications are made by logarithmic addition.

The result is shown in Figure 7.5–2, where values of K are shown enclosed in blocks.

Comment on Example 7.5–2

A combination of close-in-real poles and a zero, with a distant pole or poles, will often exhibit a root locus of this type, even with additional poles. Note that unless you locate the breakaway points at -7.28 and -8.70 you may get a very different idea of the locus. If the open loop pole at $s = -23$ is closer the origin, these breakaway points will disappear. The top branch will then not go back to the real axis but proceed upward and to the left as the closed loop pole approaches the zero.

If you desire a damping factor of 0.707 on the complex closed loop poles, draw a straight line at an angle to the negative real axis of 45°. You observe that there are three intersections with the loci or three possible gains to achieve this. Each of the three systems would exhibit very different characteristics. For the low-gain system ($K \simeq 6$), the distant pole would scarcely influence the transient response, while the zero at -3 is still at a sufficient distance (comparatively) not to greatly affect the response. Hence the system would act very much like one of second order with a low oscillation frequency, but the static gain is poor. For the medium-gain system ($K \simeq 100$), the zero is now comparatively close in, while the other pole is still so far out (at about $s = -18$) that it has little influence. The zero would cause an increased overshoot and longer settling time than for the complex poles alone. Finally, at a very high gain ($K \simeq 240$), the real pole has moved close to the zero (about $s = -3.5$), so the combination has less effect on the transient response. The static gain is now very good, and the oscillation frequency is high.

A minimum-phase system is defined as one with all zeros in the left-half plane [12]. A nonminimum phase system has some zeros in the right-half plane. Most control elements are of the minimum phase type, but occasionally you may observe a nonminimum phase type, such as a rocket. There is no difference in the plotting of the locus, but it is clear from Figure 7.5–3 that right-half-plane zeros cause some branches of the root locus to enter the right-half plane more rapidly than otherwise. Hence such systems are more likely to be unstable. Alternatively, zeros in the left-half plane tend to draw the loci into the stable region.

Some systems may be stable when the open loop function is unstable. This means that if the loop is opened, the system will be unstable, while if it is closed (normal operation) the system is stable. A very simple example is a unity negative feedback system with open loop gain

$$G = \frac{K}{(s+p_1)(s-p_2)} \qquad p_1 > 0,\ p_2 > 0$$

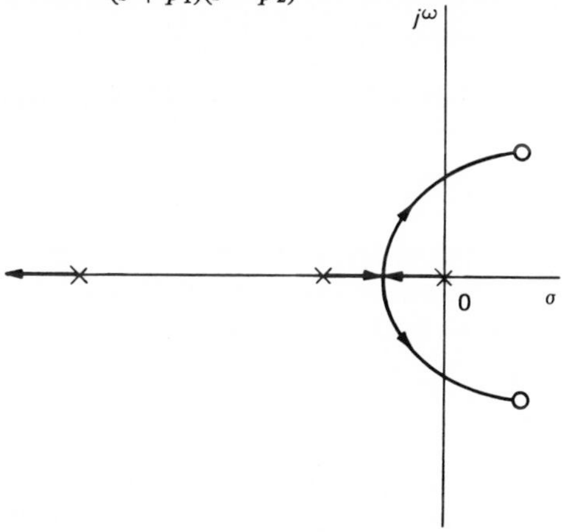

Figure 7.5–3. Root locus with right-half-plane zeros.

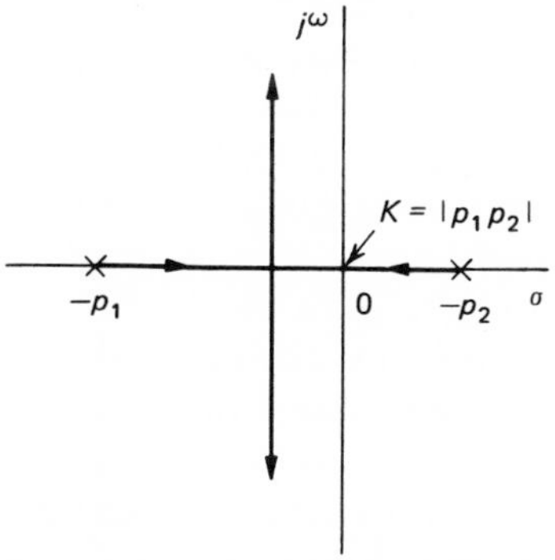

Figure 7.5–4. System open loop unstable and closed loop stable, $K > |p_1 p_2|$.

If $p_1 > p_2$, the system will be stable for any $K > |p_1 p_2|$. The root locus plot is shown in Figure 7.5–4. Many other such examples could be drawn. In general, most designers prefer stable open loop functions.

7.6 Root Locus—Positive Feedback and the Chu Plots

If we alter the sign of the feedback term in Figure 7.3–1, we get

$$\frac{C(s)}{R(s)} = \frac{G(s)}{1 - G(s)H(s)} \tag{7.6–1}$$

Obviously (7.3–5) becomes

$$G(s)H(s) = 1 \tag{7.6–2}$$

and the conditions for the root locus are

$$G(s)H(s) = |1|\epsilon^{j2k\pi} \qquad k = \text{integer} \tag{7.6–3}$$

Looking at the guidance rules, you find a few alterations in Table 7.4–1 as follows:

Rule 1. No change.

Rule 2. The intersection of the asymptotes with the real axis is the same, but the angles of the asymptotes with the real axis are $2k\pi/(n - m)$, k = integer.

Rule 3. Root loci will lie on the real axis to the right of all critical frequencies and to the left of an even number of critical frequencies.

Rule 4. No change, but not usually of much help.

Rule 5. No change, except the total angle is $2k\pi$.

Rule 6. No change.

Rule 7. No change.

Rule 8. No change.

Example 7.6–1

Repeat Example 7.5–1, except with positive feedback.

1. The open loop poles are as in Figure 7.6–1.
2. The intersection of the asymptotes is at $s_1 = -2$, as before, but the angles of the asymptotes are 0°, 120°, and −120°.

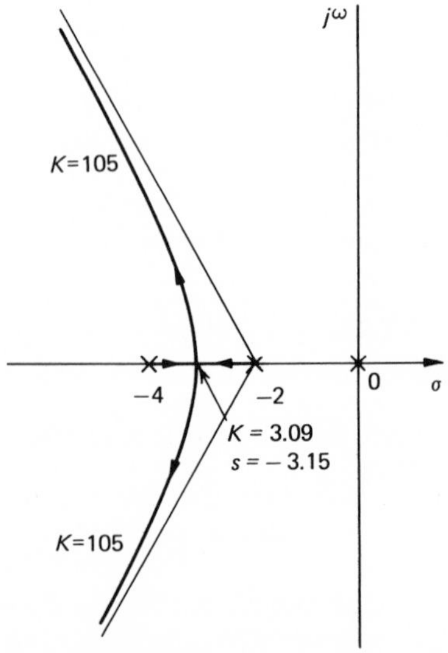

Figure 7.6–1. Root locus for $GH(s) = K/s(s + 2)(s + 4)$, positive feedback.

3. The real axis is a part of the locus between −2 and −4, and to the right of $s = 0$.
4. The system is unstable for $K > 0$ by inspection.
5. There are no complex poles or zeros.
6. Using the calculations made in Example 7.5–1, the multiple root on the locus is

$$s = -2 - \sqrt{4 - 32/12} \qquad \text{or} \qquad s \simeq -3.15$$

   Hence the solutions of $d(GH)/ds = 0$ that are not on the root locus for negative feedback may be on the root locus for positive feedback.
7. We may select any point on the positive real axis. For example, the characteristic equation is

$$s^3 + 6s^2 + 8s - K = 0$$

   and if $s = 3$, $K = 105$.

   Since $\Sigma P_k = 6$, and $P_1 = -3$, then $P_2 + P_3 = 6 + 3 = 9$. By the product rule $3P_2P_3 = 105$. Solving, $P_3 = 4.5 + j3.85$, $P_2 = 4.5 - j3.85$. The Spirule can be used to find other points on the locus, which is sketched in Figure 7.6–1.

Example 7.6–2

Plot a root locus for positive feedback for

$$GH = \frac{K}{(s + 8)(s^2 + 4s + 5)}$$

1. The open loop poles are plotted in Figure 7.6–2.
2. The asymptotes intersect at $s = -4$ at angles of 0°, 120°, and −120° with the real axis.
3. The real axis is part of the root locus between −8 and $+\infty$.
4. A root proceeds out the positive real axis as K increases, so the Routh rule is not too helpful in sketching the locus. The Routh table from the characteristic equation $s^3 + 12s^2 + 37s + 40 - K = 0$ is

1	37
12	$40 - K$
$37 - \left(\dfrac{40 - K}{12}\right)$	
$40 - K$	

   Hence the system is unstable $K > 40$, or the real root is $s = 0$ when $K = 40$. The other roots corresponding to this gain are $-6 + j1$ and $-6 - j1$.

5. The angle of a line from the real pole to the upper complex pole is about 9.5°, and of a line from the other complex pole is 90°. Hence

$$9.5^\circ + 90^\circ + \alpha = 0^\circ$$

or

$$\alpha = -99.5^\circ$$

or the root locus leaves the upper complex pole at an angle of -99.5°.

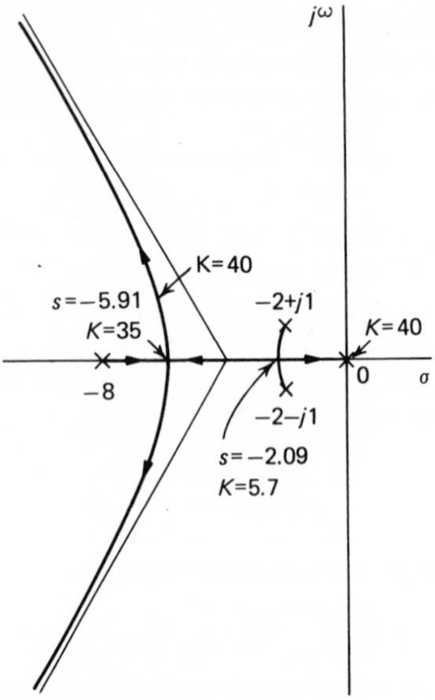

Figure 7.6–2. Root locus for $GH(s) = K/(s+8)(s^2+4+5)$, positive feedback.

6. The departure of the locus found in item 5 alerts us to the possibility of a breakaway point very near $s = -2$. A computation shows possible breakaway points at $s = -5.91$ and $s \simeq -2.09$, which are both on the locus.
7. The locus is completed as before, the sketch being shown in Figure 7.6–2.

You can see that positive feedback corresponds closely to the case of negative feedback but with $K < 0$. However, with this negative gain there will be a reversal of sign in the overall closed loop function $C(s)/R(s)$, because K will usually appear in the numerator. A sign reversal frequently occurs in amplifiers.

Feedback amplifiers of course may be analyzed by using the root locus technique. Thus is Figure 7.6–3 we depict an amplifier with forward gain G and feedback H. In the midfrequency region of amplification

$v_0 = -K_1(v_1)$, and it is often desired to make this true over as wide a frequency band as possible. Then for all frequencies,

$$v_0 = -v_1 \frac{G}{1+GH}$$

assuming no reversal of gain in H. G and H may now be adjusted to meet the required conditions.

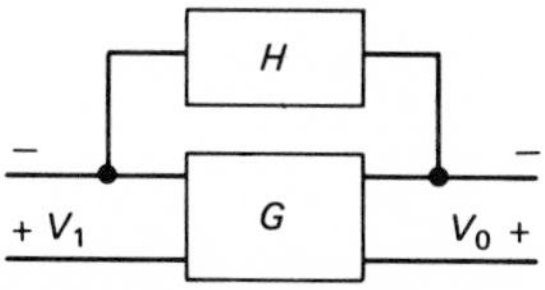

Figure 7.6–3. Amplifier with feedback.

Y. Chu proposed a more complete exploitation of the potential analogy by plotting "phase-angle" loci [13]. That is, in (7.3–7b) we allow arg $G(s)H(s)$ to take on all possible values, rather than just $(2k+1)\pi$, as in negative feedback, or $2k\pi$, as in positive feedback. Thus you set

$$G(s)H(s) = |1|\epsilon^{j\theta} \qquad \textbf{(7.6–4)}$$

with θ taking on selected values. It is easy to visualize the graph for one pole or zero. For one pole we would have a set of lines emanating from the pole as in Figure 7.6–4a, while for one zero we would have a set of lines terminating on the zero as in Figure 7.6–4b. (Here we take pole

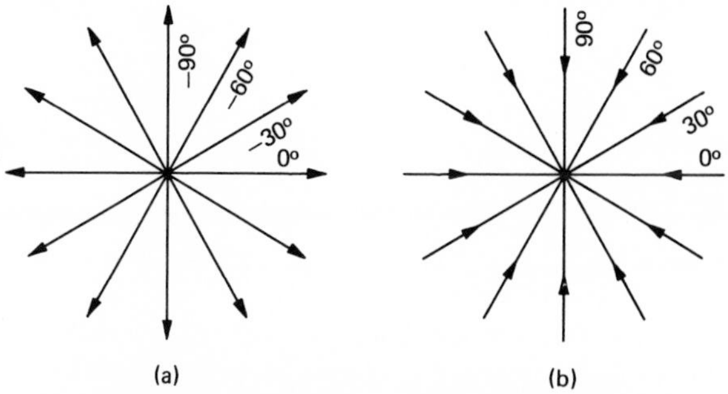

Figure 7.6–4. Basis for phase-angle plots.

angles as negative and zero angles as positive.) The phase-angle loci can be constructed by superimposing any number of pole and zero plots and finding where the total angle equals the desired angle, θ. For example, in Figure 7.6–5 we show two poles, at zero and $-a$, and two radial loci, one at $-90°$ from $-a$ and one at $-120°$ from the origin. The point of crossing is a point on the total phase-angle locus of $-210°$. By continuing this process, all phase-angle loci for increments of 30° can be drawn as in Figure 7.6–5. These loci can be added to those of additional poles or zeros, one at a time, to obtain loci for any combination. The process would become rather tedious with any large number of critical frequencies.

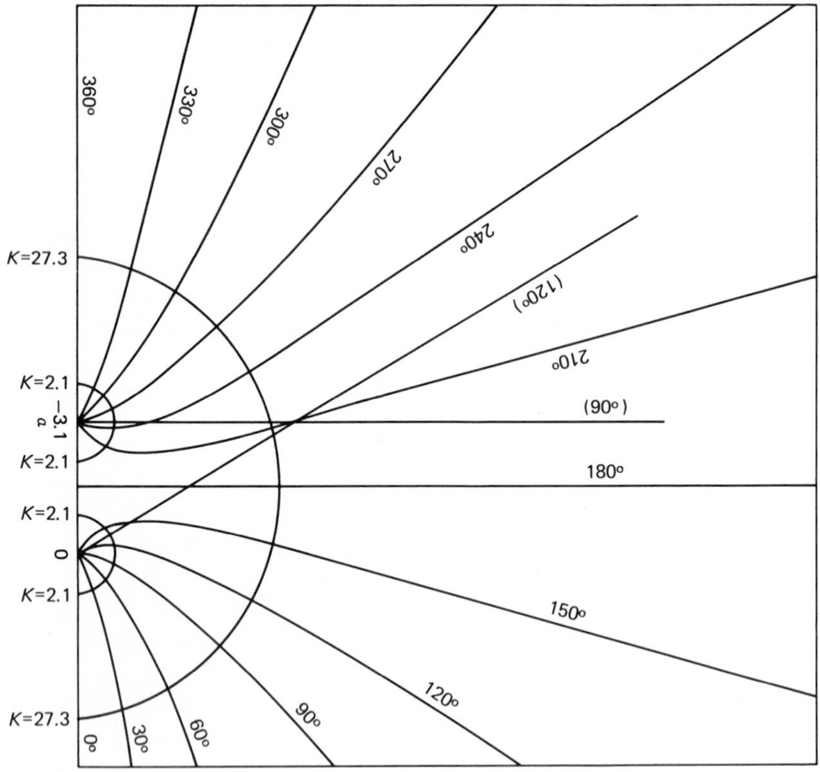

Figure 7.6–5. Phase-angle loci and gain loci for two poles.

Now for the open loop function $K/s(s+a)$, if we satisfy the magnitude requirement of (7.6–4), we can find points of constant gain K on the phase-angle loci, and connect these, as sketched in Figure 7.6–5 for two K values. It is fairly easy to sketch in the constant gain contours once the phase angle loci are constructed. If you fill in additional constant gain lines, the figure immediately becomes recognizable as a plane field plot for two positive line charges perpendicular to the plane. The phase contours correspond to the flow lines, and the gain contours correspond to the potential lines in the electrostatic case, and these contours intersect orthogonally. Similar plots can be made in the case of laminar water flow, magnetostatic fields, or steady current flow, and experience with any such field plotting assists in making the phase angle plots.

Plotting many phase-angle loci requires much more time and effort than the single root locus. Consequently, this is seldom done, but the concept may be of great assistance in visualization. The analysis of some problems using the root locus technique, as for example the case of transport lag, requires the plotting of the phase-angle loci. A digital computer can be programmed to compute these loci [14].

7.7 Root Locus for Parameters Other Than Gain

So far we have discussed the root locus with the gain K as a parameter. Although gain is an important constituent in many cases, it may not be the only factor or the most important one. Suppose that you decide that with some given configuration some K is to be preferred, and ask what happens if some pole or zero is shifted. For example, take the system

$$G(s)H(s) = \frac{K(s+z)}{s(s+p_1)(s+p_2)} \tag{7.7–1}$$

and assume that K has been fixed. Now let $p_1 = \rho + l$, where l is the original or "nominal" value of p_1 in (7.7–1) ($p_1 = l$, $\rho = 0$) and ρ is to be a variable. Then using (7.7–1) and (7.3–5) for negative feedback, we get

$$\frac{K(s+z)}{s(s+\rho+l)(s+p_2)} = -1 \tag{7.7–2}$$

Multiplying both sides by the denominator on the left and solving for ρ you get

$$K(s+z) = -s(s+l)(s+p_2) - \rho s(s+p_2)$$

$$\rho s(s+p_2) = -K(s+z) - s(s+l)(s+p_2) \tag{7.7–3}$$

Dividing both sides by the right side of (7.7–3), the result is

$$\frac{\rho s(s+p_2)}{s(s+l)(s+p_2) + K(s+z)} = -1 \tag{7.7–4}$$

Equation (7.7–4) is in the same form as (7.3–5), except that now ρ is the variable, where K was the variable previously. Hence we can plot a root locus with varying ρ to determine the effect of changing the open loop pole p_1 from its nominal value l. The hitch is that you need to know the denominator of (7.7–4) in factored form to be able to take the first step in the root locus plot or to locate the "open loop" poles. This is easily solved, however, by looking at (7.7–1) with p_1 set to its nominal value l. The characteristic polynomial of the closed loop system

$$\frac{C(s)}{R(s)} = \frac{G(s)}{1 + G(s)H(s)}$$

is $s(s + l)(s + p_2) + K(s + z)$, which is precisely the denominator of (7.7–4). Thus the needed poles to start the new locus are determined by a root locus plot using (7.7–1) with K varying, and then using the particular value of K fixed for (7.7–4). Such a root locus plot has probably already been made to determine a desired gain K, and therefore no additional work is required. The factors of the characteristic polynomial are read directly from this root locus, and you are ready to proceed to plot a root locus with ρ varying in (7.7–4). This plot will start at the poles of (7.7–4) and will have finite zeros at $s = 0$ and $s = -p_2$.

We can similarly decompose any system variable into two terms, one fixed at the nominal value and one varying, and plot a new locus for the varying term by rearranging the equation in the proper form to apply the root locus criteria.

Example 7.7–1

With negative feedback, plot the root locus for

$$G(s)H(s) = \frac{K(s + 4)}{s(s + 6)(s^2 + 4s + 8)}$$

Select a value of K such that damping factor of the closed loop complex poles is 0.5, and then find the root locus with this K fixed but vary the damping factor ζ of the complex loop poles from the present value of 0.707. Find the system poles as ζ varies.

The root locus for K varying is plotted as a heavy curve in Figure 7.7–1 with only the upper half being completed. Note that the locus crosses the asymptote and approaches it from underneath at large s values. Plotting in a radial line at an angle of 60° from the negative real axis, we find that the closed loop complex poles will be at about $s \simeq -1.11 \pm j1.92$, with a K of about 12.2. The other two roots are at about $s \simeq -1.60$ and $s \simeq -6.20$. Now look at the equation

$$\frac{12.2(s + 4)}{s(s + 6)(s^2 + (4\sqrt{2}\rho + 4)s + 8)} = -1$$

where ρ is the variation in ζ. Rearranging you get

$$\frac{4\sqrt{2}\rho s^2(s+6)}{s(s+6)(s^2+4s+8)+12.2(s+4)} = -1$$

or

$$\frac{4\sqrt{2}\rho s^2(s+6)}{(s^2+2.22s+4.92)(s+6.20)(s+1.60)} = -1$$

(We have not attempted to make the roots of the characteristic equation more accurate. Normally two-figure accuracy is the best one can get graphically.)

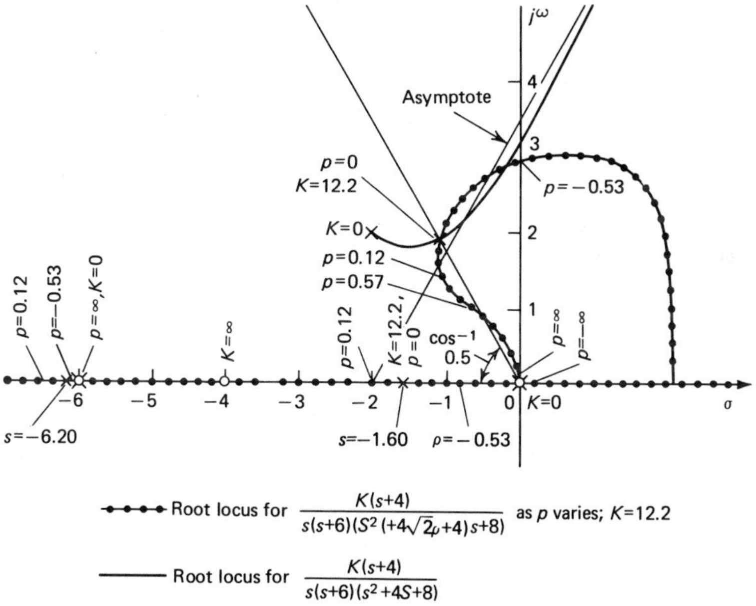

Figure 7.7–1. Root locus for a parameter other than gain, Example 7.7–1.

The new function has a double zero at zero and a zero at $s=-6$. These critical frequencies and the poles are marked on the complex plane and a new root locus plotted with ρ as a variable. In the new locus, for ρ increasing positively, one branch proceeds from the pole at $s=-1.60$ to the zero at $s=-6$ along the real axis. Another branch goes from the pole at $s=-6.20$ along the real axis to $s=-\infty$. The other two branches proceed from the complex poles in toward the double zero at $s=0$. For ρ increasing negatively, one branch moves from the pole at $s=-1.60$ to one of the zeros at the origin, and another branch goes from the pole at $s=-6.20$ to the zero at $s=-6$. The real axis to the right of the origin must be part of the locus, so the branches from the complex poles must enter a multiple root point of order 2 on the positive real axis, from which one branch proceeds inward to the second zero at the origin, while the other gives outward to infinity. In this case the multiple root point is the opposite of a breakaway point and is not easy to find analytically because a sixth-degree equation is involved, but is at about $s = 2.1$.

The portion of the root locus of most interest is that of the complex pole movement. It is seen that if the damping factor $\zeta \approx 0.707 - 0.53 = 0.177$, the system becomes unstable at the gain selected ($K = 12.2$). Note that for this locus rule 7 is of little value, because here the parameter ρ enters in the coefficient of s^3 in the fourth-degree characteristic polynomial. Rule 2 is also of not much help, because the asymptotes are along the real axis. The complete locus is sketched in Figure 7.7–1, the locus for varying ρ being drawn with small beads and the locus for varying K as a heavy curve. The locus in the lower s plane is the mirror image of that shown.

One method of ascertaining the sensitivity of a root utilizes the preceding technique. Consider, for example, the characteristic equation

$$s^2 + As + B = 0$$

with $A = 1$ and $B = 0.5$ as nominal values. If B varies,

$$s^2 + s + 0.5 + \Delta B = 0$$

or

$$\frac{\Delta B}{s^2 + s + 0.5} = -1 \quad \textbf{(7.7–5)}$$

If A varies

$$\frac{\Delta A s}{s^2 + s + 0.5} = -1 \quad \textbf{(7.7–6)}$$

One definition of root sensitivity is

$$S_{\alpha}^{P_j} = \frac{\partial P_j}{\partial \ln \alpha} = \frac{\alpha \partial P_j}{\partial \alpha} \quad \textbf{(7.7–7)}$$

$$= \lim_{\Delta\alpha \to 0} \alpha \frac{\Delta P_j}{\Delta \alpha}$$

where ΔP_j is the change in the root location for a change $\Delta\alpha$ in the element α.

If α represents the open loop pole and $\Delta\alpha$ the change, then ΔP_j may be obtained by measuring the change ΔP_j in the control ratio pole location by using a root locus plot with $\Delta\alpha$ as parameter. Thus, in (7.7–5), $\Delta\alpha = \Delta B$ and, in (7.7–6), $\Delta\alpha = \Delta A$. The change ΔP_j will in general be complex, that is, have a magnitude and direction in the s plane, both of which may be measured. The root sensitivity may be related to the Bode sensitivity defined in Chapter 1, and methods have been developed for direct computation of the root sensitivity [15].

7.8 Obtaining Desired System Performance

Rarely does a system operate satisfactorily merely by adjusting the gain K, which is the normal parameter of the root locus. Although the complex poles of the system function may be satisfactorily located, the other poles and zeros need to be observed. In Example 7.7–1 the presence of a close-in pole (at $s = -1.60$) when the damping factor of the complex poles is 0.5 and $K = 12.2$ will cause the system to be sluggish. The more distant pole and zero will not have too much effect on the step response. Furthermore, the static gain usually needs to be increased without loss of stability. Thus we usually need to add critical frequencies to the loop function to adjust the system properly. The addition of an open loop pole or zero requires a redrawing of the root locus, and at once you see the necessity for fast rough sketching of the locus during the initial design stages. We can set down a few guidelines here. With passive *RC* electric networks (or their mechanical or hydraulic equivalents), we introduce real poles and zeros in pairs. Let us look at one pair of such a combination, in which the zero is closer to the origin than the pole. In an electrical circuit, such a pair is termed a "lead" network, and its transfer function is

$$\frac{s+z_1}{s+p_1} \qquad z_1 < p_1 \tag{7.8–1}$$

You see at once that such a pair causes a loss under static conditions (as $s \to 0$) of z_1/p_1. This is not serious, as we can provide additional gain at low power levels cheaply by means of an amplifier, but it is necessary to remember to do so. In Figure 7.8–1 we redraw the system of Example 7.5–1, which, as you saw previously, became unstable at a gain K of about 48. How can you make the system more stable? If we add the lead network with critical frequencies z_1 and p_1 you see that the zero tends to pull the locus into the left-half plane as shown by the beaded locus in Figure 7.8–1. Thus for the same damping factor ζ on the system poles, we see from Figure 7.8–1 that the gain can be much greater. (It is assumed that we have already balanced the network loss with added gain p_1/z_1.) However, since the open loop zero z_1 becomes a system (control ratio) zero, the added zero brings about a more lightly damped system. Thus for the same overshoot we should reduce the ζ of the new complex poles compared to previous system poles. If the stability improvement is insufficient, we may add two or more lead pairs. These may have the same values of z_1 and p_1, in which case we have multiple open loop critical frequencies, or they may have other values. In any case, the general result is to draw the locus further into the left-half plane, or the more stable region. Figure 7.8–2 shows a possible compensation of a system with complex poles by means of two lead networks. The added poles and zeros are shown by p_1, p_2 and z_1, z_2.

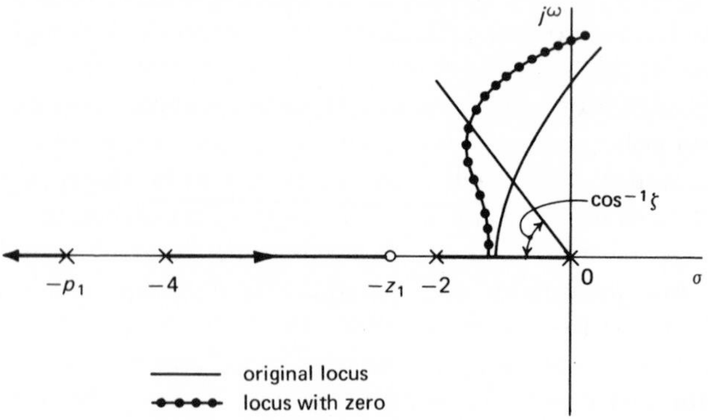

Figure 7.8–1. Root locus for $GH(s) = K/s(s+2)(s+4)$ with zero added.

If $p_1 = \alpha z_1$, $\alpha > 1$, the question of the proper value of α may arise. At first glance, it would seem best to make α very large, because the effect of the zero is then more pronounced, but we shall make clear in the next

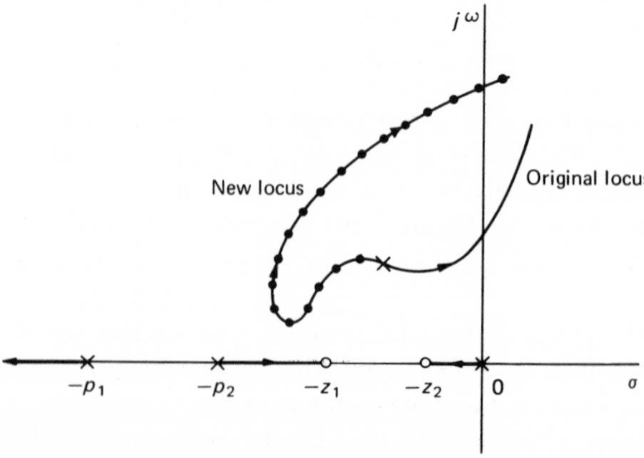

Figure 7.8–2. Adding two lead compensators to $GH(s) = K/s(s^2 + 2\zeta\omega_n s + \omega_n^2)$.

chapters that there is not much improvement for $\alpha > 10$. Beyond this point it will usually be preferable to add an additional lead pair or pairs. From Figure 7.8–1 we also see that for the same ζ that the natural frequency ω_n of the closed loop poles is greater with the added pair, and thus the bandwidth is greater. Hence the lead pair will generally allow more noise to pass through the system. Note that the zero at $-z_1$ is placed at some distance from the origin to reduce its influence on overshoot.

You may now ask: How about adding a pair with the opposite configuration, or $p_1 > z_1$? Such a pair will have the transfer function

$$\frac{p_1}{z_1}\frac{s+z_1}{s+p_1} \qquad z_1 > p_1 \tag{7.8–2}$$

The coefficient p_1/z_1 is necessary here because we assume a passive network that can have no gain as $s \to 0$. In an electrical circuit such a pair is termed a "lag" network. This pair is placed close to the origin as shown in Figure 7.8–3a. At high gain one of the roots of the characteristic equation moves around to the real axis to the left of the zero, forming a "dipole," as shown in enlarged form in Figure 7.8–3b. The other roots will move

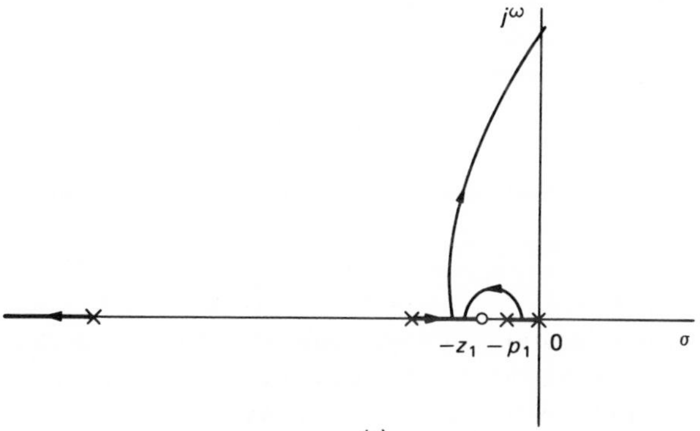

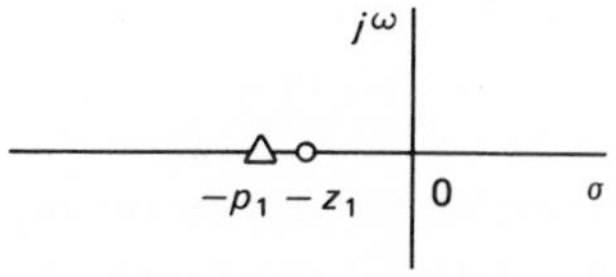

Figure 7.8–3. Formation of system dipole from a lag compensator.

out along almost the same locus as previously in the complex root region, because from a distance the $z_1 p_1$ combination effectively cancels. Thus the addition of the lag pair does not affect transient stability very much. (It may in some cases.) However, by using the lag pair we can greatly increase the static gain of the system. A convenient and simple analytical demonstration of this increase in gain will be made in Chapter 9, and a graphical explanation based on frequency analysis will be given in Chapter 8. At this point it is only necessary to see how an open loop lag pair becomes a closed loop dipole with the zero nearer the origin than the pole.

The lead and lag pairs are simple examples of more complicated transfer functions. It is possible to obtain complex poles or zeros using passive elements. Suppose, for example, that we have a pair of open loop complex poles, as in Figure 7.8–4, the location of which varies with temperature.

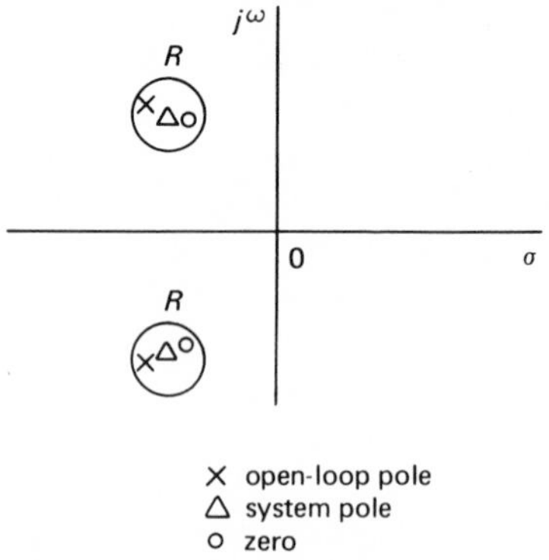

Figure 7.8–4. Confining system pole to small region.

This could be depicted by a slow movement of each pole within a region R surrounding the pole. Compensation of the system might be satisfactory if the pole is at one location, but unsatisfactory if it moves to another, or the system could be unstable in any case, owing to branch loci emanating from the poles and rapidly crossing the $j\omega$ axis.

By placing a pair of complex zeros near the center of the region, it is possible to cause branches of the root locus to proceed directly from the pole to the added zero. Thus the system poles are confined to a small area within the region R regardless of the pole movement, as shown in Figure 7.8–4. The zero position can be held constant by constructing the zero-producing device with temperature-independent precision components or by putting the device in a constant-temperature environment.

Compensation may also be achieved by cancellation, that is, by introducing a zero over an undesired pole. If the pole is in the right-half plane, this would not be satisfactory, as any change of the pole, or any error in cancellation, no matter how slight, results in instability. For a pole in the left-half plane, however, slight miscancellation (which always exists practically), may be satisfactory, because if the cancellation error is small, the result is a dipole that may not greatly affect system performance. If the pole movement is great, the root locus may be drastically altered, and the theoretical cancellation voided. As pointed out in Chapter 6, any theoretical cancellation is actually a decoupling that may cause the system to be partially uncontrollable or unobservable. The resulting internal oscillations may or may not be objectionable, but the designer should be aware of them (Figure 7.8–5).

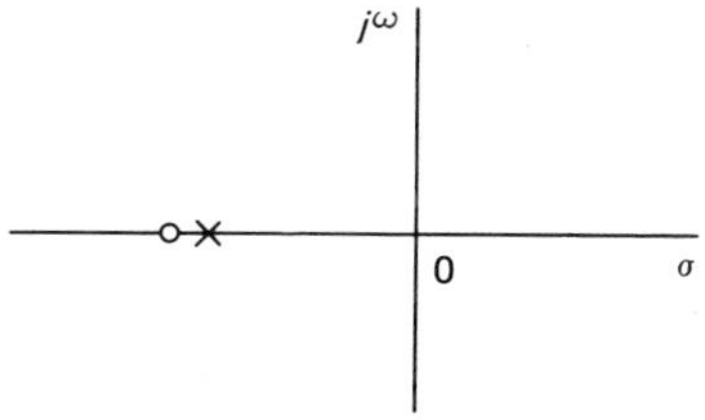

Figure 7.8–5. Result of inexact cancellation.

The compensation of the system to obtain satisfactory performance reduces to the introduction of additional poles and zeros in the open loop function *GH*. As discussed in Chapter 3, the compensation can be a tandem or an internal feedback alteration of *G* or an alteration of *H*. If, as in Figure 7.8–6a, an internal feedback *H* is used to alter the previous forward gain G_1G_2, it may be necessary to make two root locus plots. Thus one root locus map is necessary to obtain $G_2' = G_2/(1 + G_2H_1)$, as in Figure 7.8–6b, and another to obtain the overall system C/R. We discuss compensation in more detail in Chapter 9.

We have already indicated in Example 7.5–2 how to locate the complex poles to give a desire damping factor ζ. We may also locate these poles to give a desired ω_n or a desired $\zeta\omega_n$. Thus if Figure 7.8–7 represents a possible locus plotted for some varying parameter, if we draw a straight line through the origin at an angle $\psi = \cos^{-1} \zeta$, the intersection of this with the locus gives complex system poles with this damping factor, as at point 1 in Figure 7.8–7. If we wish poles with some ω_n, we draw a circle of radius ω_n, and the intersection as at point 2 is the result. Finally, if we wish a certain damping rate $\zeta\omega_n$, if we draw a straight line parallel to the $j\omega$ axis, the intersection at 3 or 3′ gives the system poles. In each case we

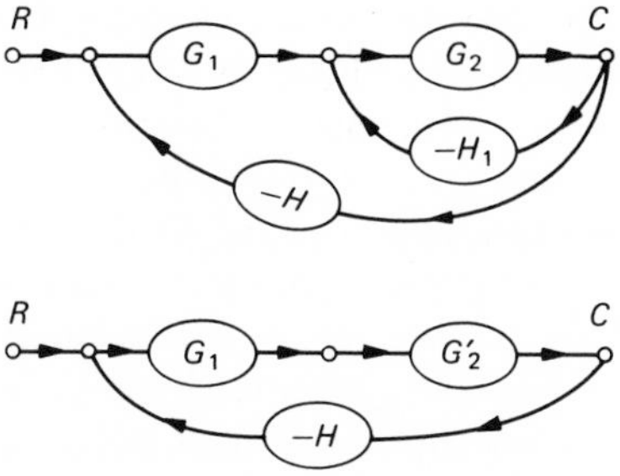

Figure 7.8–6. Reduction of inner feedback loop.

may have no intersections, or more than one intersection, as already shown in Example 7.5–2 and illustrated again in Figure 7.8–7. It is, of course, not sufficient merely to thus locate the system complex poles. You also

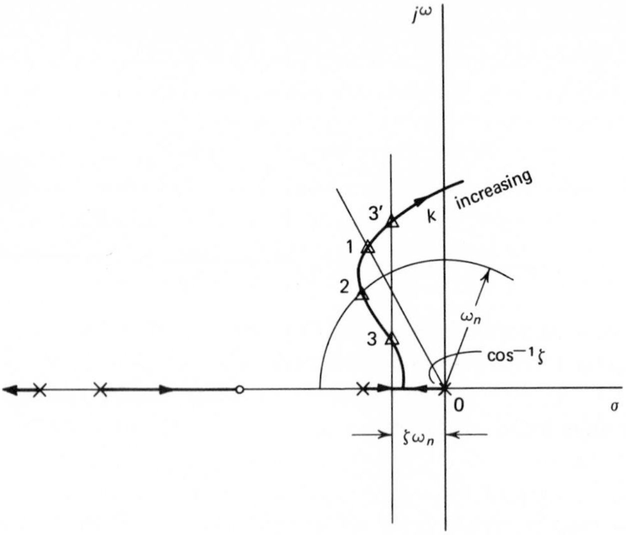

Figure 7.8–7. Locating a desired system pole 1 — ζ specified; 2 — ω_n specified; 3 — 3' $\zeta\omega_n$ specified.

need to know where the other system poles are for the same value of the parameter to ascertain the transient response. In some cases there may be two or more sets of complex poles, of which one set may be dominant.

7.9 Conclusions

The root locus offers a powerful tool to observe the movement of the system poles with the variation of some parameter. The addition of critical frequencies requires the drawing of a new root locus, so the designer requires ability to sketch the root locus rapidly, to visualize alterations in the locus, and to create new pole-zero patterns. The design method is essentially one of cut and try, although the amount of floundering is greatly reduced from blind alteration of the characteristic polynomial. Obviously you should not use great accuracy in the root locus plots during the first design stages because the design will be altered anyway. The root locus maps in our examples have been fairly accurately made because we would be criticized otherwise, but in your preliminary designs high accuracy is unnecessary and undesirable.

The chief objection to the root locus is the time and labor involved in drawing, so computers are often employed in making the plots, as suggested in Section 7.4. General-purpose analog and digital computers are both used, and special-purpose computers have been devised. The cost and time involved in using a computer must be weighed against the designer's time and cost. Again, computer use may not be warranted in the early design stages but may be necessary at the later stages. With the continued development of large-scale digital computers with remote consoles, it will become possible to obtain a root locus as a display on a cathode ray tube. Poles and zeros then may be introduced and the resulting alteration of the locus immediately observed. The designer must still be aware of the implications of the locus, however, and fundamental knowledge and experience with locus sketching will continue to be necessary.

PROBLEMS

7.1. For the following polynomials, find how many roots are in the right-half plane. Find the roots on the $j\omega$ axis if these exist.

(a) $s^5 + 3s^4 + 12s^3 + 24s^2 + 32s + 48.$
(b) $s^5 + 6s^4 + 3s^3 + 2s^2 + s + 1.$
(c) $s^3 + 3s^2 + 2s + 20.$
(d) $25s^5 + 105s^4 + 120s^3 + 122s^2 + 20s + 1.$
(e) $s^6 + 4s^5 - 4s^4 + 4s^3 - 7s^2 - 8s + 10.$
(f) $s^5 + 3s^4 + 12s^3 + 20s^2 + 35s + 25.$

7.2. Plot the root locus for negative feedback for the following open loop functions:

(a) $GH = \dfrac{K(s+5)}{s(s+3)}.$ (b) $GH = \dfrac{K(s+5)}{s^2 + 4s + 20}.$

(c) $GH = \dfrac{K}{s(s+8)}.$ (d) $GH = \dfrac{K}{s(s+3)(s^2 + 3s + 10)}.$

7.3. Plot the root locus for negative feedback for the open loop function

$$GH = \frac{K(s+3)}{(s+1)(s+5)(s+15)}$$

Find the value of K to make the control ratio $C/R = G/(1 + GH)$ have complex roots with a damping factor $\zeta = 0.5$. Write the transfer function for C/R for this case.

7.4. Plot the root locus for negative feedback for the open loop function

$$GH = \frac{K}{(s+14)(s^2 + 2s + 2)}$$

If possible, find:

(a) The value of K to make $C/R = G/(1 + GH)$ have complex roots with a damping factor $\zeta = 0.5$.

(b) The value of K to make C/R have an $\omega_n = 2$.

(c) The value of K to make C/R have a damping rate $\zeta\omega_n$ of 0.7.

Write the transfer function for C/R in each case.

7.5. Plot the root locus for positive feedback for the functions of Problem 7.2.

7.6. (a) Plot the root locus for negative unity feedback for

$$G = \frac{K}{(s+5)(s^2-4)}$$

(b) Find the value z (>0) when the term $s + z$ is placed in the numerator of G that will *just* make the system stable when $K = 50$.

(c) What is the least value of K for *any* $z > 0$ that will just make the system stable?

(d) Make $z = 1$ and replot the root locus. Write the function $G/(1 + G)$. Find K to give complex poles with $\zeta = 0.707$ and write the function $G/(1 + G)$ for this case.

7.7. If $G = K/Q(s)$, $H = (s + 5)/(s + 2)$, where $Q(s)$ has a leading coefficient of 1 and a root locus plot for $GH = -1$ shows roots at -3, -20, $-1 + j5$, and $-1 - j5$, find K and $Q(s)$.

7.8. Repeat Problem 7.7 if one root is at -2 rather than -3, all other roots the same.

7.9. Find the roots $s^3 + 3s^2 + (25/4)s + K = 0$ as K takes on all positive and negative values. [*Hint*: Plot the root locus for $K/s(s^2 + 3s + \frac{25}{4}) = -1$.]

7.10. Given $G = K/s(s^2 + 2s + 2)$, unity negative feedback.

(a) Plot a root locus and find the transfer function for $C/R = G/(1 + G)$ when $K = 2$.

(b) Find the poles of C/R as the damping factor of the open loop poles varies, $K = 2$.

(c) Find the poles of C/R as ω_n for the open loop poles varies, $K = 2$.

7.11. Given that the open loop function

$$G = \frac{K(s+5)}{s^2(s^2+6s+25)(s+16)}$$

is to be placed in a unity negative feedback system. Suggest how this might be stabilized. Sketch root loci for the cases before and after stabilization.

7.12. (a) Plot the root locus for negative feedback for $GH = K/s(s + 2)(s + 6)$.

(b) Repeat with the transfer function $\frac{1}{5}(s + 0.25)/(s + 0.05)$ added to the system.

(c) Repeat with the transfer function $10[(s + 2)/(s + 20)]$ added to the system.

(d) Compare performance of the three systems with the complex poles of the control ratio having a damping factor $\zeta = 0.707$.

7.13. Assuming you have a polynomial root-finding subroutine, consider how you might write a digital computer program to obtain a root locus.

7.14. Determine the root locus of one of the functions of Problem 7.2 analytically.

REFERENCES AND FURTHER READING

[1] W. R. Evans, Graphical Analysis of Control Systems, *Trans. AIEE*, **67** (1948), 547–551.

[2] G. J. Thaler and R. G. Brown, *Servomechanism Analysis*, McGraw-Hill, New York, 1953, Chap. 14.

[3] J. G. Truxal, *Automatic Feedback Control System Synthesis*, McGraw-Hill, New York, 1955, Chap. 4.

[4] E. J. Routh, *Dynamics of Rigid Bodies*, Dover, 1960, pp. 223–231; see also E. A. Guillemin, *The Mathematics of Circuit Analysis*, Wiley, New York, 1949, p. 395.

[5] C. H. Wilts, *Principles of Feedback Controls*, Addison-Wesley, Reading, Mass., 1960, pp. 80–81.

[6] L. D. Harris, *Introduction to Feedback Systems*, Wiley, New York, 1961, Appendix 4, pp. 351–360.

[7] J. G. Truxal, *op. cit.*, pp. 29, 34.

[8] The Spirule Company, 9728 El Venado Drive, Whittier, Calif. 90603.

[9] K. F. Teodorchik and G. A. Bendrikov, The Methods for Plotting Root Paths of Linear Systems and for Quantitative Determination of the Path Type, Proceedings of the 1960 IFAC Congress in Moscow, *Theory of Continuous Linear Control Systems* (J. F. Coales, J. R. Ragazzini, and A. T. Fuller, eds.), Butterworth, London, 1963, pp. 8–12.

[10] C. K. Wojcik, Analytical Representation of the Root Locus, *J. Basic Eng.*, **86** (1964), 37–43.

[11] V. Krishman, Semi-Analytic Approach to the Root Locus, *IEEE Trans. Auto. Control*, **11** (11), (1966), 102–108.

[12] H. W. Bode, *Network Analysis and Feedback Amplifier Design*, Van Nostrand, Princeton, N.J., 1945, pp. 117–118.

[13] Y. Chu, Synthesis of Control System by Phase-Angle Loci, *Trans. AIEE*, Part II, *Appl. Ind.*, **71** (1952), 330–339.

[14] C. J. Doda, The Digital Computer Makes Root Locus Easy, *Control Eng.*, May 1958, pp. 102–106.

[15] H. Ur, Root Locus Properties and Sensitivity Relations in Control Systems, *IRE Trans. Auto. Control*, **5** (1) (1960), 57–65.

8 Frequency Analysis

8.1 Introduction

Frequency analysis comprises one of the oldest methods for investigating control systems, growing out of similar analysis applied to amplifiers. The work of H. W. Bode, summarized in his book *Network Analysis and Feedback Amplifier Design*, provided a theoretical impetus in the 1940–1950 era [1]. Although newer methods are in vogue, frequency analysis ideas are still useful in visualization and, in many cases, quite practical. For example, the problem of testing components, subsystems, and complete systems often yields most easily to frequency analysis, and many refined instruments exist to make tests in the real frequency domain. There is no one best method for control design, and older, but useful, theories cannot be neglected.

In frequency analysis, the driving function of the system is assumed to be pure steady-state sinusoidal, with initial conditions occurring in the remote past. The investigation proceeds by varying the frequency and obtaining the ratio of output to input as a function of frequency f or, more usually, angular velocity $\omega = 2\pi f$. The time response of the system to any driving function relates to the frequency response through the Fourier transform. As discussed previously, the relation is complex, and detailed correlation often impractical. Nevertheless, knowledge of the sinusoidal response is quite useful in design, at least for lower-order systems. We have already seen in Chapter 3 the very simple connections between frequency analysis and the time response to a step function for a second-order system, and how extension may be made, at least in general, if not in detail, to higher-order systems.

8.2 Sinusoidal Steady-State Transfer Function

You are already familiar with steady-state analysis of electrical or mechanical systems. To review this briefly, we know that a sinusoidal voltage can be written as

$$v = V_m \cos(\omega t + \phi) \tag{8.2–1}$$

or

$$v = V_m \sin(\omega t + \phi + 90^\circ) \tag{8.2–2}$$

where V_m is the maximum value, ω the angular velocity, and ϕ a phase angle. Since

$$\epsilon^{j(\omega t + \phi)} = \cos(\omega t + \phi) + j \sin(\omega t + \phi) \tag{8.2–3}$$

it is convenient to express (8.2–1) as

$$v = \mathscr{R} V_m \epsilon^{j(\omega t + \phi)} \tag{8.2–4}$$

where $\mathscr{R}$ is an operator meaning "take the real part of." The object of using the exponential form is that the operations of differentiation and integration become considerably simpler with this form than with the trigonometric form, and, as a matter of fact, such operations on exponentials always yield another exponential. Next, it is not difficult to show that

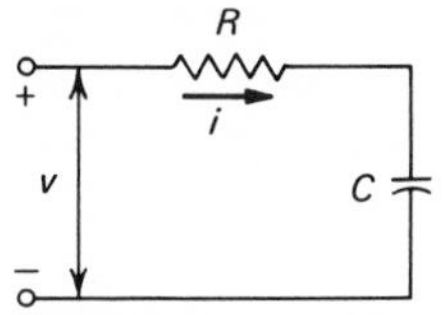

Figure 8.2–1. *RC* circuit.

the operator is commutative and can be exchanged with the integral or derivative operator in linear systems and for the type of functions of concern. Hence, for example, if we examine the circuit of Figure 8.2–1, we can write a differential equation involving y and i as

$$\frac{1}{C} \int i \, dt + Ri = v \tag{8.2–5}$$

where i and v are functions of t. It is clear that if v is given by (8.2–4), then i must also be an exponential. Assuming that $\phi = 0$ for convenience, we let $i = \mathscr{R}(I_m \epsilon^{j\omega t} \epsilon^{j\theta})$ and, interchanging operations, (8.2–5) becomes

$$\mathscr{R}\left(\frac{1}{C}\int_{-\infty}^{t} I_m \epsilon^{jx(u)}\, du + RI_m \epsilon^{jx(t)}\right) = \mathscr{R} V_m \epsilon^{j\omega t} \tag{8.2–6}$$

The solution for (8.2–6) is

$$I_m = \frac{V_m}{\sqrt{R^2 + (1/\omega C)^2}} \tag{8.2–7a}$$

$$x(t) = \omega t + \theta, \qquad \theta = \tan^{-1}\left(\frac{1}{\omega RC}\right) \tag{8.2–7b}$$

which can be verified by resubstitution in (8.2–5). Then

$$\begin{aligned} i &= \mathscr{R} I_m \epsilon^{j\omega t} \epsilon^{j\theta} \\ &= \frac{V_m}{\sqrt{R^2 + (1/\omega C)^2}} \cos(\omega t + \theta) \end{aligned} \tag{8.2–8}$$

We now introduce the concept of impedance, Z, or the ratio of v to i (sinusoidal variations only), which becomes in polar form

$$Z = \left[R^2 + \left(\frac{1}{\omega C}\right)^2\right]^{1/2} \epsilon^{j\theta} \tag{8.2–9a}$$

or in rectangular form

$$Z = R + \frac{1}{j\omega C} \tag{8.2–9b}$$

The exponential form of the voltage and current $V_m \epsilon^{j\phi} \epsilon^{j\omega t}$ and $I_m \epsilon^{j(\phi + \theta)} \epsilon^{j\omega t}$ may be considered as phasors in a complex plane whose lengths are related by the magnitude of Z in (8.2–9a) and which are separated by the angle θ. As time proceeds, the phasors rotate (conventionally counterclockwise) and the instantaneous values may be found by taking the projections on the real axis. The same development can be followed by using the projections on the imaginary axis, or using

$$v = \mathscr{I} V_m \epsilon^{j\omega(t + \phi)} \tag{8.2–10}$$

where $\mathscr{I}$ means "take the imaginary part of." It is thus possible to deal with complex phasors and to take the real or imaginary parts of these if instantaneous values are desired.

If we take the Laplace transform of (8.2–5) with zero initial conditions we obtain the steady-state relation

$$\left(\frac{1}{sC} + R\right)I = V$$

or

$$\frac{V(s)}{I(s)} = R + \frac{1}{sC} \tag{8.2–11}$$

where $I(s)$ and $V(s)$ are the transformations of i and v, and you see at once that the right side of (8.2–9b) is identical to the right side of (8.2–11) if s is replaced by $j\omega$. Hence if I is viewed as an output, and V as an input, and if both of these are exponential functions of time, (8.2–9b) gives the steady-state sinusoidal transfer function. Obviously this can be extended to linear differential equations of higher order.

In summary, if steady-state sinusoidal solutions are desired, you may use exponential driving functions, and you may find the steady-state transfer function by taking the Laplace transform using zero initial conditions, and replacing all s values by $j\omega$. The resulting transfer function is the Fourier transform of a causal system. Some authors describe this by stating that the complex variable s is confined to the $j\omega$ axis. Others indicate that this is the "real frequency" axis. There may be some terminology difficulty here, because that the word "real" means that ω is real, and the word "frequency" means $\omega = 2\pi f$. The angular velocity ω is often called frequency and you must be careful to be clear as to the meaning, else it is easy to lose a 2π factor with a resultant error by a factor of almost 10. It is also noted that the imaginary axis in the Laplace s plane becomes the real axis in the Fourier $j\omega$ plane.

If we now examine a typical transfer function such as given by (7.3–2b) and replace s by $j\omega$, we get for a sinusoidal analysis of the control system of Figure 8.3–1 the equation

$$\frac{C(j\omega)}{R(j\omega)} = \frac{K_1 \prod_{k=1}^{m} (j\omega + z_k)}{\prod_{k=1}^{n} (j\omega + P_k)} \tag{8.2–12}$$

or from (7.3–3) the equation

$$G(j\omega)H(j\omega) = \frac{K \prod_{k=1}^{m} (j\omega + z_k)}{\prod_{j=1}^{n} (j\omega + p_j)} \tag{8.2–13}$$

If you plot the poles $-p_j$ and the zeros $-z_k$ of (8.2–13) on the s plane and select some $\omega = \omega_1$, you obtain a figure such as Figure 8.2–2, where $m = 1$ and $n = 4$. You see that, as in the case of Chapter 7, the factors on the

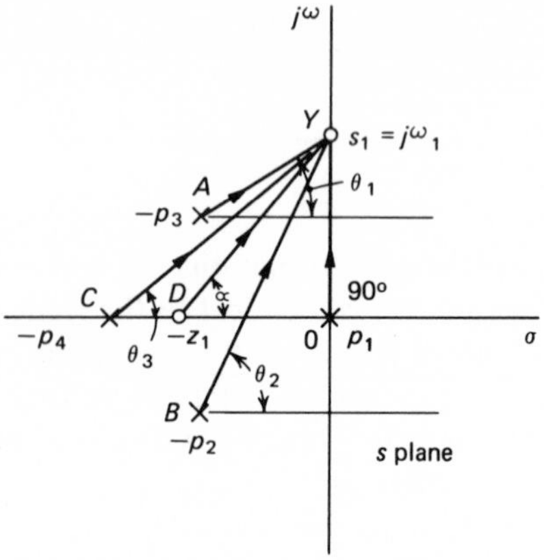

Figure 8.2–2. Poles and zeros and sinusoidal driving function.

right side of (8.2–13) are vectors from the poles and zeros to the point $s_1 = j\omega_1$, where s_1 is now confined to the $j\omega$ axis. Thus for (8.2–13) in this case we could write

$$G(j\omega)H(j\omega) = \frac{K\mathbf{DY}}{\mathbf{AY}\ \mathbf{BY}\ \mathbf{CY}\ \mathbf{OY}} \tag{8.2–14}$$

where the boldface pairs indicate vectors in the s plane. Since each vector consists of a magnitude and direction, from Figure 8.2–2 we can write (8.2–14) as

$$G(j\omega)H(j\omega) = \frac{K|\mathbf{DY}|\underline{/\alpha}}{|\mathbf{AY}|\underline{/\theta_1}|\mathbf{BY}|\underline{/\theta_2}|\mathbf{CY}|\underline{/\theta_3}|\mathbf{OY}|\underline{/90^\circ}}$$

$$= K(K_2)\underline{/\phi} \tag{8.2–15a}$$

where

$$K_2 = \frac{|\mathbf{DY}|}{|\mathbf{AY}||\mathbf{BY}||\mathbf{CY}||\mathbf{OY}|} \tag{8.2–15b}$$

$$\phi = \alpha - (\theta_1 + \theta_2 + \theta_3 + 90^\circ)* \tag{8.2–15c}$$

The symbol $\underline{/\theta}$ indicates a phase angle, or $\epsilon^{j\theta}$. The values for $GH(j\omega)$ as ω varies can therefore be obtained graphically, but more rapid methods will be described.

* One pole is at the origin in Fig. 8.2–2.

Equations (8.2–15) indicate that for any ω, the open loop function $GH(j\omega)$ has a magnitude KK_2 and a phase angle ϕ; or for a sinusoidal input to G the output from H is also sinusoidal, but the magnitude (maximum value) differs from that of the input by the factor KK_2 and the phase angle differs by ϕ. As s_1 in Figure 8.2–2 moves along the $j\omega$ axis, both K_2 and ϕ will vary, or be functions of ω.

Example 8.2–1

Let

$$G(s)H(s) = \frac{5000(s+5)}{s(s+10)(s+50)}$$

Replacing s by $j\omega$,

$$G(j\omega)H(j\omega) = \frac{5000(j\omega+5)}{j\omega(j\omega+10)(j\omega+50)}$$

$$G(j\omega)H(j\omega) = \frac{5000\sqrt{25+\omega^2}\,\underline{/\tan^{-1}(\omega/5)}}{\omega\underline{/90^\circ}\sqrt{100+\omega^2}\,\underline{/\tan^{-1}(\omega/10)}\sqrt{2500+\omega^2}\,\underline{/\tan^{-1}(\omega/50)}}$$

If ω is less than one tenth the magnitude of the smallest critical frequency, it can be neglected in calculating the magnitude (slide rule accuracy). Thus, if $\omega = 0.5$,

$$G(j\omega)H(j\omega) \simeq \frac{5000(5)\underline{/5.8^\circ}}{0.5\underline{/90^\circ}10\underline{/2.9^\circ}50\underline{/0.6^\circ}}$$

$$\simeq 100\underline{/-87.7^\circ}$$

Note that small-angle contributions cannot be neglected (although for preliminary design we have retained more accuracy than necessary). If ω is greater than 10 times the magnitude of the largest critical frequency, the pole and zero values may be neglected in calculating the magnitude on a similar basis. Hence, if $\omega = 500$,

$$G(j\omega)H(j\omega) \approx \frac{5000(500)\underline{/89.4^\circ}}{500\underline{/90^\circ}500\underline{/88.9^\circ}500\underline{/84.2^\circ}}$$

$$\approx 0.02\underline{/-173.7^\circ}$$

This example illustrates the general trend in frequency analysis of control systems; that is, the transfer function magnitude eventually becomes smaller with higher angular velocities, and the argument (arg) [or phase angle (phase)] eventually becomes more lagging. The frequency response is thus similar to that of a low pass filter. From the original function it is clear that the final phase is asymptotic to $(-90°)(n - m)$, where n and m are the degrees of the denominator and numerator polynomials, respectively. The phase at very low angular velocity equals $(-90)(r - l)$, where r and l are the powers of any $s + 0$ terms in the denominator and numerator, respectively. For example if

$$GH = \frac{Ks(s+5)}{s^3(s+5)(s^2+8s+50)}$$

$r = 3$, $l = 1$, and the phase is $-180°$ when $s = j\epsilon$, $\epsilon \to 0$. (The numerator will rarely contain such terms, which would indicate pure differentiations. Pure integration, however, is common.) The magnitude in this case approaches infinity at $s = 0$.

To obtain the sinusoidal response, then, s in the usual Laplace transform derived transfer function is replaced by $j\omega$ and ω is varied. To represent the process graphically, we need two complex planes, one for the variable s and one for the variable $GH(j\omega)$. From the previous discussion, (8.2–13) can be written

$$G(j\omega)H(j\omega) = |\mathrm{GH}|\epsilon^{j\phi} \tag{8.2–16a}$$

or

$$G(j\omega)H(j\omega) = u + jv \tag{8.2–16b}$$

where $u = |GH| \cos \phi$ and $v = |GH| \sin \phi$, and where $|GH|$, ϕ, u, and v are functions of ω. The function GH may thus be shown in the complex $u + jv$ plane while s is shown in the complex $\sigma + j\omega$ plane. In general, as s traces out a curve in its plane, a curve will also be traced in the GH plane If the function is rational, that is, a ratio of polynomials with real coefficients, there will be a one-to-one correspondence of points in both planes, and for a closed contour in the s plane there will be one corresponding closed contour in the GH plane, Moreover, angular changes in the s plane are preserved in the GH plane [2]. That is, in Figure 8.2–3, if a qualifying curve in the s plane changes at the point P by the angle ϕ, the

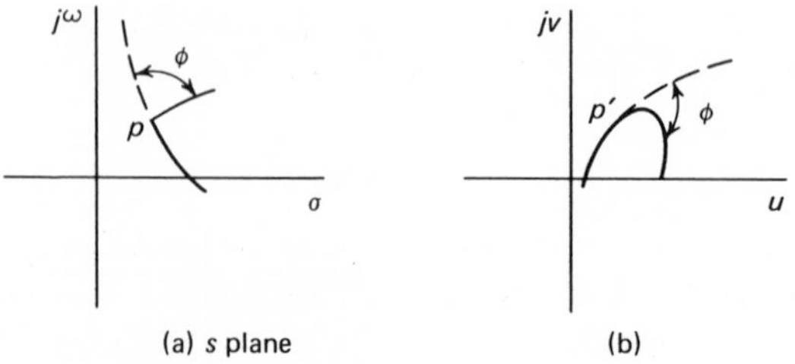

Figure 8.2–3. Preservation of angular changes in the s and $G(s)H(s)$ planes.

corresponding curve in the *GH* plane changes by the same amount at P' and in the same direction (clockwise in Figure 8.2–3). In complex variable theory this is termed "conformal mapping." Conformal mapping is very useful as a tool in solving Laplace's equation in two dimensions. Here we shall use it as an aid in plotting. For our case, the curve in the s plane in Figure 8.2–3a will lie along the $j\omega$ axis, and we will be interested in the corresponding contour in the *GH* plane. Singularities on the $j\omega$ axis must be managed by special techniques.

8.3 Nyquist Criterion

As in the root locus method, stability is of prime concern. First, you need to know if the system is stable, and, second, if it is stable, the degree of stability or the relative stability. The Nyquist criterion is a graphical method to answer these questions [3].

As shown previously, in a linear system the question of asymptotic stability reduces to ascertaining if any poles of the system lie in the right-half s plane. Referring to Figure 7.3–1, which is reproduced here as

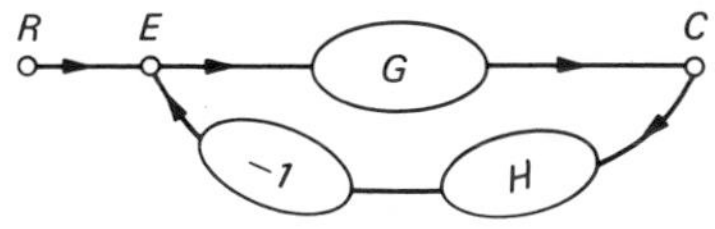

Figure 8.3–1. Feedback system.

Figure 8.3–1 for convenience, we know that the system transfer function is given by (7.3–1), repeated here:

$$\frac{C(s)}{R(s)} = \frac{G(s)}{1 + G(s)H(s)} \tag{8.3–1}$$

Obviously, again the poles of $C(s)/R(s)$ are the zeros of $1 + G(s)H(s)$, or the roots of the characteristic equation $1 + G(s)H(s) = 0$. For a $G(s)H(s)$ given by a ratio of polynomials, which has been our assumption to date, from (7.3–3)

$$1 + G(s)H(s) = 1 + \frac{K\prod_{i=1}^{m}(s + z_i)}{\prod_{j=1}^{n}(s + p_j)}$$

$$= \frac{\prod_{i=1}^{m}(s + p_j) + K\prod_{i=1}^{m}(s + z_i)}{\prod_{j=1}^{n}(s + p_j)} \tag{8.3–2}$$

The numerator of (8.3–2) is the characteristic equation, or

$$\prod_{j=1}^{n} (s + p_j) + K \prod_{i=1}^{m} (s + z_i) = \prod_{k=1}^{n} (s + P_k)$$
$$= 0 \qquad \textbf{(8.3–3)}$$

where the $-P_k$ are the control ratio system poles and it is assumed that $n > m$. We would like to know if any poles $-P_k$ lie in the right-half plane. Let us examine the right side of (8.3–2), which from (8.3–3) we rewrite as

$$\frac{\prod_{k=1}^{n} (s + P_k)}{\prod_{j=1}^{n} (s + p_j)} = 0 \qquad \textbf{(8.3–4)}$$

Suppose we have one $-P_k = P_1$ in the right-half plane, as in Figure 8.3–2, and we trace a closed contour C surrounding P_1 in the clockwise direction using a vector s_1. It is clear that that angle α of the vector $(s_1 - P_1)$ changes by 360° as the point s_1 goes around the contour once, and, from our preceding discussion, we have one corresponding closed contour C' in the $1 + GH$ plane, or ψ also changes by 360°, in the clockwise direction. The general location of C' can be found in the following argument: The left side of (8.3–4) becomes

$$\frac{(s - P_1) \prod_{k=2}^{n} (s + P_k)}{\prod_{j=1}^{n} (s + p_j)} = \frac{|s - P_1| \epsilon^{j\alpha} \prod_{k=1}^{n} (s + P_k)}{\prod_{j=1}^{n} (s + p_j)} \qquad \textbf{(8.3–5)}$$

or

$$\frac{|s - P_1| \epsilon^{j\alpha} \prod_{k=2}^{n} (s + P_k)}{\prod_{i=1}^{n} (s + p_j)} = |1 + GH| \epsilon^{j\psi} \qquad \textbf{(8.3–6)}$$

where ψ is the angle of the complex quantity $1 + GH$ in polar form.

From (8.3–6) the angle ψ changes by 360° as s_1 changes by the same amount; hence the contour C' must enclose or encircle the origin of the $1 + GH$ plane, or $\psi = 360°$, a result we anticipated in drawing Figure 8.3–2b. In pursuing this discussion, no attempt is made to limit the contour C to any particular shape; C' encircles the origin clockwise as long as C encircles P_1 clockwise. Contours C and C' will be related in shape because of the preservation of the angle rule, but we are not particularly interested in this here.

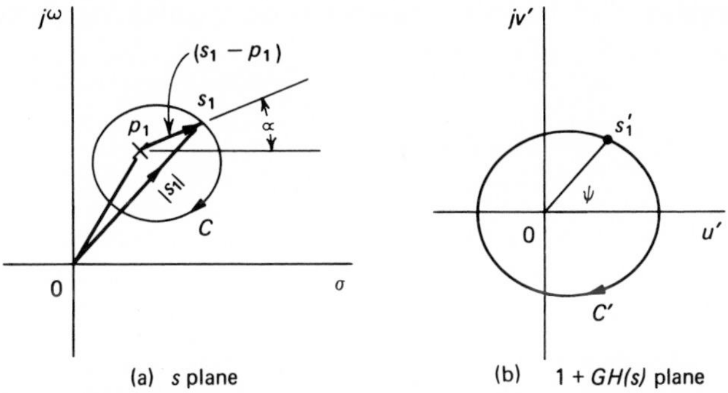

Figure 8.3–2. Encirclement of right-half-plane pole in the s plane and corresponding encirclement of the origin in the $1 + GH$ plane.

In Figure 8.3–3 one examines the contrary hypothesis—that the contour C does not enclose P_1. You can see that although the angle α changes as s_1 traces out the contour, its final value after completion of the curve is identical to its starting value. Hence from (8.3–6) the contour C' does not

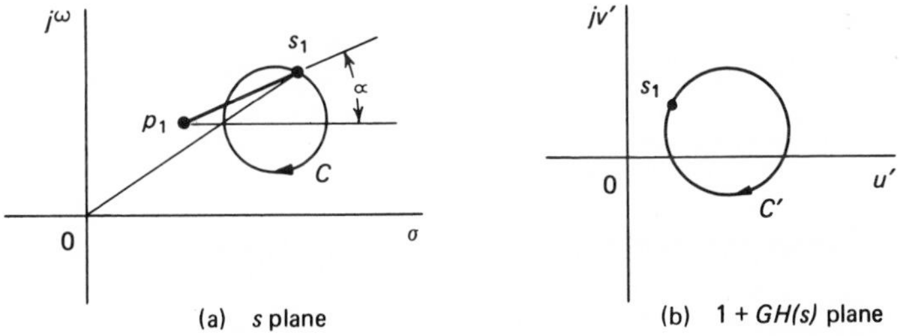

Figure 8.3–3. Pole in the s plane is not encircled and corresponding path in the GH plane.

encircle the origin in the $1 + GH$ plane. The result is easily extended to more poles in the right-half plane, for if there are two poles inside the contour C, (8.3–6) is

$$\frac{|s - P_1|\,|s - P_2|\epsilon^{j\alpha 1}\epsilon^{j\alpha 2}\prod_{k=3}^{n}(s + P_k)}{\prod_{1=1}^{n}(s + p_j)} = |1 + GH|\epsilon^{j\psi} \qquad \textbf{(8.3–7)}$$

C' encircles the origin twice, and the general rule follows that the number of clockwise encirclements of the origin by C' equals the number of poles P_r in the right-half s plane encircled by C.

Now suppose that we have one open loop singularity p_1 in the right-half plane. Then (8.3–6) becomes

$$\frac{\epsilon^{-j\gamma} \prod_{k=1}^{n} (s + P_k)}{|s - p_1| \prod_{j=2}^{n} (s + p_j)} = |1 + GH|\epsilon^{j\psi} \tag{8.3–8}$$

where γ is the angle of the $s - p_1$ vector. Because this changes to a negative angle in the numerator, as shown, the contour C' will encircle the origin of the $1 + GH$ plane in the counterclockwise direction as C proceeds in a clockwise direction.

Let N be the number of clockwise encirclements of the origin in the $1 + GH$ plane. Clearly, then, if we have P_r poles of the system function C/R in the right-half s plane and p_r poles of the open loop function GH in the right-half s plane enclosed by the clockwise-proceeding contour C, the net encirclements N of the origin of the $1 + GH$ plane will be

$$N = P_r - p_r \tag{8.3–9}$$

where N will be positive if $P_r > p_r$. The number of poles in the right-half plane p_r is assumed to be known, because we usually have the open loop function

$$GH(s) = \frac{K \prod_{i=1}^{m} (s + z_i)}{\prod_{j=1}^{n} (s + p_j)} \tag{8.3–10}$$

in factored form. The alternative case will be considered later.

To find all the poles P_r in the right-half plane, you merely stretch the contour C to include the entire right-half plane. Then Figure 8.3–4 shows a contour that will surely include all singularities in the right-half s plane. The curve follows the $j\omega$ axis from $-j\infty$ to $j\infty$, and is closed by a semi-circle of radius R, where $R \to \infty$ in the limit. We define such a contour as a "Nyquist contour" in what follows.

Next if you examine (8.3–2), you see that all has been said concerning the origin in the $1 + GH$ plane applies to the -1 point in the GH plane, Figure 8.3–5, by a shift of the origin one unit. It is much easier to examine the function GH than the function $1 + GH$. Now the rule alters slightly to: Given the s-plane Nyquist contour of Figure 8.3–4, the number of encirclements N of the point $(-1, 0)$ in the GH plane is given by the relation $N = P_r - p_r$, $P_r \geq 0$, $p_r \geq 0$. If the encirclements are clockwise, $N > 0$.

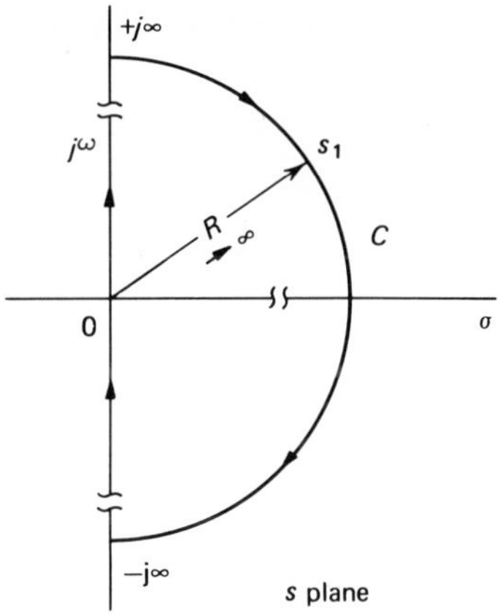

Figure 8.3–4. Nyquist contour.

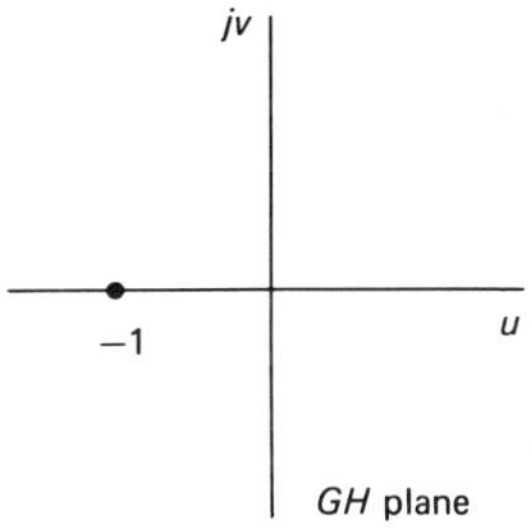

Figure 8.3–5. Encirclement of origin in the $1 + GH$ plane is equivalent to encirclement of -1 in the GH plane.

There are two minor but important points to consider. These are (1) what happens to the contour C' when $R \to \infty$ in Figure 8.3–4, and (2) how do you handle singularities on the $j\omega$ axis? In regard to point 1, the denominator of GH in (8.3–10) is almost always of higher degree than the numerator, or $n > m$. Then when s becomes large,

$$\underset{s \to \infty}{GH} = \frac{K}{s^{n-m}} \tag{8.3–11}$$

Hence as the point s_1 proceeds clockwise at a radius R the function GH proceeds counterclockwise at a radius K/R^{n-m}, and the function will have a vanishingly small circular contour at the origin as $s \to \infty$. For functions in which $n \leq m$, special effort will be required to ascertain the behavior of GH as $s \to \infty$.

In regard to point 2, it is necessary to detour around any $j\omega$ axis singularities either to the right or the left. The simplest detour contour is a small circle of radius ρ as magnified in Figure 8.3–6, where a factor of $(s+0)$ is in the denominator of (8.3–10), or we have an open loop pole at the origin. The counterclockwise detour to the right puts the pole in

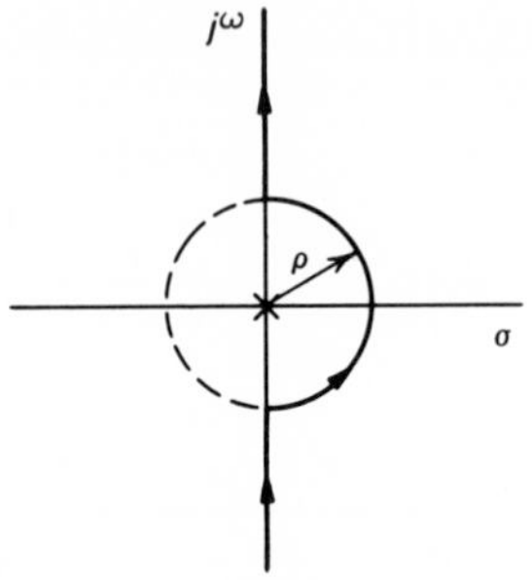

Figure 8.3–6. Nyquist contour in vicinity of $j\omega$ axis, pole at origin.

the left-hand s plane; hence it is not counted in applying rule (8.3–9). Equation (8.3–10) becomes

$$G(s)H(s) = \frac{K\prod_{i=1}^{m}(s+z_i)}{s^r\prod_{j=r+1}^{n}(s+p_j)} \qquad \textbf{(8.3–12)}$$

where $r = 1$ in Figure 8.3–6. If we let $s = \rho\epsilon^{j\alpha}$ in (8.3–12), $|GH| \to \infty$ as $\rho \to 0$, and as α goes from $-\pi/2$ to $\pi/2$, or through an angle of 180°, the function angle ψ, or arg GH, goes through an angle of 180°. The pole is in the denominator, however, so the rotation of the angle ψ is in the clockwise direction, because the rotation around the pole at the origin is counterclockwise. The contour in the GH plane thus proceeds at a radius of infinity, and clockwise through an angle of 180° as we proceed around the pole at the origin as $s \to 0$. This will result in a closure of the contour, as will be shown in some succeeding examples. Alternatively, you could bypass the pole at the origin to the left in a clockwise direction, as indicated by the dashed circle in Figure 8.3–6. Then this pole is included in the right-half-plane poles p_r, but the closure of the GH contour will be at a very large radius and 180° counterclockwise.

For a double pole at the origin, or $r = 2$ in (8.3–12), the contour of GH will go through an angle of 360° at a very large radius, and so on. There may be other open loop poles or zeros along the $j\omega$ axis. For example, there may be a factor $(s^2 + \omega_1^2)$ in the denominator of (8.3–12), resulting in poles at $\pm j\omega_1$. Each of these is bypassed in the same manner as described for a pole at the origin. If a zero z_i is on the $j\omega$ axis, a similar counterclockwise detour results in a counterclockwise curve in the GH plane, because the zero is in the numerator of GH.

Suppose that the number of poles p_r in the right-half plane is not known. Then it is necessary to do a Nyquist analysis with GH as the closed loop system function, and to continue this decomposition as often as necessary. This may come about when an inner feedback loop exists and there is uncertainty as to the stability of the open loop function making up GH.

To recapitulate, to perform a Nyquist analysis, we examine the open loop function

$$GH = \frac{K\prod_{i=1}^{m}(s+z_i)}{\prod_{j=1}^{n}(s+p_j)}$$

with s taking on all imaginary values between $-j\infty$ and $j\infty$. The resulting contour in the complex GH plane will be closed by semicircles or circles of infinite radius if any p_j lie on the $j\omega$ axis. Let N be the number of encirclements of the point -1 in the GH plane, $N > 0$ for clockwise encirclements, $N < 0$ for counterclockwise encirclements. Let p_r be the number of poles of GH in the right-half plane. Then the number of poles of the closed loop function $C/R = G/(1 + GH)$ lying in the right-half plane is given by

$$P_r = N + p_r \tag{8.3–13}$$

with

$$P_r \geq 0 \qquad p_r \geq 0$$

Any such poles result in instability of the system delinated by C/R. Note that this test checks the input-output relations of the system. If the system is uncontrollable or unobservable, interior oscillations may exist, some of which might be unstable. A system may have open loop poles p_r in the right-half plane (be open-loop-unstable) but no system poles P_r in the right-half plane (be closed-loop-stable).

If the open loop function GH has zeros in the right-half plane (non-minimum phase), these zeros do not in themselves indicate instability, because the output time constants are functions of the poles only. However, the Nyquist plot will be affected by their presence, and in general such zeros will be destabilizing, because they make the phase more lagging than if they were absent.

In control system analysis, the ability to quickly sketch the Nyquist diagram is desirable and even necessary. Just as in the root locus method, too much time would be consumed if accurate plots were made for preliminary design. The sketch may be made by calculating a few points, and guidelines, such as asymptotes. As in the root locus plot, the gain K is of primary interest, and a new Nyquist diagram is obtained for each K. Normally we are interested in the region near the point $(-1, 0)$ in the GH plane and the remainder of the contour need not be plotted. GH is a ratio of polynomials with real coefficients, so the diagram in the lower-half plane is the mirror image of that in the upper-half plane; that is, $GH(-j\omega) = GH^*(j\omega)$. Therefore only half the diagram need be plotted. Usually this is the part $0 \leq s \leq j\infty$. It may be necessary to complete the diagram to ascertain the number of encirclements of the critical point.

We now give a few examples of Nyquist plots in which we show the complete diagram. In all cases we assume the Nyquist contour in the s plane and show only the GH-plane contour.

Example 8.3–1

Plot the Nyquist diagram for

$$GH(s) = \frac{K}{(s+\alpha)(s+\beta)}$$

Letting $s = j\omega$,

$$GH(j\omega) = \frac{K}{(\alpha + j\omega)(\beta + j\omega)}$$

Then in polar form

$$GH(j\omega) = \frac{K}{(\alpha^2 + \omega^2)^{1/2}(\beta^2 + \omega^2)^{1/2}} \underline{/-\tan^{-1}(\omega/\alpha) - \tan^{-1}(\omega/\beta)}$$

When $\omega = 0$,

$$GH = \frac{K \underline{/0^\circ}}{\alpha\beta}$$

but at high frequencies

$$\lim_{\omega\to\infty} GH = \lim_{\omega\to\infty} \left| \frac{K}{\omega^2} \right| \underline{/-180^\circ}$$

These two points are sufficient to get the general trend of the diagram, although we might calculate GH for one or two other values of ω, if desired. The resultant diagram is sketched in Figure 8.3–7, first in the lower-half plane, and then by folding, into the upper-half plane. As K grows larger, the diagram retains the same shape but expands. Examining $GH(j\omega)$, there are no open loop poles in the right-half plane, or $p_r = 0$. There are no encirclements of the point -1, regardless of K; hence the system is always stable.

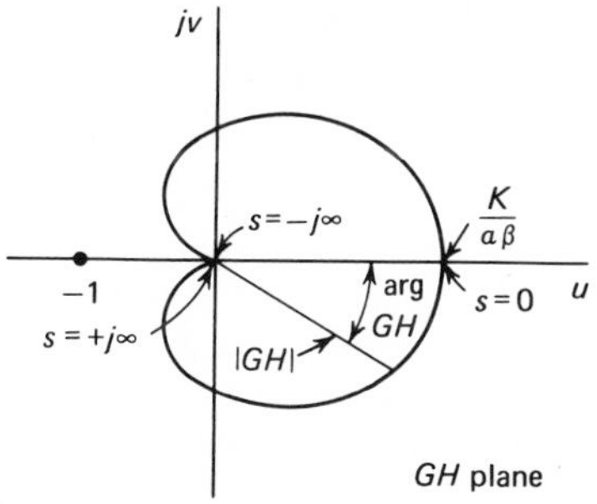

Figure 8.3–7. Contour in GH plane for Example 8.3–1.

Example 8.3–2

Plot the Nyquist diagram for

$$GH(s) = \frac{K}{s(s+\alpha)(s+\beta)}$$

Letting $s = j\omega$,

$$GH(j\omega) = \frac{K}{j\omega(\alpha + j\omega)(\beta + j\omega)}$$

$$= \frac{K}{\omega(\alpha^2+\omega^2)^{1/2}(\beta^2+\omega^2)^{1/2}} \underline{/-90^\circ - \tan^{-1}(\omega/\alpha) - \tan^{-1}(\omega/\beta)}$$

$$= \frac{K}{\omega(\alpha^2+\omega^2)(\beta^2+\omega^2)} [-\omega(\beta+\alpha) + j(\omega^2 - \alpha\beta)]$$

At very low ω values,

$$\mathscr{R}(GH) = \frac{-K(\beta+\alpha)}{(\alpha^2)(\beta^2)} \qquad \mathscr{I}(GH) \to \infty$$

and $\arg(GH) \to -90^\circ$. $\mathscr{R}(GH)$ decreases with ω, so the contour is asymptotic to a line parallel to the $j\omega$ axis through $s = -K(\beta+\alpha)/\alpha^2\beta^2$.
At very high ω values,

$$\lim_{\omega\to\infty} |GH| = 0 \qquad \lim_{\omega\to\infty} \arg GH = -270^\circ$$

We can sketch the contour as in Figure 8.3–8. This is a case of a pole on the $j\omega$ axis, so the contour is completed at a radius $R \to \infty$. Since $p_r = 0$, there is a distinct possibility for $N > 0$ if K is sufficiently large. Clearly for instability $K > \alpha^2\beta^2/(\alpha + \beta)$. The exact value for K to cause instability can be found either from the Routh-Hurwitz criterion or from Figure 8.3–8 if a diagram for some K is made. Suppose that we calculate values for $GH(j\omega)$

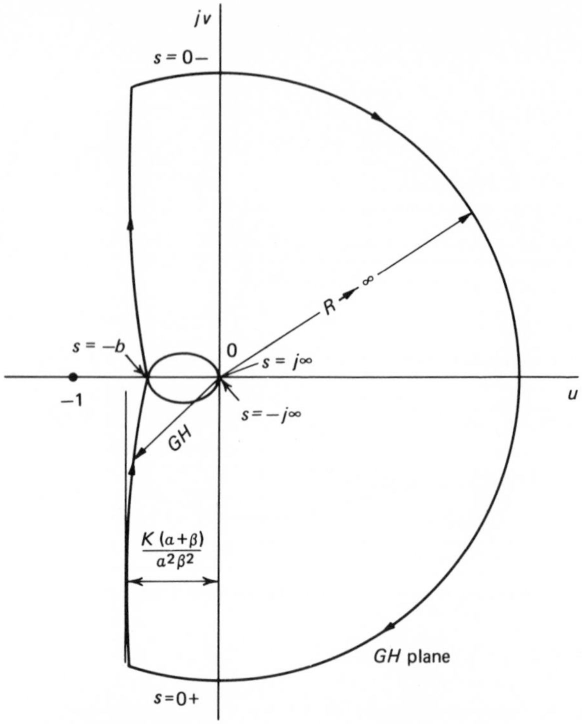

Figure 8.3–8. Contour in *GH* for Example 8.3–2.

with $K = K_1$ in the region where arg $GH = -180°$, and by plotting a curve through these points we find that it intersects the real axis at $s = -b$, $b > 0$, as in Figure 8.3–8. The system is linear, so an increase in K simply expands the diagram. Then $K_s = K_1(-1/-b) = K_1/b$, where K_s is the value of K for the system represented by $G/(1 + GH)$ to be on the verge of instability.

Example 8.3–3

Plot the Nyquist diagram for

$$GH = \frac{K}{s^2(s + \alpha)(s + \beta)}$$

Following Example 8.3–2, both the real and imaginary parts become large when $s \to 0$ and the angle at this time is $-180°$. When $s \to \infty$ the, angle is

$-360°$. Hence the GH contour resembles the sketch in Figure 8.3–9. The point -1 is encircled twice clockwise, or $N = 2$.

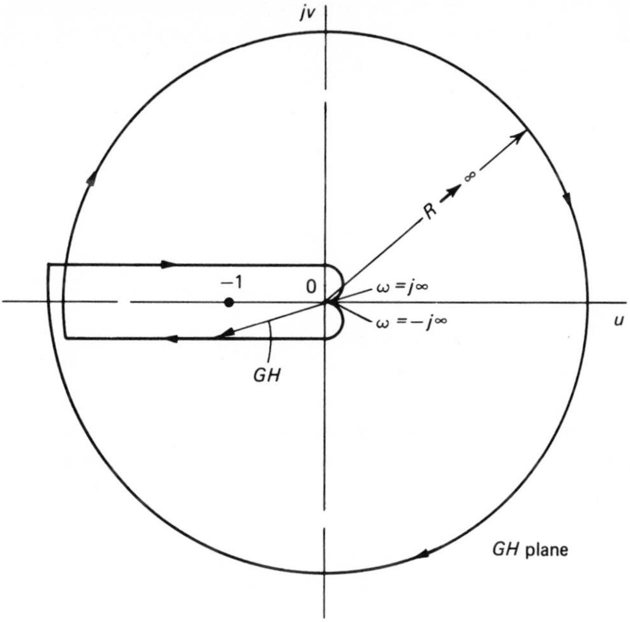

Figure 8.3–9. Nyquist diagram for Example 8.3–3.

Example 8.3–4

Plot the Nyquist diagram for

$$GH = \frac{K(s+\gamma)(s+\delta)}{s^2(s+\alpha)(s+\beta)}$$

For certain values of K, α, β, δ, and γ we may obtain a diagram such as in Figure 8.3–10, where the point -1 is not encircled. This may be seen by putting a pencil in one loop of a rubber band and the other loop over a pin stuck at the point -1. As the pencil traces out the contour from $-j\infty$ to $j\infty$ you will find that the total angle made by the rubber band sums to zero.
(We give an alternative method in Section 8.4.)

The situation of Example 8.3–4 is called "conditional stability," meaning that if the gain factor K is increased instability occurs, or if K is decreased instability occurs. In other words, instability occurs for either increase or decrease in K. Since the contour in Figure 8.3–10 expands as K increases, the point -1 will move into the inside loop L_1. Contrariwise, if K decreases, the point -1 moves into the outer loop L_2. If K decreases still more, the point -1 moves outside L_2, and the system is stable for all lower K. The root locus plot corresponding to this might appear as in Figure 8.3–11. There are other situations in which conditional stability

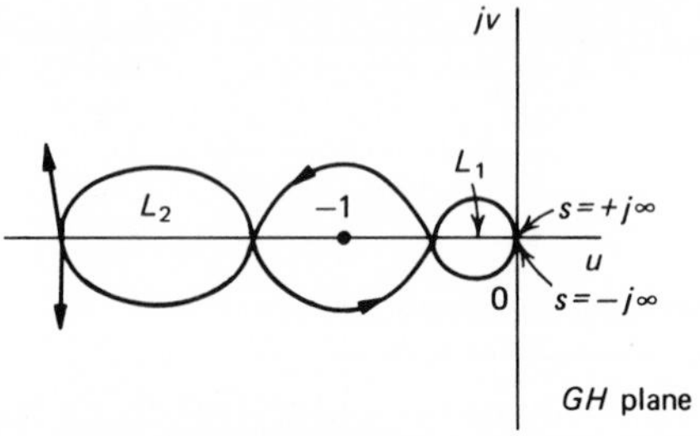

Figure 8.3–10. Nyquist diagram for Example 8.3–4.

will occur. The system will operate satisfactorily conditionally stable if the designer makes sure that K will not take on values that will cause instability or unsatisfactory operation. This he can do usually by estimating the expected loss of gain due to component aging.

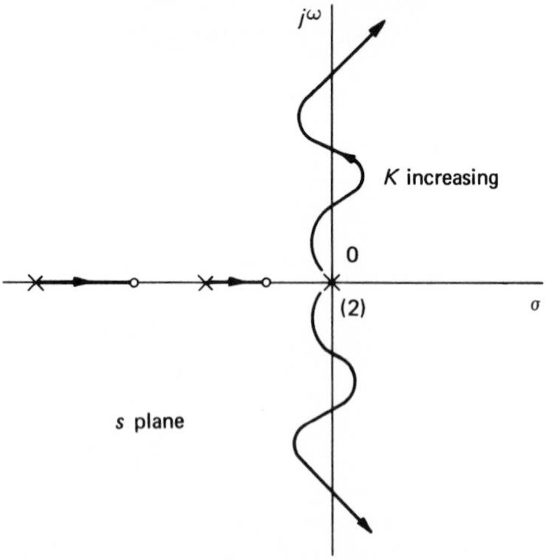

Figure 8.3–11. Possible root locus for conditionally stable system.

Example 8.3–5

Given

$$\text{(a)}\quad GH(s) = \frac{Kp(s)}{s(s+5)(s-1)} \qquad N = -1$$

$$\text{(b)}\quad GH(s) = \frac{Kp(s)}{s(s^2-6s+3)} \qquad N = 0$$

where $p(s)$ is a polynomial in s. Ascertain stability for (1) the open loop function (GH) and (2) the system function $G/(1+GH)$. For the open loop function GH, both (a) and (b) are unstable, because in the right-half s plane (a) has one pole and (b) has two poles, by inspection of the denominator in each case. For (a), $P_r = -1 + 1 = 0$; hence it is a stable closed loop. For (b) $P_r = 0 + 2 = 2$; hence the system is unstable. If in (b) $N = -2$, the system would be stable. In (b) it would not be possible for $N < -2$. (Why?)

8.4 Nyquist Criterion—Sundry Items

Section 8.3 discussed the case for negative feedback. For positive feedback the denominator of $C(s)/R(s)$ becomes $1 - GH$. The critical point is now $1 + j0$ in the GH plane and encirclements of this point are investigated; otherwise the analysis remains the same. As with the Chu plots for root locus, this can be extended to encirclements of the point $|1|\epsilon^{j\theta}$, θ taking on values of interest. Such an analysis would be unusual, because it is easier to adjust the phase angle of GH and to use the normal method.

A more interesting and profitable approach consists of investigating alternative paths in the s plane. In Figure 8.4–1 we could let s go from

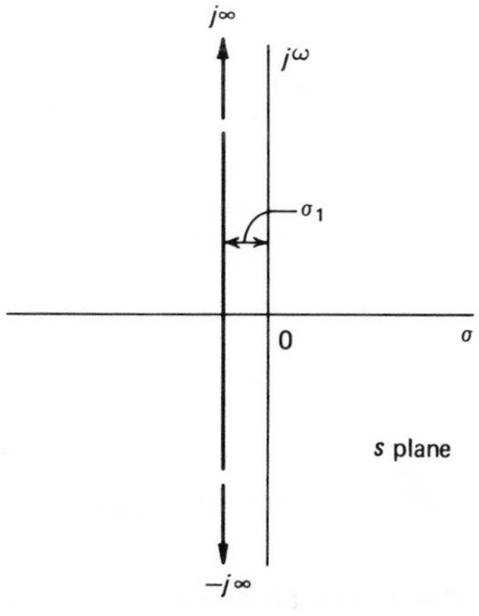

Figure 8.4–1. Alternative Nyquist path.

$-\sigma_1 - j\infty$ to $-\sigma_1 + j\infty$ along a line σ_1 units to the left of the $j\omega$ axis, closing as usual in an infinite semicircle to the right. If no poles are to the right of this line, you conclude that the transient step response damps out at a rate greater than σ_1, that is, in any output terms of the form $A\epsilon^{-\alpha t}\cos(\omega_n t + \phi)$, $\alpha > \sigma_1$. If such poles are found by encirclements of the point -1 (negative feedback) in the GH plane, then you reach the contrary conclusion. An alternative but equivalent approach is to shift the axis to the left in the s plane; that is, let $s = s' - \sigma_1$ in the transfer functions and proceed with the analysis normally. This is easy to program on a digital computer. Then, clearly, if we let σ_1 go in small steps from zero to $-\infty$, making a Nyquist analysis at each step, we shall locate the real parts of all roots of the characteristic equation. (We assume here that any roots in the right-half plane have already been located, or there are none.) Such a procedure could be automated on the digital computer.

Another path might be from the origin radially out along a line such that $s = \omega_n \epsilon^{j\theta} = \omega_n(-\cos \psi + j \sin \psi)$ or $s = \omega_n(-\zeta + j\sqrt{1 - \zeta^2})$, where $\zeta = \cos \psi$ is the damping factor ($\sigma_1 = \zeta\omega_n$), thence clockwise around the usual infinite semicircle, back along a radial line with points conjugate to the first, and into the origin (see Figure 8.4–2). Such a path would locate

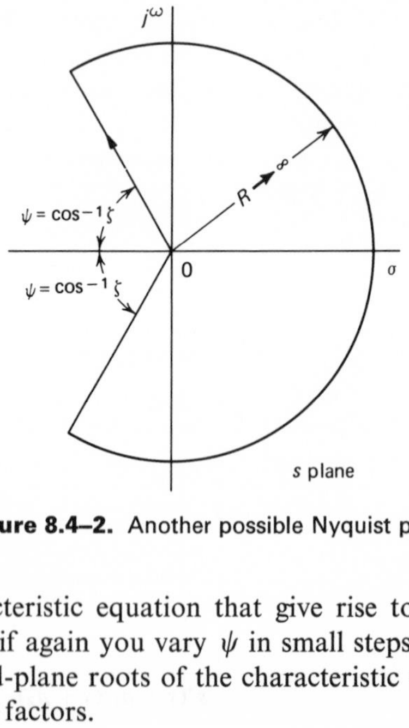

Figure 8.4–2. Another possible Nyquist path.

roots of the characteristic equation that give rise to specified damping factors. Obviously, if again you vary ψ in small steps from 0 to 90°, you classify all left-hand-plane roots of the characteristic equation as to their associated damping factors.

Other paths might be taken, such as one parallel to the real axis. A combination of these procedures would locate all left-hand-plane roots. Clearly any analysis along these lines must involve one or two specific items or must be computerized, because the Nyquist plot requires tedius calculations. Based on these ideas, a control system analysis technique originated by D. Mitrović has been developed, termed the "parameter plane" method [4, 5, 6].

The determination of encirclements of the critical point by the *GH* plane contour may be difficult to some readers for some cases. Earlier we outlined a technique using a rubber band, pin, and pencil. Another method will now be shown [7]. Consider a contour with the vector OS_1' moving in a clockwise direction in the *GH* plane (with 0 as the clock center). Sketch in the vector in various positions, from the largest positive angle at point *a* to the smallest at point *b*, as in Figure 8.4–3. Now as OS_1' moves in a counterclockwise direction with respect to 0 from *b* to *a*, erase the vector positions in the area through which it proceeds to obtain Figure 8.4–4. Then you see that any point such as *A* encircled by the contour must lie in the shaded area of Figure 8.4–4. Thus we deduce the following rule.

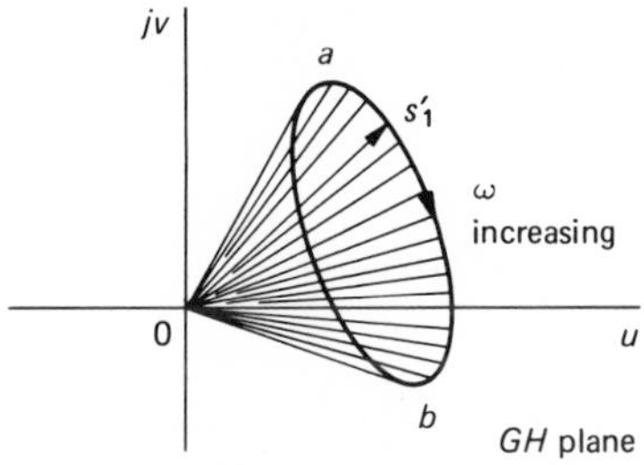

Figure 8.4–3. Shading to determine encirclements.

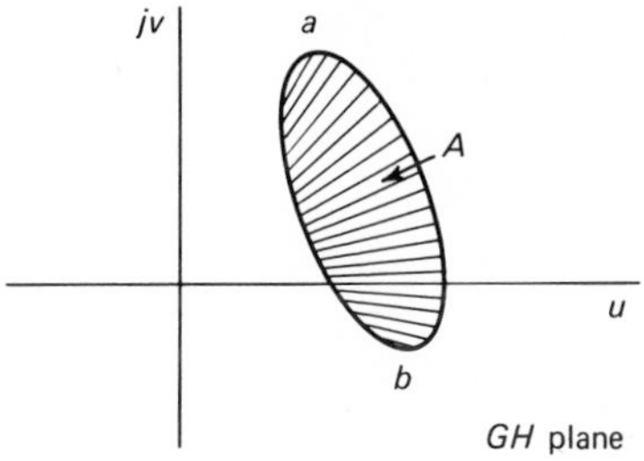

Figure 8.4–4. Conclusion of shading rule.

In following the contour in the *GH* plane in the direction of increasing angular velocity, shade to the right of the curve as you proceed. If the critical point lies within the shaded area, it is encircled clockwise; otherwise it is not. The direction of the encirclement may be determined by placing arrows on the curve in the direction of increasing frequency.

Example 8.4–1

Given

$$GH = \frac{K(s+z_1)(s+p_2)}{s^3(s+p_1)(s+p_2)}$$

in a negative feedback system. Under certain relations between z_1, z_2 and p_1, p_2, we shall get a Nyquist plot as in Figure 8.4–5. If the gain *K* is such that the critical point lies between *A* and *B* of Figure 8.4–5, then the system $G/(1 + GH)$ is stable, because the region *R* is unshaded. You again see that an effective method of stabilizing an otherwise unstable system is to introduce zeros at appropriate locations. This system is also conditionally stable.

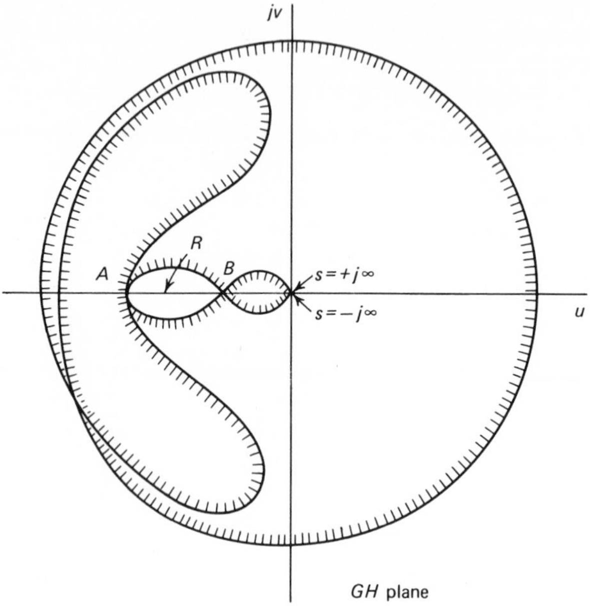

Figure 8.4–5. Use of the shading rule in Example 8.4–1.

8.5 Relative Stability

The Nyquist test for stability above tells us little more than the Routh-Hurwitz test indicates, except that the diagram may provide clues as to how to obtain stability. Also, the Routh-Hurwitz test could locate all the real parts of the left-half-plane poles by the change of variable (or axis shift) mentioned in Section 8.4 and with much less effort. However, the Nyquist diagram does give an indication of relative srability which is not provided in the Routh-Hurwitz test.

What do we mean by the term "relative stability"? For simplicity, let us assume that the system is open-loop-stable, that is, that there are no poles p_i in the right-half plane and that the feedback is negative. This is the usual situation. Then there must be no encirclements of the critical point in either direction. We shall have a situation similar to that shown in Figure 8.5–1, where the GH contour is drawn for $\omega > 0$ only. We may associate relative stability with the minimum length of the vector $1 + GH$, or to the nearness of approach of the contour to the point $(-1, 0)$. A minimum value for $|1 + GH|$ closely correlates with a maximum value for $G/(1 + GH)$, and you saw in Chapter 3 that the larger the magnitude of the sinusoidal transfer function, the more unstable is the second-order system. This effect can be more precisely delineated by use of the Nichols chart, which gives the maximum value of $|G|/|1 + GH|$, as will be shown. More useful criteria for relative stability using the Nyquist diagram itself are (1) phase margin and (2) gain margin. Because the system is on the verge of instability if the curve in Figure 8.5–1 goes through the point $(-1, 0)$, or when $GH = |1|\epsilon^{\pm j180°}$, we define the phase margin as $\phi_m = (180° + \theta)$,

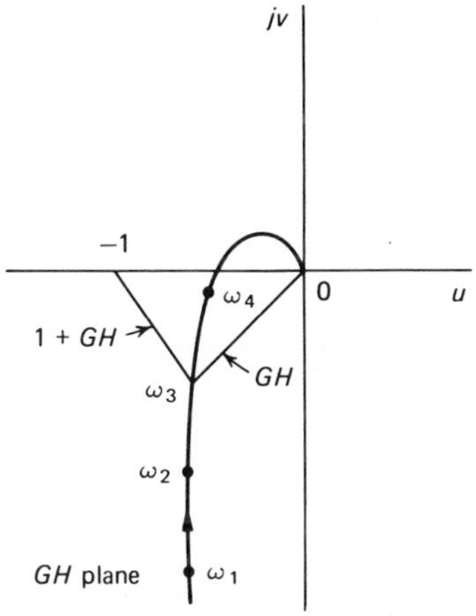

Figure 8.5–1. Nyquist diagram illustrating relative stability.

where θ is the phase angle of the vector GH when $|GH| = 1$, and the gain margin is $1/d = 1/|GH|$ when arg $GH = -180°$. Thus in Figure 8.5–2 ϕ_m is the phase margin and $1/d$ the gain margin. The two situations will occur at different angular velocities, such as ω_ϕ and ω_g. If the system is to be stable, the phase margin will usually be positive and the gain margin greater than 1. For relative stability, the region in proximity to the critical

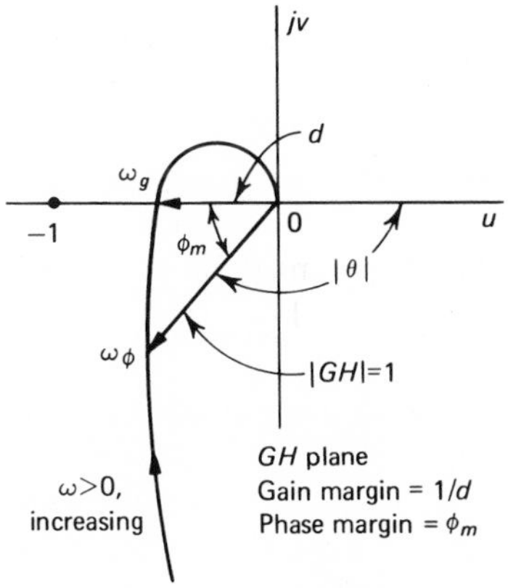

Figure 8.5–2. Gain and phase margin.

point is crucial, and the remainder of the diagram is unimportant. The curve could come into the region from other directions than in Figure 8.5–2, as shown, for example, in Figure 8.5–3. Here if we chose the length Oa, the gain margin would be less than 1 and if we chose the vector Od the phase margin would be negative. This would be a rather unusual situation for the phase margin, but not particularly unusual with respect to gain, as it represents a conditionally stable system. For such systems, we would base the definitions on the vectors Ob and Oc.

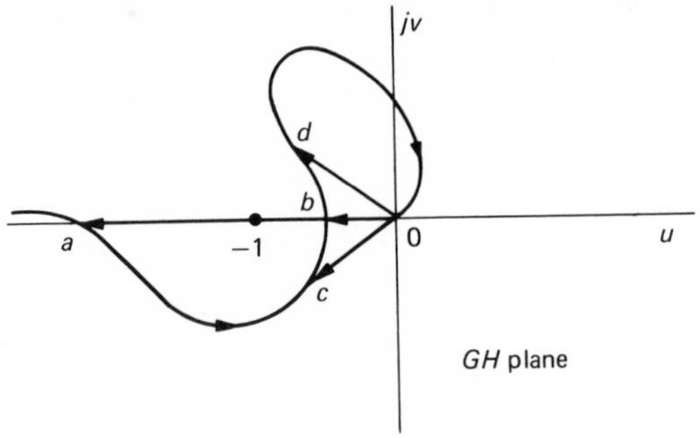

Figure 8.5–3. Unusual Nyquist diagram.

Phase margin is of importance to relative stability because in a second-order system there is close correlation between the phase margin on sinusoidal response and the overshoot on the time response to a step input. You saw in Chapter 3 that the per cent overshoot of the response to a step input depended only on the damping factor ζ (Figure 3.5–2). Similarly, the phase margin correlates with the damping factor, as we now shown in an example.

Example 8.5–1 [8]

Given a control system of unity negative feedback ($H = 1$) and

$$G = \frac{K}{s(s+p)}$$

Find the phase margin and the gain margin.

For sinusoidal analysis, the magnitude is

$$|G(j\omega)| = \frac{K}{\omega(\omega^2 + p^2)^{1/2}} \tag{8.5–1}$$

and the phase angle is

$$\arg G(j\omega) = -90° - \tan^{-1}\left(\frac{\omega}{p}\right) \tag{8.5–2}$$

The system function is

$$\frac{C}{R}(s) = \frac{G(s)}{1 + G(s)}$$

$$= \frac{K}{s^2 + ps + K} \tag{8.5–3}$$

From the characteristic polynomial $s^2 + ps + K$, we see at once that the natural frequency $\omega_n = \sqrt{K}$ and that the damping factor $\zeta = p/2\sqrt{K}$. Hence using (8.5–1),

$$|G(j\omega)| = \frac{\omega_n^2}{\omega(\omega^2 + 4\zeta^2\omega_n^2)^{1/2}} \tag{8.5–4}$$

Because the phase margin is measured when $|G| = 1$, then in (8.5–4)

$$\frac{\omega_n^2}{\omega(\omega^2 + 4\zeta^2\omega_n^2)^{1/2}} = 1 \tag{8.5–5}$$

Letting $\omega = \omega_\phi$, the angular velocity when $|G| = 1$, from (8.5–5) we obtain

$$\left(\frac{\omega_n}{\omega_\phi}\right)^4 - 4\zeta^2\left(\frac{\omega_n}{\omega_\phi}\right)^2 - 1 = 0 \tag{8.5–6}$$

The solution for $(\omega_n/\omega_\phi)^2$ is thus

$$\left(\frac{\omega_n}{\omega_\phi}\right)^2 = 2\zeta^2 \pm \sqrt{4\zeta^4 + 1} \tag{8.5–7}$$

From (8.5–1), when $\omega = \omega_n = \sqrt{K}$, $|G| < 1$, and, examining Figure 8.5–2 we see that $\omega_n > \omega_\phi$. Hence

$$\frac{\omega_n}{\omega_\phi} = (2\zeta^2 + \sqrt{4\zeta^4 + 1})^{1/2} \tag{8.5–8}$$

Using (8.5–2) we find that the phase angle when $|G| = 1$ is

$$\theta = -90° - \tan^{-1}\frac{\omega_\phi}{2\zeta\omega_n} \tag{8.5–9}$$

Combining (8.5–8) and (8.5–9), the phase margin ϕ_m is then

$$\phi_m = 90° - \tan^{-1}\frac{1}{2\zeta(2\zeta^2 + \sqrt{4\zeta^4 + 1})^{1/2}} \tag{8.5–10}$$

From Figure 3.5–2 we can find the per cent overshoot of a second-order system or a step input in terms of ζ. Then, finally, using (8.5–10) we can plot the per cent overshoot on a step input as a function of the phase margin on sinusoidal response, as shown in Figure 8.5–4.

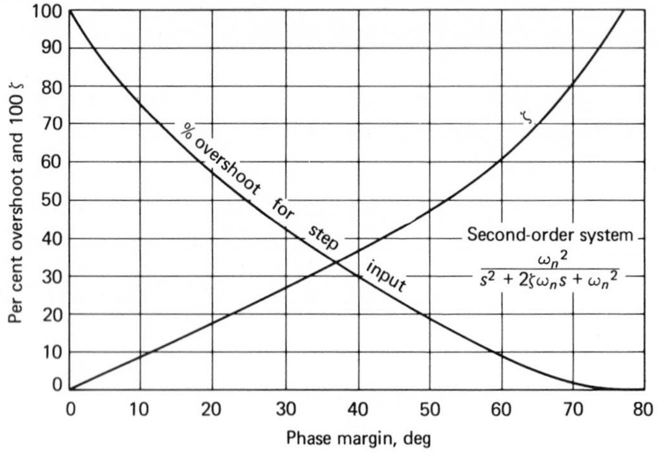

Figure 8.5–4. Damping constant and maximum overshoot as function of phase margin, second-order system.

For the second-order system when the phase angle becomes $-180°$ the gain is zero. Hence in Figure 8.5–2 the value of d is zero and the gain margin approaches infinity. (In other words, the system is never unstable.)

Pursuing the example slightly further, from (3.5–6) and (8.5–8) we find that

$$\frac{\omega_p}{\omega_\phi} = [(1 - 2\zeta^2)(\sqrt{4\zeta^4 + 1} + 2\zeta^2)]^{1/2} \qquad \textbf{(8.5–11)}$$

Hu uses (3.5–6), (8.5–11), and (3.5–7) as a basis for design for second-order systems. [8]

For higher-order systems the relation between phase margin and system performance in the time domain is not so simple, and it is easier to use the Nichols charts, as will be shown.

8.6 Bode Diagrams—Preparation

Bode suggested an alternative method of showing the sinusoidal frequency response [9]. Rather than representing the magnitude and phase angle on the complex GH plane (often termed a polar plot), he proposed drawing the magnitude and phase angle separately as functions of angular velocity on two real planes. This has advantages in the rapid preparation of the response characteristics, as you shall see, but requires two curves.

The Bode plots can best be explained by some examples. In the case of a single integrator, the transfer function is K/s, where K is a constant. The sinusoidal function is then $K/j\omega$. In the polar plot this would be depicted as in Figure 8.6–1, where the phase angle is a constant $-90°$ and the

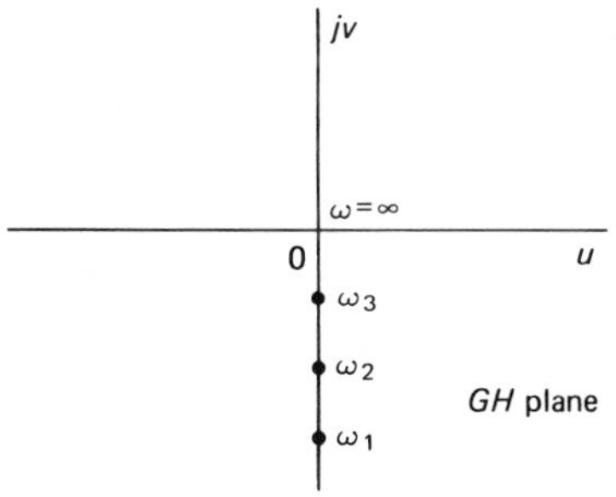

Figure 8.6–1. Nyquist diagram for $GH = K/s$, $s = j\omega$.

magnitude is inversely proportional to the angular velocity ω. Because frequency changes in systems may cover several decades, Bode proposed that the angular velocity scale be logarithmic. On the magnitude diagram we shall see that there is an advantage in also making the magnitude scale logarithmic. In the phase-angle diagram, the angle scale may be in radians or degrees—usually the latter.

Looking at the function $G(j\omega) = K/j\omega = |K/\omega|\epsilon^{-j90°}$, you see that the magnitude varies inversely with the frequency. If we take the logarithm of the function

$$\log \frac{K}{j\omega} = \log \left|\frac{K}{\omega}\right| - j90° \qquad \textbf{(8.6–1)}$$

the real part is $(\log K - \log \omega)$, which is a straight line with a slope of -1 if the independent variable $x = \log \omega$ and the dependent variable $y = \log |K/\omega|$. Since $\log (0) = -\infty$, it is not practical to have a y-axis intercept at $\omega = 0$, but we can find the value of y at some particular $\omega = \omega_1$, or $y_1 = \log |K/\omega_1|$. Hence the entire magnitude curve is a straight line proceeding through the point $(\log |K/\omega_1|, \log \omega_1)$ and at a -1 slope. For the log magnitude unit it is accepted practice to use the definition "value in db $= 20 \log G$," where db stands for decibels and G is the particular function considered for the magnitude (dependent) scale. Thus in the example, the vertical-axis scale would be in db. A decade is a change of ω by a factor of 10, giving rise to a change of magnitude by 10. Log 10 = 1, and it follows that in these units the slope of the example curve would be

-20 db per decade. It is the opinion of the author that the choice of the db for a unit of magnitude is unfortunate, because the decibel is rigorously defined as a power ratio, whereas G may be the ratio of any two quantities. Other units have been proposed, such as the "loru," where magnitude G in loru is defined as $\log |G|$. This avoids the conflict in definition of the term db and at the same time eliminates the superfluous multiplying factor 20. Thus a slope of -20 db per decade becomes -1 loru per decade. The use of the unit db in control theory is so widespread, however, it is not likely to be overturned. In this book a -1 placed by a curve will indicate a slope of -1 loru per decade or -20 db per decade, whichever is preferred. Because the number of decades between ω_2 and ω_1 is

$$N = \log_{10} \frac{\omega_2}{\omega_1} \text{ decades} \qquad \omega_2 > \omega_1 \tag{8.6–2}$$

and the number of octaves is

$$M = \log_2 \frac{\omega_2}{\omega_1} \text{ octaves} \qquad \omega_2 > \omega_1 \tag{8.6–3}$$

where an octave is a frequency ratio of 2, there are 3.32 octaves per decade. A slope of -20 db per decade is therefore a slope of about -6.02 db per octave, and hence many texts use -6 db per octave as the unit slope. You see that this is not exactly correct but is sufficiently accurate for most graphs, which usually you can read only to two places.

In the example under discussion ($G = K/j\omega$), let $K = 100$. If we let $\omega = 1$ $\log 100/1 = 2$, and the magnitude is 2 loru, or 40 db. The curve is a straight line, as in Figure 8.6–2a. It will cross the independent variable axis (0 db) when $|G| = 1$, or $\log K/\omega = 0$, whence at the crossing point $\omega = \omega_c = K$, if $K > 1$, as shown in Figure 8.6–2. The argument or phase angle is represented by a straight line with constant value $-90°$.

Because the magnitude curve has two logarithmic axis, log-log paper may be used [10]. However, it is often convenient to plot the phase on the same sheet. Hence the normal custom is to use semilog paper and compute $\log G$ for the gain curve. Four-cycle semilog paper is usually adequate for most systems. In general $|G| < 1$ as well as $|G| > 1$, so the independent axis ($\log 1 = 0$) should be sufficiently far up the paper to allow for negative $\log |G|$ values. The latter are easily found, because for $|G| < 1$, $\log |G| = -\log(1/|G|)$. For the phase-angle curve, the region of interest is usually between -90 and $-270°$, although occasionally system phase angles may become positive.

With the overall picture of the Bode curves in mind, together with the example for $G(i\omega) = K/j\omega$, let us proceed more rapidly with other factors, using as the second example

$$G = \frac{K}{s + \alpha} \tag{8.6–4}$$

or

$$G(j\omega) = \frac{K}{\alpha + j\omega} \tag{8.6–5}$$

$$= \frac{K}{\sqrt{\alpha^2 + \omega^2}} \epsilon^{-j[\tan^{-1}(\omega/\alpha)]}$$

Thus

$$\log G = \log\left[\frac{K}{\sqrt{\alpha^2 + \omega^2}} \underline{/-\tan^{-1}(\omega/\alpha)}\right] \tag{8.6–6}$$

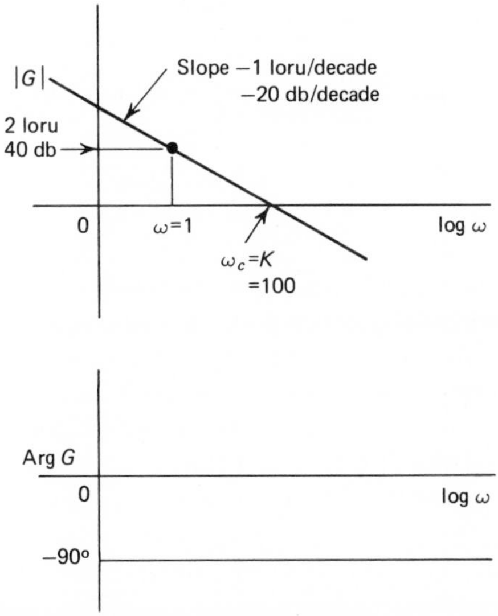

Figure 8.6–2. Bode gain and phase plots for $G = 100/s$, $s = j\omega$.

If $\omega \ll \alpha$, from (8.6–6) the magnitude is constant at the value $\log(K/\alpha)$ loru or $20 \log(K/\alpha)$ db. On the other hand, if $\omega \gg \alpha$,

$$\log |G| = \log \frac{K}{\omega}$$

which is similar to the previous example. This sloped line crosses the 0-db line at some $\omega = \omega_1$ when $K > \alpha$. The situation is shown in

Figure 8.6–3a. The straight lines representing $\log(K/\alpha)$ and $\log(K/\omega)$ intersect at $\omega = \alpha$, which is called a corner point or a "break point," as there is a change of slope here. The slopes of the lines are shown. When $\omega = \alpha$, from (8.6–5) the magnitude is

$$G = \frac{K}{\alpha\sqrt{2}} \tag{8.6–7}$$

Hence the magnitude curve is down by $\log(1/\sqrt{2})$ or 0.15 loru (3 db) from the magnitude at the point of intersection. The magnitude curve is asymptotic to the straight lines, and passes through a point 3 db lower at the intersection; hence it can be sketched in now with very little error, as shown in Figure 8.6–3a. The crossing of the gain curve with the 0-db line will be at

$$\omega_c = (K^2 - \alpha^2)^{1/2} \qquad K > \alpha$$

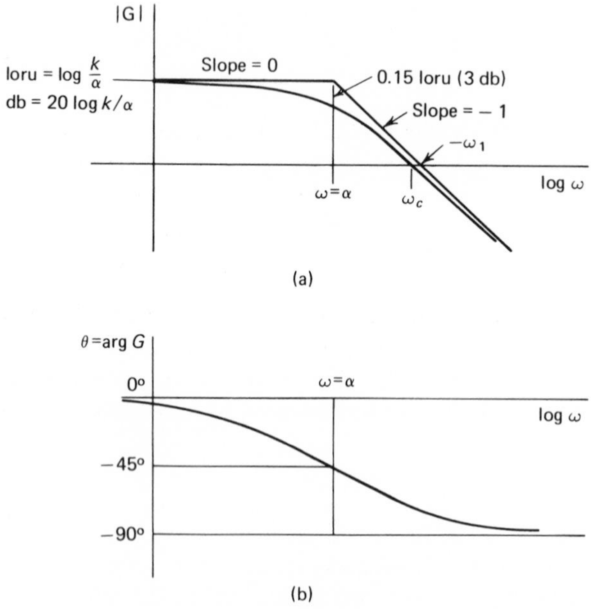

Figure 8.6–3. Bode plots for $G = K/(s+\alpha)$.

Thus ω_c occurs at a lower value of angular velocity than the straight line crossing ω_1. If $K < \alpha$, the magnitude curve never crosses 0 db and ω_c is undefined. The phase angle θ may be computed from the formula

$$\theta = -\tan^{-1}\left(\frac{\omega}{\alpha}\right) \tag{8.6–8}$$

It is clear that $\theta = 0$ for $\omega \ll \alpha$, $\theta = -90°$, $\omega \gg \alpha$ and $\theta = -45°$ for $\omega = \alpha$. Other values of θ may be computed from (8.6–8), as necessary, to give the curve sketched in Figure 8.6–3b.

Examining Figure 8.6–3a, you may ask: What happens if the frequency-independent gain K is altered? Clearly the result is an up or down movement of the curve. If K changes to K_2, the curve is merely displaced vertically up by the amount $\log(K_2/K)$ loru if $K_2 > K$, or down by the amount $\log(K/K_2)$ loru if $K_2 < K$. The phase angle is unaffected. Thus gain changes are much more easily made on a Bode chart than on a polar plot.

All functions of the type shown in (8.6–4) have similar curves, so we may prepare one set of charts for such factors, normalizing the angular velocity and adjusting K to some constant value. This is most easily done by putting (8.6–4) in different form, as

$$G = \frac{K}{\alpha[1 + (1/\alpha)s]} \qquad \textbf{(8.6–9)}$$

$$G = \frac{K_1}{1 + (1/\alpha)s} \qquad \textbf{(8.6–10)}$$

where $K_1 = K/\alpha$. The quantity $1/\alpha$ has the dimensions of time, because if we take the inverse transform of the right side of (8.6–10) we get

$$\mathcal{L}^{-1}\left[\frac{K_1}{1 + (1/\alpha)s}\right] = K_1 \varepsilon^{-t/\tau} \qquad \textbf{(8.6–11)}$$

where $\tau = 1/\alpha$ is the time constant of the system represented by G. Finally if we let $K_1 = 1$ in (8.6–10), we get a form that we can use for all factors of the type under discussion for sinusoidal analysis by letting $s/\alpha = j(\omega/\omega_n)$ where $\omega_n = \alpha$, or the breakpoint angular velocity. Thus we plot the log magnitude as

$$\log|G| = \log \frac{1}{\sqrt{1 + (\omega/\omega_n)^2}} \qquad \textbf{(8.6–12a)}$$

and the phase θ as

$$\arg G = -\tan^{-1}\left(\frac{\omega}{\omega_n}\right) \qquad \textbf{(8.6–12b)}$$

each as a function of $\log(\omega/\omega_n)$, as shown in Figure 8.6–4. These curves may now be used for any function of the type given by (8.6–5), where $K = \alpha$ with $\omega_n = \omega = 1/\tau$. The actual gain curve for any K and α may be traced from Figure 8.6–4 by displacing the figure vertically according to the given gain constant and horizontally until the value $\omega/\omega_n = 1$ on the figure occurs at the actual breakpoint $\omega = \alpha$. The actual phase curve can be traced using horizontal displacement only.

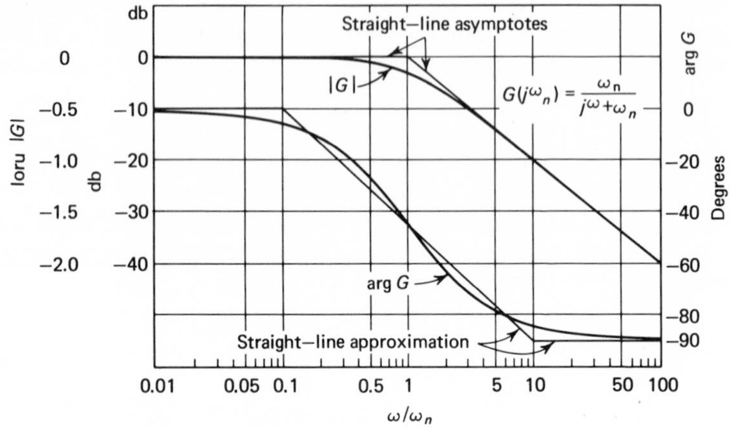

Figure 8.6–4. Magnitude (|G|) and phase (arg G) for $G(j\omega) = \alpha_n/(\omega_n + j\omega)$.

Because the straight-line asymptotes serve as guides and approximations to the magnitude curve, it is natural to inquire whether straight-line approximations exist for the phase curve in this case. One of these consists in drawing a tangent to the phase curve at the point $\omega/\omega_n = 1$ in Figure 8.6–4 [11]. Another is to draw a horizontal line at a phase angle $\theta = 0$ from $\omega = 0$ to $\omega = 0.1\omega_n$; then a straight line at a slope of $-45°$ per decade through the point where $\omega = \omega_n$, continuing to an angular velocity of $10\omega_n$, and then a horizontal line at $\theta = -90°$ to $\omega = \infty$. This three-line-segment approximation to the phase curve has a maximum error of about 6°, as shown in Figure 8.6–4. This is a sizable error, and the actual phase curve should be drawn in after the straight lines are made, using a few computed points if necessary. In using this straight-line approximation, you must also keep in mind that these line segments have two break points or corner points for each factor of the form of (8.6–9), whereas the two line segments for the magnitude curve have only one break point. This will be elaborated in a later example.

Next, if we have a function such as

$$G(s) = \frac{K}{s^n} \qquad \text{or} \qquad G(j\omega) = \frac{K}{(j\omega)^n}$$

you see from the previous discussion that for sinusoidal analysis, the magnitude curve will slope down at the rate $-n$ loru per decade ($-20n$ db per decade), and the phase angle will have a constant value of $n(-90°)$. The position of the magnitude curve vertically must again be evaluated at some particular value of angular velocity ω. It is also immediately clear that if the factor s^n is in the numerator, so that $G(s) = Ks^n$, the magnitude will slope up at a rate n loru per decade, and the phase angle will have a constant magnitude of $n(90°)$. Proceeding with factors in the numerator, if

$$G(s) = \frac{1}{\alpha}(s + \alpha)$$

you observe that the magnitude curve will be as shown in Figure 8.6–4, provided the slope is made positive rather than negative or, alternatively, the logarithmic values are changed from negative to positive in the figure. Also the phase-angle curve can be used if the angle values are similarly changed in sign. The curves are sketched in Figure 8.6–5 for completeness.

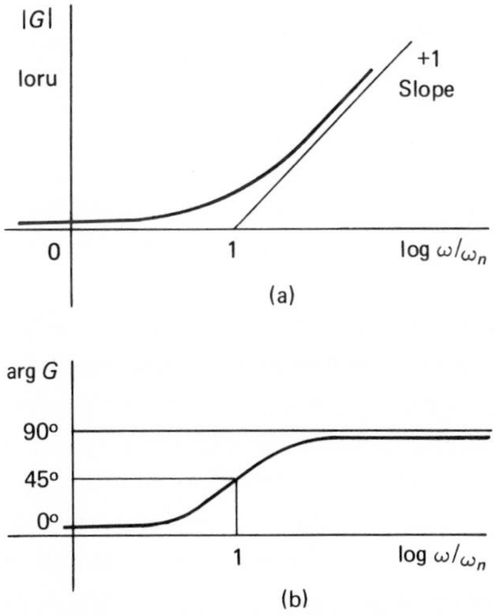

Figure 8.6–5. Bose plots for $G = (1/\alpha)(s + \alpha)$, $s = j\omega$, $\alpha = \omega_n$.

It should be clear that we shall have similar reflections of denominator factors if such factors appear in the numerator, and so the point will be belabored no more.

Now look at the function

$$G(s) = \frac{\alpha^2}{(s + \alpha)^2} \tag{8.6–13}$$

$$G(s) = \frac{1}{[1 + (1/\alpha)s]^2} \tag{8.6–14}$$

For sinusoidal analysis, you again let $s = j\omega$ and find the magnitude and phase angle of the right side of (8.6–14). From the previous discussion you see that for the magnitude the straight-line asymptotes again meet at the break point where $\omega = \alpha$, but that the slope beyond this point is -2 loru per decade (-40 db per decade); also the magnitude curve is now down 0.3 loru (6 db) from the value at the break point. The phase curve now goes from $0°$ when $\omega \ll \alpha$, to $-180°$ when $\omega \gg \alpha$, and is $-90°$ when $\omega = \alpha$.

Carrying this one step further we also need to examine the function

$$G(s) = \frac{\omega_n^2}{s^2 + 2\zeta\omega_n s + \omega_n^2} \tag{8.6–15}$$

when $s - j\omega$. Fortunately, we have already looked at this in Chapter 3, and find from (3.5–4) and (3.5–5) that

$$|G(j\omega)| = \frac{1}{[(1 - (\omega/\omega_n)^2)^2 + 4\zeta^2(\omega/\omega_n)^2]^{1/2}} \tag{8.6–16}$$

$$\arg G(j\omega) = -\tan^{-1}\left[\frac{2\zeta\omega/\omega_n}{1 - (\omega/\omega_n)^2}\right] \tag{8.6–17}$$

The Bode response plots are shown in Figures 3.5–3 and 3.5–4 and need not be repeated here. The case of the repeated root discussed just previously becomes a special case of this with $\zeta = 1$, but was discussed separately at that point to clarify the fact that the straight-line asymptotes intersect at $\omega = \omega_n$, or $\omega/\omega_n = 1$. This line is shown dashed in Figure 3.5–3, and it can be seen from this that for $\omega/\omega_n > 1$ the amplitude curve has a slope greater than -2 loru per decade if $\zeta < 1$, and a slope less than -2 loru per decade if $\zeta > 1$. The magnitude changes rapidly in the vicinity of ω/ω_n if $\zeta \ll 1$. In the limit, if $\zeta = 0$, the poles of G move to the $j\omega$ axis, or $G(s) = \omega^2/(s_n^2 + \omega_n^2)$. The magnitude becomes infinite at $\omega/\omega_n = 1$ and the phase changes from 0 at $\omega/\omega_n = 1 - \epsilon$ to $-180°$ at $\omega/\omega_n = 1 + \epsilon$, where $\epsilon > 0$ but is an arbitrarily small real number. Factors with quadratic denominators as in (8.6–13) might appear in the open loop portion of feedback systems if internal feedback paths of some sort exist.

Finally, as we know, the normal system open loop function $GH(s)$ will be a ratio of polynomials or a combination of the factors considered; that is, in general

$$GH(s) = \frac{K\prod_{i=1}^{m}(s + z_i)}{\prod_{j=1}^{n}(s + p_j)} \tag{8.6–18}$$

where some p_j may be zero and some may be complex—the latter leading to quadratic terms as in the denominator of (8.6–15) and the former to integrations in the time domain. Seldom would any z_i be zero; that is, seldom can we obtain pure differentiation in the time domain. If we take the logarithm of $GH(s)$ in (8.6–18), we get

$$\log GH(s) = \log|K| + \sum_{i=1}^{m} \log(s + z_i) - \sum_{j=1}^{m} \log(s + p_j) \qquad \textbf{(8.6–19)}$$

$$\arg GH = \sum_{i=1}^{m} \tan^{-1}\left(\frac{\omega}{z_i}\right) - \sum_{j=1}^{m} \tan^{-1}\left(\frac{\omega}{p_j}\right) \qquad \textbf{(8.6–20)}$$

Thus the magnitude curve becomes a summation of the magnitude curves for the factors and similarly for the phase curve. You now see the advantage of the logarithmic scale. The asymptotes may be drawn rapidly in the magnitude case, so this curve may be sketched very fast. In the initial design, the curve is often approximated by its asymptotes only. The phase curve takes more time, but points can be computed in a reasonable time if tabulated. We may also have straight-line guides for the phase curve, discussed previously, but the straight lines themselves are too much in error to use as they stand. Let us take a specific example.

Example 8.6–1

Let the open loop transfer function of a system have a negative feedback with $H = 1$ and forward path gain

$$G(s) = \frac{1108(s + 2)(s + 6.67)}{s(s + 0.333)(s + 0.667)(s + 33.3)(s + 200)} \qquad \textbf{(8.6–21)}$$

Find the magnitude and phase of the sinusoidal response function $G(j\omega)$ as ω varies from 0 to ∞.

If we choose four-cycle semilog paper, the lower ω value should be 0.1 and the upper value 1000 to include all breakpoints. We first compute $|G(j\omega)|$ at some low value of ω. Usually a simple value to select is $\omega < 0.1\omega_{n1}$, where ω_{n1} is the lowest breakpoint, or $\tau_{n1} = 1/\omega_{n1}$ is the largest time constant. This choice enables you to disregard all imaginary terms in any factor $j\omega + \omega_n$, $\omega_n \geq \omega_{n1}$ (slide rule accuracy), and the actual curve will have essentially the same value as the straight-line asymptote. Here 0.1 (0.333) will put you off the scale, so we choose $\omega = 0.1$ and disregard all imaginary terms except the single $j\omega$ in the denominator. This gives a point on the straight-line asymptote with the actual curve being about 1 db lower, owing to the nearby break points at 0.333 and 0.667. Then

$$|G(j0.1)| \simeq \frac{1108(2)(6.67)}{0.1(0.333)(0.667)(33.3)(200)}$$

$$\simeq 100$$

The straight line goes through a value of 2 loru or 40 db at $\omega = 0.1$ and has a slope of -1 loru per decade at this point, owing to the single $j\omega$ term in the denominator. The straight line is continued to the first break point at $\omega = 0.333$, where the slope breaks to -2, and thence to the next at $\omega = 0.667$, where the slope breaks to -3. This is continued until $\omega = 1000$. The straight lines may be easily plotted by sliding a triangle adjusted to the proper slope on a striaght edge. You need a check point at large ω to make sure you made no errors. Here let $\omega = \omega_{nz} = 500$. Now you can disregard all real terms in any factor $j\omega + \omega_n$, $\omega_n < \omega_{nz}$, and

$$|G(j500)| \simeq \frac{1108(500)^2}{(500)^5}$$

$$\simeq 8.86 \times 10^6 \quad \text{or} \quad -6 + 0.948 \text{ loru}$$

$$\simeq -5.052 \text{ loru}, \quad \text{or} \quad -101.04 \text{ db}$$

It is preferable to compute the low and high points first to see if the vertical scale is satisfactory. The plot and the check points are shown in Figure 8.6–6. The actual curve will have a maximum error of less than 1 db if it is now drawn in by inspection using the straight-line approximations.

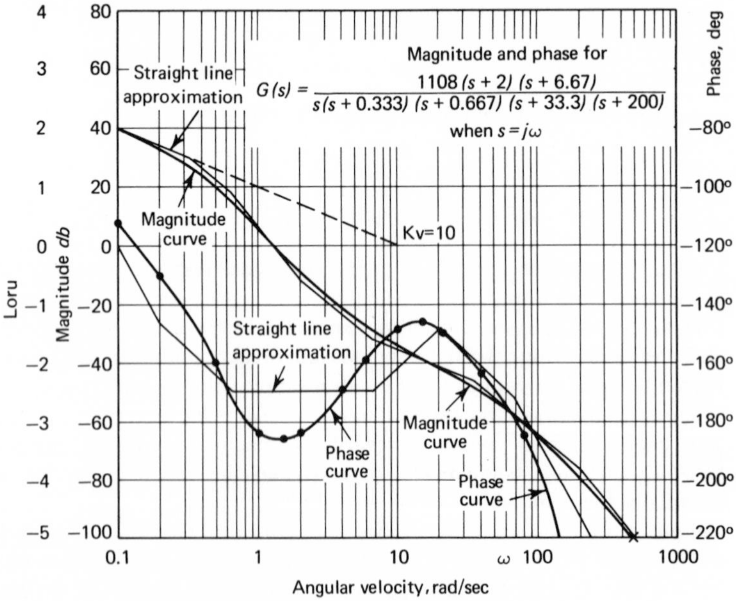

Figure 8.6–6. Figure for Example 8.6–1.

Now we need the phase-angle curve. To use the straight-line approximations, it is desirable to tabulate the break points in advance. Thus we have Table 8.6–1.

TABLE 8.6–1

Denominator			Numerator		
ω_n	$0.1\omega_n$	$10\omega_n$	ω_n	$0.1\omega_n$	$10\omega_n$
0.333	0.0333	3.33	2	0.2	20
0.667	0.0667	6.67	6.67	0.667	66.7
33.3	3.33	333			
200	20	2000			

Sketching the straight-line segments of Figure 8.6–4 we find the slopes given in Table 8.6–2.

TABLE 8.6–2

ω range		Slope
0	0.0333	0
0.0333	0.0667	−1
0.0667	0.2	−2
0.2	0.667	−1
0.667	3.33	0
3.33	6.67	0
6.67	20	1
20	66.7	−1
66.7	333	−2
3.33	2000	−1
2000	∞	0

(A slope of −1 means −45° per decade; −2, −90° per decade; and so on.) The straight lines are drawn in Figure 8.6–6. If you compute the phase angle by the formula

$$\arg G = -90^\circ - \tan^{-1}\left(\frac{\omega}{0.333}\right) - \tan^{-1}\left(\frac{\omega}{0.667}\right) - \tan^{-1}\left(\frac{\omega}{33.3}\right)$$
$$- \tan^{-1}\left(\frac{\omega}{200}\right) + \tan^{-1}\left(\frac{\omega}{2}\right) + \tan^{-1}\left(\frac{\omega}{6.67}\right)$$

the curve shown in Figure 8.6–6 results. It is obvious that the straight-line approximations are not of great use here. If the phase curve is monotonic, the straight-line approximations will be much more useful, but even here a few points need to be computed from the arctangent relation. (A similar comment is in order for the magnitude curve if it is not monotonic.)

A caution should be made to the neophyte at this point. The beginning designer tends to be less precise with the phase curve than the magnitude curve because the latter is easier to draw. Very roughly speaking, 1 or 2 degrees phase angle is as important as 1 or 2 db gain. Thus some care must be taken with the phase curve, which needs to be plotted only in the region of interest, as in Figure 8.6–6.

Occasionally you may encounter a nonminimum phase loop function, that is, one in which the zeros are in the right-half plane. Then $GH(j\omega)$ will have a term or terms of the form $(j\omega - z_i)$, $z_i > 0$, in the numerator. The magnitude curve is clearly no different than with terms of the form $(j\omega + z_i)$, $z_i > 0$, but the phase angle is drastically altered. Whereas with the left-half plane zero the associated phase angle is leading, with the right-half plane angle the associated angle is lagging. The lagging angle contributed by a $(j\omega - z_i)$ term thus makes the total angle more lagging than with the $(j\omega + z_i)$ term by twice the angle (without sign) of either. Bode thus termed the left-hand-plane zero case "minimum phase," because comparing the two situations, this results in the least phase lag.

Perhaps we have spent more time discussing a "how-to-to-it" problem than justified. However, as with the root locus, the ability to rapidly sketch the sinusoidal magnitude and phase response is important in frequency analysis and design. The Bode curves can, of course, be obtained by using a digital computer. A program to determine the overall gain and phase relations may be easily written, and with a remote station it will be possible to obtain displays of Bode curves on an oscilloscope screen by merely inputing the factors. Such capabilities imply that the important design consideration is the ability to interpret the plots, and we now turn to this aspect.

8.7 Bode Diagrams—Interpretation

The Bode plots show the open loop sinusoidal response in magnitude and phase as a function of angular velocity. If the open loop function $GH(s)$ has no poles in the right-half plane, these curves give fairly simple answers to many questions. You can see that the Bode diagrams reveal no more information than the Nyquist or polar plot; it is merely the same information in different form. Accent has been placed on the independent variable ω, but we have two charts rather than one. The magnitude curve is much easier to make, although the phase calculation is about equally difficult.

Comparing the Nyquist and Bode plots, for one thing, the effect of pure gain increase [change of K in (8.6–18)] is much more easily observed in the Bode plot. In the Bode log-amplitude plot, an increase in K results in a vertical rise in the amplitude curve by the amount log K loru or 20 log K db. Thus the frequency-independent gain for which you plot the curve is relatively unimportant; changes may be easily made by addition or subtraction. The corresponding effect in the polar plot is a radial increase or decrease, which is less easily grasped. Perhaps of equal or greater value is the fact that by using the logarithmic scale, the high-frequency region, which is the region of interest for instability, shares an emphasis equal to the low-frequency region, whereas in the polar plot the high-frequency ragion with the linear scale is derated in importance by the nature of the graph. Finally, it is fairly easy to tell from the Bode chart how the gain and phase curves will be altered by simple changes in the transfer function and hence to design simple compensation elements. The principle is straightforward; we have gain and phase curves and at least theoretically we know how we would like these to look. Hence the compensation is more easily provided by perusal of the Bode plots than from the polar plot. We shall discuss this in more detail in Chapter 9.

The gain margin and phase margin are easily found from the Bode plots. If Figure 8.7–1 represent typical magnitude and phase curves, you find the gain margin (if it exists) as shown in Figure 8.7–1a at the angular

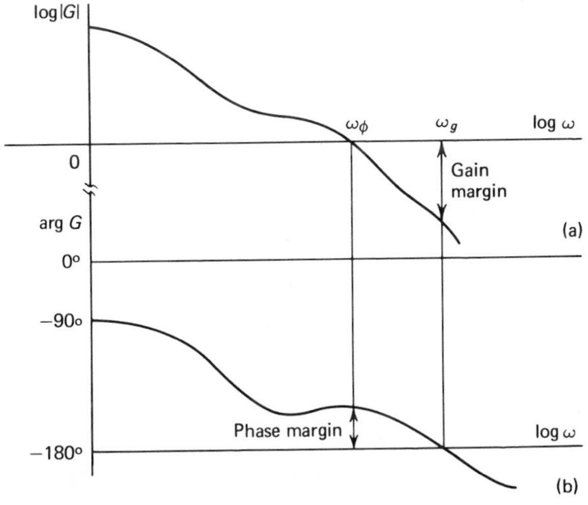

Figure 8.7–1. Gain and phase margins on Bode plots.

velocity where the phase is $-180°$, and alternatively you find the phase margin in Figure 8.7–1b at the angular velocity where the gain is 1 (0 db). Of the two, perhaps the phase margin is of more importance in judging relative stability.

The alternative task, that of finding the transfer function from experimental sinusoidal response data, is aided by the logarithmic plots. That is, if Figure 8.7–1 represents data in an experiment taken using a sinusodial driving function, you first fit the magnitude curve as well as possible with straight-line asymptotes at slopes of integral multiples (and no other) of 1 loru, or 20 db per decade. The intersections of these asymptotes determine the break points and hence the reciprocal time constants of the system. Using these, a phase curve may be calculated and compared with that obtained from the experiment. The closeness of agreement between the two curves is a measure of the astuteness in choosing the straight-line asymptotes. The method is clear but in practice may not be so straightforward. Thus it may be difficult to tell if a quadratic factor is involved and, if so, what damping factor to use. The experimental data also tends to become degraded at high frequencies, and any nonlinearities play havoc with the interpretation. Nevertheless steady-state sinusoidal frequency system identification is often simpler and more reliable than such identification using the time domain, as with a step function or by use of white noise.

Prediction of stability with the Bode plots may not be so easy as with the Nyquist diagram. For example, in Figure 8.6–6 most students would indicate that the system would be unstable (closing G through a negative unity feedback), because the phase is about $-185°$ at unity gain. So it is; but let us roughly sketch a Nyquist plot using the curves in Figure 8.6–6. Doing this you obtain Figure 8.7–2, which is not to scale. It is easy to

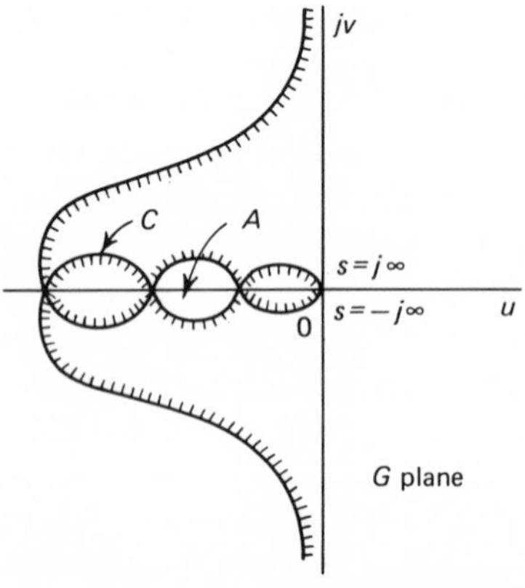

Figure 8.7–2. Nyquist plot for Figure 8.6–6.

see that the critical plot is encircled twice and hence the system is unstable. However, increasing the gain K in Figure 8.7–2 has the same effect as moving the critical point in toward the origin if you hold the figure stationary. With sufficient gain increase, the critical point moves within the region A, and the system becomes conditionally stable. Going back to the Bode plots, in Figure 8.6–6 you easily see that if the magnitude curve is pushed up by 0.6 loru (12 db), the -1 point in Figure 8.7–2 is just entering the stable region A. If the gain is increased by 2.85 loru (57 db), the -1 point in Figure 8.7–2 is just leaving the stable region A. The frequency-independent gain K for which the magnitude curve was plotted is 1108, so K may vary between the values of 4(1108) or 4432 and 707(1108), or 783,000 for conditional stability. The system will have the greatest phase margin (about 34°) in this region if the gain is increased by about 1.95 loru, or about 89 times. The system is unconditionally stable if the gain is decreased by about 0.55 loru, or dividing by about 3.5. Conditional stability is preferable from an operating standpoint, as with a gain of about 100,000, the system will have much greater static accuracy than with a gain of around 300. The gain range for conditional stability seems sufficiently great to provide a good margin against instability due to aging elements or other factors, although the transient performance will change if the gain moves very far in either direction from a nominal value of, say, 100,000. Interpretation of the Bode diagrams become somewhat more difficult in the conditionally stable case, but a Nyquist sketch clarifies the matter.

All the previous discussion assumes that the open loop function $G(s)$ or $GH(s)$ has no poles in the right-half plane. Any such poles require a somewhat more detailed look at the corresponding Nyquist plot.

Bode worked out many interesting integral relations between magnitude and phase and between the real part and the imaginary part of functions of complex quantities, which, although of great theoretical value, are not of much help to us here [12].

As one final comment on the general utility of the Bode plots, if you look at the system plots of magnitude and phase, as for example shown in Figure 8.7–1, and recall the relation between magnitude and phase for straight-line magnitude approximations, it is clear that when the magnitude is 1, or when the magnitude curve crosses the critical zero log magnitude axis, the curve slope should not be less than -1 loru per decade or -20 db per decade, or at most the critical point should not be too far from such a slope. If the slope at the critical point $\omega_c = \omega_\phi$ of Figure 8.7–1 is less than -20 db per decade, the phase angle rapidly approaches the unstable value of $-180°$. When you remember that for relative stability some phase margin is necessary, a crossing slope of -20 db per decade becomes even more momentus. This gives one good design factor. The novice when asked how to prevent instability in a feedback system almost invariably answers "lower the gain." Intuitively if we lower the gain, however, we lower the static accuracy and the sensitivity. This is quantitatively borne out by the discussion of error and sensitivity in Chapter 1. You now see that obviously a better procedure is to maintain a high gain at low frequencies but to alter the magnitude-phase relations in the high-frequency region so as to maintain an adequate phase margin. The same ideas apply to a feedback amplifier [13], except that the a-c amplifier is designed to cover some frequency band; hence a similar investigation must be made at the low-frequency end to prevent the instability leading to "motor-boating." The control system is essentially a low-pass filter, which means that either a d-c amplifier must be used or that the error signal must be modulated.

8.8 System Frequency Characteristics—The Nichols Chart

Given the open loop sinusoidal response, the next and more important question becomes "what is the overall system response?" Theoretically, if we know the system characteristics for sinusoidal driving functions at all possible frequencies, we know the response to any driving function, since using the Fourier integral such a function merely consists of a combination of sinusoidal components. The practical application of this theoretical knowledge is not so straightforward. The difficulty arises because it is necessary to take an inverse Fourier transform or to perform a convolution in the time domain. Specifically, in the first case if we let $r(t)$ be the input, $c(t)$ be the output, and $(C/R)(j\omega) = M\epsilon^{j\phi}$ be the sinusoidal transfer function of the system, we may find $c(t)$ by the following steps: (1) obtain the Fourier transform $\mathscr{F}r(t)$, (2) multiply by $(C/R)(j\omega)$, and (3) take the inverse transform $\mathscr{F}^{-1}$ of the product to obtain $c(t)$. In the second case, we may (1) find the inverse transform $I(t) = \mathscr{F}^{-1}(C/R)(j\omega)$, and (2) convole $I(t)$ with $r(t)$ to obtain $c(t)$ [14]. In either case, much work is involved. Also, using graphical methods, we know $M\epsilon^{j\phi}$ graphically and not analytically. Graphical techniques for performing the required operations are available but time consuming. Also numerical methods for approximate solutions and for the inversion of transforms have been developed [15, 16, 17] so that the problem may be solved with the aid of a digital computer. However, qualitative information is easily found and is usually helpful, at least in the first stages of design, and later a more complete analysis could be used as refinements are made. [Note: Even if fast methods for finding $c(t)$ for any $r(t)$ are available, there may be considerable speculation as to which $r(t)$'s will provide information about the actual enviroment. See the discussion in Chapter 3 concerning the philosophy of specifications.]

Because we are required to produce a design in finite time, as engineers we bear in mind the incompleteness of our knowledge but cannot wait until all the answers are available. Let us see how we may obtain the system response $M\epsilon^{j\phi}$ and what observations we may make regarding this.

The overall system response to sinusoidal driving functions, $(C/R)(j\omega) = M(\omega)\epsilon^{j\theta(\omega)}$, may be found in a form convenient for use with the polar diagram. It turns out that curves of constant M and constant θ may be drawn on the polar plot used for the open loop function GH, and that the constant M curves are circles, usually termed "M circles," while the phase curves are also circles [18]. Because we have spent so much time extolling the advantages of the Bode logarithmic plots, we shall be more interested in obtaining a form that may be used more easily with these plots. Such a form is the Nichols chart [19], which contains curves of constant M and ϕ plotted in a plane with the open loop magnitude and open loop phase used as rectangular coordinates. Then knowing the open loop function,

$$G(j\omega) = x + jy \tag{8.8–1}$$

$$G(j\omega) = |G|\epsilon^{j\theta} \tag{8.8–2}$$

we may find the closed loop function

$$\frac{C}{R}(j\omega) = \frac{G(j\omega)}{1 + G(j\omega)} \tag{8.8–3}$$

$$\frac{C}{R}(j\omega) = M\epsilon^{j\phi} \tag{8.8–4}$$

This development follows. Let

$$W = u + jv = \ln(x + jy) = \ln|G| + j\theta.$$

Then

$$\epsilon^{u} \cos v = x \tag{8.8–5}$$

$$\epsilon^{u} \sin v = y \tag{8.7–6}$$

From (8.8–3) and (8.8–4),

$$M\epsilon^{j\phi} = \frac{G}{1 + G}$$

and, from (8.8–1),

$$M\epsilon^{j\phi} = \frac{x + jy}{1 + x + jy} \tag{8.8–7}$$

Thus

$$M = \sqrt{(x^2 + y^2)/(y^2 + (x + 1)^2)} \tag{8.8–8}$$

Now using (8.8–5) and (8.8–6), you obtain

$$\epsilon^{2u}\frac{M^2-1}{M^2}+2\epsilon^u\cos v+1=0 \tag{8.8–9}$$

or, finally,

$$u=\ln\left[\frac{\cos v\pm\sqrt{\cos^2 v+(1-M^2)/M^2}}{(1-M^2)/M^2}\right] \qquad M^2\neq 1 \tag{8.8–10}$$

$$u=\ln\left(-\frac{1}{2\cos v}\right) \qquad M^2=1 \tag{8.8–11}$$

Returning to (8.8–7),

$$\phi=\arctan\frac{y}{x}-\arctan\frac{y}{x+1} \tag{8.8–12}$$

and, again applying (8.8–5) and (8.8–6), you obtain

$$\phi=v-\arctan\frac{\epsilon^u\sin v}{\epsilon^u\cos v+1} \tag{8.8–13}$$

Solving for ϵ^u,

$$\epsilon^u=\frac{\sin(v-\phi)}{\sin\phi}$$

or

$$u=\ln\frac{\sin(v-\phi)}{\sin\phi} \tag{8.8–14}$$

Using the definitions of u and v, finally,

$$|G|=\frac{\cos\theta\pm\sqrt{\cos^2\theta+M^{-2}-1}}{M^{-2}-1} \tag{8.8–15}$$

$$|G|=\frac{\sin(\theta-\phi)}{\sin\phi} \tag{8.8–16}$$

are the equations of curves of constant M and ϕ in terms of $|G|$ and θ. Usually the $|G|$ scale is in loru or db, and the θ scale is in degrees. A portion of the Nichols chart is shown in Figure 8.8–1, where the $|G|$ and θ axis are interchanged and $|G|$ and M are in db [20]. If you enter the chart with the values of $|G|$ and θ in on the straight-line coordinates, the values of magnitude and phase of the function $G/(1+G)$ are found from the curves shown. The chart thus obtains the system sinusoidal response without a factorization of the denominator $(1 + G)$. If the feedback quantity is $H(j\omega) \neq 1$,

$$\frac{C}{R}(j\omega) = \frac{G(j\omega)}{1 + GH(j\omega)} \tag{8.8–17}$$

$$\frac{C}{R}(j\omega) = \frac{1}{H(j\omega)}\left[\frac{GH(j\omega)}{1 + GH(j\omega)}\right] \tag{8.8–18}$$

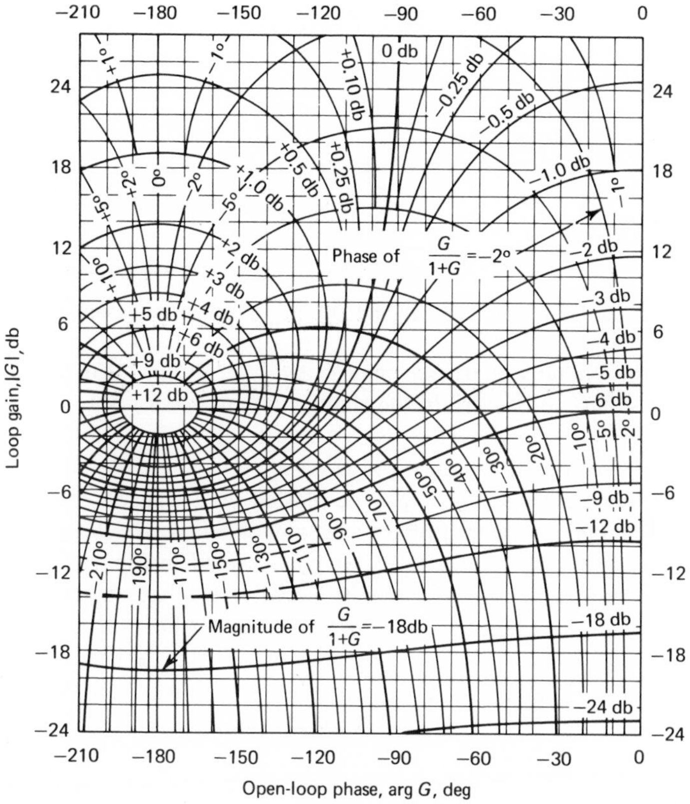

Figure 8.8–1. Nichols chart for finding gain and phase of G. (Courtesy Weston Instruments, Inc.)

Then using $GH(j\omega)$ the Nichols chart makes the transformation inside the brackets on the right side of (8.8–18), after which a further multiplication by $(1/H)(j\omega)$ is necessary to find $(C/R)(j\omega)$. The final multiplication may be done graphically by plotting the two factors on a Bode diagram. Equation (8.8–18) represents the same alteration as previously discussed to the flow diagram for changing any feedback system to one with unity feedback, as shown in Figure 8.8–2.

The Nichols chart is symmetrical about the 0° θ axis, so that, for positive θ, Figure 8.8–1 may be used by changing the signs of θ and ϕ. Occasionally this may be necessary, because in internal feedback loops the angle of GH may become positive. The equations developed previously are easily altered to describe a positive feedback system, so that the chart may be adapted to this purpose.

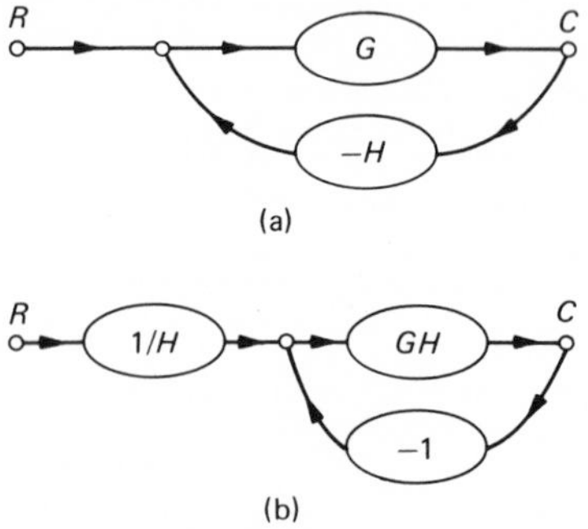

Figure 8.8–2. Flow diagrams (a) and (b) are equivalent representations of C/R.

With the Nichols chart, we may draw M contours on the open loop Bode gain plot, and ascertain the change in gain necessary to obtain some peak value of $M = M_p$. However, it is usually easier to draw the open loop characteristic curve on a prepared Nichols chart. Alternatively, the open loop characteristic GH may be plotted on a transparent paper with rectangular magnitude and phase axes and this laid over a Nichols chart made with the same scales. The idea is illustrated in Figure 8.8–3, where the open loop function G in a unity negative feedback system has been plotted on the rectangular coordinates of the Nichols chart. The points are obtained from the Bode diagrams or in some other manner, and various values of angular velocity are shown with $\omega_9 > \omega_1$. A few of the

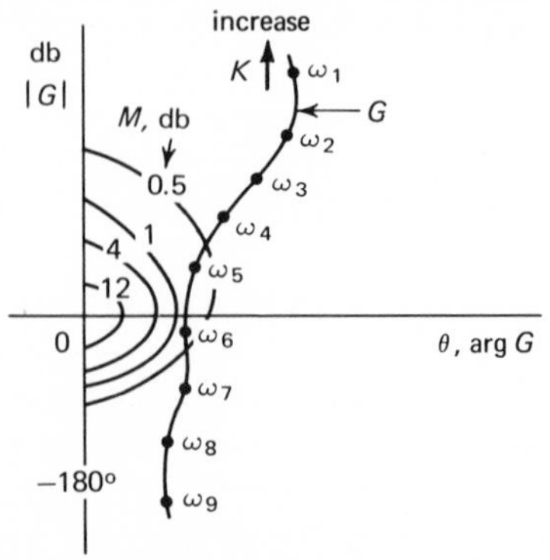

Figure 8.8–3. Change in K can be observed on the Nichols chart by moving the G curve vertically. (Courtesy Weston Instruments, Inc.)

M contours are sketched in, while the ϕ contours are omitted to permit clarity. It is clear that an increase in the frequency-independent gain factor *K* is easily made by moving the *G* or *GH* curve straight up in the direction of the arrow. Hence if the curve (or the Nichols chart) is on transparent paper, you may easily analyze the effect of a change in *K* by moving one graph sheet relative to the other. Usually an increase in gain will result in a more lightly damped system or one of less relative stability, but this is not necessarily true for conditionally stable systems.

Figure 8.8–4 shows the system of Figure 8.6–6 except that the gain has been increased by 1.95 loru or 39 db, which gives the greatest phase margin. From this figure if the gain is decreased, the maximum value of M (M_p) increases, and the system becomes more unstable. To see this, resketch the *M* curve on a Bode plot as a function of log ω as shown in Figure 8.8–5.

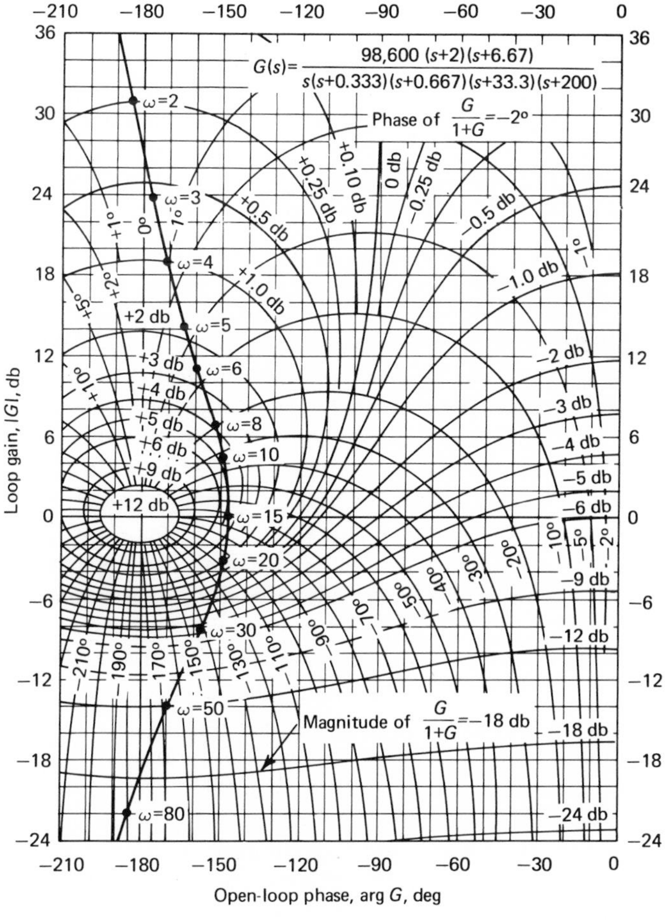

Figure 8.8–4. Nichols chart for Example 8.6–1 with $K = 98{,}6000$.

Assuming that the system operates essentially as a second-order system, because there is a relation between M_p and ζ for the sinusoidal response as shown in Figure 3.5–3 and between the overshoot and for a step function response, there is also a relation between M_p and the per cent overshoot on a step input. This is also given explicitly by (3.5–3) and (3.5–7) and shown in Figure 8.8–6. Thus if the system of Figure 8.8–4 approximates a second-order system, $M_p \simeq 5$ db, the per cent overshoot will be about 38 per cent, $\zeta \simeq 0.3$, and $\omega_p \simeq 12$ radians per second. From (3.5–10) the oscillation angular velocity ω_d is about

$$12 \frac{\sqrt{1 - 0.3^2}}{\sqrt{1 - 2(0.3)^2}}$$

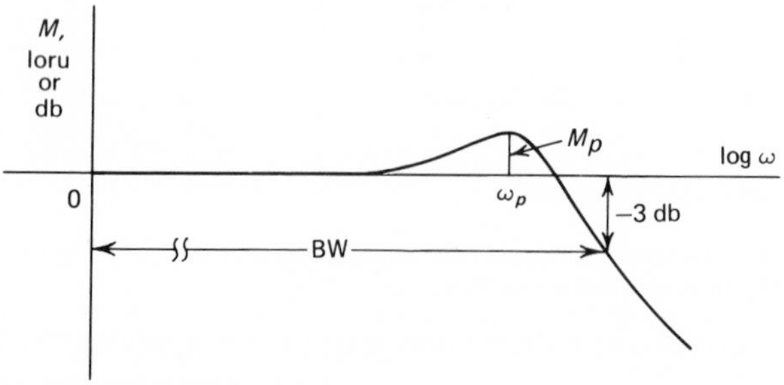

Figure 8.8–5. Definition of bandwidth, BW.

or 12.6 radians per second. The system has two zeros in the numerator, so it will not act like a second-order system but will have a faster rise time and a higher overshoot. However, the comparison with the second-order system gives at least a rough idea of the performance. Following this through, if we are to have an overshoot of less than 25 per cent, then $M_p = 2.6$ db or $\simeq 1.4$ magnitude. Hence one rule of thumb has indicated an M_p of about 1.4 as a maximum value for design. Examining Figure 8.8–4, it is also clear that if we follow the same specifications, the phase margin must be around 40°, as we also found in Figure 8.5–4, associated with Example 8.5–1. To all this we make two reservations: (1) The system is probably not of second order, and may perform differently, and (2) the desired overshoot depends on the application (specifications).

With care it would be possible to obtain straight-line asymptotic approximations to the M curve (Figure 8.8–5) and to refine these by utilizing the closed loop angle ϕ taken from the Nichols chart, using the techniques previously described. Unfortunately, the closed loop character makes this difficult, because the magnitude curve in the low-frequency region is never far from 1 or 0 db, and low-frequency break points are masked out.

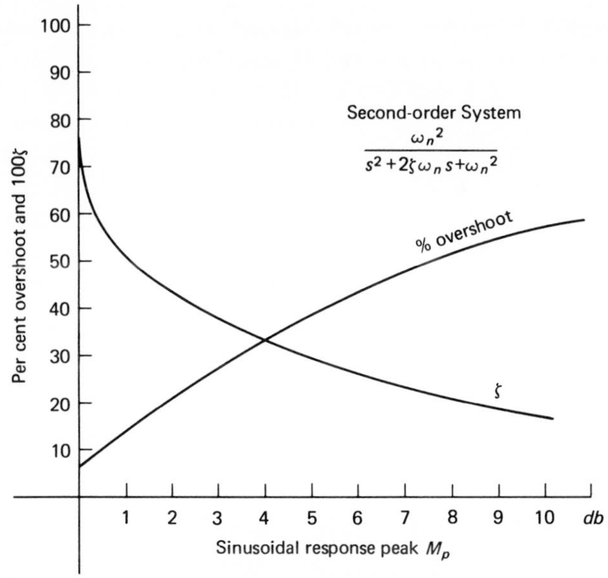

Figure 8.8–6. Damping constant and maximum overshoot as function of the peak magnitude M_p, second-order system.

Another performance criteria mentioned in Chapter 3 is the bandwidth, or the angular velocity value ω_b (or $\omega_b/2\pi$), where the magnitude M is -3 db. This is easily found from the Nichols chart. In the example of Figure 8.8–4, $\omega_b \approx 20$ radians per second. It is desirable to have a low bandwidth to reduce noise, but, as we saw in Chapter 3, ω_n in a second-order system must be large to reduce rise time. We can lower the bandwidth with a given ω_n to some extent by having a large slope beyond ω_p, or a fast cutoff rate, and this in turn can be brought about by adding distant system poles. A pole at $-p$ or beyond, where $p > 5\ \omega_n$, will not affect the transient response very much, and such poles will have almost the same values in the control ratio transfer function as in the open loop function.

8.9 Frequency Response with Internal Feedback Loops

If the system has an internal feedback loop, as in Figure 8.9–1, the inside loop must first be reduced. Thus in that fi˛ure,

$$\frac{C}{A}(s) = \frac{G(s)}{1 + GH(s)} \tag{8.9–1}$$

$$\frac{C}{A}(s) = \frac{1}{H(s)}\left[\frac{GH(s)}{1 + GH(s)}\right] \tag{8.9–2}$$

The factor within the brackets on the right of (8.9–2) can be obtained by the transformation of $GH(s)$ by the Nichols chart. This must then be multiplied by $1/H(s)$ to obtain $(C/A)(s)$. As discussed in Section 8.8, this may be done by replotting $GH/(1 + GH)$ in gain and phase on Bode diagrams, together with similar plots for $1/H$, and adding the logarithmic magnitudes and the phase angles. This is a rather lengthy, but fairly accurate, procedure. The final result must then be incorporated with G_1.

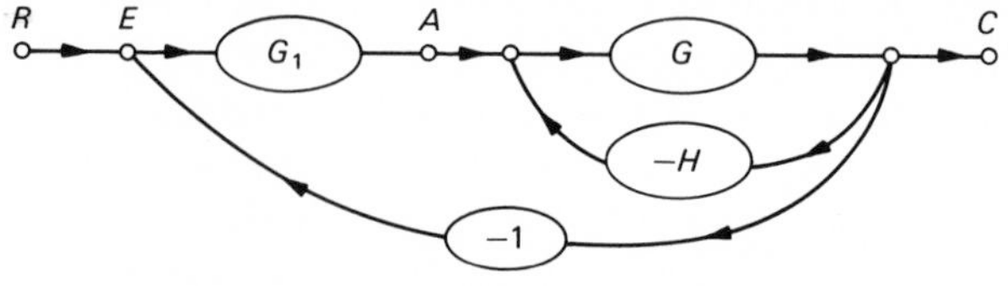

Figure 8.9–1. System with internal feedback.

This is particularly easy if $G_1 = K_1$, or pure gain, or, if G_1 is frequency-sensitive, it may be included on the same diagrams to give

$$\frac{C}{R}(s) = \frac{G_1(s)}{H(s)}\left[\frac{GH(s)}{1 + GH(s)}\right]$$

Examining (8.9–1), if $GH \gg 1$, then $(C/A)(s) \simeq 1/H(s)$. If $GH \ll 1$, then $(C/A)(s) \simeq G(s)$. Thus a crude approximation to $|(C/A)(s)|$ in (8.9–1) consists of plotting $|1/H(s)|$ and $|G(s)|$ as in Figure 8.9–2. At ω_1 and ω_2,

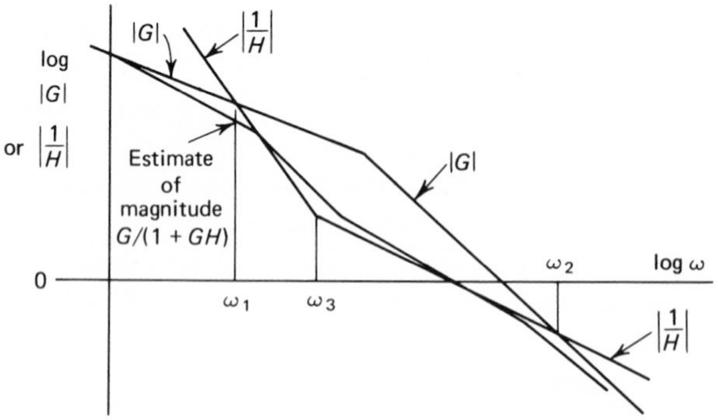

Figure 8.9–2. Straight-line approximations to $|G|$ and $|1/H|$ to obtain estimate for $G/(1 + GH)$ magnitude.

$|G| \cdot |H| = 1$, and to find $|C/A|$ we follow $|G|$ from low angular velocities to ω_1 ($G \ll 1/H$), then $|1/H|$ from ω_1 to $\omega_2(G \gg 1/H)$, and finally $|G|$ from ω_1 to high frequencies. At ω_1 and ω_2 the straight-line approximations are in error, but if the slope change at these points is only -1, all is well; we can plot in the amplitude nicely. However, if the slope chages at either point by -2 or more, then we know a quadratic factor is involved, and the damping factor ζ is unknown. Again as a rough guess, you may assume ζ to be some value, say 0.4, and draw the magnitude curve. The phase curve may be computed from the break points, as ω_1, ω_2, and ω_3 in Figure 8.9–2. Here the phase angle may be very much in error if a poor guess on ζ is made for either ω_1 or ω_2. Although the approximation is poor, it at least gives some idea as to what to make H. For example, if $G_1 = K_1$ and $|G|$ is assumed to be fixed, then the $1/H$ magnitude curve may be adjusted both in pure gain and in shape by some of our previous guides. That is, when the magnitude curve is altered by K_1 (which may be at our disposal), we would like for it to be crossing the 0-db line at a slope of -1, or have such a slope very close by the crossing point. At the same time a high gain is desired at low frequencies ($|G|$ curve). The diagram may then indicate values of break points (there may be more than one) in the $|1/H|$ characteristic, and the height (gain) of $|1/H|$ to achieve these objectives. Hence we can get some idea as to whether a feedback H can achieve the objective and some clue as to the general nature of H. Further refinement can then be made by more extensive graphical analysis or computation.

8.10 Conclusions

Frequency analysis, or analysis based on steady-state sinusoidal response, is still of importance in feedback control work. It may be of great help in the initial phases of design. As s is confined to the $j\omega$ axis, you would expect sinusoidal analysis to be less informative than the root locus, where s may vary throughout the complex plane. On the other hand, root locus alteration is probably less apparent. The approximation of the system to a second-order system will be informative, and, as the zeros of the system function are known, the system response may be predicted fairly well, but as the order of the system increases, such approximations will be of less value. The use of the Nyquist diagram and the Bode plots are basic in estimating relative stability, and it is difficult to dispense with sinusoidal analysis in experimental work because of the simplicity and accuracy of the test methods.

PROBLEMS

8.1. Sketch Nyquist diagrams for the following open loop functions (negative feedback), and determine stability.

(a) $GH = \dfrac{250}{s(s+5)}$.

(b) $GH = \dfrac{250}{s^2(s+5)}$.

(c) $GH = \dfrac{250}{s(s+5)(s+15)}$.

(d) $GH = \dfrac{250(s+1)}{s^2(s+5)(s+15)}$.

8.2. Make Bode phase and gain plots for the functions of Problem 8.1.

8.3. In the following open loop functions $(GH)(s)$, s takes on values along the $\sigma = 0$ axis from $-j\infty$ to $j\infty$. The corresponding number of revolutions made by $(GH)(s)$ around the point $-1 + j0$ are indicated. Indicate
(a) If the open loop function is stable or unstable.
(b) If the control ratio $G/(1 + GH)$ is stable or unstable.
If the problem is not consistent, indicate why.

$$\text{(a)} \quad GH = \frac{T(s)}{s(s^2 + 6s + 15)(s - 5)(s - 8)}, \quad N = -2.$$

$$\text{(b)} \quad GH = \frac{K(s - 1)R(s)}{s(s^2 - 6s + 15)(s + 5)(s + 8)}, \quad N = 1.$$

$$\text{(c)} \quad GH = \frac{Q(s)}{s(s - 1)(s + 3)(s + 6)}, \quad N = -2.$$

$$\text{(d)} \quad GH = \frac{P(s)}{(s^2 + 6s + 15)(s + 5)(s + 8)}, \quad N = 0.$$

$$\text{(e)} \quad GH = \frac{P(s)}{s^2(s + 5)(s + 8)(s + 60)}, \quad N = 2.$$

8.4. Figure P8.4 shows the excursions of GH in the GH plane as s proceeds along the Nyquist contour in the s plane. p_r represents the number of roots with positive real parts in the denominator of GH. Indicate in each case if the control ratio $G/(1 + GH)$ is stable or not, and why. (The figures are drawn from $s = -j\infty$ to $s = j0$ only, and do not necessarily represent actual systems.)

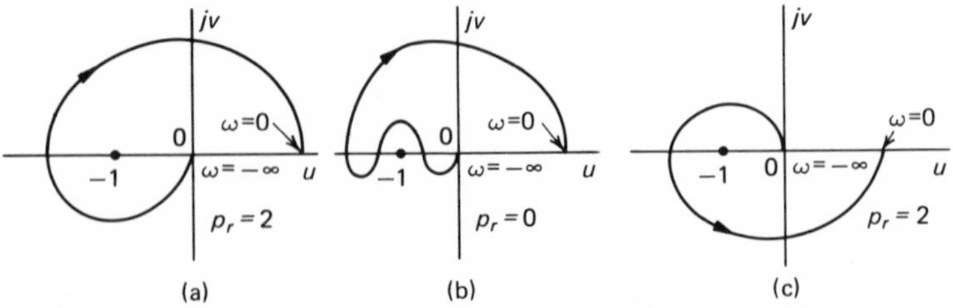

Figure P8.4.

8.5. Figure P8.5 shows a Nyquist plot of an open loop gain GH for negative feedback with a gain constant $K = 500$. Between what values of K will the system be conditionally stable? Below what K value will the system be unconditionally stable?

8.6. (a) Make Bode plots for

$$G = \frac{2083(s + 3)}{s(s^2 + 20s + 625)}$$

(b) Find the value of ω where the magnitude curve crosses 0 db (0 loru).
(c) Find the phase angle (arg G) at this same value of ω and the phase margin.

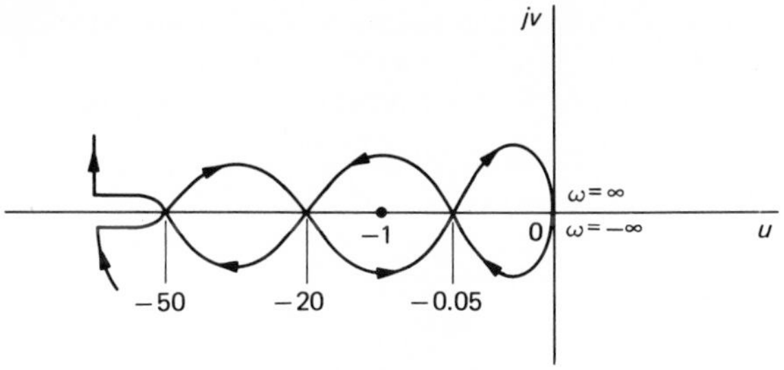

Figure P8.5.

8.7. (a) Make Bode plots for

$$G = \frac{3500}{s(s^2 + 10s + 70)}$$

(b) How much should the frequency independent gain be raised or lowered to have a phase margin of 30°?

8.8. Repeat Problem 8.7 except for

$$G = \frac{500(s + 2)}{s(s + 5)(s + 50)}$$

and a phase margin of 40°.

8.9. Make Bode phase and gain plots for

(a) $G = \dfrac{500(s + 2)}{s(s + 10)}$.

(b) $G = \dfrac{2000(s - 6)}{s(s^2 + 4s + 20)}$.

(c) $G = \dfrac{2000(s + 6)}{s(s^2 + 4s + 20)}$.

8.10. A system with unity negative feedback has

$$G = \frac{4000}{s(s + 10)(s + 40)}$$

(a) Using Bode plots and the Nichols chart, find the peak value of M_p and the approximate angular velocity ω_p at which it occurs.
(b) Find the closed loop bandwidth.

(c) Assuming the control ratio C/R is essentially a second-order system, find, for a step function input, the rise time, the per cent overshoot, the oscillation angular velocity, and the 10 per cent settling time.

8.11. A control system has a forward path gain G and an internal feedback loop H as follows:

$$G = \frac{4800}{s[s^2 + 2(0.6)(14)s + 14^2]}$$

$$H = \frac{0.15s^2}{s + 0.65}$$

The feedback is negative. It has a direct negative feedback path around the above combination GH.

(a) Find the closed loop response for the internal loop $G/(1 + GH)$, using the straight-line approximations indicated by Figure 8.9–2.

(b) From (a), using the Nichols chart, plot the overall control ratio C/R with the unity negative overall loop. Find M_p.

(c) Using the Nichols chart, or by direct calculation, find $G/(1 + GH)$ more accurately.

(d) From (c), find the control ratio C/R.

(e) Compare (b) and (d).

8.12. Given

$$G = \frac{150{,}000(s + 2.5)(s + 5)}{s(s + 0.4)(s + 0.7)(s + 50)(s + 150)}$$

(a) Using a Bode plot, find how many times the 150,000 gain figure can be increased, and also decreased, for the system to remain stable.

(b) Find the change in the 150,000 gain value to provide maximum phase margin.

(c) With the gain in (b), and using the Nichols chart, find the control ratio $C/R = G/(1 + G)$, and replot this on logarithmic paper.

(d) Using the Nichols chart, alter the frequency-independent gain and plot M_p and ω_p versus this gain figure.

8.13. Write a digital computer program to find the magnitude and phase response of a transfer function with sinusoidal input. Provide for variable quadratic and first-order factors in the numerator and denominator, and use ω as a parameter.

8.14. Write a digital computer program to find the control ratio

$$\frac{C}{R}(j\omega) = \frac{G(j\omega)}{1 + G(j\omega)} \qquad \text{with} \qquad G(j\omega) = \frac{P(j\omega)}{Q(j\omega)}$$

and where P and Q are given in factored form. Use the angular velocity ω as parameter.

REFERENCES AND FURTHER READING

[1] H. W. Bode, *Network Analysis and Feedback Amplifier Design*, Van Nostrand, Princeton, N.J., 1945.

[2] R. V. Churchill, *Introduction to Complex Variables and Applications*, McGraw-Hill, New York, 1948, pp. 135–170.

[3] —. Bode, *op. cit.* pp. 151–170. The original paper is titled Regeneration Theory, *Bell System Tech. J.*, January 1932.

[4] D. Mitrovic, Graphical Analysis and Synthesis of Feedback Control Systems, I. Theory and Analysis, II. Synthesis, III. Sampled Data Control Systems, *AIEE Trans. Appl. Ind.*, **77** (1959), 476–502.

[5] D. D. Siljak, Analysis and Synthesis of Feedback Control Systems in the Parameter Plane, *IEEE Trans. Paper* 64-398, National Electronics Conference, Chicago, October 1964.

[6] G. J. Thaler and R. G. Brown, *Analysis and Design of Feedback Control Systems*, McGraw-Hill, New York, 2nd ed., 1960, Chap. 10.

[7] L. S. Dzung, The Stability Criteria, in *Automatic and Manual Control*, Butterworth, London, 1952; see also V. Del Toro and S. R. Parker, *Principles of Control Systems Engineering*, McGraw-Hill, New York, 1960, pp. 327–328.

[8] J. P. Hu, A Method for Analyzing the Second Order Feedback Control System, *Western Electric Eng.*, April 1966, pp. 18–23.

[9] —. Bode, *op. cit.*, pp. 337–359.

[10] J. L. Bower and P. M. Schultheiss, *Introduction to the Design of Servomechanisms*, Wiley, New York, 1958, pp. 57–98.

[11] Bower and Schultheiss, *op. cit.*, pp. 83–93.

[12] Bode, *op. cit.*, pp. 303–336.

[13] L. D. Harris, *Introduction to Feedback Systems*, Wiley, New York, 1961, Chap. 6.

[14] R. Bracewell, *The Fourier Transform and Its Application*, McGraw-Hill, New York, 1965, pp. 179–180.

[15] R. E. Bellman and R. E. Kalaba, *Modern Analytic and Computational Methods in Science and Mathematics*, Vol. 4, Elsevier, Amsterdam, 1966.

[16] M. S. Corrington, Simplified Calculation of Transient Response, *Proc. IRE*, **53** (1965), 287–292.

[17] M. L. Liou, A Novel Method of Evaluating Transient Response, *Proc. IEEE*, **54** (1966), 20–23.

[18] H. Chestnut and R. W. Mayer, *Servomechanisms and Regulating System Design*, Vol. 1, Wiley, New York, 1959, pp. 250–254.

[19] H. M. James, N. B. Nichols, and R. S. Phillips, *Theory of Servomechanisms*, Vol. 25, MIT Rad. Lab. Series, McGraw-Hill, New York, 1947, and Dover, New York, 1965, pp. 179–186.

[20] Prepared Nichols charts are available from Boonshaft and Fuchs, Inc., Hatboro, Pa., and Computing Aids, Cambridge, Mass., among others.

9 System Compensation —Conventional

9.1 Steady-State Requirements

So far most of our attention in conventional analysis has been directed toward stability and relative stability. However, unless the system meets requirements under static conditions, it is unsatisfactory and a stability investigation becomes insignificant. Certain measures of static error have developed and we now explore these. As might be expected from an intuitive approach, these factors are related to the frequency-independent gain factor K.

We associate the static measures with the polynomial functions discussed in Section 1.6. These are the impulse, step ramp, and parabolic functions given in Table 9.1–1 and shown in Figure 9.1–1. These functions are convenient not only because they represent inputs found in actual practice but also because of the simple form of their Laplace transforms.

TABLE 9.1–1

Input	Time Domain	Complex Frequency Domain
Impulse	$\delta(t)$	1
Step	$u(t)$	$1/s$
Ramp	$tu(t)$	$1/s^2$
Parabolic	$\frac{1}{2}t^2u(t)$	$1/s^3$

Although eventually we are interested in the system error y_e as defined in Figure 1.5–9, we are more specifically concerned with the feedback nature of the problem. That is, the error is a known and usually simple function of the actuating signal e of Figure 1.5–9, and the actuating signal

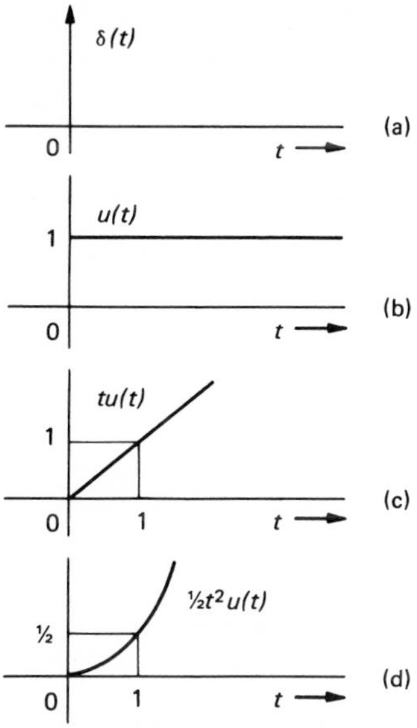

Figure 9.1–1. Input $m(t)$ functions associated with static error coefficient.

becomes the quantity of interest in analysis. Further, as has already been shown, any system with a feedback transfer function H can be reduced to an equivalent system with unity feedback. The feedback problem thus reduces to a system such as shown in Figure 9.1–2, where the forward path transfer function G includes all subsystem path factors. The actual error may easily be found from the actuating signal E shown in Figure 9.1–2 unless additional feedback loops are involved in the transfer functions between the error and this signal.

You easily see that the transfer function relation between E and R in Figure 9.1–2 is

$$\frac{E(s)}{R(s)} = \frac{1}{1 + G(s)} \tag{9.1–1}$$

or

$$E(s) = \frac{R(s)}{1 + G(s)} \tag{9.1–2}$$

If you substitute values of R in (9.1–2) you obtain the Laplace transform of the error, and if we are interested in the steady-state error, or error after a long time, we can apply the Laplace transform final value theorem. Thus

$$\lim_{t\to\infty} e(t) = \lim_{s\to 0} s\frac{R(s)}{1+G(s)} \tag{9.1–3}$$

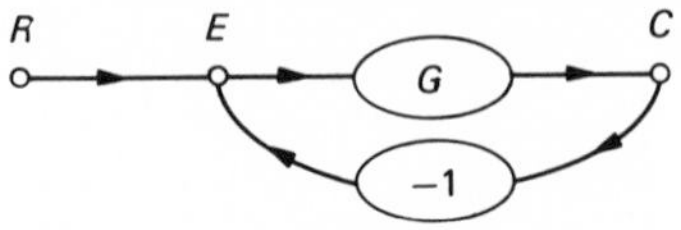

Figure 9.1–2. Elementary feedback system.

assuming that the final value theorem applies. Hence for a step function

$$\lim_{t\to\infty} e(t) = \frac{s}{s}\frac{1}{1+G(s)}\bigg|_{s=0}$$

$$= \frac{1}{1+G(s)}\bigg|_{s=0} \tag{9.1–4}$$

Now define

$$\lim_{s\to 0} G(s) = K_p \tag{9.1–5}$$

Then

$$\lim_{t\to\infty} e(t) = \frac{1}{1+K_p} \tag{9.1–6}$$

for a step function.

If $r(t)$ is a ramp function

$$\lim_{t\to\infty} e(t) = \frac{s}{s^2G(s)}\bigg|_{s=0}$$

$$= \frac{1}{sG(s)}\bigg|_{s=0} \tag{9.1–7}$$

Define

$$\lim_{s\to 0} sG(s) = K_v \tag{9.1–8}$$

Then

$$\lim_{t\to\infty} e(t) = \frac{1}{K_v} \tag{9.1–9}$$

for a ramp function.

Finally if $r(t)$ is a parabolic function, you obtain

$$\lim_{t\to\infty} e(t) = \frac{1}{s^2G(s)}\bigg|_{s=0}$$

and similarly define

$$\lim_{s\to 0} s^2G(s) = K_a \tag{9.1–10}$$

Then

$$\lim_{t\to\infty} e(t) = \frac{1}{K_a} \tag{9.1–11}$$

for a parabolic function. The quantities

$$K_p = \lim_{s\to 0} G(s)$$

$$K_v = \lim_{s\to 0} sG(s)$$

$$K_a = \lim_{s\to 0} s^2G(s)$$

are respectively called the position, velocity, and acceleration error coefficients, after the types of signals for which they apply. These values are easy to find for any system, because $G(s)$ is known. Error coefficients of higher order could be similarly defined, but these are usually sufficient.

We now classify systems as to the number of integrators in the forward path. A single integrator is represented in the complex frequency domain by $1/s$, or a pole at the origin. Hence we may write G as

$$G(s) = \frac{K\prod_{1}^{m}(s + z_i)}{s^r\prod_{r+1}^{n}(s + p_j)} \tag{9.1–12}$$

where there are r poles at the origin. Systems are then typed as shown in Table 9.1–2. Two integrators are usually the maximum number, because beyond this point the stability problem becomes very serious.

TABLE 9.1–2

r	Type
0	Zero, or 0
1	One, or 1
2	Two, or 2
⋮	

Applying the definitions for the static error coefficients, it is easy to obtain these in terms of the poles and zeros of $G(s)$. This tabulation is made in Table 9.1–3. The static error coefficients may be found from the

TABLE 9.1–3 STATIC ERROR COEFFICIENTS

System Type	K_p	K_v	K_α
0	$K\prod_1^m z_i \Big/ \prod_1^n p_j$	0	0
1	∞	$K\prod_1^m z_i \Big/ \prod_2^n p_j$	0
2	∞	∞	$K\prod_1^m z_i \Big/ \prod_3^n p_j$

Bode magnitude plot as well as from the defining equations for the type 0 system. K_p is the magnitude at zero frequency and is therefore measured from the 0-db axis to the flat slope portion of the $|G|$ curve at low frequency, as in Figure 9.1–3. For the type 1 system $K_v/\omega = 1$, where the continuation of the initial -20 db per decade slope crosses the 0-db axis. Hence $K_v = \omega_c$ in Figure 9.1–3b. Similarly, for the type 2 system, $\sqrt{K_\alpha} = \omega_c$, where ω_c is the crossing of the -2 slope, as in Figure 9.1–3c.

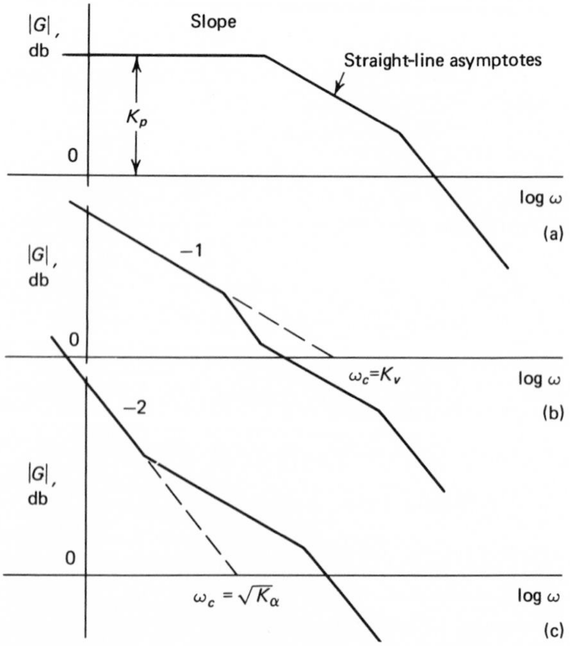

Figure 9.1–3. Static constants in terms of the magnitude plots.

It is worth discussing in more detail the meaning of the error coefficients, and we can do this using as an example a system, not necessarily practical, with an angle input and an angle output, and visualize the input and output as two dials R and C, respectively, as in Figure 9.1–4. In the type 0

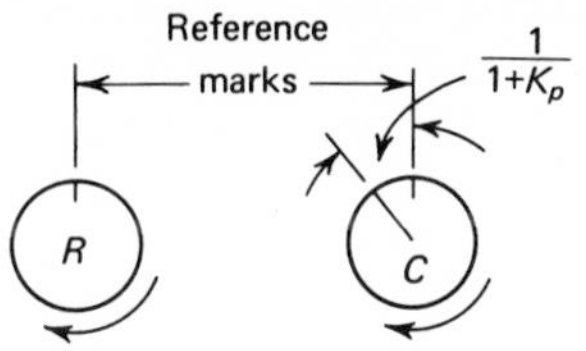

Figure 9.1–4. Illustration of error coefficients.

system, after giving the input dial a unit angular step input clockwise, this dial will remain at a fixed position, such that the index of the dial will coincide with some reference line as shown. The output dial index will in general oscillate around its corresponding reference position during the transient interval and will eventually take a fixed position $1/(1 + K_p)$ distant from the reference line. This is also shown graphically in Figure 9.1–5a. The error coefficient K_p can be made very large by making K large, so that $1/(1 + K_p)$ is small. Now if we give R a unit ramp input, or turn R at a constant velocity of 1 radian per second, using the final value theorem we see from Figure 9.1–5b that the velocity of dial C cannot equal that of

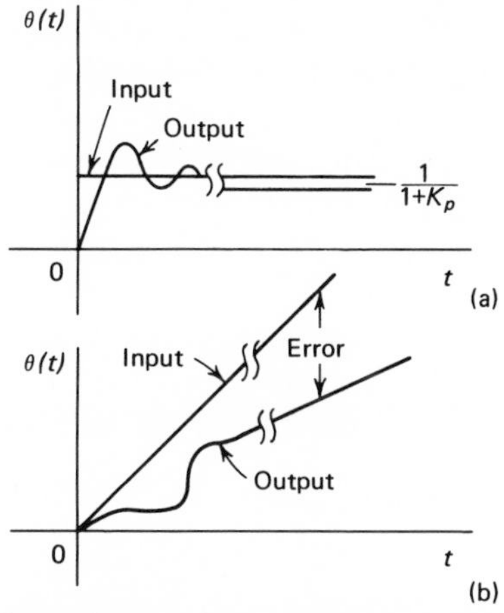

Figure 9.1–5. Errors of type 0 system.

R, or the slope of the output is less than that of the input after the transients die out. Thus dial C cannot "keep up" with R and the angular error will grow without bound. This is expressed by the relation $K_v = 0$ for this system.

Now if we have a type 1 system with one integrator, Table 9.1–3 shows that $K_p \to \infty$, and hence on a step input the position error after a long time will be zero. What happens is that any position error sensed is integrated out until it becomes zero. On a ramp input, the output dial velocity eventually will be the same as the input dial velocity, or the slopes of θ_{in}, θ_{out} will be the same. The output dial angle will be less than that of the input angle as $t \to \infty$ by the amount $1/K_v$, as in Figure 9.1–6. If you make the

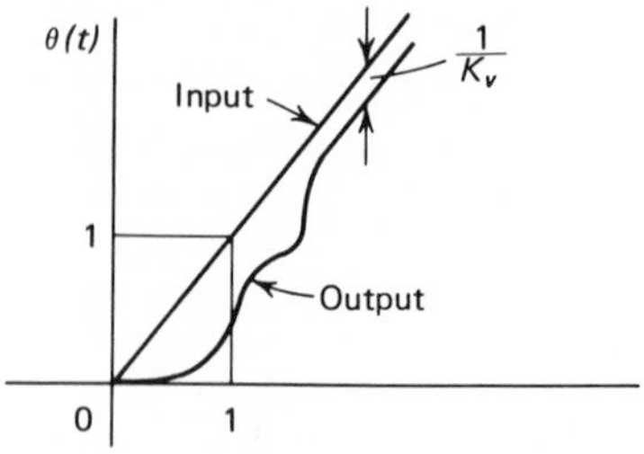

Figure 9.1–6. Error on type 1 system, velocity input.

ramp input h units rather than 1, then of course the output error becomes h/K_v, owing to the linearity of the system. On a parabolic input, the final error in the type 1 system becomes infinite.

The arguments for type 2 systems proceed in the same manner. For such a system the static error for a step or position input and for a ramp or velocity input finally becomes zero, and the static error for a parabolic input eventually is $1/K_\alpha$, and so on.

Although practical inputs will not be the simple functions discussed, it is clear that we improve static performance by making the frequency-independent gain K high. The static error coefficients K_p, K_v, and K_α of course tell little about the transient performance, which is related to the relative stability.

The sensitivity of the system with respect to changes in gain also becomes much better with increased gain. Referring to (1.7–10), which is the Bode definition of sensitivity, we find that the per unit change in C/R with per unit change in K is

$$\mathscr{S}_K^{C/R} = \frac{1}{1 + KG'} \tag{9.1–13}$$

where $KG' = G$. It is now clear that the sensitivity is a function of the complex frequency, since G' is frequency-dependent. In general $|KG'|$ will become small at high frequencies, as we have previously seen. However, the sensitivity in the low-frequency region (static or slowly changing inputs) can be made very small by making K large. The conventional design problem in terms of sinusoidal analysis is to make the low-frequency gain as large as possible while obtaining acceptable transient performance or relative stability. In terms of the root locus, we wish to make K large but to prevent the dominant complex poles from approaching too close to the imaginary axis. Any performance specification must therefore include a requirement on the static error, and this would be true regardless of the use of conventional or optimal analysis. The type of system is often fixed by other considerations, such as the practical methods of obtaining the results, and thus a specification will be made in K_p, K_v, or K_α, as required. In some cases, the system type may be changed during the operation; thus it might be type 2 on a tracking operation but type 1 on a locking operation. This could be accomplished by switching an integrator in or out.

At any rate, it is obvious that whatever compensations are introduced into the system, the frequency-independent gain K must be adjusted so that the static error specifications continue to be met.

If we know the static gain constants in terms of the open loop poles and zeros, $-p_j$ and $-z_i$, you may ask if we can find these constants in terms of the closed loop system poles and zeros $-P_j$ and $-z_i$. To that end let us expand the transfer function between actuating signal and input in a Taylor's series about zero. Then

$$\frac{E}{R}(s) = \frac{1}{1 + G(s)} \tag{9.1–14}$$

$$= C_0 + C_1 s + C_2 s^2 + \cdots \tag{9.1–15}$$

Also

$$\frac{C}{R}(s) = 1 - \frac{E}{R}(s)$$

$$= 1 - C_0 - C_1 s - C_1 s^2 - \cdots \tag{9.1–16}$$

If we have a type 0 system,

$$G(s) = \frac{K \prod_{i=1}^{m} (s + z_1)}{\prod_{j=1}^{n} (s + p_j)}$$

$$= \frac{K' \prod_{i=1}^{m} (1 + s/z_i)}{\prod_{j=1}^{n} (1 + s/p_j)} \tag{9.1–17}$$

where

$$K' = \frac{K \prod_{i=1}^{m} z_i}{\prod_{j=1}^{n} p_j} = K_p$$

Expanding (9.1–17), you obtain

$$G(s) = \frac{K'(1 + a_1 s + a_2 s^2 + \cdots)}{1 + b_1 s + b_2 s^2 + \cdots}$$

and substituting this in (9.1–14), there results

$$\begin{aligned} \frac{E}{R}(s) &= \frac{1 + b_1 s + b_2 s^2 + \cdots}{(1 + K') + (b_1 + K'a_1)s + \cdots} \\ &= \frac{1}{1 + K'} + \frac{1}{1 + K'}\left(b_1 - \frac{b_1 + K'a_1}{1 + K'}\right)s + \cdots \end{aligned} \qquad \textbf{(9.1–18)}$$

Comparing (9.1–18) and (9.1–15),

$$\begin{aligned} C_0 &= \frac{1}{1 + K'} \\ &= \frac{1}{1 + K_p} \end{aligned} \qquad \textbf{(9.1–19)}$$

For a type 1 system,

$$\begin{aligned} G(s) &= \frac{K \prod_{i=1}^{m} (s + z_i)}{s \prod_{j=2}^{n} (s + p_j)} \\ &= \frac{K' \prod_{i=1}^{m} (1 + s/z_i)}{s \prod_{j=2}^{n} (1 + s/p_j)} \end{aligned}$$

where

$$K' = \frac{K \prod_{i=1}^{m} z_i}{\prod_{j=2}^{n} p_j} = K_v$$

Again expanding,

$$G(s) = \frac{K'(1 + a_1 s + a_2 s^2 + \cdots)}{s + b_1 s^2 + b_2 s^3 + \cdots}$$

which, substituted in (9.1–14), gives

$$\frac{E}{R}(s) = \frac{s + b_1 s^2 + b_2 s^3 + \cdots}{K' + (1 + K'a_1)s + (b_1 + K'a_2)s^2 + \cdots}$$

$$= \frac{1}{K'}s + \frac{1}{K'}\left(b_1 - \frac{1 + K'a_1}{K'}\right)s + \cdots \qquad \textbf{(9.1–20)}$$

Comparing (9.1–20) with (9.1–15),

$$C_0 = 0$$

$$C_1 = \frac{1}{K'}$$

$$= \frac{1}{K_v} \qquad \textbf{(9.1–21)}$$

This could be continued to show that in general the first nonzero coefficient in (9.1–15) is the reciprocal of the static error coefficient for the corresponding order system. Succeeding coefficients of (9.1–15) are not in general zero or infinity, however, but can be found by simply dividing the characteristic polynomial (denominator) into the numerator polynomial in the order of ascending powers of s.

The coefficients C_0, C_1, and so on, of (9.1–15) are called the dynamic error coefficients, because

$$E(s) = R(s)(C_0 + C_1 s + C_2 s^2 + \cdots) \qquad \textbf{(9.1–22)}$$

Equation (9.1–22) is not particularly useful in finding $e(t)$, however, since the series formed by the product on the right side may not converge rapidly, if at all.

Now let us look at the coefficients of (9.1–16) from the Taylor's series viewpoint:

$$\frac{C}{R}(s) = \frac{K \prod_{i=1}^{m} (s + z_i)}{\prod_{j=1}^{n} (s + P_j)} \qquad \textbf{(9.1–23)}$$

If we have a type 1 system, $C_0 = 0$ and

$$\frac{C}{R}(0) = 1 \qquad \textbf{(9.1–24)}$$

From the Taylor's series expansion relations, in (9.1–16)

$$-C_1 = \frac{d}{ds}\left[\frac{C}{R}(s)\right]\Bigg|_{s=0}$$

or, from (9.1–24),

$$-C_1 = \frac{(d/ds)[(C/R)(s)]}{(C/R)(s)}\Bigg|_{s=0}$$

$$= \frac{d}{ds}\left[\ln\left(\frac{C}{R}\right)(s)\right]_{s=0}$$

Hence

$$-C_1 = \frac{d}{ds}\left(\ln K + \sum_1^m \ln(s+z_i) - \sum_1^n \ln(s+P_j)\right)\Bigg|_{s=0}$$

$$C_1 = -\left(\sum_1^m \frac{1}{s+z_i} - \sum_1^n \frac{1}{s+P_j}\right)_{s=0}$$

or

$$C_1 = \sum_1^n \frac{1}{P_j} - \sum_1^m \frac{1}{z_i}$$

Finally, since $C_1 = 1/K_v$ for a first-order system,

$$\frac{1}{K_v} = \sum_1^n \frac{1}{P_j} - \sum_1^m \frac{1}{z_i} \tag{9.1–25}$$

In terms of the open loop poles and zeros, from Table 9.1–3,

$$K_v = \frac{K\prod_{i=1}^m z_i}{\prod_{j=2}^n p_j} \tag{9.1–26}$$

Thus we have a relationship between the open loop poles and zeros and the closed loop system poles and zeros for a type 1 system. Among other things it enables us to find one system pole P_j from the open loop poles and zeros if the other system poles are known. From (9.1–25), for a single pair of complex poles as in Figure 9.1–7,

$$\frac{1}{K_v} = \frac{1}{\sigma + j\omega_d} + \frac{1}{\sigma - j\omega_d}$$

where $\omega_n = \omega_d/\sqrt{1-\zeta^2}$ and $\zeta = \omega_n/\sigma$, and where $P_1 = \sigma + j\omega_d$, $P_2 = \sigma - j\omega_d$. Hence

$$\frac{1}{K_v} = \frac{2\sigma}{\sigma^2 + \omega_d{}^2}$$

$$= \frac{2\zeta\omega_n}{\omega_n{}^2}$$

or

$$K_v = \frac{\omega_n}{2\zeta} \tag{9.1–27}$$

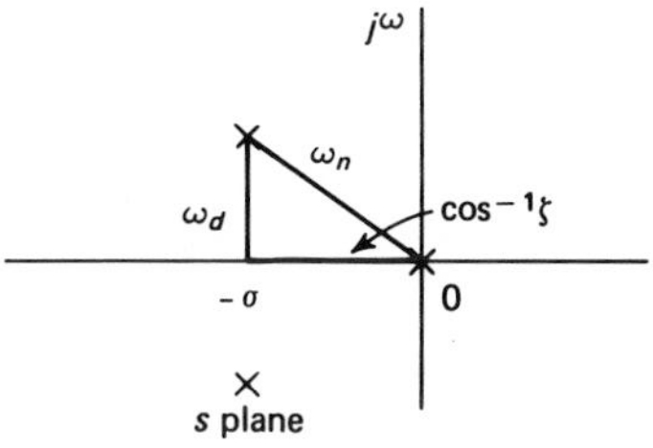

Figure 9.1–7. Complex poles.

For a pair of complex poles and a dipole, as in Figure 9.1–8,

$$\frac{1}{K_v} = \frac{2\zeta}{\omega_n} + \frac{1}{P_1} - \frac{1}{z_1}$$

$$= \frac{2\zeta}{\omega_n} + \frac{z_1 - P_1}{P_1 z_1}$$

$$= \frac{2\zeta P_1 z_1 + (z_1 - P_1)\omega_n}{\omega_n P_1 z_1} \tag{9.1–28}$$

or

$$K_v = \frac{\omega_n P_1 z_1}{2\zeta P_1 z_1 + (z_1 - P_1)\omega_n} \tag{9.1–29}$$

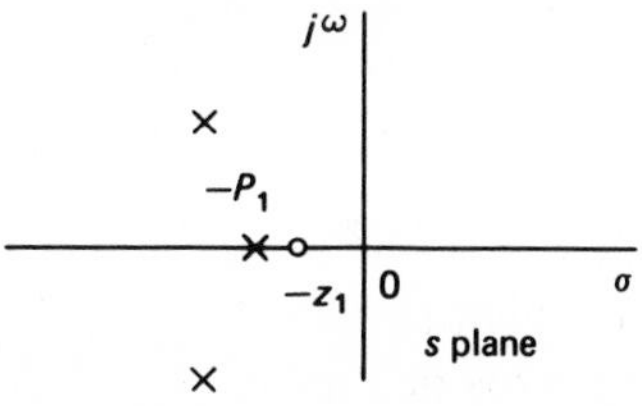

Figure 9.1–8. Complex poles and dipole.

It is clear that in the configuration of Figure 9.1–8, where $z_1 < P_1$, that the dipole reduces the value of the denominator of (9.1–29) and increases K_v.

The effect of the dipole alone from (9.1–25) is

$$|K_v| = \left| \frac{P_1 z_1}{z_1 - P_1} \right| \tag{9.1–30}$$

and if z_1 and P_1 are close together, this effect is sizable. The sign of the dipole term in (9.1–28) is such as to reduce $1/K_v$ and hence to increase K_v. There is an open loop pole at $s = 0$, so the zero z_1 must be placed close to the origin in order that the closed loop dipole will be formed, as discussed in Chapter 7. The root locus near the origin often appears as in Figure 9.1–9. As K increases, the system poles $-P_1$ and $-P_2$ move around the

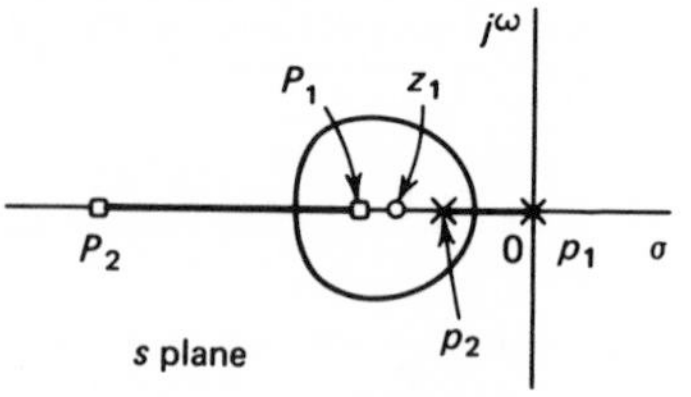

Figure 9.1–9. Formation of dipole.

zero, and $-P_1$ finally is driven close to z_1 for high K, while $-P_2$ is, hopefully, at some distance. The original combination of z_1 and p_2, called an integrating dipole, becomes the closed loop dipole of z_1P_1. If P_1 and z_1 are sufficiently close together (relative to other poles and zeros), they effect the transient response very little, because their residues almost cancel. Thus we can obtain increased K_v without greatly altering the transient response or the relative stability. Clearly also, from (9.1–25) any zeros increase K_v, while any distant poles have little effect. From (9.1–25) you also observe that it is possible to obtain a very large K_v, even $K_v \to \infty$, by adding zeros. For example, if the system has a pair of complex poles only, then $1/K_v = 2\zeta/\omega_n$, and if $z_1 = \omega_n/2\zeta$ is added, $K_v = \infty$.

The added zero increases the per cent overshoot over that encountered with the complex poles only, particularly for small damping factors. We cannot achieve a zero with a passive network without also adding a pole, so the discussion is somewhat academic unless you wish to employ active devices.

We can sum up this section by again emphasizing that the static gain must be kept large in a high-performance feedback control system. This may mean introducing zeros or dipoles in the closed loop system. If you introduce any compensating networks or devices that reduce the static gain, you must make this up by additional frequency-independent gain. Fortunately this is easy, because amplification at low power levels is simple and inexpensive. Such amplification is usually introduced immediately after the summing point of Figure 9.1–2, and operates on the low-energy-actuating signal $e(t)$. The compensating devices are also usually introduced at low-power-level points, such as prior to the amplifier or in an internal feedback loop, as this results in low-cost, light components.

9.2 Elementary Tandem Compensation Devices—Lead Networks

In this section we shall describe a few elementary compensation devices. Most of these will be electrical in nature, but you understand that it is often possible to construct hydraulic, pneumatic, or mechanical devices that perform in the same way. The electrical network is easy to make, light, and inexpensive, which probably accounts for its popularity. On the other hand, mechanical devices, although more difficult to design, may be considerably less lossy and more durable, whereas pneumatic elements are often extremely simple and inexpensive.

The general idea is, of course, to reshape the gain-phase relations in the frequency analysis approach or to alter the root locus using that technique. Thus the compensation can be quite intricate. However, we may introduce the subject with a few simple devices that will illustrate the procedure and are often sufficient. As previously indicated, in classical design we have several general types of compensation. These may be classified as (1) tandem, (2) internal feedback, and (3) parallel, as shown in Figure 9.2–1.

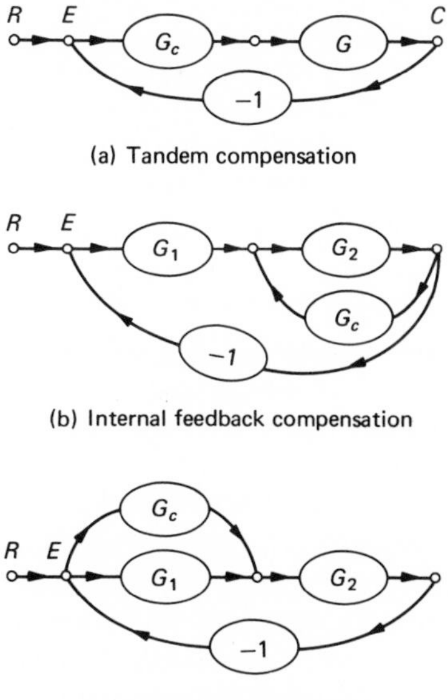

Figure 9.2–1. Various compensation schemes.

Actually in any case the compensation between R and C may be reduced to Figure 9.2–1a, but the other configurations may have advantages. There are also situations where G_c may be connected directly to R in Figure 9.2–1c or where G itself may be altered. Let us discuss tandem compensation first.

The elementary tandem compensators consists of (1) the lead network, (2) the lag network, and (3) a combination of (1) and (2). Since phase lag in the region of magnitude crossover seems to be the chief stability villain in our control drama, it seems at once to be appropriate to introduce phase lead in this region. This you may easily accomplish with an electrical network such as that shown in Figure 9.2–2. Upon writing the transfer function you find that

$$G_c = \frac{E_o}{E_i}$$

or

$$G_c(s) = \frac{s + (R_2/R_1R_2C)}{s + [(R_1 + R_2)/R_1R_2C]} \tag{9.2–1}$$

$$G_c(s) = \frac{s + z_k}{s + p_k}$$

$$= \frac{s + z_k}{s + \alpha z_k} \tag{9.2–2}$$

where

$$z_k = \frac{1}{R_1C} \qquad p_k = \frac{R_1 + R_2}{R_1R_2C} = \alpha z_k \qquad \alpha = \frac{R_1 + R_2}{R_2} \geq 1$$

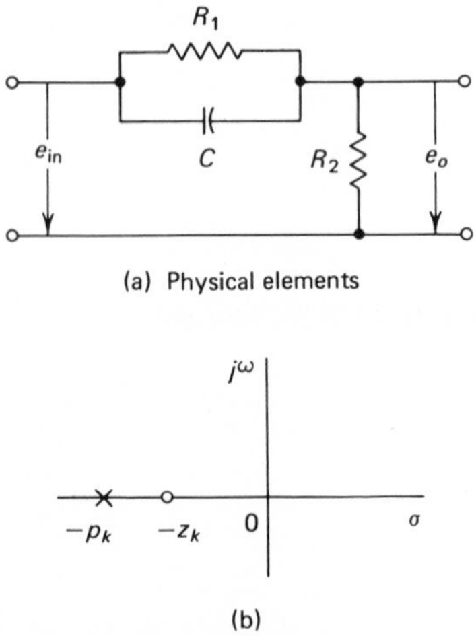

Figure 9.2–2. Lead network compensator.

The pole-zero configuration is shown in Figure 9.2–2, where the pole distance is greater than the zero distance. The sinusoidal plots are shown in Figure 9.2–3. It is noted from (9.2–2) that the magnitude at $s = 0$ is $1/\alpha$ or $R_2/(R_1 + R_2)$, or a loss of $\log(1/\alpha)$ loru. Thus if we plan to introduce the network without reducing the static error coefficient, it is necessary to increase the system gain by $(R_1 + R_2)/R_2$. The phase angle, however, constitutes the chief interest. You see from Figure 9.2–3 it is just what we want: a phase

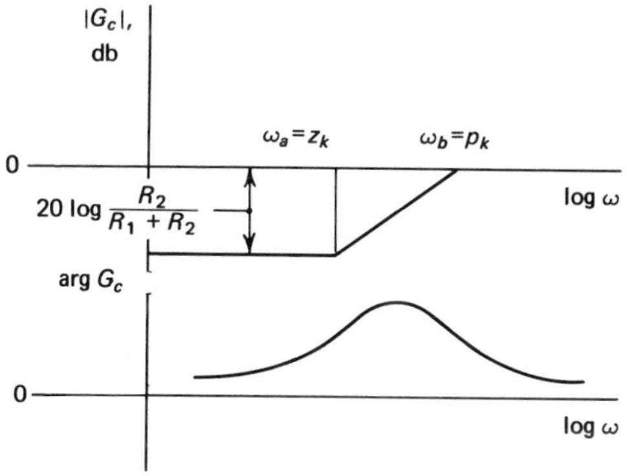

Figure 9.2–3. Lead compensator frequency characteristics.

lead or positive angle. The amount of this lead may be easily found as follows:

$$\arg G_c = \tan^{-1}\left(\frac{\omega}{z_k}\right) - \tan^{-1}\left(\frac{\omega}{\alpha z_k}\right) \quad \textbf{(9.2–3)}$$

Then

$$\frac{d \arg G_c}{d\omega} = \frac{z_k}{z_k^2 + \omega^2} - \frac{\alpha z_k}{\alpha^2 z_k^2 + \omega^2}$$

Setting this to zero to find ω_m, the point of maximum phase lead, you obtain

$$\omega_m = z_k\sqrt{\alpha} \quad \textbf{(9.2–4)}$$

$$\omega_m = \sqrt{p_k z_k} \quad \textbf{(9.2–5)}$$

Substituting this back into (9.2–3), you get

$$(\arg G_c)_m = \tan^{-1}\left(\frac{z_k\sqrt{\alpha}}{z_k}\right) - \tan^{-1}\left(\frac{z_k\sqrt{\alpha}}{\alpha z_k}\right)$$

$$= \tan^{-1}\sqrt{\alpha} - \tan^{-1}\left(\frac{1}{\sqrt{\alpha}}\right)$$

$$= \tan^{-1}\left(\frac{\alpha - 1}{2\sqrt{\alpha}}\right) \quad \textbf{(9.2–6)}$$

From (9.2–6), we prepare Table 9.2–1, which shows the variation of the maximum phase lead with $\alpha = p_k/z_k$.

TABLE 9.1–2 MAXIMUM PHASE ANGLE FOR LEAD NETWORK

α	Maximum $(\arg G)_m$, degrees	$\Delta(\arg G)_m/\Delta\alpha$
2	19.5	—
3	29.8	10.3
4	36.8	7.0
5	41.8	5.0
6	45.6	3.8
8	51.7	3.0
10	54.8	1.6
20	64.8	1
40	72.0	0.36

Equation (9.2–5) shows that the maximum phase lead comes at the geometric mean of the pole and zero. The third column in Table 9.2–1 shows the increase in phase angle with increase in α and demonstrates that increasing the pole-zero separation has progressively less beneficial results. If you remember that the gain at low frequency is $-\log \alpha$ loru, it is clear that for large phase leads it may be more desirable to have two lead compensators than to increase α. Thus if we require a phase lead of 72°, the zero frequency loss on a single unit would be 32 db, while if we use two units each with $\alpha = 4$, the loss would be 24 db. Moreover, the actual selection of component sizes in Figure 9.2–2 becomes difficult as α increases. Hence it is usual to limit α to about 10, or $p_k \leq 10z_k$, and to require an additional compensator if more phase lead is required.

Using the frequency analysis method, we make the Bode plots and add the compensator such that maximum phase lead is introduced at the magnitude crossover point of the compensated system. Since the crossover point (magnitude $|G| = 1$, or 0 db) is at relatively high angular velocity, the pole and zero making up the lead network will be relatively far from the origin of the s plane. The next example illustrates these factors.

Example 9.2–1

Given

$$G(s) = \frac{K}{s^2(s+5)}$$

in a unity negative feedback system. It is desired to design compensation to obtain a phase margin of 30° and a $K_\alpha = 1$. To obtain the required K_α, $K = 5$, and it is clear that the system is unstable with the open loop G given. If we plot the magnitude curve (sketched in Figure 9.2–4) the magnitude

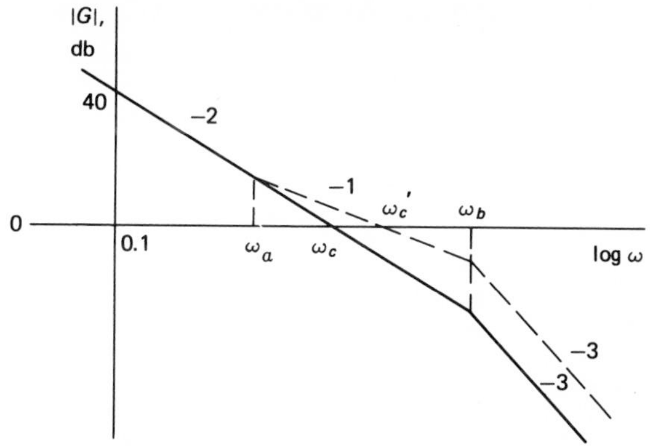

Figure 9.2–4. Bode magnitude plot for Example 9.2–1.

reaches 1 (0 db) at $\omega_c \approx 1$ radian per second. If we add a compensation of the type shown in Figure 9.2–3, except that the frequency-independent gain is increased by $(R_1 + R_2)/R_2$, the dashed line in Figure 9.2–4 shows that this results in a higher crossover point, $\omega_c' > \omega_c$. We estimate that $\omega_c' = 2$. The phase angle when $\omega = 2$ is $\arg G = -180° - \tan^{-1}(2/5) \approx -202°$. For a phase margin of 30° we therefore need a phase lead of about 52°. From Table 9.2–1 $\alpha = 10$ gives about 55°, which provides a safety factor. From (9.2–4), $z_k = 2/\sqrt{10} = 0.633$. Hence $p_1 = 10(0.633) = 6.33$. The new function with compensation then becomes

$$G_1 = \frac{50(s + 0.633)}{s^2(s + 5)(s + 6.33)}$$

where K has been increased by 10 to keep $K_v = 1$. A new Bode plot shows a $|G_1| = 1$ crossing when $\omega_c' \approx 1.7$. the phase angle at this point is $-180° - \tan^{-1}(1.7/5) - \tan^{-1}(1.7/6.33) + \tan^{-1}(1.7/0.63) \approx -145°$, which gives a phase margin $\approx 35°$. The old and new magnitude curves are shown as G and G_1, respectively in Figure 9.2–5. If a Nichols chart is required, the phase curve can be added. The compensating network is $10(s + 0.633)/(s + 6.33)$, where the gain of 10 must be supplied by an amplifier. The system is slightly overdesigned, and, if desired, a slight refinement can be made to lower α to about 9 and reduce z_1 slightly. In this connection, excessive design costs often are unwarranted, owing to incomplete knowledge of the system, nonlinearities, loose specifications, and so on.

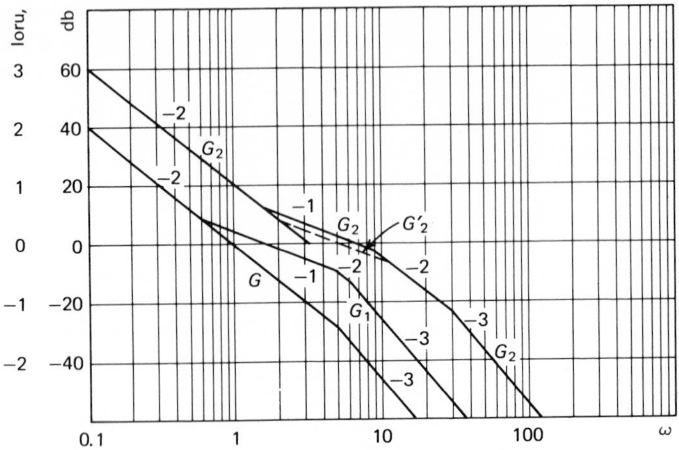

Figure 9.2–5. Bode magnitude plots for Examples 9.2–1 and 9.2–2.

Example 9.2–2

If it were required to increase K_α to 10 with the same phase margin, you see that the use of one phase lead device is insufficient. A plot of this transfer function in Figure 9.2–5 shows $\omega_c \approx 3.2$. Estimating the revised crossover point at $\omega_c' \approx 8$, you need a phase lead of about 90° for a 30° margin, and we can try two networks with $\alpha = 6$. Then let

$$G_2 = \frac{1800(s+1.5)(s+5)}{s^2(s+5)(s+9)(s+30)}$$

$$= \frac{1800(s+1.5)}{s^2(s+9)(s+30)}$$

Plotting $|G_2|$ in Figure 9.2–5, $\omega_c' \approx 6.6$ and $\arg G_2 \approx 152°$, or a phase margin of 28°. This almost meets specifications, and by increasing z_1 to about 2, a phase margin of 35° may be achieved (shown by the dashed line for G_2' in Figure 9.2–5). The method shown here is termed cancellation compensation. The validity of the cancellation depends on how well the pole and zero at $s = -5$ remain in this position. The compensating network for the revised case is

$$G_{2c} = 36\,\frac{(s+2)(s+5)}{(s+12)(s+30)}$$

while

$$G_2' = \frac{1800(s+2)}{s^2(s+12)(s+30)}$$

In forming the compensating network you need to be reminded in this case that two lead networks $(s+2)/(s+12)$ and $(s+5)/(s+30)$ in tandem will not give the G_{2c} transfer function unless the second network does not appreciably load the first.

Now we need to look at the results of the example compensations in terms of the overall closed loop system. Plotting G_1 and G_2' on a Nichols chart, we easily find that for the unity negative feedback system with G_1, the maximum magnitude M_p is about 1.56 at $\omega_p \approx 1.3$ radians per second, while for the system with G_2', which has K_α 10 times as great, $M_p \approx 1.58$ at $\omega_p \approx 4$ radians per second. The bandwidth of the second system is about 6.5, or almost three times the bandwidth of 2.2 of the first system. Thus the addition of phase lead increases the bandwidth, allowing more undesirable noise to pass.

If we assume that both systems operate essentially as second-order systems, they will both have damping factors of about 0.3, but the second system will have a faster rise time on a step input, because $\omega_{n2} \approx 3\omega_{n1}$ (assuming $\omega_n \approx \omega_p$). This seems reasonable, since K_α is larger in the second system.

As discussed in Chapter 8, the inherent difficulty of sinusoidal analysis consists in easily finding the actual location of the system poles. The characteristic equation is of fourth degree, so the factoring job is arduous if done by hand. Thus we are left with some qualitative ideas as to system performance but few actual numerical values, or, in other words, we have met the specifications, but the system may be lightly damped, particularly since a zero is present. The use of lead networks to increase the static error coefficient has drawbacks because of the bandwidth and overshoot problems, and we shall take up better methods for doing this. Sinusoidal analysis on the lead network does illustrate how this device solves the stability problem and helps to determine the regions where the compensation poles and zeros must lie.

Let us now discuss the lead network from the standpoint of the root locus. If we examine the root locus plot of a somewhat typical third-order type 1 system in Figure 9.2–6, we see that instability occurs for low K values due to the complex closed loop poles moving rapidly into the right-half plane. Recalling the potential analogy, this suggests putting a real zero to the left of $-p_2$, which will tend to keep the locus in the left-half plane for larger K values. If we can do this, then the root locus might take the appearance of the curves sketched in Figure 9.2–7, and you readily agree that the aim has been accomplished. The single zero $-z_k$ could be obtained from Figure 9.2–2 by making $R_1 = 0$. However, with the tandem compensation this would be disastrous to the system at low frequencies, because at $s = 0$ there would be no signal transmitted through the forward path and the system would be statically inoperative. It would also be possible to

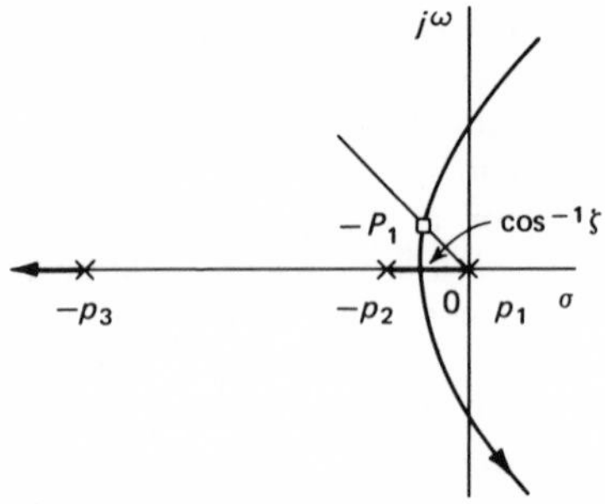

Figure 9.2–6. Root locus for third-order type 1 system.

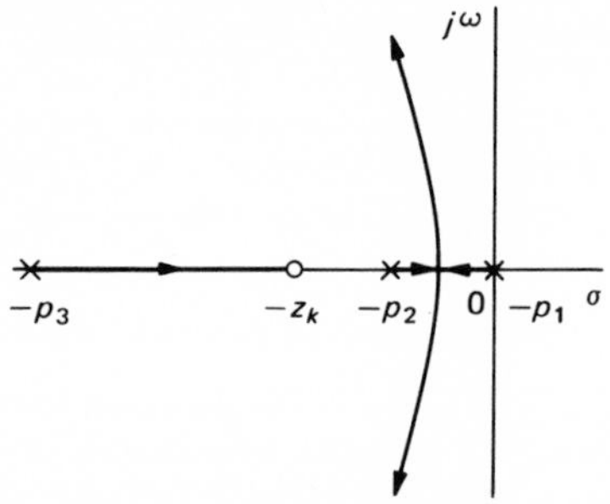

Figure 9.2–7. Root locus for system of Figure 9.2–6 with added zero $-z_k$.

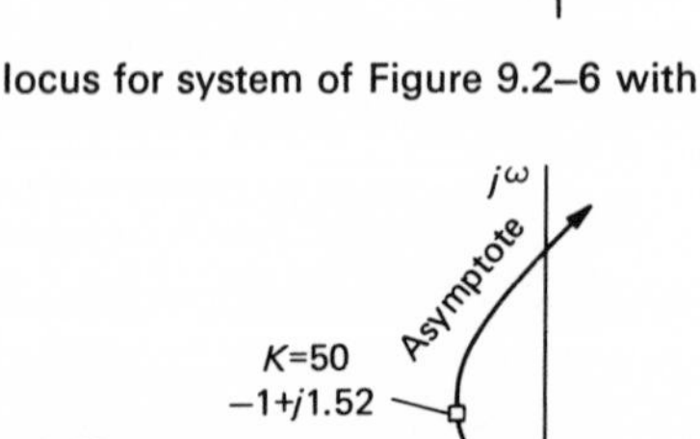

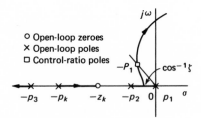

Figure 9.2–8. Root locus for system of Figure 9.2–6 with lead compensation.

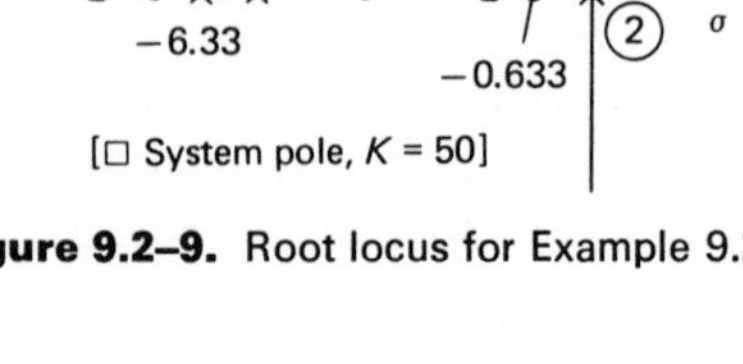

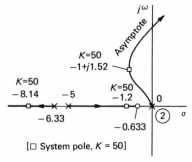

Figure 9.2–9. Root locus for Example 9.2–1.

obtain a zero (a perfect differentiator) with an active device, such as an amplifier. However, practical difficulties of drift and stability exist. In sum, using a passive network or the equivalent, we are forced to accept an additional pole furnished with Figure 9.2–2, $R_1 \neq 0$. Thus the practical compensation makes the locus of the same system appear somewhat as sketched in Figure 9.2–8.

Comparing Figure 9.2–6 with Figure 9.2–8 you note that for the same damping factor ζ, the complex system pole $-P_1$ has a larger ω_n in the compensated system than previously. Thus the response would be faster. Alternatively, for the same value of K_v, the system of Figure 9.2–8 has more relative stability than that of Figure 9.2–6. In higher-order systems it will usually be necessary to have more than one zero to achieve the desired stability.

Example 9.2–3

Again let us examine the system of Example 9.2–1, where

$$G = \frac{K}{s^2(s+5)}$$

If we provide the same compensation as used in Example 9.2–1 using frequency analysis, the poles and zeros are as shown in Figure 9.2–9, together with the compensated root locus. The closed loop poles are approximately at $s = -8.14$, $s = -1.2$, $s = -1 - j1.52$ and $s = -1 + j1.52$, as shown. The damping factor ζ is about 0.546 and ω_n is about 1.82. These compare with estimates for ω_n of about 1.58 and about 0.3 for ζ from the sinusoidal analysis. However, owing to the close-in zero at $s = -0.633$ (Figure 9.2–9), the system will probably perform very much like a second-order system, with about 0.3 damping factor. The distant pole at $s = -8.14$ affects the transient response very slightly.

Example 9.2–4

Using the G_2' of Example 9.2–2, the root locus of Figure 9.2–10 may be sketched. We do not complete it in detail, as in general it is similar to the previous root locus except the scale has been increased, resulting in a larger ω_n for the complex system poles. The original pole at $s = -5$ has been canceled by a zero at the same point.

In drawing the revised root locus we used the critical frequencies found previously. We must sketch a new root locus for each new trial compensator. Do we have any guide for the selection of the pole-zero values without

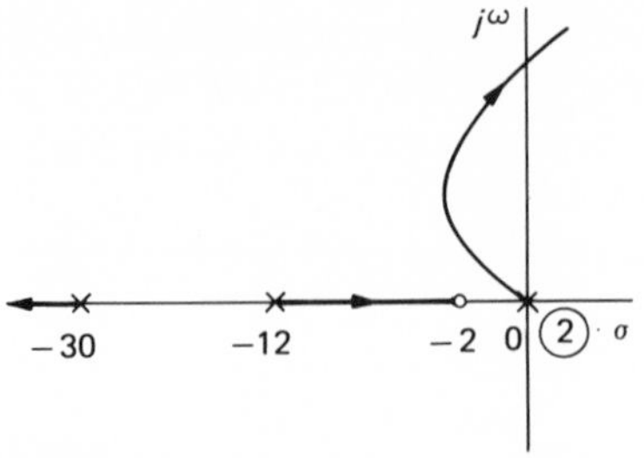

Figure 9.2–10. Root locus for Example 9.2–2.

other analysis? Several possible techniques have been suggested, some of which we now take up.

To determine preferable values for z_1 and p_1 in a lead network, one may draw auxiliary root loci with these quantities as parameters. To be specific, take for example a third-order system with

$$G(s) = \frac{K}{s(s+2)(s+10)} \tag{9.2–7}$$

and add the lead network compensator

$$G_c(s) = \alpha \frac{s + z_k}{s + \alpha z_k}$$

where the gain has been made 1 when $s = 0$. Then

$$(GG_c)(s) = \frac{\alpha K(s + z_k)}{s(s+2)(s+10)(s + \alpha z_k)} \tag{9.2–8}$$

The characteristic equation becomes

$$s^4 + (12 + \alpha z_k)s^3 + (20 + 12\alpha z_k)s^2 + (20\alpha z_k + \alpha K)s + \alpha K z_k = 0 \tag{9.2–9}$$

Rearranging to obtain the root locus form with z_k as a parameter,

$$\alpha z_k s^3 + 12\alpha z_k s^2 + 20\alpha z_k s + \alpha K z_k = -(s^4 + 12s^3 + 20s^2 + \alpha K s)$$

$$\frac{\alpha z_k(s^3 + 12s^2 + 20s + K)}{s(s^3 + 12s^2 + 20s + \alpha K)} = -1$$

$$\frac{p_k(s^3 + 12s^2 + 20s + K)}{s(s^3 + 12s^2 + 20s + \alpha K)} = -1 \tag{9.2–10}$$

The parenthetical term in the numerator of (9.2–10) is the same as the characteristic polynomial of the original system with loop gain given by

(9.2–7), while the corresponding term in the denominator is the same except that the constant differs by α. Hence if we look at (9.2–10) as a new open loop function for a root locus plot to find the roots for the characteristic equation (9.2–9), the open loop poles and zeros for (9.2–10) must lie on the root locus plotted for the original system using

$$\frac{K}{s(s+2)(s+10)} = -1$$

The zeros of (9.2–10) will lie along the original root locus at the same points where the original system poles $-p_j$ are, while the poles of (9.2–10) will be farther along the locus (in the direction of increasing K), since $\alpha > 1$. To draw the root locus of (9.2–10), then, we first locate the open loop poles and zeros by plotting the root locus of the original system. There is then one added pole at the origin in (9.2–10).

Suppose now that a minimum static coefficient K_v is specified in (9.2–7). Then K is fixed by the relation $K = K_v(2)(10)$, and the zeros for (9.2–10) are now established as shown in Figure 9.2–11. The poles then become

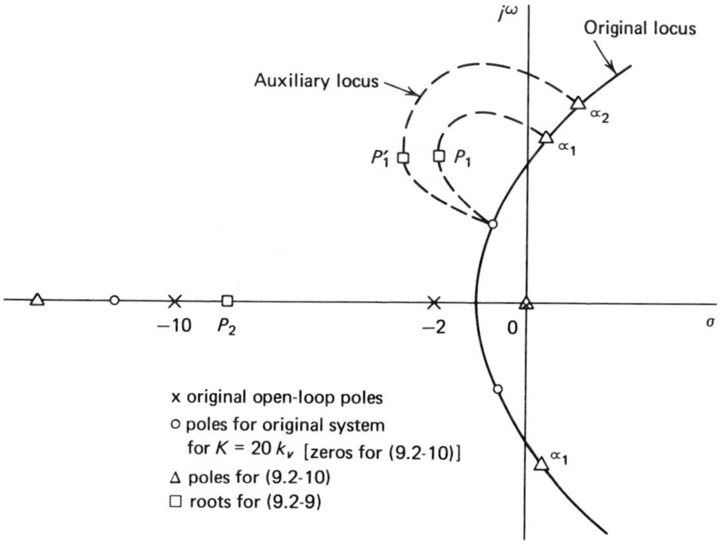

Figure 9.2–11. Auxiliary root loci to determine possible values for lead network parameters, Example 9.2–5.

fixed by α, plus a pole at the origin, and are shown for $\alpha = \alpha_1$ as diamond-shaped symbols in Figure 9.2–11. Now as p_k varies, the root locus satisfying (9.2–10) moves out into the left-half plane as shown by the dashed line (shown only in the upper-half plane in Figure 9.2–11). At the same time the pole at the origin moves along the real axis to the left, to terminate that branch at the real zero. Another real pole moves farther out the real axis, but this is at such a distance it probably can be neglected in the transient response. By a proper choice of p_k we obtain a root of (9.2–9) [or a system pole for (9.2–8)] at P_1 and a corresponding real root P_2 in Figure 9.2–11. By making $\alpha = \alpha_2$, P_1' may be obtained, and so on. As seen previously, increasing α results in progressively less movement into the left-half plane. If one lead section does not result in sufficient stability, you may fix the open loop poles of (9.2–8) by the method given, add another lead section, and proceed from these poles with an additional root locus plot in a similar manner. In such a case, the effort in plotting the loci begins to be exhausting, but the locations of all system poles and zeros are known at all times, whereas in frequency analysis we are usually in the dark on this matter.

Although the previous discussion considered third-order systems, the extension to higher-order systems is obvious. Digital computer assistance in plotting loci may be required in finalizing design, but rough sketching reveals possibilities fairly soon. As in Examples 9.2–3 and 9.2–4, frequency analysis may also be a prelude to root locus plotting. It seems clear from Figure 9.2–11 and previous experience that the single lead network section will be limited for improving stability in high-order, high-performance systems.

Another approach in root locus analysis consists in attempting to first locate a pair of complex "dominant" system poles with a desired ω_n and ζ by adding compensation. Several methods for doing this have been devised, and we shall discuss one of these later after taking up lag networks, as the method applies to both lead and lag compensation.

9.3 Elementary Tandem Compensation Devices—Lag Networks

The lag network appears as in Figure 9.3–1 and has a transfer function

$$G_c = \frac{E_o}{E_i}$$

or

$$G_c(s) = \frac{R_2}{R_1 + R_2} \frac{s + (1/R_2 C)}{s + [1/(R_1 + R_2)]C} \tag{9.3–1}$$

$$G_c(s) = \frac{1}{\alpha} \frac{s + z_c}{s + p_c}$$

$$= \frac{1}{\alpha} \frac{s + \alpha p_c}{s + p_c} \tag{9.3–2}$$

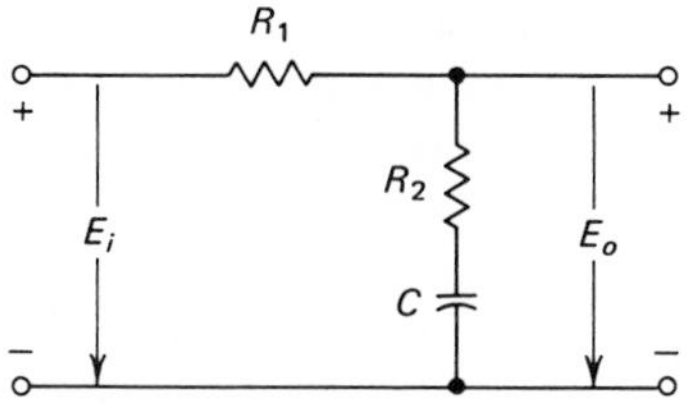

Figure 9.3–1. Lag compensator.

where $z_c = 1/R_2C = \alpha p_c$, $p_c = 1/(R_1 + R_2)C$, and $\alpha = (R_1 + R_2)/R_2 \geq 1$. The Bode plots appear as in Figure 9.3–2. The frequency analysis emphasis this time is on the magnitude characteristic. Take the situation shown in Figure 9.3–3, where the crossover of the magnitude curve for the original system G_1 at ω_c occurs at an angular velocity such that the phase margin is too small. Then if we introduce the lag characteristic such that p_c and z_c are near the origin of the s plane, ω_a and ω_b occur at low angular velocities such that the added phase lag due to the network at the angular velocity of

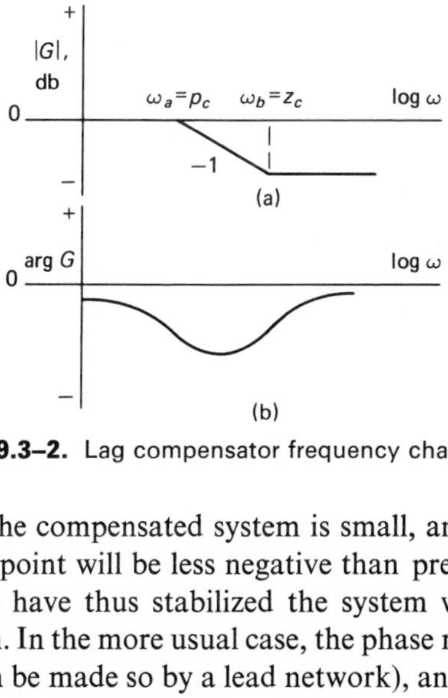

Figure 9.3–2. Lag compensator frequency characteristics.

the crossover for the compensated system is small, and the phase angle at the new crossover point will be less negative than previously (see G_2, ϕ_2, Figure 9.3–3). We have thus stabilized the system without reducing the low-frequency gain. In the more usual case, the phase margin at crossover is satisfactory (or can be made so by a lead network), and hence we can cause the new compensated magnitude to crossover 0 db at or near the same angular velocity by boosting the gain (raising the entire G_2 curve in Figure 9.3–3). Thus we increase the static error coefficient without degrading stability. The trick consists of putting z_c and p_c close enough to the s-plane origin so that very little negative angle is added to the system in the critical crossover region. The same comments as to reduction in effectiveness with increased ratio α apply to the lag network as to the lead network;

hence usually $\alpha \leq 10$. It is possible to put two lag networks in tandem, but this would be fairly rare, since if $\alpha = 10$, we can achieve a tenfold increase in K_v in Figure 9.3–3, assuming stability is satisfactory.

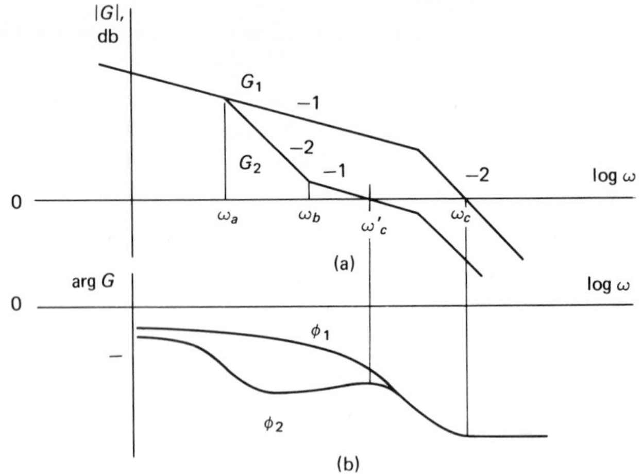

Figure 9.3–3. Effect of adding lag compensator.

From the phase-angle relation you can develop the equation

$$\omega^2 \tan \theta + \omega p_c (\alpha - 1) + \alpha p_c^2 \tan \theta = 0$$

where θ is the phase angle at ω for the given p_c and α values for the lag network. From this we calculate the relation between ω and p_c as

$$\frac{\omega}{p_c} = -\frac{\alpha - 1}{2 \tan \theta} \pm \sqrt{\left(\frac{\alpha - 1}{2 \tan \theta}\right)^2 - \alpha} \tag{9.3–3}$$

where $\tan \theta \lesseqgtr 0$. As it is desired to choose p_c so that $\omega \simeq \omega_c$, the crossover angular velocity, and such that the angle will be small there, we use the positive sign and compute ω/p_c and ω/z_c for various α values so that the lag angle will be values of 5°, 10°, and 15°. These are tabulated in Table 9.3–1.

TABLE 9.3–1 PHASE ANGLES θ FOR LAG NETWORK

	5°		10°		15°	
α	ω/p_c	ω/z_c	ω/p_c	ω/z_c	ω/p_c	ω/z_c
2	10.4	5.22	5.3	2.65	3.1	1.53
3	23.0	7.67	11.1	3.69	7.0	2.34
4	34.7	8.68	16.8	4.19	11.8	2.69
5	46.4	9.28	22.4	4.48	14.5	2.91
6	58.0	9.66	28.1	4.68	18.3	3.04
8	82.0	10.2	39.6	4.95	25.7	3.21
10	104	10.4	51.2	5.12	33.1	3.31

Example 9.3–1

Examine the negative unity feedback system with open loop gain

$$G = \frac{1500}{s(s+5)(s+30)}$$

Increase K_v by using a lag network with $\alpha = 10$, but maintain a phase margin of 35°. Assume that we add 10° phase lag with the lag network in the magnitude crossover region. From Figure 9.3–4 the present phase margin is only about 26°. For a phase margin of 35° plus 10° additional

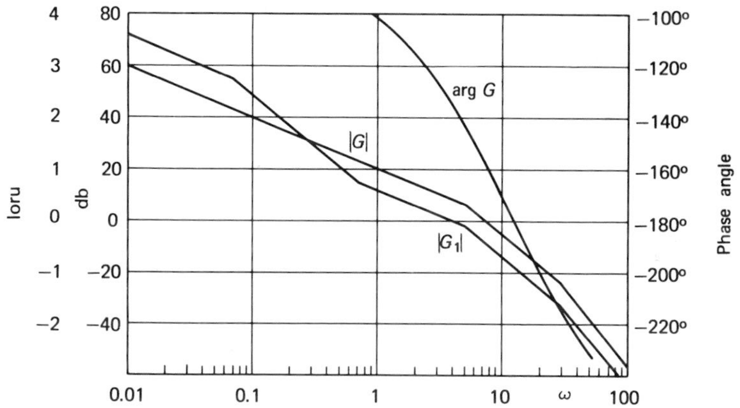

Figure 9.3–4. Bode magnitude and phase-angle plots for Example 9.3–1.

lag, the crossover must be at $\omega_c \approx 3.7$. From table 9.3–1, $\omega/p_c = 51.2$; then $p_c = 0.072$ and $z_c = 0.72$. Drawing in the compensated system with these break points through the crossover point $\omega_c = 3.7$, we see that the revised loop gain is about 0.6 loru, or 12 db, greater at low frequencies. Hence K_v is increased by a factor of 4 and this much additional gain must be supplied by an amplifier. The new open loop transfer function is

$$G_1 = \frac{600(s+0.72)}{s(s+0.072)(s+5)(s+30)}$$

If it were required to increase K_v by a factor of 10 and maintain the same phase margin, a single lag section with $\alpha \approx 25$ or two lag sections each with $\alpha \approx 5$ could be used. Alternatively, one lag section with $\alpha = 10$ and a lead section to increase the phase angle in the crossover region would also serve. The latter design would maintain the original bandwidth.

Let us now look at the same example from the root locus standpoint. Figure 9.3–5 shows a root locus sketch for the open loop transfer function

$$G = \frac{K}{s(s+5)(s+30)}$$

and Figure 9.3–6 shows the root locus sketch for the open loop transfer function

$$G_1 = \frac{K(s + 0.72)}{s(s + 0.072)(s + 5)(s + 30)}$$

The open loop pole at -5 is driven to approximately -0.85 for $K = 600$. Thus the zero at -0.72 and the system pole at -0.85 form a dipole, and

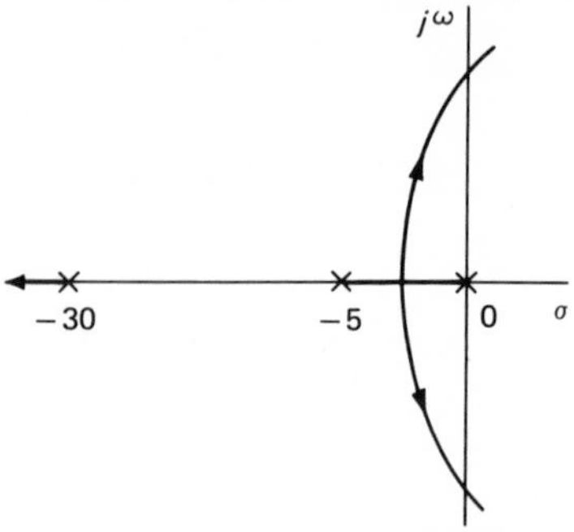

Figure 9.3–5. Root locus for Example 9.3–1.

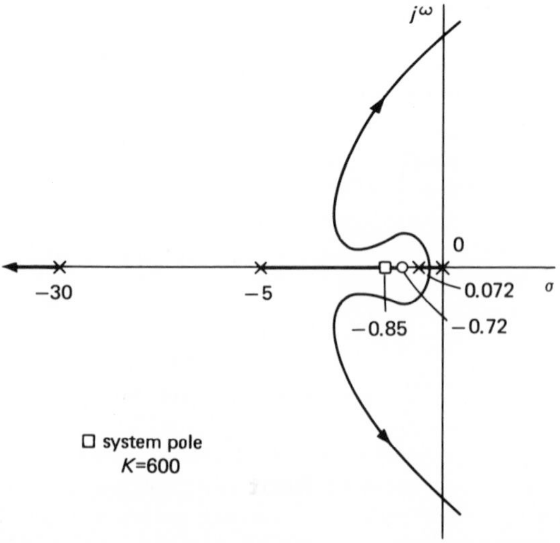

Figure 9.3–6. Root locus for Example 9.3–1 ; lag compensator added.

from (9.1–28) and the discussion of system dipoles we see why we get an increase in K_v. This dipole is formed in a slightly different manner than that illustrated in Figure 9.1–9, but the effect is the same. The root locus for large K in the complex root region in Figure 9.3–6 is almost the same as in Figure 9.3–5; hence the transient response of the two systems will be very similar.

If we wished we could combine the lag network with break points at low frequencies, with the lead network with break points at high frequencies. It is clear from the sketch of the straight-line asymptotes for the magnitude characteristic that such a network will not reduce low-frequency gain

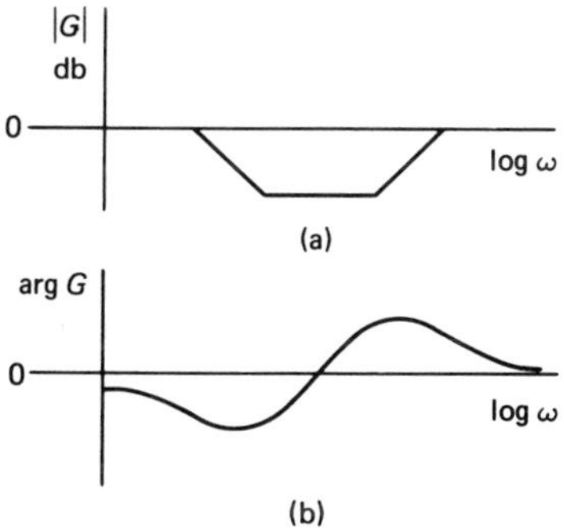

Figure 9.3–7. Lag-lead compensator frequency characteristics.

(Figure 9.3–7) if the factor α is the same for each. Such a network could be formed of the two networks in tandem (again recalling the loading caution) or approximated by the circuit of Figure 9.3–8, and would obtain the beneficial results of both if properly designed.

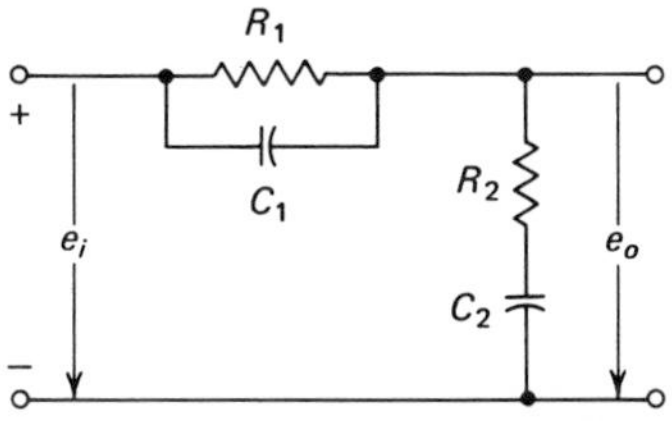

Figure 9.3–8. Electrical network to give lag-lead characteristics.

9.4 Ross-Warren Method of Root Relocation

Of the several methods of compensation using root locus principles [1, 2] we shall discuss the Ross-Warren method in detail. The basic philosophy of this method consists in selecting a pair of complex system poles that will result in the desired response and relocating the root locus of the uncompensated system such that it will pass through the poles selected. At the same time, a specified error coefficient is maintained regardless of the added compensation. We take the usual unity negative feedback system with a forward transfer function

$$G(s) = \frac{K\prod_{i=1}^{m}(s+z_i)}{s^r\prod_{j=r+1}^{n}(s+p_j)} \tag{9.4–1}$$

where K is fixed such that a specified static error coefficient κ is met, or by the relation

$$\kappa = \frac{K\prod_{i=1}^{m} z_i}{\prod_{j=r+1}^{n} p_j} \tag{9.4–2}$$

From the idea of the Chu plots, any point in the s plane is on a locus, provided we define the locus for some general angle, not necessarily 180°. Then for some point s_1 the gain constant at s_1 is given by

$$K(s_1) = \frac{|s_1|^r\prod_{n=r+1}^{n}|s_1+p_j|}{\prod_{m=1}^{m}|s_1+z_i|} \tag{9.4–3}$$

If we add a single tandem compensator to the system

$$G_c(s) = \frac{s+z_c}{s+p_c}$$

then for the compensated system, s_1 will be on some other locus and the gain constant is

$$K_c(s_1) = K(s_1)\frac{|s_1+p_c|}{|s_1+z_c|} \tag{9.4–4}$$

In Figure 9.4–1 let s_1 be the desired complex system pole, or $s_1 = \sigma_1 + j\omega_1$. Let $|s_1 + p_c| = b$ and $|s_1 + z_c| = a$, where a and b are the magnitudes defined in Figure 9.4–1. Hence in (9.4–4),

$$K_c(s_1) = K(s_1)\left(\frac{b}{a}\right) \tag{9.4–5}$$

Given a gain constant $K(s_1)$ when a locus is at s_1, the static error coefficient K_r for the system becomes

$$K_r(s_1) = K(s_1)\frac{\prod_1^m z_i}{\prod_{r+1}^n p_j} \qquad \textbf{(9.4–6)}$$

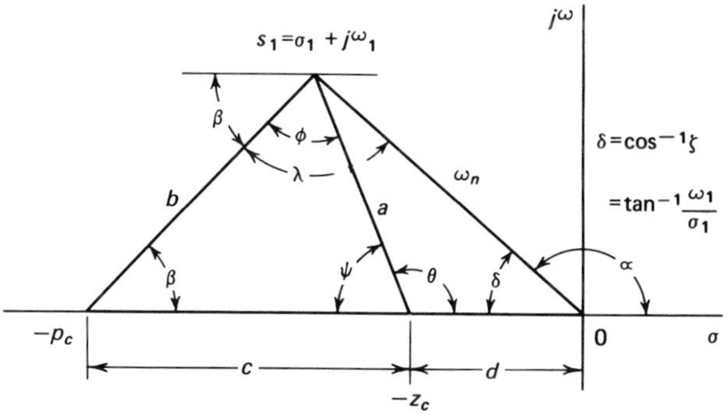

Figure 9.4–1. Defining figure for Ross-Warren method.

Similarly, given a gain constant $K_c(s_1)$ for the compensated system when a locus is at s_1, the static error coefficient $K_{rc}(s_1)$ for the system is

$$K_{rc}(s_1) = K_c(s_1)\frac{\prod_1^m z_i}{\prod_{r+1}^n p_j}\frac{z_c}{p_c}$$

and, from (9.4–5),

$$K_{rc}(s_1) = K(s_1)\frac{\prod_1^m z_i}{\prod_{r+1}^n p_j}\frac{z_c}{p_c}\frac{b}{a} \qquad \textbf{(9.4–7)}$$

If the original system is to have an error coefficient κ, and we are not to alter this, then at the point s_1 of the compensated system

$$K_{rc}(s_1) = \kappa$$

Then, from (9.4–2) and (9.4–7),

$$K\frac{\prod_1^m z_i}{\prod_{r+1}^n p_j} = K(s_1)\frac{\prod_1^m z_i}{\prod_{r+1}^n p_j}\frac{z_c}{p_c}\frac{b}{a}$$

or, finally,

$$K = K(s_1)\frac{b}{a}\frac{z_c}{p_c} \tag{9.4–8}$$

Equation (9.4–8) relates the gain at s_1 of a locus through s_1 with the original gain K, and the locations of the poles and zeros of the compensator such that the static error coefficient remains constant. We desire to shift the uncompensated 180° root locus so that the compensated 180° root locus passes through the point s_1 and at the same time gives the proper static error coefficient. We have two parameters p_c and z_c, so it seems possible that this might be done (a and b are determined once z_c and p_c are chosen for a given s_1).

From Figure 9.4–1,

$$\frac{z_c}{p_c} = \frac{d}{d+c} \tag{9.4–9}$$

and, from (9.4–8),

$$\frac{z_c}{p_c} = \frac{K}{K(s_1)}\frac{a}{b} \tag{9.4–10}$$

Solving for d using the right sides of (9.4–9) and (9.4–10),

$$d = \frac{aK(d+c)}{bK(s_1)} \tag{9.4–11}$$

From Figure 9.4–1,

$$\frac{a}{\omega_n} = \frac{\sin\delta}{\sin\theta}$$

or

$$a = \omega_n\frac{\sin\delta}{\sin\theta}$$

Also

$$\frac{d+c}{b} = \frac{\sin\lambda}{\sin\delta} \tag{9.4–12}$$

Substituting in (9.4–11), then

$$d = \frac{\omega_n \sin\delta}{\sin\theta}\frac{K}{K(s_1)}\frac{\sin\lambda}{\sin\delta}$$

or

$$d = \frac{\omega_n K}{K(s_1)}\frac{\sin\lambda}{\sin\theta} \tag{9.4–13}$$

since

$$d + c = b\frac{\sin\lambda}{\sin\delta}$$

But from Figure 9.4–1,

$$\frac{b}{\omega_n} = \frac{\sin \delta}{\sin \beta}$$

$$d + c = \frac{\omega_n \sin \delta \sin \lambda}{\sin \beta \sin \delta}$$

$$= \frac{\omega_n \sin \lambda}{\sin \beta}$$

or

$$d + c = \frac{\omega_n \sin \lambda}{\sin(\theta - \phi)} \tag{9.4–14}$$

From Figure 9.4–1, d and $d + c$ determine the pole and zero locations for the compensator network; that is, $p_c = d + c$ and $z_c = d$. You may also obtain λ in terms of ϕ as follows:

From (9.4–11),

$$\frac{K}{K(s_1)} \frac{d + c}{b} = \frac{d}{a}$$

Using (9.4–12),

$$\frac{K}{K(s_1)} \frac{\sin \lambda}{\sin \delta} = \frac{d}{a}$$

From Figure 9.4–1,

$$\frac{d}{a} = \frac{\sin(\lambda - \phi)}{\sin \delta}$$

Then

$$\frac{K}{K(s_1)} \sin \lambda = \sin(\lambda - \phi)$$

Solving for λ you get

$$\cot \lambda = \cot \phi - \frac{K}{K(s_1)} \csc \phi \tag{9.4–15}$$

From Figure 9.4–1, θ is the angle contributed by the zero in the compensating network and β is the angle contributed by the pole, which, together with the previous open loop poles $-p_j$ and zeros $-z_i$, form the total angle to place s_1 on a 180° root locus. From the geometry of the figure, $\phi = \theta - \beta$, and thus is the net angular contribution of the pole-zero combination to move the uncompensated root locus so that the compensated locus passes through s_1, or, in the language of the Chu plots, ϕ is the angle necessary to change the compensated locus for an angle of other than 180° going through s_1 to a 180° locus. Thus ϕ is the angle necessary to accomplish our aims. From Figure 9.4–1,

$$\theta = \pi + \phi - \delta - \lambda \tag{9.4–16}$$

Recalling previous design examples, you have seen that frequently one lead section will not provide sufficient lead to result in the required relative stability, or, using the present terminology, sufficient angular charge in the s plane to move the locus to the required point. If one section is insufficient, using the previous equations the locus can be moved part of the way with one section, the remainder with another, and so on. If n lead sections are identical, the previous approach gives (for each section)

$$d = \omega_n \left[\frac{K}{K(s_1)}\right]^{1/n} \frac{\sin \lambda_n}{\sin \theta_n} \tag{9.4–17}$$

$$d + c = \frac{\omega_n \sin \lambda_n}{\sin(\theta_n - \phi_n)} \tag{9.4–18}$$

where

$$\cot \lambda_n = \cot \phi_n - \left[\frac{K}{K(s_1)}\right]^{1/n} \csc \phi_n \tag{9.9–19}$$

$$\theta_n = \pi + \phi_n - \delta - \lambda_n \tag{9.4–20}$$

with

$$\phi_n = \frac{\phi}{n}$$

where ϕ is the angle required to put s_1 on the compensated root locus.

The same equations apply to a lag network or networks, because the relations between z_c and p_c were not specified. In the case of the lag network, ϕ becomes negative in Figure 9.4–1.

Returning to the lead case, you see from Figure 9.4–1 that the ultimate we can achieve with one lead section occurs when $-p_c$ goes to $-\infty$, and under this condition $\phi = \theta$. Obviously if $p_c \leq 10z_c$, we get less than this. Hence if $\theta > \phi$, a single lead section may be adequate, but if $\theta < \phi$, more lead sections are required. The number of *required* identical sections may be obtained from (9.4–10) and (9.4–20) if we chose ϕ_n the amount to be contributed by each section.

Usually the point s_1 for the complex poles is not too critical, because the specifications may be met if s_1 lies in a fairly large region. There may be some merit, then, in attempting to locate s_1 so that the minimum number of lead sections will be necessary (or that the least additional amplifier gain is required). Some preliminary sketching will reveal whether one section, say, will be adequate by using the ideas concerning the auxiliary root loci in Section 9.2.

Example 9.4–1

Take the third-order open loop gain of (9.2–7) with unity negative feedback. Make $K_v = 10$ and design for a peak overshoot ≤ 25 per cent. Then

$$G(s) = \frac{200}{s(s+2)(s+10)}$$

First we sketch the root locus for the uncompensated system as in Figure 9.4–2. When $K = 200$, the system has poles approximately at $s = -11.75$, $s = -0.125 \pm j4.14$.

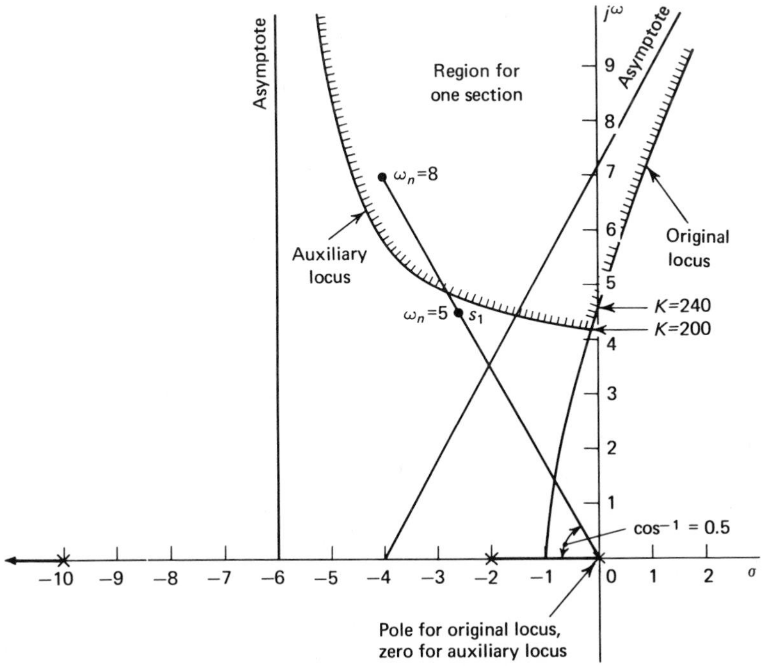

Figure 9.4–2. Root locus plots for Example 9.4–1.

For convenience let us invert (9.2–10) and simplify by assuming maximum pole-zero separation, or $\alpha = \infty$. Using (9.2–10), we obtain

$$\frac{(1/z_k)(200)s}{s^3 + 12s^2 + 20s + 200} = -1 \tag{9.4–21}$$

where all zeros but the one at the origin are at infinity. From the previous root locus, the denominator is about $(s + 11.75)(s^2 + 0.25s + 17.05)$, the complex pole of the auxiliary plot in the second quadrant is at $s \approx -0.125 + j4.14$, and there is an added zero at the origin. The asymptote for this root locus is at $\pm 90°$ and passes through the real axis at $s = -12/2 = -6$. One branch of this locus goes into the left-half plane, and another branch comes in from the pole at $s = -12.5$ along the real axis to the origin, as shown in Figure 9.4–2. The region in which one section compensation may be possible shows in Figure 9.4–2.

For a peak overshoot of 25 per cent, the damping factor ζ for only one pair of complex poles would be about 0.40. However, as we introduce a system zero with the lead compensator, more overshoot results; to be conservative, assume $\zeta \simeq 0.50$. Drawing in this ζ line in Figure 9.4–2, you see that for $\omega_n \approx 8$ the point s_1 lies in the one section region. However, if you recall that the auxiliary sketch is for infinite compensator pole-zero separation, a point anywhere on the $\zeta = 0.50$ line seems to have little margin, and it seems dubious that one section will be enough. If we go to two sections, we might reduce ω_n somewhat to keep the bandwidth down. A specification on rise time or bandwidth would place ω_n in a limited region. For the purposes of this example, let us take $\omega_n = 5$. Then the angles from the uncompensated open loop poles to the point $s_1 = -2.5 + j4.34$ are 120°, 96.5°, and 30°, or a total of 246.5°, and the distances are 5, 4.37, and 8.68. Thus the compensating networks must provide an angle $\phi \approx 66.5°$, and $K(s_1) = 5(4.37)(8.68) = 189$. From (9.4–19) for $n = 2$,

$$\cot \lambda_2 = \cot 33.25° - \left(\frac{200}{189}\right)^{1/2} \csc 33.25°$$

or

$$\lambda_2 = 109°$$

From (9.4–20),

$$\theta_2 = 180° + 33.25° - 60° - 109° \approx 44°$$

Since $\theta_2 > \phi_2$, two lead sections are adequate. From (9.4–17),

$$d = 5(1.03)\frac{\sin 109.5°}{\sin 44°} \approx 6.77$$

and, from (9.4–18),

$$d + c = \frac{5 \sin 109.5°}{\sin(44° - 33.25°)} \approx 24.8$$

Thus we obtain two networks, each with the transfer function

$$(3.67)\,\frac{s + 6.77}{s + 24.8}$$

where the gain of 3.67 for each (total 13.4) must be provided by an amplifier. The complete compensated open loop function is then

$$G = \frac{13.4(200)(s + 6.77)^2}{s(s + 2)(s + 10)(s + 24.8)^2}$$

The fundamental difficulty with the Ross-Warren method, as with all methods for picking one pair of complex "dominant" poles, is that although the complex poles are achieved, there is no control or even knowledge of the movement of the other poles until the compensator is fixed. In this example, by plotting a new root locus for the compensated function, the other poles turn out to be at about $s \approx -33.7$ and $s \approx -11.4 \pm j4.3$ (Figure 9.4–3 is a rough sketch). There is therefore an

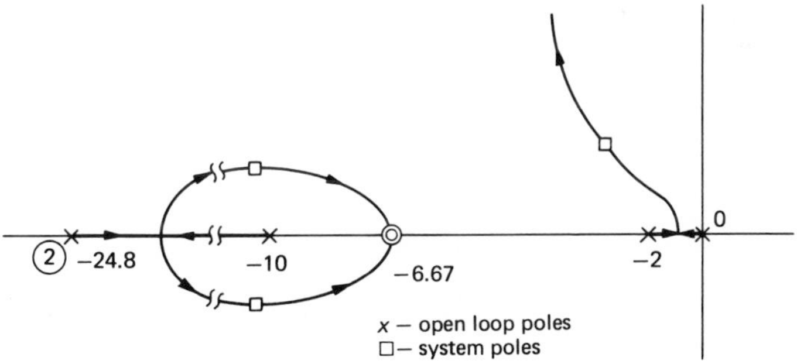

Figure 9.4–3. Root locus for Example 9.4–1.

additional pair of complex poles as well as the "dominant" complex poles, which have an imaginary part almost the same as that of the "dominant" poles at $-2.5 \pm j4.34$. Owing to the large real component, the oscillation due to the far poles will die out rapidly. There is also a double zero in the system. If the overall response is unsatisfactory, you must make another try. As previously discussed, this is a basic difficulty with most conventional analysis.

9.5 Internal Feedback Compensation

In Figure 9.5–1 assume that first we have a system (a) without the internal feedback *H*.

Let the fixed portion be $G_2 = P_2/Q_2$ and the compensator $G_c = P_c/Q_c$, where the P's and Q's are polynomials in s. Then the forward loop gain is

$$G_c G_2 = \frac{P_c P_2}{Q_c Q_2} \tag{9.5–1}$$

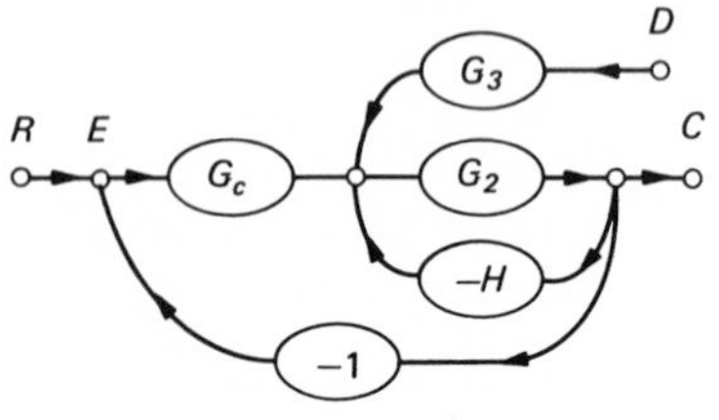

Figure 9.5–1. Internal feedback.

Now assume a system (b) with internal feedback $H = U/V$, and with altered tandem compensation $G_c' = P_c'/Q_c'$. The forward gain for (b) then becomes

$$G_c' \frac{G_2}{1 + G_2 H} = \frac{P_c'}{Q_c'} \frac{P_2 V}{P_2 U + Q_2 V} \tag{9.5–2}$$

If we wish to have C/R the same for both systems (a) and (b), with unity feedback, then

$$G_c G_2 = \frac{G_c' G_2}{1 + G_2 H} \tag{9.5–3}$$

Hence

$$\frac{P_c P_2}{Q_c Q_2} = \frac{P_c' P_2 V}{Q_c'(P_2 U + Q_2 V)}$$

or

$$P_c = P_c' V \tag{9.5–4a}$$

$$Q_c Q_2 = Q_c'(P_2 U + Q_2 V) \tag{9.5–4b}$$

Thus it is theoretically possible to put all the compensation in tandem, or part in tandem and part in internal feedback, and achieve the same control ratio.

Now look at the transfer function for C/D, where D is a disturbance. From Figure 9.5–1, using Mason's rule, for system (b),

$$\frac{C}{D} = \frac{G_3 G_2}{1 + G_2 H + G_2 G_c'}$$

However, since

$$\frac{C}{R} = \frac{G_c' G_2}{1 + G_2 H + G_2 G_c'}$$

$$\frac{C}{D} = \frac{G_3}{G_c'} \frac{C}{R} \tag{9.5–4c}$$

Equations (9.5–4) tell us that for the same control ratio (C/R) for both systems, we can greatly reduce the effect of the disturbance in system (b) compared to system (a) by making $G_c' = P_c'/Q_c'$ large. Equation (9.5–3) also indicates that if G_c becomes large, $G_2 H$ must simultaneously grow large. By manipulating G_c' and H, then, we may achieve a constant input-output ratio but improve the disturbance response, a feat that we could not accomplish using tandem compensation only. Also, although G_2 in Figure 9.5–1 is fixed, it might be possible in some cases to separate it and return an internal feedback to a point between two portions of G_2.

In addition to the reduction of disturbance output, there may be practical advantages to internal feedback. For example, in an angular position control system, a simple permanent-pole d-c generator (tachometer) can be geared to the output shaft and return to the amplifier a signal proportional to the velocity. Thus in this or similar systems, a feedback signal of the form Ks is easily obtainable. Such a derivative transfer function may be particularly helpful in a carrier-type system, where tandem compensation either requires special networks to operate on the carrier envelope, or demodulation, ordinary compensation, and remodulation. In such a system, a carrier-type signal proportional to velocity is easily generated with a two-phase machine excited by the carrier on one phase and such a signal returned to the carrier amplifier.

We have already studied tachometer feedback in Chapter 2 in connection with a second-order system. There it was clear that the feedback signal Ks altered the damping factor of the second-order system. For systems of high order, such a feedback may not be so effective. In Figure 9.5–1, if $G_2(s) = P(s)/Q(s)$, and if $H = K_1 s$, then the internal loop transfer function $G_T(s)$ is

$$G_T(s) = \frac{P(s)}{P(s)K_1 s + Q(s)} \tag{9.5–5}$$

If $P(s)$ is a constant K, or a simple factor $K(s + z_1)$, you see from (9.5–5) that the first denominator term effects only one or two terms of low degree in the characteristic equation. If $P(s)$ is of high degree, this may be harmful, not beneficial. Unfortunately, also, the fact that $Q(s)$ is of high degree may not be suspected.

Frequency analysis is fairly straightforward. As already discussed in Chapter 8, you can make a rough approximation of the loop magnitude by drawing $|1/H|$ and $|G|$ on the same log ω plot. Thus, if in Figure 9.5–1, $G_2 = K/s(s + p_1)$, we see that if a feedback H is made $K_1 s$, then the new break point is moved farther out to ω_1, as shown in Figure 9.5–2. By algebraic manipulation, the inner loop function G_T is

$$G_T = \frac{G_2}{1 + G_2 H} = \frac{K}{s(s + p_1 + KK_1)} \tag{9.5–6}$$

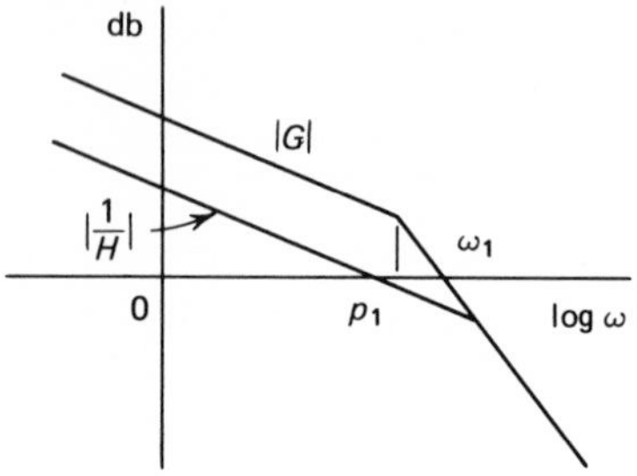

Figure 9.5–2. Tachometer-type internal feedback frequency characteristics.

The new break point is $\omega_1 = p_1 + KK_1$, compared to the old break point of p_1, or the time constant has been altered from $1/p_1$ to $1/\omega_1$. If the same K is used, the velocity constant K_v is reduced, as also shown in Figure 9.5–2. The total loop gain may be increased by G_c and, if the old K_v is desired,

$$G_c = \frac{p_1 + KK_1}{p_1}$$

Then the characteristic equation becomes

$$s^2 + (p_1 + KK_1)s + K\frac{p_1 + KK_1}{p_1} = 0 \tag{9.5–7}$$

whereas the old characteristic equation was

$$s^2 + p_1 s + K = 0 \tag{9.5–8}$$

In (9.5–8) $\zeta_1 = p_1/2\sqrt{K}$, while in (9.5–7),

$$\zeta_2 = \frac{p_1 + KK_1}{2\sqrt{K(p_1 + KK_1)/p_1}}$$

or

$$\frac{\zeta_2}{\zeta_1} = \left(\frac{p_1 + KK_1}{p_1}\right)^{1/2} \tag{9.5–9}$$

$$\frac{\omega_{n2}}{\omega_{n1}} = \left(\frac{p_1 + KK_1}{p_1}\right)^{1/2} \tag{9.5–10}$$

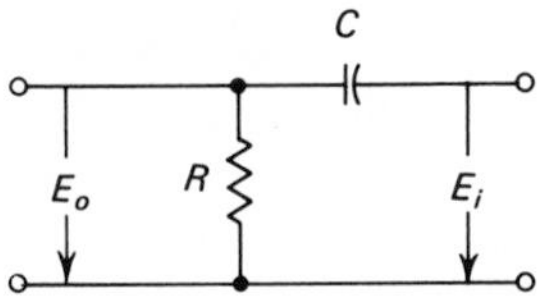

Figure 9.5–3. High-pass filter for internal feedback.

In higher-order systems we can do better with a velocity term plus a high-pass filter. Figure 9.5–3 shows one section of a simple filter that has the transfer function

$$\frac{E_0}{E_i} = \frac{s}{s + p_f} \tag{9.5–11}$$

where $p_f = 1/RC$. The filter in series with a tachometer gives the transfer function

$$H = \frac{K_1 s^2}{s + p_f} \tag{9.5–12}$$

while two filters similarly results in

$$H = \frac{K_1 s^3}{(s + p_{f1})(s + p_{f2})} \tag{9.5–13}$$

If you take a typical magnitude curve $|G|$ in Figure 9.5–4, superimpose $|1/H|$ of (9.5–12), and follow the heavy lines as shown in Figure 9.5–4 (see Chapter 8), you see that now we are achieving the proper slope at the cross-over point without effecting the low-frequency portion of $|G|$, or the static error coefficient. Similarly, for a type 2 system, you can use the characteristic of (9.5–13) effectively. By manipulating K_1 (a decrease in K_1 moves $|1/H|$ up in Figure 9.5–4) and p_f, the desired overall characteristic may be obtained. The entire heavy-line curve may then be raised by the addition of

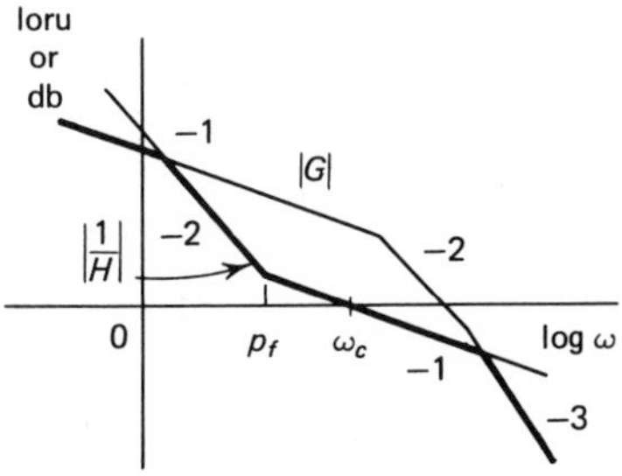

Figure 9.5–4. Typical system with *G* forward path and −*H* feedback.

frequency-independent gain in G_c (Figure 9.5–1) if required, which will of course increase K_v and ω_c. In algebraic terms, (9.5–12) and (9.5–13) put the feedback coefficient in a higher-degree term of the characteristic equation than does the velocity feedback alone.

Another philosophy is to design for C/R obtaining the compensation required as though it were all in tandem, and then portion some of this to H such that response with disturbance specifications are met, while keeping the remaining tandem compensation simple [3]. To be effective, the feedback transfer function H usually must be obtained by means of a transfer function of the type of (9.5–12) or (9.5–13).

With design using root locus we may also use the idea of the auxiliary root locus to see where the feedback may put the system poles. An example will bring out the points here.

Example 9.5–1

Given

$$G_2 = \frac{K}{s(s+2)(s+10)}$$

in Figure 9.5–1, examine possible internal feedback functions H and determine their effect.

The characteristic equation for $G_2/(1 + G_2 H)$ with $H = 1$ is

$$s^3 + 12s^2 + 20s + K = 0$$

and the root locus has already been plotted in Figure 9.4–2. If we make $H = K_1 s$, the characteristic equation becomes

$$s^3 + 12s^2 + (20 + KK_1)s + K = 0 \qquad \textbf{(9.5–14)}$$

If $K_v = 10$, $K = 200$, then you have in (9.5–14)

$$s^3 + 12s^2 + (20 + K_2)s + 200 = 0 \qquad \textbf{(9.5–15)}$$

where $K_2 = 200K_1$. In (9.5–15),

$$s^3 + 12s^2 + 20s + 200 = -K_2 s$$

or

$$\frac{K_2 s}{s^3 + 12s^2 + 20s + 200} = -1 \qquad \textbf{(9.5–16)}$$

The poles of (9.5–16) have already been determined from the root locus plot of the uncompensated system. The auxiliary root locus with K_2 as a parameter is the same as the auxiliary locus with K/z_k as a parameter in Figure 9.4–2. The two complex poles move into the left-half plane as K_2 increases, while a real pole moves in toward the origin. All these are stabilizing effects. If $K_2 \approx 69.3$, for example, we have complex system poles at $s = -3 + 4.91$ and a real pole at -6. This analysis assumes $G_c = 1$ in Figure 9.5–1. If $G_c = K_3$, then K in (9.5–14) becomes KK_3, and we redraw the auxiliary locus at a higher level in Figure 9.4–2, starting from new open loop poles.

If $H = K_1 s^2/(s + p_1)$, then the characteristic equation ($G_c = 1$) is

$$s^4 + (12 + p_1)s^3 + (20 + 12p_1 + KK_1)s^2 + (20p_1 + K)s + Kp_1 = 0$$

which is considerably more complicated. As one of the weaknesses of the locus attack is the inability to deal with more than one parameter at a time, we must fix either p_1 or K_1 for our auxiliary locus. If p_1 is fixed, we get

$$\frac{KK_1 s^2}{s^4 + (12 + p_1)s^3 + (20 + 12p_1)s^2 + (20p_1 K)s + Kp_1} = -1 \qquad \textbf{(9.5–17)}$$

for the auxiliary locus plot. Three roots of the denominator of (9.5–17) may be obtained from the root locus plot for

$$\frac{K}{s(s + 2)(s + 10)} = -1$$

while the fourth root is at $s = -p$. For the auxiliary root locus you now have a double zero at the origin and an increase of one in the open loop poles, three of which are at the same position as in the uncompensated system for a given K, and the other at the pole of the feedback network.

Note that the system has an added zero at $s = -p_1$, and poles as determined by the root locus plot using (9.5–17) for a particular K_1. Alternatively, we could fix K_1 and alter p_1.

For this system, the added complexity of the latter feedback network seems unwarranted.

9.6 Nonelectrical Compensators

As indicated previously, corrective transfer functions are not necessarily electrical networks. It is often possible to achieve the same functions with fluid or mechanical components. As an example, a pneumatic lead compensator is shown in Figure 9.6–1. For a very rapid increase in signal pressure input (high-frequency region), the diaphragm a and the rod b are pushed to the left, closing the flapper valve c, hence allowing greater output pressure to appear at f. Simultaneously the diaphragm d is pushed left, compressing the air in the left chamber, which results in increased air pressure in chamber *e*. The bellows in *e* is pushed up, thus increasing or amplifying the output pressure at *f*. For a rapid reduction in input pressure we get a reverse operation. The restriction *g* and the bellows in *e* work together such that for less rapid changes in the input signal pressure, an

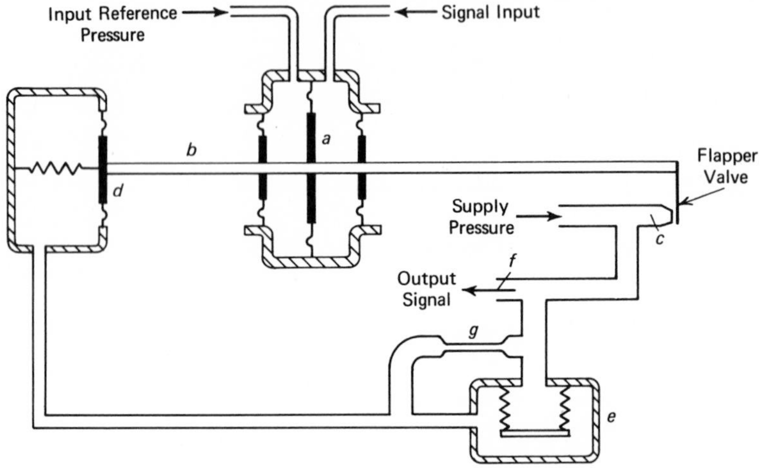

Figure 9.6–1. Pneumatic lead compensator.

equalization occurs in the chamber *e* and the output pressure is less amplified. By properly adjusting the springs, bellows, flapper valve opening, and restriction, a lead characteristic similar to that of the electrical network results. It is possible to adjust the pole and zero of the device somewhat by a change of the flapper valve, the restriction, or spring tension. Other characteristics may be obtained with pneumatic devices. Mechanical spring-mass combinations have also been made that have the advantage of much less loss (higher Q) than the corresponding network. The usual difficulty with such devices is that design is a matter of cut and try and experience, whereas you can design electrical networks in a straightforward scientific manner using a large body of information on network synthesis.

In Chapter 3 we illustrated the use of a nonelectrical compensator by a mechanical device that is applicable to a rotating shaft. This consists of two inertias, one inside the other, coupled by a viscous fluid filling the hollow space of the larger inertia. The inside inertia rotates independently of the outside inertia, being coupled to it only by the viscous fluid. The shaft is connected to the driving motor either directly, or through gears, often at the system output. As seen in Chapter 3, the design adds a system zero at the expense of a quadratic factor in the denominator, which could have real or complex roots. If the roots are real, then by proper proportioning of the constants we can obtain a lead characteristic. Other characteristics may be obtained by specifying the constants, but once installed the device is not easily altered.

9.7 Carrier System Compensation

Figure 9.7–1 shows a possible all-carrier type of system in schematic form. The two-phase motor has one phase excited by the corrected and

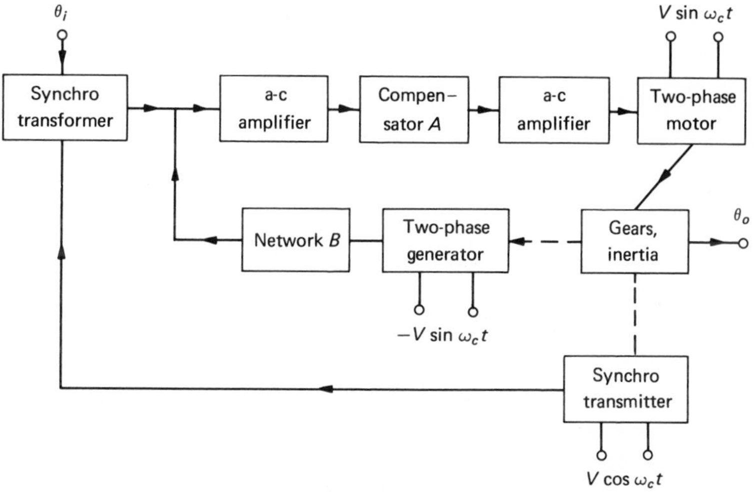

Figure 9.7–1. All-carrier-type control system.

amplified error signal and the other by a voltage $v \sin \omega_c t$, which is 90° out of phase with the carrier. Because each phase of the motor windings is placed 90 electrical space degrees apart, and the exciting voltages have a 90° electrical phase difference, the motor has a starting torque and, moreover, a direction sense; that is, it reverses when the phase of one exciting voltage changes by 180°. Because two-phase power normally is not available, the exciting voltage $v \sin \omega_c t$ is obtained from the carrier voltage $v \cos \omega_c t$ by inserting a capacitance between the motor and the carrier source. As a consequence, a full 90° shift is not obtained, so that only an approximation of two-phase operation results [4]. The two-phase generator operates on the same principle as the two-phase motor, except that the input is mechanical and the output electrical. The two synchros constitute the error-detection system and are connected by a three-wire cable. The synchrotransformer produces a carrier voltage whose amplitude is proportional to the angular difference $(\theta_i - \theta_0)$ or to the error. Hence if the error is

$e \cos \omega t$, the carrier becomes cosine-modulated and the output is of the form $e \cos \omega t \cos \omega_c t$, which is of a suppressed carrier form, as pointed out in Chapter 1. For good operation, $\omega_c > 3\omega_m$, where ω_m is the maximum error signal angular velocity and ω_c is the carrier angular velocity.

The a-c amplifiers are ordinary *RC*-coupled without special requirements—one of the reasons for the popularity of the carrier system. The synchro-error-detecting system permits continuous rotation of the output. (In translational motion an *E* type of transformer produces the same type of output.) The two-phase motor is more nonlinear and its performance is not as good as that of the d-c, hydraulic, or pneumatic motor, but it is light and inexpensive.

An actual system may have only some of the carrier-type devices shown, or the system may be a mixed carrier-conventional type. The two-phase generator has an equivalent transfer function Ks, which we have already discussed in Section 9.5. Load-type compensation as discussed in Section 9.6 or similar compensation independent of the carrier may also be used. The carrier network compensators are, however, a different matter, which we now discuss.

First, the networks *A* or *B* of Figure 9.7–1 may consist of a demodulator, corrective tandem, or feedback network, as already discussed, and remodulator. In this case we have nothing new except high-frequency noise resulting from the demodulation-remodulation process. This noise should be kept low to prevent saturation of succeeding elements, but most of it will be eliminated from the output due to the low-pass characteristics of the system. Now turn your attention to carrier-type networks, which are another affair. We desire to operate on the modulated carrier such that the envelope (error signal) is altered in the required manner. It is not possible to do this as simply as operating on the error signal itself, and we can only approximate the desired results.

We depict the problem in Figure 9.7–2, where in the left transfer function we have the usual input voltage $e(t)$, but in the right we have the modulated

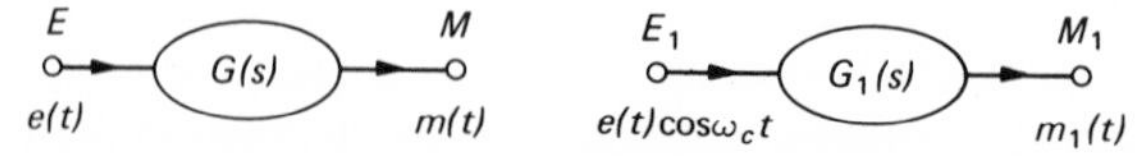

Figure 9.7–2. Transfer functions for carrier and noncarrier systems.

voltage $e(t) \cos \omega_c t$, where ω_c is the carrier angular velocity. Then we desire the equation

$$m_1(t) = m(t) \cos \omega_c t \tag{9.7–1}$$

where $m(t)$ is the output of the usual compensating network previously discussed.

Since $\cos \omega_c t = \frac{1}{2}(\epsilon^{j\omega_c t} + \epsilon^{-j\omega_c t})$, then

$$E_1(s) = \tfrac{1}{2}[E(s + j\omega_c) + E(s - j\omega_c)] \tag{9.7–2}$$

where

$$E(s) = \mathcal{L}e(t)$$

Similarly,

$$M_1(s) = \tfrac{1}{2}[M(s + \omega_c) + M(s - j\omega_c)] \tag{9.7–3}$$

where

$$\begin{aligned} M(s) &= \mathcal{L}m(t) \\ &= G(s)E(s) \end{aligned}$$

Substituting the last equation back into (9.7–3), and using (9.7–2),

$$\frac{M_1(s)}{E_1(s)} = G_1(s) = \frac{G(s - j\omega_c)E(s - j\omega_c) + G(s + j\omega_c)E(s + j\omega_c)}{E(s - j\omega_c) + E(s + j\omega_c)} \tag{9.7–4}$$

Let $s = j\omega$ and $|\omega_m| \ll |\omega_c|$, where ω_m is the maximum angular velocity for the signal input voltage $e(t)$. Then $E[j(\omega - \omega_c)] = 0$, $\omega < 0$, and $E[j(\omega + \omega_c)] = 0$, $\omega > 0$, and we get from (9.7–4)

$$\begin{aligned} G_1(j\omega) &= G[j(\omega - \omega_c)] \qquad \omega > 0 \\ &= G[j(\omega + \omega_c)] \qquad \omega < 0 \end{aligned} \tag{9.7–5}$$

Equations (9.7–5) tell us that $G_1(j\omega)$ should have the same form as $G(j\omega)$, except that the origin of the characteristic is at ω_c rather than zero, and also it is of the band-pass type, or it is an even function about ω_c. Thus a $G(j\omega)$ with lead characteristics should appear as in Figure 9.7–3 (only positive ω shown).

There are two methods presently used to obtain an approximation to (9.7–5). The first is through a frequency transformation, and the second

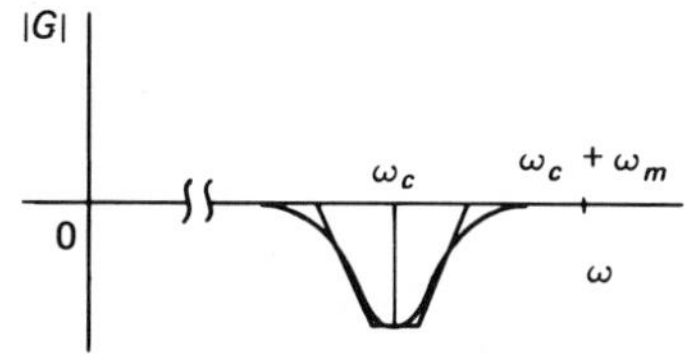

Figure 9.7–3. Lead characteristic for carrier system.

through the use of bridged-T or twin-T filters. We take up the second method first. As we desire to avoid inductances, let us investigate circuits of the type of Figure 9.7–4. If we let

$$\omega_c = \frac{1}{R_1 C_1 R_2 C_2} \tag{9.7–6}$$

the circuit is "resonant" at ω_c (has the largest attenuation at ω_c), as in Figure 9.7–3. Then in Figure (9.7–4),

$$\frac{E_2(jv)}{E_1(jv)} = \frac{1 - v^2 + jvrn}{1 - v^2 + jvn} \tag{9.7–7}$$

where

$$v = \frac{\omega}{\omega_c} \qquad r = \frac{R_1(C_1 + C_2)}{R_1(C_1 + C_2) + C_2 R_2} \qquad n = \frac{R_1(C_1 + C_2) + R_2 C_2}{R_1 C_1 R_2 C_2}$$

$$\omega_c = \frac{1}{R_1 C_1 R_2 C_2}$$

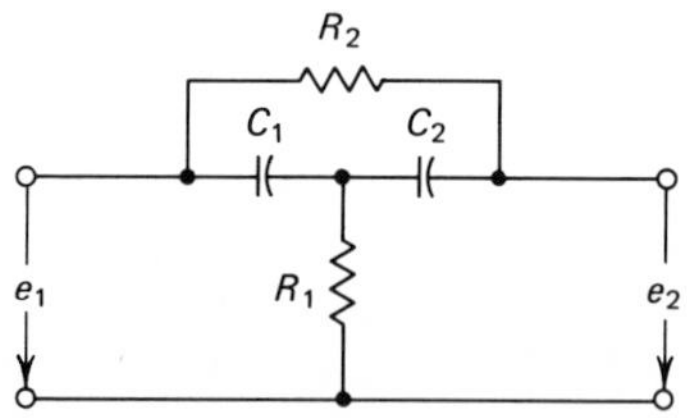

Figure 9.7–4. Bridged-T compensator.

If you plot the magnitude and phase for (9.7–7) for $\omega \geq \omega_c$, it will appear similar to that of the lead network for $\omega \geq 0$ in that case. The loss when $\omega = \omega_c$ from (9.7–7) is $[R_1(C_1 + C_2) + C_2 R_2]/R_1(C_1 + C_2)$. Unfortunately the characteristics cannot be made to coincide, the relationships of the magnitude curves being somewhat as in Figure 9.7–5 for the same maximum loss.

Parallel or twin-T networks as shown in Figure 9.7–6 may also be made to give carrier characteristics approaching that of the lead network at the expense of more elements. An extensive discussion of the design of both bridged and twin-T networks, including curves, is given in Savant [5]. The T networks will serve for tandem compensation of the lead type (network A, Figure 9.7–1), but not for the high-pass type of network B. Here a more general type of network design is required, and this may be accomplished by a frequency transformation where $j\omega$ is replaced by $p(j\omega)$. One practical transformation is given by [6]

$$p(j\omega) = \frac{j\omega}{2}\left(1 - \frac{\omega_c^2}{\omega^2}\right) \qquad \textbf{(9.7–8)}$$

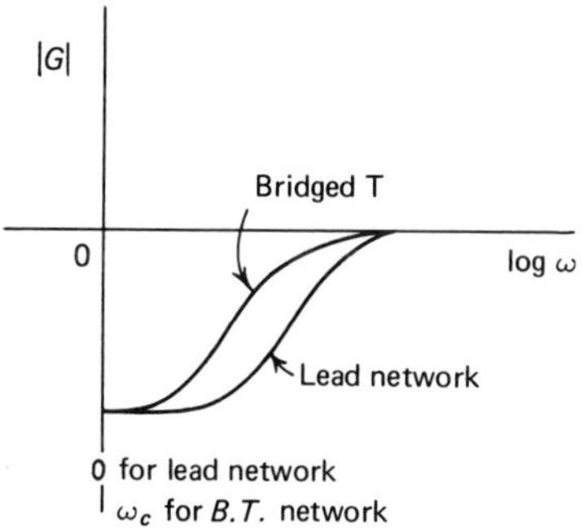

Figure 9.7–5. Comparison between lead and bridged compensators.

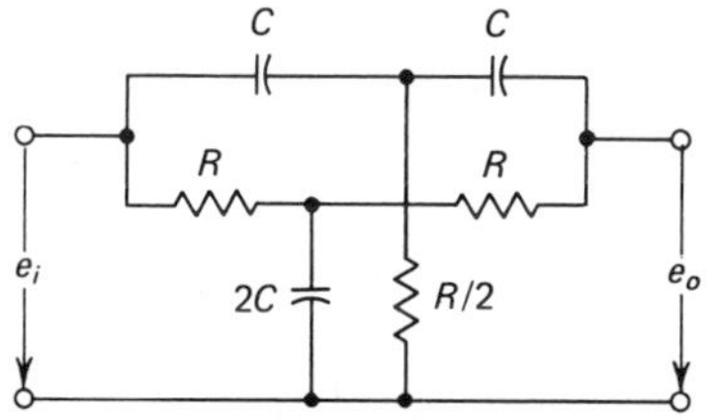

Figure 9.7–6. Twin-T-network compensator.

In using (9.7–8), the usual compensating network is designed. Then to achieve the transformation you

1. Divide each L by 2 to obtain an L'.
2. Add in series with each L' a capacitance C to resonate at ω_c; that is, $1/L'C = \omega_c^2$.
3. Divide each C by 2 to obtain C'.
4. Add in parallel with each C' an inductance to resonate at ω_c; that is, $1/LC' = \omega_c^2$.

Thus the lead network transformation appears in Figure 9.7–7a and the high-pass network transformation appears in Figure 9.7–7b. In all cases the compensation is again approximate.

The basic difficulty of carrier-type network compensation, outside of the approximate nature of the compensation, consists in the possibility that the carrier angular velocity ω_c does not remain constant. If ω_c changes, the network characteristics are no longer symmetric about ω_c, and we have little resemblance to correct compensation. A very small change may be drastic. For example, if $\omega_c = 377$ ($f = 60$ Hz), a change of only 2 per cent results in a change with respect to the band pass characteristic of over 10 per cent, because the bandwidth of the control system is probably not

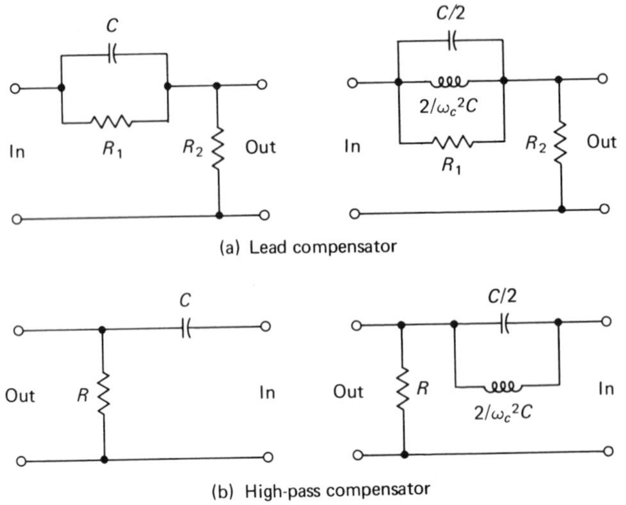

Figure 9.7–7. Compensating networks with frequency transformation.

over 30 radians per second. From Figure 9.7–3, if the midfrequency line moves this much relative to the characteristic, it is clear that the compensation scheme is virtually nullified. Hence to ensure proper compensation, particularly on space vehicles, the designer may be forced to provide a system to regulate the power-supply frequency. At this point the demodulation-remodulation idea may appear to be more practical. Recent work on the use of active elements to provide carrier compensation may result in another solution to this problem [7].

9.8 Transport Lag and Distributed Parameters

One of the more discouraging phenomena encountered in control systems is transport lag, or "dead time." Transport lag is a fixed time delay. One example is shown in Figure 9.8–1, where two rollers R_1 and R_2 actuated by a control system reduce a strip of steel S to a uniform thickness. To measure this thickness, we install an X-ray tube at X and a detector at D. The signal generated by D may then be used to activate the rolls. Because of the physical-system dimensions, it is not possible to locate the detector system on the roller axis but at some distance d in the direction of the steel motion. If the velocity of the steel is v, then the time t_e taken for the steel to go from the rollers to the detection system is $t_e = d/v$. The time delay t_e is thus fixed, and the measurements occur this much later than the action of the rollers on the steel, and we cannot correct for changes of thickness until the steel arrives at the detector system. Other examples would consist of the time taken for fluid to flow in a pipe from one point to another (as in a shower bath), the time for a relay to operate, and so on.

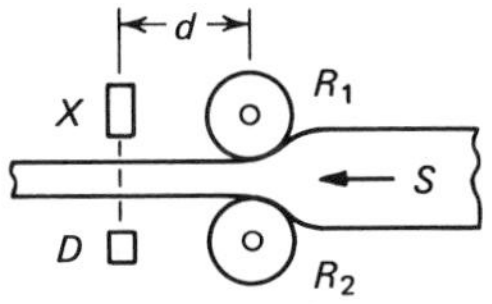

Figure 9.8–1. Rolling mill with transport lag.

If a function $f(t)$ is delayed by a time α, then the delayed function is $f(t - \alpha)$. Also, if

$$\mathscr{L} f(t)u(t) = F(s)$$

then

$$\mathscr{L} f(t - \alpha)u(t - \alpha) = F(s)\epsilon^{-\alpha s}$$

Thus if we have a linear system with an open loop transfer function $G(s)$ and add transport lag with a time delay, the new open loop transfer function is

$$G(s)G_l(s) = G(s)\epsilon^{-\alpha s}$$

Examining $\epsilon^{-\alpha s}$ through sinusoidal analysis, we let $s = j\omega$ as usual, and the second term then becomes

$$\begin{aligned} G_l(j\omega) &= \epsilon^{-j\omega\alpha} \\ &= |1|\epsilon^{-j\theta} \end{aligned} \qquad \textbf{(9.8–1)}$$

where $\theta = \omega\alpha$.

Thus the transport lag term has a magnitude of 1 and a lag phase angle of $\omega\alpha$. Consequently, if we plot $G(j\omega)$ in magnitude and phase as usual, and then add the lagging angle $\alpha\omega$ to the phase curve, we have a sinusoidal analysis picture of the system with transport lag, as shown in Figure 9.8–2. The added phase lag constantly increases as ω increases. The system therefore may be very difficult to stabilize.

Transport lag may also be analyzed with the root locus using the idea of the Chu plots. If $s = \sigma + j\omega$, $\epsilon^{-\alpha s} = \epsilon^{-\sigma\alpha}\epsilon^{-j\alpha\omega}$, then in the s plane

$$|G_t(s)| = \epsilon^{-\sigma\alpha} \tag{9.8–2a}$$

$$\arg G_t(s) = -\alpha\omega \tag{9.8–2b}$$

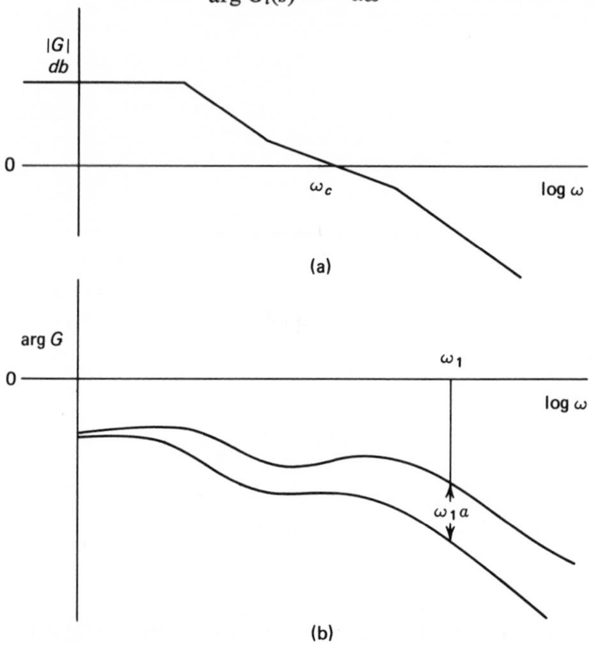

Figure 9.8–2. Sinusoidal analysis of transport lag.

Equation (9.8–2b) shows a phase angle directly proportional to ω. Hence if we plot straight lines parallel to the σ axis as in Figure 9.8–3, each line represents a constant phase of $\alpha\omega_n$ where ω_n, is the intersection on the ω axis.

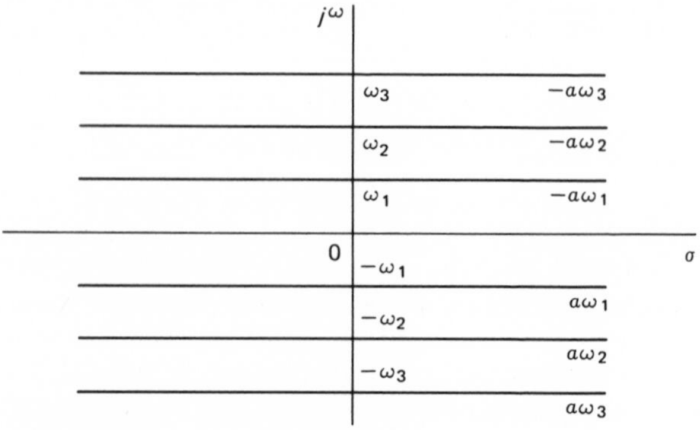

Figure 9.8–3. Lines of constant phase angle in the s plane.

To make the root locus plot, then, we must find points in the s plane where the total angle adds to 180°. For negative unity feedback,

$$\arg G(s) + \arg G_l(s) = -180°(2k+1) \qquad k = \text{integer}$$

or, in the upper-half plane,

$$\arg G(s) = 180°(2k+1) + \alpha\omega \tag{9.8–3}$$

A point s_1 may be selected on a horizontal line for $\arg G_l(s) = -\alpha\omega_1$, and moved along this line until (9.8–3) is satisfied. Alternatively, a Chu plot of $G(s)$ such as in Figure 7.6–4 for $G = K/s(s+p)$ may be superimposed on Figure 9.8–3, and points where the angles sum to the proper amount found. Needless to say, you encounter tedious work. From (9.8–3), because $\arg G(s)$ usually is negative, the root locus moves farther toward the right-half plane with transport lag. To evaluate the gain K, since

$$|G(s)||G_l(s)| = 1$$

$$|KG'(s)| = e^{\sigma\alpha} \tag{9.8–4}$$

where $KG'(s) = G(s)$ and $s = \sigma + j\omega$. Thus K depends not only on the poles and zeros of $G(s)$ but on the distance to the right or left of the $j\omega$ axis.

Example 9.8–1

In Figure 9.8–4 we have plotted the root locus of the function

$$G(s) = \frac{K}{s(s+2)}$$

for unity negative feedback, and also for an added transport lag time α with $\alpha = 0.25$, 0.5, and 1.0. Since $\epsilon^{-\alpha s}$ is multivalued, using (9.8–3) we shall get additional branches of the locus (actually an infinite number), one of which is shown in Figure 9.8–4 for $\alpha = 1.0$.

It is clear from Figure 9.8–4 that the system becomes unstable at low gain with transport lag, as the complex poles move rapidly into the right-half plane, whereas the system without transport lag was never unstable. Also, we obtain system poles producing large angular velocities, or very high frequency oscillations. If the gain is not too high, these oscillations disappear rapidly as the damping is high. Also, the low-pass nature of the system may make these inconsequential.

Lead compensation may improve the lag-angle problem of Figure 9.8–2, but unfortunately a lead network will increase the bandwidth, thus allowing more of the high-frequency oscillations to pass. A lag compensation, lowering the crossover point ω_c and reducing the bandwidth, may be helpful in some cases.

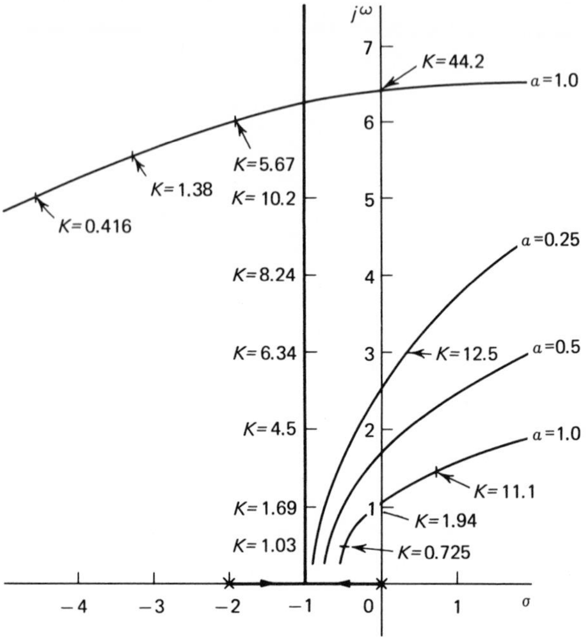

Figure 9.8–4. System for $G = K/s(s+2)$ with transport lags.

In distributed parameter systems such as highly capacitive transmission lines, we have a delay proportional to $\exp(-j\sqrt{\omega T})$, where T is a function of the line length and the per unit capacitance-resistance product. If you expand the exponential in a series,

$$\epsilon^{-\alpha s} = 1 - \alpha s + \frac{(\alpha s)^2}{2} \cdots$$

you see that both transport lag and distributed parameters have some aspects of a nonminimum phase system.

In compensating such systems, the designer may first see if there is any possibility of eliminating a transport lag or at least reducing it. Thus a redesign of some component (such as the measuring system of Figure 9.8–1) may help, or an alternative scheme may be preferable. If the situation is not too bad, then introducing simple compensation may help. In extreme cases, one compensation may consist of an internal feedback loop that gives an output essentially like the input but displaced in time by the amount of the lag. Other methods have been suggested [8].

9.9 Direct Synthesis

One method of direct synthesis, first introduced by E. A. Guillemin, derives from the expression for the system function in terms of the open loop transfer function [9]. Thus

$$\frac{C(s)}{R(s)} = \frac{G(s)}{1 + G(s)} \quad \textbf{(9.9–1)}$$

or

$$\frac{P(s)}{D(s)} = \frac{P(s)}{P(s) + Q(s)} \quad \textbf{(9.9–2)}$$

where

$$G(s) = \frac{P(s)}{Q(s)} \qquad \frac{C}{R}(s) = \frac{P(s)}{D(s)}$$

From (9.9–2),

$$Q(s) = D(s) - P(s) \quad \textbf{(9.9–3)}$$

The philosophy of design consists in first selecting a $P(s)/D(s)$ that will meet the specifications satisfactorily. Then $Q(s)$, the denominator of the open loop function, is found from (9.9–3). As s is a complex quantity, (9.9–3) would be difficult to solve, in general. However, if it is also specified that $Q(s)$ is to have real roots only, or that poles of $G(s)$ are to lie only on the negative real axis, then since the left side of (9.9–3) must have real roots, so must the right side. Hence real roots σ_i of $Q(s)$ occur when

$$D(\sigma) = P(\sigma) \quad \textbf{(9.9–4)}$$

where $s = \sigma$, a real variable. Hence if we plot $D(\sigma)$ and $P(\sigma)$ and find the intersections of these curves, $Q(s)$ is known.

The most important step in the process consists of finding a $P(s)/D(s)$ that meets all specifications. To keep the amount of work to a minimum, a suggested configuration for $P(s)/D(s)$ could consist of two complex poles, one real zero and one real pole, as in Figure 9.9–1. (Guillemin's original method considers two real poles.) Thus the proposed system function would be of the form

$$\frac{C(s)}{R(s)} = \frac{K(s + z_1)}{(s^2 + 2\zeta\omega_n s + \omega_n^2)(s + P_1)} \quad \textbf{(9.9–5)}$$

If we consider a type 1 system

$$Q(s) = s(s + p_1)(s + p_2) \qquad \textbf{(9.9–6)}$$

and apply (9.9–3) with $s = \sigma$ we get

$$(\sigma^2 + 2\zeta\omega_n\sigma + \omega_n^2)(\sigma + P_1) - K(\sigma + z_1) = \sigma(\sigma + p_1)(\sigma + p_2) \qquad \textbf{(9.9–7)}$$

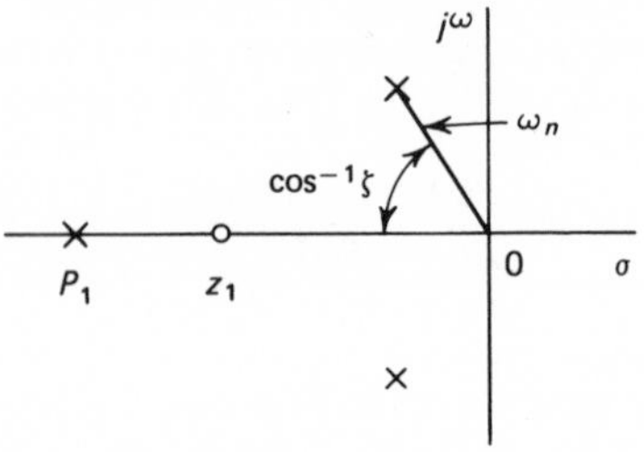

Figure 9.9–1. Configuration of system poles and zeros for direct synthesis

You can solve (9.9–4) graphically by plotting the left side and the right side and finding the intersections. We have a type 1 system, so $C(s)/R(s)|_{s=0} = 1$ and $K = \omega_n^2 P_1/z_1$. Thus (9.9–7) is true when $\sigma = 0$, satisfying one root, and the curves of (9.9–4) intersect at $\sigma = 0$. There is no guarantee that two other intersections resulting in real positive p's will occur, but if they do not, we may alter ω_n, P_1, and z_1, still maintaining requirements, until two such intersections do occur. Some sketching for (9.9–4) quickly reveals the possibilities.

Subsequent to this sketching, we may proceed analytically by multiplying out the factors on each side of (9.9–7). Thus

$$\sigma^3 + (2\zeta\omega_n + P_1)\sigma^2 + (\omega_n^2 + 2\zeta\omega_n P_1 - K)\sigma + (\omega_n^2 P_1 - Kz_1)$$
$$= \sigma^3 + (p_1 + p_2)\sigma^2 + p_1 p_2 \sigma \qquad \textbf{(9.9–8)}$$

Hence

$$\omega_n^2 P_1 - Kz_1 = 0 \qquad \textbf{(9.9–9a)}$$

$$p_1 + p_2 = 2\zeta\omega_n + P_1 \qquad \textbf{(9.9–9b)}$$

$$p_1 p_2 = \omega_n^2 + 2\zeta\omega_n P_1 - K \qquad \textbf{(9.9–9c)}$$

The first equation again evaluates K. From the other two,

$$p_1^2 - (2\zeta\omega_n + P_1)p_1 + (\omega_n^2 + 2\zeta\omega_n P_1 - K) = 0 \qquad \textbf{(9.9–10)}$$

Equation (9.9–10) can be solved by the quadratic formula to give two roots, one of which will be p_1 and the other p_2. If these roots are real and positive, as they should be from our preliminary curve sketch, we have satisfied our objective.

Example 9.9–1

For a certain system, assume the $\zeta = 0.7$ and that $\omega_n = 30$ for the complex poles; $P_1 = 100$ and $z_1 = 20$ satisfy the system requirements. Then $K = 4500$, $D(\sigma) = [\sigma^2 + 2(0.7)(30)\sigma + 900](\sigma + 100)$, and $P(\sigma) = 4500(\sigma + 20)$. A preliminary sketch of $D(\sigma)$ and $P(\sigma)$ shows that two intersections resulting in σ real and negative should occur. Then, from (9.9–10),

$$p_1^2 - 142p_1 + 600 = 0$$

or

$$p_1 = 137.6,\ 4.36$$

Hence the roots of $Q(\sigma)$ are 0, -137.6, and -4.36. Then

$$G(s) = \frac{P(s)}{Q(s)} = \frac{4500(s + 20)}{s(s + 4.36)(s + 137.6)}$$

We usually have an existing plant with some known $G_1(s)$. Thus the compensating function G_c is given by

$$G_c(s)G_1(s) = G(s)$$

or

$$G_c(s) = \frac{G(s)}{G_1(s)}$$

Assume that in the example

$$G_1(s) = \frac{3000}{s(s + 6)(s + 50)}$$

Then

$$G_c(s) = \frac{4500(s + 20)}{s(s + 4.36)(s + 137.6)} \frac{s(s + 6)(s + 50)}{3000}$$

$$= \frac{1.5(s + 20)(s + 6)(s + 50)}{(s + 4.36)(s + 137.6)}$$

We now desire to construct $G_c(s)$ using resistances and capacitances only. If so, it is clear that here we need another factor in the denominator [10]. This can be handled by adding another pole in $G_c(s)$, which in turn puts the same pole in $G(s)$. Adding the pole to $G(s)$ alters C/R, of course. However, we recall that if to the original configuration we add a pole of the order of

$6\omega_n$, the effect on the transient response will be small. Hence let us add a pole at $s = -180$. Then

$$G(s) = \frac{4500(180)(s+20)}{s(s+4.36)(s+137.6)(s+180)} \qquad \textbf{(9.9–11)}$$

Note that the addition of the pole requires a larger K or additional gain; hence the primary restriction on how large to make it concerns the question of the available amplifier gain.

The original $G(s)$ resulted from a certain $(C/R)(s)$, so the new $G(s)$ of (9.9–11) will give an altered $(C/R)(s)$. However, from our arguments concerning the transient response, the factors of the denominator of (9.9–5) will not be altered very much, or ζ, ω_n, and even p_1 will change only slightly. The last step, then, is to check the altered $(C/R)(s) = G(s)/[1 + G(s)]$, where $G(s)$ is now given by (9.9–11), to see if it still meets the specifications. This may be done by a root locus plot or factoring the new characteristic equation. If specifications are not met, the final pole can be placed at a greater distance, or the entire procedure repeated.

If the original fixed system $G_1(s)$ had a zero, the additional pole is not necessary. You can see that the higher the fixed system order, the more complex the compensator G_c becomes, as more added poles are necessary.

The final step is to synthesize $G_c(s)$ so that it may be realized by an *RC* network. This is very simple if all the poles and zeros are on the negative real axis and there are an equal number of each. If the fixed system has complex poles, then complex zeros will be required in $G_c(s)$. An *RC* synthesis is still relatively simple if these are in the left-half plane. We make the usual caution concerning network loading effects.

You may observe that we have a fairly wide choice in the configuration of Figure 9.9–1 to meet most specifications. Thus one may often put on another restriction—that one of the poles of the $G(s)$ obtained is an existing pole of the fixed plant $G_1(s)$. This simplifies the compensating network to two terms in the numerator and two terms in the denominator in Example 9.9–1. With this restriction p_1 is given and p_2 must be found in (9.9–8). To accomplish this, ζ, ω_n, p_1, and z_1 must be juggled, still maintaining specifications, and the procedure is now not straightforward.

The difficulty with this synthesis procedure lies in choosing the original configuration so as to meet the specifications, which usually include K_v, rise time, maximum overshoot, bandwidth, settling time, and so on. The outlined procedure is cut and try to a large extent, particularly if some given p_1 is to be achieved simultaneously. Lago and Hausenbauer have published curves that make the selection much easier, by allowing the designer to read off values for the pole-zero configuration that will accomplish both results, if required [11, 12].

More fundamentally, the procedural philosophy is essentially one of pole cancellation. In other words, the system is synthesized without regard to the existing plant, and unwanted poles and zeros are simply canceled out with the compensator. The cancellation consists of a decoupling and involves questions of controllability, as explained in Chapter 6. If the poles are relatively fixed, and internal oscillations damp out rapidly and are not injurious to the system, the solution may be satisfactory.

In multi-input-output systems with many couplings, unsuspected difficulties might arise. However, one can say that conventional design in the s plane usually amounts to alteration of the critical frequencies to achieve desired input-output relations, usually without regard to the internal state variables, and thus is subject to the same fundamental criticism.

9.10 Process Control

As indicated in Chapter 1, process control fundamentals differ only in detail from other control systems. One of the important details consists of the proper instruments to detect the actual outputs and to convert these to signals that may be utilized in the controller. It is not easy, for example, to obtain an accurate measure of the temperature in an open hearth furnace. Instrument manufacturers constantly work on new concepts and new designs. Here we assume the measuring instruments to be available. Figure 9.10–1 shows a typical system, where v is the command, in process control

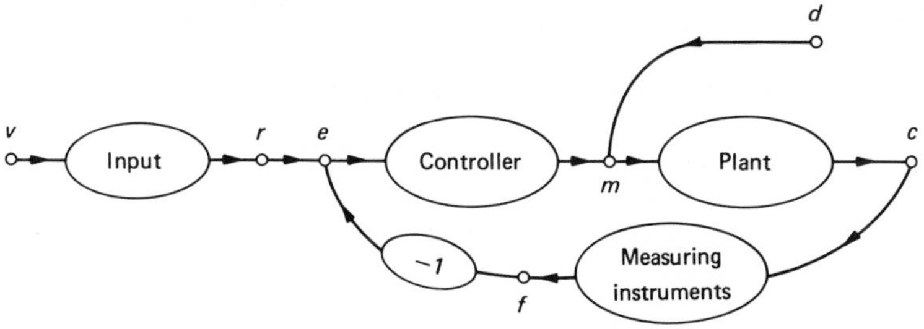

Figure 9.10.1. Typical process control system.

called the set point; e the actuating signal, which is the difference between r and f; m the manipulated variable; and c the controlled variable, f being derived from c by a measuring device. The usual requirement consists in keeping the output c at a constant value proportional to the set point regardless of the disturbance d. Normally the set point does not change during the process (except possibly during startup or shutdown), or, if it does change, the alteration is relatively slow. We concentrate interest on the controller, which corresponds to the compensation devices previously discussed. For sake of simplicity, we assume $f = c$. For this case e may be called the deviation (the deviation between c and the desired value).

Process controllers usually have three types of control: proportional, integral, and derivative (or a combination of these). Dynamically, a proportional control consists of a gain K_c between e and m in Figure 9.10–1. The linear model may be written

$$m = K_c e + K_1 \tag{9.10–1}$$

where K_c is called the proportional sensitivity and K_1 is a constant called the manual reset constant, because you may alter it manually. Clearly, from (9.10–1) a change in m is directly proportional to a change in the actuating signal m, the proportionality being K_c. The proportional band is proportional to $1/K_c$, and is often put in percentage terms. For example, if the plant were a valve regulating a fluid flow and we desire to open the valve, the proportional band might be the percentage of full scale change of the controlled variable required to operate the valve from fully shut to fully open (set point constant).

Example 9.10–1

The output m changes linearly from 0 to 20 pounds per square inch when the deviation e changes from -50 to 50°F. Find K_c.

$$K_c = \frac{20 - 0}{50 - (-50)} = 0.2 \text{ psi/deg}$$

For a unit step in e the manipulated variable m changes by K_c. For a step occurring at $t = t_1$, the change is considered to be instantaneous, as shown in Figure 9.10–2.

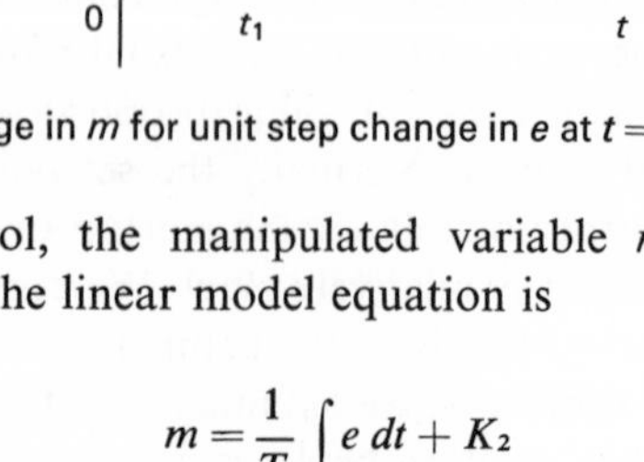

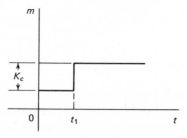

Figure 9.10–2. Change in m for unit step change in e at $t = t_1$, proportional control.

In integral control, the manipulated variable m changes at a rate proportional to e. The linear model equation is

$$m = \frac{1}{T_i} \int e\, dt + K_2 \tag{9.10–2}$$

where we call T_i the integral time and K_2 is a constant. Figure 9.10–3 shows the change in m for a unit step change in e occurring at $t = t_1$.

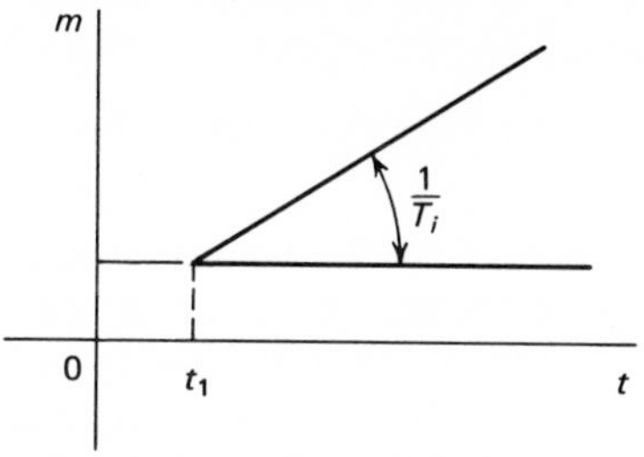

Figure 9.10–3. Change in m for unit step change in e at $t = t_1$, integral control.

Usually proportional control accompanies integral control, or the equation becomes

$$m = \frac{K_c}{T_i}\int e\,dt + K_c e + K_3 \qquad \textbf{(9.10–3)}$$

where K_3 is a constant. Both K_c and T_i are usually adjustable. Here the integral time T_i means the time taken to add an increment of response equal to the step change of response due to the proportional control alone (see Figure 9.10–4). To obtain the dynamic relation between m and e in the s domain, we drop K_3 and take the Laplace transform of (9.10–3) to get

$$M(s) = K_c\left(\frac{1}{T_i s} + 1\right)E(s)$$

or

$$\frac{M(s)}{E(s)} = K_c + \frac{K_c}{T_i s} \qquad \textbf{(9.10–4)}$$

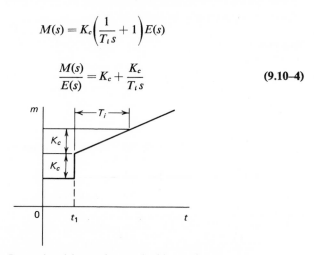

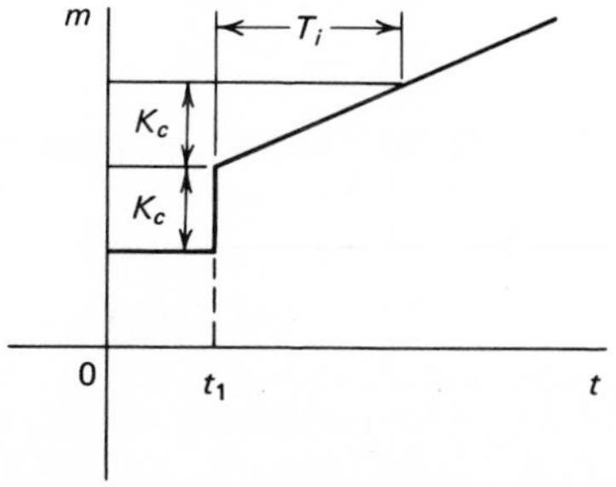

Figure 9.10–4. Proportional-integral control with step input e at $t = t_1$.

The inverse of T_i is termed the reset rate, and may be given in the number of times per minute that the proportional part is reproduced or in "repeats per minute." (Recall that time constants in process control are very large compared to those in most other control systems.)

Proportional-derivative control is defined by

$$m = K_c e + K_c T_d \frac{de}{dt} + K_4 \qquad \textbf{(9.10–5)}$$

where T_d is the derivative time and K_4 a constant. The change in m becomes influenced by the rate of change of e, and a ramp function $e(t) = K_5 t$ defines T_d. Thus in Figure 9.10–5, T_d is the amount of time the manipulated

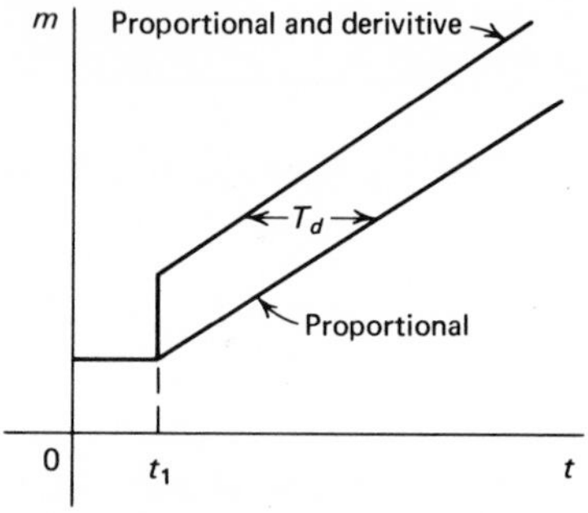

Figure 9.10–5. Proportional-derivative control with input e, starting at $t = t_1$.

variable m is shifted ahead in time compared to where it would otherwise be for proportional control alone.

Example 9.10–2

If m changes from 0 to 10 volts when e varies between -2 and 2 inches and T_d is 2 seconds, how much output is added by derivative action if e changes at the rate of 3 inches per minute?

Solution:

$$K_c = \frac{10}{4} = 2.5 \text{ volts/inch}$$

From (9.10–5),

$$\Delta m = (2.5)(2)\left(\frac{3}{60}\right)$$

$$= 0.25 \text{ volt}$$

The s-domain transfer function becomes

$$\frac{M(s)}{E(s)} = K_c(1 + T_d s) \qquad \textbf{(9.10–6)}$$

If we have all three control actions, the transfer function is obviously

$$\frac{M(s)}{E(s)} = K_c\left(1 + \frac{1}{T_i s} + T_d s\right) \tag{9.10–7}$$

The constants K_1, K_3, and K_4 may be considered to be absorbed in the set point. Equation (9.10–7) may be shown in a flow diagram by three parallel gains, the combination being in tandem with the forward path, as in Figure 9.10–6. If the derivative or integral controls are missing, these paths

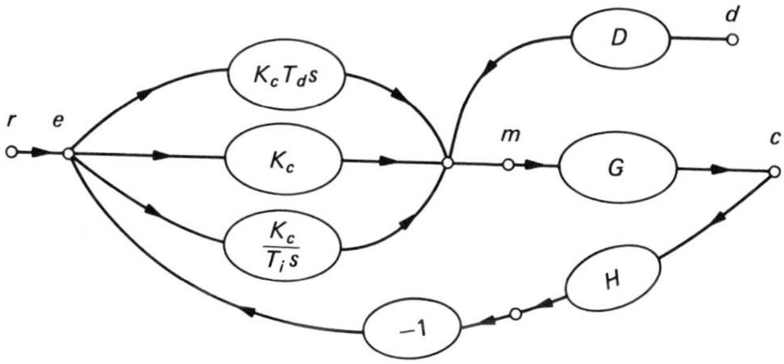

Figure 9.10–6. Transfer function flow diagram for process control.

are deleted. The plant G and feedback H must be determined by theory and measurement.

Once we have the flow diagram of Figure 9.10–6, and $G(s)$ and $H(s)$ are known, the determination of the various constants for satisfactory operation may be accomplished by any of the techniques already discussed. The solution is not straightforward, however, because the constants are interdependent. Thus we need to investigate several designs. One approach might consist of first setting K_c, the integral and derivative controls being open and then to add the other paths the improve performance, if necessary. Note that the described controller inserts tandem compensation, and we have no way to put in internal feedback. Additional devices might be obtained for this purpose, but cost may prohibit further refinements.

We have only skimmed over the surface of process control with the purpose of showing that once you develop a model of the system, design proceeds in a similar fashion to that for other systems. The same can be said of many other specialized fields. The principal difficulty in process control design resides in the fact that interconnections or couplings between other inputs and outputs may exist, some of which may not be recognized. Thus a system designed to control one variable may prove inadequate because other variables influence it. As previously indicated, this leads to the state-space approach, where many inputs and outputs must be controlled simultaneously.

PROBLEMS

9.1. A position servomechanism is to be built using a d-c shunt motor with the characteristics shown in Figure P9.1a. The system is shown in Figure 9.1b. The motor inertia is 0.8 lb-ft²; the load inertia is 5120 lb-ft²; and the data

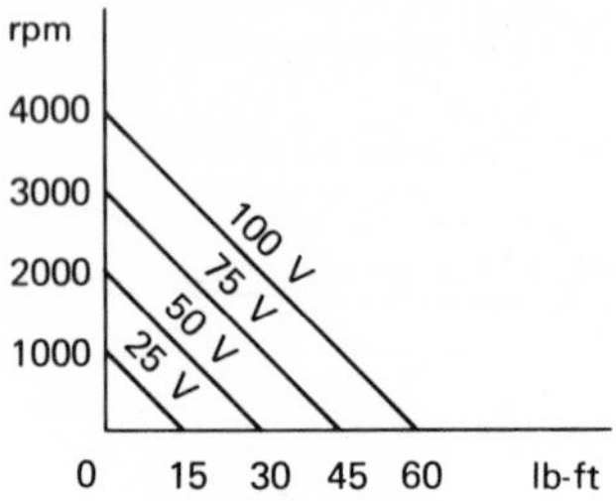

Figure P9.1a.

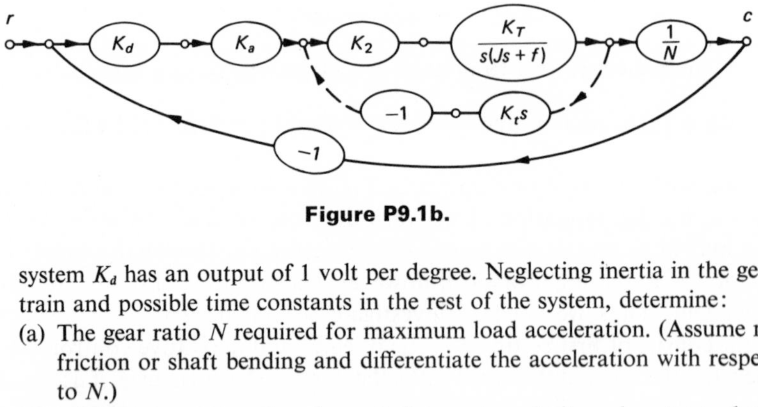

Figure P9.1b.

system K_d has an output of 1 volt per degree. Neglecting inertia in the gear train and possible time constants in the rest of the system, determine:

(a) The gear ratio N required for maximum load acceleration. (Assume no friction or shaft bending and differentiate the acceleration with respect to N.)

(b) The maximum acceleration of the motor shaft and output shaft. (Maximum motor voltage is 100 volts.)

(c) The torque that would be required for sinusoidal motion of the output shaft with a peak to peak amplitude of 10 degrees at a frequency of 1 Hz.

(d) The motor friction coefficient and time constant (including E.M.F. effect).

(e) The gain K_a required for a damping ratio (ζ) of 0.50 if $K_2 = 1$.

(f) The amplifier gain corresponding to the loop gain of (e).

(g) The steady-state error required to drive the motor at 500 rpm.

(h) Add a tachometer with transfer gain $K_t s$ and a gain K_2 as shown by the dashed lines in Figure P9.1b. Assume $K_t = 8$ volts per 1000 rpm. Find K_2 such that the altered time constant is 0.02 sec. Keeping ζ equal to 0.5 for the system complex control poles, find K_a, K_v, and the approximate step function response. Discuss.

9.2. (a) Draw the root locus of the system shown in Figure P9.2.

(b) Determine the gain K for a damping factor of 0.6 on the closed loop complex poles, and the 10 to 90 per cent rise time.

(c) It is desired to increase the gain (so as to reduce static error), lower the rise time, but retain the same damping factor. Insert a series lead network $(s + 1)/(s + 4)$ and draw the new root locus. For the revised design find K, and the approximate rise time.

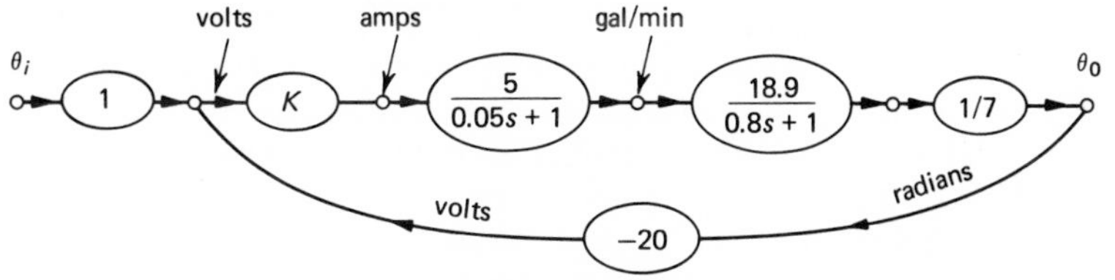

Figure P9.2.

(d) Repeat with a lead network $(s + 2)/(s + 15)$.

(e) Repeat with a lag-lead compensating network.

(f) Discuss the relative merits and (demerits) of each design.

9.3. (a) For $K = 1$ determine the gain and phase margins in the system of Figure P9.2 by drawing Bode plots. Find the closed loop characteristics from the Nichols chart.

(b) Insert a lead network of $(s + 1)/(s + 4)$ and repeat. Repeat for the lead network $(s + 2)/(s + 15)$.

(c) Insert the lag-lead network used on the root locus solution of Problem 9.2 and repeat.

(d) For (b) and (c), how much can we increase K without M_p exceeding 1.3?

(e) From the frequency analysis plot, could a better network be made than in (c), assuming the objectives are to limit the overshoot to 10 per cent, to have as fast a rise time as possible, as large a K_p as possible, but without the bandwidth becoming excessive?

(f) Discuss the relative merits of the root locus approach versus the frequency analysis approach.

9.4. The Hausenbauer-Lago curves show that for the control ratio

$$\frac{C}{R} = \frac{(2800/6.4)(s + 6.4)}{(s + 28)(s^2 + 14s + 100)}$$

the following specifications are met: BW < 30, $K_v/\text{BW} > 2$, $K_v/\omega_n = 5$, overshoot <25 per cent. The existing plant is

$$G_1 = \frac{1000}{s(s + 20)(s + 40)}$$

(a) Find the compensating function necessary in a unity negative feedback system.

(b) Add a distant pole to the function in (a) and synthesize an RC network for the resulting function G_c. Find G_1G_c.
(c) With the added pole in (b), find the new control ratio C/R. Find K_v, BW, ω_n, per cent overshoot, and the 10 to 90 per cent rise time.
(d) Make a Nichols chart of the compensated open loop function and plot M_p and BW versus the open loop gain K.
(e) Make a root locus plot of the compensated open loop G_1G_c as a function of K.

9.5. In Figure P9.1b let $K_T/sJ(s+f/J) = 12.08/s(s+2.88)$, $N = 80$, $K_d K_a = 55$, $K_2 = 1$ and omit the internal feedback $-K_t s$. Plot Bode and Nichols charts to investigate the effect of different compensating network designs.

9.6. In Problem 9.5 use the Ross-Warren method to locate system complex "control" poles at a point such that $\omega_n \geq 5$, $\zeta \geq 0.7$, while $K_v \geq 15$, if this is possible with not more than two lead sections in K_2. Find the other control ratio poles for this case, and obtain the system BW, overshoot, and rise time. If it is not possible, determine the possibilities with two lead sections.

9.7. Repeat Problem 9.6 for an open loop function

$$G = \frac{K}{s(s+3)(s+15)}$$

9.8. Investigate Figure P9.1b using a feedback of the type $K_t s^2/(s+p)$. Use both the frequency analysis and root locus methods. The object is to obtain a high K_v, low BW, and small change in $c(t)$ for a disturbance $d(t)$ inserted just ahead of K_2 in Figure P9.1b.

REFERENCES AND FURTHER READING

[1] F. Mariotti, A Direct Method of Compensating Linear Feedback Systems, *AIEE Trans. Appl. Ind.*, **80** (1961), 527–538.
[2] E. R. Ross, T. C. Warren, and G. J. Thaler, Design of Servo Compensation Based on the Root Locus Approach, *AIEE Trans. Appl. Ind.*, **79** (1960), 272–277.
[3] J. G. Truxal, *Control System Synthesis*, McGraw-Hill, New York, 1955, pp. 317–344.
[4] G. J. Murphy, *Basic Automatic Control Theory*, Van Nostrand, Princeton, N.J., 2nd ed., 1967, p. 63.
[5] C. J. Savant, Jr., *Control System Design*, McGraw-Hill, New York, 2nd ed., 1964, Appendix VI.
[6] H. W. Bode, *Network Analysis and Feedback Amplifier Design*, Van Nostrand, Princeton, N.J., 1945, pp. 211–214.
[7] Murphy, *op. cit.*, pp. 567–586.
[8] O. J. M. Smith, *Feedback Control Systems*, McGraw-Hill, New York, 1958, pp. 299–348.
[9] Truxal, *op. cit.*

[10] M. E. Van Valkenburg, *Introduction to Modern Network Synthesis*, Wiley, New York, 1960, pp. 140–156.

[11] C. R. Hausenbauer and G. V. Lago, Synthesis of Control Systems Based on Approximation to a Third Order System, *AIEE Trans. Appl. Ind.*, **77** (1958), 415–421.

[12] G. V. Lago and L. M. Benningfield, *Control System Theory*, Ronald, New York, 1962, pp. 436–454.

10 Compensation—Modern

10.1 Optimal Control in the Complex Plane

The separation of design into conventional and modern implies an arbitrary definition. The author makes this division in terms of design that optimizes some performance index or indices. One of the earliest efforts along this direction was by Phillips [1], who considered the minimization of the integral of the squared error, particularly with regard to stochastic signals and systems. Newton, Gould, and Kaiser [2] popularized this further, and today a large sector of control research investigates optimization, although some writers do not agree with the concept of optimizing one factor [3]. In this section we review some of the early approaches to optimal design.

As already discussed in Chapter 5, one idea of optimal control consists of minimizing a number J that is a function of quantities contributing to the system performance. In the first attacks on this problem the obvious thing to minimize seemed to be a function of the error. For example, if we consider the usual simple system that comprises a forward gain G with unity negative feedback, as in Figure 10.1–1, the error can be expressed as

$$e(t) = r(t) - c(t) \qquad \textbf{(10.1–1)}$$

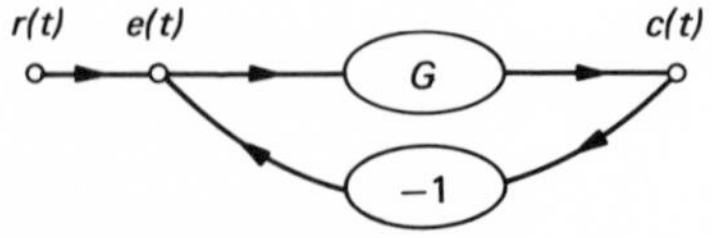

Figure 10.1–1. Unity negative feedback system.

If $r(t)$ is a step function, with no initial conditions, $c(t)$ could appear as in Figure 10.1–2. Then the shaded area might be a fair measure of the system performance. Thus we select

$$J = \int_0^\infty |e(t)|\, dt \tag{10.1–2}$$

as the quantity to be minimized. From (10.1–2) J is a functional that depends on the history of $e(t)$ and not on just one value.

The integral of the magnitude turns out to be a difficult index with which to deal analytically, but the squared error becomes more tractable and expresses almost the same idea. Hence we select a criterion

$$J = \int_{-\infty}^{\infty} (e(t))^2\, dt \tag{10.1–3}$$

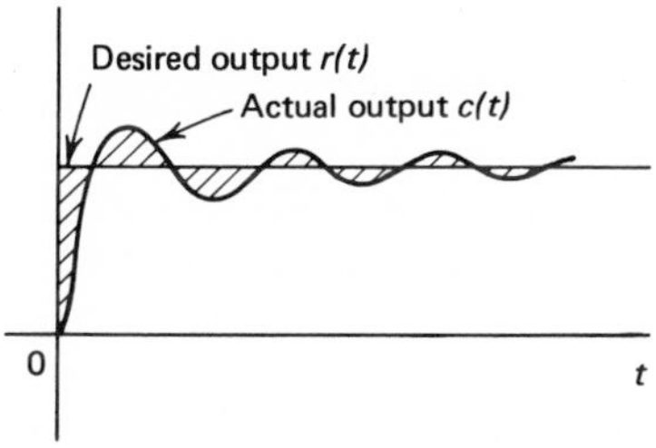

10.1–2. Integral error performance criterion.

where the signal is considered to go for all time. If $e(t)$ starts at time $t = 0$, the lower limit may be changed to zero.

In the selection of a criteria J to be minimized, we abandon specifications pertaining to overshoot, bandwidth, rise time, static error, and so on, and put all our faith in the one measure J. It is true that in the process of minimizing J we may achieve reasonable performance from other standpoints, but these results are by-products of the main effort. There is thus a heavy responsibility in selecting the form of J, and only experience can tell if our choice was a good one.

One method for attacking the index given by (10.1–3) is through Parseval's theorem. Let us investigate the integral

$$J = \int_{-\infty}^{\infty} x_1(t) x_2(t)\, dt$$

and write $x_2(t)$ in terms of its inverse Fourier transform. Then

$$J = \frac{1}{2\pi j} \int_{-\infty}^{\infty} x_1(t) \left[\int_{-j\infty}^{j\infty} X_2(s) \epsilon^{st}\, ds \right] dt$$

If $x_1(t)$ and $x_2(t)$ meet the conditions for Fourier transformable functions, we may exchange the order of integration to obtain

$$J = \frac{1}{2\pi j} \int_{-j\infty}^{j\infty} X_2(s)\, ds \int_{-\infty}^{\infty} x_1(t) \epsilon^{st}\, dt$$

The second integral is $X_1(-s)$, so we then obtain Parseval's theorem:

$$\int_{-\infty}^{\infty} x_1(t) x_2(t)\, dt = \frac{1}{2\pi j} \int_{-j\infty}^{j\infty} X_1(s) X_2(-s)\, ds \qquad \textbf{(10.1–4)}$$

If the lower limit of the left integral in (10.1–4) is zero [$x_1(t)$, $x_2(t) = 0$, $t < 0$], then $X_1(s)$ and $X_2(s)$ are Laplace transforms with fewer restrictions on the time functions. The integration in the complex plane must be from $s = \sigma - j\infty$ to $s\,\sigma = +j\infty$, where σ defines the region of convergence of the Laplace transform.

Using this theorem, then the index J of (10.1–3) with lower limit zero becomes

$$J = \int_{-j\infty}^{j\infty} E(s) E(-s)\, ds \qquad \textbf{(10.1–5)}$$

where $E(s)$ is the Laplace transform of $e(t)$.

In the system of Figure 10.1–1,

$$\begin{aligned} E(s) &= \frac{R(s)}{1 + G(s)} \\ &= \frac{R(s) Q(s)}{P(s) + Q(s)} \\ &= \frac{N(s)}{D(s)} \end{aligned} \qquad \textbf{(10.1–6)}$$

where $G(s) = P(s)/Q(s)$, $D(s) = P(s) + Q(s)$, and $N(s) = R(s)Q(s)$, with $P(s)$, $Q(s)$, and $R(s)Q(s)$ being polynomials in s. Hence (10.1–5) manipulates into the relation

$$J = \int_{-j\infty}^{j\infty} \frac{N(s)}{D(s)} \frac{N(-s)}{D(-s)}\, ds \qquad \textbf{(10.1–7)}$$

The integral on the right in (10.1–7) may be found by integration in the complex plane. Fortunately, however, G. R. MacLane has evaluated this integral for various polynomials $N(s)$ and $D(s)$ and these values have been tabulated [4]. We show a few of these results in Table 10.1–1. The formula for J_n rapidly becomes more complex with increasing n.

TABLE 10.1–1

Value for J_n using (10.1–7) where:
$D(s) = d_n s^n + d_{n-1}s^{n-1} + \cdots + d_0$
$N(s) = c_{n-1}s^{n-1} + \cdots + c_0$
$J_1 = \dfrac{c_0^2}{2d_0 d_1}$
$J_2 = \dfrac{c_1^2 d_0 + c_0^2 d_2}{2d_0 d_1 d_2}$
$J_3 = \dfrac{c_2^2 d_0 d_1 + (c_1^2 - 2c_0 c_2) d_0 d_3 + c_0^2 d_2 d_3}{2d_0 d_3(-d_0 d_3 + d_1 d_2)}$

The next task is to minimize J by altering parameters. Analytically this can be done by a set of k equations of the form

$$\frac{\partial J}{\partial p_i} = 0$$

where p_i, $i = 1, 2, \ldots, k$ are parameters. Such equations usually would be difficult to solve. An alternative method would consist of plotting J for vairous values of each parameter in turn, and "homing" in on a minimum using these plots. Let us take two examples.

Example 10.1–1

Given $G(s) = K/s(s + p)$ in a unity negative feedback system, with a step input $r(t) = Au(t)$. Find K such that the squared error criteria are minimized.
$R(s) = A/s$, and thus

$$E(s) = A\frac{s + p}{s^2 + ps + K}$$

From Table 10.1–1, $d_2 = 1$, $d_1 = p$, $d_0 = K$, $c_1 = 1$, and $c_0 = p$. Hence

$$J_2 = A^2\frac{K + p^2}{2Kp}$$

$$= \frac{A^2}{2}\left(\frac{1}{p} + \frac{p}{K}\right)$$

From the last equation it is evident that

$$\min J_2 = J_2^* = \frac{A^2}{2}\frac{1}{p}$$

when $K = \infty$.

The system is stable for all $K > 0$; hence we have an acceptable result in that sense. However, the system would be highly underdamped and unsatisfactory in other respects with a large K. The use of the criteria here is thus helpful only in that it tells us to use the largest K possible subject to limitations on underdamping or that we cannot apply the optimal results blindly.

If p can be varied, then

$$\frac{\partial J_2}{\partial p} = \frac{A^2}{2}\left(-\frac{1}{p^2} + \frac{1}{K}\right) = 0$$

or $p = \sqrt{K}$. Then

$$J_2^* = \frac{A^2}{\sqrt{K}}$$

The complex poles of the characteristic equation thus have a damping factor $\zeta = 0.5$. In general, the use of the squared error criteria results in a more lightly damped system than might be selected using other performance indices.

Example 10.1–2

In Figure 10.1–3

$$G = \frac{K}{s(s + p_1)}$$

$$G_c = \frac{K_1}{s + p_2}$$

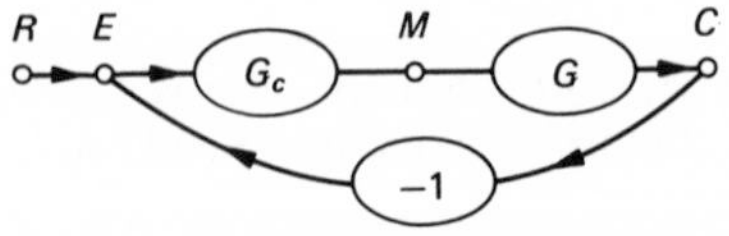

Figure 10.1–3. Feedback system with tandem compensation for Example. 10.1–2

Minimize $J_a = \int_0^\infty e^2(t)\, dt$ for a unit step input $u(t)$ subject to the constraint that

$$J_b = \int_0^\infty m^2(t)\, dt \le k_m, \qquad \text{a constant}$$

The constraint here is an energy-type constraint. We may solve this problem by minimizing

$$J_a + \lambda J_b$$

where λ is a Lagrange multiplier. Here

$$E(s) = \frac{1}{s}\frac{s(s+p_1)(s+p_2)}{KK_1 + s(s+p_1)(s+p_2)}$$

$$= \frac{s^2 + (p_1+p_2)s + p_1p_2}{s^3 + (p_1+p_2)s^2 + p_1p_2 s + KK_1}$$

Hence $d_3 = 1$, $d_2 = p_1 + p_2$, $d_1 = p_1p_2$, $d_0 = KK_1$, $c_2 = 1$, $c_1 = p_1 + p_2$, and $c_0 = p_1p_2$, and, from Table 10.1–1,

$$J_a = \frac{p_1p_2 KK_1 + KK_1(p_1^2 + p_2^2) + (p_1p_2)^2(p_1+p_2)}{2KK_1p_1p_2(p_1+p_2) - 2(KK_1)^2}$$

$$M(s) = E(s)G_c(s)$$

$$= \frac{K_1(s+p_1)}{s^3 + (p_1+p_2)s^2 + p_1p_2 s + KK_1}$$

Hence $d_3 = 1$, $d_2 = p_1 + p_2$, $d_1 = p_1p_2$, $d_0 = KK_1$, $c_2 = 0$, $c_1 = K_1$, and $c_0 = K_1p_1$, and, from Table 10.1–1,

$$J_b = \frac{K_1[KK_1 + p_1^2(p_1+p_2)]}{2K[-KK_1 + p_1p_2(p_1+p_2)]}$$

As we have two equations, we may vary two parameters at a time, or (K, K_1), (K, p_1), (K, p_2), and so on. Suppose that K_1 and p_2 are the free parameters. Then

$$\frac{\partial(J_a + \lambda J_b)}{\partial K_1} = 0$$

$$\frac{\partial(J_a + \lambda J_b)}{p_2} = 0$$

Any attempt to carry this out soon bogs down in some rather complicated algebra. Probably a simpler approach consists of plotting J_b for some values of K_1 and p_2 to see for what range of these parameters $J_b \le k_m$. Then K_1 and p_2 values in this range may be used to plot J_a curves to determine a minimum, if such exists.

More recently Chang has shown that for a type 1 system with step input, and where the criteria to be minimized is $J_a + k^2J_b$, where k is a constant and J_a and J_b are as in Example 10.1–2, that the optimal system in this sense may be found by a root locus plot with $(K/k)^2$ as a parameter [5]. Omitting the derivation here, his results give the following procedure:

1. For the existing system

$$G(s) = \frac{K \prod_{i=1}^{m} (s + z_i)}{\prod_{j=1}^{n} (s + p_j)} \qquad n > m$$

find new poles $-P_i$ and zeros $-Z_i$ for a "root square" locus by the equations

$$Z_i = z_i^2 \qquad i = 1, m$$

$$P_j = p_j^2 \qquad j = 1, n$$

2. Plot a root locus for

$$\left(\frac{K}{k}\right)^2 \frac{\prod_{i=1}^{m} (\Omega + Z_i)}{\prod_{j=1}^{n} (\Omega + P_j)} = -1 \tag{10.1–8}$$

The roots Q_j, $j = 1$ to n, of the characteristic equation for (10.1–8) are found at values of $(K/k)^2$ along the loci. $(K/k)^2$ may be chosen to (1) result in a desired K_v, (2) result in a desired rise time, (3) place a desired relative weighting on J_b as compared to J_a, or in other ways.

3. The system function is then

$$\frac{C(s)}{R(s)} = \frac{K_1 \prod_{i=1}^{m} (s + z_i)}{\prod_{j=1}^{n} (s + q_j)} \tag{10.1–9}$$

where $q_j = \pm\sqrt{-Q_j}$ with the sign selected so that q_j is in the left-half plane, and

$$K_1 = \frac{\prod_{i=1}^{n} q_i}{\prod_{j=1}^{m} z_j} = \frac{K}{k}$$

4. The compensated open loop function is then found as

$$G_0(s) = \frac{(C/R)(s)}{1 - (C/R)(s)}$$

or

$$\frac{1}{G_0(s)} = \frac{1}{(C/R)(s)} - 1 \tag{10.1–10}$$

Example 10.1–3

In Figure 10.1–3 let the fixed portion of the system be $G = K/s(s+1)(s+5)$. Make a root-square-locus plot.

Here $P_1 = -1$, $P_2 = -25$, and $P_3 = 0$. Then we make a plot for $(K/k)^2/\Omega(\Omega+1)(\Omega+25)$, as shown in Figure 10.1–4. As examples of roots, when

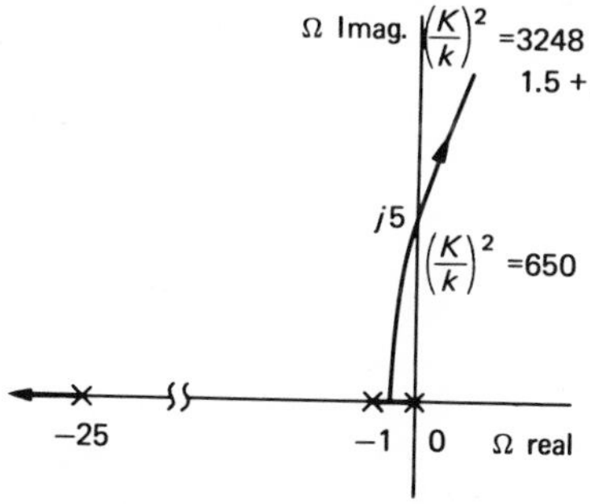

Figure 10.1–4. Root-square locus for Example 10.2–1.

$(K/k)^2 = 650$ the characteristic equation is $(\Omega^2+25)(\Omega+26) = 0$, and when $(K/k)^2 = 3248$ the characteristic equation is $(\Omega+29)(\Omega^2 - 3\Omega + 112) = 0$. To select K/k, we have some possible alternatives as follows:

1. If we wish to make K a given value (that already furnished by G, for example), then k could be picked to give the desired emphasis to the second term of $J_a + k^2 J_b$. The greater k, the more the relative effect of the $J_b = \int_0^\infty m^2(t)\,dt$ term, and hence the less m can be.
2. We can choose K/k to give a desired static constant K_v.
3. We can choose a pole q_i that will result in a desired rise time.

(There are other possibilities, such as a choice for bandwidth.) For choice (3), Chang suggests that the nearest pole be about π/t_p radians per second from the origin, where t_p is the time required to first reach 95 per cent of its final value (step input), or the nearest Q_i should be at a distance of about $(\pi/t_p)^2$. In this case, assume the specified $t_p = 0.95$ sec. Then $Q_i = \pi^2/0.95^2 \approx 11$, which is met when $(K/k)^2 \approx 3428$ from the root-square locus.

Then

$$Q_1 \approx -29.2$$

$$Q_2 \approx 1.6 + j10.8$$

$$Q_3 \approx 1.6 - j10.8$$

$$q_1 \approx 5.4$$

$$q_2 \approx 2.16 - j2.5$$

$$q_3 \approx 2.16 + j2.5$$

or

$$\frac{C}{R}(s) = \frac{58.7}{(s+5.4)(s^2+4.325s+10.92)}$$

The open loop function is then

$$G_0(s) \approx \frac{58.7}{s(s^2 + 9.725s + 34.25)}$$

and, finally,

$$G_c(s) \approx \frac{58.7(s + 1)(s + 5)}{K(s^2 + 9.725s + 34.25)}$$

[If $(C/R)(s)$ does not meet the t_p specifications, a slight alteration may be necessary.] From $G_0(s)$, $K_v \approx 1.71$. If you wished to increase K_v, you could add a dipole to C/R without greatly affecting the transient response (and hence J_a or J_b). Next, we can select k to place the desired emphasis on the kJ_2 term. Once k is selected, K becomes fixed, because $(K/k)^2 \approx 3428$. This design may force us to add (or subtract) gain from the original fixed portion of the system, but this is dictated by our desire to minimize $(J_a + k^2J_b)$. Obviously normally it would be poor design to increase the gain of the plant unless we had some control over this portion, that is, unless we could obtain a larger motor, for example. The design would then have to be reconsidered in the light of economics, weight, and so on. Alternatively, if K for the existing G is adequate, we could make a check to see if k seems reasonable.

To check Chang's optimal design, 16 systems were investigated. The optimal design in his sense was checked on the analog computer against a design using the Lago-Hausenbauer method (Chapter 9), making the 95 per cent rise time t_p about the same for each system. Four configurations for $G(s)$ were taken, as follows:

$$G_1 = \frac{K}{s(s + 1)(s + 5)}$$

$$G_2 = \frac{K}{s(s + 1)(s + 2)}$$

$$G_3 = \frac{K(s + 2)}{s(s + 1)(s + 5)}$$

$$G_4 = \frac{K(s + 2)}{s(s^2 + 6s + 13)}$$

In all systems both the per cent overshoot and J_a were less in the optimal system. For systems with about the same K_v (no dipole added), the same results occurred [6].

We observe that this technique again results in pole-zero cancellation, and that $G_c(s)$ no longer necessarily has poles on the real axis, thus requiring a more complicated compensator. Chang states that the inclusion of the energy-type constraint causes a system to operate better, because the constraint tends to keep the input out of the saturation range [7]. We do know that large inputs tend to saturate any system and force a departure in operation from linear theory prediction.

10.2 Calculus of Variations

Optimization in the complex plane as described in Section 10.1 primarily concerns itself with single input-output systems, and utilizes the transfer function concept. Modern control theory relies heavily on the state-space idea, and as this came to the fore, efforts were made to optimize indices that involved multivariable systems.

Up to now you may have observed that we have said little about whether an optimal system is of the open loop type or the feedback type. A strong case was made for the feedback system in Chapter 1, and indeed most present control systems probably are of this type. In the state-space approach, however, there is no predilection for either type. Assuming that everything can be predicted, that is, that the signals are known deterministically or the probability distribution is known if the signals are random, that the system will operate in a known fashion, and that disturbances are known, the open loop system may prove better (and certainly cheaper) than the feedback system. One of the chief advantages of the feedback idea, however, is that it provides considerable assistance to the controller by transferring the information regarding unpredictable events. In setting up the state-space equations, the designer is free to choose the desired configuration. If he wishes to optimize a performance index, however, the methods he uses may result in one or the other type of system. Three general methods for optimization have been studied and research continues in these areas. These are (1) calculus of variations (including Hölder's inequality) [8, 9], (2) dynamic programming [10], and (3) Pontryagin's principle [11].

The first, calculus of variations, inherently results in an open loop type of system. The method of calculus of variations has been known for some time and has been successfully used to solve a number of maximization problems. There are numerous objections to it, as perhaps best outlined by Bellman [10]. Nevertheless, it is still applied to many problems, sometimes using steepest-ascent methods of computation. Notable among these are trajectories in physical space for vehicles that minimize some variable such as fuel consumption or time.

Dynamic programming, furthered most by Bellman, is an attack on the problem that relies on a computer and might be said to lean more on a pragmatic computational approach than on an analytic approach, although this does not imply that the theory is not rigorous.

Pontryagin's principle, developed by the Russian mathematician L. S. Pontryagin, is essentially an extension of the calculus of variations but is less restrictive as to the type of control functions. Using dynamic programming or Pontryagin's principle one obtains the result as a closed loop or feedback system; that is, the control function **m** is found naturally as a function of the state **x** as well as of the time t. Fundamentally, all three methods are similar, but utilize differing viewpoints. Although Pontryagin's principle inherently seems more satisfying to the average engineer, it is not amiss to discuss briefly the calculus of variations before going into this. We shall keep the development to an exposity level without great rigor.

The calculus of variations as applied in control systems consists of minimizing a performance index

$$J = \int_{t_0}^{t_f} F(\dot{\mathbf{x}}, \mathbf{x}, t)\, dt \qquad \textbf{(10.2–1)}$$

where F is some function of the state variables, their derivatives, and possibly time. Usually the lower limit of the integral can be taken as zero, and often $t_f \to \infty$. The performance index of Section 10.1 is a special case of this general definition. The index J must be minimized subject to the system state-space equations

$$\dot{\mathbf{x}} = \mathbf{f}(\mathbf{x}, \mathbf{m}, t) \qquad \textbf{(10.2–2a)}$$

$$\mathbf{y} = \mathbf{g}(\mathbf{x}, \mathbf{m}, t) \qquad \textbf{(10.2–2b)}$$

The situation stated in this form is known as the Lagrange problem.

For the moment let us consider a one-dimensional or scalar system with $t_0 = 0$ and without the constraints (10.2–2) for simplicity. Figure 10.2–1

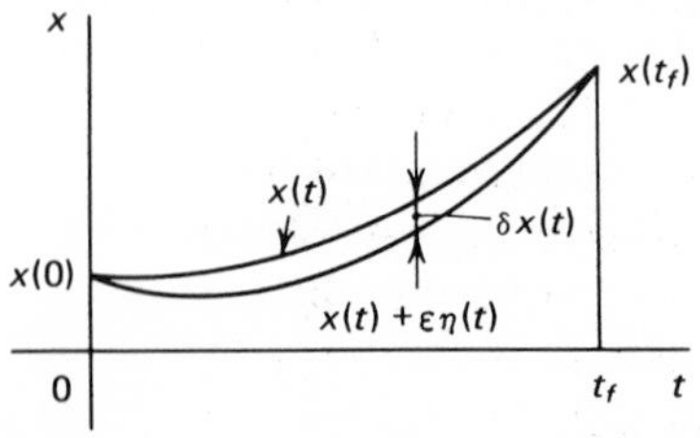

Figure 10.2–1. Neighboring trajectories.

shows a trajectory $x(t)$ in state space from $x(0)$ to $x(t_f)$ (both specified), and a possible neighboring trajectory $x(t) + \epsilon\eta(t)$, where we believe $x(t)$ to be $x^*(t)$, the trajectory minimizing (10.2–1), ϵ is a constant, and $\eta(t)$ is an arbitrary function of t except that $\eta(0) = \eta(t_f) = 0$. For the minimizing trajectory, $J = J^*$ and for a neighboring trajectory

$$J(\epsilon) = \int_0^{t_f} F(x + \epsilon\eta, \dot{x} + \epsilon\dot{\eta}, t)\, dt \tag{10.2–3}$$

where x, $\dot{x}$, η, and $\dot{\eta}$ are functions of t.

If $x(t) = x^*(t)$ or $x(t)$ is truly an optimal trajectory, then

$$\frac{d}{d\epsilon} J(\epsilon) \bigg|_{\epsilon=0} = 0$$

Assuming the function F is such that we may change the order of differentiation and integration, we find from (10.2–3) that

$$\frac{dJ(\epsilon)}{d\epsilon} = \int_0^{t_f} \left(\frac{\partial F}{\partial x} \eta + \frac{\partial F}{\partial \dot{x}} \dot{\eta} \right) dt = 0$$

where the arguments of F have been dropped. Now integrate the second term by parts to obtain the equation

$$\int_0^{t_f} \left[\frac{\partial F}{\partial x} \eta - \frac{d}{dt} \left(\frac{\partial F}{\partial \dot{x}} \right) \eta \right] dt + \left(\frac{\partial F}{\partial \dot{x}} \eta \right)_0^{t_f} = 0 \tag{10.2–4}$$

The last term in (10.2–4) equals zero, because $\eta(0) = \eta(t_f) = 0$. Then

$$\int_0^{t_f} \left[\frac{\partial F}{\partial x} - \frac{d}{dt} \left(\frac{\partial F}{\partial \dot{x}} \right) \right] \eta(t)\, dt = 0$$

As $\eta(t)$ is arbitrary, we get the famous Euler-Lagrange equation

$$\frac{\partial F}{\partial x} - \frac{d}{dt} \frac{\partial F}{\partial \dot{x}} = 0 \tag{10.2–5}$$

For an n-dimensional system the equations

$$\frac{\partial F}{\partial x_i} - \frac{d}{dt} \frac{\partial F}{\partial \dot{x}_i} = 0 \qquad i = 1, 2, \ldots, n \tag{10.2–6}$$

must be true all along the optimal trajectory $\mathbf{x}^*(t)$. If F is not a function of t, then

$$F - \dot{x}_i \frac{\partial F}{\partial \dot{x}_i} = \text{constant} \qquad i = 1, 2, \ldots, n \tag{10.2–7}$$

Example 10.2–1

Find the equation of the path giving the shortest distance between two points on a sphere. We use spherical coordinates a, ϕ, and θ, as shown in Figure 10.2–2. Then $J = \int ds$ and

$$J = \int [(a \cos \phi \, d\theta)^2 + (a \, d\phi)^2]^{1/2}$$

$$= \int \left[(a \cos \phi)^2 + \left(a \frac{d\phi}{d\theta} \right)^2 \right]^{1/2} d\theta$$

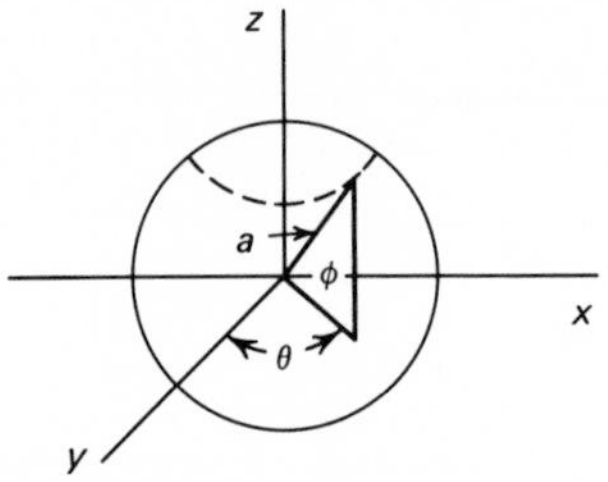

Figure 10.2–2. Coordinates for Example 10.2–1.

and F is the integrand. Here ϕ takes the place of x and $d\phi/d\theta = \dot{\phi}$ replaces $\dot{x}$ in (10.2–6). Now $\partial F/\partial \dot{\phi} = [(a \cos \phi)^2 + a\dot{\phi}^2]^{-1/2} a^2 \dot{\phi}$, and, as F is independent of t, we may use (10.2–7). After some algebra, you get

$$\dot{\phi} = \cos^2 \phi (K \cos \phi - 1)^{1/2}$$

where K is a constant. The solution to this is

$$\phi = \tan^{-1}[K \sin(\phi + \delta)]$$

where K and δ are determined by the end points.

You can readily show that the intersection of a plane through the origin and the sphere is the same equation, or the shortest path is a great circle on the sphere.

The Euler-Lagrange equations are necessary for a minimum but in some cases we may need a number of other tests. The first of these is the Weierstrass-Erdmann corner condition. A "corner" is a point at which $\mathbf{x}(t)$ is discontinuous. If a discontinuity in x_j occurs at $t = t'$, then the corner conditions are

$$\left. \frac{\partial F}{\partial \dot{x}_j} \right|_{t=t'_-} = \left. \frac{\partial F}{\partial \dot{x}_j} \right|_{t=t'_+} \quad \textbf{(10.2–8a)}$$

$$\left. \left(F - \sum_{i=1}^{n} \frac{\partial F}{\partial \dot{x}_i} \right) \right|_{t=t'_-} = \left. \left(F - \sum_{i=1}^{n} \frac{\partial F}{\partial \dot{x}_i} \right) \right|_{t=t'_+} \quad \textbf{(10.2–8b)}$$

The question as to whether J constitutes a maximum, minimum, or some other stationary point also must be answered, as in ordinary calculus. Thus if we define the first variation as

$$\delta J = \left.\frac{\partial J}{\partial \epsilon}\right|_{\epsilon=0}$$

and the second variation as

$$\delta^2 J = \left.\frac{\partial^2 J}{\partial \epsilon^2}\right|_{\epsilon=0}$$

and so on, then

$$J(\epsilon) = J^*(0) + \epsilon\delta J + \frac{\epsilon^2}{2}\,\delta^2 J + \cdots$$

whence if $J^*(0)$ is a minimum, $\delta^2 J \geq 0$. Expansion of $\delta^2 J$ then gives the Legendre necessary condition

$$\frac{\partial^2 F}{\partial \dot{x}^2} \geq 0 \qquad t_0 \leq t \leq t_f \tag{10.2–9}$$

Equation (10.2–9) also depends on the Jacobi condition for a continuous function that we do not pursue here. For the multivariable case the Legendre condition requires that

$$\frac{\partial^2 F}{\partial \mathbf{x}^2} = \frac{\partial^2 F}{\partial x_i\, \partial x_j}$$

be positive semidefinite.

Finally, Weierstrass pointed out that the Euler-Lagrange equations assume that the variations $\delta x = \epsilon\eta$ and $\delta\dot{x} = \epsilon\dot{\eta}$ both approach zero simultaneously. The variation of the trajectory for this situation is termed "weak." If we consider only the variation in x, and let the slope $\dot{x}$ do what it will, then we might get a different minimum. We call this "strong" variation.

Assume that we believe that $x(t)$ in Figure 10.2–3 is the optimal trajectory, but we investigate an alternative trajectory $y(t)$, where $y(t)$ is defined as follows:

$$\begin{aligned}
&x(t) && \text{for } 0 \leq t \leq t_1 \\
&f_1(t) = x(t_1) + m(t - t_1) && \text{for } t_1 \leq t \leq \alpha \\
&f_2(t) = x(t) + \frac{\beta - t}{\beta - \alpha}\,[x(t_1) + m(\alpha - t_1) - x(\alpha)] && \text{for } \alpha \leq t \leq \beta \\
&x(t) && \text{for } \beta \leq t \leq t_f
\end{aligned}$$

The trajectory $y(t)$ has an (arbitrary) slope m at t_1, and $f_2(t)$ is such that it rejoins $x(t)$ at $t = \beta$ (we assume $\alpha \leq \beta \leq t_f$). Let J_x and J_y be the respective performance indices for the $x(t)$ and $y(t)$ trajectories. Then if $J_x = J^*$,

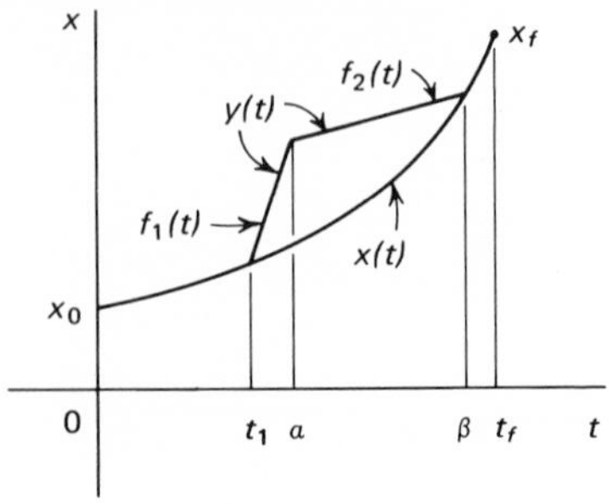

Figure 10.2–3. Neighboring trajectories for strong variation.

$J_y \geq J_x$. Expanding the performance index integrals and using the Euler-Lagrange equations, it is not difficult to show that a necessary condition for $\mathbf{x}(t) = \mathbf{x}^*(t)$ in the multidimension case is for $E \geq 0$, where

$$E = F(\mathbf{x}, \mathbf{q}, t) - F(\mathbf{x}, \dot{\mathbf{x}}, t) - \frac{\partial}{\partial \dot{\mathbf{x}}} [F(\mathbf{x}, \dot{\mathbf{x}}, t)](\mathbf{m} - \dot{\mathbf{x}}) \qquad \textbf{(10.2–10)}$$

and $\mathbf{m}$ is an arbitrary vector. Note that the slope of the neighboring trajectory $y(t)$ does not approach that of $x(t)$, although the magnitudes of $x(t)$ and $y(t)$ are in a restricted neighborhood.

Bliss demonstrates that if the equality conditions are removed from the Legendre and the Weierstrass conditions and that if the given necessary conditions are met otherwise, then sufficiency is established [12]. Although meeting all the necessary conditions guarantees an optimal trajectory, if some are not met, there exists no formula for locating the optimal, which then we can approach only by a hunt and seek procedure.

So far we have not included the fact that the system dynamics restrict the state-space variables. The easiest way to include the constraint of the state-space equations is to adjoin them to the function F using a Lagrange multiplier. For the multivariable case, we adopt the Lagrange multiplier vector $\mathbf{p}(t)$. Then (10.2–2a) may be expressed as $\dot{\mathbf{x}} - \mathbf{f}(\mathbf{x}, \mathbf{m}, t) = \mathbf{0}$, and we treat the problem of minimizing the functional

$$J_1 = \int_0^{t_f} F_1 \, dt$$

or

$$J_1 = \int_0^{t_f} (F(\mathbf{x}, \dot{\mathbf{x}}, t) + \mathbf{p}^T(t)[\dot{\mathbf{x}}(t) - \mathbf{f}(\mathbf{x}, \mathbf{m}, t)]) \, dt \qquad \textbf{(10.2–11)}$$

in the same way we previously worked with J. $\mathbf{p}(t)$ must be determined such that (10.2–11) holds.

Example 10.2–2

Given the plant $\dot{x} = m$, as in Figure 10.2–4, find the control m such that the trajectory goes from $x(0) = x_0$ to $x(t_f) = x_f$ and minimizes the performance index

$$J = \int_0^{t_f} (\alpha^2 x^2 + \beta^2 m^2)\, dt$$

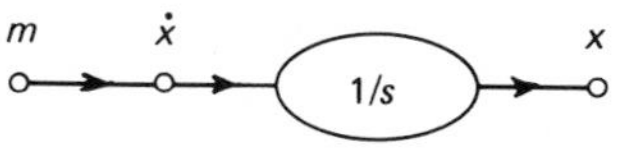

Figure 10.2–4. System for Example 10.2–2.

Solution:

$$F_1 = \alpha^2 x^2 + \beta^2 m^2 + p(\dot{x} - m)$$

We alter the previous development slightly by considering m an additional variable, and apply (10.2–6).

Then

$$\frac{\partial F_1}{\partial x} - \frac{d}{dt}\frac{\partial F_1}{\partial \dot{x}} = 0$$

gives

$$2\alpha^2 x - \dot{p} = 0$$

and

$$\frac{\partial F_1}{\partial m} - \frac{d}{dt}\frac{\partial F_1}{\partial \dot{m}} = 0$$

gives

$$2\beta^2 m - p = 0$$

The second equation shows that $p = 2\beta^2 m$, and substituting in the first equation we find that

$$\alpha^2 x - \beta^2 \dot{m} = 0$$

or

$$\dot{m} - \frac{\alpha^2}{\beta^2} x = 0$$

Transforming, we obtain

$$sM(s) - m(0) - \gamma^2 X(s) = 0$$

where $\gamma = \alpha/\beta$. Transforming the plant equation, there results

$$sX(s) - x_0 = M(s)$$

Substitution gives the equation

$$s^2 X(s) - \gamma^2 X(s) = sx_0 + m(0)$$

or

$$X(s) = \frac{m(0)}{s^2 - \gamma^2} + \frac{sx_0}{s^2 - \gamma^2}$$

Then

$$x(t) = \frac{m(0)}{\gamma} \sinh \gamma t + x_0 \cosh \gamma t$$

$$x_f = \frac{m(0)}{\gamma} \sinh \gamma t_f + x_0 \cosh \gamma t_f$$

or

$$m(0) = \gamma \frac{x_f - x_0 \cosh \gamma t_f}{\sinh \gamma t_f}$$

$$x^*(t) = x_0 \cosh \gamma t + \frac{x_f - x_0 \cosh \gamma t_f}{\sinh \gamma t_f} \sinh \gamma t$$

$$m^*(t) = \dot{x}^*(t)$$

$$= \gamma x_0 \sinh \gamma t + \gamma \frac{x_f - x_0 \cosh \gamma t_f}{\sinh \gamma t_f} \cosh \gamma t$$

If we allow t_f to approach infinity in the performance index, then

$$m^*(t) = \gamma x_0(\sinh \gamma t - \cosh \gamma t)$$

$$x^*(t) = x_0(\cosh \gamma t - \sinh \gamma t)$$

In these cases, the optimal control $m^*(t)$ is given in the open loop form, as a function of x_0 and t. However, we can find x_0 in terms of $x^*(t)$, and get a feedback system. Thus

$$x_0 = \frac{1}{\cosh \gamma t - \coth \gamma t_f \sinh \gamma t} \left[x^*(t) - \frac{x_f}{\sinh \gamma t_f} \sinh \gamma t \right]$$

and substitution in the relation for $m^*(t)$ gives $m^*(t)$ as a function of the present value $x^*(t)$ or a feedback relation. If $t_f \to \infty$, this becomes very simple, or

$$m^*(t) = -\gamma x^*(t)$$

The resultant system is shown in Figure 10.2–5.

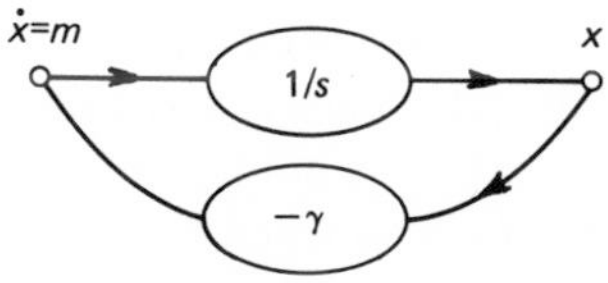

Figure 10.2–5. Optimal system for Example 10.2–2 as $t_f \to \infty$.

Inspection of the results of the example show that for a fixed x_f and t_f the control is linear but time-varying, even though the original system was stationary. If $t_f \to \infty$, the resulting system becomes linear and fixed. In this case, however, we take a very long time to reach x_f. The factor $\gamma = \alpha/\beta$ shows the relative weight we wish to place on the control. If γ is large, then the size of m is relatively unimportant, and large control magnitudes will result, while x will tend to stay near zero. A small γ makes m important and reduces the optimal control size. These observations turn out to be generally true for linear plants with the type of performance index selected.

We have not checked the solution of Example 10.2–2 with the other necessary conditions. This may often turn into a horrendous task and constitutes one of the chief objections to the calculus of variations approach. Discontinuities in the control $\mathbf{m}(t)$ raise other difficulties, which can be resolved more readily with the Pontryagin principle.

Another class of problem arises if one or both of the end points of the trajectory are not specified, but we may require the trajectory to reach a surface in state space. The classic Brachistochrone problem of determining the least time trajectory for a falling mass to go from the origin to a given straight line in two-dimensional space is an example (see Figure 6.4–4). For this situation we need an added condition, called the transversality condition.

Assume that $\mathbf{x}(0)$ is given but $x_i(t_f)$ is unspecified for i taking on any number of values $\leq n$. Then the arbitrary function $\eta(t)$ can be made zero at $t = 0$, but $\eta_i(t_f)$ cannot be made zero where $x_i(t_f)$ is not specified. Further, t_f itself may not be specified; that is, we may be required to reach a specified surface.

In the multidimensional case, (10.2–4) takes the form

$$\int_0^t \left[\frac{\partial F}{\partial x_i}\eta_i - \frac{d}{dt}\left(\frac{\partial F}{\partial \dot{x}_i}\right)\eta_i\right] dt + \left(\frac{\partial F}{\partial \dot{x}_i}\eta_i\right)_0^{t_f} = 0$$

If $\eta_i(t_f) \neq 0$, then obviously to make the Euler-Lagrange equations hold we require that

$$\left.\frac{\partial F}{\partial \dot{x}_i}\right|_{t=t_f} = 0 \tag{10.2–12}$$

for those $x_i(t)$ whose end points $x_i(t_f)$ are unspecified. [A similar relation would hold at $t = 0$ for any unspecified $x_i(0)$.]

If the end point $\mathbf{x}(t_f)$ in state space is given implicitly by specifying that it lie on a surface, other conditions hold. For simplicity, assume the scalar case and that the surface (curve) is given by

$$\phi[x(t_f), t_f] = 0$$

but that t_f is not specified. Consider variations in t_f, $x(t)$, and $\dot{x}(t)$ by amounts δt_f, $\delta x(t)$, and $\delta \dot{x}(t)$, respectively, where these variations are as defined previously. Then

$$\begin{aligned} J^* - J &= \int_0^{t_f+\delta t_f} F(x + \delta x, \dot{x} + \delta \dot{x}, t)\, dt - \int_0^{t_f} F(x, \dot{x}, t)\, dt \\ &= \int_0^{t_f} F(x + \delta x, \dot{x} + \delta \dot{x}, t)\, dt + \int_{t_f}^{t_f+\delta t_f} F(x + \delta x, \dot{x} + \delta \dot{x}, t)\, dt \\ &\quad - \int_0^{t_f} F(x, \dot{x}, t)\, dt \end{aligned}$$

If δt_f is small, the second term becomes $F|_{t=t_f}\,\delta t_f$, while the first and third terms may be combined to give

$$\int_0^{t_f} \left(\frac{\partial F}{\partial x}\, \delta x + \frac{\partial F}{\partial \dot{x}}\, \delta \dot{x} \right) dt$$

where we have dropped the function arguments. Repeating the former ploy, the second term in the last integral is integrated by parts, or

$$\int_0^{t_f} \left(\frac{\partial F}{\partial x}\, \delta x + \frac{\partial F}{\partial \dot{x}}\, \delta \dot{x} \right) dt = \left.\frac{\partial F}{\partial \dot{x}}\, \delta x \right|_0^{t_f} + \int_0^{t_f} \left(\frac{\partial F}{\partial x} - \frac{d}{dt}\frac{\partial F}{\partial \dot{x}} \right) \delta x\, dt$$

The Euler-Lagrange equations must be satisfied along the optimal trajectory; hence the last integral is zero. If $\delta x = 0$ at $t = 0$, we get

$$J^* - J = \left.\left(F\, \delta t_f + \frac{\partial F}{\partial \dot{x}}\, \delta x \right)\right|_{t=t_f}$$

From Figure 10.2–6 you see that since t_f changes as the trajectory intersects the surface $\phi = 0$, that δx_f cannot be taken at t_f but that

$$\delta x_f \simeq \delta x \bigg|_{t=t_f} + \dot{x}(t_f)\delta t_f$$

Then

$$J^* - J \simeq \left(F - \dot{x}\frac{\partial F}{\partial \dot{x}}\right)\bigg|_{t=t_f} \delta t_f + \frac{\partial F}{\partial \dot{x}}\bigg|_{t=t_f} \delta x_f$$

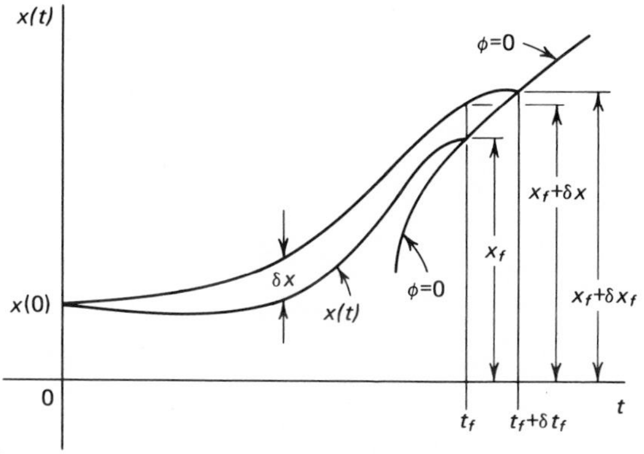

Figure 10.2–6. Neighboring trajectories, end point specified to lie on surface $\phi = 0$.

If $J = J^*$, the right side of the last equation goes to zero, or

$$\left(F - \dot{x}\frac{\partial F}{\partial \dot{x}}\right)\bigg|_{t=t_f} \delta t_f + \left(\frac{\partial F}{\partial \dot{x}}\right)\bigg|_{t=t_f} \delta x_f = 0 \qquad \textbf{(10.2–13a)}$$

Also, $\delta\phi = 0$ at t_f, or

$$\frac{\partial \phi}{\partial x_f}\,\partial x_f + \frac{\partial \phi}{\partial t_f}\,\delta t = 0 \qquad \textbf{(10.2–13b)}$$

Similar equations may be developed for a free starting point at $t = 0$. If the system is multivariable, then (10.2–13) hold for each state-space variable x_i, $i = 1, 2, \ldots, n$.

For the system with dynamic constraints, for any $x_i(t_f)$ free, then

$$\frac{\partial F_1}{\partial \dot{x}_i}\bigg|_{t=t_f} = p_i(t_f) = 0 \qquad \textbf{(10.2–14)}$$

Hence if $\mathbf{x}(t_f)$ is free, $\mathbf{p}(t_f) = \mathbf{0}$ for this case, or the Lagrange multiplier vector is zero at the end point.

In some cases, the performance index may be $J = F(x_f, t_f)$, or we are interested in minimizing some function of an end point. This is called the Meyer problem, and may be altered into the Lagrange problem by the addition of a variable or solved directly.

This very brief view of the calculus of variations would need more exposition for adequate application, but it provides a background for the principle of Pontryagin, which we now examine.

10.3 Pontryagin's Principle

We continue our expository approach. The general optimal control problem may be stated as follows:

1. Given a plant or subsystem described by a set of dynamic performance equations with state-space variables.
2. Find the plant input **m** that will minimize some performance index J.
3. Subject to constraints.

We have already discussed the performance index in some detail. Usually this is of the form

$$J = \int_{t_0}^{t_f} F(\mathbf{x}, \mathbf{m}, \mathbf{r})\, dt \tag{10.3–1}$$

where F is some function of the state variable **x**, the input **m**, and the reference **r**, and where all these may be functions of time. The limits t_0 and t_f are starting and final times, respectively. As pointed out before, the function F often is some sort of quadratic form, such as the square of the error.

The state-space expression for the dynamic performance of the plant also has been explored rather thoroughly. The linear stationary relation is of the form

$$\dot{\mathbf{x}} = \mathbf{A}\mathbf{x} + \mathbf{B}\mathbf{m} \tag{10.3–2}$$

while more generally

$$\dot{\mathbf{x}} = \mathbf{f}(\mathbf{x}, \mathbf{m}, \mathbf{t}) \tag{10.3–3}$$

The output **y** is assumed to be simply related to the state variable **x**.

The constraints have received some attention in Chapter 9. The imposition of a constraint often leads to a nonlinear solution. There are two general types of constraints: (1) input constraints on **m** and (2) state-space constraints on **x**. Constraints on **m** may consist of limits on the magnitude of **m**, such as $\|\mathbf{m}\| \leq L$, where L is a constant or limits on the total effort such as

$$\int_{t_0}^{t_f} \|\mathbf{m}\|^2 \, dt \leq L$$

or others, and combinations of these. State-space constraints mean that certain regions of the state space are forbidden. For example, in trying to land in the opposite side of the moon, obviously a rocket must avoid the vicinity of the moon itself on all sides except where the landing is desired, as in Figure 10.3–1.

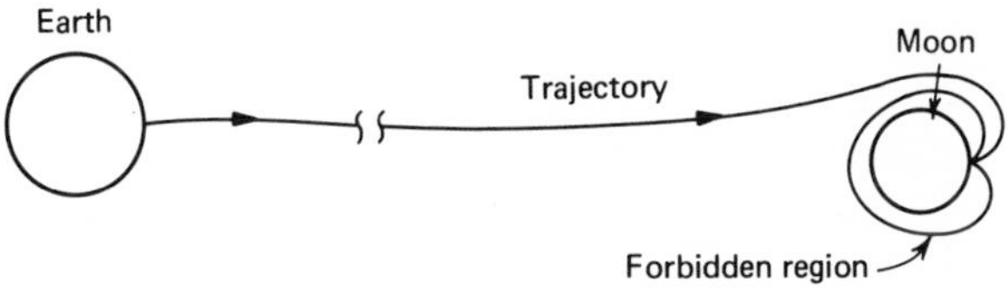

Figure 10.3–1. Constraints in state space—earth to moon trajectory.

The Pontryagin principle can be given in general terms by augmenting the state space. That is, let $x_1, x_2, \ldots, x_n$ be the variables that span the state space necessary to describe the dynamics of the plant as given by (10.3–2) or (10.3–3), and add the variable x_0, where x_0 will usually be concerned with the minimization. The principle states that in achieving a state-space trajectory starting at $t = t_0$ and finishing at $t = t_f$ the control m^* that minimizes

$$J = \sum_{i=0}^{n} c_i x_i(t_f) \tag{10.3–4}$$

maximizes the Hamiltonian

$$H = \sum_{i=0}^{n} p_i f_i \tag{10.3–5}$$

where

$$\dot{x}_i = f_i(\mathbf{x}, \mathbf{m}^*) \tag{10.3–6}$$

$$\dot{p}_i = -\sum_{j=0}^{n} \frac{\partial f_j}{\partial x_i} p_j \bigg|_{\mathbf{m}=\mathbf{m}^*} \tag{10.3–7}$$

In this formulation, $i = 0, 1, 2, \ldots, n$, and the c_i are constants. The performance index is a linear combination of the (augmented) state variables. The boundary conditions are as follows:

Let $x_i(t_f)$, $i = 0, 1, \ldots, k$, $k \leq n$ be not fixed (open). Then $p_i(t_f)$, $i = 0, 1, \ldots, k$ are given by

$$p_i(t_f) = -c_i \tag{10.3–8}$$

Let $x_i(t_f)$, $i = k+1, k+2, \ldots, n$, be fixed. Then $p_i(t_f)$, $i = k+1, k+2, \ldots, n$ are open. Finally, if t_f is open, then

$$H(t_f) = \sum_{i=1}^{n} p_i(t_f) x_i(t_f) = 0 \tag{10.3–9}$$

Equations (10.3–6) and (10.3–7) may be written

$$\dot{\mathbf{x}} = \nabla_{\mathbf{p}} H^* \tag{10.3–10}$$

$$\dot{\mathbf{p}} = -\nabla_{\mathbf{x}} H^* \tag{10.3–11}$$

respectively [13]. (See Appendix A for the definition of ∇.)

The restrictions on the control $\mathbf{m}^*$ are not onerous, piecewise continuous controls such as shown in Figure 10.3–2, for example, being admissible.

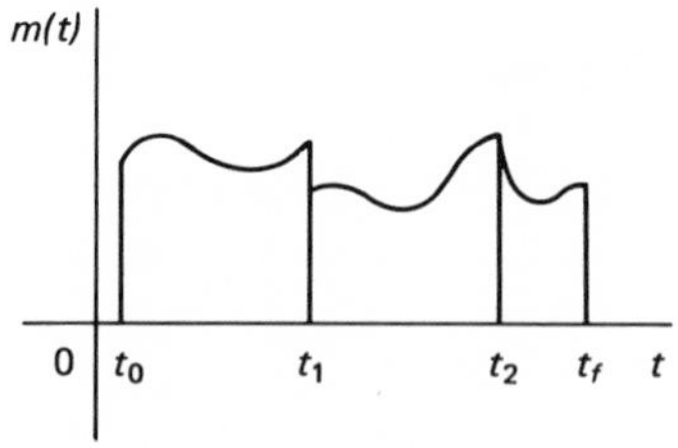

Figure 10.3–2. Type of control possible for Pontryagin principle.

Such discontinuous control functions are difficult to handle using the calculus of variations. We may illustrate the entire control system by Figure 10.3–3, where $\mathbf{r}$ is the reference (more exactly, the desired output), $\mathbf{m}$ the control, $\mathbf{x}$ the state variable, and $\mathbf{y}$ the output. P is the plant, described by the dynamic equations and G the controller to be designed. We assume

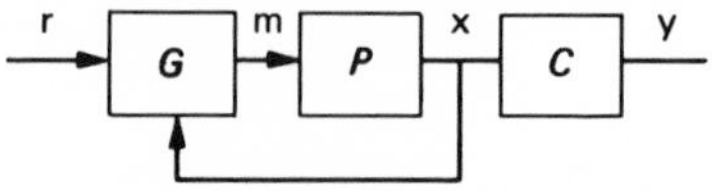

Figure 10.3–3. Schematic diagram for optimal control problem.

that only a design ensuring a desired **x** is required. There will be feedback paths between **x** and G, and in adaptive systems the output **y** may be used to determine the plant dynamics. For purposes of further investigation we can classify the optimal problem into several categories:

1. The regulator. In this system the reference **r** is a constant, which is usually assumed to be the equilibrium point. With the system initially displaced (for example by a disturbance), return the system to the equilibrium point so as to minimize the performance index.
2. The servomechanism. Here **r** is a time function, either random or deterministic. Keep the output **y** close to the desired value as time progresses, and minimize the performance index.
3. Terminal control. It is desired to minimize a function of the error at the final time t_f, such as $\|\mathbf{x}(t_f) - \mathbf{r}(t_f)\|^2$, where t_f is often specified.
4. Minimum time. The initial and final states are specified, and it is desired to minimize t_f.
5. Minimum fuel. Transfer the system from an initial to a final state using a minimum amount of fuel.

Other categories could be made but these will suffice for now. Let us give an example of the Pontryagin principle as applied to a regulator problem ($\mathbf{r} = \mathbf{0}$).

Example 10.3–1

Given the dynamic system

$$\ddot{y} + 2a\dot{y} + y = m$$

minimize

$$J = \int_{t_0}^{t_f} (y^2 + \lambda m^2)\, dt$$

where λ is given.

Conditions: No constraints, t_f fixed and $y(t_f)$ open.
Solution: Let $y = x_1$ and write the plant dynamics as

$$\dot{x}_1 = x_2$$

$$\dot{x}_2 = -x_1 - 2ax_2 + m$$

Let the augmented state variable be x_0, where

$$\dot{x}_0 = x_1^2 + \gamma m^2$$

Then, from (10.3–4), $c_0 = 1$.

Thus $f_0 = x_1^2 + \lambda m^2, f_1 = x_2, f_2 = -x_1 - 2ax_2 + m$, and

$$H = p_0(x_1^2 + \lambda m^2) + p_1(x_2) + p_2(-x_1 - 2ax_2 + m)$$

From (10.3–7),

$$\dot{p}_0 = -\frac{\partial H}{\partial x_0} = 0$$

$$p_0(t_f) = -c_0 = -1$$

Hence

$$p_0 = -1$$

Then we wish to find a control m that will maximize

$$H = -(x_1^2 + \lambda m^2) + p_1(x_2) + p_2(-x_1 - 2ax_2 + m)$$

From (10.3–5) we set $\partial H/\partial m = 0$ to get

$$m^* = \frac{1}{2\lambda} p_2$$

We might pause and remark that if there were constraints on the control m, we would immediately have an involved relation for m^* at this point. With no constraints, then

$$\dot{x}_1 = \left.\frac{\partial H}{\partial p_1}\right|_{m=m^*} = x_2$$

$$\dot{x}_2 = \left.\frac{\partial H}{\partial p_2}\right|_{m=m^*}$$

$$= -x_1 - 2ax_2 + \frac{1}{2\lambda} p_2$$

These are the dynamic equations again with $m = m^*$. Also, from (10.3–7),

$$\dot{p}_1 = -\frac{\partial H^*}{\partial x_1} = 2x_1 + p_2$$

$$\dot{p}_2 = -\frac{\partial H^*}{\partial x_2} = -p_1 + 2ap_2$$

These four differential equations can be expressed in vector form by letting $z_1 = x_1$, $z_2 = x_2$, $z_3 = p_1$, and $z_4 = p_2$. Then

$$\dot{\mathbf{z}} = \mathbf{C}\mathbf{z}$$

where

$$\mathbf{C} = \begin{bmatrix} 0 & 1 & 0 & 0 \\ -1 & -2a & 0 & 1/2\lambda \\ 2 & 0 & 0 & 1 \\ 0 & 0 & -1 & 2a \end{bmatrix}$$

We now find a solution for $\mathbf{z}$ using the initial conditions $z_{10} = x_{10}$ and $z_{20} = x_{20}$. However, we do not know the initial conditions $z_{30} = p_{10}$ and $z_{40} = p_{20}$. What we do know are the final conditions on $\mathbf{p}$ at t_f which in this case are $p_1(t_f) = p_2(t_f) = 0$ from (10.3–8). Thus we conclude that Pontryagin's principle results in twice as many ordinary differential equations as the order of the system, and that we have a two-point boundary problem; some variables are known at t_0 and others at t_f. This causes some difficulties. In this case, we can solve for $\mathbf{z}$ by finding the transition martix, or

$$\mathbf{z} = \mathbf{\Phi}(t - t_0)\mathbf{z}_0$$

and letting $z_3 = z_4 = 0$ when $t = t_f$. Thus

$$0 = \Phi_{31}x_1(t_0) + \Phi_{32}x_2(t_0) + \Phi_{33}p_1(t_0) + \Phi_{34}p_2(t_0)$$

$$0 = \Phi_{41}x_1(t_0) + \Phi_{42}x_2(t_0) + \Phi_{43}p_1(t_0) + \Phi_{44}p_2(t_0)$$

where $\Phi_{ij} = \Phi_{ij}(t_f - t_0)$, and the subscripts refer to the components of the transition matrix $\mathbf{\Phi}(t_f - t_0)$.

These equations may now be solved for $p_2(t_0)$, and the optimal control m^* is

$$m^* = \frac{1}{2\lambda} p_2(t)$$

where t is substituted for t_0, $t_0 \leq t \leq t_f$. m^* will be linear but time-varying, or

$$m^*(t) = \frac{1}{2\lambda} [k_1(t)x_1(t) + k_2(t)x_2(t)]$$

As m is dependent on x_1 and x_2, it is a feedback control system.

We should pause here for a moment to make some general remarks and tie this discussion to Section 10.2. First, the vector $\mathbf{p}$, called the costate or adjoint vector, is closely related to the Lagrangian multipliers of the calculus of variations and in fact can be considered in this light. Equation (10.3–7) also corresponds to the adjoint equation discussed in Chapter 5, and hence the p_i constitute a kind of "reverse" time set relative to the x_i. The Hamiltonian H is closely analogous to the Hamiltonian of classical mechanics. In fact, partial differential equations developed from the Pontryagin principle are called the Hamilton-Jacobi equations. The advantages of Pontryagin's principle is that all the additional conditions of the calculus of variations are contained and that discontinuous control functions may be handled without difficulty. (We have skimmed over many of the finer points, however.)

We now outline a proof of the Pontryagin principle, using the scalar case. The proof follows Dorato and Drenick [13]. (For a proof using vectors see Athans and Falb [14].)

Given a performance index

$$J = cx(t_f) \tag{10.3–12}$$

and a plant

$$\dot{x} = f(x, m) \tag{10.3–13}$$

minimize J using an admissible control m for $x(0)$ specified but $x(t_f)$ free.

First, we follow the calculus of variations approach and then point out the Pontryagin alternative. As in Section 10.2, assume a variation in the control from the optimal control $m^*(t)$ such that

$$m(t) = m^*(t) + \epsilon\eta(t) \qquad 0 \leq t \leq t_f \tag{10.3–14}$$

where $m^*(t)$ and $\epsilon\eta(t)$ are as shown in Figure 10.3–4, with $\eta(0) = \eta(t_f) = 0$ but $\eta(t)$ being an arbitrary bounded function otherwise. As $x(t_f)$ depends on $m(t)$, J is a functional with respect to m, and takes on the minimum J^*

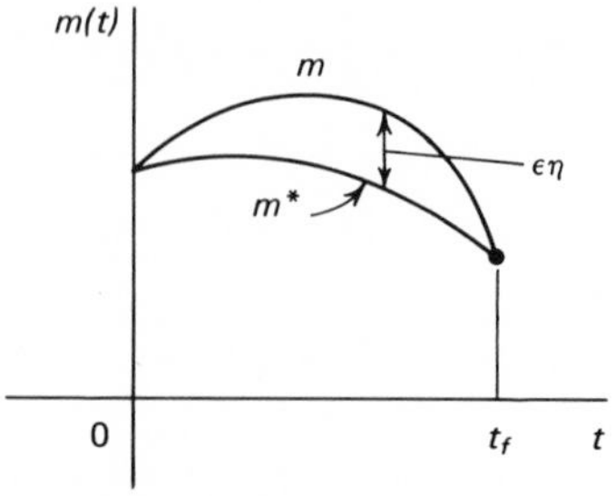

Figure 10.3–4. Optimal control—variational calculus approach.

when $m = m^*$. Using (10.3–14), J becomes a function of ϵ, and J^* must occur when $\epsilon = 0$. Hence

$$\left.\frac{dJ(\epsilon)}{d\epsilon}\right|_{\epsilon=0} = 0$$

or

$$\left.\frac{\partial J(\epsilon)}{\partial \epsilon}\, d\epsilon\right|_{\epsilon=0} = 0 \tag{10.3–15}$$

From (10.3–12),

$$\frac{\partial J(\epsilon)}{\partial \epsilon} = c\,\frac{\partial x(t_f, \epsilon)}{\partial \epsilon} \tag{10.3–16}$$

and, from (10.3–13),

$$\frac{\partial \dot{x}}{\partial \epsilon} = \frac{d}{dt}\frac{\partial x}{\partial \epsilon} = \frac{\partial f}{\partial x}\frac{\partial x}{\partial \epsilon} + \frac{\partial f}{\partial m}\frac{\partial m}{\partial \epsilon}$$

$$= \frac{\partial f}{\partial x}\frac{\partial x}{\partial \epsilon} + \frac{\partial f}{\partial m}\eta \tag{10.3–17}$$

Equation (10.3–17) is linear in the variable $\partial x/\partial \epsilon$ if $\partial f/\partial x$ and $\partial f/\partial m$ are evaluated with $m(t) = m^*(t)$. For an initial condition,

$$\left.\frac{\partial x}{\partial \epsilon}\right|_{t=0} = 0 \tag{10.3–18}$$

since $x(0)$ is specified. Then the solution of (10.3–17) is

$$\frac{\partial x(t_f, \epsilon)}{\partial \epsilon} = \int_0^{t_f} \phi(t_f, \tau)\,\frac{\partial f}{\partial m}\,\eta(\tau)\, d\tau \tag{10.3–19}$$

where $\phi(t_f, \tau)$ is the transition matrix (here a scalar) for the homogeneous equation. Owing to the form of (10.3–13), $\phi(t_f, \tau)$ will be time-varying.

Using (10.3–12), then,

$$\frac{\partial J(\epsilon)}{\partial \epsilon} = \int_0^{t_f} c\phi(t_f, \tau)\,\frac{\partial f}{\partial x}\,\eta(\tau)\, d\tau \tag{10.3–20}$$

Now let $p(t)$ be a new variable such that

$$\dot{p} = \frac{\partial f}{\partial x}\,p \tag{10.3–21}$$

where $\partial f/\partial x$ is evaluated at $m = m^*$ and $p(t_f) = -c$. Because (10.3–21) is the adjoint of (10.3–17) without the driving function, the solution is

$$p(t_f) = \phi^{-1}(t_f, t)p(t) \qquad \textbf{(10.3–22)}$$

whence (10.3–20) becomes

$$\frac{\partial J(\epsilon)}{\partial \epsilon} = \int_0^{t_f} p(\tau) \frac{\partial f}{\partial m} \eta(\tau)\, d\tau \qquad \textbf{(10.3–23)}$$

Finally, because $\eta(\tau)$ is arbitrary,

$$p(\tau) \frac{\partial f}{\partial m}\bigg|_{m=m^*} = 0 \qquad \textbf{(10.3–24)}$$

If we adopt the definition $H = pf(x, m)$, then you get

$$\frac{\partial H}{\partial m}\bigg|_{m=m^*} = 0 \qquad \textbf{(10.3–25)}$$

This completes the proof outline using the calculus of variations approach. Equations (10.3–13), (10.3–21), and (10.3–25) constitute the principle.

To permit greater flexibility in the variable $\eta(t)$, Pontryagin considers the variation shown in Figure 10.3–5, where $m(t)$ follows $m^*(t)$ for $t_1 \le t$ and

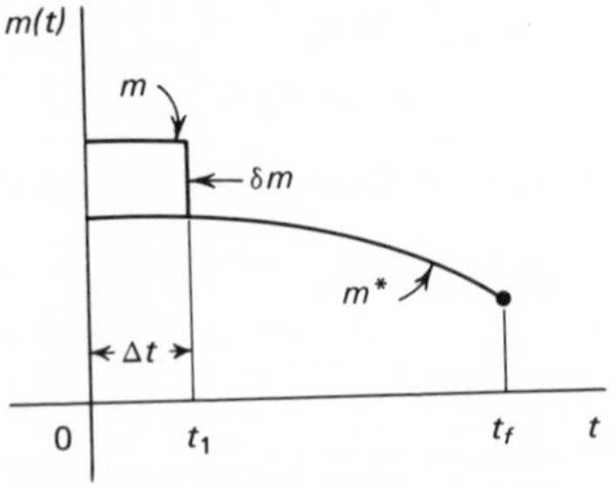

Figure 10.3–5. Optimal control—Pontryagin approach.

t_f, but is not the same for $0 \le t \le t_1$, where $t_1 = \Delta t$ if $t_0 = 0$. Again optimality is characterized by

$$J(m) \ge J^*(m)$$

or

$$c\,\delta x(t_f) \ge 0 \qquad \textbf{(10.3–26)}$$

where $\delta x(t_f) = x(t) - x^*(t_f)$.

The change $\delta x(t_1)$ brought about by the variation in m of Figure 10.3–5 is given to first-order terms in Δt by

$$\delta x(t_1) = f(x, m) - f(x, m^*)\Big|_{t=0} \Delta t \tag{10.3–27}$$

Using a Tayler's series, if we linearize the perturbed equation about the optimal trajectory (see Chapter 6), we get the equation

$$\frac{d}{dt}(\delta x) = \frac{\partial f}{\partial x}\Bigg|_{m=m^*} \delta x$$

which has the solution

$$\delta x(t_f) = \phi(t_f, t_1)\delta x(t_1) \tag{10.3–28}$$

Substituting (10.3–28) and (10.3–27) into (10.3–26) we find that

$$c\phi(t_f, t_1)(f(x, m) - f(x, m^*))\Big|_{t=0} \Delta t \geq 0 \tag{10.3–29}$$

Again let $p(t)$ satisfy the relation

$$\dot{p} = -\frac{\partial f}{\partial x}\Bigg|_{m=m^*} p$$

with $p(t_f) = -c$. Then

$$p(t_f) = \phi^{-1}(t_f, t)p(t_1) \tag{10.3–30}$$

$$p(t_1)(f(x, m) - f(x, m^*))\Big|_{t=0} \Delta t \leq 0 \tag{10.3–31}$$

Finally let $H = pf(x, m)$ and $t_1 \to 0$ while $\Delta t \neq 0$. Then

$$[H(m) - H(m^*)]_{t=0} \leq 0 \tag{10.3–32}$$

The origin of the time scale ($t = 0$) is arbitrary, so (10.3–32) indicates that H is a maximum along the optimal trajectory.

The crux of the Pontryagin approach, resulting in (10.3–32), is that we find it only necessary to obtain an absolute maximum H with respect to the control m, and we avoid the derivative situation of (10.3–25), which applies only to problems where the minimizing control is interior to a constraint set Ω. Since m may jump from one boundary of Ω to another, discontinuous controls are included in the Pontryagin principle.

10.4 Linear System with Quadratic Performance Index

Because this text concerns itself primarily with linear systems, let us look at such a system with a special performance index. The solution for this situation has been developed as follows [15].

Let the performance index be a quadratic form, or

$$J = \int_0^{t_f} \tfrac{1}{2}(\mathbf{x}^T\mathbf{Q}\mathbf{x} + \mathbf{m}^T\mathbf{R}\mathbf{m})\,dt \qquad (10.4\text{–}1)$$

where **Q** and **R** are positive definite, and let the controllable plant dynamics be

$$\dot{\mathbf{x}} = \mathbf{A}\mathbf{x} + \mathbf{B}\mathbf{m} \qquad (10.4\text{–}2)$$

and assume no constraints. **A**, **B**, **Q**, and **R** may be time-varying. Then

$$H = \mathbf{p}^T(\mathbf{A}\mathbf{x} + \mathbf{B}\mathbf{m}) - \tfrac{1}{2}(\mathbf{x}^T\mathbf{Q}\mathbf{x} + \mathbf{m}^T\mathbf{R}\mathbf{m}) \qquad (10.4\text{–}3)$$

To maximize H, set $\nabla_{\mathbf{m}} H = \mathbf{0}$, or

$$\begin{bmatrix} \dfrac{\partial H}{\partial m_1} \\ \dfrac{\partial H}{\partial m_2} \\ \vdots \\ \dfrac{\partial H}{\partial m_i} \end{bmatrix} = \mathbf{0}$$

Then

$$\nabla_{\mathbf{m}}(\mathbf{p}^T\mathbf{B}\mathbf{m}) - \nabla\mathbf{p}(\tfrac{1}{2}\mathbf{m}^T\mathbf{R}\mathbf{m}) = \mathbf{B}^T\mathbf{p} - \mathbf{R}\mathbf{m} = \mathbf{0}$$

Hence

$$\mathbf{m} = \mathbf{m}^* = \mathbf{R}^{-1}\mathbf{B}^T\mathbf{p} \qquad (10.4\text{–}4)$$

From (10.3–11),

$$\dot{\mathbf{p}} = -\nabla_x H$$

Hence

$$\dot{\mathbf{p}} = -\mathbf{A}^T\mathbf{p} + \mathbf{Q}\mathbf{x} \qquad (10.4\text{–}5)$$

We can combine (10.4–2) and (10.4–4) to get

$$\dot{\mathbf{x}} = \mathbf{Ax} + \mathbf{BR}^{-1}\mathbf{B}^T\mathbf{p} \tag{10.4–6}$$

and finally put (10.4–5) and (10.4–6) together as follows:

$$\begin{bmatrix} \dot{\mathbf{x}} \\ \dot{\mathbf{p}} \end{bmatrix} = \begin{bmatrix} \mathbf{A} & \mathbf{BR}^{-1}\mathbf{B}^T \\ \mathbf{Q} & -\mathbf{A}^T \end{bmatrix} \begin{bmatrix} \mathbf{x} \\ \mathbf{p} \end{bmatrix} \tag{10.4–7}$$

The variables **p** and **x** in (10.4–5) through (10.4–7) are for the optimal trajectory, or **p*** and **x***, but we omit the superscript for brevity and continue in this fashion. Equation (10.4–7) may be solved as before. However, if we let

$$\mathbf{p} = \mathbf{Kx} \tag{10.4–8}$$

where **K** is a new matrix [16], substitution in (10.4–5) gives

$$\dot{\mathbf{K}}\mathbf{x} + \mathbf{K}\dot{\mathbf{x}} = -\mathbf{A}^T\mathbf{Kx} + \mathbf{Qx} \tag{10.4–9}$$

Using (10.4–6) to eliminate $\dot{\mathbf{x}}$, we then obtain

$$\dot{\mathbf{K}}\mathbf{x} + \mathbf{KAx} + \mathbf{KBR}^{-1}\mathbf{B}^T\mathbf{Kx} + \mathbf{A}^T\mathbf{Kx} - \mathbf{Qx} = \mathbf{0} \tag{10.4–10}$$

Since this holds for all **x**,

$$\dot{\mathbf{K}} + \mathbf{KA} + \mathbf{KBR}^{-1}\mathbf{B}^T\mathbf{K} + \mathbf{A}^T\mathbf{K} - \mathbf{Q} = 0 \tag{10.4–11}$$

If $\mathbf{x}(t_f)$ is not specified, from (10.3–9)

$$\mathbf{p}(t_f) = \mathbf{0}$$

and hence

$$\mathbf{K}(t_f) = \mathbf{0}$$

Other boundary conditions may be obtained from the Pontryagin principle.

Equation (10.4–11) gives a set of nonlinear differential equations of the Riccati type. Only in very simple cases may they be solved analytically. However, if **A**, **B**, **Q**, and **R** are constant, the system is controllable, and $t_f \to \infty$, then (10.4–10) becomes [17]

$$\mathbf{KA} + \mathbf{A}^T\mathbf{K} + \mathbf{KBR}^{-1}\mathbf{B}^T\mathbf{K} - \mathbf{Q} = \mathbf{0} \tag{10.4–12}$$

This results in a set of algebraic equations that may be solved if the system order is not too high. The optimal control is

$$\mathbf{m}^* = \mathbf{R}^{-1}\mathbf{B}^T\mathbf{Kx} \tag{10.4–13}$$

Example 10.4–1

Given the plant

$$\dot{x}_1 = x_2$$
$$\dot{x}_2 = m$$
$$y = x_1$$

Minimize the performance index of (10.4–1) for a regulator system with

$$\mathbf{Q} = \begin{bmatrix} \alpha_{11} & 0 \\ 0 & \alpha_{22} \end{bmatrix} \qquad \mathbf{R} = \begin{bmatrix} 1 & 0 \\ 0 & \gamma \end{bmatrix}$$

if $t_f \rightarrow \infty$. Owing to the form of J, $\mathbf{x}$ eventually goes to $\mathbf{0}$, but how it proceeds depends on $\mathbf{Q}$ and $\mathbf{R}$.

Solution:

$$\mathbf{A} = \begin{bmatrix} 0 & 1 \\ 0 & 0 \end{bmatrix} \qquad \mathbf{B} = \begin{bmatrix} 0 & 0 \\ 0 & 1 \end{bmatrix}$$

Let

$$\mathbf{K} = \begin{bmatrix} k_{11} & k_{12} \\ k_{21} & k_{22} \end{bmatrix}$$

Then, using (10.4–12),

$$\begin{bmatrix} 0 & k_{11} \\ 0 & k_{12} \end{bmatrix} + \begin{bmatrix} 0 & 0 \\ k_{11} & k_{21} \end{bmatrix} + \frac{1}{\gamma} \begin{bmatrix} k_{11} & k_{12} \\ k_{21} & k_{22} \end{bmatrix} \begin{bmatrix} 0 & 0 \\ 0 & 1 \end{bmatrix} \begin{bmatrix} k_{11} & k_{12} \\ k_{21} & k_{22} \end{bmatrix} - \begin{bmatrix} \alpha_{11} & 0 \\ 0 & \alpha_{22} \end{bmatrix} = \mathbf{0}$$

This gives four equations as follows:

(a) $$\frac{k_{12}k_{21}}{\gamma} - \alpha_{11} = 0$$

(b) $$k_{11} + \frac{k_{12}k_{22}}{\gamma} = 0$$

(c) $$k_{11} + \frac{k_{21}k_{22}}{\gamma} = 0$$

(d) $$k_{12} + k_{21} + \frac{k_{22}^2}{\gamma} - \alpha_{22} = 0$$

Equations (b) and (c) show that $k_{12} = k_{21}$†. Substitution in the remainder of the equations results in

$$k_{12} = \sqrt{\alpha_{11}\gamma} \qquad k_{22} = [\alpha_{22}\gamma - 2\gamma\sqrt{\alpha_{11}\gamma}]^{1/2}$$

$$k_{11} = -[\alpha_{11}\alpha_{22} - 2\alpha_{11}\sqrt{\alpha_{11}\gamma}]^{1/2}$$

We have a question as to the proper signs to use for the square roots, but let us defer this for the moment. The optimal control from (10.4–13) is

$$m^* = \frac{1}{\gamma}(k_{12}x_1 + k_{22}x_2)$$

or we have a feedback system as in Figure 10.4–1. It is clear from Figure 10.4–1 that the feedback paths must be real and negative for stability. This

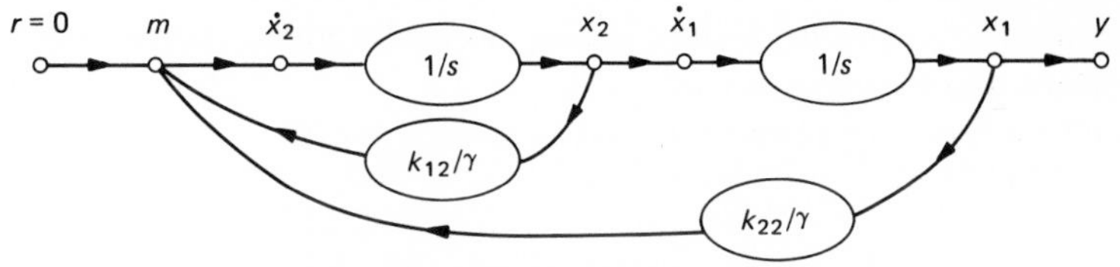

Figure 10.4–1. System for Example 10.4–1.

resolves the ambiguities in signs previously mentioned. (See also reference [14].) The system can now be described by the equations

$$\dot{x}_1 = x_2$$

$$\dot{x}_2 = \frac{1}{\gamma}k_{12}x_1 + \frac{1}{\gamma}k_{22}x_2$$

and the characteristic equation becomes

$$s^2 - \frac{1}{\gamma}k_{22}s - \frac{1}{\gamma}k_{12} = 0$$

or

$$s^2 + \left(\frac{\alpha_{22}}{\gamma} + 2\sqrt{\frac{\alpha_{11}}{\gamma}}\right)^{1/2} s + \sqrt{\frac{\alpha_{11}}{\gamma}} = 0$$

assuming the positive sign is needed in the parentheses to give a real quantity. Then we have a system where

$$\omega_n = \left(\frac{\alpha_{11}}{\gamma}\right)^{1/4}$$

$$\zeta = \left(\frac{1}{4}\sqrt{\frac{\alpha_{22}^2}{\alpha_{11}\gamma}} + \frac{1}{2}\right)^{1/2}$$

† Athans and Falb show that **K** is symmetric in general.

You see that the second-order damping factor $\zeta \geq \sqrt{0.5}$. This result has been proved in general by Kalman for any second-order system [18]. Greater damping is provided by α_{22}.

In Example 10.4–1 the question may arise: What do we make α_{11}, α_{22}, γ, or in general how do we select the matrix elements in the quadratic forms of the performance index? In the example, we could select α_{11} and γ on the basis of a desired ω_n and α_{22} for further damping. However, this seems a little like defeating the purpose of the performance index, although we would have some simultaneous notion of the relative weights we are giving the error (distance from the origin) and the effort, because the **Q** and **R** give some sort of measure of this relation. This lack of a scientific method for choosing the matrix elements (even assuming the quadratic form to be meaningful) reveals one of the Achilles' heels of optimal control theory.

Athans and Falb give a method for putting the servomechanisms problem into a regulator problem for some situations [19].

10.5 Optimal Time Control

Completing a trajectory in minimum time is certainly very meaningful in some situations. We give an example of this case and also show how discontinuous controls arise. (The example appears in reference [11] and in many other papers.)

Example 10.5–1

Consider the dynamic equations

$$\dot{x}_1 = x_2$$

$$\dot{x}_2 = m$$

with the performance index $J = t_f$, $x_1(t_f) = x_2(t_f) = 0$, and the constraint $|m| \leq 1$. In words, we wish to find a trajectory such that the force m brings a unit mass from any given point x_0 at $t = 0$ in state space to the origin in the least possible time if the magnitude of m is limited.

Solution:

$$J = \int_0^{t_f} 1\, dt$$

Then

$$\dot{x}_0 = 1 \qquad c_0 = 1$$

$$H = p_0 + p_1 x_2 + p_2 m$$

$$\dot{p}_0 = -\frac{\partial H}{\partial x_0} = 0$$

$$p_0(t_f) = -c_0 = -1$$

or

$$H = -1 + p_1 x_2 + p_2 m$$

Then

$$\dot{p}_1 = -\frac{\partial H}{\partial x_1} = 0$$

$$\dot{p}_2 = -\frac{\partial H}{\partial x_2} = -p_1$$

Hence $p_1 = k_1$, $p_2 = k_2 - k_1 t$, where k_1 and k_2 are constants. Thus

$$H = -1 + k_1 x_2 + (k_2 - k_1 t)m$$

To maximize H by varying m it is necessary to make the last term positive and as large as possible. Hence, if p_2 is negative, m should be negative, and vice versa, and, since $|m| \leq 1$, $m^* = \operatorname{sgn} p_2 = \operatorname{sgn}(k_2 - k_1 t)$. The sgn function is shown in Figure 10.5–1. If $m = 1$, then

$$\dot{x}_2 = 1$$

or

$$x_2 = t + A$$

$$x_1 = \frac{t^2}{2} + At + B$$

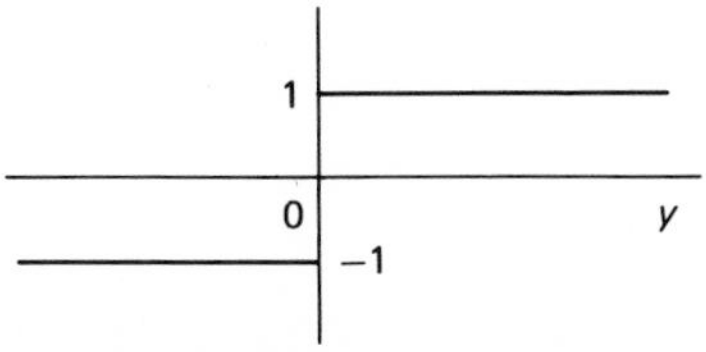

Figure 10.5–1. Function sgn *y*.

where A and B are constants, or

$$x_1 = \tfrac{1}{2}(x_2)^2 + D \tag{10.5–1}$$

where $D = B - A^2/2$. Similarly, when $m = -1$,

$$x_1 = -\tfrac{1}{2}(x_2)^2 + E \tag{10.5–2}$$

where E is another constant. Equations (10.5–1) and (10.5–2) describe sets of parabolas as shown in Figures 10.5–2 and 10.5–3.

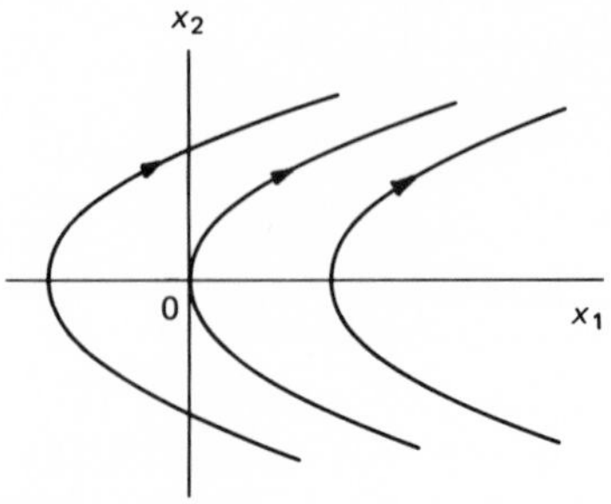

Figure 10.5–2. Trajectories for Example 10.5–1, $m = 1$.

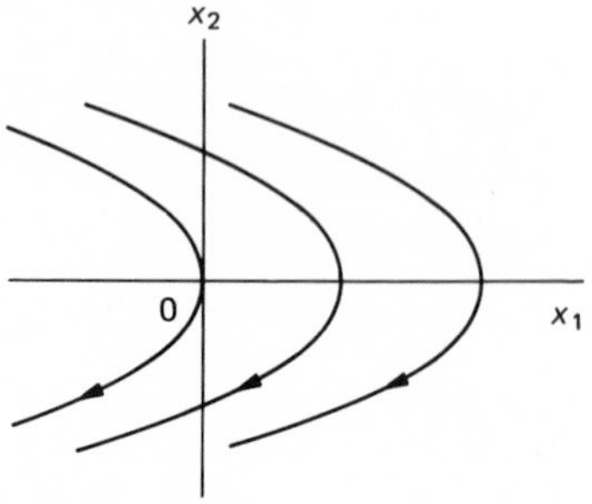

Figure 10.5–3. Trajectories for Example 10.5–1, $m = -1$.

From $m^* = \operatorname{sgn}(k_2 - k_1 t)$, in any interval $0 \leq t \leq t_f$ there can be at most two values of m, because $k_2 - k_1 t$ can change sign once at most in this interval. Hence if we start at some initial point x_0 such that $m = 1$, we must proceed along one of the parabolas in Figure 10.5–2 until we reach another parabola on which $m = -1$ in Figure 10.5–3 and which goes directly to the origin. Continuing this reasoning, we get a family of trajectories as in Figure 10.5–4. The line *aob* is a "switching" line; that is, at the

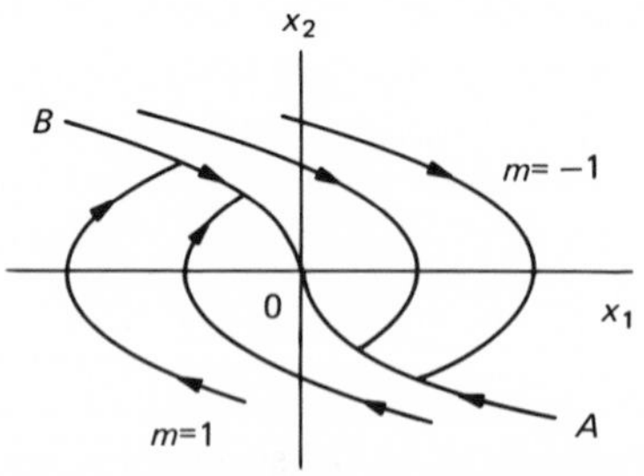

Figure 10.5–4. Optimal time trajectories for Example 10.5–1.

values of x_1 and x_2 along this line, m must change from 1 to -1 if $\mathbf{x}_0$ is below AOB, and vice versa if $\mathbf{x}_0$ is above AOB. This line has the equations

$$x_1 = \tfrac{1}{2}(x_2)^2 \qquad x_2 \leq 0$$

$$x_1 = -\tfrac{1}{2}(x_2)^2 \qquad x_2 \geq 0$$

Hence if we measure x_1 and x_2, the above equations tell us when to change the control m from full on one way to full on the other. The system expressed in this parametric manner is of the feedback type, because the control depends on x_1 and x_2. We could also express the system as an open loop type by putting the switching curves in terms of the time variable t. The constants D and E would be determined by the initial condition x_0. Figure 10.5–5

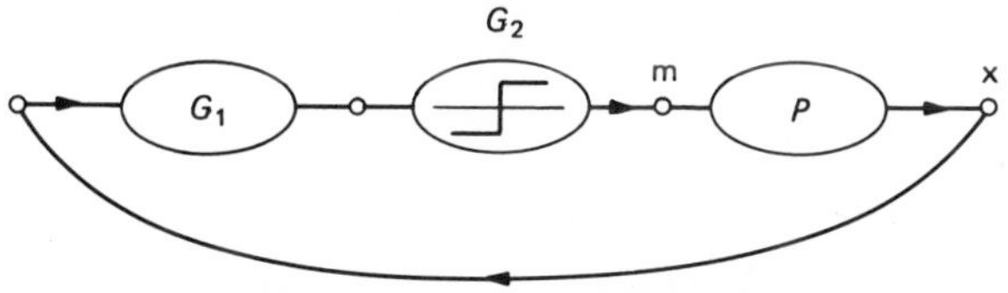

Figure 10.5–5. System for Example 10.5–1.

shows the general arrangement for using the feedback approach. The controller G is shown in two parts, G_2, which is a sgn function generator (such as a relay), and G_1, which receives the measurements of x_1 and x_2, finds the region of space, adjusts the sign of the sgn generator accordingly, and changes sign on the switching curve. In general, G_1 would therefore be some sort of computer.

Many optimal controls resolve into the type discussed if the control magnitude is limited. In practical cases saturation always limits the output of a device, so an optimal control is frequently one that is on full in one direction or the other. This simple but effective system is termed the "bang-bang" system. The control device may be a simple relay that applies full power to obtain maximum output torque, in one direction or the other. The fly in the sweets consists in reversing the relay at exactly the correct time (or when the state-space variables reach the correct value). Even from our simple example we can see that this is not easy. In a multidimensional system, the switching curve becomes a hypersurface in state space. If the computations in G_1 are performed using the Pontryagin principle, the two-point boundary problem will be formidable, and the computational time could be excessive. It may be possible to make many of the computations beforehand and to store polynomial approximations in the computer. In any case, these computational difficulties form the present barrier to widespread application of the optimal system.

An alternative to the completely nonlinear bang-bang system consists of a two-phase system such that full power is applied when the error is large, and the system is nonlinear, while when the error is small or the system is near the origin, it operates as a linear system. Such a control is of the "sat" variety, as shown in Figure 10.5–6. The computational difficulties of course still remain.

If the end points in the maximum problem are variable, then transversality relations are necessary, just as for the calculus of variations approach. In this case, if we must reach a specified hypersurface it turns out that the first m components of the costate vector $\mathbf{p}$ must be orthogonal to any

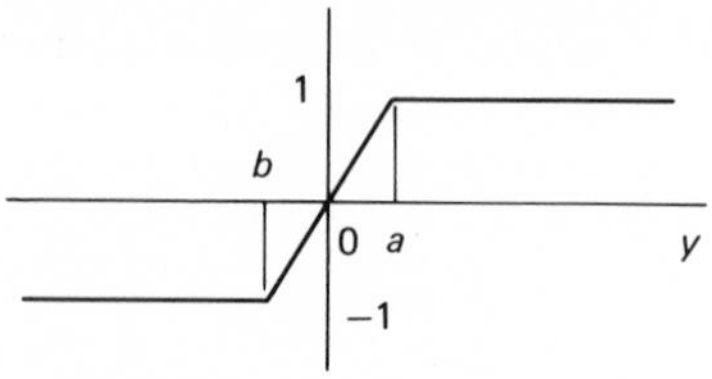

Figure 10.5–6. Function sat y.

vector tangent to the m-dimensional hypersurface at the point where the trajectory reaches the surface. In three-dimensional terms, the $\mathbf{p}$ vector has the direction of the gradient (but points inward).

10.6 State-Variable Approach—Miscellaneous

For a single input-output controllable and observable system described by

$$\dot{\mathbf{x}} = \mathbf{A}\mathbf{x} + \mathbf{b}m \qquad \textbf{(10.6–1a)}$$

$$y = \mathbf{C}\mathbf{x} \qquad \textbf{(10.6–1b)}$$

and with a performance index of the type

$$J = \frac{1}{2}\int_0^\infty (\mathbf{x}^T\mathbf{Q}\mathbf{x} + m^2)\,dt \qquad \textbf{(10.6–2)}$$

Kalman finds a simple condition in the complex s plane [20]. If

$$\mathbf{Q} = \mathbf{q}\mathbf{q}^T \quad (\mathbf{Q} \text{ symmetric})$$

then

$$m = \mathbf{k}^T\mathbf{x} \qquad \textbf{(10.6–3)}$$

where

$$\mathbf{k} = \mathbf{K}^T\mathbf{b}$$

$$\mathbf{A}^T\mathbf{K} + \mathbf{K}\mathbf{A} + Kbb^TK - \mathbf{q}\mathbf{q}^T = 0 \qquad \textbf{(10.6–4)}$$

This is the same as (10.4–12) for the particular case. In addition, Kalman shows that this is equivalent in the complex plane to a condition

$$|1 + \mathbf{k}^T\hat{\boldsymbol{\phi}}(s)\mathbf{b}|^2 = 1 + |\mathbf{q}^T\hat{\boldsymbol{\phi}}(s)\mathbf{b}|^2 \tag{10.6–5}$$

where $\hat{\boldsymbol{\phi}}(s) = (s\mathbf{I} - \mathbf{A})^{-1}$. Since for zero initial conditions,

$$\mathbf{x}(s) = \hat{\boldsymbol{\phi}}(s)\mathbf{b}m(s)$$

$$\frac{Y(s)}{M(s)} = \mathbf{C}\hat{\boldsymbol{\phi}}(s)\mathbf{b}$$

Then if we let $H_1 = \mathbf{k}^T\mathbf{x}/\mathbf{C}\mathbf{x}$ be an "equivalent" feedback function, (10.6–5) becomes

$$|1 + G(s)H_1(s)|^2 = 1 + |\beta(s)|^2 \tag{10.6–6}$$

where $\beta(s) = \mathbf{q}^T\hat{\boldsymbol{\phi}}(s)\mathbf{b}$. Since $|\beta(s)| \geq 0$, then

$$|1 + G(s)H_1(s)| \geq 1 \tag{10.6–7}$$

Equation (10.6–7) indicates that for the performance index chosen, the return difference must be at least 1. Figure 10.6–1 shows the situation with

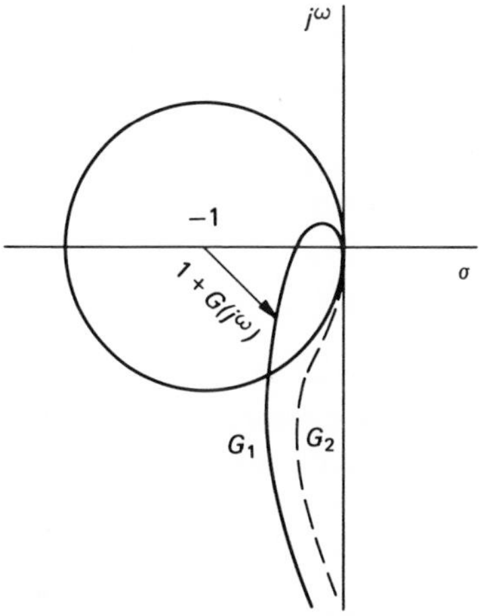

Figure 10.6–1. Comparison of s-plane plots for conventionally compensated system G_1 and optimal system G_2.

$H_1 = -1$ for simplicity. The solid curve (G_1) depicts a possible conventionally compensated system, with adequate relative stability. The dashed curve (G_2) indicates a possible optimal system, which must avoid the circle of unit radius with center at -1. Clearly, (10.6–7) is a severe requirement. For one thing, the optimal system must be stable at all gains. This is not possible unless all state variables are fed back [21]. Although the optimal system might not be achieved, at least it might serve as a comparison for the other designs, however.

Kalman also shows that Chang's root-square-locus design (Chapter 9) is a special case of (10.6–5) [18].

Several authors have shown that observable and controllable optimal systems that meet certain requirements must be stable. This may be done by using the performance index as a Lyapunov function [22]. Certainly if it is possible to get the system from one point to another in state space it is stable. If the integrand of the loss function is zero at $\mathbf{x}(t_f)$, asymptotic stability may be proved.

From an economic standpoint, the process control industry seems to offer one of the most fruitful areas for optimal control. Most of these systems are of the regulator type. Douglas has published a design for a stirred-tank reactor. His procedure goes as follows:

1. Reduce the large number of variables to those (about 10) which are the most important. This makes the problem manageable to some degree.
2. Linearize the system about some operating point. This allows a solution that is possibly practical.
3. Consider nonlinear operation based on step 2, using cut and try regular techniques.

By greatly reducing the time for a process, Douglas shows how may extensive savings are possible. Such model studies also often reveal large capital investments to be unnecessary [23].

10.7 Summary and Critique of State-Space Analysis

State-space techniques have become dominant in research since World War II. The great majority of the current literature involves analysis using equations of state. As previously discussed, this is due to the growing complexity of control systems and inability to extend the older concepts to multi-input-output systems or to achieve optimal designs by direct methods. The mathematics of vector spaces offers powerful generalization tools with which we can attack the otherwise unwieldy problems, and, coupled with the growing use of computers, hope exists that ever larger systems will become tractable.

We have of course only touched on a very small part of the knowledge in this area. The effort has been to enable you to be sufficiently grounded in the fundamentals of state-space theory so that you can start reading the current literature, indicate something of the large scope of the problems, and to arouse interest in these. We have not discussed many aspects, such as random processes, and the theory of information flow. In fact, one of the striking things concerning control systems is the broadness of the problems, and the intimate connections with many other fields, such as information theory and general system theory. There seems to be no limit to the interdisciplinary investigations associated with control.

In spite of all the advances in theory and of the large volume of research being done using the state-space approach, it is fairly safe to say that at this point in time the state-space approach has not achieved great success in practical control systems. There are several reasons for this:

1. The approach is relatively new and unfamiliar to the older generation of designers.
2. The theory has been developed and carried on primarily by mathematicians and acceptance and application by engineers has lagged.
3. The computational aspects of synthesis are formidable. The largest and fastest of modern computers are incapable of solving, in the time required, most large-scale optimal problems using any of the three techniques mentioned. The occurrence of a two-point boundary problem with a large number of nonlinear equations, as in the Pontryagin principle, indicates the size and difficulty of the issue.
4. Generally the state variables are not directly available.

We are thus in a transition period when the theory offers much but has not yet produced extensive achievements in practical application. Even if we could easily apply optimal methods, however, we eventually come back to the question of the performance specifications and their relation to system quality. As shown, most optimal theory so far consists in minimizing a performance index involving the square of some quantity as, for example, the error after a step input. The design then certainly minimizes this index, but the next task is to evaluate the overall performance. The squared error index places a great deal of weight on the value of the error shortly after the step input is initiated and when such error is inevitable. The design may thus result in a long decaying tail with little area as in curve 1 in Figure 10.7–1. If we are interested in quickly reducing $|e(t)|$ to zero, however, we might better consider curve 2, which brings the error to zero more rapidly but may have slightly greater total area. The index for this design might be

$$J = \int_0^\infty t^2 e^2(t)\, dt$$

As another example, it might be preferable not to make a system time optimal if we can save fuel thereby and still not increase the time greatly.

Furthermore, a reasonable design might not follow a linear combination of two indices. Some progress has been made in application by using approximations. For example, if a performance index changes slowly in the vicinity of the minimum, it may be possible to design a control with a

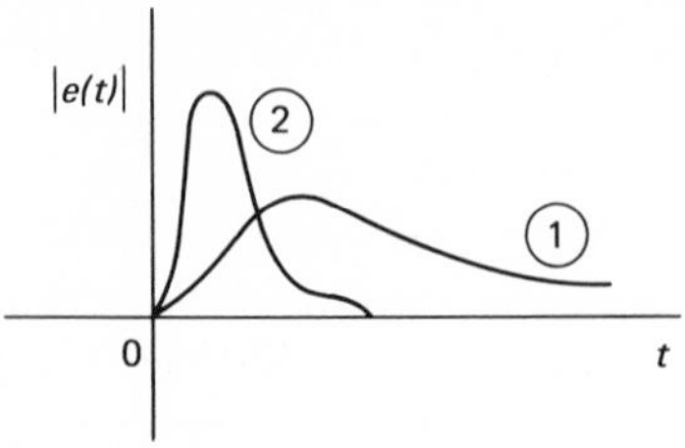

Figure 10.7–1. Comparison of possible error functions.

simple switching surface that will not have a minimum index but will give an index sufficiently close to the minimum and at the same time be practically realizable [24]. Solutions to many such problems are not analytic and again involve cut and try designs using computers. It is also very difficult to escape the conventional ideas of rise time, overshoot, and bandwidth in any design.

One concludes therefore that in the last analysis you cannot avoid value judgments in design. An optimal system design may be used as a base or norm for comparing other designs, but there will always exist different criteria for each application, some of which may be too subtle or intangible for mathematical expression. For this the engineer can breathe a sigh of relief, for the machine cannot make such judgments.

There still remains much to be done, and the boundaries are limitless. It is hoped that you have been sufficiently stimulated to meet the challenge of application of state-space concepts, or to devise an alternative approach, if necessary.

PROBLEMS

10.1. Given a system with a forward path gain $G = K(Ts + 1)/s^2$ and unity negative feedback. If the input is a unit step function, find K to minimize the integral squared error performance index

$$J = \int_0^\infty (e)^2 \, dt$$

for a given T. Repeat for T with a given K. Comment on stability and relative stability.

10.2. In Figure P10.2, $r = au(t)$. Investigate the minimization of

$$J_1 = \int_0^\infty e^2\, dt$$

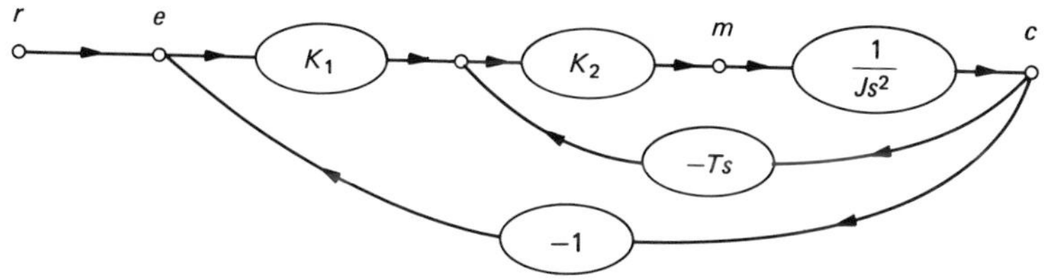

Figure P10.2.

subject to the constraint

$$\int_0^\infty m^2\, dt \leq N$$

for the following case:
(a) T, J fixed, K_1, K_2 variable.
Comment on stability and relative stability.

10.3. Make a root-square-locus plot for a unity negative feedback system with a forward path gain

$$G = \frac{K}{s(s+1)(s+5)}$$

Select various values of K/k for Chang's optimal design (Section 10.1), and check the resulting systems as to
(a) Per cent overshoot.
(b) t_p, time to 95 per cent of final value.
(c) Values of $\int_0^\infty e^2\, dt$.
(d) Values of $\int_0^\infty m^2\, dt$.
(e) Velocity constant, K_v.

10.4. Compare conventional designs (Chapter 9) with those of Problem 10.3.

10.5. (a) Find the equation of the path giving the shortest distance between two points in a plane.
(b) Find the equation of the path giving the shortest distance between two points on a cylinder.

10.6. Figure P10.6 shows a mass in sliding along a smooth curve under the force of gravity. Find the curve that will get the particle from the origin to the line $y = -x + 5$ in the shortest time (downward y is taken as positive for convenience). *Hint:*

$$t = \int [(dx^2 + dy^2)/2gy]^{1/2}.$$

Also the curve will be perpendicular to the line at the point of contact.

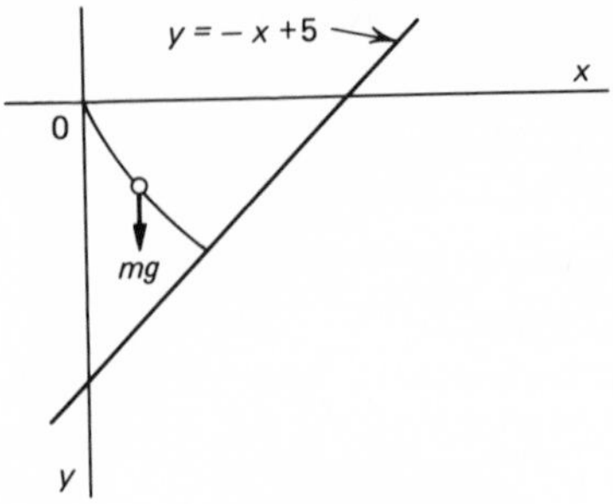

Figure P10.6.

10.7. In Figure P10.7, find the voltage $v(t)$ necessary to raise the capacitor voltage from v_0 at $t = 0$ to v_f at $t = t_f$ and simultaneously make the energy losses in R a minimum. Find the energy loss $W = RC^2\int_0^{t_f}\dot{v}_c^2\,dt$ and the energy added to the capacitor.

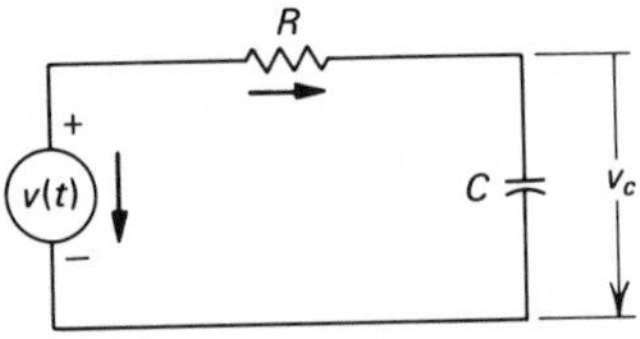

Figure P10.7.

10.8. Given the system $\ddot{x} = m$, $x(0) = 0$, and $\dot{x}(0) = 2$, no constraints on m. Find the control m^* that will minimize the performance index $J = \int_0^1 m^2\,dt$ and also make $x(1) = \dot{x}(1) = 0$, if this is possible. Express m^* as a function of $x(0)$ and $\dot{x}(0)$ (open loop law) and as a function of $x(t)$ and $\dot{x}(t)$ (closed loop law). *Answer:*

$$m^* = -\left[\frac{6}{(1-t)^2}\,x(t) + \frac{4}{(1-t)}\,\dot{x}(t)\right]$$

10.9. Given the system

$$\dot{\mathbf{x}} = \mathbf{A}\mathbf{x} + \mathbf{b}u$$

where $|u| \leq 1$, show that to take the system from $\mathbf{x}(0)$ to the origin and minimize the performance index

$$J = \frac{1}{2}\int_0^\infty [(\mathbf{x}, \mathbf{Q}\mathbf{x}) + cu^2]\,dt$$

requires the control $u^* = \text{sat}[(1/c)\mathbf{p}^T\mathbf{b}]$.

10.10. Given the system $\dot{\mathbf{x}} = \mathbf{Ax} + \mathbf{Bm}$, where

$$\mathbf{A} = \begin{bmatrix} 0 & 1 \\ -b & -a \end{bmatrix} \qquad \mathbf{B} = \begin{bmatrix} 0 & 0 \\ 0 & 1 \end{bmatrix}$$

$(a/2)^2 - b > 0, a < 0, b > 0.$
The control is limited, or $|m| \leq 1$. It is desired to obtain a control which will bring the system to the origin in the least time.
(a) Find and sketch the region where the system can be brought to the origin.
(b) Sketch the switching lines in this region.
(*Hint:* Take $m = 1$ and -1 and find the trajectories about the singular points (with control) $\pm 1/b$.)

REFERENCES AND FURTHER READING

[1] H. M. James, N. B. Nichols, and R. S. Phillips, *Theory of Servomechanisms*, Vol. 25, MIT Rad. Lab. Series, McGraw-Hill, New York, 1947, and Dover, New York, 1965, pp. 308–370.
[2] G. C. Newton, Jr., L. A. Gould, and J. F. Kaiser, *Analytical Design of Linear Feedback Controls*, Wiley, New York, 1957.
[3] R. Oldenburger, *Optimal Control*, Holt, New York, 1966.
[4] Newton, Gould, and Kaiser, *op. cit.*, Appendix E.
[5] S. S. L. Chang, *Synthesis of Optimal Control Systems*, McGraw-Hill, New York, 1961, pp. 11–35.
[6] R. L. Morrell, A Comparison of Optimal and Conventional Control Systems, M.S. thesis, Utah State University, Logan, 1965.
[7] Chang, *op. cit.*
[8] L. E. Elsgolic, *Calculus of Variations*, Pergamon, London, 1962.
[9] G. M. Kranc and P. E. Sarachik, An Application of Functional Analysis to the Optimal Control Problem, Trans. ASME, *J. Basic Eng.*, **85** (1963), 143–150.
[10] R. Bellman, *Adaptive Control Processes—A Guided Tour*, Princeton Univ. Press, Princeton, N.J., 1961.
[11] L. S. Pontryagin, V. G. Boltyanskii, R. V. Gamkrelidze, and E. F. Mischenko, *The Mathematical Theory of Optimal Processes*, Wiley (Interscience), New York, 1962.
[12] G. A. Bliss, *Lectures on the Calculus of Variations*, Univ. Chicago Press, Chicago, 1946, Phoenix edition, 1961.
[13] P. Dorato and R. F. Drenick, *Optimal Control Theory—A Short Course*, Brooklyn Polytechnic Institute, Brooklyn, N.Y., 1963.
[14] M. Athans and P. L. Falb, *Optimal Control*, McGraw-Hill, New York, 1966.
[15] P. M. De Russo, R. J. Roy, and C. M. Close, *State Variables for Engineers*, Wiley, New York, 1965, pp. 557–558.
[16] M. Athans and P. L. Falb, *Optimal Control*, McGraw-Hill, New York, 1966, pp. 758–760.
[17] *Ibid.*, pp. 771–782.

[18] R. E. Kalman, When is a Linear Control System Optimal? *J. Basic Eng.*, **86** (1964), 51–60.
[19] Athans and Falb, *op. cit.*, pp. 804–814.
[20] Kalman, *op. cit.*
[21] D. G. Schultz and J. L. Melsa, *State Functions and Linear Control Systems*, McGraw-Hill, New York, 1967.
[22] L. K. Timothy and B. E. Bona, *State Space Analysis: An Introduction*, McGraw-Hill, New York, 1968, Chap. 12.
[23] J. M. Douglas, The Use of Optimization Theory to Design Simple Multivariable Control Systems, *Chem. Eng. Sci.*, **21** (1966), 519–532.
[24] W. L. Nelson, On the Use of Optimization Theory for Practical Control System Design, *IEEE Trans. Auto. Control*, **9** (1964), 469–477.
[25] M. Athans, The Status of Optimal Control Theory and Applications for Deterministic Systems, *IEEE Trans. Auto. Control*, **11** (1966), 580–596. (This reference has an extensive list of other references.)
[26] L. Lapidus, *Optimal Control of Engineering Processes*, Ginn-Blaisdell, Boston, 1967.
[27] C. T. Leondes "Advances in Control Systems," Vol. I, 1964, Vol, II, Vol. III, Vol. IV, 1966, Vol. V, 1967, Academic Press, New York.

11 Discrete Time Systems

11.1 Introduction

In an analogical sense, the difference equation bears the same relation to the discrete time system as the differential equation to the continuous time system. The difference equation expresses the connection between a sequence of values for some quantity. In general this can be written

$$x(t_{k+1}) = f[x(t_k), m(t_k), t_k] \qquad k = 0, 1, 2, \ldots \tag{11.1–1}$$

where x is the quantity under consideration, m is some input, and t_n is the nth time interval. If the sequence occurs at intervals of time that are a constant period T apart, then (11.1–1) may be altered to

$$x(k+1) = f[x(k), m(k), k] \qquad k = 0, 1, 2, \ldots \tag{11.1–2}$$

where $t_{k+1} - t_k = T$, and the functional notation now refers to the value of the discrete function x at the appropriate interval. Discrete time functions have values only at these particular intervals, and are not defined elsewhere (see Chapter 1).

As with continuous time systems, again we have linear versus nonlinear, fixed versus time-varying, causal versus noncausal, and dynamic versus nondynamic systems. If the system is linear, f in (11.1–1) becomes a linear function, and if fixed, is not a function of t_k. We imply by (11.1–1) that the system is dynamic and causal.

Systems utilizing sequences of quantities that are known only at discrete times are called sampled-data systems. This implies that signals are "sampled" at intervals, and utilized by the system to obtain the desired results. Figure 11.1–1 shows a possible sampling switch, in which the signal to the left is sampled by a switch opening and closing in some manner. In general, more than one such switch will exist in the system. Usually the switches are considered to remain closed for a very short period compared to the open time T_k, so that the function to the right is known only at discrete time intervals T_k apart. If all switches open and close together, and

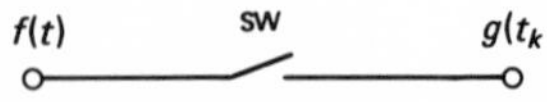

Figure 11.1–1. Sampling switch for sampled-data systems.

at a constant time interval ($T_k = T$), we term the sampling conventional or synchronous. Constant rate sampling where the switches do not operate at the same time is called nonsynchronous, and if the switches operate at different rates, you designate the system as multirate. Finally, the switches may operate in a random fashion.

One type of ideal switch is assumed to stay closed for a time τ and open a time T, where $\tau \ll T$. Using the designations of Figure 11.1–1, the pulses obtained from such a sampler might appear as in Figure 11.1–2. Then we

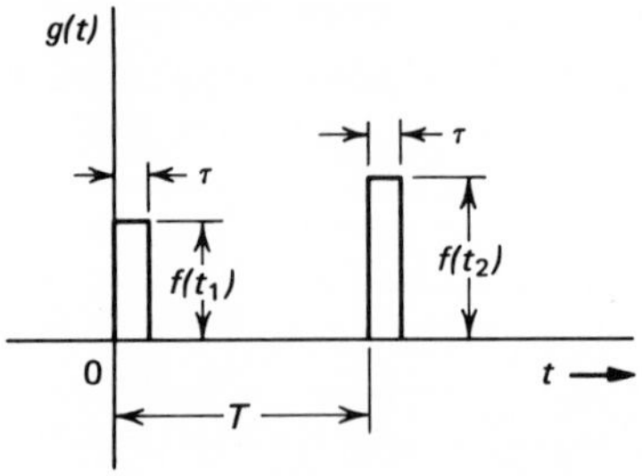

Figure 11.1–2. Pulses obtained from ideal sampler switch.

may assume that if τ is much less than any time constants in the system supplied by $g(t_k)$ that the pulses become essentially impulses of amount $f(t_k)\tau$. Thus

$$g(t_k) = \tau \sum_{k=0}^{\infty} f(kT)\delta(t - kT)$$

The factor τ is a constant gain that may be included in the system following the sampler. Hence we take the output of the sampler to be

$$g(t_k) = f^*(t) = \sum_{k=0}^{\infty} f(kT)\delta(t - kT) \qquad \textbf{(11.1–3)}$$

and imply that the sampler gain becomes a part of the succeeding system. (In problems and examples, we assume this gain factor to be included in the given system gains.) If another sampling switch immediately follows the first, complications may arise in the assumption of an impulse [1], but normally some sort of smoothing circuit intervenes.

Using this convention, if in Figure 11.1–3a $f(t)$ is the sampler input, then Figure 11.1–3b represents the output, with the value of each impulse

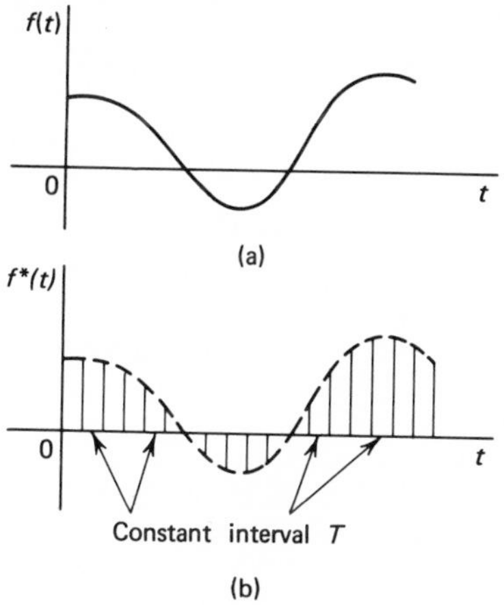

Figure 11.1–3. Sampled input (a) and output (b), for $T \gg \tau$. Switch gain included in following device.

representing the function value at that instant. Some authors assume other sampler outputs but we shall take (11.1–3) as defining our sampling switch for constant T [2].

In this chapter we shall concern ourselves primarily with constant rate synchronous systems that are linear, dynamic, and causal. Such a system may be described by the linear difference equation

$$y(k+n) + d_1 y(k+n-1) + \cdots + d_{n-1} y(k+1) + d_n y(k)$$
$$= b_0 m(k+j) + \cdots + b_{j-1} m(k+1) + b_j m(k) \quad \mathbf{(11.1\text{–}4)}$$

If the coefficients d_i and b_i in (11.1–4) are independent of the interval, then the system is stationary or fixed. In a manner analogous to analysis of the continuous time system, we may also describe a linear system by means of matrix notation, which, as before, becomes of particular value when more than one input or output exists, or write

$$\mathbf{x}(k+1) = \mathbf{A}\mathbf{x}(k) + \mathbf{B}\mathbf{m}(k) \quad \mathbf{(11.1\text{–}5a)}$$

$$\mathbf{y}(k) = \mathbf{C}\mathbf{x}(k) + \mathbf{D}\mathbf{m}(k) \quad \mathbf{(11.1\text{–}5b)}$$

where the matrices **A** and **B** will be functions of the sampling interval T (and if time-varying, also of k).

Difference equations are much simpler in many respects than differential equations. In particular, questions of continuity and differentiability do not arise in difference equations; the values are only known at discrete times. Again, solutions proceed in a very analogous manner but involve terms such as $\mathbf{A}^k$ rather than terms such as $\epsilon^{\mathbf{A}t}$. Having already studied functions of $\mathbf{A}$ in Chapter 5, these solutions should be easy to digest. Transform theory proves useful for continuous linear fixed systems, so we expect similar results here and find the Z transform in discrete time system to be the analog of the $\mathscr{L}$ transform in continuous time systems.

The close ties between difference and differential equations come about rather naturally, because if you take the differential equation

$$\frac{d\mathbf{x}}{dt} = \mathbf{A}_1\mathbf{x}(t) + \mathbf{B}_1\mathbf{m}(t) \tag{11.1–6}$$

and make the approximation

$$\frac{d\mathbf{x}}{dt} \simeq \frac{\mathbf{x}(t+h) - \mathbf{x}(t)}{h}$$

where h is a small time increment, then (11.1–6) takes the form

$$\begin{aligned}\mathbf{x}(t+h) &= h[\mathbf{A}_1\mathbf{x}(t) + \mathbf{B}_1\mathbf{m}(\mathbf{t})] + \mathbf{x}(t) \\ &= (h\mathbf{A}_1 + \mathbf{I})\mathbf{x}(t) + h\mathbf{B}_1\mathbf{m}(t)\end{aligned} \tag{11.1–7}$$

Equation (11.1–7) may then be rewritten in terms of the values of $\mathbf{x}$ at each interval by letting $\mathbf{x}(t_0) = x(0)$, $x(t_0 + h) = \mathbf{x}(1)$, and so on, to obtain the equation in the form of (11.1–5a).

Sampled-data systems arise naturally from the use of quantized processors, such as digital computers. Because information does not continuously enter the system, you would expect that the performance of such a system might be poorer, particularly during the periods when no data enters than for the continuous system. Also you might expect that the faster the sampling rate (the smaller the period T), the more closely the continuous system might be approached. Generally this is true, although in a few specific cases the sampled-data system is superior. However, the sampled-data system may be good enough for our purpose, and the use of a digital computer also raises exciting possibilities. The fact that the usual control system contains energy-storage devices means that the entering signal becomes smoothed, permitting an operation that might otherwise not be possible.

11.2 Conventional Solution of Difference Equations

For differential equations it is often convenient to introduce an operator $p = d/dt$, and for difference equations a corresponding difference operator Δ, where

$$\Delta y(k) = y(k+1) - y(k) \tag{11.2–1}$$

may be used. However, it turns out that a more useful operator for the solution of difference equations is the shifting operator E, where

$$E[y(k)] = y(k+1) \tag{11.2–2}$$

The relation between these operators is obviously furnished by

$$\Delta y(k) = (E - 1)y(k)$$

or

$$\Delta = E - 1$$

Corresponding to the difference operator Δ, there also exists an anti-difference operator Δ^{-1}, which is an analog to the integral. Δ^{-1} has usefulness in expressing sums in closed form [3].

From definition (11.2–2),

$$E^2[y(k)] = E[Ey(k)] = y(k+2)$$

and, continuing,

$$E^n y(k) = y(k+n)$$

Then (11.1–4) may be written

$$(E^n + d_1 E^{n-1} + \cdots + d_n)y(k) = (b_0 E^j + b_1 E^{j-1} + \cdots + b_j)m(k) \tag{11.2–3}$$

For a stationary system, the d_i and b_i are independent of k. Taking a stationary homogenous system, then

$$(E^n + d_1 E^{n-1} + \cdots d_n)y(k) = 0 \tag{11.2–4}$$

and you postulate a solution of the form

$$y(k) = r^k$$

Since $E^j y(k) = y(k+j) = r^{(j+k)} = r^j r^k$, substitution into (11.2–4) gives the characteristic equation

$$r^n + d_1 r^{n-1} + \cdots + d_n = 0 \tag{11.2–5}$$

which will have n roots, $r_1, r_2, \ldots, r_n$. The solution to (11.2–4) then becomes

$$y(k) = K_1 r_1^k + K_2 r_2^k + \cdots + K_n r_n^k \qquad \textbf{(11.2–6)}$$

where $K_1, K_2, \ldots, K_n$ are constants determined by n successive values of y_k.

You see that this process is entirely parallel to the continuous case, where solutions of the form e^{st} are postulated. Similarly, if not all the roots are distinct, you get the solution for a root r_i repeated n times as

$$y(k) = K_1 r_i^k + K_2 k r_i^k + \cdots + K_{n+1} k^{n+1} r_i^k \qquad \textbf{(11.2–7)}$$

If a root r_j is complex, or $r_j = R\epsilon^{j\theta}$, then $r_{j+1} = R\epsilon^{-j\theta}$ and

$$y(k) = CR^k \cos(k\theta + \phi) \qquad \textbf{(11.2–8)}$$

where C and ϕ are constants.

Example 11.2–1

Find the solution to the difference equation

$$y(k+3) + 3y(k+2) + 7y(k+1) + 5y(k) = 0 \qquad \textbf{(11.2–9)}$$

Using the differencing operator,

$$(E^3 + 3E^2 + 7E + 5)y(k) = 0$$

and the characteristic equation is

$$r^3 + 3r^2 + 7r + 5 = 0.$$

This has roots

$$r_1 = -1$$

$$r_2 = \sqrt{5}\epsilon^{j\theta}$$

$$r_3 = \sqrt{5}\epsilon^{-j\theta}$$

where $\theta = \tan^{-1} 2$. Then

$$y(k) = K_1(-1)^k + C\sqrt{5} \cos(k\theta + \phi) \qquad \textbf{(11.2–10)}$$

K_1, C, and ϕ depend on three values of $y(k)$; for example, $y(0)$, $y(1)$, and $y(2)$. Note that given $y(0)$, $y(1)$, and $y(2)$, any $y(k)$ could be determined by using (11.2–9) as a recursion formula first for $y(3)$, then for $y(4)$, and so on. However, (11.2–10) gives $y(k)$ in a closed form. If only a few low-order $y(k)$ values are needed, the recursion method may be simpler, particularly if the original equation is nonlinear or nonstationary.

The solution of (11.2–3) now proceeds again in an analogous fashion; that is, using undetermined coefficients or variation of parameters. However, just as with the continuous time case we found it advantageous to go to the Laplace transform, we now find it advantageous to use the Z transform.

11.3 Z-Transform Solution for Stationary Systems

The one-sided Z transform is defined as

$$Z[f(k)] = \sum_{k=0}^{\infty} f(k)z^{-k} \tag{11.3–1}$$

where f is a function of k and $k \geq 0$.

Then if $Z[f(k)] = F(z)$,

$$\begin{aligned} Z[Ef(k)] &= Z[f(k+1)] \\ &= f(1) + f(2)z^{-1} + f(3)z^{-2} + \cdots \\ &= z[F(z) - f(0)] \end{aligned} \tag{11.3–2}$$

$$\begin{aligned} Z[\Delta f(k)] &= Z[f(k+1)] - Z[f(k)] \\ &= (z-1)[F(z) - f(0)] \end{aligned} \tag{11.3–3}$$

Continuing with (11.3–2),

$$Z[E^n f(k)] = z^n F(z) - z^n f(0) - z^{n-1} f(1) - \cdots - zf(n-1) \tag{11.3–4}$$

Additional properties of the Z transform may be obtained, just as for the Laplace transform. As in the Laplace transform case, possibly the most useful property in solving difference equations with constant coefficients is the "convolution" property, which states that

$$Z\left[\sum_{k=0}^{n} f_1(n-k)f_2(k)\right] = F_1(z)F_2(z) \tag{11.3–5}$$

You also may obtain tables of Z transforms similar to those for Laplace transforms, and extensive tables of this kind are available [4, 5, 6]. In consulting such tables, you are warned that contrary to the uniformity of

Laplace transform tables, little such standardization exists for Z-transform tables. Thus some are shown as functions of k and some as functions of t ($t = kT$). In some tables z is used; in others, z^{-1}. Other authors define the Z transform in terms of positive powers of z [see (11.3–1)], with still other results. Once you overcome the notational barrier, the tables become fairly easy to use. For example, you can find the transform of $f(k) = u(k)$, or a step function occurring at the zeroth interval, from (11.3–1). Thus

$$Z[u(k)] = z^{\circ} + z^{-1} + z^{-2} + \cdots = \frac{1}{1 - z^{-1}}$$

which also may be written

$$Z[u(k)] = \frac{z}{z-1}$$

Similarly,

$$Z(k) = \frac{z^{-1}}{(1 - z^{-1})^2} = \frac{z}{(z-1)^2}$$

$$Z(t) = Z(kT)$$

$$= TZ(k)$$

or

$$Z(t) = \frac{Tz}{(z-1)^2}$$

Each of these forms may be convenient for the problem at hand. We shall deal primarily with systems having the independent variable time t; Table 11.3–1 presents a few Z transforms for functions of $t = kT$, where k is the interval number and T the time period between intervals. That is, we make a scale change, letting $k = kT$ in definition (11.3–1).

If the difference equations are given as functions of the interval k, as in (11.2–9), make $T = 1$ in Table 11.3–1 for $F(z)$. Alternatively, if available Z-transform tables are given as functions of k, and the equations as functions of t, replace t by t/T in the equations, making the required scale change before utilizing the tables. Figure 11.3–1 shows the effect of the scale change if $T = \frac{1}{2}$ second. (T is not necessarily rational.)

You note in Table 11.3–1 a given region of convergence. Examining the Z transform of $u(k) = z^0 + z^{-1} + z^{-2} + \cdots$, for example, it is clear that in this power series convergence requires $|z| > 1$. The convergence region becomes of importance in inverting a function in the z domain using contour integration, just as knowledge of the convergence region may be

TABLE 11.3–1 A FEW Z TRANSFORMS

$f(kT)$	$F(z)$	Region of Convergence
$\delta(kT)$*	z^{-0}	$\|z\| > 0$
$\delta(kT - nT)$*	z^{-n}	$\|z\| > 0$
$u(kT)$	$\frac{1}{1 - z^{-1}}$	$\|z\| > 1$
a^{kT}	$\frac{1}{1 - a^T z^{-1}}$	$\|z\| > a^T$
kT	$\frac{Tz^{-1}}{(1 - z^{-1})^2}$	$\|z\| > 1$
$(kT)^2$	$\frac{T^2 z^{-1}(1 + z^{-1})}{(1 - z^{-1})^3}$	$\|z\| > 1$
ϵ^{akT}	$\frac{1}{1 - z^{-1}\epsilon^{aT}}$	$\|z\| > \epsilon^{aT}$
$\sin \alpha kT$	$\frac{z^{-1} \sin \alpha T}{1 - 2z^{-1} \cos \alpha T + z^{-2}}$	$\|a\| > 1$
$\cos \alpha kT$	$\frac{z^{-1}(z^{-1} - \cos \alpha T)}{1 - 2z^{-1} \cos \alpha T + z^{-2}}$	$\|z\| > 1$

*Recall that the sampling switch actually has a closed interval time τ, $\tau \ll T$.

necessary in the inversion of the Laplace transform utilizing contour integration. For the one-sided Z transform, the region of convergence is the z plane outside a circle enclosing all the poles of $F(z)$, with $f(k) = 0$ for $k < 0$ [7].

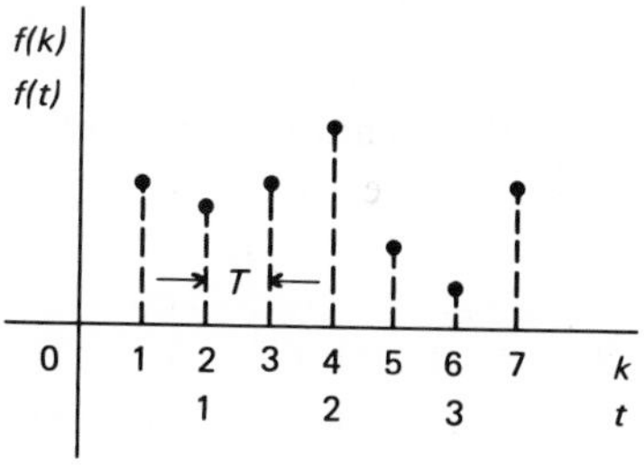

Figure 11.3–1. Change of scale in discrete time system.

It is not difficult to show that [4]

$$Z[f(k-n)u(k-n)] = z^{-n}F(z) \tag{11.3–6}$$

Equation (11.3–6) states that multiplication of $F(z)$ by z^{-1} causes a unit delay (a delay of one interval) in the corresponding function $f(k)$, z^{-2} causes two units delay, and so on. Thus $1/z$ in the z domain is analogous to $1/s$ in the s domain, and a unit delay in a discrete time system corresponds to an integrator in the continuous time system. Therefore you may draw flow diagrams for the discrete time system just as previously, but with unit delay devices replacing integrators if the system is expressed as a function of k, or delays of T if the system is a function of kT.

A more direct relation may be made between the z domain and the s domain by considering

$$\mathscr{L}[f(t-T)u(t-T)] = e^{-Ts}F(s) \tag{11.3–7}$$

In words, this states that a delay of T seconds in the time domain results from multiplication by e^{-Ts} in the s domain. Comparing (11.3–6) with $n = 1$ and (11.3–7), and taking a sample period T, you see that since we have a delay of one unit in each case,

$$z = \epsilon^{Ts} \tag{11.3–8}$$

Equation (11.3–8) is often used to define the z transform [8]. The interrelation of the s and z transforms enables the writing of transfer functions in the z domain directly from known transfer functions in the s domain. Formally, if $F(s)$ is the transfer function in the s domain, then

$$F(z) = \sum_{1}^{n} \left[\text{residues of } \frac{F(s)}{1 - \epsilon^{sT}z^{-1}} \text{ at the poles of } F(s) \right] \tag{11.3–9}$$

n being the number of poles of $F(s)$. Equation (11.3–9) holds if

$$\frac{1}{2\pi j} \int_{c-j\infty}^{c+j\infty} \frac{F(s)\, ds}{1 - \epsilon^{sT}z^{-1}}$$

equals (11.3–9) but not otherwise. It will generally be true for $F(s) = P(s)/Q(s)$ if $Q(s)$ is of higher degree than $P(s)$, both being polynomials in s. (See Appendix A for contour integration procedure [9].) The system may be known in transfer function form in the s domain, so you may find this a simpler way of obtaining the z transform than using the t or k relation. Table 11.3–2 gives a few of these relations (see also [10, 11]).

TABLE 11.3–2

$F(s)$: Transfer Function, s Domain	$Z_s[F(s)]$: Transfer Function, z Domain
$\dfrac{1}{s}$	$\dfrac{1}{1-z^{-1}}$
$\dfrac{1}{s+a}$	$\dfrac{1}{1-\epsilon^{-aT}z^{-1}}$
$\dfrac{a}{s(s+a)}$	$\dfrac{z^{-1}(1-\epsilon^{-aT})}{(1-z^{-1})(1-\epsilon^{-aT}z^{-1})}$
$\dfrac{b-a}{(s+a)(s+b)}$	$\dfrac{z^{-1}(\epsilon^{-aT}-\epsilon^{-bT})}{(1-\epsilon^{-aT}z^{-1})(1-\epsilon^{-bT}z^{-1})}$
$\dfrac{b}{(s+a)^2+b^2}$	$\dfrac{\epsilon^{-aT}(\sin bT)z^{-1}}{1-2\epsilon^{-aT}(\cos bT)z^{-1}+\epsilon^{-2aT}z^{-2}}$
$\dfrac{a}{s^2+a^2}$	$\dfrac{(\sin aT)z^{-1}}{1-2(\cos aT)z^{-1}+z^{-2}}$
$\dfrac{s}{s^2+a^2}$	$\dfrac{1-(\cos aT)z^{-1}}{1-2(\cos aT)z^{-1}+z^{-2}}$

Example 11.3–1

Find the transfer function in the z domain of a sampled-data system with sampling rate $T=\pi/8$ if the transfer function of the system in the s domain is

$$G(s)=\frac{K(s+2)}{s(s+1)(s^2+2s+5)}$$

Using partial fractions,

$$G(s)=K\left(\frac{2/5}{s}-\frac{1/4}{s+1}-\frac{3/20s+11/20}{s^2+2s+5}\right)$$
$$=K[F_1(s)+F_2(s)+F_3(s)+F_4(s)]$$

$F_3(s)$ may be found from (11.3–9) as follows:

$$-\frac{20}{3}F_3(z)=\left.\frac{s}{(s+1-j2)(1-\epsilon^{sT}z^{-1})}\right|_{s=-1-j2}$$
$$+\left.\frac{s}{(s+1+j2)(1-\epsilon^{sT}z^{-1})}\right|_{s=-1+j2}$$
$$=\frac{1-\sqrt{5}/2\,z^{-1}\epsilon^{-T}\sin(2T+\theta)}{(1-2\epsilon^{-T}z^{-1}\cos 2T+\epsilon^{-2T}z^{-2})}\qquad \theta=\tan^{-1}2$$
$$=\frac{1-0.715z^{-1}}{1-0.954z^{-1}+0.456z^{-2}}\qquad \text{(slide rule accuracy)}$$

providing we did not make any mistakes.

$F_4(z)$ may be found from Table 11.3–2 as

$$F_4(z) = -\frac{11}{20}\frac{1}{2}\left(\frac{\epsilon^{-T}\sin 2Tz^{-1}}{D}\right)$$

where D is the previous denominator. $F_1(z)$ and $F_2(z)$ for the first two terms come directly from Table 11.3–2.

Then $G(z) = P(z)/Q(z)$, where $P(z)$ and $Q(z)$ are polynomials in z. If repeated roots of $F(s)$ exist, obtaining the residues follows the same rules as for s-domain residues in determining the Laplace transform [12].

Three methods exist for inverting the z transform. The first consists of putting $F(z)$ into partial fraction form and inverting each term using a table or applying the second method. The second technique utilizes integration in the complex z domain and in the third you divide out the polynomials term by term. The last method may be the easiest if only a few values are desired, but the first or second are usually necessary if a closed expression is desired. The partial fraction idea should be clear, so we proceed to the second method.

It can be shown that the Z-transform inversion, if it exists, is given by

$$f(k) = \sum \text{residues of } F(z)z^{k-1} \tag{11.3–10}$$

the residues being taken at all poles of $F(z)z^{k-1}$. Note that in some cases $F(z)z^{k-1}$ may have a pole at zero, $k \geq 0$, even though $F(z)$ does not have one there. We now illustrate the inversion process and the solution of difference equations using the z transform by some examples.

Example 11.3–2

Given $(E^2 + 3E + 2)y(k) = m(k)$. Find the solution for $y(k)$ if (a) $m(k) = u(k)$; (b) $m(k)$ consists of two unit impulses, one at $k = 0$ and one at $k = 1$; and (c) $m(k) = ku(k)$. $y(0) = 1$, $y(1) = 2$ in all cases.

Solution:

Transforming, you obtain

$$(z^2 + 3z + 2)y(z) = M(z) + z^2y(0) + zy(1) + zy(0)$$

or

$$Y(z) = \frac{M(z) + z^2 + 3z}{(z+2)(z+1)}$$

(a) $m(k) = u(k), \quad M(z) = 1/(1 - z^{-1}).$

(b) $m(k) = \delta(k) + \delta(k-1), \quad M(z) = 1 + z^{-1}.$

(c) $m(k) = ku(k), \quad M(z) = z^{-1}/(1 - z^{-1})^2.$

For (a),

$$Y(z) = \frac{z}{(z-1)(z+2)(z+1)} + \frac{z^2}{(z+2)(z+1)} + \frac{3z}{(z+2)(z+1)}$$

Expressing in partial fractions,

$$Y(z) = \frac{1/6}{z-1} - \frac{2/3}{z+2} + \frac{1/2}{z+1} - \frac{4}{z+2} + \frac{1}{z+1} + \frac{6}{z+2} - \frac{3}{z+1} + 1$$

$$Y(z) = \frac{1/6}{z-1} + \frac{4/3}{z+2} - \frac{3/2}{z+1} + 1$$

$$= z^{-1}\left(\frac{1/6}{1-z^{-1}}\right) + z^{-1}\left(\frac{4/3}{1+2z^{-1}}\right) - z^{-1}\left(\frac{3/2}{1+z^{-1}}\right) + 1$$

Then

$$y(k) = \tfrac{1}{6}(1)^{k-1}u(k-1) + \tfrac{4}{3}(-2)^{k-1}u(k-1) - \tfrac{3}{2}(-1)^{k-1}u(k-1) + 1$$

If you write $Y(z)$ as two polynomials,

$$Y(z) = \frac{z^3 + 2z^2 - 2z}{z^3 + 2z^2 - z - 2}$$

and divide the denominator into the numerator, you get

$$\begin{array}{r|l} & 1 + 0 - z^{-2} + 4z^{-3} - 9z^{-4} + \cdots \\ \hline z^3 + 2z^2 - z - 2 & z^3 + 2z^2 - 2z \\ & \underline{z^3 + 2z^2 - z - 2} \\ & \quad -z + 2 \\ & \quad \underline{-z - 2 + z^{-1} + 2z^{-2}} \\ & \qquad 4 - z^{-1} - 2z^{-2} \end{array}$$

The first five coefficients of the quotient agree with the values of $y(k)$ above for $k = 0$, 1, 2, 3, and 4. The division method provides a check against the other method and is easy to perform.

One expansion method for the terms due to the initial conditions consists of finding $G(z)/z$ in partial fractions and multiplying by z. If $G(z)$ consists of the last two terms of the previous $Y(z)$, this gives

$$\frac{G(z)}{z} = \frac{z}{(z+2)(z+1)} + \frac{3}{(z+2)(z+1)}$$

or

$$G(z) = \frac{2z}{z+1} - \frac{z}{z+2}$$

Hence the response due to these terms is

$$y(k) = 2(-1)^k - 1(-2)^k$$

This response will be the same for all forcing functions.

To illustrate the use of the residue method, again take the initial condition terms. Then for the first term,

$$y(k) = \text{residues of } \frac{z^2 z^{k-1}}{(z+2)(z+1)} \qquad \text{at } z = -2, \quad z = -1$$

$$= -1(-1)^k + 2(-2)^k$$

For the second term,

$$y(k) = \text{residues of } \frac{3zz^{k-1}}{(z+2)(z+1)} \qquad \text{at } z = -2, \quad z = -1$$

$$= 3(-1)^k - 3(-2)^k$$

Then the transient response is

$$y(k) = 2(-1)^k - 1(-2)^k$$

which produces the same results.

Proceeding to the input of (b), since the transient response is as before, we solve for an input of $\delta(k)$. Then for the forced response,

$$Y(z) = \frac{1}{(z+2)(z+1)}$$

or

$$Y(z) = \frac{1}{z+1} - \frac{1}{z+2}$$

or

$$y(k) = (-1)^{k-1}u(k-1) - 1(-2)^{k-1}u(k-1)$$

The input of the second term, $\delta(k-1)$, gives an $M(z)$ of z^{-1}. Hence the previous output is merely displaced by one interval. Then the total output due to the forcing function $\delta(k) + \delta(k-1)$ is

$$y(k) = (-1)^{k-1}u(k-1) + (-1)^{k-2}u(k-2) - (-2)^{k-1}u(k-1) - (-2)^{k-2}u(k-2)$$

For the input of (c),

$$Y(z) = \frac{z}{(z-1)^2(z+2)(z+1)}$$

Since the pole at 1 is of the second order, using the residue theorem (Appendix A), we get

$$y_1(k) = \left[\frac{d}{dz}\frac{z^k}{(z+2)(z+1)}\right]_{z=1}$$

$$= \frac{k}{6}\,u(k-1) - 5/36$$

The residue of $Y(z)z^{k-1}$ at $z = -2$ is

$$y_2(k) = \left[\frac{z^k}{(z-1)^2(z+1)}\right]\Bigg|_{z=-2}$$

$$= -\tfrac{1}{9}(-2)^k$$

The residue of $Y(z)z^{k-1}$ at $z = -1$ is

$$y_3(k) = \left[\frac{z^k}{(z-1)^2(z+2)}\right]\Bigg|_{z=-1}$$

$$= \tfrac{1}{4}(-1)^k$$

Then the response due to the (c) forcing function is

$$y(k) = -\frac{5}{36} - \frac{1}{9}(-2)^k + \frac{1}{4}(-1)^k + \frac{k}{6}\,u(k-1),\; k \geq 0$$

If the forced response is to be written as a function of time, then

$$y(t) = -\frac{5}{36} - \frac{1}{9}(-2)^{t/T} + \frac{1}{4}(-1)^{t/T} + \frac{t}{6T}\,u\left(\frac{t}{T} - 1\right)$$

where T is the sampling period.

You should note that the inverse transform may not be unique if δ functions exist [13].

At this point it is also important to point out that the output of a system as given by the Z transform is valid only at the sampling instants. In other words, the discrete variable, if expressed as a function of time t, is meaningful only at discrete times, and not valid anywhere else. We illustrate this forcefully with the following example.

Example 11.3–3

In Figure 11.3–2 the input to the circuit may be considered to be a train of pulses $e_1^*(t) = \sum_{k=0}^{\infty} e(t)\,\delta(t - kT)$. Find the output $e_2(t)$ if $e_1(t)$ is a unit step function $u(t)$.

The transfer function of the network in the s domain is $a/(s+a)$. Then from Table 11.3–2 the transfer function in the z domain is $a/(1-\epsilon^{-aT}z^{-1})$. From Table 11.3–1 the input in the z domain is $1/(1-z^{-1})$. Hence the output is given by

$$e_2^*(t) = Z^{-1}\left[\frac{az^2}{(z-1)(z-\epsilon^{-aT})}\right]$$

$$= \frac{a}{1-\epsilon^{-aT}}(1-\epsilon^{-aT}\epsilon^{-at}) \qquad \textbf{(11.3–11)}$$

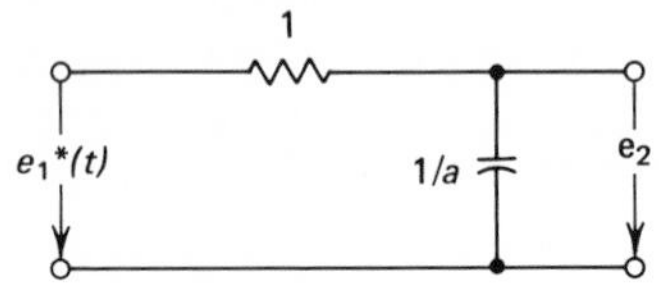

Figure 11.3–2. Circuit for Example 11.3–3.

If we apply the Laplace transform method to the problem, using the shift operator ϵ^{-sT}, the actual output may be found. Figure 11.3–3 shows by the stepped solid lines the actual output for a capacitor of 1 farad, a sampling rate of 1 sec, and a unit step input. The dashed line connects the points

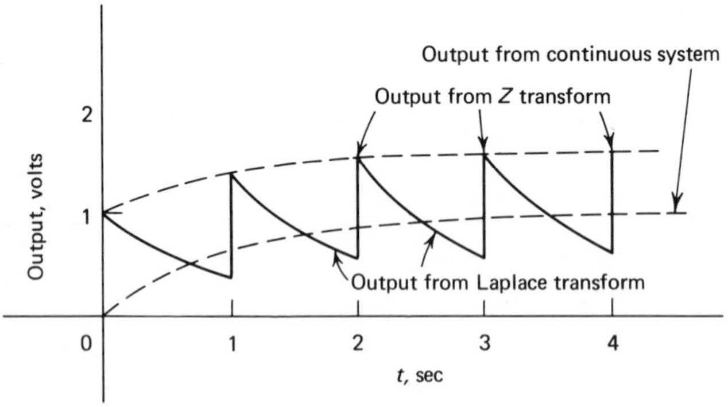

Figure 11.3–3. Output from the system of Figure 11.3–2, Example 11.3–3.

given by the Z transform at $k = 0, 1, 2, 3$, and 4 sec. Clearly the Z-transform method indicates nothing of the output between sampling instants. If the system were oscillatory, high-frequency oscillations could exist during the sampling interval which the Z-transformed output would not reveal.

The possibility of "hidden" responses shown by Example 11.3–3 may be investigated by the "modified" Z transform or the "advanced" Z transform, which consider pseudo sampling intervals less than the actual interval [14, 15]. We do not go into these here but point out the necessity of investigation before completion of the design. Normally the low-pass nature of a dynamic system precludes high-frequency oscillations, but this is not guaranteed, particularly if the system bandwidth is large. The possibility of a sinusoidal output undetected by the Z transform also exists if the sinusoidal period coincides with the sampling period. Practically, this is not too likely, but discretion again calls for investigation of outputs during the interval.

Figure 11.3–3 also shows the output if the system is continuous. The large difference here lies in the assumption that the sampled data is a series of impulses (each of constant value in this example) and arises primarily from the impulse at $t = 0$. If half the value of the impulse at $t = 0$ is taken, the output using the Z transform will approximate the output from a continuous system more closely.

In order to "smooth" the sampled data, a smoothing device often may be used with systems. One such consists of a "zero-order hold," or clamp that holds or maintains the sample value during the interval until the next sample, and so on. The approximation to $f(t)$ is clearly better than a train of impulses, as shown by Figure 11.3–4. A first-order hold gives further

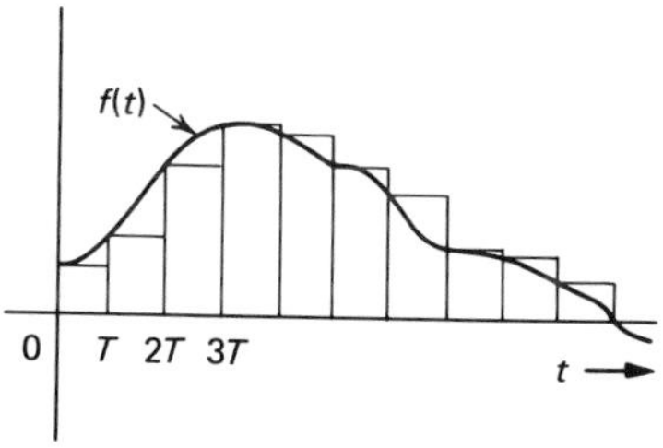

Figure 11.3–4. Zero-order hold used with sampler.

refinement, in that the slope of the function at the sampling instant is maintained until the next sample time, and so on. The zero-order hold usually provides sufficient smoothing without undue complexity. Its characteristic in the s domain is that of a pulse of unit height and of width T, or

$$G_h(s) = \frac{1 - \epsilon^{-Ts}}{s} \qquad \textbf{(11.3–12)}$$

where T is the sampling period.

If you desire the Z transform of a system with a hold unit, you must be cautioned concerning (11.3–9), because $(1 - \epsilon^{-Ts})$ has a pole at $s = -\infty$, and the residue condition is not met.

Example 11.3–4

Let

$$G(s) = \frac{1-\epsilon^{-Ts}}{s}\,\frac{2}{s(s+2)}$$

Find the Z-transformed transfer function.

Solution: A simple approach is to write $G(z)$ as

$$G(z) = (1 - z^{-1})Z_s\left[\frac{2}{s^2(s+2)}\right]$$

From tables, or using the residue theorem,

$$G(z) = \frac{1}{z-1} - \frac{1-\epsilon^{-2}}{2(z-\epsilon^{-2})}$$

An incorrect result is obtained by using (11.3–9) directly on $G(s)$.

If $e^*(t)$ represents the sampler output, that is, if

$$e^*(t) = \sum_{k=0}^{\infty} e(kT)\delta(t-kT)$$

then it is not difficult to show that

$$E^*(s) = \frac{1}{T}\sum_{k=-\infty}^{\infty} E(s+jk\omega_c) \qquad \textbf{(11.3–13)}$$

where $\omega_c = 2\pi/T$ is the sampler angular velocity [8].

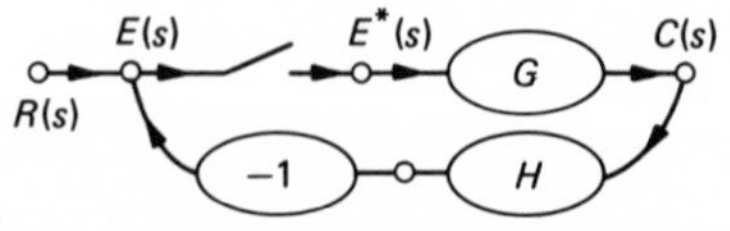

Figure 11.3–5. One possible linear sampled-data system.

If a linear sampled-data system appears as in Figure 11.3–5, then the output $C(s)$ is given by

$$C(s) = E^*(s)G(s)$$

But

$$E^*(s) = R^*(s) - (HG)^*(s)E^*(s)$$

Hence

$$C(s) = \frac{R^*(s)G(s)}{1 + (HG)^*(s)} \tag{11.3–14}$$

From our previous study, the poles of $C(s)/R^*(s)$ must lie in the left-half plane for asymptotic stability. However, from (11.3–13) these poles are not only at the zeros of $1 + GH(s)$ but lie at points $jk\omega_c$ separated from them. Thus if the zeros of $1 + GH(s)$ were at $s = -1 \pm j1$, say, the poles of $C(s)$ would be at $s = 1 \pm j1$ and $-1 \pm j(1 + k\omega_c)$, where k takes on all integral values from $-\infty$ to ∞. Hence the pole-zero pattern repeats in strips of width ω_c in the s plane. Six of these infinitely many poles show in Figure 11.3–6. It is

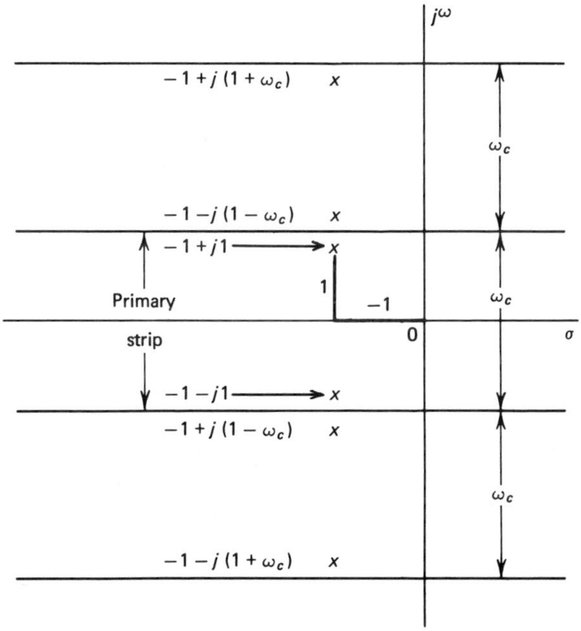

Figure 11.3–6. Repetition of pole pattern in sampled-data system.

also clear from Figure 11.3–6 that the maximum signal angular velocity for $r(t)$ must be less than $\frac{1}{2}\omega_c$, as otherwise we get an interference of modulated signal frequencies. Now since $z = \epsilon^{st}$, when $s = j\omega$,

$$z = \epsilon^{j\omega/\omega_c} \tag{11.3–15}$$

or the primary strip of width ω_c maps into a circle of unit radius in the z plane. However, owing to the multiplicity of the angle, all other s-plane strips similarly map into the unit circle in the z plane, multiple s-plane poles coinciding on the z plane. The output of the system described by (11.3–14) at the sampling instants is

$$C(z) = \frac{R(z)G(z)}{1 + (HG)(z)} \tag{11.3–16}$$

For asymptotic stability, the poles of $C(z)/R(z)$ must therefore lie within the unit circle in the z plane, and their distance from the origin is a measure of the relative stability. Bear in mind that $G(z)$ does not mean $G(s)$ with z replacing s. Strictly speaking, we should use a different symbol than $G(z)$. However, this is common practice in the literature, and we are running out of symbols. By $G(z)$ we mean the operator represented by G in Figure 11.3–5 in the z domain. We continue use of such parallel symbols subsequently.

11.4 Discrete Time Systems in State Space

In a manner analogous to that used in continuous systems, a discrete time system may be written in a state-space form. For linear systems, a change of variable may be utilized, or a flow diagram may assist.

Example 11.4–1

Draw a flow diagram and write state-space equations for the difference equation

$$y(k+3) + 4y(k+2) + 3y(k+1) + y(k)$$
$$= m(k+3) + 2m(k+2) + m(k+1) + 3m(k)$$

One scheme consists in transforming the difference equation to the z domain, giving

$$(z^3 + 4z^2 + 3z + z)Y(z) = (z^3 + 2z^2 + z + 3)M(z)$$

or

$$\frac{Y(z)}{M(z)} = \frac{1 + 2/z + 1/z^2 + 3/z^3}{1 + 4/z + 3/z^2 + 1/z^3}$$

The latter equation allows us to draw the flow diagram of Figure 11.4–1, where the nodes $X_1(z)$, $X_2(z)$, and $X_3(z)$ are selected as shown. The integrators in the continuous system (transfer functions $1/s$ in the s domain) become delays ($1/z$ in the z domain) as previously discussed, thus making the nodes entering these units zX_i if the leaving node is X_i. From the denominator of the Z-domain transfer function and Mason's rule, we can immediately fill in the feedback elements as shown. However, the forward path elements are not so obvious, but applying Mason's rule we get

$$\frac{Y(z)}{M(z)} = \frac{a/z^3 + (b/z^2)(1 + 4/z) + (c/z)(1 + (4/z) + 3/z^2) + d\Delta}{\Delta}$$

$$= \frac{(a + 4b + 3c + d) + (b + 4c + 3d)z + (c + 4d)z^2 + dz^3}{z^3 + 4z^2 + 3z + 1}$$

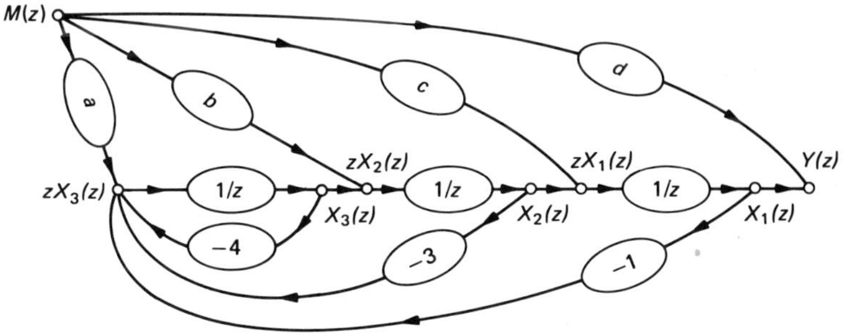

Figure 11.4–1. Flow diagram for Example 11.4–1.

Comparing with the z-transformed equation,

$$d = 1$$
$$c = -4d + 2 = -2$$
$$b = -4c - 3d + 1 = 6$$
$$a = -4b - 3c - d + 3 = -16$$

From the flow diagram, you then obtain

$$zX_1 = X_2 - 2M$$
$$zX_2 = X_3 + 6M$$
$$zX_3 = -X_1 - 3X_2 - 4X_3 - 16M$$
$$Y = X_1 + M$$

Returning to the k domain,

$$\mathbf{x}(k + 1) = \mathbf{A}\mathbf{x}(k) + \mathbf{B}\mathbf{m}(k) \quad \textbf{(11.4–1a)}$$

$$\mathbf{y}(k) = \mathbf{C}\mathbf{x}(k) + \mathbf{D}\mathbf{m}(k) \quad \textbf{(11.4–1b)}$$

where

$$\mathbf{A} = \begin{bmatrix} 0 & 1 & 0 \\ 0 & 0 & 1 \\ -1 & -3 & -4 \end{bmatrix} \qquad \mathbf{B} = \begin{bmatrix} -2 \\ 6 \\ -16 \end{bmatrix}$$

$$\mathbf{C} = [1 \quad 0 \quad 0] \qquad \mathbf{D} = [1]$$

Alternatively, we may use the standard form of Chapter 5. From (5.8–3) you get

$$\begin{bmatrix} 1 & 0 & 0 & 0 \\ 4 & 1 & 0 & 0 \\ 3 & 4 & 1 & 0 \\ 1 & 3 & 4 & 1 \end{bmatrix} \begin{bmatrix} d \\ b_1 \\ b_2 \\ b_3 \end{bmatrix} = \begin{bmatrix} 1 \\ 2 \\ 1 \\ 3 \end{bmatrix}$$

Solving,

$$d = 1$$

$$4d + b_1 = 2 \qquad \text{or} \qquad b_1 = -2$$

$$3d + 4b_1 + b_2 = 1 \qquad \text{or} \qquad b_2 = 6$$

$$d + 3b_1 + 4b_2 + b_3 = 3 \qquad \text{or} \qquad b_3 = -16$$

This gives the same results as (11.4–1). To put (11.4–1) in the time domain, substitute kT for k and $(k+1)T$ for $k+1$. You may also use any of the other state-space forms discussed in Chapter 4.

If we take the state-space equation

$$\boldsymbol{\phi}(k+1) = \mathbf{A}\boldsymbol{\phi}(k) \qquad \boldsymbol{\phi}(0) = \mathbf{I} \tag{11.4–2}$$

with $\mathbf{A}$ independent of k (stationary system), and postulate the solution

$$\boldsymbol{\phi}(k) = \mathbf{A}^k$$

Substitution into (11.4–2) shows that this is indeed a correct result. Hence for the undriven system

$$\mathbf{x}(k+1) = \mathbf{A}\mathbf{x}(k) \qquad \mathbf{x}(k_0) = \mathbf{x}_0$$

the solution is

$$\mathbf{x}(k) = \boldsymbol{\phi}(k - k_0)\mathbf{x}_0 \tag{11.4–3}$$

As in the continuous-time case, we term $\boldsymbol{\phi}(k)$ the transition matrix of the system. For the nonstationary system, $\boldsymbol{\phi}$ is a function of both k and k_0 and (11.4–3) alters to

$$\mathbf{x}(k) = \boldsymbol{\phi}(k, k_0)\mathbf{x}_0 \tag{11.4–4}$$

For the stationary driven system,

$$\mathbf{x}(k+1) = \mathbf{A}\mathbf{x}(k) + \mathbf{B}\mathbf{m}(k) \tag{11.4–5}$$

By starting with $k = 0$, and proceeding iteratively, it is not difficult to show that the solution becomes

$$\mathbf{x}(k) = \mathbf{A}^{(k-k_0)}\mathbf{x}_0 + \sum_{j=k_0}^{k-1} \mathbf{A}^{(k-j-1)}\mathbf{B}\mathbf{m}(j) \qquad \textbf{(11.4–6)}$$

Equation (11.4–6) is the analog of the integral equation for the forced continuous-time system.

If the system is in state-space form, we may apply any of the techniques already discussed in Chapters 4 and 5, in particular diagonalization and spectral representation. If an nth-order system is represented by

$$\mathbf{x}(k+1) = \mathbf{A}\mathbf{x}(k) + \mathbf{B}\mathbf{m}(k) \qquad \textbf{(11.4–7a)}$$

$$\mathbf{y}(k) = \mathbf{C}x(\mathbf{k}) + \mathbf{D}m(k) \qquad \textbf{(11.4–7b)}$$

and n distinct eigenvalues exist, we may diagonalize the $\mathbf{A}$ matrix by first making a change of variable $\mathbf{x}(k) = \mathbf{T}\mathbf{w}(k)$, where $\mathbf{T}$ is the modal matrix (not necessarily normalized).

Then (11.4–7a) becomes

$$\mathbf{T}\mathbf{w}(k+1) = \mathbf{A}\mathbf{T}w(k) + \mathbf{B}\mathbf{m}(k)$$

and premultiplying by $\mathbf{T}^{-1}$ you get

$$\mathbf{w}(k+1) = \mathbf{\Lambda}\mathbf{w}(k) + \mathbf{T}^{-1}\mathbf{B}\mathbf{m}(k) \qquad \textbf{(11.4–8a)}$$

$$\mathbf{y}(k) = \mathbf{C}\mathbf{T}\mathbf{w}(k) + \mathbf{D}\mathbf{m}(k) \qquad \textbf{(11.4–8b)}$$

Again, if the jth row of $\mathbf{T}^{-1}\mathbf{B}$ contains all zeros, the jth mode is uncontrollable, while if the ith column of $\mathbf{CT}$ contains all zeros, the ith mode is unobservable. All these matters move over naturally from the continuous system. However, we must keep clear that the matrices of (11.4–8) hold true only at discrete instants.

11.5 Finding $\phi(k)$, and $\mathbf{H}(k)$,

As in the continuous case, we may compute $\phi(k)$ in various ways as follows: (1) Cayley-Hamilton technique, (2) Z-transform method, (3) flow diagram, and (4) diagonalization or spectral representation. We wish to find $\mathbf{A}^k$ rather than ϵ^{At}, using the ideas discussed in Chapter 5.

Example 11.5–1

Find $\phi(k)$ for the difference equation

$$y(k+2) + 3y(k+1) + 2y(k) = 0$$

Solution: One $\mathbf{A}$ matrix is

$$\mathbf{A} = \begin{bmatrix} 0 & 1 \\ -2 & -3 \end{bmatrix}$$

and the characteristic equation is $\lambda^2 + 3\lambda + 2 = 0$, giving eigenvalues $\lambda = -1$, $\lambda = -2$. Using the remainder polynomial procedure of Chapter 5 with the Cayley-Hamilton theorem,

$$\lambda_1^k = (-1)^k = \alpha_0 + \alpha_1\lambda_1$$

or

$$(-1)^k = \alpha_0 - \alpha_1$$

$$\lambda_2^k = (-2)^k = \alpha_0 + \alpha_1\lambda_2$$

or

$$(-2)^k = \alpha_0 - 2\alpha_1$$

Solving for α_0 and α_1, $\alpha_0 = 2(-1)^k - (-2)^k$, $\alpha_1 = (-1)^k - (-2)^k$. Then

$$\mathbf{A}^k = \alpha_0\mathbf{I} + \alpha_1\mathbf{A}$$

$$\mathbf{A}^k = \begin{bmatrix} 2(-1)^k - (-2)^k & (-1)^k - (-2)^k \\ -2[(-1)^k - (-2)^k] & -(-1)^k + 2(-2)^k \end{bmatrix}$$

You could use the Sylvester expansion theorem also.

In case 2, if you take the Z transform of (11.4–5), you get

$$z\mathbf{X}(z) - z\mathbf{x}(k_0) = \mathbf{AX}(z) + \mathbf{BM}(z)$$

Letting $\mathbf{M}(z) = \mathbf{0}$, then

$$(z\mathbf{I} - \mathbf{A})\mathbf{X}(z) = z\mathbf{x}(k_0)$$

$$\mathbf{X}(z) = (z\mathbf{I} - \mathbf{A})^{-1}z\mathbf{x}(k_0)$$

$$\mathbf{\Phi}(z) = (z\mathbf{I} - \mathbf{A})^{-1}z$$

or

$$\boldsymbol{\phi}(k) = \mathbf{A}^k = Z^{-1}[(z\mathbf{I} - \mathbf{A})^{-1}z] \tag{11.5–1}$$

where Z^{-1} means take the inverse Z transform.

Example 11.5–2

Using the $\mathbf{A}$ matrix of Example 11.5–1,

$$(z\mathbf{I} - \mathbf{A}) = \begin{bmatrix} z & -1 \\ 2 & z+3 \end{bmatrix}$$

$$(z\mathbf{I} - \mathbf{A})^{-1} = \begin{bmatrix} z+3 & -2 \\ 1 & z \end{bmatrix}^T \left(\frac{1}{z^2 + 3z + 2}\right)$$

$$= \begin{bmatrix} \dfrac{z+3}{(z+1)(z+2)} & \dfrac{1}{(z+1)(z+2)} \\ \dfrac{-2}{(z+1)(z+2)} & \dfrac{z}{(z+1)(z+2)} \end{bmatrix}$$

Then

$$\mathbf{A}^k = Z^{-1}[(z\mathbf{I} - \mathbf{A})^{-1}z] = \Sigma \text{ residues of } (z\mathbf{I} - \mathbf{A})^{-1}z^k$$

or

$$\mathbf{A}^k = \begin{bmatrix} 2(-1)^k - (-2)^k & (-1)^k - (-2)^k \\ -2(-1)^k - (-2)^k & -(-1)^k + 2(-2)^k \end{bmatrix}$$

which checks with the previous example.

Note that the analogy with the Laplace transform case breaks down slightly here. You may use the Fadeeva method of matrix inversion for larger-order systems, which proceeds just as outlined in Chapter 6. Furthermore, the inversion of the Z transform may proceed by an interative division process unless a closed form is desired, as discussed previously.

For case 3 we may use a simulation diagram analogously to the method used in continuous systems. Since

$$\mathbf{x}(k) = \boldsymbol{\Phi}(k)\mathbf{x}(k_0)$$

$$x_i(k) = \sum_{j=1}^{n} \phi_{ij}(k)x_j(k_0) \tag{11.5-2}$$

Then a unit initial condition on x_l, all other state variables having zero initial conditions, gives a response of $\phi_{il}(k)$ at x_i. Because a delay unit results in a multiplication by z^{-1} in the z domain, if we put an impulse at the front of the lth unit delay, we get $z^{-1}\Phi_{il}(z)$. From (11.5–1),

$$z^{-1}\boldsymbol{\Phi}(z) = (z\mathbf{I} - \mathbf{A})^{-1} \tag{11.5-3}$$

Hence an impulse into the jth delay results in $z^{-1}\Phi_{ij}$ at the output of the ith delay. In other words, $(z\mathbf{I} - \mathbf{A})^{-1}$ is obtainable in a similar fashion to $(s\mathbf{I} - \mathbf{A})^{-1}$ in the continuous case, but since in the z-transform case, (11.5–3) holds, $\mathbf{A}^k = z(z\mathbf{I} - \mathbf{A})^{-1}$.

Example 11.5–3

Using the same system as in Example 11.5–1, Figure 11.5–1 shows the flow diagram in the z domain. If we number the delays as shown, and use Mason's rule, then

$$z^{-1}\Phi_{11} = \frac{(1/z)(1 + 3/z)}{1 + (3/z) + 2/z^2} = \frac{z + 3}{z^2 + 3z + 2}$$

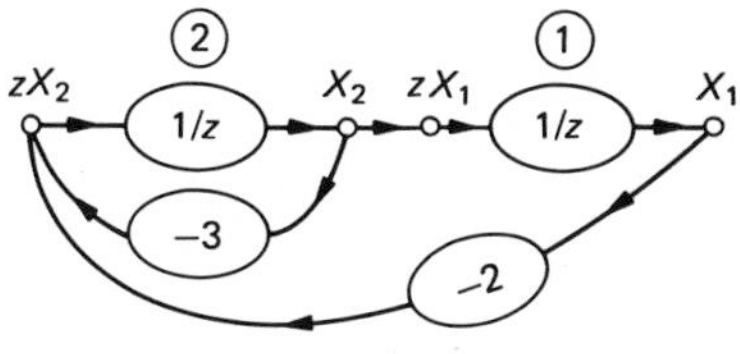

Figure 11.5–1. Flow diagram for Example 11.5–3.

which results from the transfer function in the z domain between nodes zX_1 and X_1. Similarly,

$$z^{-1}\Phi_{12} = \frac{1}{z^2 + 3z + 2}$$

$$z^{-1}\Phi_{21} = \frac{-2}{z^2 + 3z + 2}$$

$$z^{-1}\Phi_{22} = \frac{z}{z^2 + 3z + 2}$$

Hence

$$\phi(k) = \mathbf{A}^k = Z^{-1}\begin{bmatrix} \dfrac{z(z+3)}{(z+1)(z+2)} & \dfrac{z}{(z+1)(z+2)} \\ \dfrac{-2z}{(z+1)(z+2)} & \dfrac{z^2}{(z+1)(z+2)} \end{bmatrix}$$

which checks the previous results.

For case 4, let us find the modal matrix and diagonalize **A**.

Example 11.5–4

Using the system of Example 11.5–1 again, we can immediately write down the (unnormalized) matrix **T**, since **A** is in the proper form to be diagonalized by a Vandermonde matrix. Then with $\lambda_1 = -1$ and $\lambda_2 = -2$,

$$\mathbf{T} = \begin{bmatrix} 1 & 1 \\ -1 & -2 \end{bmatrix} \qquad \mathbf{T}^{-1} = \begin{bmatrix} 2 & 1 \\ -1 & -1 \end{bmatrix}$$

Now in the original difference equation,

$$\mathbf{x}(k+1) = \mathbf{A}\mathbf{x}(k)$$

a change of variable $\mathbf{x}(k) = \mathbf{T}\mathbf{w}(k)$ gives

$$\mathbf{T}\mathbf{w}(k+1) = \mathbf{A}\mathbf{T}\mathbf{w}(k)$$

and premultiplication by $\mathbf{T}^{-1}$ results in

$$\mathbf{w}(k+1) = \mathbf{\Lambda}\mathbf{w}(k)$$

or

$$w_1(k+1) = -1w_1(k)$$

$$w_2(k+1) = -2w_2(k)$$

From these decoupled equations you immediately see that

$$w_1(k) = (-1)^k w_1(0)$$

$$w_2(k) = (-2)^k w_2(0)$$

or

$$\mathbf{w}(k) = \begin{bmatrix} (-1)^k & 0 \\ 0 & (-2)^k \end{bmatrix} \mathbf{w}(0)$$

since

$$\mathbf{x}(k) = \mathbf{T}\mathbf{w}(k) \qquad \mathbf{w}(0) = \mathbf{T}^{-1}\mathbf{x}(0)$$

$$\mathbf{x}(k) = \begin{bmatrix} 1 & 1 \\ -1 & -2 \end{bmatrix} \begin{bmatrix} (-1)^k & 0 \\ 0 & (-2)^k \end{bmatrix} \begin{bmatrix} 2 & 1 \\ -1 & -1 \end{bmatrix} \mathbf{x}(0)$$

or

$$\mathbf{x}(k) = \begin{bmatrix} 2(-1)^k - (-2)^k & (-1)^k - (-2)^k \\ -2(-1)^k + 2(-2)^k & -(-1)^k + 2(-2)^k \end{bmatrix} \mathbf{x}(0)$$

As this is a solution to the equation, the matrix on the right is $\mathbf{A}^k$.

The spectral representation involves a very similar analysis.

As in the continuous situation, for a stationary system we may define a transfer function matrix $\hat{\mathbf{H}}(z)$ and an impulse response matrix $\mathbf{H}(k)$.* Writing the system equations as

$$\mathbf{x}(k+1) = \mathbf{A}\mathbf{x}(k) + \mathbf{B}\mathbf{m}(k)$$

$$\mathbf{y}(k) = \mathbf{C}\mathbf{x}(k) + \mathbf{D}\mathbf{x}(k)$$

and transforming, you get

$$z\mathbf{X}(z) - z\mathbf{x}(0) = \mathbf{A}\mathbf{X}(z) + \mathbf{B}\mathbf{M}(z) \qquad \textbf{(11.5–4a)}$$

$$\mathbf{Y}(z) = \mathbf{C}\mathbf{X}(z) + \mathbf{D}\mathbf{M}(z) \qquad \textbf{(11.5–4b)}$$

Solving (11.5–4) you obtain

$$\mathbf{Y}(z) = \mathbf{C}(z\mathbf{I} - \mathbf{A})^{-1}z\mathbf{x}(0) + [\mathbf{C}(z\mathbf{I} - \mathbf{A})^{-1}\mathbf{B} + \mathbf{D}]\mathbf{M}(z) \qquad \textbf{(11.5–5)}$$

Defining the transfer function matrix as

$$\hat{\mathbf{H}}(z) = \mathbf{Y}(z)\mathbf{M}^{-1}(z)$$

with $\mathbf{x}(0) = 0$, then

$$\hat{\mathbf{H}}(z) = \mathbf{C}(z\mathbf{I} - \mathbf{A})^{-1}\mathbf{B} + \mathbf{D}$$

or

$$\hat{\mathbf{H}}(z) = \mathbf{C}\boldsymbol{\Phi}(z)z^{-1}\mathbf{B} + \mathbf{D} \qquad \textbf{(11.5–6)}$$

* $\mathbf{H}(k)$ is analogous to $\mathbf{W}(t)$ in Chapter 6.

Taking the inverse transform,

$$\mathbf{H}(k) = \mathbf{C}\boldsymbol{\phi}(k-1)\mathbf{B} \qquad k \geq 1 \tag{11.5–7a}$$

$$\mathbf{H}(k) = \mathbf{D} \qquad k = 0 \tag{11.5–7b}$$

Equations (11.5–7) result from two considerations; (1) the z^{-1} in (11.5–6) provides a delay of one unit and $\boldsymbol{\phi}(k)$, $k < 0$, is undefined; and (2) the impulse nature of $\mathbf{H}(k)$ makes $\mathbf{D}$ the only transmission vehicle at $k = 0$. Again the analogy with the continuous-time system is very close but not exact.

The transfer function matrix $\hat{\mathbf{H}}(z)$ may be found by (11.5–6) or by using a flow diagram.

Example 11.5–5

Given

$$\mathbf{x}(k+1) = \mathbf{A}\mathbf{x}(k) + \mathbf{B}\mathbf{m}(k)$$

$$\mathbf{y}(k) = \mathbf{C}\mathbf{x}(k) + \mathbf{D}\mathbf{m}(k)$$

where

$$\mathbf{A} = \begin{bmatrix} -1 & 1 \\ -1 & -2 \end{bmatrix} \qquad \mathbf{B} = \begin{bmatrix} 1 \\ 2 \end{bmatrix} \qquad \mathbf{C} = [2 \quad 1] \qquad \mathbf{D} = \mathbf{0}$$

find $\hat{\mathbf{H}}(z)$ and $\mathbf{H}(k)$.

Solution:

$$(z\mathbf{I} - \mathbf{A}) = \begin{bmatrix} z+1 & -1 \\ 1 & z+2 \end{bmatrix}$$

$$(z\mathbf{I} - \mathbf{A})^{-1} = \begin{bmatrix} z+2 & 1 \\ -1 & z+1 \end{bmatrix} \frac{1}{z^2 + 3z + 3}$$

Then

$$\hat{\mathbf{H}}(z) = \frac{[2 \quad 1]}{z^2 + 3z + 3} \begin{bmatrix} z+2 & 1 \\ -1 & z+1 \end{bmatrix} \begin{bmatrix} 1 \\ 2 \end{bmatrix}$$

or

$$\hat{\mathbf{H}}(z) = \frac{4z + 9}{z^2 + 3z + 3}$$

A flow diagram is shown in Figure 11.5–2.

Using Mason's rule on the single input-output system of Figure 11.5–2,

$$\Delta = 1 - \left(-\frac{1}{z} - \frac{2}{z} - \frac{1}{z^2}\right) + \frac{2}{z^2} = 1 + \frac{3}{z} + \frac{3}{z^2}$$

Then

$$\frac{Y(z)}{M(z)} = \frac{(2/z)(1+2/z) - (1/z^2) + (4/z^2) + (2/z)(1+1/z)}{\Delta}$$

or

$$\hat{\mathbf{H}}(z) = \frac{4z+9}{z^2+3z+3} = \frac{4z+9}{(z+3/2+j\sqrt{3}/2)(z+3/2-j\sqrt{3}/2)}$$

Hence

$$\mathbf{H}(k) = \Sigma \text{ residues of } \hat{\mathbf{H}}(z)z^{-1}z^k$$

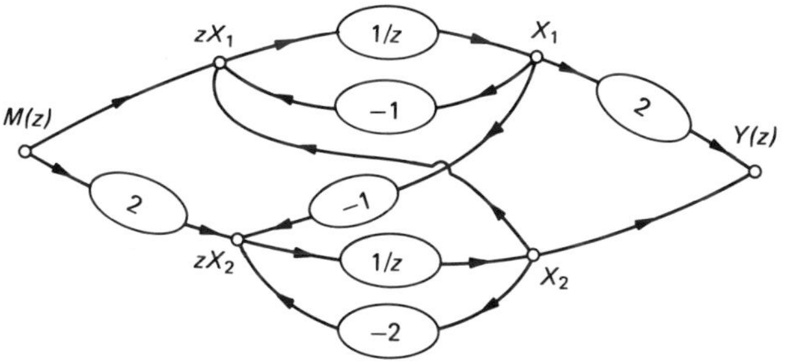

Figure 11.5–2. Flow diagram for Example 11.5–5.

Division of $(4z+9)$ by (z^2+3z+3) gives $4z^{-1} - 3z^{-2} - 7z^{-3} + \cdots$. Since from this the residues at $k = 0$ sum to zero, we proceed to the other residues to find $\mathbf{H}(k)$ in closed form as

$$\mathbf{H}(k) = 2\sqrt{7}(\sqrt{3})^{k-1} \sin[(k-1)\theta + \phi] \qquad k \geq 1$$

where

$$\tan\theta = \frac{1/2}{-\sqrt{3}/2} \qquad \tan\phi = \frac{2/\sqrt{7}}{-\sqrt{3}/\sqrt{7}}$$

Uncontrollable and/or unobservable modes cause cancellations in the transfer function matrix, or, in other words, $\hat{\mathbf{H}}(z)$ specifies only the controllable and observable portion of the system. If the system is time-varying, the transition and impulse response matrices will be functions of kT, or k, depending on the variable. Analytic solutions usually will not be possible. If $\mathbf{A}(k)$ can be expressed as $\mathbf{A}_0 + \mathbf{A}_1(k)$, and if $\mathbf{A}_1(k)$ consists of a small perturbation on $\mathbf{A}_0$, then $\boldsymbol{\phi}(k, k_0)$ may be found by an iteration process [17]. In general, a computer solution becomes necessary. For nonlinear systems, matrices cannot be used at all.

If a zero-order hold, or clamp, is used, then for fixed systems special but interesting relations may be developed as follows. Let

$$\dot{\mathbf{x}}(t) = \mathbf{A}\mathbf{x}(t) + \mathbf{B}\mathbf{m}(t) \tag{11.5–8}$$

represent a fixed system with a signal that is constant between sampling instants that are T units of time t apart. From the work in continuous time systems, the solution is

$$\mathbf{x}(t) = \exp(\mathbf{A}t)\mathbf{x}(0) + \int_0^t \exp(\mathbf{A}(t - \lambda)\mathbf{B}\mathbf{m}(\lambda)\, d\lambda \tag{11.5–9}$$

assuming $t_0 = 0$. If $t = (k + 1)T$, then

$$\begin{aligned}\mathbf{x}(k+1)T &= \exp \mathbf{A}(k+1)T\mathbf{x}(0) + \int_0^{(k+1)T} \exp[\mathbf{A}(k+1)T - \lambda]\mathbf{B}\mathbf{m}(\lambda)\, d\lambda \\ &= \exp \mathbf{A}T\left[\exp(\mathbf{A}kT)\mathbf{x}(0) + \int_0^{kt} \exp[\mathbf{A}(kT - \lambda)]\mathbf{B}\mathbf{m}(\lambda)\, d\lambda\right] \\ &\quad + \int_{kt}^{(k+1)T} \exp[\mathbf{A}(k+1)T - \lambda]\mathbf{B}\mathbf{m}(\lambda)\, d\lambda\end{aligned}$$

or, from (11.5–9),

$$\mathbf{x}(k+1)T = \exp(\mathbf{A}T)\mathbf{x}(kT) + \int_{kt}^{(k+1)T} \exp[\mathbf{A}(k+1)T - \lambda]\mathbf{B}\mathbf{m}(\lambda)\, d\lambda$$

If $\mathbf{m}(t)$ is constant, or $\mathbf{m}(t) = \mathbf{m}(kT)$ for $kT \le t \le (k + 1)T$, then the last equation becomes

$$\mathbf{x}(k+1)T = \exp(\mathbf{A}T)\mathbf{x}(kT) + \mathbf{m}(kT) \int_{kt}^{(k+1)T} \exp(\mathbf{A}(k+1)T - \lambda]\mathbf{B}\, d\lambda$$

Letting $w = (k + 1)T - \lambda$, you then get

$$\mathbf{x}(k+1)T = \exp(\mathbf{A}T)\mathbf{x}\,(kT) + \mathbf{m}(kT) \int_0^T \exp(\mathbf{A}w)\mathbf{B}\, dw$$

Finally,

$$\mathbf{x}(k+1) = \hat{\mathbf{A}}\mathbf{x}(k) + \hat{\mathbf{B}}\mathbf{m}(k) \tag{11.5–10}$$

where

$$\hat{\mathbf{A}} = \exp(\mathbf{A}T) = \boldsymbol{\phi}(T)$$

$$\hat{\mathbf{B}} = \int_0^T \exp(\mathbf{A}w)\mathbf{B}\,dw = \int_0^T \boldsymbol{\phi}(w)\mathbf{B}\,dw$$

Equation (11.5–10) is a difference equation giving $\mathbf{x}(k)$ at the sampling instants for a sampled-data system with a clamp type (zero-hold) smoothing device.

Example 11.5–6

Analyze the system of Figure 11.5–3 where the switch sw is an ideal sampling device with period T and h is a zero-order hold.

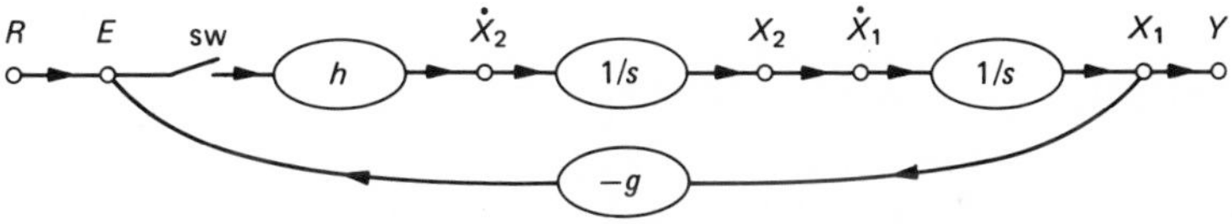

Figure 11.5–3. Flow diagram for Example 11.5–6.

Solution: The equation for the system in Figure 11.5–3 is

$$\dot{x}_1 = x_2$$

$$\dot{x}_2 = m$$

where m is the piecewise constant input given by sampling $r - gx_1$. Then in (11.5–8)

$$\mathbf{A} = \begin{bmatrix} 0 & 1 \\ 0 & 0 \end{bmatrix} \qquad \mathbf{B} = \begin{bmatrix} 0 \\ 1 \end{bmatrix}$$

Hence

$$\boldsymbol{\phi}(t) = \begin{bmatrix} 1 & t \\ 0 & 1 \end{bmatrix}$$

$$\hat{\mathbf{A}}(t) = \begin{bmatrix} 1 & T \\ 0 & 1 \end{bmatrix}$$

$$\hat{\mathbf{B}} = \int_0^T \begin{bmatrix} 1 & w \\ 0 & 1 \end{bmatrix} \begin{bmatrix} 0 \\ 1 \end{bmatrix} dw = \begin{bmatrix} T^2/2 \\ T \end{bmatrix}$$

The difference equation is then given by (11.5–10), or

$$\mathbf{x}(k+1) = \begin{bmatrix} 1 & T \\ 0 & 1 \end{bmatrix} \mathbf{x}(k) + \begin{bmatrix} T^2/2 \\ T \end{bmatrix} \mathbf{m}(k)$$

Since $\mathbf{m}(k) = r(k) - gx_1(k)$, the discrete system becomes

$$\mathbf{x}(k+1) = \mathbf{A}_1\mathbf{x}(k) + \mathbf{B}_1 r(k)$$

$$\mathbf{y}(k) = \mathbf{C}\mathbf{x}(k)$$

where

$$\mathbf{A}_1 = \begin{bmatrix} 1 - T^2g/2 & T \\ -Tg & 1 \end{bmatrix} \qquad \mathbf{B}_1 = \begin{bmatrix} T^2/2 \\ T \end{bmatrix} \qquad \mathbf{C} = [1 \quad 0]$$

Using the z transform,

$$(z\mathbf{I} - \mathbf{A}_1)^{-1} = \begin{bmatrix} z-1 & T \\ -Tg & \dfrac{2z + T^2g - 2}{2} \end{bmatrix} \frac{2}{2z^2 + (T^2g - 4)z + T^2g + 2}$$

From this we could find $\boldsymbol{\phi}(k)$, if desired. If we are interested only in the output y, then

$$\hat{\mathbf{H}}(z) = C(z\mathbf{I} - \mathbf{A}_1)^{-1}\mathbf{B}_1$$

$$= \frac{2T^2(z/2 - (1/2) + 1)}{2z^2 + (T^2g - 4)z + (T^2/g) + 2}$$

If $T = g = 1$,

$$\hat{\mathbf{H}}(z) = \frac{\frac{1}{2}(z+1)}{z^2 - 3z/2 + 3/2}$$

Since the characteristic equation gives $z = 3/4 \pm j\sqrt{15}/4$, $|z| = \sqrt{24}/4$, which is greater than 1. The poles of $\hat{\mathbf{H}}(z)$ lie outside the unit circle in the z plane and the system is unstable.

If there is an input $2 - (0.5)^k$, then

$$Y(z) = \frac{\frac{1}{2}z^2(z+1)}{(z-1)(z-0.5)[z^2 - (3z/2) + 3/2]}$$

and $y(k) = (-3/4)(0.5)^k - (9/8)(C^k/b)\sin k\theta + (15/8)(C^{k-1}/b) \sin[(k-1)\theta]$ $u(k-1)$ where $C = \sqrt{3/2}$, $b = \sqrt{15}/4$, and $\tan\theta = \sqrt{15}/(-3)$.

If we use the method suggested by Figure 11.3–5 and (11.3–16), the hold device has the transform $(1 - \epsilon^{-Ts})/s$. Hence

$$G(s) = \frac{1 - \epsilon^{-Ts}}{s^3} \qquad GH(s) \frac{k(1 - \epsilon^{-Ts})}{s^3}$$

$$G(z) = \frac{T^2}{2}\frac{z^{-1} - z^{-3}}{(1 - z^{-1})^3} \qquad GH(z) = \frac{T^2k}{2}\frac{z^{-1} - z^{-3}}{(1 - z^{-1})^3}$$

Then

$$\frac{Y(z)}{R(z)} = \frac{G(z)}{1 + GH(z)}$$

which gives the same $\hat{\mathbf{H}}(z)$ as before.

You clearly see that obtaining closed analytic expressions for these systems becomes a most difficult task. Once the system is in the form of a difference equation, such as (11.5–10), however, the solution for any interval may be obtained by iteration, which is a task performed rapidly and accurately by digital computer (or by analog systems using delays). Thus as in the continuous system, for a problem of any magnitude a computer is a necessity. Therefore, perhaps the main purpose of our examples is to emphasize this fact and to familiarize you with the mathematical nomenclature and concepts.

11.6 Conventional Analysis of Discrete Time Systems

Conventional analysis here covers much the same territory as in continuous-time systems. Fundamentally, we have the questions of static accuracy, stability, and relative stability. Stability for the linear system involves checking the roots of the characteristic equation, to see that they lie within the unit circle. For a characteristic equation of second order this is not difficult, as Truxal [18] shows that for a second-degree polynomial $p(z)$ the requirements are

$$|p(0)| < 1 \qquad p(1) > 0 \qquad p(-1) > 0$$

Example 11.6–1

$p(0)$ for the polynomial of Example 11.5–6, $2z^2 + (T^2g - 4)z + (T^2/g) + 2$ is $T^2/g + 2$. Hence the system cannot be stable for any $g > 0$. The other tests also eliminate $g < 0$. This is not surprising, because the system has two integrators in tandem.

For polynomials of higher degree, we may adopt the transformation

$$z = \frac{w+1}{w-1} \tag{11.6–1}$$

which maps the z plane into the w plane, with the area inside the circle $z = \epsilon^{j\theta}$ becoming the left-half w plane. We may then apply the Routh criteria in the w plane.

Example 11.6–2

Check the characteristic equation

$$z^3 + 3z^2 + 2z + 1 = 0$$

for roots outside the unit circle. Using (11.6–1), you get

$$\frac{7w^3 + w^2 + w - 1}{(w-1)^3}$$

Examining the numerator polynomial the Routh array is

$$\begin{array}{rr} 7 & 1 \\ 1 & -1 \\ 8 & \\ -1 & \end{array}$$

There is one change of sign; hence one root of the original characteristic equation lies outside the unit circle in the z plane.

The transformation of (11.6–1) can be used to bring all the frequency analysis techniques to bear. That is, once the system is transformed from the z domain into the w domain, Bode plots, Nichols charts, and so on, may be used, because the w plane is the same as the s plane in normal frequency analysis. Two disadvantages exist: (1) The transformation involves considerable algebra, and (2) the determination of a compensating network in the original system may be difficult. Tou discusses this technique [19].

You can apply the root locus directly in the z domain. The criteria now involves a crossing of the unit circle, but since the method is graphical, this involves little more effort than the use of the root locus in the s plane. Before we give an example, it should be pointed out that the position of the sampler switch or switches may alter the form of the control ratio expression in the z domain, particularly if feedback occurs. Thus, if Figure 11.3–5 applies, (11.3–16) is correct, and $(HG)(z)$ would be our starting point. However if Figure 11.6–1 represents the system, then (11.6–2) results, while with Figure 11.6–2, (11.6–3) should be used. The control ratio for Figure 11.6–1 is

$$\frac{C(z)}{R(z)} = \frac{G(z)}{1 + H(z)G(z)} \tag{11.6–2}$$

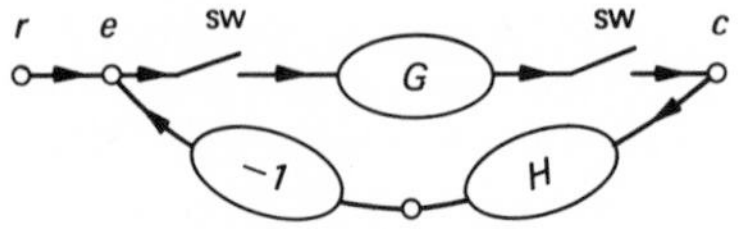

Figure 11.6–1. Flow diagram for Equation (11.6–2).

The $C(z)$ for Figure 11.6–2 is

$$C(z) = \frac{G_2(z)(RG_1)(z)}{1 + (GH_1G_2)(z)} \tag{11.6–3}$$

$(HG)(z)$ means find the z transform corresponding to HG, while $H(z)G(z)$ means take the product of $H(z)G(z)$; the expressions are not the same. The z transform thus depends on the sampler switch location(s). We now proceed to an example of a root locus in the z plane.

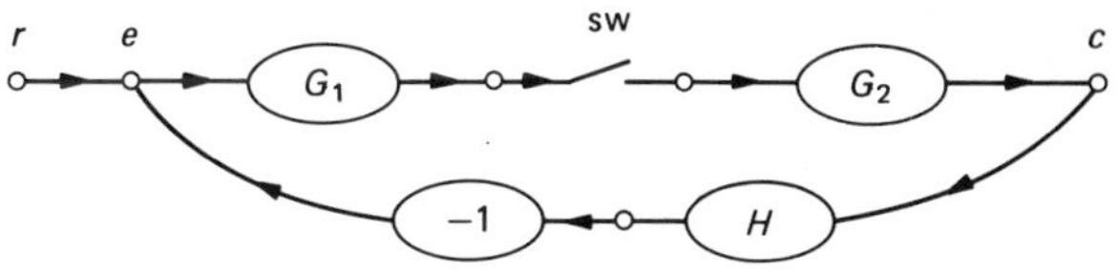

Figure 11.6–2. Flow diagram for Equation (11.6–3).

Example 11.6–3

In Figure 11.6–3 find the value of K for instability if $T = 0.8$ sec and the z transform corresponding to $1/(s + a)^2$ is $Tz\epsilon^{-aT}/(z - \epsilon^{-aT})^2$.

Solution:

$$G(s) = \frac{K}{s} - \frac{K}{(s + 1)^2} - \frac{K}{s + 1}$$

$$G(z) = \frac{Kz[z(-\epsilon^{-T} - T\epsilon^{-T} + 1)] + \epsilon^{-2T} + T\epsilon^{-T} - \epsilon^{-T}}{(z - \epsilon^{-T})^2(z - 1)}$$

If $T = 0.8$,

$$G(z) = \frac{0.190Kz(z + 0.590)}{z^3 - 1.90z^2 + 1.103z - 0.203} \quad \text{(slide rule accuracy)}$$

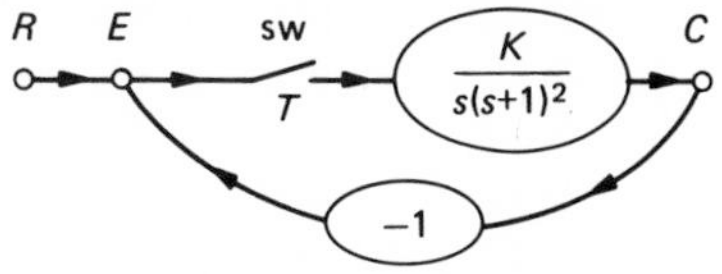

Figure 11.6–3. System for Example 11.6–3.

The characteristic equation for the control ratio C/R is therefore $z^3 - (1.90 - 0.190K)z^2 + (1.103 + 0.112K)z - 0.203 = 0$. $G(z)$ has zeros at 0 and -0.590, two poles at $z = 0.450$ and one pole at $z = 1$. We use the z plane, so some of the s-plane root locus rules do not apply, but most do.

The breakaway points are at about $z = 0.77$ and $z = -2.30$, both of which are on the locus. Routh's rule cannot be used directly, but from a sketch you see that when K is such that the locus crosses the unit circle, the poles must be conjugate complex and have a magnitude of 1, or we find $p_1 = \epsilon^{j\theta}$, $p_2 = \epsilon^{-j\theta}$. Then $p_1 p_2 p_3 = -0.203$ from the characteristic equation, or $-p_3 = 0.203$. Dividing the factor $z - 0.203$ out of the characteristic equation, $K \approx 1.6$ and the other two roots occur at $z \simeq 0.696 \pm j0.715$. Figure 11.6–4

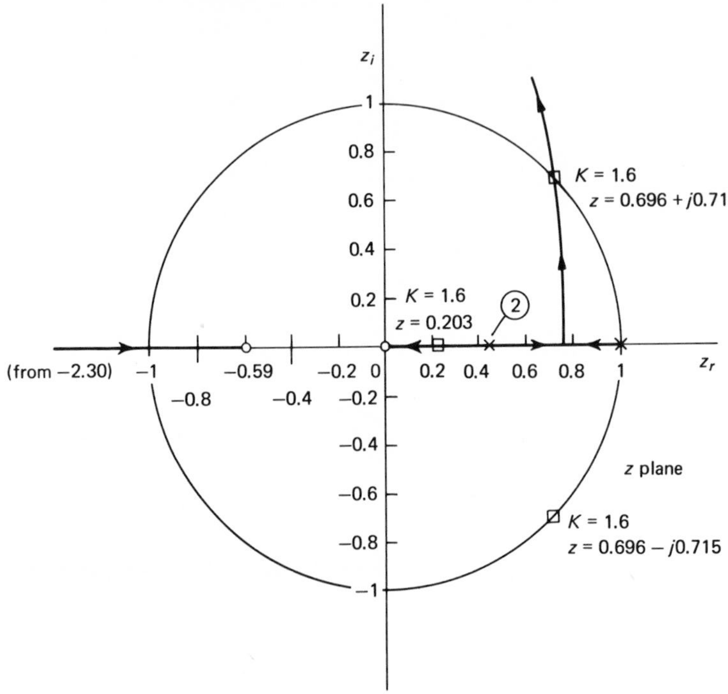

Figure 11.6–4. Root locus for Example 11.6–3.

shows part of the locus. The two branches in the complex z plane continue to the left until they meet again on the real axis at $z = -2.30$. Because $z = \epsilon^{sT}$, when $z = \epsilon^{j\theta}$, $sT = j\omega T$ or $\omega T = \theta$. In this case $T = 0.8$ and $\theta \simeq 0.8$ radian when $K \simeq 1.6$; hence the angular velocity of oscillation of the sampled-data system is about 1 radian per second when on the verge of instability. Note again, we know nothing as to system performance between sampling instants without further analysis.

Design for specific dominant complex pole locations utilizing the root locus may be accomplished by drawing the locus of points representing specified ω_n, ζ, or $\zeta\omega_n$ values in the z plane, and finding where the root locus crosses these curves. A line of constant $\zeta\omega_n$ in the s plane as in Figure 11.6–5a maps into a circle in the z plane as shown in Figure 11.6–5b, while a line depicting a constant damping factor $\zeta = \cos\theta$ maps into the logarithmic spiral

$$z = \exp\left[\frac{-\zeta\omega}{\sqrt{1-\zeta^2}} + j\omega T\right]$$

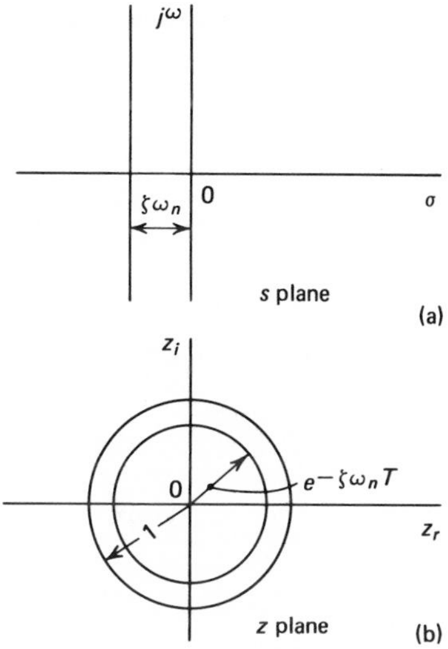

Figure 11.6–5. Mapping from the *s* to the *z* plane for $s = \zeta_n\omega + j\omega$.

If only poles in the primary strip of Figure 11.3–6 are considered, then a line of constant damping factor ζ as in Figure 11.6–6a maps into the spiral of Figure 11.6–6b, where $z_a = z_b = -\exp(-\zeta\omega_c/2\sqrt{1-\zeta^2})$. For a circle of constant radius ω_n in the s plane $\omega_n \le \omega_s/2$, the transformation is given by $z = \exp(\omega_n T\epsilon^{j\theta})$ or $z = \exp(\omega_n T\cos\theta)\exp(j\omega_n T\sin\theta)$. The circle of Figure 11.6–7a is shown in Figure 11.6–7b for various values of ω_n.

Design using the root locus becomes largely a cut and try procedure; that is, if the system does not perform correctly, you introduce compensation as in the continuous situation and draw a new root locus, and so on. Experience assists but does not solve all cases. The use of a direct synthesis procedure, such as the Lago-Hausenbauer approach, does not seem usually possible, because if an appropriate open loop $G(z)$ function can be obtained, there is no guarantee that this can be physically realizable as a continuous time network [that $G(s)$ can be constructed].

The root locus may be used to investigate the alteration of some component other than gain, just as in the continuous case. However, an analysis of the sample period T by this procedure becomes difficult due to the fact that T is involved both as a multiplier and as an exponent. Straightforward redrawing of the locus with a new T therefore seems simpler.

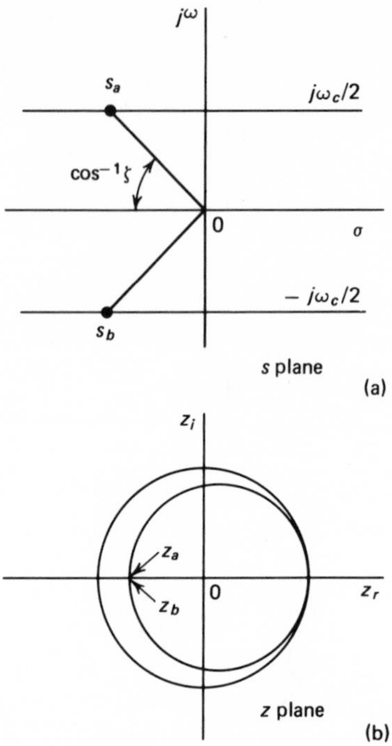

Figure 11.6–6. Mapping from the s to the z plane for constant ζ.

You may conduct analysis in the z plane using the Nyquist diagram. For example, examining the function

$$(HG)(z) = \frac{z^2 + 0.5}{z^2 + z + 1}$$

we take a Nyquist path in the z plane around the unit circle, and returning at infinity, as in Figure 11.6–8a. The corresponding path in the $(HG)(z)$ plane is as shown in Figure 11.6–8b. The point $(-1, 0)$ is not enclosed, so $1 + (HG)(z)$ has no zeros outside the unit circle in the z plane. If poles or zeros exist along the real axis between c and d in Figure 11.6–8a, they must be bypassed as in the s-plane case. By taking various Nyquist paths, all the zeros of $1 + (HG)(z)$ could be located analogous to the possibilities discussed in Chapter 8 for continuous-time systems.

The Nyquist diagram for $G^*(s)$ can also be used. This reduces to finding a series expression for $G^*(s)$ and approximating this by a finite number of terms. From (11.3–13), since

$$G^*(s) = \frac{1}{T} \sum_{k=-\infty}^{\infty} G(s + jk\omega_c) \qquad \textbf{(11.6–4)}$$

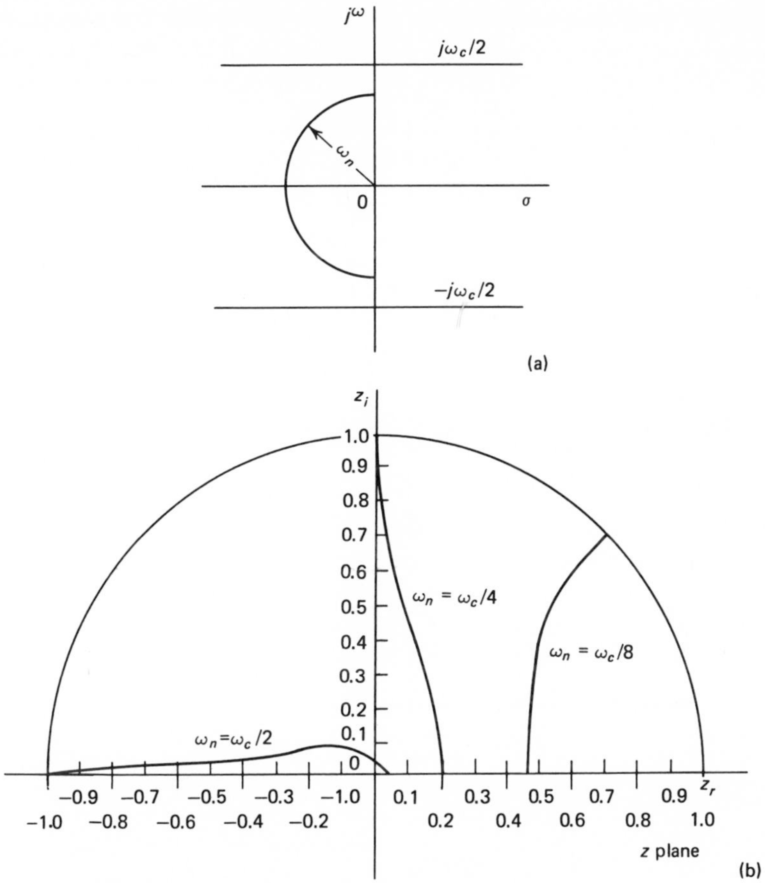

Figure 11.6–7. Mapping from the *s* to the *z* for constant ω_n.

then, for example,

$$G^*(j1) = \frac{1}{T}[G(j1) + G(j(1 - \omega_c)) + G(j(1 + \omega_c)) + G(j(1 - 2\omega_c)) + G(j(1 + 2\omega_c)) + \cdots]$$

If $T = 1$, or $\omega_c = 2\pi$, then the terms in the series diminish rapidly, because $G(j\omega)$ normally has the characteristics of a low-pass filter. By using the first three terms, say, the characteristics for $G^*(j\omega)$ may be plotted fairly rapidly and the usual Nyquist criteria of stability and relative stability applied. Similarly, Bode plots could be prepared. The process is procedurally straightforward but vastly tedious without computer support. The parameter plane method also may be used in discrete time systems [20].

As discussed previously, if the signals in the system are broken into Fourier components, the highest angular velocity that can be passed without distortion is one half the angular velocity of the sampler rate, as the

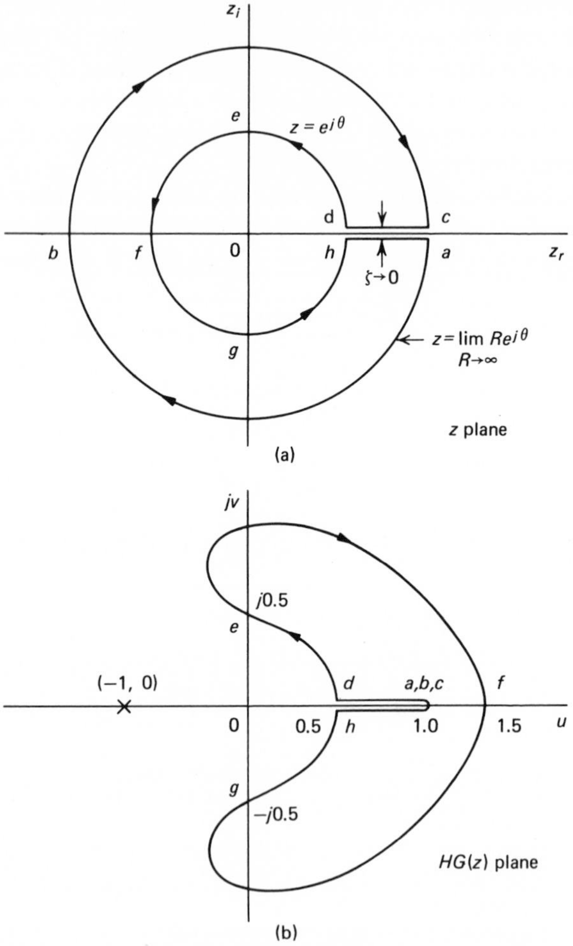

Figure 11.6–8. Nyquist diagram for $HG(z) = (z^2 + 0.5)/(z^2 + z + 1)$.

sampling process is essentially one of modulation. Thus meaningful signals should not have angular velocities greater than $2\pi/2T = \pi/T$, or in Example 11.6–3, of π radians per second. Hence rapid changes in the input will not be properly transmitted unless the sampling period is short, which agrees with our intuition. On the other hand, if we go back to the s-plane analysis you recall that the system poles and zeros occur in strips ω_c in width. Hence to prevent the poles in the strips beyond the primary strip of Figure 11.3–6 from influencing system performance, the bandwidth of the system must be sufficiently low relative to ω_c that these poles do not enter substantially into the picture, and we should have a sharp cutoff at high frequencies. If we make the bandwidth about $\omega_c/2$, then the multiple complex poles will have little effect, but high-frequency signals will also be attenuated.

Although at first blush it would seem that the shorter the sampling period T the better the stability, this is not necessarily true, and, although it would similarly seem that smoothing by means of a hold system would improve performance, this may not be true either. Each system must be analyzed in full, and generalizations are risky [21].

The static coefficients for a sampled-data system are similar to those for a continuous-time system. For a unity negative feedback, system with forward path gain $G(z)$, these coefficients may be defined as follows:

$$K_p = \lim_{z \to 1} G(z) \tag{11.6–5a}$$

$$K_v = \frac{1}{T} \lim_{z \to 1} [(z-1)G(z)] \tag{11.6–5b}$$

$$K_a = \frac{1}{T^2} \lim_{z \to 1} [(z-1)^2 G(z)] \tag{11.6–5c}$$

Then the steady-state error ($t \to \infty$) using the final value theorem becomes

$$\frac{1}{1+K_p} \quad \text{for a step input}$$

$$\frac{1}{K_v} \quad \text{for a ramp input}$$

$$\frac{1}{K_a} \quad \text{for a parabolic input}$$

as in the continuous case. The error here, however, is taken at the sampling instants and nowhere else. These relations are found easily by using the formula

$$\frac{E(z)}{R(z)} = \frac{1}{1+G(z)}$$

applying the inputs in turn, and taking the limits as $z \to 1$. This implies a configuration as in Figure 11.3–5 with $H = 1$.

11.7 State-Space Analysis of Discrete Time Systems

Discrete time systems may be optimized using the same principles as discussed in Chapter 6 for continuous-time systems. Any digital computer solution actually employs discrete time techniques even if the problem originally was stated in a continuous-time framework. Dynamic programming is uniquely suited to discrete time systems, as the basic formulation depends on dividing the state space into discrete points and optimizing a trajectory that connects particular points in this discretized space. Conceptually, dynamic programming is not difficult to understand [22]. However, the number of arithmetic operations, although vastly reduced from the number required for a blind search for an optimum by taking all possible trajectories, still increases with the state-space dimension as an exponent. Specifically, if we have a one-dimensional space, we divide the desired observation time into N equal intervals (or create an N-stage process), and let the state variable have r possible discrete values (see Figure 11.7–1). In a

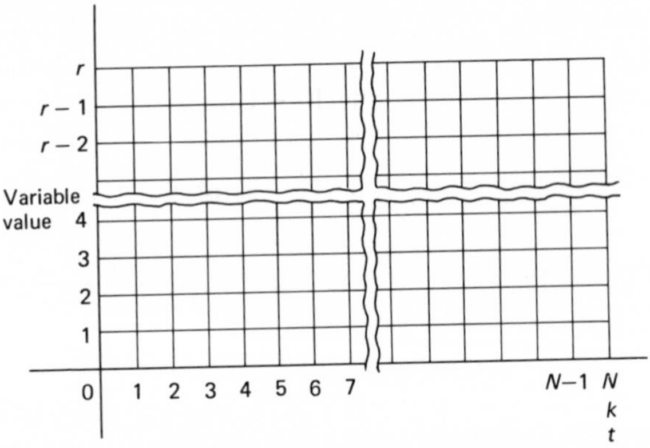

Figure 11.7–1. Dividing a space into discrete stages and values.

blind search for a trajectory from $k = 0$ to $k = N$ that optimizes some performance index, at each stage we have r possible decisions as to the next step. The total number of decisions d will therefore be approximately

$$d \simeq r^N \tag{11.7–1}$$

and, if there are n dimensions,

$$d \simeq r^{nN} \tag{11.7–2}$$

Very loosely, dynamic programming states that no matter how we arrive at some point, we shall make the next decision such as to optimize the trajectory. More rigorously, the principle of optimility states that a policy optimal over the interval 0 to $N - 1$ is optimal over any subinterval η to $N - 1$, where $0 \leq \eta < N - 1$.

Using the optimal principle, something like r^2 decisions must be made at each stage (except the first and last), and hence for a one-dimensional problem,

$$d \simeq Nr^2 \tag{11.7–3}$$

or for n dimensions,

$$d \simeq Nr^{2n} \tag{11.7–4}$$

The number N has been removed as an exponent in (11.7–4) as compared to (11.7–2), but for an n of any size, (11.7–4) is still formidable.† In addition, a large amount of storage is required to keep track of the optimization index values. In sum, dynamic programming requires much larger and faster computers than presently available for problems of any size. In the meantime, Pontryagin's principle and the calculus of variations can be used with success in some cases.

In this section, let us discuss a type of optimization called "deadbeat" performance. For this performance we require the system to respond to a step function input such that the output reaches the desired value as rapidly as possible and without overshoot. Let the system be given as in

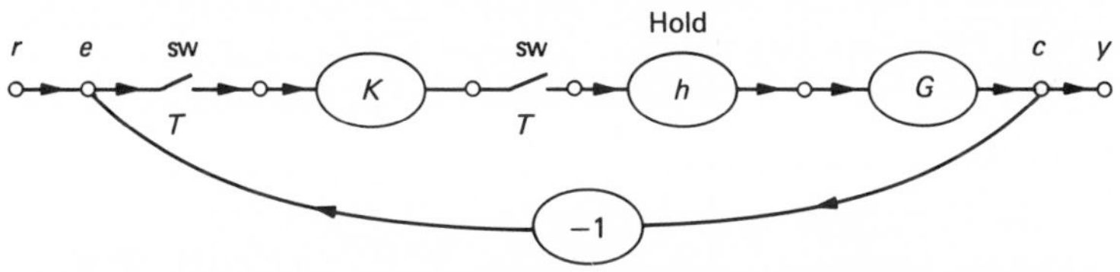

Figure 11.7–2. Controller with variable gain K for deadbeat control.

Figure 11.7–2, where h is a zero-order hold and the digital controller has a variable gain K. The system of Figure 11.7–2 has been analyzed in Section 11.5, which gives the discrete system as

$$\mathbf{x}(k+1) = \mathbf{A}_1\mathbf{x}(k) + \mathbf{B}_1 r(k) \tag{11.7–5a}$$

$$\mathbf{y}(k) = \mathbf{C}\mathbf{x}(k) \tag{11.7–5b}$$

where

$$\mathbf{A}_1 = \hat{\mathbf{A}} - [\mathbf{B}_1 : \mathbf{0}]$$

$$\mathbf{B}_1 = \hat{\mathbf{B}}$$

$$\hat{\mathbf{A}} = \boldsymbol{\phi}(T)$$

$$\hat{\mathbf{B}} = \int_0^T \boldsymbol{\phi}(w)\mathbf{B}\, dw$$

† Bellman calls this "the curse of dimensionality" [23].

$\boldsymbol{\phi}(t)$ is the transition matrix, and $\mathbf{B}$ and $\mathbf{C}$ the corresponding system matrices for the forward path elements KG in Figure 11.7–2. If $K_k = m(kT)/e(kT)$ is a function of the stage, or $K_k = K(kT)$, then $\boldsymbol{\phi}$ is a function of K_k. Consequently $\mathbf{A}_1$ and $\mathbf{B}_1$ are also functions of K_k, or $\mathbf{A}_1 = \mathbf{A}_1(K_k, T)$ and $\mathbf{B}_1 = \mathbf{B}_1(K_k, T)$. For a deadbeat response,

$$y(nT) = x_1(nT) = r(nT) \quad \textbf{(11.7–6a)}$$

$$x_2(nT) = x_3(nT) = \cdots x_n(nT) = 0 \quad \textbf{(11.7–6b)}$$

Equations (11.7–6) imply that the system response will reach the desired value in n stages, n being the order of the system. We assume the system to be linear, controllable, observable, and with no constraints [24]. Equations (11.7–5) and (11.7–6) determine the K values required. The equations for K_0, K_1, and so on, are nonlinear in general, but may be solved analytically if the order of the system is not too great.

Example 11.7–1

Let G of Figure 11.7–2 be

$$G(s) = \frac{1}{s(s+1)}$$

and find K_k for deadbeat performance.

Solution: The forward path continuous-time transfer function G (including K_k) may be written in state-space form as

$$\dot{x}_1 = x_2$$

$$\dot{x}_2 = -x_2 + K_k e$$

or

$$\mathbf{A} = \begin{bmatrix} 0 & 1 \\ 0 & -1 \end{bmatrix} \qquad \mathbf{B} = \begin{bmatrix} 0 \\ K_k \end{bmatrix}$$

Introducing the sampler, hold, and feedback,

$$\hat{\mathbf{A}} = \boldsymbol{\phi}(T) = \begin{bmatrix} 1 & 1 - \epsilon^{-T} \\ 0 & \epsilon^{-T} \end{bmatrix}$$

$$\hat{\mathbf{B}} = \begin{bmatrix} K_k(T + \epsilon^{-T} - 1) \\ K_k(1 - \epsilon^{-T}) \end{bmatrix}$$

$$\mathbf{A}_1 = \begin{bmatrix} 1 - K_k(T + \epsilon^{-T} - 1) & 1 - \epsilon^{-T} \\ K_k(\epsilon^{-T} - 1) & \epsilon^{-T} \end{bmatrix}$$

If $T = 1$,

$$\mathbf{A}_1 = \begin{bmatrix} 1 - 0.368K_k & 0.632 \\ -0.632K_k & 0.368 \end{bmatrix}$$

$$\mathbf{B}_1 = \begin{bmatrix} 0.368K_k \\ 0.632K_k \end{bmatrix}$$

Then using (11.7–5a), and assuming zero initial conditions [$\mathbf{x}(0) = \mathbf{0}$], and a unit step input, or $r(0) = 1$, we get

$$x_1(1) = 0.368K_0$$

$$x_2(1) = 0.632K_0$$

Again applying (11.7–5a) as a recursion relation, with the conditions of (11.7–6),

$$\begin{bmatrix} 1 \\ 0 \end{bmatrix} = \begin{bmatrix} 1 - 0.368K_1 & 0.632 \\ -0.632K_1 & 0.368 \end{bmatrix} \begin{bmatrix} 0.368K_0 \\ 0.632K_0 \end{bmatrix} + \begin{bmatrix} 0.368K_1 \\ 0.632K_1 \end{bmatrix}$$

or

$$1 = (1 - 0.368K_1)(0.368K_0) + (0.632)^2 K_0 + 0.368K_1$$

$$0 = (-0.632)(0.368)K_0 K_1 + (0.368)(0.632)K_0 + (0.632)K_1$$

Solving, $K_0 = 1.58$, $K_1 = -1.39$, The digital controller must supply the gain K_0 when $k = 0$ and gain K_1 when $k = 1$. Hence its characteristic in the z domain is

$$\frac{M(z)}{E(z)} = \frac{K_0 e(0) + K_1 e(1) z^{-1}}{e(0) + e(1) z^{-1}}$$

$$= \frac{1.58 - (1.39)(0.418)z^{-1}}{1 + 0.418z^{-1}}$$

$$= \frac{1.58 - 0.582z^{-1}}{1 + 0.418z^{-1}}$$

Since $x_2(2) = 0$, no further change in x_1 occurs for $k > 2$.

The example illustrates the general fact that an nth-order linear controllable discrete system of this type may be taken between any two points in state space in n steps. The reason for this is that if the system is controllable, n linearly independent vectors may be generated in n steps and hence form a basis in the n-dimensional space. Furthermore, if the control effort is unconstrained, the vectors may be extended to any length. We can make this plausible by pointing to the example, where the first vector $\mathbf{v}_1$ generated has components

$$\mathbf{v}_1 = \begin{bmatrix} 0.582 \\ 1.0 \end{bmatrix}$$

and

$$\mathbf{v}_2 = \begin{bmatrix} 0.418 \\ -1.0 \end{bmatrix}.$$

$\mathbf{v}_1$ and $\mathbf{v}_2$, being linearly independent, form a basis for the two-dimensional space in this case. It is also clear that T can be selected such that the system may be uncontrollable.

The variable-gain concept for deadbeat performance easily may be extended to the case of a single nonlinearity in the forward path. Usually the number of required steps will be greater than the order of the system in this case, because the vectors generated by the control will be restricted in length.

Much more can be said, and has, concerning discrete system design. In general, the same comments made at the conclusion of Chapter 10 apply here. Much remains to be done before state-space design becomes widespread.

PROBLEMS

11.1. Solve the following difference equations:

(a) $y(k+2) + 5y(k+1) + 6y(k) = 0$; $y(0) = 0$, $y(1) = 1$.

(b) $y(k+3) + 6y(k+2) + 11y(k+1) + 6y(k) = 0$; $y(0) = y(1) = 1$, $y(2) = 2$.

(c) $y(k+3) + 3y(k+2) + 7y(k+1) + 5y(k) = 0$; $y(0) = y(1) = 0$, $y(2) = 1$.

(d) $y(k+2) + 5y(k+1) + 6y(k) = (-1)^k$; $y(0) = y(1) = 0$.

(e) $y(k+2) + 5y(k+1) + 6y(k) = \cos k(\pi/2)$; $y(0) = y(1) = 0$.

11.2. Find the Z transforms of the following functions of kT:

(a) $1 - \epsilon^{-akT}$.
(b) $\epsilon^{-akT} - \epsilon^{-bkT}$.
(c) $\epsilon^{-akT} \cos bkT$.
(d) $\epsilon^{-akT} \sin bkT$.
(e) $\sinh akT$.

11.3. Find the inverse Z transforms of the following functions of z:

(a) $$\frac{z}{(z+1)(3z^2+1)}.$$

(b) $$\frac{z}{z^2-z+1}.$$

(c) $$\frac{2z^2+z}{(z-1)(z^2-z+1)}.$$

11.4. (a) Show that the following Z-transform pairs are true:

$$a^k \cos kb \leftrightarrow \frac{z^2 - a\cos bz}{z^2 - 2a\cos bz + a^2}$$

$$a^k \sin kb \leftrightarrow \frac{a \sin bz}{z^2 - 2a\cos bz + a^2}$$

(b) From (a) find the inverse Z transform of

$$\frac{Cz^2 + Dz}{z^2 - 2a\cos bz + a^2}$$

where C and D are constants.

11.5. Draw simulation diagrams for the following systems:

(a) $y(k+3) + 6y(k+2) + 11y(k+1) + 6y(k) = m(k+1) + m(k)$.

(b) $$\frac{Y(z)}{M(z)} = \frac{3z^2+4z+2}{z^5+3z^4+8z^3+12z^2+36z+98}.$$

(c) $y_1(k+2) + 5y_1(k+1) + 4y_2(k+1) + y_1(k) = m_1(k)$
$y_2(k+2) + 6y_2(k+1) + 2y_1(k+1) + y_1(k) + 3y_2(k) = m_2(k)$.

(d) $y(k+3) + 6y(k+2) + 4y(k+1) + 8y(k) = m(k+3) + 3m(k+2)$ $+ 2m(k+1) + m(k)$.

11.6. Find $\boldsymbol{\phi}(k)$ for the following systems by any two methods:
(a) $y(k+2) + 6y(k+1) + 8y(k) = 0$.
(b) $\mathbf{x}(k+1) = \mathbf{A}\mathbf{x}(k)$, where

$$\mathbf{A} = \begin{bmatrix} 0 & -3 \\ 2 & -5 \end{bmatrix}$$

(c) As in (b), with

$$\mathbf{A} = \begin{bmatrix} 0 & 2 & 0 \\ 0 & 0 & -4 \\ -1 & 3 & 6 \end{bmatrix}$$

(d) As in (b), with

$$\mathbf{A} = \begin{bmatrix} 0 & 1 \\ -5 & -3 \end{bmatrix}$$

11.7. Find the transfer function matrix $\hat{\mathbf{H}}(z)$ for the systems of Problem 11.5.

11.8. Figure P11.8 shows a system with a zero-order hold h.

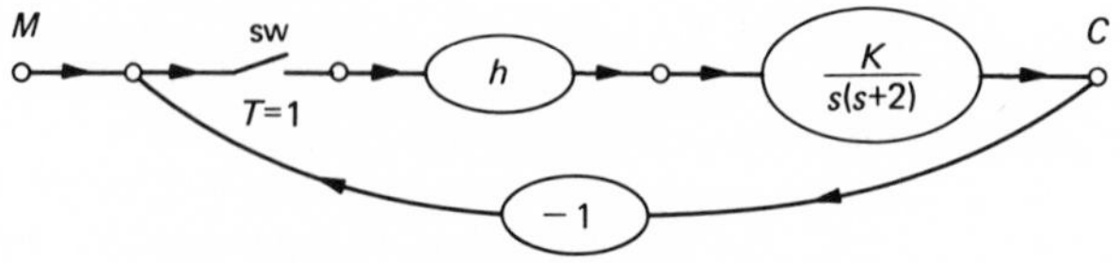

Figure P11.8.

(a) For $K = 2$ find for the output $c(k)$ at the sampling instants using the Z transform.

(b) Repeat (a) except use the method outlined in Example 11.5–6.

11.9. Draw a root locus for the system of Figure P11.8 and find the limiting value of K for stability of the discrete time system.

11.10. Determine the limiting value of K for stability in Problem 11.9 using the Routh array.

11.11. Find the K_k necessary for deadbeat performance in Figure 11.7–2 except that

$$G = \frac{1}{(s+1)(s+2)}$$

REFERENCES AND FURTHER READING

[1] R. K. Cavin, III, D. L. Chenoweth, and C. L. Phillips, The Z Transform of an Impulse Function, *IEEE Trans. Auto. Control*, **12** (1) (1967), 113.

[2] C. H. Wilts, *Principles of Feedback Control*, Addison-Wesley, Reading, Mass., 1960, pp. 196–203.

[3] K. Miller, *An Introduction to the Calculus of Finite Differences and Difference Equations*, Holt, New York, 1960.

[4] J. R. Ragazzini and G. F. Franklin, *Sampled Data Control Systems*, McGraw-Hill, New York, 1958.

[5] J. T. Tou, *Digital and Sampled Data Control Systems*, McGraw-Hill, New York, 1959.

[6] Wilts, *op. cit.*

[7] P. M. De Russo, Rob. J. Roy, and C. M. Close, *State Variables for Engineers*, Wiley, New York, 1965, p. 173.

[8] J. G. Truxal, *Control System Synthesis*, McGraw-Hill, New York, 1955, pp. 508–517.

[9] De Russo, Roy, and Close, *op. cit.*, pp. 164–167.
[10] Ragazzini and Franklin, *op. cit.*
[11] B. C. Kuo, *Analysis and Synthesis of Sampled-Data Control Systems*, Prentice-Hall, Englewood Cliffs, N.J., 1963.
[12] R. V. Churchill, *Modern Operational Mathematics in Engineering*, McGraw-Hill, New York, 1944.
[13] Truxal, *op. cit.*, p. 512.
[14] Truxal, *op. cit.*, pp. 515–517.
[15] Tou, *op. cit.*, pp. 184–198.
[16] Truxal, *op. cit.*, pp. 502–503.
[17] De Russo, Roy, and Close, *op. cit.*, p. 434.
[18] Truxal, *op. cit.*, pp. 523–524.
[19] Tou, *op. cit.*, pp. 465–579.
[20] D. Mitrović, Graphical Analysis and Synthesis of Feedback Control Systems, III. Sampled-Data Feedback Control Systems, *AIEE Trans. Appl. Ind.*, **77** (1959), 497–503.
[21] Wilts, *op. cit.*, pp. 213–218.
[22] O. I. Elgerd, *Control Systems Theory*, McGraw-Hill, New York, 1967, pp. 456–467.
[23] R. Bellman, *Adaptive Control Processes—A Guided Tour*, Princeton Univ. Press, Princeton, N.J., 1961, p. 94.
[24] Tou, *op. cit.*, pp. 118–121.

Appendix A

Fourier and Laplace Transforms

The Fourier transform may be defined as

$$F(\omega) = \int_{-\infty}^{\infty} f(t)\epsilon^{-j\omega t}\, dt \tag{A-1}$$

In (A–1) $f(t)$ must be single-valued and satisfy the Dirichlet conditions: (1) a finite number of discontinuities in a finite interval, (2) a finite number of points at which it reaches infinity in this interval, and (3) a finite number of maxima and minima in the interval. Most functions of engineering concern meet these conditions. Further, $f(t)$ must be such that

$$\int_{-\infty}^{\infty} |f(t)|\, dt \tag{A-2}$$

converges. If these conditions are met, then the inverse transform is

$$f(t) = \frac{1}{2\pi j}\int_{-\infty}^{\infty} F(\omega)\epsilon^{j\omega t}\, d(j\omega) \tag{A-3}$$

The Fourier transform may be viewed as the limiting case of the Fourier series as the period of the fundamental becomes very long. The modern approach, however, simply defines the transform by (A–1) [1, 2]. Table A–1 gives a few Fourier transform properties and Table A–2 some transforms.

TABLE A–1 PROPERTIES OF THE FOURIER TRANSFORM

Function	Transform	
$x(t)$	$X(\omega)$	(a)
$X(t)$	$x(-\omega)$	(b)
$x(at)$	$\frac{1}{\|a\|} X\left(\frac{\omega}{a}\right)$	(c)
$x(t - t_0)$	$\epsilon^{-j\omega t_0} X(\omega)$	(d)
$\epsilon^{j\omega_0 t} x(t)$	$X(\omega - \omega_0)$	(e)
$\frac{d_n}{dt^n} x(t) \quad \left[\text{if } \sum_{m=0}^{n-1} \frac{d^m}{dt^m} x(t) = 0, \ t \to \infty\right]$	$(j\omega)^n X(\omega)$	(f)
$\int_{-\infty}^{t} x_1(\lambda) x_2(t - \lambda)\, d\lambda$	$X_1(\omega) X_2(\omega)$	(g)
$x(t) \cos \omega_0 t$	$\frac{1}{2}[X(\omega - \omega_0) + X(\omega + \omega_0)]$	(h)

TABLE A–2 A FEW FOURIER TRANSFORMS

$f(t)$	$F(\omega)$
$\delta(t)$	1
$\sum_{n=-\infty}^{\infty} \delta(t - nT)$	$\frac{2\pi}{T} \sum_{n=-\infty}^{\infty} \delta\left(\omega - \frac{2\pi n}{T}\right)$
$\epsilon^{j\omega_0 t}$	$2\pi\delta(\omega - \omega_0)$
$\cos \omega_0 t$	$\pi[\delta(\omega - \omega_0) + \delta(\omega + \omega_0)]$
$\sin \omega_0 t$	$\frac{\pi}{j}[\delta(\omega - \omega_0) - \delta(\omega + \omega_0)]$
$-\tau/2 \qquad \tau/2 \ \ t \to$	$\frac{\tau \sin(\omega\tau/2)}{\omega\tau/2}$
$\epsilon^{-a\|t\|}$	$\frac{2a}{a^2 + \omega^2}$
$\|t\|$	$\frac{-2}{\omega^2}$
$\epsilon^{-t^2/2}$	$\sqrt{2\pi}\, \epsilon^{-\omega^2/2}$
$\epsilon^{-\alpha t^2}$	$\sqrt{\pi/\alpha}\, \epsilon^{-\omega^2/4\alpha}$

Fourier transforms from Laplace transforms: Given $x(t)$, Laplace transform $F(s)$, Fourier transform $X(\omega)$:

(a) For $x(t) = 0$, $t \leq 0$; $X(\omega) = F(j\omega)$.
(b) For $x(t) = 0$, $t \geq 0$; $X(\omega) = F_R(-j\omega)$, where $x_R(t) = x(-t)$.
(c) In general, apply (a) to $x(t)$, $t \geq 0$, (b) to $x(t)$, $t \leq 0$.

Fourier transforms are extensively used in communications theory. The difficulty imposed by the convergence requirement may be overcome in some cases by special techniques, but the control engineer usually prefers the Laplace transform, which solves this problem by replacing $\epsilon^{-j\omega t}$ by $\epsilon^{-(\sigma+j\omega)t} = \epsilon^{-st}$ in definition (A–1), or, in other words, inserts a weighting function $\epsilon^{-\sigma t}$ that forces the integral

$$\int_0^{\infty} |f(t)|\epsilon^{-\sigma t}\, dt \tag{A–4}$$

to converge for most $f(t)$ of engineering interest. Then the Laplace transform and its inverse becomes

$$F(s) = \int_{-\infty}^{\infty} f(t)\epsilon^{-st}\, dt \tag{A–5}$$

$$f(t) = \frac{1}{2\pi j}\int_{\sigma_a - j\infty}^{\sigma_a + j\infty} F(s)\epsilon^{st}\, ds \tag{A–6}$$

Definition (A–5) and equation (A–6) are for a two-sided Laplace transform. Usually the history of the function from $t = -\infty$ to some (arbitrary) $t = 0$ may be expressed in terms of initial conditions at $t = 0$. It is then sufficient to use the one-sided transform and its inverse

$$F(s) = \int_0^{\infty} f(t)\epsilon^{-st}\, dt \tag{A–7}$$

$$f(t) = \frac{1}{2\pi j}\int_{\sigma_a - j\infty}^{\sigma_a + j\infty} F(s)\epsilon^{st}\, ds \tag{A–8}$$

The value of σ_a in (A–6) and (A–8) must be such that convergence of (A–5) [or (A–7)] is assured for all $s = \sigma + j\omega$, where $\sigma < \sigma_a$. The value of σ necessary to cause convergence is termed the region of convergence. Equation (A–8) indicates that the integration in the complex s plane must be along a straight line σ_a units to the right of the $j\omega$ axis, as in Figure A–1. A few properties of the Laplace transform are shown in Table A–3 and a few transforms in Table A–4. In Table A–3, (i) may not exist, and (j) depends on the analyticity of $sF(s)$ on the $j\omega$ axis and in the right-half s plane.

Properties (d), (e), and (h) are the most important. That is, differentiation and integration in the time domain become algebraic processes in the s domain, while convolution transforms into a product relation. The procedure in solving a linear differential equation then reduces to transforming

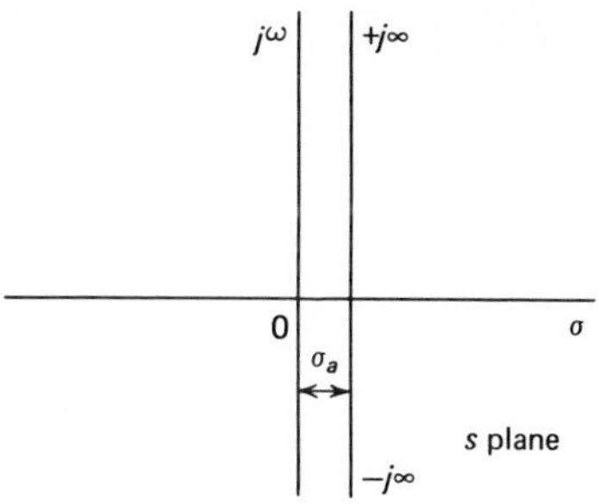

Figure A–1. Path of integration for inverse Laplace transform.

TABLE A–3 PROPERTIES OF THE LAPLACE TRANSFORM

Function	Transform	
$f(t)$	$F(s)$	(a)
$af(t)$	$aF(s)$	(b)
$\frac{d}{dt} f(t)$	$sF(s) - f(0_+)$	(c)
$\frac{d^2}{dt^2} f(t)$	$s^2F(s) - sf(0_+) - \frac{df}{dt}(0_+)$	(d)
$\int_{-\infty}^{t} f(\lambda)\,d\lambda$	$\frac{F(s)}{s} + \frac{1}{s}\lim_{t\to 0+}\int_{-\infty}^{t} f(\lambda)\,d\lambda$	(e)
$\epsilon^{-at}f(t)$	$F(s+a)$	(f)
$f(t/a)$	$aF(as)$	(g)
$\int_0^t f_1(t-\lambda)f_2(\lambda)\,d\lambda$	$F_1(s)F_2(s)$	(h)
$\lim_{t\to 0} f(t)$	$\lim_{s\to\infty} sF(s)$	(i)
$\lim_{t\to\infty} f(t)$	$\lim_{s\to 0} sF(s)$	(j)

it into the s domain, making algebraic manipulations, and transforming it back. Note that if all initial conditions are zero, s has practically the same meaning as the operator $p = d/dt$.

The usual difficulty comes in inverting the transform to get the final

TABLE A–4 A FEW LAPLACE TRANSFORMS

$f(t)$	$F(s)$	Region of Convergence
$\delta(t)$	1	$\sigma > -\infty$
$u(t)$	$\frac{1}{s}$	$\sigma > 0$
t	$\frac{1}{s^2}$	$\sigma > 0$
$\frac{t^{n-1}}{(n-1)!}$	$\frac{1}{s^n}$	$\sigma > 0$
ϵ^{-at}	$\frac{1}{s+a}$	$\sigma > -a$
$t\epsilon^{-at}$	$\frac{1}{(s+a)^2}$	$\sigma > -a$
$\sin \alpha t$	$\frac{\alpha}{s^2+\alpha^2}$	$\sigma > 0$
$\cos \alpha t$	$\frac{s}{s^2+\alpha^2}$	$\sigma > 0$
$\epsilon^{-at} \sin \alpha t$	$\frac{\alpha}{(s+a)^2+\alpha^2}$	$\sigma > -a$
$\epsilon^{-at} \cos \alpha t$	$\frac{s+a}{(s+a)^2+\alpha^2}$	$\sigma > -a$

result in the time domain (although in control work this often does not become necessary). From Figure A–2 it is easy to see that if the integral $\int F(s)\epsilon^{st}$ along the circle of radius R approaches zero as $R \to \infty$, then (A–8) equals the integral taken around the closed path of Figure A–2. It is not

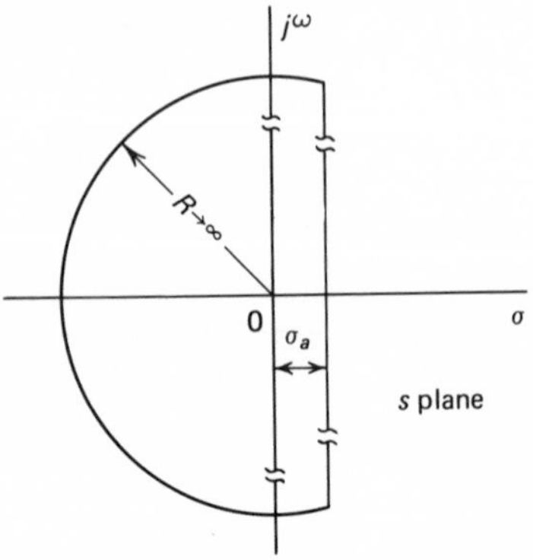

Figure A–2. Contour for integrating in the complex s plane.

hard to show that this will be true if $\lim_{s\to\infty}|F(s)| \leq K|1/s|$, where $K < \infty$. Since most control systems come under this restriction, we may use this conclusion, remembering that sometimes it may not be true [3]. If the closed path integral equals (A–8), then we may at once apply Cauchy's residue theorem, which gives

$$f(t) = \sum \text{residues of the finite poles of } F(s)\epsilon^{st} \qquad t > 0$$

The residue b_{-1} of an nth-order pole at $s = s_k$ is given by

$$b_{-1} = \frac{1}{(n-1)!}\left[\frac{d^{n-1}}{ds^{n-1}}(s - s_k)^n F(s)\epsilon^{st}\right]_{s=s_k} \qquad \textbf{(A–9)}$$

Where $n = 1$, this reduces to

$$b_{-1} = [(s - s_k)F(s)\epsilon^{st}]_{s=s_k} \qquad \textbf{(A–10)}$$

or

$$b_{-1} = \left[\frac{P(s)\epsilon^{st}}{(d/ds)Q(s)}\right]_{s=s_k} \qquad \textbf{(A–11)}$$

where $F(s) = P(s)/Q(s)$.

You may then accomplish the inversion procedure by either (1) reducing $F(s)$ into partial fractions and looking up the inverse transforms in a table, or (2) using the residue relation [perhaps with (1)].

A usual problem engineers have with the Laplace transform concerns the initial conditions. Usually the initial time $t = t_0$ may be made $t = 0$ without loss of generality. The question then becomes: Do you take the initial conditions as existing just before $t = 0$, or just after $t = 0$? Most texts take these conditions as just after $t = 0$, or as zero is approached from the right in Figure A–3. Thus we write $f(0_+)$, where this means $\lim_{\epsilon\to 0} f(0 + \epsilon)$,

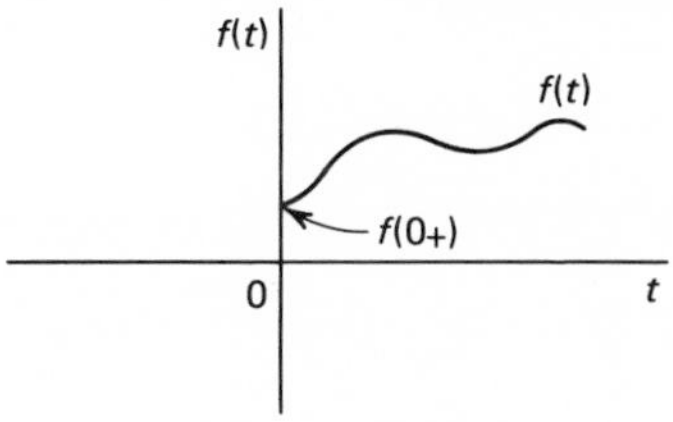

Figure A–3. $f(0+)$ means $\lim_{\epsilon\to 0} f(0+\epsilon)$, $\epsilon > 0$.

where $\epsilon > 0$. As the given initial conditions usually imply a situation just before $t = 0$ or $f(0_-)$, it is necessary to find $f(0_+)$ from $f(0_-)$. Normally, this can be done from physical considerations, that is, by looking at the energy-storage devices.

In electrical systems, two continuity relations exist: (1) continuity of flux linkages, or $\sum L_1 i_1 = \sum L_2 i_2$, and (2) continuity of charge, or $\sum q_1 = \sum q_2$, where the subscripts refer to the before and after situations, respectively. If only one inductor exists, (1) then reduces to the continuity of current in an inductor, or the common expression "current in an inductor cannot change instantaneously." If only one capacitor exists, (2) reduces to the continuity of capacitor voltage. In mechanical systems, the analog of (1) is the continuity of momentum, $\sum M_1 v_1 = \sum M_2 v_2$, and of (2) the continuity of distance, $\sum x_1 = \sum x_2$. In fluids we have the continuity of the quantity of the fluid, and so on. All these involve general inertia effects.

The relations may also be found by integration of the differential equation from $t = 0_-$ to $t = 0_+$.

Example A–1

Given

$$J\frac{d^2c}{dt^2} + B\frac{dc}{dt} + Kc = Wr(t) + Y\frac{dr(t)}{dt} \tag{A–12}$$

Find $c(0_+)$ and $dc/dt|_{0_+}$ in terms of the conditions at $t = 0_-$.

Solution: Integrate over the interval from $t = 0_-$ to $t = 0_+$. Then

$$J\left(\frac{dc}{dt}\bigg|_{t=0_+} - \frac{dc}{dt}\bigg|_{t=0_-}\right) + B[c(0_+) - c(0_-)] + K\int_{0_-}^{0_+} c\,dt = W\int_{0_-}^{0_+} r(t)\,dt + Y[r(0_+) - r(0_-)] \tag{A–13}$$

Integrate again to obtain

$$J[c(0_+) - c(0_-)] + B\int_{0_-}^{+} c\,dt + K\iint_{0_-}^{0_+} c\,dt^2 = W\iint_{0_-}^{0_+} r(t)\,dt^2 + Y\int_{0_-}^{0_+} r(t)\,dt \tag{A–14}$$

The integral relations in (A–13) and (A–14) are zero, owing to the infinitesimally small interval. Hence

$$J\left(\frac{dc}{dt}\bigg|_{t=0_+} - \frac{dc}{dt}\bigg|_{t=0_-}\right) + B[c(0_+) - c(0_-)] = Y[r(0_+) - r(0_-)]$$

$$J[c(0_+) - c(0_-)] = 0$$

In the Laplace transform, the driving function $r(t)$ is assumed to be zero before $t = 0$, because the lower limit of the Laplace integral is zero. We must be given $c(0_-)$ and $dc/dt\,|_{t=0_-}$ and $r(t)$, $t \geq 0$. Hence $c(0_+)$ and $dc/dt\,|_{t=0_+}$ may be found. The second relation involves the continuity-of-momentum principle. By continued integration, a differential equation of any order may be reduced.

The initial condition problem becomes acute with impulse inputs, $r(t) = \delta(t)$, and higher-order singularity functions. Using the Laplace transform method, $\mathscr{L}\delta(t) = 1$, which is simple enough, but since the impulse instantaneously injects energy into the system, the continuity laws seem to be violated. This may be overcome by assuming that the impulse $f(t) = \delta(t)$ occurs at $\lim_{\Delta\to 0}[f(0 + \Delta)]$, while $f(0_+)$ occurs at $\lim_{\epsilon\to 0}[f(0) + \epsilon]$, where $\Delta > \epsilon$. This trick may be justified by finding the response to a pulse of height $1/\tau$ and width τ for various τ, as τ becomes smaller. In the limit, as $\tau \to 0$, the response will have a value at $t = 0 + \Delta$, $\Delta \to 0$, but just before $\Delta = 0$ it will not have a value at $t = 0$. Again this accentuates the peculiarities of the impulse function. From the standpoint of the control engineer, an important attribute of the impulse input consists of the fact that since $\delta(t) = 1$, the impulse response of a system is the same as the system function in the s domain. Hence we define the system transfer function as being the impulse response in the s domain.

Example A–2

In Figure A–4 sw_2 and sw_3 have been closed for a long time and sw_1 has been open. At $t = 0$, sw_1 closes and sw_2 and sw_3 open without sparking. Find $i(t)$.

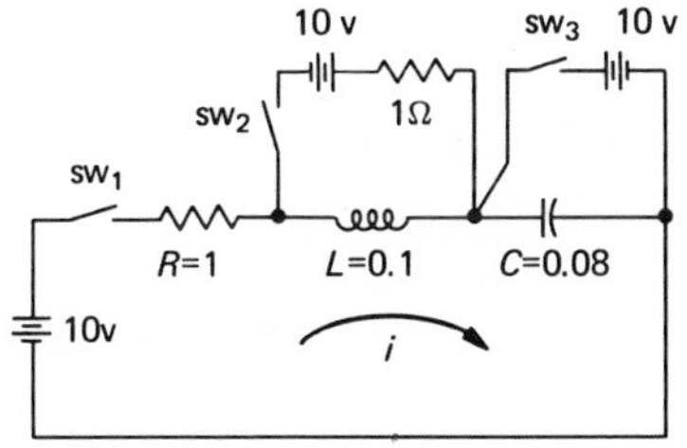

Figure A–4. Circuit for Example A–2.

Solution: The integrodifferential equation (after sw_1 closes) is

$$L\frac{di}{dt} + Ri + \frac{1}{C}\int i\,dt = m(t)$$

Inserting values, you get

$$0.1\frac{di}{dt} + i + 12.5\int_{-\infty}^{t} i\,d\lambda = 10u(t)$$

From Figure A–4 at $t = 0_-$ the current through L is -10 amperes (i is reference), and the voltage across C is -10 volts (clockwise reference). From $L_1 i_1 = L_2 i_2$, $i(0_+) = -10$ and from $q_1 = q_2$, $v_c(0_+) = -10$. Then transforming, we get

$$\left(0.1s + 1 + \frac{12.5}{s}\right) I(s) - 0.1i(0_+) + \frac{1}{s}\, v_c(0_+) = \frac{10}{s}$$

$$(s^2 + 10s + 125)I(s) = 100 - 10s + 100$$

$$I(s) = \frac{-10(s - 20)}{(s + 5 + j10)(s + 5 - j10)}$$

The residue at one pole is

$$b_{-1} = \frac{-10(s-20)}{s + 5 - j10}\,\epsilon^{st}\Bigg|_{s=-3-j10}$$

$$= \frac{-(25 + j10)\epsilon^{-5t}\epsilon^{-j10t}}{2j}$$

The residue at the other pole is

$$b_{-1} = \frac{-10(s-20)}{s + 5 + j10}\,\epsilon^{st}\Bigg|_{s=-5+j10}$$

$$= \frac{(25 - j10)\epsilon^{-5t}\epsilon^{j10t}}{2j}$$

The summation of the residues becomes

$$(26.94)\epsilon^{-5t}\left[\frac{\epsilon^{j(10t-\theta)} - \epsilon^{-j(10t-\theta)}}{2j}\right]$$

or $$i = 26.94\epsilon^{-5t}\sin(10t - \theta) \qquad \theta = \tan^{-1}\left(\frac{10}{25}\right)$$

Example A–3

In Figure A–5, $m(t)$ is an impulse of value 2 and $v_c(0_+) = 1$ with polarity as shown. Find $v_c(t)$.

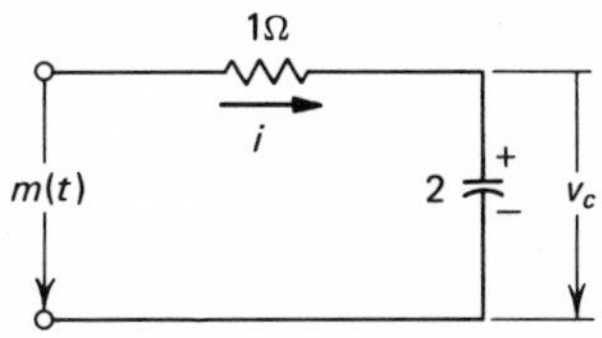

Figure A–5. Circuit for Example A–3.

Solution: Since $i = C(dv_c/dt)$,

$$RC\frac{dv_c}{dt} + v_c = m(t)$$

or

$$2\frac{dv_c}{dt} + v_c = \delta(t)$$

Since the voltage across the capacitance is continuous and we follow the suggestion of applying the impulse just after $t = 0_+$, on transforming we get

$$(2s + 1)V_c(s) = 2 + 2v(0_+)$$

$$V_c(s) = \frac{4}{2s + 1}$$

$$= \frac{4}{2(s + 0.5)}$$

or

$$v_c(t) = 2\epsilon^{-0.5t}$$

Note that at $t = 0$, $v_c = 2$. The impulse has instantaneously put one additional volt across the capacitor, or injected an energy of 1 joule. But then the impulse is an unusual (philosophically one might even say transcendental) function.

It might be pointed out that it is unnecessary to use the $t = 0_+$ convention. By redefining the transform of the impulse, you may start from $t = 0_-$. If $f(t)$ is discontinuous $t > 0$, the Laplace transform may still be used, and added terms apply at each discontinuity. The inverse transform gives the average of the two values at a discontinuity. However, it is usually simpler to (1) think of such a function as a sum of continuous functions (which is valid since superposition applies), or (2) to make a time shift to the discontinuity and start with a new time origin at that point and with a new initial-condition problem.

One should also mention that the Fourier and Laplace transforms are but special cases of other possible transforms. Transforms that are useful for certain boundary conditions are the Mellin, Hankel, Hilbert, Euler, and others [4].

Laplace transforms may be used on time-varying systems but usually are of no great assistance [5].

It is desirable that the control systems student have some understanding of Laplace transform theory, but the author feels that it is not necessary (as a control systems student) for him to go into the subject exhaustively in an introductory controls course, as otherwise he has no time to put on problems specific to controls. Too much effort can be spent on a mathematically fascinating technique.

REFERENCES AND FURTHER READING

[1] A. Papoulis, *The Fourier Integral and Its Applications*, McGraw-Hill, New York, 1962.
[2] R. Bracewell, *The Fourier Transform and Its Applications*, McGraw-Hill, New York, 1965.
[3] G. C. Newton, Jr., L. A. Gould, and J. F. Kaiser, *Analytical Design of Linear Feedback Controls*, Wiley, New York, 1957, Appendix A.
[4] Bracewell, *op. cit.*
[5] P. M. De Russo, R. J. Roy, and C. M. Close, *State Variables for Engineers*, Wiley, New York, 1965.
[6] R. J. Schwarz and B. Friedland, *Linear Systems*, McGraw-Hill, New York, 1965,
[7] M. F. Gardner, and J. L. Barnes, *Transients in Linear Systems*, Wiley, New York, 1942 (this reference has extensive tables).
[8] R. V. Churchill, *Introduction to Complex Variables and Applications*, McGraw-Hill, New York, 1948.
[9] R. V. Churchill, *Fourier Series and Boundary Value Problems*, McGraw-Hill, New York, 1941.
[10] R. V. Churchill, *Modern Operational Mathematics in Engineering*, McGraw-Hill, New York, 1944.
[11] D. K. Cheng, *Analysis of Linear Systems*, Addison-Wesley, Reading, Mass., 1959.
[12] *Standard Mathematical Tables*, The Chemical Rubber Co., Cleveland, Ohio, 14th ed., 1965, pp. 359–368 (includes tables).
[13] M. R. Spiegel, *Laplace Transforms*, Schaum, New York, 1965.
[14] P. A. McCollum and B. F. Brown, *Laplace Transform Tables and Theorems*, Holt, New York, 1965.

(Most of the introductory control texts listed at the end of Chapter 1 contain a discussion of the Laplace transform.)

Appendix B

Elements of Matrix Analysis

B.1 Nomenclature

A matrix, written **A** or sometimes a_{ij}, is defined as a rectangular array of elements a_{ij}, or

$$\mathbf{A} = \begin{bmatrix} a_{11} & a_{12} & \cdots & a_{1n} \\ a_{21} & a_{22} & \cdots & a_{2n} \\ \cdots & \cdots & \cdots & \cdots \\ a_{m1} & a_{m2} & \cdots & a_{mn} \end{bmatrix} \tag{B–1}$$

A matrix with m rows and n columns is referred to as an $(m \times n)$-order matrix. In particular, if $m = n$ the matrix is square of order n, and if $n = 1$, the matrix is called a column matrix or a vector. The vector **a** is

$$\mathbf{a} = \begin{bmatrix} a_1 \\ a_2 \\ \vdots \\ a_n \end{bmatrix} \tag{B–2}$$

The number of components of a vector is referred to as the dimension of the vector, thus **a** in (B–2) is an n-dimensional vector. Sometimes a vector may be written column $[a_1 \; a_2 \cdots a_n]$ to save space.

B.2 Matrix Algebra

Let **A**, **B**, and **C** be matrices with components a_{ij}, b_{ij}, and c_{ij}, respectively, where the index i designates the row, and the index j the column.

The following algebraic operations are defined:

1. Addition of two matrices, $\mathbf{C} = \mathbf{A} + \mathbf{B}$:

$$c_{ij} = a_{ij} + b_{ij} \tag{B–3}$$

2. Multiplication of a scalar b with a matrix $\mathbf{A}$: $\mathbf{C} = b\mathbf{A}$:

$$c_{ij} = ba_{ij} \tag{B–4}$$

3. Multiplication of matrix $\mathbf{A}$ with a matrix $\mathbf{B}$: $\mathbf{C} = \mathbf{AB}$:

$$c_{ij} = \sum_{k=1}^{n} a_{ik} b_{kj} \tag{B–5}$$

where n is the number of columns of $\mathbf{A}$ and the number of rows of $\mathbf{B}$. If $\mathbf{A}$ is $m \times n$ and $\mathbf{B}$ $n \times p$, $\mathbf{C}$ is $m \times p$. For example:

$$\begin{bmatrix} a_{11} & a_{12} \\ a_{21} & a_{22} \end{bmatrix} \begin{bmatrix} b_{11} & b_{12} \\ b_{21} & b_{22} \end{bmatrix} = \begin{bmatrix} c_{11} & c_{12} \\ c_{21} & c_{22} \end{bmatrix}$$

where

$$\begin{aligned} c_{11} &= a_{11}b_{11} + a_{12}b_{21} \\ c_{12} &= a_{11}b_{12} + a_{12}b_{22} \\ c_{21} &= a_{21}b_{11} + a_{22}b_{21} \\ c_{22} &= a_{21}b_{12} + a_{22}b_{22} \end{aligned}$$

Division in matrix algebra is undefined.

B.3 Notes and Definitions

1. To sum two matrices the matrices must be of the same size, that is they must both be $m \times n$ matrices, and to form the product of two matrices, the number of columns in the $\mathbf{A}$ matrix must equal the number of rows in the $\mathbf{B}$ matrix.
2. In general, $\mathbf{AB} \neq \mathbf{BA}$.
3. The product of a matrix with a vector is always a vector; thus

$$\begin{bmatrix} a_{11} & a_{12} & \cdots & a_{1n} \\ a_{21} & a_{22} & \cdots & a_{2n} \\ \vdots & & & \\ a_{m1} & \cdots & \cdots & a_{mn} \end{bmatrix} \begin{bmatrix} x_1 \\ x_2 \\ \vdots \\ x_n \end{bmatrix} = \begin{bmatrix} y_1 \\ y_2 \\ \vdots \\ y_n \end{bmatrix} \tag{B–6}$$

where

$$y_i = \sum_{k=1}^{n} a_{ik} x_k \qquad i = 1, 2, \ldots, n$$

Thus the matrix **A** may be considered as a linear transformation of the vector **x** into the vector **y**.

4. The product of a matrix **a** with $m = 1$ and a vector **b** is always a one-dimensional vector (scalar), that is,

$$[a_1 a_2 \cdots a_n]\begin{bmatrix} b_1 \\ b_2 \\ \vdots \\ b_n \end{bmatrix} = [c] \qquad \textbf{(B–7)}$$

where

$$c = \sum_{k=1}^{n} a_k b_k$$

Alternatively, **ba** is an $n \times n$ matrix.

5. Ordinary operations of calculus on matrices are transferred to the elements of the matrix; thus

$$\int_0^T \mathbf{A}(t)\,dt = \mathbf{C} \text{ signifies } c_{ij} = \int_0^T a_{ij}(t)\,dt \qquad \textbf{(B–8)}$$

$$\frac{d}{dt}\mathbf{A}(t) = \mathbf{C} \text{ signifies } c_{ij} = \frac{d}{dt}a_{ij}(t) \qquad \textbf{(B–9)}$$

6. From the basic operations it can be shown that the following algebraic properties are true:

$$(\mathbf{AB})\mathbf{C} = \mathbf{A}(\mathbf{BC}) \qquad \text{(associative property)} \qquad \textbf{(B–10a)}$$

$$(\mathbf{A}+\mathbf{B})\mathbf{C} = \mathbf{AC}+\mathbf{BC} \qquad \text{(distributive property)} \qquad \textbf{(B–10b)}$$

$$\mathbf{A}(\mathbf{B}+\mathbf{C}) = \mathbf{AB}+\mathbf{AC} \qquad \textbf{(B–10c)}$$

7. The following are special matrices.

a. *Diagonal matrix:*

$$\begin{bmatrix} x_1 & 0 & 0 & \cdots \\ 0 & x_2 & 0 & \\ 0 & 0 & x_3 & \\ \vdots & & & \end{bmatrix} \qquad \textbf{(B–11)}$$

or sometimes, $\mathrm{diag}(x_1, x_2, x_3, \ldots)$.

b. *Identity matrix:*

$$\mathbf{I} = \begin{vmatrix} 1 & 0 & 0 & \cdots \\ 0 & 1 & 0 & \\ 0 & 0 & 1 & \\ \vdots & & & \end{vmatrix} \qquad \textbf{(B–12)}$$

Note that the identity matrix is a special case of the diagonal matrix and has the property that for a square matrix **A**

$$\mathbf{IA} = \mathbf{AI} = \mathbf{A}$$

c. *Symmetric and skew symmetric matrices:* A symmetric matrix $\mathbf{A}_S$ is defined by the condition

$$a_{ij} = a_{ji} \tag{B–13a}$$

and a skew-symmetric (sometimes called antisymmetric) matrix $\mathbf{A}_a$ is defined by the condition

$$-a_{ij} = a_{ji} \tag{B–13b}$$

d. *The zero matrix*, written **0**, is defined as a matrix whose elements are all zero, and has the property that $\mathbf{0} + \mathbf{A} = \mathbf{A}$.
e. *Equivalent matrices:* Two matrices are equivalent if one is obtained from the other by a sequence of elementary transformations. An elementary transformation consists of (1) an interchange of two rows, (2) the multiplication of every element in a row by a scalar, (3) the addition of elements in one row to another row [(3) may follow (2)], and (4) the same operations on the columns. Equivalent matrices have the same order and rank (see below).
f. *Similar matrices:* If a matrix $\mathbf{B} = \mathbf{Q}^{-1}\mathbf{AQ} = \mathbf{PAP}^{-1}$, where $\mathbf{Q} = \mathbf{P}^{-1}$ and is nonsingular, **B** is defined to be similar to **A**.

8. Trace **A** or $\text{tr}[a_{ij}]$ is defined as the sum of the leading diagonal $(i = j)$ elements of **A**, or $\sum_{i=1}^{n} a_{ii}$.

B.4 Determinants: Rank

A determinant is a number that is associated with a square $(n \times n)$ matrix **A**, written det **A** or sometimes $|\mathbf{A}|$. One method of evaluating a determinant of **A** uses the row expansion

$$\det \mathbf{A} = \sum_{i=1}^{n} a_{ki} C_{ki} \tag{B–14}$$

where k is any one of the integers from 1 to n, and where C_{ki} represents the *cofactor* of the element a_{ki}. C_{ki} is defined as the determinant of the matrix that results if the kth row and ith column of the **A** matrix are struck out, multiplied by a sign term $(-1)^{k+1}$. The cofactor without the sign term is referred to as a minor. Thus det **A**, where

$$\mathbf{A} = \begin{bmatrix} 1 & 0 & 2 \\ 3 & 4 & 5 \\ 1 & 1 & 1 \end{bmatrix} \tag{B–15}$$

is given by (expanding along the first row)

$$\det \mathbf{A} = (-1)^2 \cdot 1 \cdot \begin{vmatrix} 4 & 5 \\ 1 & 1 \end{vmatrix} + (-1)^3 \cdot 0 \cdot \begin{vmatrix} 3 & 5 \\ 1 & 1 \end{vmatrix} + (-1)^4 \cdot 2 \cdot \begin{vmatrix} 3 & 4 \\ 1 & 1 \end{vmatrix}$$

which becomes

$$\det \mathbf{A} = (4 - 5) + 0 + 2(3 - 4) = -3 \tag{B–16}$$

If the value of det **A** is zero, then the matrix is said to be *singular*.

A matrix $\mathbf{A} \neq \mathbf{0}$ has rank r if at least one of its r square minors $\neq$ zero while every $(r + 1)$ square minor, if any, is zero. If an $n \times n$ matrix is non-singular, its rank $r = n$.

B.5 Inverse, Adjoint Matrices

The inverse of a square $(n \times n)$ matrix **A** is given by

$$\mathbf{A}^{-1} = \frac{1}{\det \mathbf{A}} \begin{bmatrix} C_{11} & C_{21} & C_{31} & \cdots \\ C_{12} & C_{22} & C_{32} & \\ C_{13} & C_{23} & C_{33} & \\ \vdots & & & \end{bmatrix} \tag{B–17}$$

where the C_{ij} represents the cofactors of matrix **A**; C_{12} is the cofactor of a_{12}, and so on. The inverse has the property that $\mathbf{A}^{-1}\mathbf{A} = \mathbf{A}\mathbf{A}^{-1} = \mathbf{I}$. $\mathbf{A}^{-1}$ does not exist if the matrix **A** is singular. The inverse of a 2×2 matrix **A**, where

$$\mathbf{A} = \begin{bmatrix} a_{11} & a_{12} \\ a_{21} & a_{22} \end{bmatrix} \tag{B–18}$$

is, from (B–17),

$$\mathbf{A}^{-1} = \begin{bmatrix} a_{22} & -a_{12} \\ -a_{21} & a_{11} \end{bmatrix} \frac{1}{a_{11}a_{22} - a_{12}a_{21}} \tag{B–19}$$

The adjoint matrix of **A** is given by

$$\mathbf{Adj\ A} = [C_{ji}] \tag{B–20}$$

where C_{ij} is a cofactor of a_{ij}. Thus in (B–17) **Adj A** is given by the right-hand matrix, and

$$\mathbf{A}^{-1} = \frac{\mathbf{Adj\ A}}{\det \mathbf{A}} \tag{B–21}$$

or

$$\frac{\mathbf{A\ Adj\ A}}{\det \mathbf{A}} = \mathbf{I} \tag{B–22}$$

The adjoint matrix of **A** in (B–18) is the right-hand matrix in (B–19). **Adj A** may be found from **A** by (a) replacing each element a_{ij} by its cofactor and (b) transposing the result (see below).

For large matrices, an inversion method more adaptable to a digital computer will be presented later.

It can be shown that

$$(\mathbf{AB})^{-1} = \mathbf{B}^{-1}\mathbf{A}^{-1} \tag{B–23}$$

If **AB** = **I**, then **B** is called a right inverse of **A**. If **BA** = **I**, **B** is a left inverse.

B.6 Special Operations on Matrices

1. The transpose of a matrix **A**, written $\mathbf{A}^T$, is defined as

$$\mathbf{C} = \mathbf{A}^T \tag{B–24}$$

where

$$c_{ij} = a_{ji}$$

The transpose operation changes all the rows of a matrix into columns. Thus, for example, for the matrix

$$\mathbf{A} = \begin{bmatrix} a_{11} & a_{12} \\ a_{21} & a_{22} \end{bmatrix} \tag{B–25}$$

$\mathbf{A}^T$ is given by

$$\mathbf{A}^T = \begin{bmatrix} a_{11} & a_{21} \\ a_{12} & a_{22} \end{bmatrix} \tag{B–26}$$

If $\mathbf{A}$ is symmetric, $\mathbf{A}^T = \mathbf{A}$. It can also be shown that

$$(\mathbf{AB})^T = \mathbf{B}^T\mathbf{A}^T \tag{B–27}$$

2. The norm $\|\mathbf{a}\|$ of a vector $\mathbf{a}$ represents a measure of the length of $\mathbf{a}$ with the following properties:

(a) $$\|\mathbf{a}\| > 0 \qquad \text{for } \mathbf{a} \neq \mathbf{0}$$
(b) $$\|\mathbf{a}\| = 0 \qquad \text{for } \mathbf{a} = \mathbf{0}$$
(c) $$\|\mathbf{a} + \mathbf{b}\| \leq + \|\mathbf{a}\| + \|\mathbf{b}\|$$
(d) $$\|\alpha\mathbf{a}\| = \alpha\|\mathbf{a}\|$$

Many realizations of a norm are possible. Two common norms are

$$\|\mathbf{a}\| = (a_1^2 + a_2^2 + \cdots + a_n^2)^{1/2} \tag{B–28}$$

$$\|\mathbf{a}\| = |a_1| + |a_2| + \cdots \tag{B–29}$$

Both the above norms satisfy the basic properties (a) to (d). The norm given in (B–28) may be expressed in terms of the transpose operation, or

$$\|\mathbf{a}\| = (\mathbf{a}^T\mathbf{a})^{1/2} \tag{B–30}$$

3. *A bilinear form* W in $\mathbf{x}$ and $\mathbf{y}$ is defined as

$$W = \mathbf{x}^T\mathbf{A}\mathbf{y} = \sum_{i=1}^{n}\sum_{k=1}^{n} a_{ik}x_i y_k \tag{B–31}$$

and a *quadratic form* in $\mathbf{x}$ is defined as

$$W = \mathbf{x}^T\mathbf{A}\mathbf{x} = \sum_{i=1}^{n}\sum_{k=1}^{n} a_{ik}x_i x_k \tag{B–32}$$

where $\mathbf{A}$ is a square-symmetric matrix. A quadratic form is said to be positive definite if $W > 0$ for $\mathbf{x} \neq \mathbf{0}$. A square-symmetric matrix is said to be positive definite if its corresponding quadratic form is positive definite. A test for positive definition is the satisfaction of the inequalities

$$a_{11} > 0, \begin{vmatrix} a_{11} & a_{12} \\ a_{21} & a_{22} \end{vmatrix} > 0, \begin{vmatrix} a_{11} & a_{12} & a_{13} \\ a_{21} & a_{22} & a_{23} \\ a_{31} & a_{32} & a_{33} \end{vmatrix} > 0, \ldots \tag{B–33}$$

The matrix $\mathbf{A}$ is semidefinite if $W \geq 0$ for $\mathbf{x} \neq \mathbf{0}$. It is negative definite if $W < 0$, $\mathbf{x} \neq \mathbf{0}$, and so on.

Also, if the roots of the characteristic equation (eigenvalues) of a matrix are distinct and positive, the matrix is positive definite.

The gradient of $W(\mathbf{x})$ with respect to $\mathbf{x}$ is a vector, denoted $\nabla_{\mathbf{x}} W$ and is defined to be

$$\nabla_{\mathbf{x}} W = \begin{bmatrix} \dfrac{\partial W}{\partial x_1} \\ \dfrac{\partial W}{\partial x_2} \\ \vdots \\ \dfrac{\partial W}{\partial x_n} \end{bmatrix} \tag{B–34}$$

When $W(\mathbf{x}) = \mathbf{x}^T \mathbf{A} \mathbf{x}$,

$$\nabla_{\mathbf{x}} W = 2\mathbf{A}\mathbf{x}$$

For a bilinear form,

$$\nabla_{\mathbf{x}}(\mathbf{x}^T \mathbf{A} \mathbf{y}) = \mathbf{A}\mathbf{y} \tag{B–35}$$

$$\nabla_{\mathbf{y}}(\mathbf{x}^T \mathbf{A} \mathbf{y}) = \mathbf{A}^T \mathbf{x} \tag{B–36}$$

These equations may be verified by direct computation of

$$\frac{\partial W}{\partial x_i}, \quad \frac{\partial W}{\partial y_i}, \ldots$$

B.7 Partitioned Matrices

It is sometimes convenient for algebraic reasons to subdivide (partition) a given matrix into various submatrices. Thus a matrix $\mathbf{A}$ may sometimes be written

$$\mathbf{A} = \left[\begin{array}{c|c} \mathbf{A}_{11} & \mathbf{A}_{12} \\ \hline \mathbf{A}_{21} & \mathbf{A}_{22} \end{array}\right] \tag{B–37}$$

where the various elements $\mathbf{A}_{ij}$ are matrices. The matrix properties and operations carry over to the partitioned case, except that care must be taken when multiplication is involved since $\mathbf{AB} \neq \mathbf{BA}$.

Thus, if **A** were written as in (B–37), and **B** similarly,

$$\mathbf{AB} = \left[\begin{array}{c:c} \mathbf{A}_{11}\mathbf{B}_{11} + \mathbf{A}_{12}\mathbf{B}_{21} & \mathbf{A}_{11}\mathbf{B}_{12} + \mathbf{A}_{12}\mathbf{B}_{22} \\ \hdashline \mathbf{A}_{21}\mathbf{B}_{11} + \mathbf{A}_{22}\mathbf{B}_{21} & \mathbf{A}_{21}\mathbf{B}_{12} + \mathbf{A}_{22}\mathbf{B}_{22} \end{array}\right]$$

$\mathbf{A}_{11}$, $\mathbf{A}_{12}$, $\mathbf{A}_{21}$, $\mathbf{A}_{22}$, $\mathbf{B}_{11}$, $\mathbf{B}_{12}$, $\mathbf{B}_{21}$, and $\mathbf{B}_{22}$ obviously must be of the correct dimensions to perform the operation.

One example of the use of partitioned matrices is in the elimination of a group of vector components. Thus if a system of equations can be written

$$\begin{bmatrix} y_1 \\ y_2 \\ \vdots \\ y_k \\ 0 \\ 0 \end{bmatrix} = \begin{bmatrix} a_{11} & a_{12} & \cdots \\ a_{21} & a_{22} & \\ a_{31} & & \\ \cdot & & \\ \cdot & & \\ \cdot & & \end{bmatrix} \begin{bmatrix} x_1 \\ x_2 \\ \cdot \\ \cdot \\ \cdot \\ x_n \end{bmatrix} \tag{B–38}$$

then we can make the partition

$$\left[\begin{array}{c} \mathbf{y}_1 \\ \hdashline \mathbf{0} \end{array}\right] = \left[\begin{array}{cc} \mathbf{A}_{11} & \mathbf{A}_{12} \\ \hdashline \mathbf{A}_{21} & \mathbf{A}_{22} \end{array}\right] \left[\begin{array}{c} \mathbf{x}_1 \\ \hdashline \mathbf{x}_2 \end{array}\right] \tag{B–39}$$

where

$$\mathbf{y}_1 = \begin{bmatrix} y_1 \\ \vdots \\ y_k \end{bmatrix}, \qquad \mathbf{x}_1 = \begin{bmatrix} x_1 \\ \vdots \\ x_k \end{bmatrix}, \qquad \mathbf{x}_2 = \begin{bmatrix} x_{k+1} \\ \vdots \\ x_n \end{bmatrix}$$

and $\mathbf{A}_{11}$ is $k \times n$, $\mathbf{A}_{12}$ is $k \times (n - k - 1)$, $\mathbf{A}_{21}$ is $(n - k - 1) \times n$, and $\mathbf{A}_{22}$ is $(n - k - 1) \times (n - k - 1)$. This is convenient for the elimination of the variables x_{k+1} to x_n. Thus one may now write

$$\begin{aligned} \mathbf{y}_1 &= \mathbf{A}_{11}\mathbf{x}_1 + \mathbf{A}_{12}\mathbf{x}_2 \\ \mathbf{0} &= \mathbf{A}_{21}\mathbf{x}_1 + \mathbf{A}_{22}\mathbf{x}_2 \end{aligned} \tag{B–40}$$

which then yields

$$\mathbf{y}_1 = [\mathbf{A}_{11} - \mathbf{A}_{12}\mathbf{A}_{22}^{-1}\mathbf{A}_{21}]\mathbf{x}_1 \tag{B–41}$$

B.8 Linear Equations

Matrix equations can be written much as ordinary algebraic ones, if the special rules of matrix manipulation are observed. A set of n simultaneous linear equations in n variables might be represented as

$$\mathbf{Ax} = \mathbf{y} \tag{B–42}$$

where $\mathbf{x}$ and $\mathbf{y}$ are vectors and $\mathbf{A}$ is the square matrix. Division is not defined, so to solve for $\mathbf{x}$ multiply both sides by $\mathbf{A}^{-1}$ to get

$$\mathbf{A}^{-1}\mathbf{Ax} = \mathbf{A}^{-1}\mathbf{y}$$

or

$$\mathbf{Ix} = \mathbf{A}^{-1}\mathbf{y} \tag{B–43}$$

$$\mathbf{x} = \mathbf{A}^{-1}\mathbf{y}$$

Finding the inverse of a matrix therefore solves a set of linear equations.

B.9 Vector Inner Product. Vector Outer Product

The inner product (scalar product) of two vectors of the same dimension may be defined as

$$(\mathbf{x}, \mathbf{y}) = \sum_{i=1}^{n} x_i y_i \tag{B–44}$$

$$= \mathbf{y}^T\mathbf{x}$$

If $\mathbf{x}$ and $\mathbf{y}$ are complex, substitute $\mathbf{x}^*$ for $\mathbf{x}$ in (B–44). $(\mathbf{x}, \mathbf{y})$ is often written $\langle \mathbf{x}, \mathbf{y} \rangle$ (see outer product).

Hence

$$(\mathbf{x}, \mathbf{x}) = \sum_{i=1}^{n} x_i x_i \tag{B–45}$$

$$= \mathbf{x}^T\mathbf{x}$$

This is the square of the vector norm of (B–30).

Two vectors $\mathbf{x}$ and $\mathbf{y}$ with real components are defined to be orthogonal if

$$(\mathbf{x}, \mathbf{y}) = 0 \tag{B–46}$$

If the vectors have complex components, the definition is

$$(\mathbf{x}, \mathbf{y}^*) = 0 \tag{B–47}$$

where y^* is the conjugate of $\mathbf{y}$.

A set of real vectors that are mutually orthogonal [or $(\mathbf{x}^i, \mathbf{x}^j) = 0$, $i \neq j$], and normalized such that $(\mathbf{x}^i, \mathbf{x}^i) = 1$, have the property such that if any vector

$$\mathbf{x} = \sum_{i=1}^{m} c_i \mathbf{x}^i$$

then

$$c_i = (\mathbf{x}, \mathbf{x}^i) \tag{B-48}$$

$$(\mathbf{x}, \mathbf{x}) = \sum_{i=1}^{m} c_i^2 \tag{B-49}$$

The vector outer product (dyadic product) of an n-dimensional vector $\mathbf{x}$ and an m-dimensional vector $\mathbf{y}$ is

$$\mathbf{x} > < \mathbf{y} = \mathbf{x}\mathbf{y}^T = \begin{bmatrix} x_1 y_1 & x_1 y_2 & \cdots & x_1 y_m \\ x_2 y_2 & x_2 y_2 & & \\ \vdots & & & \\ x_n y_1 & x_n y_2 & \cdots & x_n y_m \end{bmatrix} \tag{B-50}$$

If $\mathbf{x}$ and $\mathbf{y}$ are complex, substitute $\mathbf{y}^*$ for $\mathbf{y}$ in (B–50).

B.10 Eigenvalues and Eigenvectors

If

$$\mathbf{A}\mathbf{x} = \lambda \mathbf{x} \tag{B-51}$$

where λ is a real number, λ is defined as an eigenvalue (proper value, characteristic value) of $\mathbf{A}$, and $\mathbf{x}$ is defined as an eigenvector (proper vector; invariant vector) of $\mathbf{A}$.

Transposing $\mathbf{A}\mathbf{x}$ to the right side in (B–51), λ values may be found by

$$[\lambda \mathbf{I} - \mathbf{A}] = \mathbf{0}$$

For λ to have nontrivial values in this homogeneous equation,

$$\det[\lambda \mathbf{I} - \mathbf{A}] = 0 \tag{B-52}$$

Equation (B–52) is called the characteristic equation $\phi(\lambda) = 0$ of A.

Two similar matrices have the same eigenvalues, and if $\mathbf{y}$ is an eigenvector of $\mathbf{B} = \mathbf{Q}^{-1}\mathbf{A}\mathbf{Q}$ corresponding to an eigenvalue λ_i of $\mathbf{B}$, then $\mathbf{x} = \mathbf{Q}\mathbf{y}$ is an eigenvector of $\mathbf{A}$.

The eigenvectors may be found by substituting the eigenvalues back in (B–51). If the eigenvalues are all distinct, then each eigenvector is proportional to the nonzero columns of the matrix $\mathbf{Adj}[\lambda_i \mathbf{I} - \mathbf{A}]$, $i = 1, n$. The modal matrix is a matrix with the eigenvectors as columns. For example, if

$$\mathbf{A} = \begin{bmatrix} -3 & 2 \\ 2 & 0 \end{bmatrix}$$

$$\det[\lambda\mathbf{I} - \mathbf{A}] = (\lambda + 3)(\lambda) - 4 = \lambda^2 + 3\lambda - 4 = 0$$

or $\lambda_1 = 1$, $\lambda_2 = -4$,

$$\mathbf{B} = \mathbf{Adj}[\lambda\mathbf{I} - \mathbf{A}] = \begin{bmatrix} \lambda & 2 \\ 2 & \lambda + 3 \end{bmatrix}$$

Then for λ_1,

$$\mathbf{B} = \begin{bmatrix} 1 & 2 \\ 2 & 4 \end{bmatrix}$$

and for λ_2,

$$\mathbf{B} = \begin{bmatrix} -4 & 2 \\ 2 & -1 \end{bmatrix}$$

Hence the modal matrix is

$$\begin{bmatrix} 1 & 2 \\ 2 & -1 \end{bmatrix}$$

and the eigenvectors are $\begin{bmatrix} 1 \\ 2 \end{bmatrix}$ and $\begin{bmatrix} 2 \\ -1 \end{bmatrix}$ (not normalized). As the eigenvectors are specified only as to direction, vectors with components proportional to these are acceptable. The eigenvectors may be normalized, if desired, by making their magnitudes 1.

The Caley-Hamilton theorem states that every square matrix $\mathbf{A}$ satisfies its characteristic equation $\phi(\lambda) = 0$; that is, $\phi(\mathbf{A}) = \mathbf{0}$. The polynomial of minimum degree $m(\lambda)$ with a leading coefficient of 1 such that $m(\mathbf{A}) = \mathbf{0}$ is termed the minimum polynomial of $\mathbf{A}$. If the minimum polynomial and the characteristic polynomial of $\mathbf{A}$ are the same, the matrix $\mathbf{A}$ is called nonderogatory. The minimum polynomial may be found by canceling the common factors of

$$(\lambda\mathbf{I} - \mathbf{A})^{-1} = \frac{\mathbf{B}(\lambda)}{\phi(\lambda)}$$

where $\phi(\lambda) = \det(\lambda\mathbf{I} - \mathbf{A})$, to give [1, 2]

$$(\lambda\mathbf{I} - \mathbf{A})^{-1} = \frac{\mathbf{C}(\lambda)}{m(\lambda)}$$

If $\mathbf{D}(\lambda) = [\lambda\mathbf{I} - \mathbf{A}]$ is of order n and rank r, it may be shown that $\mathbf{D}(\lambda)$ may be reduced by means of elementary transformations (including multiplying any row by a polynomial) to the Smith normal form [2]

$$\mathbf{S}(\lambda) = \begin{bmatrix} f_1(\lambda) & 0 & \cdots & 0 & \cdots & 0 \\ 0 & f_2(\lambda) & \cdots & 0 & \cdots & 0 \\ \vdots & & & & & \\ 0 & 0 & \cdots & f_r(\lambda) & \cdots & 0 \\ 0 & 0 & \cdots & 0 & \cdots & 0 \end{bmatrix} \tag{B–53}$$

where each $f_i(\lambda)$ is a polynomial in λ with a leading coefficient of 1 and divides evenly into $f_{i+1}(\lambda)$.

The $f_i(\lambda)$ of (B–53) are called similarity invariants of $\mathbf{A}$, and the minimal polynomial $m(\lambda)$ is the $f_i(\lambda)$ of highest degree. The characteristic polynomial $\phi(\lambda)$ is $m(\lambda)$ [factors of $m(\lambda)$]. For any similarity invariant $f_k(\lambda) = \lambda^k + a_{k-1}\lambda^{k-1} + \cdots + a_1\lambda + a_0$, there is a companion matrix

$$\mathbf{C}_f = \begin{bmatrix} 0 & 1 & 0 & \cdots & 0 & 0 & 0 \\ 0 & 0 & 1 & \cdots & 0 & 0 & 0 \\ \vdots & & & & & & \\ 0 & 0 & 0 & \cdots & 0 & 1 & 0 \\ 0 & 0 & 0 & \cdots & 0 & 0 & 1 \\ -a_0 & -a_1 & -a_2 & \cdots & -a_{k-3} & -a_{k-2} & -a_{k-1} \end{bmatrix} \tag{B–54}$$

C_f is nonderogatory with a characteristic polynomial $f_k(\lambda)$. (Some authors call C_f^T the companion matrix.)

If a matrix $\mathbf{C}$ with n distinct eigenvalues λ_1 is in the form of (B–54), it may be diagonalized by the Vandermonde matrix

$$\mathbf{V} = \begin{bmatrix} 1 & 1 & \cdots & 1 \\ \lambda_1 & \lambda_1 & \cdots & \lambda_n \\ \lambda_1^2 & \lambda_2^2 & & \lambda_n^2 \\ \vdots & & & \\ \lambda_1^{n-1} & \lambda_2^{n-1} & \cdots & \lambda_k^{n-1} \end{bmatrix} \tag{B–55}$$

or

$$\mathbf{C} = \mathbf{V}\mathbf{\Lambda}\mathbf{V}^{-1} \tag{B–56}$$

Where

$$\mathbf{\Lambda} = \begin{bmatrix} \lambda_1 & & & & 0 \\ & \lambda_2 & & & \\ & & \lambda_3 & & \\ & & & \ddots & \\ 0 & & & & \lambda_n \end{bmatrix}$$

B.11 Matrix Inversion on a Digital Computer

One method of inverting a matrix uses a variation of the Gaussian elimination method. This is outlined as follows:

Augment **A** by the identity matrix **I** of the same rank, thus:

$$\mathbf{B} = [\mathbf{A} : \mathbf{I}] \tag{B–57}$$

The ith row of (B–57) is associated with

$$\sum_{k=1}^{n} a_{ik} x_k = b_i \tag{B–58}$$

and the entire **B** therefore represents the set of equations

$$\sum_{k=1}^{n} a_{1k} x_k = b_i \qquad i = 1, 2, \ldots, n \tag{B–59}$$

Suppose we alter matrix **B** by elementary transformations such that we obtain the matrix

$$[\mathbf{I} : \mathbf{C}] \tag{B–60}$$

(B–60) thus represents the set of equations

$$x_i = \sum_{k=1}^{n} c_{ik} b_k \qquad i = 1, 2, \ldots, n \tag{B–61}$$

Then (B–61) represents solutions to (B–58), and **C** is the inverse of **A**, or

$$\mathbf{C} = \mathbf{A}^{-1}$$

To change the partitioned matrix in (B–57) to that of (B–60), we can (1) multiply any row of **B** by a constant, and (2) add or subtract any row, element by element, to any other row. This is similar to solving a set of simultaneous linear equations.

To illustrate on a 2 × 2 matrix,

$$\mathbf{B} = \begin{bmatrix} a_{11} & a_{12} & 1 & 0 \\ a_{21} & a_{22} & 0 & 1 \end{bmatrix}$$

1. Divide the first row by a_{11} to obtain a 1 in place of a_{11}, to get

$$\begin{bmatrix} 1 & \dfrac{a_{12}}{a_{11}} & \dfrac{1}{a_{11}} & 0 \\ a_{21} & a_{22} & 0 & 1 \end{bmatrix}$$

2. Multiply the first row by a_{21} and subtract from the second row to get

$$\begin{bmatrix} 1 & \dfrac{a_{12}}{a_{11}} & \dfrac{1}{a_{11}} & 0 \\ 0 & \dfrac{a_{11}a_{22} - a_{12}a_{21}}{a_{11}} & -\dfrac{a_{21}}{a_{11}} & 1 \end{bmatrix}$$

3. Divide the second row by a_{22} to get

$$\begin{bmatrix} 1 & \dfrac{a_{12}}{a_{11}} & \dfrac{1}{a_{11}} & 0 \\ 0 & 1 & \dfrac{-a_{21}}{a_{11}a_{22} - a_{12}a_{21}} & \dfrac{a_{11}}{a_{11}a_{22} - a_{12}a_{21}} \end{bmatrix}$$

4. Multiply the second row by a_{12}/a_{11}, and subtract from the first row to get

$$\begin{bmatrix} 1 & 0 & \dfrac{a_{22}}{a_{11}a_{22} - a_{12}a_{21}} & \dfrac{-a_{12}}{a_{11}a_{22} - a_{12}a_{21}} \\ 0 & 1 & \dfrac{-a_{21}}{a_{11}a_{22} - a_{12}a_{21}} & \dfrac{a_{11}}{a_{11}a_{22} - a_{12}a_{21}} \end{bmatrix}$$

It is easily verified that the right matrix in this partitioned matrix is the inverse of

$$\begin{bmatrix} a_{11} & a_{12} \\ a_{22} & a_{22} \end{bmatrix}$$

The elimination process requires about n^2 multiplications compared to about n^3 multiplications using the determinate method. Hence it is much faster. We must be sure that a_{11}, a_{22}, and so on, are not zero. It would be wasteful of memory space in a computer to store the identity matrix **I**. One way we can avoid this is by setting up an auxiliary vector for temporary storage and replacing elements of **A** as computed. For example, in step 2 above, row 1 can be stored in the temporary storage, multiplied by a_{21}, and subtracted from row 2 while the original row 1 resulting from step 1 remains stored in **A**.

There are, of course, many other methods of inverting a matrix. (See, for example, pivotal condensation, reference [8], pp. 207–210.)

REFERENCES AND FURTHER READING

[1] K. S. Kunz, *Numerical Analysis*, McGraw-Hill, New York, 1957.

[2] L. A. Pipes, *Matrix Methods for Engineering*, Prentice-Hall, Englewood Cliffs, N.J., 1963.

[3] R. W. Hamming, *Numerical Methods for Scientists and Engineers*, McGraw-Hill, New York, 1962.

[4] F. R. Gantmacher, *The Theory of Matrices*, Vols. I and II, Chelsea, New York, 1959.

[5] R. Bellman, *Introduction to Matrix Analysis*, Princeton Univ. Press, Princeton, N.J., 1962.

[6] P. Dorato and R. F. Drenick, *Optimal Control Theory—A Short Course*, Brooklyn Polytechnic Institute, Brooklyn, N.Y., 1963.

[7] L. P. Huelsman, *Circuits, Matrices and Linear Vector Spaces*, McGraw-Hill, New York, 1963.

[8] P. M. De Russo, R. J. Roy, and C. M. Close, *State Variables for Engineers*, Wiley, New York, 1965.

Appendix C

Analog and Digital Computers

C.1 Analog Computers

Most present-day analog computers are based on the electronic amplifier of Figure C.1–1. Assume that the amplifier has a voltage output to input

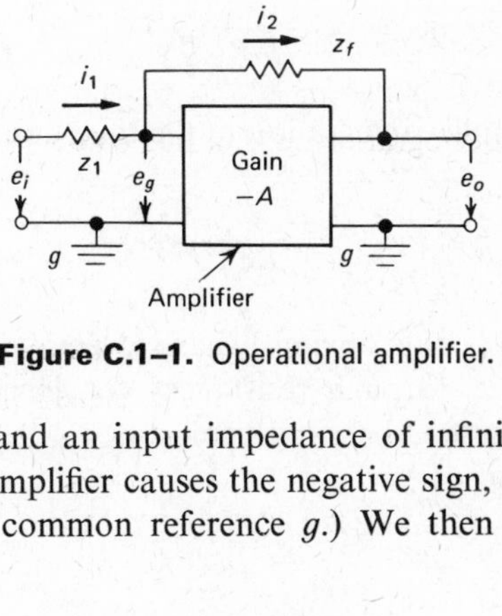

Figure C.1–1. Operational amplifier.

ratio (gain) of $-A$ and an input impedance of infinity. (Convenience in construction of the amplifier causes the negative sign, or voltage inversion with respect to the common reference g.) We then have the following equations:

$$e_o = -Ae_g \tag{C.1–1}$$

$$i_1 = i_2$$

or

$$\frac{e_i - e_g}{Z_1} = \frac{e_g - e_o}{Z_f} \tag{C.1–2}$$

Rearranging (C.1–2),

$$e_g\left(\frac{1}{Z_1}+\frac{1}{Z_f}\right)-\frac{e_o}{Z_f}=\frac{e_i}{Z_1}$$

and substituting (C.1–1), we get

$$-\frac{e_o}{A}\left(\frac{Z_1+Z_f}{Z_1Z_f}\right)-\frac{e_o}{Z_f}=\frac{e_i}{Z_1}$$

If $|A| \gg (Z_1+Z_f)/Z_1Z_f$, then

$$e_o=-\frac{Z_f}{Z_1}e_i \tag{C.1–3}$$

If $Z_1 = R_1$ and $Z_f = R_2$, where both R_1 and R_2 are constant resistances (independent of frequency), then

$$e_o=-\frac{R_f}{R_1}e_i \tag{C.1–4}$$

If $Z_1 = R_1$ and $Z_f = 1/C_f s$ (a capacitance), then in the s domain

$$E_o=-\frac{1}{R_1C_f s}E_i \tag{C.1–5}$$

Equation (C.1–5) implies integration in the time domain, or

$$e_o=-\frac{1}{R_1C_f}\int e_i(t)\,dt \tag{C.1–6}$$

In Figure C.1–1, we could obviously have several voltages e_i connected to the amplifier input e_g through resistances R_i. Hence for the case that $Z_f = R_f$, we get Figure C.1–2, and here

$$e_o=-R_f\sum_{i=1}^{n}\frac{1}{R_i}e_i \tag{C.1–7}$$

In Figure C.1–2 we have changed the diagram slightly in that the voltage reference (usually ground) has been omitted but understood to exist. The symbol for the amplifier, a triangle with the apex in the direction of the output, is fairly standard. This diagram may be further simplified as shown in Figure C.1–3, where the gains $g_i = R_f/R_i$, $i = 1, n$ are shown as numbers above the input lines. The amplifier used in this manner is known as a

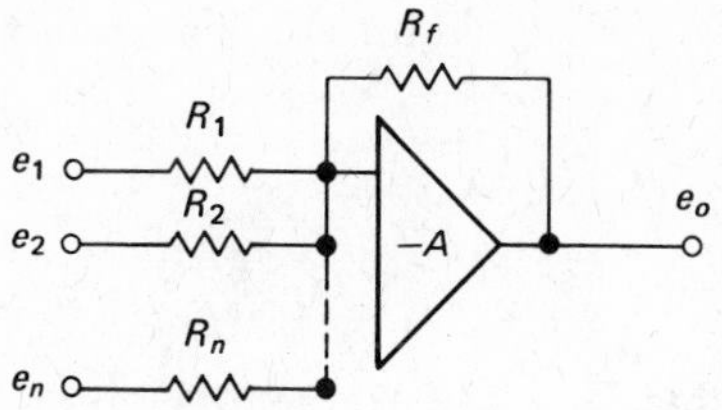

Figure C.1–2. Operational amplifier with number of inputs used as summer.

summer, and we use the symbol of Figure C.1–3 to depict this. The summing unit multiplies each input by a constant and adds these to form the output.

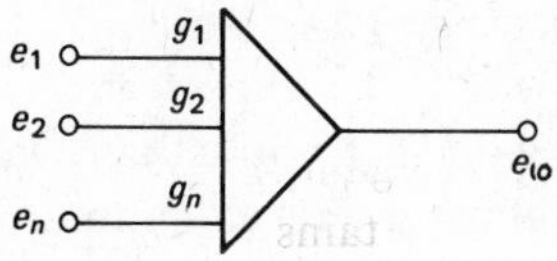

Figure C.1–3. Summer—schematic.

Similarly, if $Z_f = C_f s_1$, then we have Figure C.1–4, which gives

$$e_o = -\frac{1}{C_f} \sum_{i=1}^{n} \left(\frac{1}{R_i} \int e_i \, dt \right) \tag{C.1–8}$$

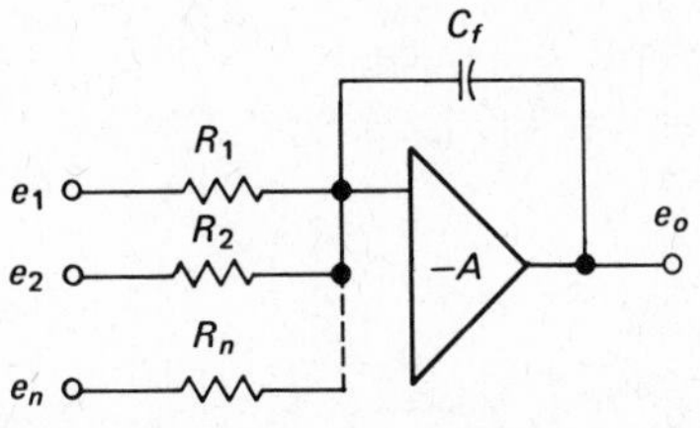

Figure C.1–4. Operational amplifier with number of inputs used as integrator.

Figure C.1–4 may be further simplified to Figure C.1–5. We use Figure C.1–5 to represent an integrator.

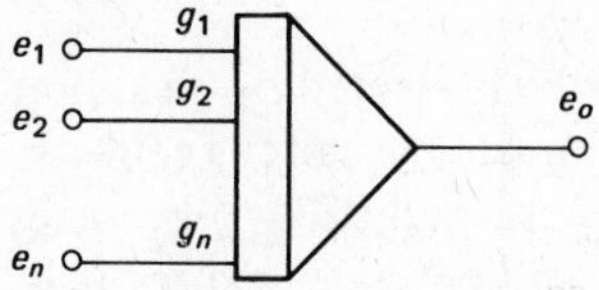

Figure C.1–5. Integrator—schematic.

If $Z_1 = C_1 s$ and $Z_f = R_f$, then the amplifier of Figure C.1–1 becomes a differentiator, or

$$e_o = -\frac{C_1}{R_f}\frac{de_i}{dt}$$

Because of noise problems, however, the differentiator is seldom used. By making Z_1 and Z_f more complicated networks, it is possible to get a variety of transfer functions between e_o and e_i (see, for example, reference [1], Chapter 13). By using the complex s domain, you may easily work out these relations for any combination desired.

A few words need to be said about the basic assumption that $|A| \gg (Z_1 + Z_f)/Z_1Z_f$. First, this requires that the impedance levels be high enough for negligible loading of the amplifier. Usually, the resistors are 100,000 ohms or over, while the capacitors are seldom larger than 1 microfarad. Second, the gain A is not actually independent of frequency, because the amplifier contains physical components. Hence A falls off at high frequencies, which means that when a number of such amplifiers are connected in feedback arrangements, oscillations may occur. Normally, however, the assumption is quite good. ($|A|$ is usually at least 10^6 or 10^7.) The amplifier must also be of the direct-coupled variety, because amplification must occur at zero frequency. This requirement causes problems of drift, and the amplifier power supply must be carefully designed. Special circuits, however, give very low drift rates. (See reference [2], Appendix.)

Besides the summer and the integrator, we need a device for multiplication by a constant. This is a simple potentiometer, as in Figure C.1–6, where

$$e_o = \left(\frac{R_o}{R_t}\right) e_i \tag{C.1–9}$$

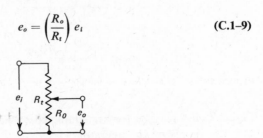

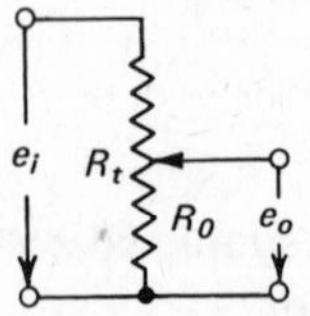

Figure C.1–6. Potentiometer used as multiplier by a number less than 1.

The ratio (R_0/R_t) may be measured by a calibrated dial on the potentiometer. Since the potentiometer usually is followed by other devices, normally a loading effect exists, and (C.1–9) becomes only approximate. We therefore usually set the potentiometer after it is in the circuit by direct measurement of e_o and e_i. (Modern digital voltmeters make this a very simple procedure.) The potentiometer is schematically shown in Figure C.1–7 with the multiplication shown as a_i ($a_i \leq 1$).

We are now ready to put these components together to solve a linear differential equation with constant coefficients. For example, take the equation

$$\frac{d^3y}{dt^3} + 5\frac{d^2y}{dt^2} + 4\frac{dy}{dt} + 10y = 0 \tag{C.1–10}$$

Rearranging,

$$\frac{d^3y}{dt^3} = -5\frac{d^2y}{dt^2} - 4\frac{dy}{dt} - 10y \tag{C.1–11}$$

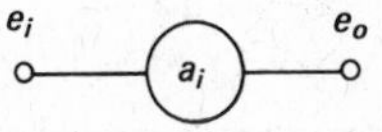

Figure C.1–7. Multiplier (<1)—schematic.

Assume that we have the quantity d^3y/dt^3. Then a single integration gives d^2y/dt^2, two integrations give dy/dt, and three integrations result in y. Remembering that each integrator reverses the sign of the input, Figure C.1–8 results.

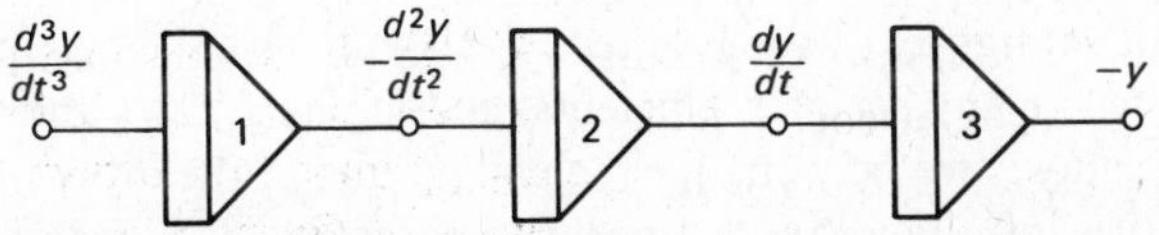

Figure C.1–8. Three integrations of d^3y/dt^3 give y (with sign reversal).

Now, (C.1–11) tells us that if we have $-5(d^2y/dt) - 4(dy/dt) - 10y$, we have d^3y/dt^3. Hence Figure C.1–9 will solve the original differential equation, because we bring these quantities back to the first integrator. Summer 4 gives y from $-y$, and normally would not be required, while summer 5 is

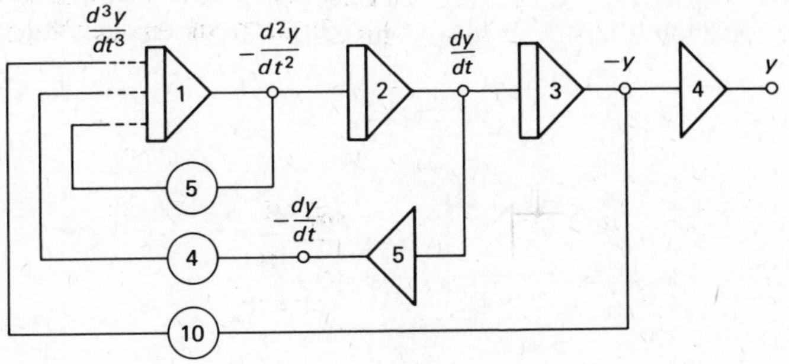

Figure C.1–9. Analog solution of $d^3y/dt^3 + 5(d^2y/dt^2) + 4(dy/dt) + 10y = 0$.

required to give the necessary sign for (C.1–10). Practically, Figure C.1–9 cannot serve, however, because our multipliers have a gain factor of less than 1. Remembering that each amplifier has multiplication possibilities, we may rearrange Figure C.1–9 to Figure C.1–10, which is now a practical

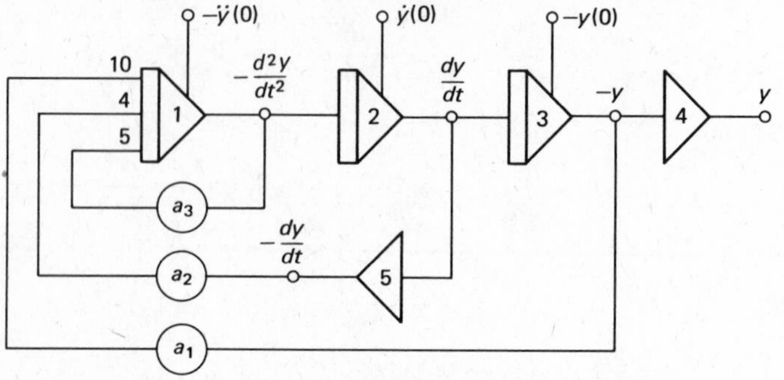

Figure C.1–10. Practical analog solution of $(d^3y/dt^3)+a_3(d^2y/dt^2)+a_2(dy/dt)+a_1=0$.

setup where all potentiometers a_i are set to 1. This seems a little ridiculous until you remember that the coefficients in the original differential equation likely will not be nice integers in practical cases but are known to perhaps three significant figures. Thus Figure C.1–10 will solve the original differential equation for any set of coefficients, as long as a_1, a_2, and a_3 are 1 or less. Furthermore, we may change the gain of any of the other amplifiers so that multiples of the outputs of the integrators of Figure C.1–10 will result, so it is always possible to accomplish this requirement.

The electronic amplifier may be arranged in one of two ways: (1) with fixed gain input or (2) with plug-in capacitors and resistors. The latter type is more flexible but may require a longer setup time. In the former case it is desirable to be able to convert a summer to an integrator, or vice versa.

Figure C.1–10 shows that initial conditions on d^2y/dt^2, dy/dt, and y are necessary to get a solution. We accomplish this physically by a circuit somewhat as shown in Figure C.1–11. In this figure E represents a voltage that is

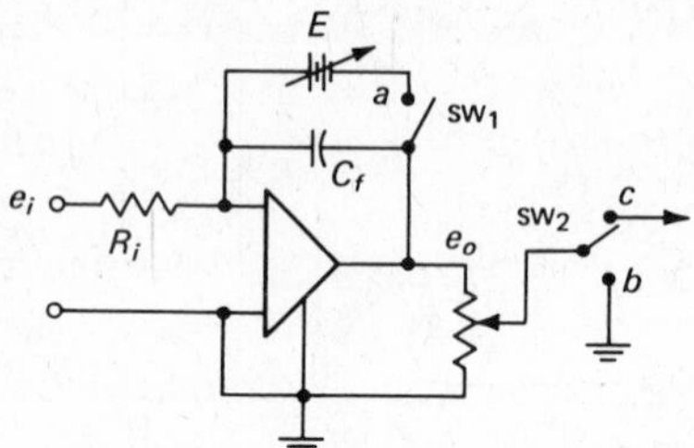

Figure C.1–11. Obtaining initial conditions on integrator.

variable in magnitude and polarity. Before $t = 0$, sw_1 is connected to terminal a, and the amplifier is isolated by connecting sw_2 to b (ground). At $t = 0$, sw_1 opens and sw_2 closes to c_1, which connects to the remaining circuit. Thus the amplifier output at $t = 0$ may be made the correct amount by premeasuring e_o while adjusting E. The actual circuit will be considerably more complicated, and in modern computers the switches consist of electronic circuits that may operate several hundred times a second. (This results in so-called "rep-op" operation, which permits the solution of differential equations with two boundary conditions or a display on an oscilloscope.)

Figure C.1–10 still does not represent a practical arrangement, as two things are still needed: (1) time scaling and (2) magnitude scaling. The problem must be timed-scaled to allow the results to be recorded in some way. The solution cannot be allowed to take all day, but, on the other hand, we must consider the response of our recorder. Inexpensive modern ink-type or heat-sensitive paper recorders will respond to frequencies up to about 100 Hz, although more expensive light-sensitive paper recorders go up to around 5000 Hz. Higher speeds may be shown on an oscilloscope by repeating the solution or by using a retentative-type screen. The roots of the characteristic equation are difficult to determine, so the frequencies of oscillation of the solution (or the time constants) may not be known. However, you may make a first guess and have the circuit time scaled by letting $\tau = \alpha t$ in the original differential equation. Then

$$\frac{d^n y}{dt^n} = \alpha^n \frac{d^n y}{d\tau^n}$$

Thus, in our example, if $\alpha = 10$ (the analog computer solution will be 0.1 the rate of the original problem, or the solution will be slowed down), then in (C.1–10),

$$10^3 \frac{d^3 y}{d\tau^3} + 5.10^2 \frac{d^2 y}{d\tau^3} + 40 \frac{dy}{d\tau} + 10y = 0$$

or

$$\frac{d^3 y}{d\tau^3} + 0.5 \frac{d^2 y}{d\tau^2} + 0.04 \frac{dy}{d\tau} + 0.01y = 0$$

We now solve the new equation in τ time on the computer. Because the value y may have been any quantity (pressure, force, distance, and so on) in the original equation but is represented in volts on the electronic computer, we need a magnitude conversion from the original quantity to volts. Furthermore, because of the physical limitations of the amplifiers, their outputs must be kept within certain limits. The upper limit is set by amplifier saturation (linear amplification limit), and the lower limit by the noise level. These upper and lower magnitude limits are often 100 and 1 volts, respectively. To achieve this, we usually do not get out y, dy/dt, and so on, but some multiples of these as required to reach the objectives of maintaining the specified limits (still satisfying the differential equation).

The amplifier output excursions are not exactly known in advance, so we must again make an intelligent guess at the solution limits and revise the amplitude scaling if the solution demonstrates a faulty guess. Thus both the time scaling and magnitude scaling may be changed before you obtain a final solution. Normally this is not difficult, but careful bookkeeping of changes does become necessary.

If the differential equation has a driving function, you introduce this into the proper integrator. Thus if the right side of (C.1–10) is $f(t)$, then we add $f(t)$, properly time and magnitude scaled, to the input of amplifier 1 of Figure C.1–9. The function $f(t)$ usually may be obtained by simulation of a differential equation on the analog computer itself, or it may be obtained from an external generator (see Chapter 4).

As shown in Chapter 4, the state-space variables are not unique, so many analog simulations are possible. Thus we may use the Kalman forms, the normal form, or many other forms, as desired. One simulation may be preferable to another in a certain situation.

Solution of nonlinear or time-varying equations by the analog computer becomes (conceptually) easy. We need a few additional tools as follows: (a) function multipliers, (b) nonlinear function generators, and (c) time function generators.

The function multiplier gives the product of two functions. This device is commercially available as an electronic unit or it may be simulated over a limited range by a nonlinear element. The function and time generators may be simulated by resistors and diodes. The generation of a time-varying function may be more difficult and require some sort of mechanical-electrical device, such as a cam-controlled rotating servomechanism. Time and magnitude scaling becomes extremely important in such systems. The reader will find many appropriate devices in the references listed. Many standard units are available commercially.

Modern analog computers may have the amplifiers connected, and the potentiometers set, from a central console, or in more costly installations, by program through a digital computer. Such installations save much time and, more important, many errors. In connecting over a dozen amplifiers, you can well appreciate that the chances of error in connections or settings becomes very large and the checking of solutions mandatory.

C.2 Digital Computers

A simplified schematic diagram of the digital computer is shown in Figure C.2–1. The heart of the digital computer is the memory, which is a

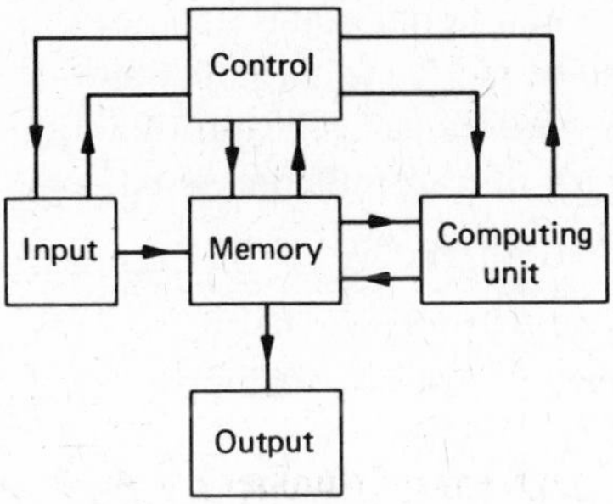

Figure C.2–1. Digital computer schematic.

device for storing numbers. Many types of memories have been used, such as magnetic drums, mercury delay lines, diode flip-flops, photographic films, and electronic tube storage units. The memory designer strives to obtain a very large memory in a small space, and with a short access time,

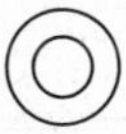

Figure C.2–2. Magnetic core for memory.

that is, a short time to enter or retrieve a number. One type of memory that is currently popular but may soon be obsolete consists of an assembly of magnetic cores, or doughnuts. A magnetic core is shown in Figure C.2–2 and consists of a special magnetic material that may be magnetized in either one of two directions, or senses. That is, the north pole is either above the paper in Figure C.2–2, or below. One induces the magnetization by means of a current-carrying wire that passes through the hole of the doughnut, the direction of the current determining the polarity of the magnetization. A sufficiently strong current flips the core into either one state or the other. Thus we have a binary counter, which has either a value 0 or 1 in binary terms. The state of the core magnetization is "read out" by another wire through the hole. In one type of memory, four doughnuts constitute one arabic (base 10) digit. Thus in Figure C.2–3 the digits in our

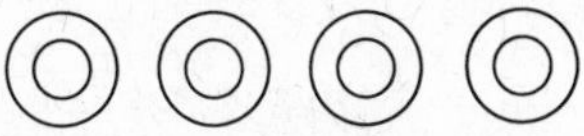

Figure C.2–3. Four magnetic cores can represent one digit.

normal base 10 arithmetic might be represented by the cores in the states shown in Table C.2–1.

For a shift of decimal, another set of four cores would be necessary for the second digit, and so on. You note that not all possible states of the cores are used; that is, five additional states are possible. Hence another core can be added that will be put in such a state that the total binary count will be "even." Then when we transmit the information, an even count is some measure of the accuracy of transmission. A sixth core provides a sign, 0 for

TABLE C.2–1 STATES OF CORES IN FIGURE C.2–3

	Cores			
Base 10 Number	4	3	2	1
0	0	0	0	0
1	0	0	0	1
2	0	0	1	0
3	0	0	1	1
4	0	1	0	0
5	0	1	0	1
6	0	1	1	0
7	0	1	1	1
8	1	0	0	0
9	1	0	0	1

positive, 1 for negative. Thus for an eight-digit number we require 48 cores. A memory of 30,000 numbers, which is about that required for many large control problems, therefore requires about 1.5 million cores.

The memory is divided into cells or storage locations, each location containing a number (frequently consisting of eight significant digits). Each cell has an address, or a number indicating the location, similar to a house address. These addresses run sequentially; thus in a hypothetical machine of 10,000 locations, the addresses would start at 0000, continue through 0001, 0002, and so on, through 9999. If a number is to be inserted or retrieved from memory, the address must be known and given.

A program consists of a series of commands recognized by the machine that will effectuate the required solution. A two-number code may indicate the command. Thus, if we wish to add two numbers designated as *A* and *B*, if *A* were located at address 0005 and *B* at 0100, we might have the set of commands given in Table C.2–2. In this set, the accumulator means the

TABLE C.2–2

Machine Code	English Code
(1) 01 0000 0000	Clear accumulator
(2) 02 0000 0005	Put *A* in accumulator
(3) 07 0100 0000	Add *A* to *B*
(4) 52 0300 0000	Put result in 0300

arithmetic or computing unit of Figure C.2–1. A more efficient use of such a code might be the command 21 0005 0100, which might mean "add the contents of 0005 (A) to the contents of 0100 (B) and store the result ($A + B$) into 0005." This action erases the previous contents of 0005, A, and puts $C = A + B$ in its place. If you did not wish to erase A, you should store it at a new location previously. A command such as 52 0005 0111 might store the contents of 0005 (A) into address 0111; then the previous command might be given. There would be codes for multiplication, subtraction, division, storage, retrieval, decimal shifting, and so on. Any operation may be broken down into a series of such basic commands, so all we need to do to accomplish any problem is to put the necessary commands in the proper order or to write a program. Because the program consists of numbers of 10 digits each, it may also be stored in memory. The machine is then instructed to start at the first command and proceed sequentially through the commands, unless a special transfer command, which causes the machine to jump to a new place in the program, is encountered. This type of machine is called a "stored program" machine, and practically all modern machines are of this type. Hence part of the memory contains the program, and part of it contains the numbers or data with which we work.

A machine language program might consist of 100 to 500 commands such as

```
05 0301 0296
02 1213 0301
06 1512 1213
     ⋮
```

To write such a program would drive the average engineer insane. To keep track of the command structure might not be so bad, but to know the location of the data at all times becomes almost impossible. Machine designers recognized this early and developed special languages such as Fortran, using the machine itself to generate the machine language program. Such programs are termed "compilers" or "assemblers." In this usage, we go to the machine twice; first, to translate the Fortran commands into machine language commands, and, second, to actually run the problem. Figure C.2–4 shows these steps. Thus in Figure C.2–4 the compiler is inserted or "loaded" into the memory, and the Fortran language program, called the "source program," becomes the data for the compiler. The results of this step is the "object program," which now has the machine language form previously shown. The object program is then loaded into a computer (not necessarily the same one), the numerical data is loaded, and the results are hopefully forthcoming in step 2. Once you obtain a correct object program in permanent form (punched cards), step 1 may be by-passed, and this is usually done, because step 1 may consume much more computer time than step 2.

The Fortran (or other) source program must obviously conform to certain rules as determined by the structure of the compiler. However, these requirements need not be onerous; the Fortran language symbols and rules may be learned very quickly. Step 1 thus relieves the programmer of keeping track of the data and all the machine commands. The Fortran language is written in a style very intelligible to the usual engineer; thus if A, B, and C represent pneumonic addresses of data known to the machine,

$$ZVT = [(A + B) * C]**2$$

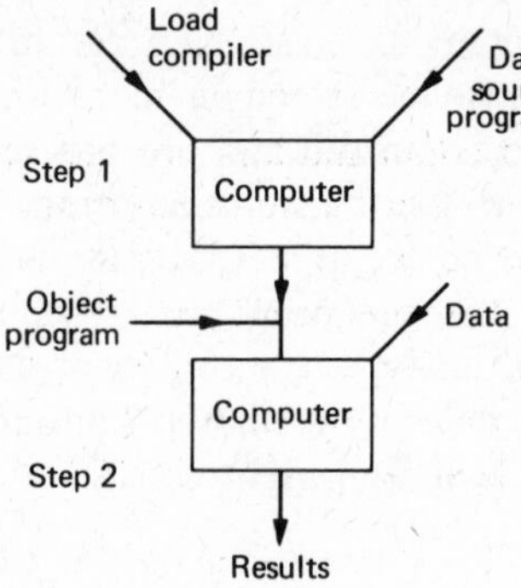

Figure C.2–4. Two-step process used with compiler languages on digital computer.

means: Find the result of $[(A + B)C]^2$ and store this at an address called ZVT. Because humans remember pneumonic names better than numbers, such addresses have much greater significance. In translating this single statement in step 1, the compiler will produce many machine language commands, and it will assign a machine language (number) address to ZVT and remember this correspondence for all subsequent commands. Basic Fortran consists of about 15 types of statements and is thus considerably easier to learn than a foreign language. Chapter 4 shows a Fortran program for solving a quadratic. Other compilers exist for special uses, such as accounting.

Much of the drudgery of programming has been removed by prewritten programs or subroutines available on call. The programmer simply names the subroutine and the variables to be used, and the computing system does the rest. Such programs consist of matrix inversion, differential equation solving, all sorts of functions, and so on. However, the programmer must put together the logic required for his particular situation, and this may be the really difficult part of the task.

Going back to Figure C.2–1, the memory of the machine must be supplemented by the other units to perform the functions described. The computing unit may be considered a glorified desk calculator but of enormously higher speed (one addition in about 2 microseconds). The control consists of the functions necessary to cause all the other units to work together smoothly. Of greater interest to the engineer-user are the input-output devices.

The original input is usually on punched cards, although occasionally paper tape may be used. The punched card is the usual 80-column card originated by IBM. In the case of Fortran, each card will have one Fortran statement punched into it. A special card punch code converts the statements to holes properly located on the card. Most of us are now familiar with this through checks or other such documents. The holes in the cards are converted into electrical impulses by a card-reading device and then loaded into the memory. In modern high-speed machines, card reading takes too much time, so the card information is first converted into magnetic type data, which may be read much more rapidly. The programmer need not be concerned with the details of this step, however. The output usually consists of printed sheets about 30 inches wide, although punched card or magnetic tape output may also be obtained. Again, the output may be first produced on a magnetic device and converted to printing by a separate machine. Usually the programmer worries only about the inputed cards and the output printed sheets. In more recent designs, a separate machine plots the output in the form of curves or displays curves on an oscilloscope tube. These outputs frequently have more meaning to the engineer than a printed page. Inputs may be placed into the machine by a remote card reader, typewriter console, or even by means of a cathode-ray gun directed at an oscilloscope tube face. We may expect in the future to have comparatively rapid access to the computer and almost immediate results. Thus design will be freed of numerical work, allowing the exploration of more possibilities, taking into consideration more variables and resulting in greater creativity. Most of the routine problems will be accomplished by machine.

The basic differences and advantages of the analog and digital computers are discussed in Chapter 4. In some situations they may be combined into what is termed a " bybrid " machine, which utilizes the advantages of each.

REFERENCES AND FURTHER READING

[1] V. Del Toro and S. R. Parker, *Principles of Control Systems Engineering*, McGraw-Hill, New York, 1960.

[2] G. J. Murphy, *Basic Automatic Control Theory*, Van Nostrand, Princeton, N.J., 1st ed., 1957; 2nd ed., 1967.

[3] G. A. Korn and T. M. Korn, *Electronic Analog Computers*, McGraw-Hill, New York, 1st ed., 1952; 2nd ed., 1956.

[4] C. L. Johnson, *Analog Computer Techniques*, McGraw-Hill, New York, 2nd ed., 1963.

[5] G. A. Korn and T. M. Korn, *Electronic Analog and Hybrid Computers*, McGraw-Hill, New York, 1964.

[6] N. R. Jenness, *Analog Computation and Simulation; Laboratory Approach*, Allyn & Bacon, Boston, 1965.

[7] N. R. Scott, *Analog and Digital Computer Technology*, McGraw-Hill, New York, 1960.

[8] R. S. Ledley, *Digital Computer and Control Engineering*, McGraw-Hill, New York, 1960.

[9] R. K. Richards, *Arithmetic Operations in Digital Computers*, Van Nostrand, Princeton, N.J., 1955.

[10] J. Jeenel, *Programming for Digital Computers*, McGraw-Hill, New York, 1959.

[11] G. W. Evans and C. L. Perry, *Programming and Coding for Automatic Digital Computers*, McGraw-Hill, New York, 1961.

[12] G. K. Douthwaite and W. L. Dunn, *Introductory Engineering Problems by Computer Methods*, Pacific Books, Palo Alto, Calif., 1965.

[13] G. Hellmut, *Fortran II and IV for Engineers and Scientists*, Macmillan, New York, 1966.

[14] Dimitry and T. Mott, Sr., *Introduction to Fortran IV Programming*, Holt, New, York, 1966.

[15] D. McCracken, *A Guide to Fortran IV Programming*, Wiley, New York, 1965.

See also references for Chapter 4.

Index